SUFFOCATING MOTHERS

D0023758

SUFFOCATING MOTHERS

FANTASIES OF MATERNAL ORIGIN IN SHAKESPEARE'S PLAYS, *HAMLET* TO *THE TEMPEST*

JANET ADELMAN

Routledge □ New York   London

Published in 1992 by

Routledge
an imprint of
Routledge, Chapman & Hall, Inc.
29 West 35 Street
New York, NY 10001

Published in Great Britain by

Routledge
11 New Fetter Lane
London EC4P 4EE

© 1992 by Routledge, Chapman & Hall, Inc.

Printed in the United States of America

All rights reserved. No part of this book may be reprinted or reproduced or
utilized in any form or by any electronic, mechanical or other means, now
known or hereafter invented, including photocopying and recording, or in
any information storage or retrieval system, without permission in writing
from the publishers.

Library of Congress cataloging in publication data

Adelman, Janet.
  Suffocating mothers : fantasies of maternal origin in
Shakespeare's plays, Hamlet to the Tempest / Janet Adelman.
    p. cm.
  Includes bibliographical references and index.
  ISBN 0-415-90038-7 (HB)   ISBN 0-415-90039-5 (PB)
    1. Shakespeare, William, 1564–1616—Knowledge—Psychology.
  2. Shakespeare, William, 1564–1616—Characters—Mothers.
  3. Masculinity (Psychology) in literature.   4. Mothers and sons in
  literature.   5. Psychoanalysis and literature.   6. Body, Human, in
  literature.   7. Fantasy in literature.   I. Title.
  PR3065.A37   1991
  822.3'3—dc20   91-29716
                                                            CIP

British Library cataloguing in publication data

Adelman, Janet
  Suffocating mothers : fantasies of maternal origin
  in Shakespeare's plays, Hamlet to The Tempest.
  I. Title
  822.33

  ISBN 0-415-90038-7
  ISBN 0-415-90039-5 pbk

To my father, who taught me that there was nothing I couldn't think about,

To my husband, whose loving support has made this project possible at every stage since its inception,

To my sons, who have patiently listened to me say "when the book is finished" for as long as they have been alive,

And to the memory of my mother.

CONTENTS

Acknowledgments

This book has been a long time in the making. The first finished essay incorporated into it—the essay on *Coriolanus*—was written in 1975–76; the first ruminations about Gertrude's role in *Hamlet* and in Shakespeare's career start turning up in my lecture notes in 1972. During all these years, I have incurred a great many debts; it is a pleasure to record the most public and nameable of them here, though I am keenly aware of all those that I have left out.

Throughout this book's long inception, I have been blessed in my friends and in institutional support of various kinds. The University of California has given me sabbatical leave time, sabbatical supplements in the form of Humanities Research Fellowships, research grants, and travel funds. At a crucial moment (1976–77), the American Council of Learned Societies gave me the study fellowship that enabled me to pursue my psychoanalytic interests in London at Hampstead Clinic and Tavistock Clinic; both of these clinics generously allowed me to sit in on seminars for trainees and to learn from conversation with their faculty and students. At another crucial moment (1982–83), a fellowship from the Guggenheim Foundation gave me the leisure (and the confidence) to confront the blank pages of what would become the central chapters on *Hamlet* and on *King Lear*. And from the start, my students and colleagues in the Department of English have provided me with an extraordinarily challenging and supportive atmosphere in which to work. My developing interest in psychoanalytic criticism was nurtured by several years' worth of wonderful conversations with Brent Cohen, my student, co-teacher, and dear friend, whose loss to the profession during the lean years I still mourn. Carol Christ, my oldest friend and intellectual comrade in the department, first made me realize that psychoanalysis might provide me with a language for what I had been unable to talk about in my work on *Antony and Cleopatra*.

Among the many other colleagues who have enriched my life at Berkeley from the start, I think especially of Alex Zwerdling, Jonas Barish, and Paul Alpers; as department chair and the first to read many of these pages, Paul Alpers's respectful and affectionate skepticism gave me just what I needed to go on.

During the early stages of work, I was both exhilarated and challenged by a wonderful group of people working in the areas of feminist and psychoanalytic criticism of Shakespeare; my debt to Coppélia Kahn, Murray Schwartz, Gayle Greene, Peter Erickson, Meredith Skura, and Carol Neely will be obvious on every page. My debt to Carol Neely in fact predates our work in feminism and Shakespeare: first at Smith College and then at Yale, Carol always went before me, demonstrating how to think passionately and lucidly about literature. Long conversations with Jane Flax and with Nancy Chodorow enabled me to take certain kinds of personal and intellectual risks in my thinking and writing; their continuing friendship is one of the wonderful side-effects of my excursion into psychoanalysis. At several crucial moments, C. L. Barber was there to encourage me; more than anyone else, he was the "good enough mother" that enabled this book, as he enabled the work of a whole generation of psychoanalytic critics. William Germano has been everything I could have dreamed of in an editor, and more: his belief in this project and his willingness to wait for it sustained me in the final years; his friendship is one of its most unexpected benefits. And above all, there are four dear friends—Elizabeth Abel, Stanley Cavell, Madelon Sprengnether, and Richard Wheeler—who have been gracious presences in my head throughout the writing of this book, enabling it even when we had not had an audible conversation in months. I could not have written this book without imagining them as its readers; in a deep sense, it was written for, and to, them.

A Note on Texts

All references to the following plays are to the Arden Shakespeare editions (London: Methuen):

1 Henry VI, ed. Andrew S. Cairncross (1962)

2 Henry VI, ed. Andrew S. Cairncross (1957)

3 Henry VI, ed. Andrew S. Cairncross (1964)

King Richard III, ed. Antony Hammond (1981)

Hamlet, ed. Harold Jenkins (1982)

Troilus and Cressida, ed. Kenneth Palmer (1982)

Othello, ed. M. R. Ridley (1958)

All's Well That Ends Well, ed. G. K. Hunter (1959)

Measure for Measure, ed. J. W. Lever (1965)

King Lear, ed. Kenneth Muir (1959)

Macbeth, ed. Kenneth Muir (1972)

Coriolanus, ed. Philip Brockbank (1976)

Timon of Athens, ed. H. J. Oliver (1959)

Antony and Cleopatra, ed. M. R. Ridley (1954)

Pericles, ed. F. D. Hoeniger (1963)

Cymbeline, ed. J. M. Nosworthy (1955)

The Winter's Tale, ed. J. H. P. Pafford (1963)

The Tempest, ed. Frank Kermode (1954)

With the exception of *The Two Noble Kinsmen*, references to all other plays and poems are to *William Shakespeare: The Complete Works*, gen. ed. Alfred Harbage (Baltimore, Md.: Penguin Books, 1969); references to *The Two Noble Kinsman* are to the Signet edition, ed. Clifford Leech (New York: New American Library, 1977).

Sections of Chapter 3 are adapted from " 'This is and is not Cressid': The Characterization of Cressida," first published in *The (M)other Tongue: Essays in Feminist Psychoanalytic Interpretation,* ed. Shirley Nelson Garner, Claire Kahane, and Madelon Sprengnether (copyright © 1985 by Cornell University); used by permission of the publisher, Cornell University Press.

Sections of Chapter 4 are taken from "Bed Tricks: On Marriage as the End of Comedy in *All's Well That Ends Well* and *Measure for Measure,*" first published in *Shakespeare's Personality,* ed. Norman N. Holland, Sidney Homan, and Bernard J. Paris (copyright © 1990 The Regents of the University of California); used by permission of the publisher, University of California Press.

Sections of Chapter 6 are taken from " 'Anger's My Meat': Feeding, Dependency, and Aggression in *Coriolanus,*" first published in *Shakespeare: Pattern of Excelling Nature,* ed. David Bevington and Jay L. Halio (Cranbury, N.J.: Associated University Presses, Inc., 1978) and reprinted in slightly revised form in *Representing Shakespeare: New Psychoanalytic Essays,* ed. Murray M. Schwartz and Coppélia Kahn (Baltimore, Md.: Johns Hopkins University Press, 1980), and from " 'Born of Women': Fantasies of Maternal Power in *Macbeth,*" first published in *Cannibals, Witches, and Divorce: Estranging the Renaissance,*" ed. Marjorie Garber (Baltimore, Md.: Johns Hopkins University Press, 1987); they are reprinted here by permission of the publishers.

1

INTRODUCTION

In *King Henry VI, Part 3*, the man who will make himself into Richard III pauses for a moment on his way to the throne to meditate on the origins of his unstable desire. If the crown eludes him, he tells us, he will turn to love, and "make [his] heaven in a lady's lap" (3.2.148); but desire for the crown itself turns out to be compensatory, for

> Love foreswore me in my mother's womb:
> And, for I should not deal in her soft laws,
> She did corrupt frail Nature with some bribe,
> To shrink mine arm up like a wither'd shrub;
> To make an envious mountain on my back,
> Where sits Deformity to mock my body;
> To shape my legs of an unequal size;
> To disproportion me in every part,
> Like to a chaos, or unlick'd bear-whelp
> That carries no impression like the dam.
> And am I then a man to be belov'd?
> O monstrous fault to harbour such a thought!
> Then, since this earth affords no joy to me
> But to command, to check, to o'erbear such
> As are of better person than myself,
> I'll make my heaven to dream upon the crown.
> (3.2.153–68)

This seems to me an extraordinary moment: in it we hear—I think for the first time in Shakespeare—the voice of a fully developed subjectivity, the characteristically Shakespearean illusion that a stage person has interior being, including motives that he himself does not fully understand. As Richard gropes to explain himself to himself, the perfect circularity of the reasoning—he wants love because he can't have the

1

crown, he wants the crown because he can't have love—mimics the self-enclosed processes of his mind, and the hitherto political becomes psychological: aggressive masculine ambition—the unexplained norm of the history plays until now—becomes de-naturalized, problematized, itself in need of explanation. And the explanation Richard gives himself turns on his construction of a psychic myth of origins, a past that will account for who he is: Shakespeare creates his subjectivity in effect as psychoanalysis does, by locating the origins of the self in this re-imagined past.

I take this moment as the point of origin for my exploration of masculinity and the maternal body in Shakespeare because the origin that Richard imagines for himself turns crucially on that body: if Richard is the first fully developed male subject in Shakespeare, and if he speaks fully for the first time here, what he speaks about is the origin of his aggression in the problematic maternal body.[1] Misshapen in the womb by a triply maternal figure—Mother, Love, and Nature combined—he considers his deformed body and its consequences her "monstrous fault." Already withered in her womb, he cannot make his heaven in another lady's lap, and so he will remake himself in the image of a commanding and overbearing political ambition, finding his masculine potency through the substitute heaven of the crown:

> I'll make my heaven to dream upon the crown;
> And whiles I live, t'account this world but hell,
> Until my misshap'd trunk that bears this head
> Be round impaled with a glorious crown.
> And yet I know not how to get the crown,
> For many lives stand between me and home.
> (3.2.168–73)

But his fluid fantasy remakes the crown itself in the image of the lady's lap: strikingly, it is his deformed trunk—not his head—that is to be round impaled with the crown, "home" again within its enclosure. And the return home is always dangerous; no sooner has the crown been made into a substitute womb than it too turns against him, its protective pales transformed into the thorns that now impale him:[2]

> And I,—like one lost in a thorny wood,
> That rents the thorns and is rent with the thorns,
> Seeking a way, and straying from the way;
> Not knowing how to find the open air,
> But toiling desperately to find it out—
> Torment myself to catch the English crown:
> And from that torment I will free myself,
> Or hew my way out with a bloody axe.
> (3.2.174–81)

In an imagistic nightmare, the crown and the obstacles to the crown collapse into one another: womb and crown coalesce with the thorny wood as Richard is returned to its dangerous enclosure. Entrapped within this enclosure, he becomes a suffocating fetus once more, returned to the womb that would deform him and toiling desperately to find the open air. And once again, his only recourse is to the counter-violence through which he would redefine himself: returned to the site of maternal origin, he would hew his way out, giving birth to himself through the rent of a violent caesarian section and freeing himself from the suffocating maternal matrix.[3]

Within the context of Richard's actions, his explanatory fantasy seems wholly factitious: his violence has already been well established as part of his contest with his siblings to please his father. But this fantasy emerges only after his father's death, as though that death had deprived Richard of his father's protection and thrust him back toward his mother; and, factitious or not, in defining masculine violence—indeed, masculine survival—as a turning against the maternal body, it predicts the peculiar turn of Richard's violence away from common familial enemies and toward the matrix of his own family. No longer content to act for his family, from this moment on Richard is increasingly determined to become "myself alone" (3 Henry VI, 5.6.83); and he becomes himself alone by hewing and hacking his way through the maternal body and the matrix of relationships it engenders,[4] swilling the "warm blood" of England "like wash, and mak[ing] his trough / In the embowell'd bosoms" of its citizens, "prey[ing] on the issue of his mother's body" (Richard III, 5.2.9–10, 4.4.57).[5]

And in doing so, Richard acts on behalf of a masculinity that has been threatened throughout the four plays of the sequence. For Richard's fantasy of maternal malevolence is not his alone; it condenses and localizes a whole range of anxieties about masculinity and female power in this sequence,[6] from its early warnings about the fatherless realm in which there will be "none but women left to wail the dead" (1 Henry VI, 1.1.51) to its final vision of nemesis in the form of Margaret, whose hunger for revenge is cloyed as one by one the mothers' sons "drop into the rotten mouth of death" (Richard III, 4.4.61–62, 4.4.2). These anxieties are sometimes localized in particular female characters at particular moments: in the witch Joan, whose command over the French ensures their effeminacy, in the Margaret who dandles Henry VI like a baby (2 Henry VI, 1.3.145) and then takes on the aspect of Medea,[7] "drain[ing] the life-blood of the child, / To bid the father wipe his eyes withal" (3 Henry VI, 1.4.138–39), and finally in Richard's literal mother, who tries to "smother" her son in the breath of bitter words, who would have "intercepted" him "by strangling [him] in her accursed womb" (*Richard III*, 4.4.133, 137–38). But they are more often diffused over the whole surface of the text, free-floating particles of a nightmare the plays can neither quite confront nor dismiss: the nightmare of a femaleness that can weaken and contaminate masculinity, a "thirsty" earth-mouth that can "gape open wide and eat him quick" (*3 Henry VI*, 2.3.15; *Richard III*, 1.2.65), a womb that is a "bed of death," smothering its children in "the swallowing gulf / Of dark forgetfulness and deep oblivion" (*Richard III*, 4.1.53; 3.7.127–28).[8] Through this imagery of engulfment and swallowing suffocation—imagery that returns us to our starting point in Richard's fantasy of suffocation—the womb takes on a malevolent power quite divorced from the largely powerless women who might be supposed to embody it,[9] and divorced as well from the imagined particulars of Richard's psyche. And just this disembodiedness marks the source of its power: because it is not embodied in any individual woman in whom it might be contained and controlled, the maternal malevolence of these plays invokes a primitive infantile terror derivative from the period when the mother or her surrogate was not seen as a whole and separate person, when she—or the body-parts through which she was imagined—had the power to make or unmake the world and the self for her child.

This terror finds its psychological locus in the despoiling maternal origin that haunts Richard III in the shape of his own misshapen body; and as always, the infantile fantasies that Shakespeare invokes to empower his fictions would themselves have been shaped by the actual conditions of infancy and reformulated in adulthood according to the terms provided by his culture. This was, first of all, a culture in which infants routinely died,[10] in which they began life—if they were lucky enough to live—hungry, and often stayed hungry. Since mothers' milk was believed to be unwholesome during the period immediately after childbirth, a period that could last for a few days or as much as a month, the newborn was often fed on pap or wine and sugar unless a wet-nurse could be found immediately;[11] and the wet-nurses to whom children were routinely sent were notorious for having contaminated or insufficient milk.[12] Wet-nursing itself was sometimes tantamount to murder: even aside from the "killing nurses" who allegedly tended to the very poor, children put out to nurse were twice as likely to die as those nursed by their mothers, through the effects of disease or neglect, or sometimes deliberate malice.[13] If the infant survived, the period of infancy was both dangerous and long: poor nutrition and perhaps rickets sometimes delayed the appearance of teeth—and hence weaning and the routine eating of solid food—until the child was two or three;

similar conditions sometimes restricted the child's mobility, delaying the onset of walking also until two or three.[14] What we know of the actual conditions that shape infantile fantasy suggests, that is, that many would have experienced a prolonged period of infantile dependency, during which they were subject to pleasures and dangers especially associated with nursing and the maternal body.

For the custom of wet-nursing apparently did not break the hold of the mother on the imagination; even when it was most successful, the fact of wet-nursing in itself might be reconstructed by the child or the adult as a sign of maternal abandonment. Here is Stephen Guazzo's account of a child speaking to his mother in 1581: "You bore me but nine months in your belly, but my nurse kept me with her teats the space of two years. . . . So soon as I was born, you deprived me of your company, and banished me your presence."[15] Guillimeau's *The Nursing of Children* approvingly quotes one of the Gracchi: "I know (Mother) that you bore me nine moneths in your wombe, yet that was out of necessitie, because you could do no otherwise; but when I was borne, then you forsooke me, and my Nurse-mother willingly entertained me, carried me three yeares in her armes, and nourished mee with her owne blood." Guillimeau concludes, with Aulus Gellius, that there is "no difference between a woman that refuses to nurse her own childe, and one that kils her child, as soone as shee hath conceived; that shee may not be troubled with bearing it nine months in her wombe. For why may not a woman with as good reason, deny to nourish her childe with her blood, in her wombe, as to deny it her milke being borne?"[16] Wet-nursing merely gave the child two psychic sites of intense maternal deprivation rather than one: first, the original maternal rejection signaled by wet-nursing itself; and then the weaning—routinely by the application of wormwood or another bitter-tasting substance to the nipple[17]—and abrupt separation from the nurse-mother he or she might have known for two or three years.

If the child had had a difficult and prolonged infancy, the culture provided him or her with plenty of directives about who to blame: for many, the actual conditions of infancy would have intersected with cultural representations of the female body to mark that body as the site of deformation and vulnerability. Fortune was traditionally represented as a disappointing or unreliable nurse;[18] for Quarles, the maternal body becomes the metaphor for all the dissatisfactions of the world. Radically revising Isaiah 66.11 ("ye may suck, and be satisfied with the breasts of her consolations") by inserting a crucial *not* ("ye may suck, but not be satisfied with the breast of her consolation"), Quarles chooses the infected breast as the emblem of the world's plenty that makes him poor ("Inopem me copia fecit"):

What, never fill'd? Be thy lips screw'd so fast
  To th'earth's full breast? . . .
    Ah, fool, forbear; thou swallowest at one breath
Both food and poison down! thou draw'st both milk
        and death.

....

  There's nothing wholesome where the whole's infected.
  Unseize thy lips; earth's Milk's a ripen'd core,
That drops from her disease, that matters from her sore.
               (*Emblems*, I. 12)[19]

Here milk—even healthy milk—becomes pus, the sign of infection that "matters" from earth's sore—and so, for that matter, does matter.[20] For matter itself is the diseased inheritance of the female body: the myth that made Eve responsible for the Fall and hence for the mortal body is played out in miniature in any ordinary birth. The womb was traditionally understood as the entrance to death and the site of mortality: after his gruesome contemplation of the womb as a potential tomb for the unborn baby, Donne concludes that those who manage to be born are not much better off than those who die *in utero*, for "we have a winding sheet in our Mothers wombe, which growes with us from our conception, and wee come into the world, wound up in that *winding sheet*, for wee come to *seeke a grave*."[21] The body is this winding sheet, made in—and derived from—the mother's body: neither popular nor scientific embryologies could wholly rid themselves of the Aristotelian dualities linking the male with spirit or form and the female with matter, as though mortality itself were the sign of hereditary deformation by the female.[22]

Both actual conditions and current beliefs—beliefs that of course influenced the conditions, as in the condemnation of the mother's first milk as noxious—thus conspired to locate the child's vulnerability in the body of the nurse/mother. Richard's fantasy of having been deformed in his mother's womb is less grotesque in this context; in fact it reiterates the belief that the mother could literally deform fetuses through her excessive imagination, her uncontrollable longings, her unnatural lusts.[23] And his fantasy of suffocation in the womb is no more than scientific fact: many understood birth itself as the fetus's response to the inadequate supply of air or food in the womb; and the most popular midwifery of the day sounds remarkably like Richard or his mother when it attributes spontaneous abortion to the mother's "excesse feeding and surfetting, by the which the byrth is suffocate and strangled in the belly" (*The birth of mankinde*, p. 135).[24] Guillimeau suggests that the mother could in fact choose to "intercept" her baby, in effect strangling the fetus in the womb, if she did not want the bother of bearing it for nine months.[25] The mother could of course poison the baby once it was born—Joan's father regrets that her mother had not given her a litte ratsbane with her milk (*1 Henry VI*, 5.4.27–29)—but she might not need to: for her milk itself was believed to be a derivative of menstrual blood—"nothing else but blood whitened"[26]—which was still held by some to be poisonous.[27] Nurses could transmit literal diseases, and apparently often did, but they could also transmit their own noxious qualities to the child; books on the care of children therefore urge extreme caution in the selection of nurses.[28] Leontes implies that femaleness itself might be one such undesirable characteristic, transmitted through the milk that is whitened female blood: separating his son from his wife, he tells her, "I am glad you did not nurse him: / Though he does bear some signs of me, yet you / Have too much blood in him" (*The Winter's Tale*, 2.1.56–58).

Too much female blood. Culturally constructed as literally dangerous to everyone, the maternal body must have seemed especially dangerous to little boys: fed *in utero* on her menstrual blood and then on the milk that was its derivative, he had too much of her blood in him.[29] Contemporary object-relations psychoanalysis locates differentiation from the mother as a special site of anxiety for the boy-child, who must form his specifically masculine selfhood against the matrix of her overwhelming femaleness;[30] how much more difficult and anxiety-ridden this process must have been if the period of infantile dependency—with all its pleasures and dangers—was prolonged, and if the body itself, in all its vulnerability, could later be understood as the inheritance from her contaminating female matter. Cultural practice in fact formalized both the "femaleness" of the boy-child and the need to leave that femaleness behind in order to become a man, enforcing the equation of masculine identity with differentiation from the mother through its own differentiating ceremony. Until the little boy came of age as a man, he was dangerously close to the maternal body, dangerously undistinguished from "the baby of a girl" (*Macbeth*, 3.4.105)—the girl-baby—Macbeth protested against in himself: dressed like a girl, tended almost entirely by women, his nurse/mother's milk and his mother's tears still in him, his voice "small as an eunuch, or the virgin voice / That babies lull asleep" (*Coriolanus*, 3.2.114–15), he was too much his mother's son; and his passage to manhood was marked by taking him out of the undifferentiated "female" clothing of childhood, "breeching" him, and removing him to the care of men.[31]

"Tears then for babes; blows and revenge for me!" (*3 Henry VI*, 2.1.86): it is no wonder that so many of Shakespeare's adult men anxiously note the presence of woman's tears in themselves, no wonder that Richard should wish to hew his way out of the suffocating maternal body; though anyone might be swallowed up by the nurse-mother from whom separation is always only imperfectly achieved, for the man, merger with the female would mean the end of his hard-won masculine selfhood. And yet, this body sings a siren-song of return to her children, pulling them back toward oneness and the imagined satisfaction of their hunger, dissolving masculinity and masculine bonds. In *1 Henry VI*, Joan works her witchcraft on Burgundy by making him see his attack on France as an attack on the maternal body ("Behold the wounds, the most unnatural wounds / Which thou thyself hast given her woeful breast" [3.3.50–51]) and then offering—in Shakespeare's most Spenserian line—to convert that attack into blissful return ("Come, come, return; return, thou wandering lord" [3.3.76]); the result is his turn from Talbot and manly England to the effeminate French. And Margaret's bewitching of Suffolk apparently has the same source; though he initially sees in her a chance to rule the king (*1 Henry VI*, 5.5.107–8), by the time of his exile, her hold over him has been bizarrely redefined:

> If I depart from thee I cannot live;
> And in thy sight to die, what were it else
> But like a pleasant slumber in thy lap?
> Here could I breathe my soul into the air,
> As mild and gentle as the cradle-babe
> Dying with mother's dug between his lips.
> (*2 Henry VI*, 3.2.387–92)[32]

Death and the mother's body coalesce in his image of union; and the grim image of Margaret parading around the stage with his head in her arms (4.4) suggests what happens to the men who succumb to its allure.

After the death of Suffolk, the longing for return to the maternal body is not heard again in the *Henry VI* plays or in *Richard III*; except perhaps for his bogus attempt to win Queen Elizabeth as mother,[33] it certainly is not heard in Richard himself, who manages to use women only as political pawns or scapegoats, reducing them to helpless victims as though to compensate for his original nightmare of maternal malevolence. Nor is that nightmare heard again in Richard; Shakespeare in fact deflects its terror away from him, following Richard's own lead and undoing the powerful subjectivity he had developed in *3 Henry VI*. For Richard himself empties himself out in *Richard III*, doing away with selfhood and its nightmare origins and remaking himself in the shape of the perfect actor who has no being except in the roles he plays. He had predicted this solution in his soliloquy of *3 Henry VI*, 3.2, where his actor's pride in shape-shifting—"I can add colours to the chameleon, / Change shapes with Proteus for advantages" (*3 Henry VI*, 3.2.191–93)—seemed clearly a defensive response to his fear that his shape and his selfhood had been given him, fixed by his deformation in his mother's womb; and by the time of *Richard III*, he seems to have achieved this erasure of selfhood.[34] There, the vestiges of Richard's old selfhood surface only in the particular pleasure he takes in enacting its fragments—the victimized innocent child, the man whose arm has been withered up by women—*as roles*, in effect redoing his nightmare as farce (*Richard III*, 1.3.143, 2.2.153, 3.4.68–71).

But even while Shakespeare suggests the etiology of Richard's transformation into an actor, he participates in the erasure of Richard's intolerable selfhood: in *Richard III*, our attention is directed more to Richard's theatrical machinations than to any imagined subjectivity behind his roles; even in Richard's spectacular final soliloquy (5.3.178–204), the effect is less of a psyche than of diverse roles confronting themselves across the void where a self should be. And Shakespeare similarly participates in Richard's violent unmaking of the maternal body that is the point of origin of his selfhood: though Richard's violence is always deplored, its action is nonetheless replicated in a dramatic structure that moves women from positions of power and authority to positions of utter powerlessness, and finally moves them off the stage altogether.[35] Even Margaret is in the end rendered powerless. For much of the play, the maternal malevolence deflected from Richard's psyche is generalized and enacted through her witchlike power: her hunger for revenge becomes the play's aesthetic principle as her curses determine its action, predicting each catastrophe.[36] But—having summed up maternal malevolence in her—Shakespeare dispenses with it easily, banishing her before the final catastrophe is complete: after 5.1, she goes unmentioned, and aesthetic control of the play passes into the hands of the benevolent God who works through Richmond.

The selfhood of Richard as Shakespeare develops it in *3 Henry VI*—the masculine selfhood embedded in maternal origin—is the stuff of tragedy; and Shakespeare is not yet ready to write that tragedy. In its retreat from this selfhood and in its containment of maternal power, *Richard III* in fact predicts the shape of Shakespeare's career. There are powerful maternal figures in Shakespeare's earliest plays: aside from Margaret and her psychic kin, there is the horrific devouring mother in *Titus Andronicus*,[37] in whose presence all identity and all family bonds dissolve; and there is the benign and purified mother of

Comedy of Errors, in whose presence masculine identity and the family can safely be reconstituted. But after these plays, mothers virtually disappear: in the plays before *Hamlet*, masculine identity is constructed in and through the absence of the maternal.[38] Except for Romeo—who leaves his family behind as he comes on stage for the first time—and for the multiple sons of *King John*, Shakespearean sons have no mothers. The case of *King John* is in fact diagnostic of Shakespeare's retreat in the face of maternal power: though he begins the play with two warring mothers, each in her own way powerful both politically and dramatically, he kills both of them off in act 4—with an abruptness that borders on the ludicrous (4.2.120–23)—in order to recuperate masculinity at the end of the play. For mothers and sons cannot co-exist in his psychic and dramatic world: and his solution is to split his world in two, isolating its elements—heterosexual bonds in the comedies and *Romeo and Juliet*, father-son bonds in the histories and *Julius Caesar*—from each other and from the maternal body that would be toxic to both.

But the mother occluded in these plays returns with a vengeance in *Hamlet*; and it is the thesis of this book that the plays from *Hamlet* on all follow from her return. For the masculine selfhood discovered and deflected in Richard III—selfhood grounded in paternal absence and in the fantasy of overwhelming contamination at the site of origin—becomes the tragic burden of Hamlet and the men who come after him. And they do not bear the burden alone: again and again, it is passed on to the women, who must pay the price for the fantasies of maternal power invested in them. In the chapters that follow, I will explore these fantasies and their cost.

2

MAN AND WIFE IS ONE FLESH:
HAMLET AND THE CONFRONTATION WITH
THE MATERNAL BODY

In *Hamlet*, the figure of the mother returns to Shakespeare's dramatic world, and her presence causes the collapse of the fragile compact that had allowed Shakespeare to explore familial and sexual relationships in the histories and romantic comedies without devastating conflict; this collapse is the point of origin of the great tragic period. The son's acting out of the role of the father, his need to make his own identity in relationship to his conception of his father—the stuff of *1 and 2 Henry IV* and *Julius Caesar*—becomes deeply problematic in the presence of the wife/mother: for her presence makes the father's sexual role a disabling crux in the son's relationship with his father. At the same time, the relations between the sexes that had been imagined in the comedies without any serious confrontation with the power of female sexuality suddenly are located in the context of the mother's power to contaminate, with the result that they can never again be imagined in purely holiday terms. Here again, *Hamlet* stands as a kind of watershed, subjecting to maternal presence the relationships previously exempted from that presence.[1]

From the perspective of *Hamlet*, the father-son relationships of the earlier plays begin to look like oedipal dramas from which the chief object of contention has been removed. Both the *Henry IV* plays and *Julius Caesar* manage their sophisticated psychological explorations in effect by denying that women have anything to do with these explorations, ultimately by denying the complications that the mother poses for the father-son relationship. Before *Hamlet*, this relationship tends to be enacted in the political rather than the domestic sphere, and in the absence of women. Insofar as the triangulated conflict characteristic of oedipal material makes its way into these plays, the triangle is composed of a son and two fathers, not of a son and his parents; the son's identity is defined by his position between the fathers, not between

11

father and mother. The *Henry IV* plays and *Julius Caesar* both strikingly represent the defining act of the son's manhood as the process of choosing between two fathers; in both, the son attempts to become fully himself by identifying with the true father rather than the false, an identification signaled by the son's willingness to carry out the true father's wish that the false father be disowned or killed. But the choice becomes increasingly problematic in these plays. In *1 and 2 Henry IV*, it is a relatively easy matter for Hal to kill off that "father ruffian" Falstaff (*1 Henry IV*, 2.4.254) by exiling him, thus becoming "father" to his brothers (*2 Henry IV*, 5.2.57) and the embodiment of his father's spirit (*2 Henry IV*, 5.2.125); in this cross-generational alliance, he becomes himself in effect by choosing to become his father. Although we may feel that he has diminished himself in his choice, the plays do not finally encourage us to wish other choices on him or to dwell at length on the selfhood he has lost. The choice and its outcome are far more complex in *Julius Caesar*, where becoming oneself by becoming one's ancestral father necessitates killing off—literally, not symbolically—a much more ambiguously powerful father than Falstaff. Brutus is pushed toward conspiracy partly by his desire to live up to the image of his great ancestor and namesake, Junius Brutus, the slayer of tyrants (see, for example, 1.2.158; 1.3.82, 146; 2.1.53, 322). But immediately after Brutus has killed the man whom he himself sees as "the foremost man of all this world" (4.3.22), his enabling ancestral father drops out of the play; reference to him entirely disappears. In place of this father, the figure of Caesar increasingly comes to loom like a paternal ghost over the play, obliterating the memory of the heroic father on whom Brutus had hoped to found his selfhood. This interchange of fathers neatly poses one aspect of Brutus's tragic dilemma: Brutus kills one father apparently to satisfy the wishes of another, only to discover that he has slain the wrong father, that the dead father is not only more powerful but more powerfully his; only in killing Caesar—only as Caesar says "Et tu, Brutus?"—does he come to realize his position as Caesar's son and hence to suffer the disabling guilt that is the consequence of parricide.[2]

The triangulated choice between two fathers that is characteristic of these plays is at the center of *Hamlet*; here, as in the earlier plays, assuming masculine identity means taking on the qualities of the father's name—becoming a Henry, a Brutus, or a Hamlet—by killing off a false father. Moreover, the whole weight of the play now manifestly creates one father true and the other false. Nonetheless, the choice is immeasurably more difficult for Hamlet than for his predecessors; for despite their manifest differences, the fathers in *Hamlet* keep threatening to collapse into one another, annihilating in their collapse the son's easy assumption of his father's identity. The initiating cause of this collapse is Hamlet's mother: her failure to serve her son as the repository of his father's ideal image by mourning him appropriately is the symptom of her deeper failure to distinguish properly between his father and his father's brother.[3] Even at the start of the play, before the ghost's crucial revelation, Gertrude's failure to differentiate has put an intolerable strain on Hamlet by making him the only repository of his father's image, the only agent of differentiation in a court that seems all too willing to accept the new king in place of the old. Her failure of memory—registered in her undiscriminating sexuality—in effect defines Hamlet's task in relation to his father as a task of memory: as she forgets, he inherits the burden of differentiating, of idealizing and making static the past; hence the ghost's insistence on remembering (1.5.33, 91) and the degree to which Hamlet registers his failure to avenge his father as a failure of memory (4.4.40). Hamlet had promised the ghost to remember him in effect by becoming him, letting his father's commandment live all alone within his brain; but the intensity of Hamlet's need to idealize in the face of his mother's failure makes his father inaccessible to him as a model, hence disrupts the identification from which he could accomplish his vengeance. As his memory of his father pushes increasingly in the direction of idealization, Hamlet becomes more acutely aware of his own distance from that idealization and hence of his likeness to Claudius,[4] who is defined chiefly by his difference from his father. Difference from the heroic ideal represented in Old Hamlet becomes the defining term common to Claudius and Hamlet: the very act of distinguishing Claudius from his father— "no more like my father / Than I to Hercules" (1.2.152–53)—forces Hamlet into imaginative identification with Claudius. The intensity of Hamlet's need to differentiate between true father and false thus confounds itself, disabling his identification with his father and hence his secure identity as son.

If Gertrude's presence in *Hamlet* undoes the strategy by which father-son relations are protected in the Lancastrian tetralogy and in *Julius Caesar*, it simultaneously undoes the strategy that protects sexual relations in the romantic comedies: in *Hamlet*, both kinds of relationship are in effect contaminated by their relocation in the presence of the mother. Maternal absence is as striking in these comedies as in the tetralogy. And if, in the histories, this absence functions to enable the son's assumption of his father's identity, here it functions to protect comic possibility itself by sustaining the illusion that the endlessly appealing girls of the comedies will never become fully sexual women and hence will never lose their androgynous charm: having no mothers, they need not become mothers. Despite the degree to which marriage is the ostentatious goal of Shakespeare's romantic comedies, these plays rarely look forward to the sexual consummation that seals marriage; even *A Midsummer Night's Dream* does so only in the context of a series of magical protections against danger. The comedies tend rather to deflect attention away from female sexuality through a variety of devices: through a comic closure that defers consummation, through the heroine's sometimes unresolved transvestitism or allusion to the male actor who will remain when the play is over and costumes are removed, even through the insistent cuckoldry jokes—jokes that serve both to deflect the imagined sexual act away from the male wooer and to defer it into the indefinite future, where, as Lavatch will say in a different mood, "the knaves come to do that for me which I am aweary of" (*All's Well*, 1.3.41). The absence of fully imagined female sexuality is, I think, what enables the holiday tone of these plays; that sexuality is for Shakespeare the stuff of tragedy, not comedy.

The female sexuality largely absent from the comedies invades *Hamlet* in the person of Gertrude, and, once there, it utterly contaminates sexual relationship, disabling holiday. In her presence, Hamlet sees his task as the disruption of marriage itself: "I say we will have no mo marriage" (3.1.149), he says to Ophelia as she becomes contaminated in his eyes, subject to the same "frailty" that names his mother.[5] As he comes to identify himself with his cuckolded father—his "imaginations are as foul / As Vulcan's stithy" (3.2.83–84)—he can think of Ophelia only as a cuckold-maker, like his mother: "if thou wilt needs marry, marry a fool; for wise men know well enough what monsters you make of them" (3.1.139–41). Moreover, Ophelia fuses with Gertrude not only as potential cuckold-maker but also as potential mother:

> Get thee to a nunnery. Why, wouldst thou be a breeder of sinners?
> I am myself indifferent honest, but yet I could accuse me of such
> things that it were better my mother had not borne me. (3.1.121–24)

The implicit logic is: why would you be a breeder of sinners like me? In the gap between "breeder of sinners" and "I," Gertrude and Ophelia momentarily collapse into one figure. It is no wonder that there can be no more marriage: Ophelia becomes dangerous to Hamlet insofar as she becomes identified in his mind with the contaminating maternal body, the mother who has borne him.

Hamlet thus redefines the son's position between two fathers by relocating it in relation to an indiscriminately sexual maternal body that threatens to annihilate the distinction between the fathers and hence problematizes the son's paternal identification; at the same time, the play conflates the beloved with this betraying mother, undoing the strategies that had enabled marriage in the comedies. The intrusion of the adulterous mother thus disables the solutions of history and comedy as Shakespeare has imagined them; in that sense, her presence initiates tragedy. But how can we understand the mother whose presence has the capacity to undermine the accommodations to which Shakespeare had come? Why should the first mother powerfully present in Shakespeare since the period of his earliest works be portrayed as adulterous? Why should her adulterous presence coincide with the start of Shakespeare's great tragic period?

Given her centrality in the play, it is striking how little we know about Gertrude; even the extent of her involvement in the murder of her first husband is left unclear. We may want to hear her shock at Hamlet's accusation of murder—"Almost as bad, good mother, / As kill a king and marry with his brother"(3.4.28–29)—as evidence of her innocence;[6] but the text permits us to hear it alternatively as shock either at being found out or at Hamlet's rudeness. The ghost accuses her at least indirectly of adultery[7] and incest—Claudius is "that incestuous, that adulterate beast" (1.5.42)—but he neither accuses her of nor exonerates her from the murder. For the ghost, as for Hamlet, her chief crime is her uncontrolled sexuality; that is the object of their moral revulsion, a revulsion as intense as anything directed toward the murderer Claudius. But the Gertrude we see is not quite the Gertrude they see. And when we see her in herself, apart from their characterizations of her, we tend to see a woman more muddled than actively wicked; even her famous sensuality is less apparent than her conflicted solicitude both for her new husband and for her son.[8] She is capable from the beginning of a certain guilty insight into Hamlet's suffering ("I doubt it is no other but the main, / His father's death and our o'er-hasty marriage" [2.2.56–57]). Insofar as she follows Hamlet's instructions in reporting his madness to Claudius (3.4.189–90; 4.1.7), she seems to enact every son's scenario for the good mother, choosing his interests over her husband's. But she may of course believe that he is mad and think that she is reporting accurately to her husband; certainly her courageous defense of her husband in their next appearance together— where she bodily restrains Laertes, as 4.5.122 specifies—suggests that she has not wholly adopted Hamlet's view of Claudius. Here, as elsewhere, the text leaves crucial aspects of her action and motivation open.[9] Even her death is not quite her own to define. Is it a suicide designed to keep Hamlet from danger by dying in his place?[10] She knows that Claudius has prepared the cup for Hamlet, and she shows unusual determination in disobeying Claudius's command not to drink it ("Gertrude, do not drink. / I will, my lord" [5.2.294–95]). In her last moment, her thoughts seem to be all for Hamlet; she cannot spare Claudius even the attention it would take to blame him ("O my dear Hamlet! / The drink, the drink! I am poison'd" [5.2.315–16].) Muddled, fallible, fully human, she seems ultimately to make the choice that Hamlet would have her make. But even here she does not speak clearly; her character remains relatively closed to us.

The lack of clarity in our impressions of Gertrude contributes, I think, to the sense that the play lacks, in Eliot's famous phrase, an "objective correlative."[11] For the character of Gertrude as we see it becomes for Hamlet—and for *Hamlet*—the ground for fantasies quite incongruent with it; although she is much less purely innocent than Richard III's mother, like that mother she becomes the carrier of a nightmare that is disjunct from her characterization as a specific figure. This disjunction is, I think, the key to her role in the play and hence to her psychic power: her frailty unleashes for Hamlet, and for Shakespeare, fantasies of maternal malevolence, of maternal spoiling, that are compelling exactly as they are out of proportion to the character we know, exactly as they seem therefore to reiterate infantile fears and desires rather than an adult apprehension of the mother as a separate person.

These fantasies begin to emerge as soon as Hamlet is left alone on stage:

> O that this too too sullied flesh would melt,
> Thaw and resolve itself into a dew,
> Or that the Everlasting had not fix'd
> His canon 'gainst self-slaughter. O God! God!
> How weary, stale, flat, and unprofitable
> Seem to me all the uses of this world!
> Fie on't, ah fie, 'tis an unweeded garden
> That grows to seed; things rank and gross in nature
> Possess it merely. That it should come to this!
> But two months dead. . .
>
> (1.2.129–38)

This soliloquy establishes the initial premises of the play, the psychic conditions that are present even before Hamlet has met with the ghost and has been assigned the insupportable task of vengeance. And what Hamlet tells us in his first words to us is that he feels his own flesh as sullied and wishes to free himself from its contamination by death, that the world has become as stale and unusable to him as his own body, and that he figures all this deadness and staleness and contamination in the image of an unweeded garden gone to seed—figures it, that is, in the familiar language of the fall. And he further tells us that this fall has been caused not by his father's death, as both Claudius and Gertrude seem to assume in their conventional consolations, but by his mother's remarriage,[12] the "this" he cannot specify for fourteen lines, the "this" that looms over the soliloquy, not quite nameable and yet radically present, making his own flesh— "this . . . flesh"—dirty, disrupting his sense of the ongoing possibility of life even as it disrupts his syntax.

Hamlet's soliloquy is in effect his attempt to locate a point of origin for the staleness of the world and his own pull toward death, and he discovers this point of origin in his mother's body. He tells us that the world has been transformed into an unweeded garden, possessed by things rank and gross, because his mother has remarried. And if the enclosed garden—the garden unpossessed—traditionally figures the Virgin Mother, this garden, full of seed, figures his mother's newly contaminated body: its rank weeds localize what Hamlet will later call the "rank corruption" of her sexuality (3.4.150–51), the "weeds" that will grow "ranker" if that sexuality is not curbed (3.4.153–54).[13] In this highly compacted and psychologized version of the fall, death is the sexualized mother's legacy to her son: maternal sexuality turns the enclosed garden into the fallen world and brings death into that world by making flesh loathsome.[14] If Hamlet's father's death is the first sign of mortality, his mother's remarriage records the desire for death in his own sullied flesh. For in the world seen under the aegis of the unweeded garden, the very corporality of flesh marks its contamination: Hamlet persistently associates Claudius's fleshiness with his bloated sexuality—transforming the generalized "fatness of these pursy times" (3.4.155) into the image of the "bloat king" tempting his mother to bed (3.4.184)—as though in its grossness flesh was always rank, its solidity always sullied.[15]

The opening lines of the soliloquy point, I think, toward a radical confrontation with the sexualized maternal body as the initial premise of tragedy, the fall that brings death into the world: Hamlet in effect rewrites Richard III's sense that he has been spoiled in his mother's womb as the condition of mortality itself. The structure of *Hamlet*—and, I will argue, of the plays that follow from *Hamlet*—is marked by the struggle to escape from this condition, to free the masculine identity of both father and son from its origin in the contaminated maternal body. Hamlet's father's death is devastating to Hamlet—and to Shakespeare—partly, I think, because it returns Hamlet to this body, simultaneously unmaking the basis for the son's differentiation from the mother and the heroic foundation for masculine identity that Shake-

speare had achieved in the histories.[16] As in a dream, the plot-conjunction of father's funeral and mother's remarriage expresses this return:
it tells us that the idealized father's absence releases the threat of
maternal sexuality, in effect subjecting the son to her annihilating
power. But the dream-logic of this plot-conjunction is also reversible;
if the father's death leads to the mother's sexualized body, the mother's
sexualized body, I will argue, leads to the father's death. For the
conjunction of funeral and marriage simultaneously expresses two
sentences for the son: both "My idealized father's absence leaves me
subject to my mother's overwhelming power," and "The discovery of
my mother's sexuality kills my idealized father for me, making him
unavailable as the basis for my identity." This fantasy-conjunction thus
defines the double task of Hamlet and of Shakespeare in the plays to
come: if Hamlet attempts both to remake his mother as an enclosed
garden in 3.4 and to separate the father he idealizes from the rank
place of corruption, Shakespearean tragedy and romance will persistently work toward the de-sexualization of the maternal body and the
recreation of a bodiless father, untouched by her contamination.

A small psychological allegory at the beginning of the play—the
exchange between Horatio and Marcellus about the ghost's disappearance—suggests what is at stake in this double task. The first danger
in *Hamlet* is the father's "extravagant and erring spirit" (1.1.159)
wandering in the night, the father who is—Horatio tells us—"like a
guilty thing" (1.1.153).[17] As though in a kind of ghostly aubade, this
father vanishes at the sound of the cock, who "with his lofty and shrill-
sounding throat / Awake[s] the god of day" (1.1.156–57). At the
approach of the sun-god, the guilty father is banished; and Marcellus's
christianizing expansion of this conjunction explicates his banishment:

> It faded on the crowing of the cock.
> Some say that ever 'gainst that season comes
> Wherein our Saviour's birth is celebrated,
> This bird of dawning singeth all night long;
> And then, they say, no spirit dare stir abroad,
> The nights are wholesome, then no planets strike,
> No fairy takes, nor witch hath power to charm,
> So hallow'd and so gracious is that time.
>
> (1.1.162–69)

Through an incipient pun, Marcellus transforms the god of day into
the Son who makes the night wholesome because he is born from the
mother's de-sexualized body; and the dangers he protects against are
increasingly identified not only with the father's guilty spirit but with

the dark female powers of the night. The sequence here—from guilty thing, to sun-god, to the Son whose birth banishes the witch—follows the logic of a purifying fantasy: the female body of the night can be cleansed only as the guilty father gives way to the sun-god, allowing for the emergence of the purified Son.[18]

The exchange between Horatio and Marcellus predicts both Hamlet's confrontation with the night-dangers of the female body and the fantasy-solution to that confrontation: it establishes the Son born of a bodiless father and a purified mother as the only antidote to her power. And it specifically predicts Hamlet's need to remake his father as Hyperion, his attempt to find a safe basis for his own identity as son in the father he would remake pure. As though in response to this initial encounter with the impure father, the initial strategy of both Hamlet (in the soliloquy) and *Hamlet* is to split the father in two,[19] deflecting his guilt onto Claudius and reconstituting him in the form of the bodiless sun-god:

> That it should come to this!
> But two months dead—nay, not so much, not two—
> So excellent a king, that was to this
> Hyperion to a satyr.
>
> (1.2.137–40)

The identification of Old Hamlet with Hyperion makes him benignly and divinely distant, separate from ordinary genital sexuality and yet immensely potent, his sexual power analogous to God's power to impregnate the Virgin Mother (often imaged as Spirit descending on the sun's rays) and to such Renaissance mythologizings of this theme as the operation of the sun on Chrysogonee's moist body (*The Faerie Queene*, 3.6.7). Ordinary genital sexuality then becomes the province of Claudius the satyr: below the human, immersed in the body, he becomes everything Hyperion/Old Hamlet is not, and the agent of all ill.

This work of splitting is already implicit in Hamlet's initial image of his mother's body as fallen garden, for that image itself makes a physiologically impossible claim: if Claudius's rank and gross possession now transforms the garden that is the mother's body, then it must not before have been possessed. Insofar as the soliloquy expresses Hamlet's sense of his mother's body as an enclosed garden newly breached, it implies the presence of a formerly unbreached garden; the alternatives that govern Hamlet's imagination of his mother's body are the familiar ones of virgin and whore, closed or open, wholly pure or wholly corrupt. And the insistence that the garden has just been transformed functions to exonerate his father, separating him from his mother's sexualized body: it is the satyr Claudius, not the sun-god father, who has violated the maternal space. Literalized in the plot, the splitting of the father thus evokes the ordinary psychological crisis in which the son discovers the sexuality of his parents, but with the blame handily shifted from father onto another man as unlike father as possible—and yet as like, hence his brother; in effect, the plot itself serves as a cover-up, legitimizing disgust at paternal sexuality without implicating the idealized father. But thus arbitrarily separated, these fathers are always prone to collapse back into one another. The failure to differentiate between Old Hamlet and Claudius is not only Gertrude's: the play frequently insists on their likeness even while positing their absolute difference;[20] for the sexual guilt of the father—his implication in the mother's body—is its premise, its unacknowledged danger. Even Hamlet's attempt to imagine a protective father in the soliloquy returns him to this danger:

> So excellent a king, that was to this
> Hyperion to a satyr, so loving to my mother
> That he might not beteem the winds of heaven
> Visit her face too roughly. Heaven and earth,
> Must I remember? Why, she would hang on him
> As if increase of appetite had grown
> By what it fed on; and yet within a month—
> Let me not think on't . . .
>
> (1.2.139–46)

This image of parental love is so satisfying to Hamlet in part because it seems to enfold his mother safely within his father's protective embrace: by protecting her against the winds of heaven, he simultaneously protects against her, limiting and controlling her dangerous appetite. But as soon as that appetite has been invoked, it destabilizes the image of paternal control, returning Hamlet to the fact of his father's loss: for Gertrude's appetite is always inherently frightening, always potentially out of control; as the image of the unweeded garden itself implied, it has always required a weeder to manage its over-luxuriant growth.[21] The existence of Gertrude's appetite itself threatens the image of the father's godlike control; and in his absence, Gertrude's appetite rages, revealing what had been its potential for voraciousness all along. Having sated herself in a celestial bed, she now preys on garbage (1.5.55–57); and her indifferent voraciousness threatens to undo the gap between then and now, virgin and whore, Hyperion and satyr, on which Hamlet's defensive system depends. Despite the ghost's insistence on the difference, sating oneself in bed and preying on garbage sound suspiciously like the same activity: the imagery of devouring common to both tends to flatten out the distinction. "Could you on this fair mountain leave to feed / And batten on this moor?" Hamlet asks his mother (3.4.66–67), insisting again on a difference that seems largely without substance, inadvertently collapsing the distance between the idealized and the debased versions of Gertrude's appetite and hence between the brothers she feeds on. But in fact the strenuousness of the opposition between them has indicated their resemblance all along: what they have in common is an appetite for Gertrude's appetite; and her appetite can't tell the difference between them.

The ghost's revelation of Gertrude's adultery is horrifying not only because it reveals that she has not been faithful to him—her rapid remarriage has already done that—but also because it threatens to undo the structure of difference that Hamlet has had to maintain in order to keep his father and Claudius apart. For if Gertrude's appetite for the two men is the same, then Old Hamlet is as fully implicated in her sexuality as Claudius. Hence in part Hamlet's shock when he meets the father he has idealized so heavily: when Old Hamlet appears to his son, not in his mind's idealizing eye (1.2.185) but in the dubious form of the ghost, he reveals not only Claudius's but also his own "foul crimes done in [his] days of nature" (1.5.12). The fathers Hamlet tries so strenuously to keep separated keep threatening to collapse into one another; even when he wants to kill one to avenge the other, he cannot quite tell them apart. In 3.3, on his way to his mother's closet, he comes across Claudius praying, a ready-made opportunity for revenge. But knowing that his father has committed foul crimes, and seeing Claudius praying, Hamlet becomes so unsure that there is an essential difference between them that he worries that God might send the wrong man to heaven. Even as he describes Claudius's murder of his father to himself, he conflates it imagistically with his father's crimes: "A took my father grossly, full of bread, / With all his crimes broad blown, as flush as May" (3.3.80–81). Claudius's and Old Hamlet's crimes become equally broad-blown, as the two sinful fathers merge linguistically: the imagery of the rank garden, of over-luxuriant and swollen growth, has passed from Claudius to Old Hamlet, the "blossoms" of whose sin (1.5.76) are now broad-blown and flush. The highly charged word *grossly* registers this failure of differentiation: it hovers indeterminately between the two men, attaching itself first to Claudius (Claudius killed Old Hamlet grossly) and then to Old Hamlet (who died in a gross and unsanctified state); and in its indeterminacy, it associates both Claudius and Old Hamlet with the gross possession of Gertrude's unweeded garden.[22]

Ultimately Hyperion and the satyr refuse to stay separated, so that Hamlet—and *Hamlet*—have to do and redo the distinction over and over again. Whatever Hamlet's original intentions in approaching his mother in 3.4, his most immediate need after the crisis of differentiation in 3.3 is to force her to acknowledge the difference between the two fathers ("Hamlet, thou hast thy father much offended. / Mother, you have my father much offended" [3.4.8–9]). But even as he attempts to force this acknowledgment, he repeats the crisis of differentiation in yet another form. He presents her (and us) with two pictures initially indistinguishable and linguistically collapsed into one another: "Look here upon this picture, and on this, / The counterfeit presentment of two brothers" (3.4.53–54). As he begins the work of distinguishing between them all over again, the sense of counterfeit presentment becomes descriptive not only of the portraits as works of art but of his own portraiture, his own need both to present and to counterfeit these potentially similar false coins. Once again his father becomes a god, with "Hyperion's curls, the front of Jove himself, / An eye like Mars" (3.4.56–57); and Claudius becomes a "mildew'd ear / Blasting his wholesome brother" (3.4.64–65). But his words undermine the distinction he would reinstate: the most significantly contaminated ear in the play belongs to Old Hamlet.

Finally, the myth of his father as Hyperion cannot be sustained; and its collapse returns both father and son to the contaminated maternal body. No longer divinely inseminating, the sun-god becomes deeply implicated in matter in Hamlet's brutal parody of incarnation:

> Ham. If the sun breed maggots in a dead dog, being a good
> kissing carrion—Have you a daughter?
>
> Pol. I have, my lord.
>
> Ham. Let her not walk i' th' sun. Conception is a blessing, but as
> your daughter may conceive—friend, look to't.
>
> (2.2.181–86)[23]

Here is male spirit wholly enmeshed in female matter, kissing it, animating it with a vengeance; and—unlike the Son's—this conception is no blessing. If Marcellus's fantasy condenses father and son in a protective dyad, father and son here collapse into one another in their contamination: "Let her not walk i' th' sun," Hamlet warns Polonius; and his bitter pun locates the father-god's contamination in his own flesh. For this conception relocates the son in the dead matter of the unweeded garden: the horrific image of conception as the stirring of maggots in a corpse makes the son himself no more than one of the maggots, simultaneously born from and feeding on death in the maternal body.[24]

In the myth of origins bitterly acknowledged here, the son is wedded

to death by his conception, spoiled by his origin in the rank flesh of
the maternal body; and there is no idealized father to rescue him from
this body. This fantasy of spoiling at the site of origin is, I think, the
under-text of the play; it emerges first in muted form as Hamlet waits
for the appearance of his ghostly father and meditates on the dram of
evil that ruins the noble substance of man. When Hamlet hears the
drunken revel of Claudius's court, he first fixes blame on Claudius for
the sense of contamination he feels: "They clepe us drunkards, and
with swinish phrase / Soil our addition" (1.4.19–20). But as he continues, his bodily language rewrites the source of contamination, increasingly relocating it in the female body. "Indeed it takes / From our
achievements, though perform'd at height, / The pith and marrow of
our attribute" (1.4.20–22): through the imagery, the soiling of the
male body—its pith and marrow emptied out at the height of performance—is grotesquely equated with intercourse and its aftermath.[25]
And this shadowy image of the male body spoiled by the female in
intercourse predicts the rest of the speech, where the role of spoiler is
taken not by Claudius and his habits but by an unnamed and unspeci-
fied female body that corrupts man against his will:

> So, oft it chances in particular men
> That for some vicious mole of nature in them,
> As in their birth, wherein they are not guilty
> (Since nature cannot choose his origin),
>   . . . these men,
> Carrying, I say, the stamp of one defect,
> Being Nature's livery or Fortune's star,
> His virtues else, be they as pure as grace,
> As infinite as man may undergo,
> Shall in the general censure take corruption
> From that particular fault.
>   (1.4.23–36, *passim*)

As Hamlet imagines man struggling against his one defect—the mark
of his bondage to a feminized Nature or Fortune—the origin he cannot
choose increasingly becomes not only the site but the agent of corruption. Even as Hamlet unorthodoxly proclaims man not guilty in his
birth, that is, he articulates his own version of original sin: here, as in
Richard III's fantasy of himself deformed by Nature in his mother's
womb (*3 Henry VI*, 3.2.153–64), man is spoiled in his birth by birth
defects not of his own making, and he takes corruption from that
particular fault.

    Fall/fault/foutre: the complex bilingual pun registers the fantasy that
moves under the surface of Hamlet's meditation. For *fault* allusively

collapses the female genitals with the act of intercourse that engendered the baby there, and then collapses both with the fall and original sin:[26] through its punning formulations, original sin becomes literally the sin of origin.[27] "Virtue cannot so inoculate our old stock but we shall relish of it" (3.1.117–18): formed and deformed in his mother's womb, man takes his corruption from that particular fault. Hamlet is indeed "to the manner born" (1.4.15), as he says at the start of his meditation: "It were better my mother had not borne me," he tells Ophelia (3.1.123–24); but he is "subject to his birth" (1.3.18).[28]

This subjection of male to female is, I think, the buried fantasy of *Hamlet*, the submerged story that it partly conceals and partly reveals; in its shift of contaminating agency from Claudius to the female body as the site of origin, Hamlet's meditation seems to me to be diagnostic of this fantasy. The poisoning of Old Hamlet is ostentatiously modeled on Cain's killing of Abel; Claudius cannot allude to his offense without recalling "the primal eldest curse upon't" (3.3.37). But this version of Cain and Abel turns out in part to be a cover for the even more primal story implicit in the unweeded garden, the prior explanation for the entrance of death into the world: the murder here turns not on the winning of a father's favor but on the body of a woman; and Old Hamlet is poisoned in his orchard-garden (1.5.35; 3.2.255) by the "serpent" who wears his crown (1.5.39).[29] On the surface of the text, that is, the story of Adam and Eve has been displaced, the horrific female body at its center occluded: Eve is conspicuously absent from the Cain-and-Abel version of the fall. But if the plot rewrites the fall as a story of fratricidal rivalry, locating literal agency for the murder in Claudius, a whole network of images and associations replaces his literal agency with Gertrude's, replicating Eve in her by making her both the agent and the locus of death. Beneath the story of fratricidal rivalry is the story of the woman who conduces to death, of the father fallen not through his brother's treachery but through his subjection to this woman; and despite Gertrude's conspicuous absence from the scene in the garden, in this psychologized version of the fall, the vulnerability of the father—and hence of the son—to her poison turns out to be the whole story.[30]

In an astonishing transfer of agency from male to female, malevolent power and blame for the murder tend to pass from Claudius to Gertrude in the deep fantasy of the play.[31] We can see the beginnings of this shift of blame even in the Ghost's initial account of the murder, in which the emotional weight shifts rapidly from his excoriation of Claudius to his much more powerful condemnation of Gertrude's sexuality. And in "The Murder of Gonzago," Hamlet's version of his father's tale, the murderer's role is clearly given less emphasis than the

Queen's: Lucianus gets a scant six lines, while her protestations of undying love motivate all the preceding dialogue of the playlet. Moreover, while the actual murderer remains a pasteboard villain, the Queen's protestations locate psychic blame for the murder squarely in her. "None wed the second but who kill'd the first," she tells us (3.2.175). In her formulation, remarriage itself is a form of murder: "A second time I kill my husband dead, / When second husband kisses me in bed" (3.2.179–80). We know that Hamlet has added some dozen or sixteen lines to the play (2.2.535), and though we cannot specify them, these protestations seem written suspiciously from the point of view of the child, whose mother's remarriage often seems like her murder of the image of his father. When Hamlet confronts his mother in her closet immediately after his playlet, he confirms that he at least has shifted agency from Claudius to her: his own killing of Polonius is, he says, "A bloody deed. Almost as bad, good Mother, / As kill a king and marry with his brother" (3.4.28–29). Given the parallel with his killing of Polonius, "as kill a king" first seems to describe Claudius's act; but when the line ends with "brother" rather than "queen" or "wife," the killing attaches itself irrevocably to Gertrude, playing out in miniature the shift of agency from him to her. For Claudius's crime is nearly absent here: in Hamlet's accusation, Claudius becomes the passive victim of Gertrude's sexual will; she becomes the active murderer.

And the play itself is complicit with Hamlet's shift of agency: though the degree of her literal guilt is never specified, in the deep fantasy of the play her sexuality itself becomes akin to murder. The second of the Player Queen's protestations—"A second time I kill my husband dead / When second husband kisses me in bed"—implicitly collapses the two husbands into one and thus makes the equation neatly: when her husband kisses her, she kills him. But this is in fact what one strain in the imagery has been telling us all along. As Lucianus carries the poison onstage in "The Murder of Gonzago," he addresses it in terms that associate it unmistakably with the weeds of that first unweeded garden:

> Thou mixture rank, of midnight weeds collected,
> With Hecate's ban thrice blasted, thrice infected,
> Thy natural magic and dire property
> On wholesome life usurps immediately.
> (3.2.251–54)

Even as we see him poison the Player-King, the language insists that the poison is not his but hers, its usurpation on wholesome life derivative not from Claudius's political ambitions but from the rank weeds

(3.4.153–54) of Gertrude's body. Its "mixture rank" merely condenses and localizes the rank mixture that is sexuality itself:[32] hence the subterranean logic by which the effects of Claudius's poison on Old Hamlet's body replicate the effects of venereal disease, covering his smooth body with the lazarlike tetter, the "vile and loathsome crust" (1.5.71–72) that was one of the diagnostic signs of syphilis.[33]

In Lucianus's words, the poison that kills Old Hamlet becomes less the distillation of a usurping fratricidal rivalry than the distillation of the horrific female body, the night-witch against whom Marcellus had invoked the protection of the Saviour born from a virgin birth; cursed by Hecate, it is in effect the distillation of midnight itself, the "witching time" when "hell itself breathes out / Contagion to this world" (3.2.379–81). The play here invokes the presence of an unbounded nightmare night-body, breathing out the contagion of her poison; and it gives shape to this horrific night-body through a curious and punning repetition. Horatio tells Hamlet that the ghost first appeared "in the dead waste and middle of the night" (1.2.198); and Hamlet repeats his phrase when he questions Rosencranz and Guildenstern about their relations with the lady Fortune:

> *Ham.* Then you live about her waist, or in the middle of her favours?
> *Guild.* Faith, her privates we.
> *Ham.* In the secret parts of Fortune? O, most true! She is a strumpet.
>
> (2.2.232–36)

"Waste" and "waist" coalesce in the dangerous middle of this strumpet;[34] and the idealized father turns out to be horribly vulnerable to the poison of her rank midnight weeds. For however mild-mannered Gertrude may be as a literal character, in fantasy she takes on the aspect of this night-body, herself becoming the embodiment of hell and death: the fires in which Hamlet's father is confined, the fires that burn and purge the foul crimes done in his days of nature (1.5.11–13), merely reproduce the fire of the "rebellious hell" that burns in her bones (3.4.82–88).[35] In anticipation of Lear's anatomy—"there's hell, there's darkness, / There is the sulphurous pit" (*King Lear*, 4.6.129–30)—punishment and crime coalesce: death is not only the consequence of sexuality but also its very condition.

This anatomy is in its own way perfectly orthodox; it condenses the story of the fall by making female sexuality itself the locus of death:

> Surely her house tendeth to death, & her paths unto the dead. All thei that go unto her, returne not againe, nether take they holde of the waies of life.

> For she hathe caused manie to fall downe wounded, and the strong
> men are all slayne by her. Her house is the waie unto the grave, which
> goeth downe to the chambers of death. (*The Geneva Bible*, Proverbs,
> 2:18–19, 7:26–27)

Every encounter with the "strange woman" of Proverbs—and all
women are sexually strangers—is thus a virtual reliving of the fall into
mortality. But female sexuality in *Hamlet* is always maternal sexuality:
Gertrude's is the only fully sexualized female body in the play, and we
experience her sexuality largely through the imagination of her son. In
Hamlet, that is, Shakespeare re-understands the orthodox associations
of woman with death by fusing the sexual with the maternal body, re-
imagining the legacy of death consequent upon the fall as the legacy
specifically of the sexualized maternal body. And except in the saving
case of the Virgin Mother, the maternal body is always already sexual,
corrupted by definition. The mother's body brings death into the world
because her body itself is death: in the traditional alignment of spirit
and matter, the mother gives us the stuff—the female matter—of our
bodies and thus our mortality.[36] Birth itself thus immerses the body in
death: hence the power of Hamlet's grotesque version of conception
as the stirring of maggots in dead matter. Through this fusion of the
sexual with the maternal body and the association of both with death,
Shakespeare in effect defamiliarizes the trope of the "womb of earth"
(1.1.140): death and sexuality are interchangeable in this psychologized version of the fall because both lead back to this maternal body.
Hence also Shakespeare's punning equation of death and the maternal
body in his reformulation of the Biblical source of danger: in the deep
fantasy of the play, the deadly woman of *Proverbs*—"thei that go unto
her, returne not againe"—is one with Hamlet's "undiscover'd country,
from whose bourn / No traveller returns" (3.1.79–80).[37]

Both death and sexuality return the traveler to the undiscovered
country, familiar and yet utterly foreign, of the maternal body itself;
and in *Hamlet*, this body is always threatening to swallow up her
children, to absorb them back within her bourn, undoing their own
boundaries. Death itself is a hell-mouth, swallowing Old Hamlet up
between its "ponderous and marble jaws" (1.4.50), bringing him and
Polonius "not where he eats, but where a is eaten" (4.3.19), where all
are subject to "my Lady Worm" (5.1.87); and Gertrude is death's
mouth, indiscriminately devouring her husbands "as if increase of
appetite had grown / By what it fed on" (1.2.144–45). In this grotesquely oral world, everything is ultimately meat for a single table.
Hence I think the slight *frisson* of horror beneath Hamlet's wit as he
describes "the funeral bak'd meats" that "Did coldly furnish forth the

marriage tables" (1.2.180–81): we are never sure just what it is that is being consumed in the ceremonies of death and sexual union imagined here. And this momentary confusion is diagnostic of the play's fusion of eating and death and sex: in *Hamlet*, the turn toward the woman's body is always felt as the return to the devouring maternal womb, with all the potential not only for incestuous nightmare but for total annihilation implied by that return.

Hence, I think, the logic of the play's alternative name for poison: "union" (5.2.269, 331).[38] For "union" is just another version of Hecate's "mixture rank," the poison that kills Old Hamlet: each is the poisonous epitome of sexual mixture itself and hence of boundary danger, the terrifying adulteration of male by female that does away with the boundaries between them.

> *Ham.* Farewell, dear mother.
>
> *Claud.* Thy loving father, Hamlet.
>
> *Ham.* My mother. Father and mother is man and wife, man and wife is one flesh; so my mother.
>
> (4.3.52–55)

In this fantasy, it does not matter whether Hamlet is thinking of his father or of his incestuous stand-in; all sexuality—licit or illicit—is imagined as an adulterating mixture. And in this rank mixture, the female will always succeed in transforming the male, remaking him in her image, "for the power of beauty will sooner transform honesty from what it is to a bawd than the force of honesty can translate beauty into his likeness" (3.1.111–14). The imagined concourse of male honesty and female beauty ends in the contamination of the male by the female, his translation into a version of her. No wonder Marcellus associates the danger of invasion with the sweaty activity that makes "the night joint-labourer with the day" (1.1.81), obliterating the distinction between the realm of the witch-mother and that of the sun-god father; no wonder Hamlet is so intent upon keeping his father's commandment—or perhaps his father himself—all alone within his brain, "unmix'd with baser matter" (1.5.104).[39]

For Hamlet is ultimately subject to the same adulterating mixture; the sexual anxiety registered through the play's two names for poison, like the incestuous marriage at its center, both covers and expresses a more primitive anxiety about the stability and security of individuating boundaries that finds its focus in Hamlet himself. Promiscuous mixture and boundary contamination everywhere infect this play, from its initial worry about invasion to its final heap of poisoned bodies: in a psychic world where boundaries cannot hold, where the self is invaded, its pales and forts broken down, its pith and marrow extracted, where mother-aunts and uncle-fathers (2.2.372) become indistinguishably one flesh, where even camels become weasels become whales (3.2.367–73), identity itself seems on the point of dissolving or being swallowed up. And the overwhelming use of images of oral contamination and oral annihilation to register these threats to the self suggests their origin in the earliest stages of emergent selfhood, when the nascent self is most fully subject to the mother's fantasied power to annihilate or contaminate. Hence, I think, the centrality of Gertrude: for the play localizes its pervasive boundary panic in Hamlet's relationship with his mother, whose contaminated body initially serves him as the metaphor for the fallen world that has sullied him. And the selfhood that Hamlet constructs in response to this threat becomes the crux of the play: withdrawing himself from the sullying maternal body of the world, Hamlet retreats into what he imagines as an inviolable core of selfhood that cannot be known or played upon (1.2.85; 3.2.355–63), constructing an absolute barrier between inner and outer as though there were no possibility of uncontaminating communication between them; unable to risk crossing this boundary in any creative way, through any significant action in the world, he fantasizes crossing it through magical thinking—imagining the revenge that could come "with wings as swift / As meditation" (1.5.29–30) or through the power of his horrid speech (2.2.557)—or he mimes crossing it from within the extraordinary distance of his withdrawal, taking up a variety of roles not to engage the world but to keep it at bay.[40] Hence in part his intense admiration for Horatio, who plays no roles and seems impervious to outer influence, who is "not a pipe for Fortune's finger / To sound what stop she please" (3.2.70–71);[41] here as elsewhere, Hamlet figures the threat to (masculine) inner integrity as the sexualized female, aligning it with the strumpet Fortune in whose secret parts corrupt men live (2.2.232–36), as though all such threats were derivative from his unreliable mother's body. But there is no exemption from this body for Hamlet, no pure and unmixed identity for him; like honesty transformed into a bawd, he must eventually see the signs of her rank mixture in himself:

> Why, what an ass am I! This is most brave,
> That I, the son of a dear father murder'd,
> Prompted to my revenge by heaven and hell,
> Must like a whore unpack my heart with words
> And fall a-cursing like a very drab,
> A scullion!
>
> (2.2.578–83)

He himself is subject to his birth: he would imagine himself the unmixed son of an unmixed father, but the whore-mother in him betrays him, returning him to his own mixed origin, his contamination by the sexual female within.[42]

The first mother to reappear in Shakespeare's plays is adulterous, I think, because maternal origin is in itself felt as equivalent to adulterating betrayal of the male, both father and son; *Hamlet* initiates the period of Shakespeare's greatest tragedies because it in effect rewrites the story of Cain and Abel as the story of Adam and Eve, relocating masculine identity in the presence of the adulterating female. This rewriting accounts, I think, for Gertrude's odd position in the play, especially for its failure to specify the degree to which she is complicit in the murder. Less powerful as an independent character than as the site for fantasies larger than she is, she is preeminently mother as other, the intimate unknown figure around whom these fantasies swirl. She is kept ambiguously innocent as a character, but in the deep fantasy that structures the play's imagery, she plays out the role of the missing Eve: her body is the garden in which her husband dies, her sexuality the poisonous weeds that kill him, and poison the world—and the self—for her son. This is the psychological fantasy registered by the simultaneity of funeral and marriage: the reappearance of the mother in *Hamlet* is tantamount to the death of the idealized father because her presence signals his absence, and hence the absence of the son's defense against her rank mixture, her capacity to annihilate or contaminate; as in Marcellus's purifying fantasy, what the idealized father ultimately protects against is the dangerous female powers of the night. The boy-child masters his fear of these powers partly through identification with his father, the paternal presence who has initially helped him to achieve separation from his mother; but if his father fails him—if the father himself seems subject to her—then that protective identification fails. This is exactly the psychological situation at the beginning of *Hamlet*, where Hamlet's father has become unavailable to him, not only through the fact of his death but through the complex vulnerability that his death demonstrates. This father cannot protect his son; and his disappearance in effect throws Hamlet into the domain of the engulfing mother, awakening all the fears incident to the primary mother-child bond. Here as in Shakespeare's later plays, the loss of the father turns out in fact to mean the psychic domination of the mother: in the end, it is the specter of his mother, not his uncle-father, who paralyzes his will. The Queen, the Queen's to blame.

This shift of agency and of danger from male to female seems to me characteristic of the fantasy-structure of *Hamlet* and of Shakespeare's imagination in the plays that follow. The ghost's initial injunction sets as the prime business of the play the killing of Claudius; he specifically asks Hamlet to leave his mother alone, beset only by the thorns of conscience (1.5.85–87). But if Gertrude rather than Claudius is to blame, then Hamlet's fundamental task shifts; simple revenge is no longer the issue. Despite his ostensible agenda of revenge, the main psychological task that Hamlet seems to set himself is not to avenge his father's death but to remake his mother:[43] to remake her in the image of the Virgin Mother who could guarantee his father's purity, and his own, repairing the boundaries of his selfhood. Throughout the play, the covert drama of reformation vies for priority with the overt drama of revenge, in fact displacing it both from what we see of Hamlet's consciousness and from center stage of the play: when Hamlet accuses himself of lack of purpose (3.4.107–10), of failing to remember his father's business of revenge (4.4.40), he may in part be right. Even as an avenger, Hamlet seems motivated more by his mother than by his father: when he describes Claudius to Horatio as "he that hath kill'd my king and whor'd my mother" (5.2.64), the second phrase clearly carries more intimate emotional weight than the first. And he manages to achieve his revenge only when he can avenge his mother's death, not his father's: just where we might expect some version of "rest, perturbed spirit" to link his killing of Claudius with his father's initial injunction, we get "Is thy union here? / Follow my mother" (5.2.331–32).

This shift—from avenging the father to saving the mother— accounts in part for certain peculiarities about this play as a revenge play: why, for example, the murderer is given so little attention in the device ostensibly designed to catch his conscience, why the confrontation of Hamlet with Gertrude in the closet scene seems much more central, much more vivid, than any confrontation between Hamlet and Claudius. Once we look at "The Murder of Gonzago" for what it is, rather than for what Hamlet tells us it is, it becomes clear that the playlet is in fact designed to catch the conscience of the queen: its challenge is always to her loving posture, its accusation "A second time I kill my husband dead / When second husband kisses me in bed." The confrontation with Gertrude (3.4) follows so naturally from this attempt to catch her conscience that Hamlet's unexpected meeting with Claudius (3.3) feels to us like an interruption of a more fundamental purpose. Indeed, Shakespeare stages 3.3 very much as an interruption: Hamlet comes upon Claudius praying as he is on his way to his mother's closet, worrying about the extent to which he can repudiate the Nero in himself; and we come upon Claudius unexpectedly in the same way.

That is: the moment that should be the apex of the revenge plot—the potential confrontation alone of the avenger and his prey—becomes for the audience and for the avenger himself a lapse, an interlude that must be gotten over before the real business can be attended to.[44] It is no wonder that Hamlet cannot kill Claudius here: to do so would be to make of the interlude a permanent interruption of his more fundamental purpose. Not even Hamlet could reasonably expect to manage his mother's moral reclamation immediately after he has killed her husband.

Nor would that avenging death regain the mother whom Hamlet needs: once his mother has been revealed as the fallen and possessed garden, she can be purified only by being separated from her sexuality. This separation is in fact Hamlet's effort throughout 3.4. In that confrontation, Hamlet first insists that Gertrude acknowledge the difference between Claudius and Old Hamlet, the difference her adultery and remarriage had undermined. But after the initial display of portraits, Hamlet attempts to induce in her revulsion not at her choice of the wrong man but at her sexuality itself, the rebellious hell that mutines in her matron's bones (3.4.82–83), the "rank corruption, mining all within" (3.4.150). Here, as in the play within the play, Hamlet recreates obsessively, voyeuristically, the acts that have corrupted the royal bed, even when he has to subject his logic and syntax to considerable strain to do so:

> Queen   What shall I do?
>
> Ham.   Not this, by no means, that I bid you do:
> Let the bloat King tempt you again to bed,
> Pinch wanton on your cheek, call you his mouse,
> And let him, for a pair of reechy kisses,
> Or paddling in your neck with his damn'd fingers,
> Make you to ravel all this matter out
> That I essentially am not in madness,
> But mad in craft.
>   (3.4.182–90)

There has to be an easier way of asking your mother not to reveal that your madness is an act. "Not this, by no means, that I bid you do": Hamlet cannot stop imagining, even commanding, the sexual act that he wants to undo. Moreover, the bloated body of this particular king is not particular to him: it is the sexualized male body, its act any sexual act. The royal bed of Denmark is always already corrupted, already a couch for luxury, as Hamlet's own presence testifies. "Go not to my uncle's bed" (3.4.161), Hamlet tells his mother; but his disgust at the incestuous liaison rationalizes a prior disgust at all sexual concourse, as his attempt to end the specifically incestuous union rationalizes an attempt to remake his mother pure by divorcing her from her sexuality.

Act 3 scene 4 records Hamlet's attempt to achieve this divorce, to recover the fantasied presence of the asexual mother of childhood, the mother who can restore the sense of sanctity to the world her sexuality has spoiled: his first and last word in the scene is "mother" (3.4.7; 3.4.219). And in his own mind at least, Hamlet does seem to achieve this recovery. He begins the scene by wishing that Gertrude were not his mother ("would it were not so, you are my mother" [3.4.15]); but toward the end, he is able to imagine her as the mother from whom he would beg—and receive—blessing:

> Once more, good night,
> And when you are desirous to be blest,
> I'll blessing beg of you.
> (3.4.172–74)

This mother can bless Hamlet only insofar as she herself asks to be blessed by him, signaling her conversion from husband to son and inverting the relation of parent and child; Hamlet is very much in charge even as he imagines asking for maternal blessing. Nonetheless, coming near the end of Hamlet's long scene of rage and disgust, these lines seem to me extraordinarily moving in their evocation of desire for the maternal presence that can restore the sense of the world and the self as blessed.[45] And the blessedness they image is specifically in the relation of world and self: as mother and son mirror each other, each blessing each, Shakespeare images the reopening of the zone of trust that had been foreclosed by the annihilating mother. For the first time, Hamlet imagines something coming to him from outside himself that will neither invade nor contaminate him: the recovery of benign maternal presence for a moment repairs the damage of the fall in him, making safe the boundary-permeability that had been a source of terror. Toward the end of the scene, all those night-terrors are gone: Hamlet's repeated variations on the conventional phrase "good night" mark his progression from rage at his mother's sexuality to repossession of the good mother he had lost. He begins with "Good night. But go not to my uncle's bed. . . . Refrain tonight" (3.4.161, 167), attempting to separate her from her horrific night-body; but by the end—through his own version of Marcellus's purifying fantasy—he has succeeded in imagining both her and the night wholesome. If he begins by wishing Gertrude were not his mother, he ends with the poignant repeated leave-taking of a child who does not want to let go of the mother who now keeps him safe: "Once more, good night . . . So again, good night. . . . Mother, good night indeed. . . . Good night, mother" (3.4.172, 179, 215, 219).

In the end, we do not know whether or not Gertrude herself has been morally reclaimed; it is the mark of the play's investment in Hamlet's fantasies that, even here, we are not allowed to see her as a separate person. To the extent that she looks into the heart that Hamlet has "cleft in twain" (3.4.158) and finds the "black and grained spots" (3.4.90) that he sees there, she seems to accept his version of her soiled inner body; in any case, her response allows him to think of his initial Nero-like aggression—speaking daggers though using none (3.2.387)—as moral reclamation. But as usual in this play, she remains relatively opaque, more a screen for Hamlet's fantasies about her than a fully developed character in her own right: whatever individuality she might have had is sacrificed to her status as mother. Nonetheless, though we might wonder just what his evidence is, Hamlet at least believes that she has returned to him as the mother he can call "good lady" (3.4.182). And after 3.4, her remaining actions are ambiguous enough to nourish his fantasy: though there are no obvious signs of separation from Claudius in her exchanges with him, in her last moments she seems to become a wonderfully homey presence for her son, newly available to him as the loving and protective mother of childhood, worrying about his condition, wiping his face as he fights, even perhaps intentionally drinking the poison intended for him.

In the end, whatever her motivation, he seems securely possessed of her as an internal good mother; and this possession gives him a new calm about his place in the world and especially about death, that domain of maternal dread. Trusting her, he can begin to trust in himself and in his own capacity for action; and he can begin to rebuild the masculine identity spoiled by her contamination. For his secure internal possession of her idealized image permits the return of his father to him, and in the form that he had always wanted: turning his mother away from Claudius, Hamlet wins her not only for himself but also for his father—for his father conceived as Hyperion, the bodiless godlike figure he had invoked at the beginning of the play. If her sexuality had spoiled this father, her purification brings him back; after 3.4, the guilty father and his ghost disappear, replaced by the distant heavenly father into whom he has been transformed, the one now acting through the sign of the other: "Why, even in that was heaven ordinant. / I had my father's signet in my purse" (5.2.48–49). Unexpectedly finding this sign of the father on his own person, Hamlet in effect registers his repossession of the idealized father within; and, like a good son, Hamlet can finally merge himself with this father, making His will his own. But though we may feel that Hamlet has achieved a new calm and self-possession, the price is high: for the parents lost to him at the beginning of the play can be restored only insofar as they are entirely separated from their sexual bodies. This is a pyrrhic solution to the problems of embodiedness and familial identity; it does not bode well for Shakespeare's representation of sexual union, or of the children born of that union.

In creating for Hamlet a plot in which his mother's sexuality is literally the sign of her betrayal and of her husband's death, Shakespeare recapitulates the material of infantile fantasy, playing it out with a compelling plot logic that allows its expression in a perfectly rationalized, hence justified, way. Given Hamlet's world, anyone would feel as Hamlet does—but Shakespeare has given him this world.[46] And the world Shakespeare gives him sets the stage for the plays that follow:[47] from *Hamlet* on, all sexual relationships will be tinged by the threat of the mother, all masculine identity problematically formed in relationship to her. For despite Hamlet's tenuous recovery of his father's signet ring through the workings of Providence, the stabilizing father lost at the beginning of *Hamlet*—the father who can control female appetite, who can secure pure masculine identity for his son—cannot be brought back from the dead; the ambiguities that attend the bodiless father-Duke of *Measure for Measure* merely serve to make paternal absence visible, underscoring at once the need for his control over the sexuality that boils and bubbles like a witch's cauldron in Vienna and the desperate fictitiousness of that control. The plays that follow *Hamlet* enact and re-enact paternal absence in shadowy and fragmentary form—in the sick king of *All's Well*, in Lear's abdication, in the murder of Duncan, the fatherlessness of Coriolanus, the weakness of Cymbeline; and they thrust the son into the domain of maternal dread inhabited by all the avatars of strumpet fortune—the wicked wives, lovers, daughters, mothers and stepmothers, the witches and engulfing storms—that have the power to shake his manhood (*King Lear*, 1.4.306).

The central elements of the fantasy of maternal power in *Hamlet* will recur in a variety of forms, with first one and then another becoming most prominent; they will sometimes be the psychic property of a single character from whom Shakespeare distances himself, and sometimes find embodiment in the play as a whole in ways that suggest Shakespeare's complicity in them. Despite Shakespeare's sometimes astonishing moments of sympathetic engagement with his female characters, his ability to see the world from their point of view, his women will tend to be like Gertrude, more significant as screens for male fantasy than as independent characters making their own claim to dramatic reality; as they become fused with the mother of infantile need, even their fantasized gestures of independence will be read as the signs of adulterous betrayal. And the women will pay heavily for the fantasies—both of destruction and of cure—invested in them. For their sexual bodies will always be dangerous, the sign of the fall and original sin, the "disease that's in my flesh" (*King Lear*, 2.4.224), "the imposition . . . / Hereditary ours" (*The Winter's Tale*, 1.2.74–75): as they enter into sexuality, the virgins—Cressida, Desdemona, Imogen—will be transformed into whores, their whoredom acted out in the imaginations of their nearest and dearest; and the primary antidote to their power will be the excision of their sexual bodies, the terrible revirginations that Othello performs on Desdemona, and Shakespeare on Cordelia. For the emergence of the annihilating mother in *Hamlet* will call forth a series of strategies for confining or converting her power. Hamlet's desire for the return of the virgin mother who can bless him, undoing the effects of the fall, will be played out in Cordelia's return to Lear, Thaisa's return to Pericles, Hermione's return to Leontes, each of whom must first suffer for her participation in sexuality. And in the absence of these purified figures, parthenogenetic fantasies of exemption from the "woman's part" (*Cymbeline*, 2.4.174) will seem to offer protection against maternal malevolence. Enunciating his desire to "stand / As if a man were author of himself / And knew no other kin" (*Coriolanus*, 5.3.35–37), Coriolanus speaks for all those who would not be born of woman (*Macbeth*, 4.1.80), undoing the subjection to birth that Hamlet discovered in himself. But the problematic maternal body can never quite be occluded or transformed: made into a monster or a saint, killed off or banished from the stage, it remains at the center of masculine subjectivity, marking its unstable origin. For the contaminated flesh of the maternal body is also home: the home Shakespeare's protagonists long to return to, the home they can never quite escape.

In the chapters that follow, I will trace the consequences of this body's reappearance in *Hamlet*, both for the construction of male identity and for the representation of women. The plays central to the next two chapters—*Troilus and Cressida* and *Othello*, and *All's Well That Ends Well* and *Measure for Measure*—focus on the dangerous return home to the maternal body through the representation of sexual union, as though explicating Hamlet's failed relationship with Ophelia: *Troilus* and *Othello* play out the deeply ambivalent desire for erotic return to that body and the recoil from desire; *All's Well* and *Measure* play out the extraordinary contortions and contrivances through which the return might provisionally be made safe. In the plays central to the following two chapters—*King Lear*, and *Macbeth* and *Coriolanus*—Shakespeare shifts ground, recasting in them the primary relationship of Hamlet to his mother: *Lear* records the horrific discovery of the suffocating mother at the center of masculine authority and the terrible vengeance taken on her; *Macbeth* and *Coriolanus* record the attempt to create an autonomous masculinity in the face of this discovery. In the plays central to the next chapter—*Timon of Athens* and *Antony and Cleopatra*—Shakespeare exposes this masculinity in its most naked form and then attempts to move beyond it, reimagining both sexual union and masculine identity in a new relation to the maternal as it is invested in Cleopatra; and the final alliance of his own creativity with hers opens the way toward the romances. But even the romances—the subject of the final chapter—bear the signs of Shakespeare's continuing ambivalence toward the maternal body: if the sanctified mother who can bless is recovered in Thaisa and Hermione, the witch-mother reemerges in Cymbeline's Queen and in Sycorax; and as though in answer to the beginning of *Hamlet*, paternal authority can be recovered only in her absence, in the shrunken realm Prospero founds on her banishment.

3

"Is Thy Union Here?":
Union and Its Discontents in
Troilus and Cressida and *Othello*

As Hamlet forces Claudius to drink from the cup that has been poisoned by his "union" (5.2.269), he punningly makes Claudius's death the consequence of the poisonous sexual union that has haunted the play: "Is thy union here? / Follow my mother" (5.2.331–32). In Hamlet's pun, the poison in the cup figures the danger of union itself, deadly in *Hamlet* because it is always imagined as a return to the maternal body, as "follow[ing] my mother"; imagined thus, consummation will always threaten to annihilate the boundaries of masculine selfhood. But the union so dreaded is also intensely desired; and if *Hamlet* plays out the dread, *Troilus and Cressida* and *Othello* play out the desire. Both Troilus and Othello derive the language of their desire from Hamlet's initial response to his mother's body, rewriting his wish to lose his bodily boundaries in death—to melt, thaw, and resolve himself into a dew (1.2.129–30)—as the lover's wish for fusion with the beloved;[1] and both eventually recoil from that desire as though it were death indeed. Early in his career, Shakespeare had figured the dangers of erotic return to the maternal body through Venus, who tells the infantilized Adonis, "Here come and sit, where never serpent hisses / And being set, I'll smother thee with kisses" (11. 17–8); and as though responding to Venus's buried pun, both Troilus and Othello break away from the suffocating matrix, each in his own way recovering his manhood by taking a terrible vengeance on the woman in whom it is represented.

The dangerous desire for union that informs these two plays is curiously adumbrated in "The Phoenix and the Turtle," probably written around the time of *Hamlet* and *Troilus and Cressida* and published in 1601. Here Shakespeare gives us his most unambiguous expression of desire for a union so powerful that it annihilates boundaries, transforming identity itself:

> So they loved as love in twain
> Had the essence but in one;
> Two distincts, division none:
> Number there in love was slain.
>
> Hearts remote, yet not asunder;
> Distance, and no space was seen
> 'Twixt this turtle and his queen . . .
>
> Property was thus appalled,
> That the self was not the same;
> Single nature's double name
> Neither two nor one was called.
>
> Reason, in itself confounded,
> Saw division grow together,
> To themselves yet either neither,
> Simple were so well compounded;
>
> That it cried, "How true a twain
> Seemeth this concordant one!
> Love hath reason, reason none,
> If what parts can so remain."
> (ll. 25–48, *passim*)

In its refiguring of the horrific "one flesh" of *Hamlet*, the poem retrospectively recreates—by recording the demise of—an impossible dual unity in which identities are simultaneously merged and preserved, memorializing a perfect fusion that confounds ordinary distinctions of distance ("Distance, and no space was seen / 'Twixt the turtle and his queen") and identity ("Property was thus appalled, / That the self was not the same"). This is the stuff of lovers' paradoxes—the "we two being one" by which Donne easily explicates the "Phoenix riddle" in "The Canonization" (ll. 23–24); and yet the celebratory language here is extraordinarily abstract, forbidding us to imagine any ordinary union. In fact this perfect union seems to depend on the language of abstraction insofar as that language promises an escape from the realm of the body altogether; for this union is imagined not only in its own demise but also specifically in the absence of the fleshly consummation that the paradox usually serves to glorify. Unlike Donne's sexualized "tapers," who "at our own cost die" ("The Canonization", l. 21), the "mutual flame" here is specifically nonsexual; these two are fled

Leaving no posterity:
  'Twas not their infirmity,
  It was married chastity.

These lovers do not "die and rise the same" as Donne's do ("The
Canonization, l. 26); although Shakespeare reassures us about their
sexual adequacy—" 'Twas not their infirmity"—he makes their child-
lessness the sign not only of their self-containment but also of their
ideal chastity, hence of their status as ideally two and one. Given its
central position in the threnos, their married chastity comes to seem
not an aberration but the necessary condition of their perfect union.

In celebrating the union the loss of which it laments, the poem
reconstructs the conditions under which this union—or, it turns out,
any idealized union—can be maintained. In Shakespeare's rewriting of
the lovers' paradox, that is, the fusion of identities that had been so
threatening in *Hamlet* is recuperated by excluding the sexual answer
to the "phoenix riddle."[2] So much is in fact promised by the title,
with its odd miscegenation of dove and phoenix, the one traditionally
coupled and associated with love, the other unique and hence associated with a form of self-reproduction that by definition excludes cou-
pling.[3] Even as Shakespeare assembles the funeral procession, he reiterates the exclusion implicit in the title and explicit in the threnos: he
specifically counts out all those without "chaste wings" (l. 4), specifically counts in the crow "that thy sable gender mak'st / With the breath
thou giv'st and tak'st" (11. 18–19). Only eagle and crow are specified
as mourners, and the appearance of the low-class and somewhat sinis-
ter crow would seem on the face of it to constitute a breach of decorum.
Shakespeare risks this breach in order to substantiate "chaste": the
crow reproduces without sexual activity,[4] perhaps even without sexual
difference, insofar as both give and take; he is thus the perfect mourner
for this chaste couple, the one whose arrival allows the anthem to
commence (l. 21). Chastity is here the condition of celebratory song,
as it is the condition of these lovers' benign mutuality.

The paradoxes that animate "The Phoenix and the Turtle" are as
much emotional as intellectual; they rest, I think, on its fusion of lovers'
language with an insistence on absolute chastity. That is: the poem
appeals intensely to the desire for fusion in the relation of male and
female at the same time that it makes fusion contingent on escaping
any bodily form of relatedness. We cannot have what the poem makes
us want, not here, not ever; only death enables so mutual a flame. In
its elegiac retrospection, the poem fixes us in its "tragic scene," presenting the object of desire as always already lost. Moreover, the
paradox through which the lovers' language here is both the mark of

desire and the condition limiting its fulfillment is at the heart of *Troilus and Cressida* and *Othello*, shaping their tragic scenes; if the poem gives us an idealized union from which sexuality is banished, the plays enact the consequences of seeking this union through sexuality. Both *Troilus and Cressida* and *Othello* locate the fracture of the sexual union at the moment of its consummation; both, moreover, figure that fracture as the simultaneous soiling of, and soiling by, a maternal presence. In that sense, the intense desire for union expressed in both plays is heir to the psychic world of *Hamlet*, with its horror of the "one flesh," its identification of the Fall with the soiled maternal body; and the etherialized union of "The Phoenix and the Turtle" is the desperate antidote to that world.

Hence, I think, Troilus's virtual rewriting of the poem's paradoxes when he is confronted by the ocular evidence of Cressida's uncontrolled sexuality, her defection to Diomed:

> This is, and is not, Cressid.
> Within my soul there doth conduce a fight
> Of this strange nature, that a thing inseparate
> Divides more wider than the sky and earth;
> And yet the spacious breadth of this division
> Admits no orifex for a point as subtle
> As Ariachne's broken woof to enter.
> (5.2.145–51)

Troilus's discovery of the place where "reason can revolt / Without perdition" (5.2.143–44) replays the poem's confounding of reason in the register of tragic loss: looking at Cressida, he turns the poem's paradoxes of perfection inside out, finding in her duplicitous body both "distance, and no space" and the self that "was not the same." Hence, while the poem celebrates the mystery that something two—as two as a phoenix and a turtle— could be one, Troilus laments that something one can be two, both Cressida and not Cressida, union and not union. "Property was thus appalled"; his discovery of duplicity threatens to unmake the "rule in unity itself" (5.2.140). And his language of division and orifex suggests that this discovery is simultaneous with the discovery of Cressida's self-divisive sexuality: as he gazes at her sexualized body, the divison that is no division, the orifex that is no orifex, begin to become anatomically localized, as though her orifice were itself the defining condition of fractured union. Troilus turns the paradoxes of "The Phoenix and the Turtle" inside out because he comes at them in effect from the other side: if the poem manages to celebrate a union perfect in the absence of sexuality, the play names sexuality—

specifically female sexuality—as that which destroys union. And if *Troilus and Cressida* rewrites the lovers' paradoxes of the poem, *Othello* rewrites its elegiac mode, enacting in its end a skewed version of its flight into death.[5] For the poem's solutions cannot be the solutions of the tragedies, where escape from the body is not so easily achieved.

In *Hamlet*, the horror of the "one flesh" is released by the play's initiating image of a disrupted marriage. When Shakespeare moves from *Hamlet* to *Troilus and Cressida*, he rewrites that disrupted marriage as the debilitating ground of being: displaced from the center of its own story, separated from its literal human agents, urgently voiced only in Hector's evocation of the "moral laws / Of nature and of nations" (2.2.185–86) that he has already decided to disavow, the broken marriage that leads to the fall of Troy nonetheless decisively shapes the play. *Troilus and Cressida* is informed by the same nostalgia for past order—in which meaning and identity are fixed—as *Hamlet*; and as in *Hamlet*, the cornerstone of this order is patriarchal marriage. Hence the metaphoric appropriateness of the terms in which Ulysses warns about the destruction of hierarchical order, terms that reenact analogically the destroyed marriage of *Hamlet*:

> And therefore is the glorious planet Sol
> In noble eminence enthron'd and spher'd
> Amidst the other; whose med'cinable eye
> Corrects the influence of evil planets,
> And posts like the commandment of a king,
> Sans check, to good and bad. But when the planets
> In evil mixture to disorder wander,
> What plagues and what portents, what mutiny,
> What raging of the sea, shaking of earth,
> Commotion in the winds, frights, changes, horrors,
> Divert and crack, rend and deracinate
> The unity and married calm of states.
>   (1.3.89–100)

Marriage here epitomizes the ordered unity about to be fragmented; and as in *Hamlet*, marriage depends on the strength of a nearly godlike paternal authority. Like Hamlet's own Hyperion-father, who had "an eye like Mars to threaten and command" (3.4.56, 57), this Sol's eye "posts like the commandment of a king, / Sans check"; and like Hamlet's father, this "glorious planet Sol" loses his authority when he is subjected to a planetary version of *Hamlet*'s "mixture rank" (3.2.251), the "evil mixture" that rends the married calm of states.[6]

In moving from Denmark to Troy, Shakespeare in effect rewrites the broken marriage of *Hamlet* as originary cultural history; and as in *Hamlet*, broken marriage leads to the domain of the weakened or dead father and the sexualized mother. In *Hamlet*, the death of the reverend father, "old grandsire Priam" (*Hamlet*, 2.2.460, 470, 475), had served to model for Hamlet his own sense of the loss of authoritative paternal presence; and though the literal death of Priam is indefinitely deferred in *Troilus and Cressida*, the sense of his absence is nonetheless diffused throughout the plot, registered not only in his insignificance even when he is present[7] but also in the play's debunking of all its cultural forefathers—a debunking that renders them as impotent as Old Fortinbras or Polonius, as imperfect as Hamlet fears his father is. And, as *Hamlet* would predict, the father's absence here releases the horrific presence of the strumpet-mother. In a characteristic shift of agency from male to female, the First Player's narrative in fact makes this strumpet, rather than the male avenger, responsible for Priam's death: as soon as Pyrrhus's "bleeding sword" has fallen on Priam, Pyrrhus vanishes from the narrative altogether, his place taken by the "strumpet Fortune" to whom blame is displaced (2.2.487–89). Prompted by Hamlet—"Say on, come to Hecuba" (2.2.497)—the First Player invokes the antidote to this strumpet, the good mother who can keep her husband's memory alive by mourning for him properly: in *Hamlet*, Hecuba serves as reassurance, as the model of the beneficent mother Hamlet hopes to find—or to make—in Gertrude. But this potentially restorative figure is strikingly missing from *Troilus and Cressida*'s version of the matter of Troy. In fact Hecuba herself never appears on stage; and insofar as she is present by allusion, her presence is sexualized and trivialized by her association with Helen (1.2.1), her laughter at Helen's sexual banter (1.2.144–45), and her promotion of her daughter's sexual relation with Achilles, where she is emblematically reduced to the function of bawd, trading tokens between the illicit lovers (5.1.38). This mother could not restore paternal presence or make milch the eyes of heaven (*Hamlet*, 2.2.513); she herself is corrupted by her association with—not her differentiation from—this play's version of the strumpet Fortune, now named Helen.

In its weakening of the reverend father and sexualizing of the restorative mother, *Troilus and Cressida* plays out Hamlet's initial relationship to his parents. The absence of protective parental figures joined in marriage leaves the play—in *Hamlet*'s terms—squarely in the realm of the strumpet Fortune, with no escape: Helen's contaminated body thus becomes its dominant image, the locus that defines its representations of war and love. Here war itself is imagined as the consequences of a contaminating sexual contact, equivalent to the syphilitic skin disease that runs rampant on Old Hamlet's smooth body when Claudius poisons him; and Helen is the source of this disease, the "contaminated carrion" whose every drop of blood has cost lives (4.1.72), virtually a literalization of Hamlet's deadly "good kissing carrion" (*Hamlet*, 2.2.182). As the spokesman for the syphilitic point of view, the bastard Thersites insists that we make the connection: "The vengeance on the whole camp—or rather, the Neapolitan bone-ache; for that methinks is the curse depending on those that war for a placket" (2.3.18–21). His response to Troilus's declaration of war on Diomedes—"Lechery, lechery, still wars and lechery! Nothing else holds fashion. A burning devil take them!" (5.2.193–95)—moreover identifies the fires of venereal disease with the fires that will burn Troy—an identification eerily borne out by Cassandra's prophecy: "Our firebrand brother Paris burns us all. / Cry, Trojans, cry! A Helen and a woe: / Cry, cry! Troy burns, or else let Helen go" (2.2.111–13). The plots of love and war come together in Helen's body; and insofar as the play itself persistently associates its own performance with a kind of syphilitic impotence, it too is bred out of Helen's "whorish loins" (4.1.64).[8]

Yet Helen herself is scarcely present in the play, and then present in ways that suggest her mere vacuity. She appears only once, near the literal center of the play, in 3.1; and then "the mortal Venus, the heartblood of beauty, love's visible soul" (3.1.31–32) amuses herself by flirting and giggling at Pandarus's dirty song. Her absence throughout the play and her vacuity here, at its center, make her emblematic of the sense of absence or hollowness at the core that pervades this play, where there is no center from which meaning can radiate, where high rhetoric, exalted sentiments, heroic battles, even the logic of the plot itself, perpetually seem on the point of collapsing into meaninglessness.[9] Like the fusty nut that is Thersites's image for Achilles's intelligence (2.1.103) or the putrefied core of the gorgeous armor Hector pursues (5.8.1), the center of corruption here is uncannily empty, as though the universal wolf had already eaten up himself and delivered the play into nothingness (1.3.124), a contaminating emptiness unsuccessfully masked by gorgeous self-assertion. At the end of her central scene, when Helen prepares to "do more / Than all the island kings—disarm great Hector" (3.1.149–50), she becomes radically identified with the "most putrefied core, so fair without" (5.8.1) that will fatally disarm Hector at the play's end, robbing this world not only of the possibility of heroic action but of the possibility of fixed meaning itself. Like Hamlet in his first soliloquy, that is, *Troilus and Cressida* associates the meaninglessness of its world with the sexual corruption of a woman's body and enacts this association first in the body of Helen and then in Cressida.[10]

This is the world that Troilus inherits, the world of broken marriage in which his desire for Cressida must attempt to find a place. It is, above all, a world in which identity itself has become meaningless, in which fragmentation and annihilation have replaced the "unity and married calm" Ulysses nostalgically depicts, where each entity was defined by its place in a harmonious whole.[11] Hence "fragment" Thersites (5.1.8) is the legitimate spokesman for this ruptured world, heir to its broken marriage: bastard himself, he is fittingly identified as the product of the sexualized female body, soiled son of a soiled mother, a "bitch-wolf's son" (2.1.10), a "stool for a witch" (2.1.44), a "whoreson cur" (2.1.42). In his astonishing exchange with the bastard son of Priam, Thersites comes close to identifying the whore his mother with the whore who is the cause of the war:

> I am a bastard, too: I love bastards. I am bastard begot, bastard instructed, bastard in mind, bastard in valour, in everything illegitimate. One bear will not bite another, and wherefore should one bastard? Take heed: the quarrel's most ominous to us—if the son of a whore fight for a whore, he tempts judgement.
>
> (5.7.16–22)

As the emblematic bastard son of Helen, the present-absent whore/mother of the play, Thersites appropriately figures the fragmentation of this world, its subjection to meaninglessness and annihilation.

Troilus and Cressida is, like *Hamlet*, a confrontation with the soiled maternal body that makes life meaningless, played out in the relationship of Troilus and Cressida. All the nostalgia for spoiled unity that permeates the play is vested in Troilus: he enacts the nostalgic desire for wholeness articulated by Ulysses and diffused throughout the plot; he bears the burden of its disappointment. Through his sexual union with Cressida, I shall argue, he seeks to regain a fantasy of wholeness by merging with a "repured" maternal presence. But as "The Phoenix and the Turtle" suggests, the union he desires must by definition exclude sexuality: for sexuality as a way back to an idealized unity fails in its own enactment, leads only to Helen, making the beloved herself one with the soiled maternal body.[12] The plot in fact problematically literalizes this logic, making Cressida a whore virtually as soon as the sexual relationship is consummated. In the process, Cressida loses her status as a fully articulated subject and becomes merely the object of the male gaze that constitutes her as a whore; and the extent to which

she becomes merely the creature of Troilus's needs suggests the extent
to which Shakespeare himself is invested in the fantasy he expresses
through Troilus.

When Troilus responds to the sight of Diomed's Cressida by crying
out "This is, and is not, Cressid" (5.2.145) we feel, as so often in this
play of divisions, a divided duty. On the one hand, we are bound to
respond to Troilus's attempt to preserve his illusions at any cost as
mad, a near psychotic denial of an obvious reality. On the other hand,
Troilus's words trouble us partly because they respond to something
that *we* have found troubling about Cressida: and insofar as they echo
our dim sense that this is not Cressida, we find ourselves caught up in
his psychosis.[13] I shall argue that we are at this moment divided against
ourselves because, at the deepest level, *Troilus and Cressida* enacts
Troilus's fantasies, hence ensnaring us in them even as it encourages
our distance from him: as Cressida becomes Diomed's, in an important
sense she ceases to be her own creature; as she becomes Diomed's, she
becomes oddly the creature of Troilus's needs. In fact, the shift in her
status that Troilus articulates here is earlier registered in a change not
so much in her character as in the means by which she is characterized
and hence in the relationship that we as well as Troilus have toward
her. For Cressida's famous inconstancy is accompanied by a radical
inconsistency of characterization; and both occur at once because both
are reflections of the same fantasy.

Critics frequently dismiss Cressida as "the wanton of tradition,"[14]
but when we first meet her, we feel her presence not as a stereotype
but as a whole character. Throughout 1.2 we are encouraged to speculate about her motives; and by the end of the scene we seem to have
established a privileged relationship with her. After our discomfort
with Troilus's self-indulgent romanticizing and poeticizing (1.1.55–
59, 100–104), we are likely to find Cressida's literalizing and deflating
wit refreshing;[15] she at least is not wallowing in imaginary lily beds.
And in the process of engaging us by her wit, Cressida calls attention
to its psychic function and hence to her status as a whole character
whose psychic processes may legitimately concern us: she relies, she
tells Pandarus, on her wit to defend her wiles (1.2.265–66). In taking
up Pandarus's metaphor of defense, she suggests the defensive function
of her wit as a means of warding off serious emotion with all its threats,
perhaps especially the threat of sexual vulnerablity implicit in her image
of pregnancy (1.2.272–75). On the other hand, we may notice that she
seems to regard sexuality itself as a defense when she tells us that she
will lie on her back to defend her belly (1.2.265); given our knowledge

of the story, we may even begin to speculate that her view of sexuality as a defense will play a role in her defection to Diomedes. At the same time as she keeps Pandarus at bay, she teases us to question her; and just as we are speculating about her motives, she suddenly reveals herself, and to us alone. Her soliloquy confirms our sense that her chief concern is with her vulnerability and her means of defense against it: her entire strategy is directed toward gaining control over Troilus, her entire assumption that he will no longer love her once he has possessed her. In a declaration of passion filled with calculation, a statement of love from which Troilus himself is notably absent, replaced by abstract dicta about the typical behavior of men, in couplets so constricted that they suggest a fundamental niggardliness of the self, Cressida reveals the way in which her awareness of the crippling malaise of this world, the gap between expectation and performance,[16] colors her own expectations about Troilus and hence her behavior; she is coy because "men prize the thing ungain'd more than it is" (1.2.294). It is an understatement to say that she has no sense of her own intrinsic worth. She seems to have internalized the principle of valuation that rules this society, the principle implied by Troilus's question, "What's aught but as 'tis valued?" (2.2.53). Echoing the commercial language that so infects human relationships throughout the play, she identifies herself as a thing, in fact seems to identify herself with her "thing," and tells us that this thing gains its value not through any intrinsic merit but through its market value, determined by its scarcity. Beneath the deflating tendencies of her wit, then, the soliloquy reveals her vulnerability, her dependence on the love of men to establish her value even for herself, and her sense that her best defense lies in holding off, concealing her own desires. And whatever we may feel about the self thus revealed, we feel that it *is* a self: the very structure of the scene—ending in her soliloquy—establishes in us a keen sense both of Cressida's inwardness and of our own privileged position as the recipient of her revelations.

By the end of this scene, then, we have established not only some sense of Cressida but also the expectation that we will be allowed to know her as a full character, that she will maintain her relationship with us. And the scenes in Troy do not, for the most part, disappoint us. Although they contain no private revelations like that which concluded 1.2, they continually focus our attention on Cressida's inwardness by making us question her motives. When next we see her in 3.2 she amplifies our sense that fear, especially fear of betrayal, defines her relationship not only to Troilus but also to herself (3.2.66–71); throughout 3.2 she seems terribly divided between impulses toward a self-protective and manipulative coyness and impulses toward a self-revelation that feels to her like dangerous self-betrayal. Given her vision of a world in which "things won are done" (1.2.292), in which her coy refusal seems the necessary basis for Troilus's faith, she cannot simply make herself known. She can be true to herself only by hiding herself; by revealing herself, she fears that she has committed a self-betrayal that will be the model for Troilus's betrayal of her: "Why have I blabb'd? Who shall be true to us / When we are so unsecret to ourselves?" (3.2.123–24). But even as she chides herself for her apparent loss of self control, she ends with a plea ("Stop my mouth") that both Troilus and Pandarus seem to take as the coquette's coy request for a kiss. As though in response to Troilus's suspicion, her reply to his kiss stresses the authenticity of her loss of control: " 'Twas not my purpose thus to beg a kiss. / I am asham'd. O heavens, what have I done? / For this time I will take my leave, my lord" (3.2.136–38). In her fear of self-betrayal, Cressida tries to leave Troilus in order to separate herself from her "unkind" self, the unnatural and unreliable self that has betrayed her, making her Troilus' fool:

> *Troil.* What offends you, lady?
>
> *Cress.* Sir, mine own company.
>
> *Troil.* You cannot shun yourself.
>
> *Cress.* Let me go and try.
> I have a kind of self resides with you,
> But an unkind self, that itself will leave
> To be another's fool. I would be gone:
> Where is my wit? I know not what I speak.
> (3.2.142–49)

She can see love only as the unkind self's foolish self-abandonment; and the loss of her defensive wit seems to leave her utterly vulnerable.[17] Troilus's reply to this perilous self-revelation is devastating: "Well know they what they speak that speak so wisely" (l. 150). He cannot believe in—almost cannot hear—what she has said. And in the face of his continued assumption that she is in control, that her self-revelation, like her request that her mouth be stopped, is part of the coquette's craft, she herself is brought to challenge the authenticity of her loss of control, hence of her unkind, loving self: "Perchance, my lord, I show more craft than love, / And fell so roundly to a large confession / To angle for your thoughts" (ll. 151–53). For Cressida at this moment, as for Troilus, there are only two choices: she is either a loving fool or a crafty coquette. And in the context created both by her own fears and by Troilus's expectations, there is no true choice. She re-establishes her dignity both for herself and for Troilus by retreating from self-revelation and from love: regaining her wit, she suggests that even her loss of self may be self-controlled, simultaneously fulfilling Troilus's expectation that she will be a stereotypical coquette and defending herself against her own fears of self-betrayal. Her retreat from her unkind self here may strike us as oddly prophetic of her later defection from Troilus; in the vow at the end of the scene, Cressida strikingly imagines herself as stereotypically false rather than true. Cressida's unkind self does not emerge again in 3.2. In fact, the whole scene moves toward the increasing distance and contrivance reflected in the final vows, in which each of the triad threatens to become no more than his or her name,[18] threatens, that is, to lose depth of character, to become merely stereotypical. That is: if we see Cressida as a stereotypi-cal coquette in 3.2, we also see her taking on this role in response to specific psychological pressures; we are never allowed to see her merely as an uncomplicated type-character.

Whether or not we feel that we understand Cressida in 3.2, and whatever the terms of our understanding, the scene clearly focuses on her inner state. Our most intense engagement is with her: throughout the scene, Troilus does indeed seem "simpler than the infancy of truth" (3.2.168) compared to her. Her next appearance, in 4.2, continues this intense engagement. In abandoning the caution of her 1.2 soliloquy, Cressida has shown more love than craft; and with the consummation of their union, she feels herself defenseless, as though her self-betrayal threatens to turn at any moment into Troilus's betrayal of her. As Troilus attempts to leave her to preserve the secrecy of their union, she asks poignantly, "Are you aweary of me?" (4.2.7). Then, as though she wishes magically to prolong their sexual relationship by undoing it, she adds, "O foolish Cressid, I might have still held off, / And then you would have tarried" (4.2.17–18). This scene is in the normal pattern of Shakespearean morning-after scenes in which the woman typically wishes to hold the man with her, while the man asserts the necessities of the outside world. But both Romeo and Antony seem to have more pressing reasons for leaving than Troilus; and neither Juliet nor Cleopatra responds to the parting with the sense of betrayal, and with the analysis of betrayal, that Cressida expresses here. Immediately after the consummation, that is, the lovers seem already separate, as Cressida had feared. And the rest of the scene—indeed, the rest of the plot—in some sense constitutes an objective correlative to that separateness. The entrance of Pandarus underscores the breach in the lovers' union. Cressida knows that her "naughty mocking uncle" (4.2.25) will mock her. But by the end of their exchange, she feels herself mocked by Troilus too: "You smile and mock me, as if I meant naughtily" (l. 38). Troilus laughs (l. 39); and though the lovers leave the stage together, he indeed seems more allied with Pandarus than with Cressida.[19] At this point, the plot moreover makes the separation between them both literal and dramatic: Aeneas brings the news of the political trade-off that sends Cressida to the Greeks; and the lovers respond to his news not together but separately. We do not see them together again in this scene. Moreover, as the lovers respond separately to the news of separation, the tensions of the opening of the scene are clarified. Troilus responds rather easily to the news of the exchange, accepting it as a *fait accompli* ("Is it so concluded?" [4.2.68]), philosophizing upon it as though Cressid were merely one of his "achievements" ("How my achievements mock me!" [4.2.71]), and making arrangements to meet this new necessity while preserving honor (4.2.72–73), all without any show of overwhelming emotion.[20] Given Troilus's ready acceptance of the news, Cressida's response to it is doubly impressive: the extremity of her grief, her assertion that nothing but Troilus matters to her, and her refusal to accept the separation ("I will not go from Troy" [4.2.112]) make her response not only the most powerful assertion of her love for Troilus but also one of the most emotionally charged moments in the play.

When the lovers are reunited after this brief separation, the tone of passionate expostulation has passed from Cressida to Troilus: he makes the speeches, while she replies with a numb repeated questioning of the necessity of separation (4.4.29, 30, 31, 54), concluding finally by asking, "When shall we see again?" (4.4.56). During the opening movement of the scene, that is, she seems painfully resistant to the bare fact of separation, while he embellishes it rhetorically, acquiescing. The emotional focus of the scene then moves from the acknowledgment of separation to Troilus's fears about Cressida's fidelity and her pained and puzzled responses to those fears. She responds first with surprise and indignation (4.4.58, 73), then with the fear that he does not love her (4.4.81), and finally with a question that reflects her shaken faith not only in Troilus but also in herself: "Do you think I will?" (4.4.91). The last words that we hear her speak to Troilus recall her own fear of betrayal: "My lord, will you be true?" (4.4.99). And these two questions— "Do you think I will?"; "My lord, will you be true?"— are the last we hear from Troilus's Cressida. We have been engaged throughout with Cressida's fears and her defenses against them; but suddenly, at the moment she is about to part from Troilus, she recedes from us. As Troilus and Diomed quarrel over her, she stands silent, as though she has become merely the object of their competitive desire,[21] as though she has no voice of her own.

This sudden move into opacity remains constant for the rest of the play. In the next scene (4.5), when she kisses the Greek camp generally, she speaks her first words only after she has been kissed by Agamemnon, Nestor, Achilles, and Patroclus; her banter seems both a response to Greek expectations about her and a return to the earlier mode of 1.2, that is, to a sexual wit that serves an essentially defensive function. But we are given no reassuring soliloquy to enable us to support this understanding; she simply exits, distressingly, with Diomed. She seems suddenly to have passed beyond us as she has passed from Troilus to Diomed. Ulysses's assessment of her as merely a daughter of the game (4.5.63) is disquieting partly because it offers us an explanation for her behavior just when we are feeling the need for one, in the absence of one by Cressida herself. Ulysses's commentary asks us to see someone that we have seen as a whole character, someone whose inwardness we alone have been privy to, as a mere character type, a person with no conflict or inwardness at all: and Shakespeare does nothing to qualify Ulysses's appraisal.[22] The Cressida with whom we have been engaged simply does not allow us to understand her, here or later in the play. We may speculate that she leaves Troilus because his suspicion of her and his relatively easy acquiescence in the separation make her feel unknown and unloved. We may think that she leaves him because she fears that he will leave her, in order to ensure that she will be actively in control of her fate rather than the passive victim of his will. We may note her entire vulnerability in this society and her reliance on the opinion of men to determine her value even for herself and hence speculate that she adopts Troilus's view of her capacity for fidelity to prove his expectations right. We may locate the basis for her actions in her own pleasure in the excitement of the chase, her use of sexuality as a defense, even her genetic predisposition to treason, inherited from her father—and probably an actress will have to attempt some such construction in order to play the part at all. But after 4.4, the play gives us no place to ground our speculation: exactly when we most need to understand what Cressida is doing, we are given no enlightenment; and we are, moreover, forced to acknowledge our distance from Cressida by the very theatrical structure through which we see her. In 5.2 we are allowed to see Cressida only through the intervening commentary of Troilus, Ulysses, and Thersites. Instead of being especially privy to her thoughts, as we were in 1.2, we become merely one more spectator to her new status as devalued object; indeed, we take our places as the furthest removed of the spectators as we watch Thersites watching Ulysses watching Troilus watching Cressida. The consequence is that Cressida seems to betray *us* at the same time as she betrays Troilus; our relationship with her is broken off as sharply as Troilus's.

This abrupt shift in the mode of characterization, and hence in the distance between character and audience, seems to me to override any argument about Cressida's consistency or inconsistency as her allegiance shifts from Troilus to Diomedes: we know so little about her at this moment that we can no longer judge her as a whole character. But the timing of the shift may give us a way of understanding it, even if we can't understand her. In changing our relationship to Cressida, in making her radically unknowable as she leaves Troilus and moves toward the Greek camp, the play makes her status as subject contingent on her relationship with Troilus: separated from him, she becomes irreducibly other; and her sexual betrayal is the sign of her status as opaque object.[23] This is Troilus's reading of her; when she gives herself to Diomed, she demonstrates to him that she is both unknowable and unpossessable. At this moment, he can make sense of her only by imagining that she has been split in two, into his pure Cressida and Diomed's soiled one; even Cressida seems to participate in his fantasy when she offers as her only explanation for her actions her own helpless sense that she is split ("Troilus, farewell! One eye yet looks on thee, / But with my heart the other eye doth see" [5.2.106–7]). But since we have already watched her become newly opaque when she separates from Troilus and takes up her new sexual position in the Greek camp, our experience of her prepares for his; the shift in the mode through which Cressida is characterized encourages us to participate in Troilus's sense that Cressida is split and moreover that her splitting is the consequence of her sexual infidelity. In its characterization of Cressida, that is, the play anticipates Troilus's final vision of Cressida, making her radically unknowable and unpossessable for us as she separates from Troilus and becomes sexually other. In the process, Cressida is made to act out a dreamlike conjunction of sexuality, separation, and infidelity—a conjunction more the consequence of the fantasies that Troilus brings to their sexual union than the consequence of her own character.

What, then, are those fantasies? From the first, Troilus's desire for Cressida is invested with the power of a nostalgic longing for, and fear of, union with an overpoweringly maternal figure. From the first, he wants to believe in Cressida's power and his own weakness; from the first, he associates his love with his own infantilization. When we first meet him, he is luxuriating in the enervating effects of love, an enervation described in terms that suggest the loss of his adult masculinity:

> . . . I am weaker than a woman's tear,
> Tamer than sleep, fonder than ignorance,
> Less valiant than the virgin in the night,
> And skilless as unpractis'd infancy.
> (1.1.9–12)

Throughout, he associates love with the powerlessness and the innocent—or willfully ignorant—trust of an infant; even in the midst of
telling Cressida that he does not believe that women can be constant,
he claims to be naive, "as true as truth's simplicity, / And simpler than
the infancy of truth" (3.2.167–68). His initial imagination of the sexual
act is given shape by images that suggest a return to the blissful and
dangerous fusion of infancy: it is feeding on an exquisitely purified
nectar; its consummation simultaneously promises and threatens a
delicious death in which distinction itself—both the capacity to distinguish and the separate identity so distinguished—will be lost, and
boundaries will dissolve:[24]

> I am giddy: expectation whirls me round.
> Th'imaginary relish is so sweet
> That it enchants my sense: what will it be
> When that the wat'ry palate tastes indeed
> Love's thrice-repured nectar? Death, I fear me,
> Sounding destruction, or some joy too fine,
> Too subtle-potent, tun'd too sharp in sweetness
> For the capacity of my ruder powers.
> I fear it much; and I do fear besides
> That I shall lose distinction in my joys,
> As doth a battle, when they charge on heaps
> The enemy flying.
>
>   (3.2.16–27)

Troilus gives us none of the images of penetration that we might expect;
instead, he imagines the sexual act as wallowing, tasting, dissolving.
With an intensity unequaled in Shakespeare's plays, he records the
ambivalent desire for a fusion in which individual identity will be lost:
here love *is* death, a joy too sharp in sweetness, a battle, a swooning
destruction in which one's powers are lost. No wonder that Troilus
invokes Pandarus as Charon to ferry him to this ambiguous land of
the dead (3.2.9–11); for he imagines the sexual act not in phallic but
in oral terms,[25] not as the mark of adult male sexuality but as the
dangerous return to the infant's first union with a nurturing maternal
figure, the union out of which the adult self must be painfully differentiated, distinguished.

Insofar as Troilus's union with Cressida is an attempt to recapture
infantile fusion with an idealized—"repured"—maternal figure, the
rupture of the union threatens to soil the idea of the pure mother
herself:

Troil.   Was Cressid here?

Ulyss.   I cannot conjure, Trojan.

Troil.   She was not, sure.

Ulyss.	Most sure she was.
Troil.	Why, my negation hath no taste of madness.
Ulyss.	Nor mine, my lord: Cressid was here but now.
Troil.	Let it not be believ'd for womanhood.
	Think, we had mothers; do not give advantage
	To stubborn critics, apt, without a theme
	For depravation, to square the general sex
	By Cressid's rule: rather, think this not Cressid.
Ulyss.	What hath she done, prince, that can soil our mothers?
Troil.	Nothing at all, unless that this were she.

(5.2.124–34)

Like Posthumus (*Cymbeline*, 2.4.153–59), Troilus immediately associates the infidelity of his beloved with the infidelity of his mother. Ulysses's puzzled question insists on the association and clarifies the fantasy that shapes it: for Troilus, Cressida has the power to soil a mother figure so universal that she becomes "the general sex," all "our mothers." Troilus's desperate attempt to split Cressida from herself is, first of all, an attempt to keep this figure pure: if this is not Cressida, then the mother remains unsoiled. But as Troilus continues, the act of splitting serves to preserve not only the idealized mother but Troilus's fantasy of union with her and the sense of wholeness based on that union:[26]

> This she?—No, this is Diomed's Cressida.
> If beauty have a soul, this is not she;
> If souls guide vows, if vows be sanctimonies,
> If sanctimony be the gods' delight,
> If there be rule in unity itself,
> This is not she.

(5.2.136–41)

At stake for Troilus is a union so essential that its dissolution is felt as a threat to the very "rule of unity" itself (5.2.140), so essential that he will attempt to maintain it by invoking even "the rule of unity" against itself: here that rule—the guarantor of individual identity insofar as it postulates that a thing must be itself and not something else—guarantees not Cressida's identity but her separation from herself, in the service of a larger unity. To preserve the idea of his union with Cressida, he thus divides "a thing inseparate . . . more wider than the sky and earth" (5.2.147–48), splitting Cressida in two, separating his own Cressida from Diomed's. For Troilus, that is, the idea of union overrides any sense of Cressida as a person separate from himself; Cressida becomes simply that with whom he is united and hence ceases to be herself at the moment the union dissolves.[27]

But this is clearly an impossible position to maintain; not even Troilus can manage the degree of unreason necessary to insist forever that Cressida is not herself. As he continues, Troilus's language reveals the strain, becoming dense in its struggle to affirm and deny separation simultaneously:

> This is, and is not, Cressid.
> Within my soul there doth conduce a fight
> Of this strange nature, that a thing inseparate
> Divides more wider than the sky and earth;
> And yet the spacious breadth of this division
> Admits no orifex for a point as subtle
> As Ariachne's broken woof to enter.
> (5.2.145–51)[28]

There is division in a thing inseparate, but it is a division that is no division, an orifex without orifex. At this moment a sexual horror threatens to break through Troilus's language of reason contending against itself. His words suggest a barely contained and nightmarish version of his one sexual encounter with Cressida: his encounter with the woof that he has broken, the thing inseparate that divides, the subtle point that enters— or does not enter—this no-orifex, reminiscent of the joy "too subtle-potent" that earlier threatens to dissolve distinction (3.2.22).[29] And at the moment that he imagines this "orifex," the act of splitting fails, and he is left irrevocably with the image of a soiled Cressida and the fragmentation of the universe that had depended on her:

> Instance, O instance! strong as Pluto's gates:
> Cressid is mine, tied with the bonds of heaven.
> Instance, O instance! strong as heaven itself:
> The bonds of heaven are slipp'd, dissolv'd, and loos'd;
> And with another knot, five-finger-tied,
> The fractions of her faith, orts of her love,
> The fragments, scraps, the bits, and greasy relics
> Of her o'er-eaten faith are given to Diomed.
> (5.2.152–59)

"Fractions," "orts," "fragments," "scraps," and "bits": all diagnostically proclaim the breaking of wholeness into pieces as equivalent to the spoiling of food. This is what the tasting of "love's thrice-repured nectar" has come to, what Cressida herself has come to, in Troilus's imagination: as idealized mother to his infant love, she is the source of both wholeness and nurturance; and with her loss, wholeness and nurturance are spoiled at once. Her failure to live out Troilus's fantasy of union with a nurturing maternal figure thus simultaneously fractures his world and turns her to a greasy relic.

When Troilus cries out that the bonds of heaven are loos'd, he rewrites Ulysses's planetary analogy ("The heavens themselves . . . Observe degree" [1.3.85–6]); at this moment, the sense of fragmentation that pervades the play is given its locus in the individual psyche, expressed as the response to the soiling of a maternal presence. Ulysses asks what Cressida has done that can soil our mothers. We might answer that she has betrayed Troilus's fantasy of union with her, demonstrating her status as promiscuous other, not simply the creature of his desire. But we might also answer that Cressida is the creature not of her own needs but of Troilus's, that she is utterly responsive to his expectations, and that she in fact acts for him. His insistence on his own remarkable truth in love is from the start accompanied by doubts about Cressida's capacity for fidelity:

> O that I thought it could be in a woman—
> As, if it can, I will presume in you—
> To feed for aye her lamp and flames of love;
> To keep her constancy in plight and youth,
> Outliving beauty's outward, with a mind
> That doth renew swifter than blood decays!
> Or that persuasion could but thus convince me
> That my integrity and truth to you
> Might be affronted with the match and weight
> Of such a winnow'd purity in love—
> How were I then uplifted! But alas,
> I am as true as truth's simplicity,
> And simpler than the infancy of truth.
>
> (3.2.156–68)

Even as he imagines tasting Cressida as a repured nectar, he imagines her as unfaithful. Through all his protestations of the simplicity of his truth and the strained purity of his love (4.4.23), Troilus gives us the impression of an underlying hopelessness, as though he knows all along that the straining in his love cannot repurify a nectar already hopelessly contaminated. His desire to be uplifted by love is phrased in the subjunctive, dependent on his conviction that he will always be disappointed. In fact his status as the embodiment of "truth"—"as true as Troilus" (3.2.180])—depends on his imagining his truth put to the test, imagining it as an infantile and foolish response—"simpler than the

infancy of truth"—to the fact of female infidelity.[30] Here, as in Agamemnon's initial speech, the "persistive constancy" of men is tried not
in Fortune's love but in her frown (1.3.21–30). Hence Troilus's images
of the infant purity of his love always encode a fantasy of his own
victimization: to imagine himself as an infant in love *is* to imagine
himself betrayed by his own infantlike simplicity and trust.

Troilus needs to imagine a Cressida who betrays him; and insofar
as his expectation that she will be false spoils Cressida's trust in herself
and him in 3.2 and 4.2, his need in part creates her infidelity. (One can
hardly imagine a speech more calculated to create infidelity in a beloved
than 3.2.156–68; and in fact Cressida in response immediately imagines herself as false [3.2.182–94]). But for the most part, the play does
not seem to hold Troilus responsible for Cressida's betrayal; in fact
the plot shifts the blame from Troilus to Cressida, making both of
them unproblematically live up to their names. It is doubly striking,
then, that Troilus himself assigns blame somewhat differently in the
Trojan Council scene: the Troilus who needs to imagine Cressida
betraying him, who insists on his own extraordinary truth, tells us
there that male sexual satiety, not female infidelity, is the soiling agent.
His argument for keeping Helen depends on an extraordinary analogy—extraordinary not least because Troilus himself seems unaware
of its relevance to his approaching union with Cressida:[31]

> I take today a wife, and my election
> Is led on in the conduct of my will:
> My will enkindled by mine eyes and ears,
> Two traded pilots 'twixt the dangerous shores
> Of will and judgement—how may I avoid,
> Although my will distaste what it elected,
> The wife I choose? There can be no evasion
> To blench from this and to stand firm by honour.
> We turn not back the silks upon the merchant
> When we have soil'd them, nor the remainder viands
> We do not throw in unrespective sieve
> Because we now are full.
>
> (2.2.62–73)

On the verge of union with Cressida, Troilus imagines a marriage from
which he will wish to "blench" or retreat; he expects to "distaste" his
choice. In this fantasy, sexual satiety leads to indifference or even
disgust very much as Cressida had predicted (1.2.291–96); and the
terms of the disgust are precisely those in which Troilus will later
respond to Cressida's betrayal of him: the distasted wife is associated
with soiled silks and leftover food no longer desirable *because we now*

are full. The analogies of the Trojan Council scene ground Troilus's responses to Cressida in 5.2—and hence ground Cressida's infidelity—in a male sexual process that first soils its object (thus reducing its value) and then kills desire itself, making it distaste what it had chosen as it achieves satiety. That is, Troilus's response to Cressida's infidelity in 5.2 strikingly reiterates his Trojan Council speech, but with the onus shifted from him to her: the soil in 5.2 is the result not of his shifting desire but of her action; she is distasted, made into leftover food, not because he is now full, but because she has broken her faith.

The conjunction of Troilus's speech to the Trojan Council with his response to Cressida in the Greek camp suggests that the failure of this sexual union is as much the product of Troilus's desire as it is of Cressida's falsehood: even as he approaches union with Cressida for the first time, he anticipates a desire to separate from her; 3.2, in which the lovers meet to consummate their union, is in fact full of the sense of separation, and not only in the lovers' final disquieting vows. Almost as soon as they begin to speak of love, they speak of inevitable disappointment:

> *Troil.* This is the monstruosity in love, lady: that the will is infinite, and the execution confined: that the desire is boundless, and the act a slave to limit.
>
> *Cress.* They say all lovers swear more performance than they are able, and yet reserve an ability that they never perform: vowing more than the perfection of ten, and discharging less than the tenth part of one.
>
> (3.2.79–87)

Cressida's response, with its submerged metaphorics of reserving and discharging, specifies the anxiety about sexual performance already implicit in Troilus's claim that the only monster in Cupid's pageant is the lover himself, who vows more than he can possibly do (ll. 72–79); she invokes the dynamic of failed performance that Pandarus has already established ("Words pay no debts, give her deeds; but she'll bereave you o'th'deeds too, if she call your activity in question" [3.2.55–57]). But Troilus's anticipated disappointment goes deeper: his words point beyond her joke at the expense of male sexual bravado toward the melancholy awareness that the sexual act can never live up to expectation—that the "imaginary relish" (3.2.17) will in fact always prove sweeter than the act itself. And this inevitable disappointment will be a consequence not of male impotence, not even of choosing the wrong woman, but of something in the nature of sexual experience itself as he conceives it, a limitation at the very heart of limitless desire.

The will is infinite and the execution confined, the desire boundless and the act a slave to limit: the monstrous discrepancy is not only between boundless desire and limited performance, but between a desire for boundlessness and a sense of limit or boundary confirmed by the sexual act. Even at the very site that seems to promise—or to threaten—boundless fusion, one will find only limitation, only the otherness of the other; seeking union, one will find separation.[32] Hence in part the dream-logic through which—even at the cost of some temporal confusion—the separation of the lovers is arranged just at the moment of their consummation.[33]

The play records a profound ambivalence toward this separation at the heart of consummation. On the one hand, Troilus laments his loss of union with an intensity that marks it as essential to his own sense of wholeness; on the other, he founds his masculine identity on its loss. The ending of the play, in which Troilus rearms himself after the defection of Cressida, answers to the logic of his first disarming: if he soils Cressida, transforming her into the image of the contaminated maternal body, she has from the beginning threatened to soil him, dissolving his masculine identity through her contaminating femaleness. When we first see him—"Call here my varlet, I'll unarm again" (1.1.1)—love has disarmed him, leaving him "weaker than a woman's tear, /. . . Less valiant than the virgin in the night, / And skilless as unpractis'd infancy" (1.1.9–12); here Helen's literal disarming of Hector is metaphorized and psychologized, given its basis in masculine fears of emasculation. Even as it locates soilure in the accomplishment of the male sexualized will, the Trojan Council speech hints at this fear through a submerged metaphorics that associates the dangers of this accomplishment with the passage between two "dangerous shores" (2.2.65). Since Troilus has already imagined his coming to Cressida as crossing a "wild and wand'ring flood" (1.1.102) and will again evoke the image of dangerous watery crossing when he calls on Pandarus-Charon to give him "waftage" to her (3.2.9), the speech again seems obscurely anticipatory of their sexual union, evoking Cressida's presence in those shores even as it establishes Troilus's desire to leave her. The deep fantasy shaping Troilus's metaphor seems to associate intercourse with the boat trapped between menacing shores, giving Troilus's generalized fear of engulfment—his fear that he will lose distinction in his joys (3.2.25)—its specific physiological locus.[34] Under these circumstances, it's no wonder that Troilus is concerned with standing firm by honor—an honor that he cannot maintain if he "blenches" from his wife.[35]

Immediately after the consummation, Troilus acts out this desire to blench from her, leaving Cressida's bed with what seems to her unnecessary haste (4.2.1–18). At the same time, he attempts to transfer his own infant vulnerability to Cressida in language striking for its incipient violence:[36]

> Sleep kill those pretty eyes,
> And give as soft attachment to thy senses
> As infants empty of all thought.
>   (4.2.4–6)

But Cressida does not become a reassuringly passive infant. Instead, the plot comes to Troilus's rescue, enabling him to blench from his wife and still stand firm by honor, to leave behind his infantilized and feminized self, founding his masculine identity on separation from her. Even while 3.3 arranges the lamented separation of the lovers, it portrays an Achilles who is urged to break the bonds of Cupid that keep him effeminate (ll. 206–24); and the enforced separation achieves just this end for Troilus. Moreover, Cressida's betrayal conveniently makes this separation permanent; it enables Troilus to move from the position of trusting infant—or weeping woman— into ruthless manhood. He manages this transformation before our eyes, in response to Cressida's betrayal:

> *Troil.* The fragments, scraps, the bits, and greasy relics
>   Of her o'er-eaten faith are given to Diomed.
>
> *Ulyss.* May worthy Troilus be half attach'd
>   With that which here his passion doth express?
>
> *Troil.* Ay, Greek; and that shall be divulged well
>   In characters as red as Mars his heart
>   Inflam'd with Venus. Never did young man fancy
>   With so eternal and so fix'd a soul.
>   Hark, Greek: as much as I do Cressid love,
>   So much by weight hate I her Diomed.
>   That sleeve is mine that he'll bear on his helm;
>   Were it a casque compos'd by Vulcan's skill
>   My sword should bite it.
>   (5.2.158–70)

With the spoiling of the repured nectar, Troilus will seek another source of food, his frustrated oral desires becoming oral rage: "My sword should bite it." And this transfer from dependency to aggression—as in *Coriolanus*—confers manhood upon him. Betrayed love now fuels his hate: the lover Mars becomes the god of war, his inflamed and wounded heart the sign of the damage he shall inflict. Picking up his sword again, he undoes his initial emasculation by love.

When we next see Troilus, he is vigorously defending his newly regained masculinity against Hector's insistence that he is too young for war. Just as Hector tells Andromache and Cassandra that his own honor requires him to fight, Troilus enters, and Hector asks him, "How now, young man; mean'st thou to fight today?" (5.3.29); and before Troilus has had a chance to answer, Hector attempts to dissuade him:

> No, faith, young Troilus; doff thy harness, youth.
> I am today i'th'vein of chivalry:
> Let grow thy sinews till their knots be strong
> And tempt not yet the brushes of the war.
> Unarm thee, go; and doubt thou not, brave boy,
> I'll stand today for thee and me and Troy.
> (5.3.31–36)

With their extraordinary insistence on Troilus's youth, Hector's words rewrite Troilus's story, replacing its narrative of escape from the effeminizing power of love—"I will disarm again"—with a narrative about the development from youth to full manhood.[37] But this rewriting requires rewriting Troilus's status as warrior: the first story requires a Troilus who has already fought—one cannot be disarmed by love unless one has previously been armed; the second requires a Troilus who is a virgin warrior, whose sinews' knots are not yet strong, who has not yet tempted the brushes of the war. In its treatment of Troilus as warrior, that is, the play here conflates a developmental narrative (in which young Troilus emerges into fierce manhood) with a narrative of escape from emasculation (in which love has disarmed an already accomplished warrior).[38] Troilus's odd response to Hector further conflates these two narratives, making both turn on escape from the female; he answers Hector not by insisting that he is old enough to fight but by attacking Hector's "vice of mercy" (l. 37), a vice that he explicitly associates with his mother:

> Let's leave the hermit pity with our mother;
> And when we have our armours buckled on
> The venom'd vengeance ride upon our swords,
> Spur them to ruthful work, rein them from ruth!
> ... Hector, then 'tis wars.
> (5.3.45–49, *passim*)

He now defines his own manliness as leaving an effeminized youth behind, as absolute separation from the female within and without: he will no longer be the trusting infant, no longer "weaker than a woman's tear"; and his ruthlessness will be the mark of this separation.[39] As

Troilus makes himself into a murderous automaton, he institutionalizes the breaking of bonds, erecting the terrible isolation and fragmentation he had felt at Cressida's betrayal into the principle of masculinity and locating that principle in separation from his mother. Troilus conflates the narrative in which he leaves Cressida with the narrative in which he leaves his mother because for him the two narratives are one: he had approached Cressida as though she were a source of idealized nurturance; he had felt the soiling of his mother in her betrayal; now he leaves his mother in leaving her. Hence when Hector later praises him—"O, well fought, my youngest brother!" (5.6.12)—we hear the accents of an accomplished initiation rite, the passage into full manhood.[40]

Troilus's adult manhood is thus founded on Cressida's betrayal of him: that betrayal enables him to achieve a particularly brutal form of individuation, a hyper-masculine identity postulated as leaving the mother behind. The morning-after story of betrayal and loss thus simultaneously obscures and enables a developmental story, in which masculine identity requires sexual disappointment, requires the trans- formation of the lover's oral neediness—his fantasy of tasting the repured nectar—into his martial prowess ("My sword should bite it"). But this requirement itself comes, I think, from the nature of Troilus's desire, particularly from the extent to which it is a response to the psychological conditions of the play. I have earlier suggested that the play vests the disappointed longing for union in the figure of Troilus: in imagining sexual union as a retrieval of infantile fusion with the mother as repured nectar, Troilus is in effect attempting to undo the fragmentation that is the legacy of the absent or soiled mother. His passion is accordingly doubly idealizing, expressing not only desire for an ideal—repured—maternal object but also desire for a total fusion that will undo fragmentation, the fusion of "The Phoenix and the Turtle" or of Milton's spirits ("If Spirits embrace, / Total they mix" [*Paradise Lost*, 8.626–27]): idealizing in both object and aim. But these sexualized idealizations must inevitably fail, inevitably lead to their own debasements: insofar as the object is idealized, it will inevita- bly be contaminated by its participation in sexuality; insofar as the aim is idealized, it will be impossible to enact in the body.[41] Impossible, and terrifying: enacted in the body, fusion would be indistinguishable from annihilation, from Hamlet's horrific "one flesh." The contamina- tion of both object and aim by the sexual act thus enforces the broken union: hence perhaps the logic that makes the lovers' separation simul- taneous with their consummation. For once the desire for fusion with an ideal maternal presence has become sexualized, separation is the only out: seeking escape from fragmentation, Troilus drives himself further toward it.[42]

Insofar as the mother with whom Troilus would unite is the idealized "repured" mother, the very act that seems to promise union with her soils her and hence turns her into a version of the contaminating whore; and insofar as the attempt to enact total fusion in the body is successful in fantasy, it leads to fears of effeminization and annihilation so deep that they cause a defensive recoil from fusion itself. Both these movements are enshrined in the plot: the transformation of the idealized mother into a whore is played out in Cressida's infidelity with Diomedes; Troilus's recoil from fusion is played out in the process by which he gains his manhood by leaving the hermit pity with his mother. But the plot enshrines one movement only by obscuring the other. The play fleetingly registers Troilus's desire for separation through Cressida's poignant question, "Are you aweary of me?" (4.2.7) and through the ease with which he gives her up; but for the most part separation is displaced from any naturalistic basis in Troilus's desire and is instead enacted in a plot that in effect protects Troilus by having others act for him. Calchas and Agamemnon obligingly agree on trading Antenor for Cressida, thus achieving the separation that Troilus had imagined himself wanting during the Trojan Council;[43] and in Cressida's betrayal, the plot similarly comes to his rescue, making the separation final, representing his psychic necessities as though they were her fault.[44] Her character is in effect sacrificed to his: leaving him so that he can leave her, Cressida becomes a whore to keep him pure; hence the opacity of her motives as she leaves him. Act 4, scene 5, the scene in which Cressida comes to the Greek camp, in fact contains the traces of this exchange: soon after Ulysses directs us to see Cressida as no more than a daughter of the game (4.5.55–63), he directs us— in puffery that exceeds even Pandarus's—to see Troilus as a matchless hero. Neither account tallies with what we've seen of the characters: as Cressida is debased, Troilus is idealized. In fact, the parallelism of the speeches suggests the extent to which she is debased so that he can be idealized, the extent to which his status as masculine hero depends on her status as whore. In the end, it is easier—for Troilus and for Shakespeare—to call Cressida whore than to acknowledge the painful paradoxes at the heart of the love-plot: that vesting one's sexual desire in a pure object inevitably soils that object; that masculine identity is defined by separation from the very union it seems to seek.

The transfer of blame from male to female just below the surface in *Hamlet* has thus become the surface in *Troilus and Cressida*: Cressida is to blame for the failure of romantic love, as Helen is for the war in Diomed's account ("For every false drop in her bawdy veins / A Grecian's life hath sunk" [4.1.70–71]). But it is, after all, the Trojans and

Greeks who kill one another by agreeing to go on fighting over Helen: the men of this play need Helen, as they need Cressida's betrayal with Diomed, in order to go on concealing their own contamination from themselves. And although Shakespeare undermines Diomed's account of Helen, revealing the extent to which the men use Helen as a "theme of honour and renown" (2.2.200) for a war they wish to perpetuate, he is nonetheless largely complicit in the concealments of the love plot: Troilus is protected from the contaminating effects of his own sexuality by a plot that gives him Cressida's betrayal and the convenient presence of a Diomed who legitimates his sense of Cressida as split into pure and impure; and Shakespeare participates in this solution insofar as he too splits Cressida, writing her "whore" after she is spoiled by sexual contact. But Shakespeare does not rest here; and in *Othello*, when he returns to the working out of the same fantasies, we are asked to become critical of the process of splitting itself: instead of being enacted by the play, the split is enacted only in the mind of Othello as he is tutored by Iago.[45] Both plays enact the contamination of a maternal figure through sexuality; both are versions of the morning-after fantasy in which the madonna is transformed into the whore. But now Shakespeare redefines the source of corruption, locating it not in the unstable female body but in the diseased male imagination:[46] Othello's need for Cassio, his rush to believe his wife a whore as soon as they have consummated their union,[47] explicate Troilus's covert need for Diomed—and Shakespeare's own need to write Cressida whore. But no matter how fervently Othello writes Desdemona whore, Shakespeare does not: though she pays for Othello's fantasy with her life, Desdemona remains largely independent of it, innocent not only of the crime Othello imagines but also of the fantasies that infect him. Her independence—her refusal to turn whore to suit Othello's needs— marks the extent to which Shakespeare's revision of *Troilus and Cressida* in *Othello* was an attempt to dissociate himself from the fantasies that motivate Cressida's betrayal.

The beginning of *Othello* cites the end of *Troilus and Cressida* as though to call attention to this process of revision. At the end of *Troilus and Cressida*, disillusioned by Cressida's betrayal, Troilus leaves the hermit pity with his mother to forge a ruthless martial identity; at the beginning of *Othello*, Othello leaves his martial identity behind to encounter maternal pity in the form of Desdemona ("She lov'd me for the dangers I had pass'd, / And I lov'd her that she did pity them" [1.3.167–68]). And as with Troilus, martial identity is defined as leaving childhood behind. "Since these arms of mine had seven years' pith, / Till now some nine moons wasted, they have us'd / Their dearest action in the tented field" (1.3.83–85), Othello tells the assembled Senate; in specifying his youth—the "seven years' pith" of his arm—Othello makes his entry into the tented field simultaneous with his coming of age as a man-child. And describing the course of his love to the Senate, he casts it as a return to the childhood he has left behind: in bracketing his career as a soldier, Othello calls attention to the homology between the period before he entered the tented field and the "nine moons wasted" since he left it; the reference to the nine moons shapes this homology as rebirth into the realm of female generativity, with all its vulnerabilities. Making himself susceptible to Desdemona's pity, that is, Othello unmakes the basis for his martial identity, exchanging it for one dependent on her. And in the exchange, the self-sufficiency and isolation that had been the mark of his masculine identity—heard for example in the vast and lonely landscape of his narrative to Desdemona and named in Lodovico's late reference to him as "the noble Moor, whom our full senate / Call all in all sufficient" (4.1.260–61)—give way before his new need for her love. This new need frames itself as a return to childhood in part because it reawakens the sense of vulnerability that Othello had managed to conceal from himself through his identity as a soldier: in effect, the relationship with Desdemona spoils Othello's self-sufficiency, reconstructing ordinary human need as a lack or gap in the self, a massive hunger that can only be filled by something outside him, something moreover frightening exactly because it is outside him and hence not wholly subject to his control. Now his sense of harmonious wholeness—his "perfect soul" (1.2.31)—will be perilously vested not in himself but in Desdemona's perfection; he will now feel himself as imperfect, dependent on her wholeness to repair the gaps in his own being.[48] Leaving his martial identity behind, he makes of Desdemona the idealized center of his being, the principle of order: when he loves her not, "chaos is come again" (3.3.92–93).

When Othello names Desdemona his stay against chaos, his love-language is infused with the intensity of infantile need for the maternal presence that orders its world. Both the intensity of this need and its entanglement with his desire for Desdemona are given psychological grounding in his account of the handkerchief. At the center of his story of the talisman that guarantees male desire (3.4.57–58) is the figure of his dying mother: "she dying, gave it me, / And bid me, when my fate would have me wive, / To give it her" (3.4.61–63); his desire for Desdemona traces its lineal descent from this figure. But like the hand-kerchief itself, his mother can appear only as a figure for her own loss: only as she is dying, only after Desdemona is already lost to Othello. Othello's one link to the past effaced by his martial identity, his one maternal possession, thus encodes maternal loss in its history. And in telling Desdemona the story of this loss, Othello performs an act of revisionary autobiography, reshaping his origin and hence his sense of himself in accordance with the new sense of dependency that comes with the possibility of her loss. He had initially presented himself as the child only of fathers ("I fetch my life and being / From men of royal siege" [1.2.21–22]); his past—for us as for Desdemona—was composed only of the signs of his maleness, his heroic capacity to do and to suffer. His reference here to his dying mother is a destabilizing insertion into this previous tale, qualifying his purely male origin and making visible the childhood occluded by his entry into the tented field. And this destabilization rewrites that abrupt entry into manhood: partly because it is temporally unmoored, the story encoded in the handkerchief seems to me a re-remembering of the same point of transition, redefining the move into manhood as the consequence of maternal death.[49] This redefinition retrospectively makes sense of one of the oddities of the narrative through which Othello won Desdemona: the extent to which he describes not his heroic exploits among men but his sufferings in the strange and desolate landscape of maternal deprivation, its vast and empty caves and rocks peopled by strangers and cannibals (1.3.140–45). Thus re-understood, abandonment becomes the burden of his tale and helps to explain both his terrible hunger for Desdemona and the terrible speed with which he believes that she, too, has abandoned him.

As Othello's love for Desdemona is infused with the language of infantile need, his loss of her is infused with the language of maternal abandonment:[50]

> There, where I have garner'd up my heart,
> Where either I must live, or bear no life,
> The fountain, from the which my current runs,
> Or else dries up, to be discarded thence. . .
> (4.2.58–61)

Insofar as he makes her the nurturant source of his being, chaos must come again when he is discarded thence. And he will inevitably be discarded thence: the more fully Othello seeks his own perfection in Desdemona, the more fully he constructs her as the principle that nourishes him, the more fully the sexual act that consummates their union will spoil her perfection and hence his; here, as in *Troilus and Cressida*, sexuality will become the sign of separation and loss, the sign of his having been cast out. The whole of his exchange with Desdemona demonstrates Othello's terrible conflict between his intense desire for fusion with the woman he idealizes as the nurturant source of his being and his equally intense conviction that her participation in sexuality has contaminated her and thus contaminated the perfection that he has vested in her:

> *Oth.*   to be discarded thence,
> Or keep it as a cistern, for foul toads
> To knot and gender in!. . .
>
> *Des.*   I hope my noble lord esteems me honest.
>
> *Oth.*   O, ay, as summer's flies, are in the shambles,
> That quicken even with blowing:
> O thou black weed, why art so lovely fair?
> Thou smell'st so sweet, that the sense aches at thee,
> Would thou hadst ne'er been born!
>
>   (4.2.61–71)

As in *Troilus and Cressida*, the sexual act that had seemed to promise access to this nurturant source of being instead contaminates it, turning Desdemona into spoiled food as it has turned Cressida into "remainder viands" (*Troilus and Cressida*, 2.2.71; 5.2.156–59). Obsessively, Othello's mind turns on food contaminated by sexual contact: the fountain/garner transformed into the cistern where toads knot and gender,[51] the meat in the shambles—in a return to Hamlet's grotesque image for conception (*Hamlet*, 2.2.181–82)—become the breeding ground for flies. And once again, as in both *Troilus and Cressida* and *Hamlet*, responsibility for the soiling of this maternal body must be displaced, performed by a Claudius, a Diomed, a Cassio; as with Hamlet's and Troilus's, Othello's disgust at duplicitous sexuality covers disgust for sexuality *per se*, the sexuality that threatens to "corrupt and taint" (1.3.271) his business from the start. However passionately Othello looks forward to enjoying the fruits of his purchase (2.3.9), that consummation changes them both in his imagination.[52] After it, Desdemona can no longer be the vessel of his perfection: broken, soiled, she mirrors him not as the idealized pure mother who would reflect the essential wholeness and whiteness of his soul but rather as the reflection of his own contaminating and contaminated blackness;[53] the anguish of "O thou black weed" marks the extent to which they have now blackened one another in his imagination. Hence the logic by which Othello acknowledges his own sexual arousal—"the sense aches at thee"—even as he tries to disown the sexuality that has blackened Desdemona.

The handkerchief maintains its hold over Othello's imagination partly insofar as it records the moment at which this idealized maternal figure is lost. A miniature representation of the wedding sheets,[54] "spotted with strawberries" (3.3.442) as those "lust-stain'd" sheets are "spotted" with "lust's blood" (5.1.36), it is a talisman that guarantees both virginity and its loss in the act of consummation. And the loss of the handkerchief itself only reconfirms what is lost in that act: as Othello's mother enters the play only by allusion to the moment of her death, the handkerchief becomes imaginatively present to Othello only in its absence, and only after he believes Desdemona lost to him. The handkerchief thus comes doubly to stand for the loss of the perfect object of desire. But how are we to understand the handkerchief's simultaneous encoding of maternal loss and marital consummation? Or—put differently—why does the act of consummation registered in the handkerchief fuse Desdemona with the mother already lost to Othello, finally requiring Desdemona's dead body as the counterpart to his mother's?

As Othello elaborates the history of the handkerchief, its magical power to stabilize male desire turns increasingly on the magical power of long-dead women:

> that handkerchief
> Did an Egyptian to my mother give . . .
> . . . there's magic in the web of it;
> A sibyl, that had number'd in the world
> The sun to make two hundred compasses,
> In her prophetic fury sew'd the work;
> The worms were hallow'd that did breed the silk,
> And it was dyed in mummy, which the skilful
> Conserve of maidens' hearts.
>   (3.4.53–73, *passim*)

In Othello's version of its history—true emotionally for him whether or not it is literally true—the weaving of the handkerchief reaches back through an unbroken line of female descent; if the dying mother is at the center of its magic, her presence is oddly diffused, exfoliated through the Egyptian charmer, the sibyl, the maidens. And the final magical ingredients of the handkerchief seem to me to define the series and hence the power of the handkerchief as erotic emblem. Like the wedding sheets, the handkerchief itself commemorates both virginity and its loss, encoding in its weave the tension between breeding and hallowedness, sexuality and the sacred:[55] its silk is bred from hallowed worms; the very spots that signify consummation are made from mummy, conserved from the hearts of dead virgins. As Othello embroiders the story of the handkerchief, its power is increasingly defined by this tension; in the end, the dying mother's hold over her son's imagination, like the virginal sibyl's, merges with the magic of the dead maidens. And as the maternal power of the lost handkerchief is increasingly defined by virginity, the handkerchief increasingly becomes a fetishistic representation of specifically maternal virginity as the impossible condition of male desire, the condition always already lost.[56] As fetish, the handkerchief magically defends against acknowledgement of the primary loss, the separateness signaled by the mother's sexuality[57]; and as fetish, it can finally do nothing more than exhibit the loss it attempts magically to compensate for. Hence the centrality of the mother to the erotics of the handkerchief: like Troilus feeling his mother's soil in Cressida's or Posthumus assuming that his wife's infidelity implies his mother's and lamenting the "woman's part" in making men, the conjunctions in Othello's story of the handkerchief make his dying mother equivalent to the site of loss, her womb the first place of betrayal. This is the logic according to which Othello associates the loss of Desdemona not only with her birth (4.2.71) but also with his own, with his mother's gestation of him: "Even then this forked plague is fated to us, / When we do quicken" (3.3.280–81). The consummation with Desdemona can only duplicate this first betrayal, spoiling again the perfect maternal figure already spoiled and hence spoiling the fantasy of perfect union with her.

Contaminated, Othello's mother can only be dead to him; like the fetishistic handkerchief itself, she can epitomize only her own loss. And the maternal death variously encoded in the handkerchief is similarly both the sign of loss and the denial of loss: the mummy conserved of dead maidens' hearts recapitulates the mother's dead body and at the same time magically preserves her lost virginity, ensuring male desire. In its complex weave of consummation, virginity, and death, that is, the handkerchief enunciates both the limiting condition of male desire and the impossibility of that condition, thus anticipating Desdemona's end: if virginity is the ground of Othello's desire, death is its only preservative. Through the consummation, Desdemona and the dying mother become one, fused as the perfect ambiguity of Othello's "her"[58] had predicted: "She dying, gave it me, / And bid me, when my fate would have me wive, / To give it her." In Desdemona's death, the transmission of the handkerchief becomes perfectly circular: the talisman that comes from the dying mother is returned to her through the dead body of the wife. And as the mother is preserved in the dead maidens, so Desdemona's death serves not only to punish but to preserve her, returning her to her status as maiden/mother and making her Othello's alone, in the terrible love-death that consummates the play.

Othello's first images for Desdemona's death turn on the nurturance he has been denied: if she has spoiled the fountain/garner, he will retaliate by recording the oral spoilage on her body, chopping her into messes (4.1.196) or poisoning her (4.1.203–4). But under Iago's tutelage, he comes to think of the murder as a ritual of repurification, strangling her "in her bed, even the bed she hath contaminated" (4.1.203–4), on the very wedding sheets that witness the contamination. As he oscillates between the two forms of murder, the act becomes for him the psychic equivalent of doing and undoing the moment of consummation:[59] approaching her, he imagines a bloody killing that reenacts it ("Thy bed, lust-stain'd, shall with lust's blood be spotted" [5.1.36]); but faced with her sleeping body, he decides instead on the form of murder that will restore it to its unmarred condition, in which no blood is shed (5.2.3). In the end, doing and undoing—consummation and purifying murder—become one in his imagination: bloodlessly "pluck[ing] the rose" (5.2.13), he simultaneously takes and restores her virginity. For only death can restore her to the state in which it is safe to love her; only when she is "cold as her chastity" (5.2.276–77), when there is "no more moving" (5.2.94), can he let himself be moved by her. Imagining her sleeping body as her own funerary statue, the pure white "monumental alabaster" (5.2.5) that memorializes her death, he can safely acknowledge his own desire: "Be thus, when thou art dead, and I will kill thee, / And love thee after" (5.2.18–19).[60] Thus preserved, she can be all his: the purifying murder undoes the sexuality that was the mark of her separateness from him. Once her death has fulfilled the condition of the handkerchief, he can merge with her on their marriage bed, safely reconsummating their union in the love-death: "I kiss'd thee ere I kill'd thee, no way but this, / Killing myself, to die upon a kiss" (5.2.359–60).

At the same time that Othello's murder of Desdemona repurifies her in his imagination, it allows him to recuperate the masculine identity that he had lost in abandoning the tented field, the identity that union with her had always threatened;[61] the love-death becomes safe for Othello only after he has both repurified Desdemona and redefined himself as a man through violent action. Even as Othello first vested his heroic perfection in Desdemona, he registered uneasiness at this new housing of his selfhood, the "circumscription and confine" in which he had newly located his "unhoused free condition" (1.2.26–27). When he first speaks to the Senate of leaving this condition, his language reflects his anxiety at entering the arena of female generativity: "Since these arms of mine had seven years' pith, / Till now some nine moons wasted, they have us'd / Their dearest action in the tented field" (1.3.83–85). The deeply ambiguous "wasted," referring indiscriminately both to "moons" and to "these arms of mine," encapsulates his sense of danger, condensing a complex of fears: that the time away from war has been a waste of time; that the pith of his soldier's arm has wasted away through its peacetime leisure; ultimately that his involvement in the feminized realm of peace and generativity—the realm of the "nine moons" bound up with Desdemona's loving maternal pity—will destroy his masculine identity. These are the fears that Othello will articulate more clearly when Desdemona's request to accompany him in his wars elicits his somewhat hysterical denial that sexuality will "corrupt and taint" his business, so disabling his masculinity that housewives will be able to make a skillet of his helm (1.3.271–72); and they are the fears played out as the play charts his return to ruthless masculinity.

In *Othello* as in *Troilus and Cressida*, both the soiling of the maternal object and the initial threat to masculinity require a recoil back into the world of men, leaving women and their dangerous pity behind. The story of the handkerchief seems retrospectively to define Othello's first entry into the masculine realm of the tented field as a consequence of maternal death; now Desdemona's apparent betrayal—like Cressida's real one—enables his return in fantasy to the male identity that he had left in succumbing to her maternal pity. His obsessive vengeance enables that return: it is always directed toward the troubling female body, not toward the male friend who has apparently betrayed him; it is always a sign of solidarity with a male community, a way to break the hold of the female over him. Replacing his marriage to Desdemona with a "sacred vow" (3.3.468) of mock-marriage to Iago,[62] hardening his heart against the pity that had been the sign of Desdemona's love and hence of his susceptibility to her (4.1.177–96), killing her on behalf of the other men she might betray (5.2.6), he rejoins that community, undoing the threat that would make a skillet of his helm. And once Desdemona is dead, Othello can return in fantasy to the world of his fathers, the world in which desire is controlled by men, not women: now the handkerchief becomes the sign of paternal—not maternal—legacy: it is now "an antique token / My father gave my mother" (5.2.218). And only here, after he has murdered his wife, does the play allow us fully to imagine him as a soldier, giving us a moment of his heroic past to seize on; it specifies his martial identity for the first time as he turns his soldier's weapon upon himself, replicating that moment in Aleppo once where he took "the circumcised dog, / And smote him thus" (5.2.356–57). Even Othello's death thus enacts this resumption of his masculinity: apparently endlessly supplied with masculine weapons, he returns via suicide to a purely martial mode.

Once death has restored both Desdemona's idealized chastity and Othello's idealized masculinity, Othello can redefine their deaths as lovers' union, dying upon a kiss. But this redefinition is Othello's, not the play's. Hamlet and Troilus had both associated sexual union with death ("Is thy union here?" [*Hamlet*, 5.2.331]; "Death, I fear me" [*Troilus and Cressida*, 3.2.20]); but only Othello willingly substitutes death for union, purchasing thereby not the fruits of love but escape from unbearable tension. And despite his final anguish, this escape seems to give Othello what he has wanted all along. Meeting Desdemona on Cyprus, before the consummation of their marriage, he tells us as much:

> O my soul's joy,
> If after every tempest come such calmness,
> May the winds blow, till they have waken'd death,
> And let the labouring bark climb hills of seas,
> Olympus-high, and duck again as low
> As hell's from heaven. If it were now to die,
> 'Twere now to be most happy, for I fear
> My soul hath her content so absolute,
> That not another comfort, like to this
> Succeeds in unknown fate.
>
> (2.1.184–93)

The anticipation of sexual union—represented in the climbing and ducking of the labouring ship—here awakens Othello's longing for the death that can simultaneously represent and forestall the dangers of consummation.[63] And this is the death Othello chooses at the end: a death that maintains the purity of an idealized sexual union, replacing consummation with its own symbolic enactment.

In its own way, then, the ending of *Othello* enacts the etherealized union of "The Phoenix and the Turtle," where death is the only way to solve the paradoxes of desire and hence the only possible route to consummation; but the play questions this solution by enacting it as tragedy, specifically as the tragic consequence of male sexual fantasy. Unlike *Romeo and Juliet*, where the love-death is shared between the protagonists and hence largely accepted by the audience, *Othello* makes it plain that this love-death is the psychic property of the men, its enactment something that Cassio, Iago, and Othello do to Desdemona.[64] Although Desdemona calls for her wedding sheets to be laid on what she suspects will be her deathbed (4.2.106; 4.3.24–25), the equation of love and death does not come naturally to her; she must learn it, unwillingly, from Othello. When the lovers meet on Cyprus, Desdemona's passionate rejoinder to Othello's desire to die—"The heavens forbid / But that our loves and comforts should increase, / Even as our days do grow" (2.1.193–95)—defines the differences between them.[65] Othello ambivalently desires love as an absolute, an end point of perfection in which the self dissolves; his sexual imagination tends toward the stasis of death both as the epitome of loss of self in symbiotic union with a maternal figure and as a way of keeping both the object and the imagined moment of consummation perfect. But Desdemona has no desire to die. She flatly rejects Othello's implied equation, allying love not with stasis but with generative process. The exchange encapsulates the play's exploration of the difference not only between Othello and Desdemona but between male and female sexual dynamics and hence between the male and female sexual imagination: the male end-stopped, figured by stasis and death; the female unbounded, figured as part of a larger process of generation. The final love-death can thus represent consummation for him, but not for her: for her, "That death's unnatural, that kills for loving" (5.2.42). In the tragic lodging of the bed (5.2.364), Shakespeare plays out this difference, specifically plays out its tragic consequences for the woman forced to participate in the male fantasy against her will.

Shakespeare's portrayal of the love-death, like his portrayal of Desdemona throughout, marks his attempt to dissociate himself from this fantasy. And the attempt is at least partly successful: in *Othello*, Shakespeare gives us—uniquely among the tragedies—a woman who can be both frankly sexual and utterly virtuous, who can moreover combine in herself sexual appetite and maternal nurturance without becoming whorish or overwhelming, except in the imagination of her husband. With her fidelity and her devotion to process, Desdemona in fact points the way toward *The Winter's Tale*, where female sexuality will again be associated with nurturant growth and change, and again opposed by the male desire for stasis and control. There, the male protagonist will finally learn to submit himself to the generative flux registered in Polixenes's "nine changes of the watery star" (*The Winter's Tale*, 1.2.1, itself a revised version of Othello's "some nine moons wasted"); and the female protagonist will outlive his fantasy of stasis, returning from the statue-like condition—the "monumental alabaster"—in which he has imprisoned her. But Othello cannot yet safely trust to this benign female realm of generation; and before Shakespeare can write *The Winter's Tale*, he himself will have to embrace some of the openness and flux of the romance form.[66] For the moment, his formal and psychological allegiance is with the end-stopped genre of tragedy: even while he diagnoses the male pathology that leads to Desdemona's death, his own aesthetic designs require her dead body as fully as Othello does.

Even here, that is, Shakespeare is not wholly able to dissociate himself from the psychic patterns that sanctify women or write them whore; ultimately, *Othello* rewrites the dilemmas of *Troilus and Cressida* without fully resolving them. Though Desdemona remains entirely virtuous and to that extent exempt from Othello's fantasy, she is in the end subject to a containment as stringent as Cressida's; sexually vibrant and independent as she is at first, she is finally made to conform not only to Othello's control but to Shakespeare's. The virtuous self-assertion that is initially attractive in her is made to seem increasingly problematic as it increasingly impinges on the realm of Othello's military competence, as her badgering increasingly threatens his male autonomy; and after her initial display of power—perhaps in retaliation for it—her virtue is increasingly redefined as her wifely obedience, her fidelity to the ideal of wifely perfection.[67] Still as loving and faithful to Othello as she has been all along, the quality of her love changes, becoming allied with an otherworldly sweetness, a helpless self-abnegation that makes her tragically obedient to her husband's fancies (3.3.89–90), however dangerous they may be to her. In this mood, she will put on those wedding sheets and prepare to die on them. Her mysterious final words—"Nobody, I myself, farewell: / Commend me to my kind lord" (5.2.125–26)—register the absorption of her self into his, even as they shift the blame from her kind lord to the "I" who has become nobody; they therefore function simultaneously to mark the extent of her tragedy and to reassure Shakespeare's audience—and perhaps Shakespeare himself—that her potentially dangerous self-assertion has been curbed, hence that she fully deserves the sanctity that the play finally bestows on her.[68]

But insofar as her virtue is thus redefined, Shakespeare's containment of Desdemona fuses with Othello's: her sanctification reassuringly links female virtue with self-sacrifice, enabling the pathos of the final scenes and hence the male audience's vicarious participation in the love-death.[69] Contained, she becomes safe for that audience to adore, as she is now safe for Othello to adore. And her containment here signals Shakespeare's renewed investment in the fantasies that guide Troilus and Othello and hence predicts the fate of the women in the tragedies that follow from *Othello*. In them, the qualities momentarily brought together in Desdemona will be violently split apart and demonized. Female power *per se* will be dangerous: in Goneril and Regan, Lady Macbeth and Volumnia, sexuality will become the sign of villainy, maternity the sign of overwhelming destructive power. In Shakespeare's own reiteration of the fantasy that destroys Desdemona, only absolutely a-sexual maternity will now be tolerable; the possibilities for virtuous femininity will shrink to the dimensions of the sanctified Cordelia, the virginal daughter/mother dead in her father's arms. Only Cleopatra—on the verge of romance—will remain to some extent exempt from these splittings; through them, the other tragedies will all take their vengeance on the figures of women, in effect paying them back for Desdemona's wholeness, the wholeness finally intolerable both to Othello and to Shakespeare.

4

MARRIAGE AND THE MATERNAL BODY: ON MARRIAGE AS THE END OF COMEDY IN *ALL'S WELL THAT ENDS WELL* AND *MEASURE FOR MEASURE*

In the midst of Hamlet's attack on Ophelia, he cries out to Ophelia, "I say we will have no mo marriage" (*Hamlet*, 3.1.149). Fusing mother with beloved in his diatribe, he proclaims an end to the institution of marriage itself, giving us a graphic emblem for the need to come to terms with the sexualized maternal body before embarking on the establishment of a new family through marriage. In their own ways, *Troilus and Cressida* and *Othello* play out the end to marriage proclaimed by Hamlet: both record the impossibility of return to the mother's body through sexual union. But patriarchal society nonetheless demands this return: before the son can take his place in that society, he must remake himself as a father; patriarchal authority itself passes from fathers to sons only through the problematic medium of the mother's body. The problem comedies—written roughly at the same time as *Troilus and Cressida* and *Othello*—seem to me ways of attempting to deal with this necessity: through the separations and recombinations recorded in their plots, they figure both the recoil from sexual union and the desperate remedies that might make marriage possible again.

Like Troilus and Othello, Bertram and Angelo are presented as virgins, facing what is in effect their first sexual experience; and that experience again takes the shape of a morning-after fantasy, in which a virgin is violated and then abandoned, psychically transformed into a whore. The morning-after fantasy of contamination and abandonment embedded in each play marks what makes these comedies problematic *as comedies*: under the aegis of this fantasy, marriage—and with it, comedy—becomes impossible. This is in fact the situation at the beginning of both problem comedies, where both protagonists rush out of wedlock toward illegitimate union, desiring only where they do not wed, wedding where they do not desire. And in an extraordinary move, Shakespeare enables marriage again not by evading but by following out the logic of the morning-after fantasy, in effect enshrining it in the plot. In these plays the psychological splittings that govern the fates of Cressida and Desdemona are literalized and enacted: whereas Troilus and then Othello split one woman in two—Troilus finding both his own and Diomed's Cressida in the one body of Cressida, Othello seeing in Desdemona "the cunning whore of Venice, / That married with Othello" (4.2.91–92)—Bertram and Angelo negotiate their sexual desire between two women, one of whom (Diana/Isabella) is apparently violated and shamed, becoming the repository of sexual soiling, the other of whom (Helena/Mariana) mysteriously remains unsoiled and hence—eventually—available for marriage. Split apart and then violently yoked together through the device of the bed trick, the women in *All's Well* and *Measure for Measure* simultaneously illustrate the fundamental incompatibility between marriage and male desire and provide a magical solution to it: the final scenes of both plays depend on something akin to a theatrical exorcism, where sexual contamination is first attached to the supposedly violated virgins and then banished as the virtual wives return and the truth is revealed. And through this two-body accommodation to the morning-after fantasy, Shakespeare is able to turn the tragic endings of *Troilus and Cressida* and *Othello* toward comedy, though comedy of a problematic sort.

In both plays, the bed trick is thus the primary device through which desire is regulated, both legitimized and relocated in the socially sanctioned bond of marriage. Through a version of homeopathic cure,[1] the two bodies of the bed trick allow both Bertram and Angelo to enact fantasies in which a virgin is soiled—one nearly a nun, the other a Diana—only to find out that their sexual acts have in fact been legitimate, that the soiling has taken place only in fantasy. The bed tricks thus offer to save Bertram and Angelo from their own fantasies: presented with legitimate sexuality as a *fait accompli*, they might go on to accept the possibility that they have been tricked into, the possibility of desire within marriage. So much, at least, is promised by Helena's brief glance at the kindness with which Bertram unknowingly used her (*All's Well*, 5.3.304) and by Mariana's wistful "They say best men are moulded out of faults" (*Measure*, 5.1.437). But given the status of the bed tricks as tricks and the unwilling husbands' failure to give much evidence that they have in fact been transformed, that promise seems frail indeed. And insofar as the bed tricks betray the desires of the male protagonists in curing them, they tend to become less a vehicle for the working out of impediments to marriage than a forced and conspicuous emblem for what needs working out. As such, their comic solutions suggest why it is that marriage has become for Shakespeare literally the end of comedy.

The bed tricks thus stand at the center of what is problematic about sexual relations in these plays. Comparison with Shakespeare's source for the bed trick can help us gauge their peculiar valence. In *The Palace of Pleasure*, William Painter's translation of Boccaccio's *Decameron* (Day 3, Story 9), the bed trick is a rather well-mannered and genial affair, repeated often and with affection. We are specifically told that the count (equivalent to Bertram) "at his uprising in the morning . . . used many courteous and amiable words and gave diverse fair and precious jewels."[2] But all this friendliness has been edited out of Shakespeare's versions; the potentially curative mutuality of Painter's account is entirely absent. In both *All's Well* and *Measure for Measure*, the emphasis on speed and silence (*All's Well*, 4.2.58; *Measure*, 3.1.247–48) transform it utterly, so that it becomes the epitome not only of the dark waywardness of desire but also of its depersonalization, the interchangeability of the bodies with which lust plays (*All's Well*, 4.4.24–25). Moreover, these bed tricks are portrayed as one-night stands that the male protagonists have no desire to repeat, and not only for reasons of dramatic compression. Both Bertram and Angelo recoil immediately from the object of desire, losing interest in their virgins as soon as they are ravished; for both, the fantasied act of despoiling virginity seems to be the only source of sexual desire. Thus transformed, these bed tricks do not bode well as cures. The psychic violence of their proposed solutions merely illustrates the seriousness of the disease: the extent to which sexuality here is a matter of deception on the one side and hit-and-run contamination on the other underscores the deep incompatibility that separates sexuality from marriage.[3]

When Montaigne treats this incompatibility in "Upon Some Verses of Virgil," he names it incest: "Nor is it other then a kinde of incest, in this reverent alliance and sacred bond [of marriage], to employ the effects and extravagant humor of an amorous licentiousness."[4] In so naming the tension between the sacred and the sexual, Montaigne comes close to identifying the psychological dynamic of these plays, in which the soiling potentiality of sexuality is understood within a familial context, associated with the prohibitions surrounding the boy-child's first fantasies of soiling a sacred space. These are the terms through which Hamlet understands Claudius's literally incestuous relationship with his mother: under the impact of his new knowledge of maternal sexuality, the enclosed garden-paradise that was his mother's body becomes for him the fallen and unweeded garden, possessed by things rank and gross. Insofar as Troilus and Othello associate Cressida and Desdemona with that maternal body, sexual union is for them as for Hamlet the contamination of a sacred maternal space: the soiling of a mother (*Troilus and Cressida*, 5.2.133), the transformation of the garner into a cistern where toads knot and gender (*Othello*, 4.2.58–63). Between them, *All's Well* and *Measure for Measure* provide a complex exploration of the forces that disrupt union in *Troilus and Cressida* and *Othello*; the central actions of both are exfoliations of Hamlet's dilemma, difficult attempts to clear a space for marriage in the face of his terrible knowledge.

In their own ways, both Bertram and Angelo act out the conflict Montaigne depicts, locating their "amorous licentiousness" in the illicit, far from family bonds; and yet sexual desire brings each of them home, to the problematic maternal body and to its traces in the self. *All's Well* analyzes male flight from a woman who has become nearly indistinguishable from the mother and the desperate measures necessary to render her safe and pure; *Measure for Measure* analyzes sexual desire *per se* as a return to contaminated maternal origins and reinvents the bodiless and all-seeing father who can control its dangers. Both problem comedies attempt in effect to legitimize desire, enabling a diminished version of the marriage Hamlet has lost; but the defensive measures they must undertake to enable marriage remain more striking than the marriages they achieve. The marriages that end these comedies fail to satisfy the desires of either the characters or the audience; and their failure marks the extent to which Hamlet's prohibition remains in force and hence the extent to which comedy is no longer a viable genre for Shakespeare.[5]

All's Well begins with the promise of a son separating from his mother, going to seek a new father and new possibilities for manhood elsewhere; here, as in *Troilus*, manhood initially seems a function of leaving the mother behind. But the achievement of manhood is notoriously problematic in a world of dead and dying fathers; and this mother is an imposing figure, one who cannot easily be left behind. Initially, she seems a comedic version of Gertrude,[6] undoing Gertrude's tragic faults both through her right remembrance of her husband and through her willingness to "deliver" her son from her (1.1.1), permitting him to find his manhood elsewhere. But even with her permission, Bertram does not fully succeed in leaving her; although she herself is kept innocent of agency, other women act for her, relentlessly bringing Bertram home. Almost as soon as Bertram has left, the Countess has given her endorsement and her ambiguous strength to Helena's Parisian project ("What I can help thee to, thou shalt not miss" [1.3.251]); and by the end of the play she seems more concerned with Helena's interests than with Bertram's, crying out for justice against Helena's assumed murderer as though the primary suspect were not her son (5.3.153), enthusiastically confirming the damning evidence of the ring (5.3.194–98). The Countess, Helena, the Widow, Diana: all force Bertram's return to Rosillion and the identity he had attempted to leave behind. In effect, the Countess's binding maternal power is extended through this partly unspoken alliance of women;[7] whatever her intentions as an isolated character—intentions, like Helena's, kept deliberately shadowy—in the end the play has come full circle, and Bertram has, through her surrogates, been restored to her.

Shakespeare in fact manages his sources in a way that foregrounds this psychic process: the figure of the Countess and the crucial association of her with Helena are his additions to Boccaccio/Painter. With this alteration, Shakespeare makes Bertram's flight from marriage to Helena the consequence not only of the generalized threat to manhood posed by woman—"That man should be at woman's command, and yet no hurt done!" (1.3.89–90)—but of the specific conditions allying Helena with his mother.[8] For Bertram, Helena has virtually no existence apart from his mother; his only words to her before the scene of their enforced marriage are a parenthesis within his farewell to his mother ("Be comfortable to my mother, your mistress, and make much of her" [1.1.73–74]). This marriage is intolerable to him partly because it collapses exactly the distinctions that would enable Bertram's individuated manhood, the distinctions preserved and reinforced by the incest taboo.[9] Even as the king asserts his power to make and unmake distinctions of class, he inadvertently invokes the loss of distinction that is at the root of Bertram's psychic as well as his social panic:

> Strange it is that our bloods,
> Of colour, weight, and heat, pour'd all together,
> Would quite confound distinction, yet stands off
> In differences so mighty.
> (2.3.118–21)

Bred by his father (2.3.114), identified with his mother both by her position in the Rosillion household and by her sexual power over his surrogate father (1.1.6),[10] in herself Helena confounds distinctions; mingling blood with her[11] would necessarily bring down (2.3.112) both his masculine and his social standing.

Bertram's flight from Helena, and his attraction to a woman decidedly outside his family structure, represent his attempts to repeat the separation of the first scene, founding his masculinity in escape from his mother and the threat posed by marriage to one so closely identified with her. And his problem is peculiarly complicated by the death of his father: here, as in the beginning of *Hamlet*, a father is newly dead and a son is exhorted to live up to his image. From the first, Bertram's masculine identity is the subject of anxious speculation on the part of his mother and the king, speculation expressed as the desire that he be like his father in moral parts as well as shape (1.1.57–58; 1.2.21–22); the repeated emphasis has the effect of establishing Bertram's distance from this idealized figure. And the surrogate father on whom Bertram might newly found his adult identity is very little help: weakened, he presides over an effeminate court where "no sword [is] worn / But one to dance with," where Bertram would serve merely as "forehorse to a smock" (2.1.30, 33). Himself saved only by Helena's power, the king cannot serve as the basis for Bertram's masculinity; instead of enabling separation from the mother, he would enforce a return to her through Helena. The very figure who should enable separation confounds it: hence in part the significance of the king's surprising appearance at Rosillion in the last scene. In the series of curious removes from the court, none required by the plot or given any explanation, kingly authority itself is decentered, relocated finally in the mother's realm; in resuming his adult status only there, and only under the aegis of this father, Bertram is returned to the point of origin.

In leaving his mother and Helena and the effeminate court of his surrogate father, Bertram seems to achieve manhood of a kind on the battlefield, as Troilus does. But socially sanctioned manhood in this play entails a return to, not a separation from, one's mother. Bertram can take his place as a man within this social structure only insofar as he can be reconciled with his mother and the king, and hence with the woman they have chosen for him; these are the only terms on which he can in effect become his father, claiming adulthood and hence his paternal legacy. Bertram himself unwittingly encodes Helena's power in his "passport" to her, simultaneously setting his own achievement of paternity as the condition of his resumption of adult status in France and making her the place-holder of his masculine identity: "When thou canst get the ring upon my finger, which never shall come off, and show me a child begotten of thy body that I am father to, then call me husband; but in such a 'then' I write a 'never' " (3.2.56–59). Only her body can show him forth as a legitimate father; her acquisition of the ring that is "an honour 'longing to our house" (4.2.42), passed "from son to son some four or five descents / Since the first father wore it" (3.7.24–25), is the sign of her status as place-holder to his paternal legacy, the sign therefore of her intervention in what had been imagined as a purely male line of descent. In this world of weakened fathers,

Helena presides over the transmission of adult masculinity. But women's bodies always function thus: her showing forth of the ring and of her own pregnant body in the last scene rewrites the parthenogenetic fantasy embedded in the ring's history, redefining the transmission of male honor—and male identity—as inevitably contingent on the female body.

The complicated exchange of rings in the bed trick and its unraveling in the final scene reiterate Helena's intervention and thus her power. Bertram initially supposes that he is in control of the ring's transmission, and therefore of the sexual ring-play. After claiming that his father's ring "shall never come off," Bertram lightly trades it for what he supposes is the "ring" of Diana's chastity ("Mine honour's such a ring" [4.2.45]).[12] But it is of course Helena's "ring," not Diana's, that he gets in the dark, Helena, not Bertram, who is always in charge of the exchange. Her control—the disruptive power of her "ring"—is moreover literalized in the ring she places on his finger, the ring that we eventually find out had belonged to the king. The weightiness of this second ring in the last scene comes as a surprise to us, since the earlier emphasis on Bertram's ring has encouraged us to believe that it would be the spring on the trap set for Bertram; but in the end, Helena's ring—not Bertram's—initiates the series of puzzles that can be solved only by her return. In effect, we find out in the last scene, Bertram has traded his father's ring for his surrogate father's, through the medium of Helena's body. But this surrogate father himself stands for the vulnerability of male authority, its subjection to a saving female power; and the ring that the king gives Helena, and she gives Bertram, is the token not of kingly power *per se* but of Helena's power over that power, her capacity to command the king's help. In substituting this ring—the sign of her power over the play's last remaining masculine authority— for Bertram's father's, Helena displaces his father's authority with her own, making Bertram as fully dependent on her as the king had been: in the end, only her reappearance can solve the riddle of the bed trick, releasing Bertram from a potential death sentence and restoring him to his adult identity. Even as she meets the conditions he has set, that is, Helena demonstrates not his power over her but her power over him.

In making Helena's sexual potency—she could "araise King Pippen" (2.1.75)—rescue both the king and Bertram, Shakespeare initially seems to be rewriting the Helen of *Troilus and Cressida*, in effect making a woman's sexual powers curative rather than corrupting; he in fact alludes to this Helen near the start of the play (1.3.66–76). But despite the overt attempt to make sexuality curative, suspicion of sexuality remains the dominant emotional fact of the play; even here, where Shakespeare attempts, Pandarus-like, to bring two together, we are left with a sense of failure about the sexual act and with a final queasiness about the getting of children. It does not prove easy to turn disease into cure by fiat; and in vesting its cures in the figure of Helena, the play reawakens fears of male submission that are distinctly part of the disease. Despite her self-abnegation, even despite our confusion about her purposes,[13] she ends up in control of the plot; and her bed trick fails to detoxify or legitimize sexuality partly insofar as it becomes one more instance of man at woman's command (1.3.89), and hence merely confirmation of the loss of male control that had been a terrifying potentiality of sexual union all along.[14] Far from confirming Bertram's masculinity in his triumph over a young virgin, this bed trick merely exhibits the failure of his autonomy publicly. Even as he attempts to define his manhood by locating sexual desire in a world apart from his mother and surrogate father, Bertram thus finds himself returned to their choice: flee as he might, there is no escaping Helena. Both in the plot logic that returns Bertram to Helena and in the conflicted portrayal of Helena herself, Shakespeare seems to me to embody a deep ambivalence of response toward the mother who simultaneously looks after us and threatens our independence, the mother whose power is frighteningly diffuse, there where we least expect it. Astonishing both for her willfulness and her self-abnegation, simultaneously far below Bertram's sphere and far above it, apparently all-powerful in her weakness, present even when Bertram most thinks that he has escaped her, triumphantly proclaiming her maternity at the end, Helena becomes the epitome of the maternal power that binds the child, especially the male child, who here discovers that she is always the woman in his bed.

In returning him to the woman he would flee, the bed trick reiterates the dilemma that has motivated his flight in the first place; in attempting to legitimate desire, it succeeds only in restating the utter incompatibility between male autonomy and female desire, between male sexuality and the constraints of the family. And as the purification ritual of the last scene unfolds, the bed trick increasingly enables marriage less by legitimating sexual union than by magically doing away with it altogether. The complex series of doings and undoings in the last scene functions, I think, to deflect shame away from Helena's pregnant body, in effect allowing her to appear as the secular equivalent of the virgin mother. Insofar as Bertram returns to marriage with her, that marriage is protected from the incompatibility that Montaigne called incest not because Bertram has been able to achieve the separation of wife and mother but because sexuality itself is occluded.

Throughout the final scene, the stress is on the undoing of the defiling sexual act, not on the potentially saving conception. Like the final scene of *Measure for Measure*, this scene takes the form of a shaming ritual;[15] and in both plays, the most prominent shaming is reserved for the sexually corrupt male. But in both plays that ritual turns on the production and subsequent shaming of the supposedly violated virgin; and the man's release from shame is in the end dependent less on his coming to terms with his own guilt than on the double process through which his shame is first transferred to the apparently wronged woman and then exorcised by the appearance of the legitimate sexual partner. The peculiar insistence on Diana's shaming illustrates this process. Just before Helena appears in the last scene, Diana says, "He knows himself my bed he hath defil'd; / And at that time he got his wife with child" (5.3.294–95). In effect, she separates the mental from the physical components of the sexual act, Bertram's intentions from his deed, ascribing the shame and soil to herself in order to leave Helena pure and hence available to rescue Bertram from his shame. Her words identify her role here as substitute strumpet, the figure onto whom both Bertram and the play can displace the sense of sexuality as defiling. Displace and then disavow: with the appearance of Helena, the shame that has been ascribed to Diana first intensifies—in the reference to her defiled bed—and then disappears, ostensibly carrying the taint attached to sexuality along with it. Apparently, that is, the play evokes sexual shame only to dispel it.

But in the process of undoing shame here, *All's Well* comes close to undoing the sexual act itself. As Diana repudiates her shame, whatever it was that happened in that bed is done and undone in our imaginations, as the ring—emblematic of the sexual encounter—is given ("this was it I gave him, being abed" [5.3.227]) and ungiven ("I never gave it him" [5.3.270]). The business of the ring underlines the extent to which this portion of the last scene takes on the configurations of a ritual of doing and undoing, from which the soiled Diana emerges pure, transformed from "strumpet" into "maid" (5.3.286–87). The play strikingly asks us to imagine her as contaminated and then repurified; and she emerges pure insofar as the bed trick deflects the sexual act away from her. But the bed trick manages to deflect the sexual act away from her without fully attaching it to Helena; as we witness the multiple undoings of the last scene, the sexual act itself becomes increasingly elusive, as though it had not happened at all, not with Diana and not with Helena. In separating Bertram's intentions from his deed, Diana's last words—the riddle to which the appearance of Helena is the solution—virtually define that deed out of existence, rescuing not only herself but also Bertram and Helena from its contamination. "He knows himself my bed he hath defil'd; / And at that time he got his wife with child": her riddle splits the sexual act into an imaginary defilement and a miraculous conception. Defiling one woman, Bertram impregnates another; through the magical transference of the riddle, Diana gets the taint and Helena gets the child. The prestidigitation of Diana's riddle—itself the exfoliation of the bed trick—brings the promised birth of Bertram's child as close to virgin birth as the facts of the case will allow.[16]

But this is apparently what Bertram has wanted all along: he has already told us that he will accept Helena as his wife only when she can prove herself in effect a virgin mother, that is, prove that she is with child by him without his participation in the sexual act. Helena's puzzling words on her entrance mark her collusion with this fantasy-miracle: " 'Tis but the shadow of a wife you see; / The name and not the thing" (5.3.301–2). In a culture in which marriage consisted of a series of stages and was often regarded as final only when it was consummated,[17] the distinction Helena makes between name and thing implies that the marriage is unconsummated even as her next words— "when I was like this maid / I found you wondrous kind" (5.3.303– 4)—insist on the fact of consummation. Enabling marriage both by her successful sexual manipulation of Bertram and by her insistence that she is wife in name only, Helena manages to fulfill in her body the conditions that will allow Bertram to return to Rosillion and his paternal legacy. But how can she do both at once? The puzzling doubleness of this moment is in fact characteristic of the representation of Helena throughout and signals the intense ambivalence toward female sexuality that informs the play.[18] Nearly from the beginning, we have been invited to see Helena both as a miraculous virgin and as a deeply sexual woman seeking her will: thus the early dialogue with Parolles, in which we see her meditating simultaneously on how to defend her virginity and on how to lose it to her liking (1.1.110–51); and thus the double presentation of her cure of the king, where her miraculous power depends equally on her status as heavenly maid and on the problematic sexuality that could "araise King Pippen" (2.1.75). Given this doubleness, she seems to fulfill the conditions of her own description of the Countess's youth, when "your Dian / Was both herself and love" (1.3.207–8). But Helena is no stable mix of Venus and Diana;[19] as in the dialogue with Parolles, the contrary impulses fail to cohere. The incoherence implicit in Helena is I think played out in the figure of Diana; her contradictory roles serve both to localize and to contain the conflicting elements of strumpet and virgin in Helena. As Helena chooses Bertram at court, she imagines herself shifting allegiance from Diana to Venus (2.3.74–76)—and a few scenes later, the aptly named Diana comes on stage for the first time. Her emergence as a character only after Helena has renounced her allegiance to the goddess whose name she bears suggests the complexity of her role: if the play vests the sense of sexuality as soiling in her, it also vests Helena's virginity in her. Both as the bearer of sexual shame and as the preserver of virginity, she functions as a split off portion of Helena herself,[20] and hence as the repository for the unstable incompatibilities within her and within the play.

The dissonance between Helena's various roles seems to me less the sign of an idealized union of love and chastity than the sign of a deep anxiety about female power, especially sexual power. Insofar as the play locates cure in Helena, that is, it enables male sexual desire and male identity only under the aegis of an elusively powerful woman; the equivocal desexualization of her throughout, like Shakespeare's various equivocations about the extent to which she is in charge of her own plot, is in part his attempt to manage the anxiety generated by the spectacle of man so utterly at woman's command. Partly as a consequence, Helena carries very little sense of the miraculous with her when she returns to life; unlike Hermione, or even to some extent Hero, she comes as the answer to a riddle, not the answer to a prayer. And like her return from the dead, her pregnancy seems a bogus miracle, less a promise of new life than a desperate attempt to fulfill the impossible condition governing desire within marriage for Bertram. The buried fantasy of Helena as Venus/Diana, the secular equivalent to the Virgin Mother, seems to me the play's pyrrhic solution to the problem of legitimizing sexuality, relocating it within sacred family bonds. Insofar as it enables this fantasy, the bed trick permits Bertram's safe return to Helena and Rosillion partly by wishing away the sexuality that makes that return dangerous. For the ending can restore Bertram's patrimony and his family bonds only insofar as it equivocates about Helena's pregnancy and hence about her body as the point of transmission of his male identity, making her into a dubious virgin mother to protect him from the consequences of her dangerous power.

There are no mothers in *Measure for Measure*; but there is another pregnant body. It is no accident that the unborn child of *All's Well*, who epitomizes the conflicted attempt to bring sexual desire back into the bonds of the family, reappears at the start of *Measure for Measure* as the product of an illicit union, the sign of sin who condemns its parents by proclaiming their sexuality publicly. The transformation of the pregnant Helena into the pregnant Juliet typifies the relation between the two plays: the sexual queasiness that lies behind Bertram's flight from both Helena and Diana is given much fuller expression in

Measure for Measure, with the consequence that the getting of children is the problem, not the purported solution. Here the bed trick cures nothing; it is written in effect from the point of view of Diana, designed overtly to preserve virginity, not to consummate a potentially saving sexual union. The very distinction between licit and illicit sexuality on which *All's Well* depends has broken down in *Measure*, at least until Mariana appears halfway through the play;[21] as this world is initially presented to us, all sexuality is illicit and enforces its own death sentence, whether through Angelo's restitution of the law condemning fornication or through the disease that seems its inevitable attendant. In this play's literalization of the pun that identifies death and orgasm,[22] sexuality becomes the original sin that brings death into the world; the bawd appropriately becomes the executioner. Even the marriages that traditionally end comedy in festivity have here become the punishment for sexual sin. No wonder Helena must be transformed into Juliet; no wonder the baby Juliet carries is not a hope for the future but "the sin you carry" (2.3.19).

The Duke's identification of the baby as "the sin you carry" confounds the illicit act with the product of the act, making the baby itself the bearer of its parents' sin; its sin is derived from its corrupt origin. And though the Duke addresses a Juliet whose sexual union was not fully legitimate, his terms would not be very different if her baby were the product of a perfectly legitimate union. For the Duke—as for the play—disgust at life is expressed as disgust at the facts of human dependency and the corruption inherited at its source. When the Duke condemns Pompey's life for its dependence on illicit sexual transactions, his language undermines the distinction between legitimacy and illegitimacy, unwittingly evoking the corruptness of all our origins:

> Say to thyself,
> From their abominable and beastly touches
> I drink, I eat, array myself, and live.
> Canst thou believe thy living is a life,
> So stinkingly depending?
> (3.2.22–26)

In this psychic lexicon, there is no room for legitimate sexuality: sexual touch *per se* is abominable and beastly; and since we all live from these touches, we are all stinkingly dependent. Hence the degree to which the Duke's question to Pompey—"Canst thou believe thy living is a life, / So stinkingly depending?"—reiterates the logic of his attempt to dissuade Claudio from life: for both, "all th'accommodations that thou bear'st / Are nurs'd by baseness" (3.1.14–15).[23] Both are stinkingly dependent; and in both instances, the language of sexual origin and maternal dependence carries the weight of the Duke's disgust, as though the facts of conception and maternal nursery were in themselves enough to turn one away from life.

Measure for Measure equivocally attempts to make life livable by simultaneously affirming and denying this origin. On the face of it, the play seems to enforce its acknowledgment: Angelo and Isabella are severely punished for their attempt to claim exemption from ordinary sexual processes. For both these baffled puritans, sexuality becomes the sign of bondage to the sexual family, hence literally the sign of their original sin; violently brought face to face with their own sexuality, both are forced to take their places in the bodily family.[24] Isabella is emphatically made to acknowledge the claims of her biological sisterhood even as she tries to immure herself in a spiritual family of sisters and mothers; both Angelo and Isabella are shamed and manipulated into wedlock in the end. The extremity of their self-exposure and degradation seems to me in part the mark of Shakespeare's strenuous attempt to separate himself from the bearers of the impossible fantasy of escape from the sexual body. But even while the play enforces the claims of the biological family in the persons of Angelo and Isabella, it accords the Duke himself the powers of an all-seeing spiritual father, apparently exempt from bodily needs; even as Isabella and Angelo are vindictively brought to recognize their origins and thus their human natures, a muted version of the fantasy of escape from sexual origins is reiterated and vested in the Duke. As the Duke increasingly puts himself in charge of matters of marriage and generation, in the last scene liberally bestowing new life as though he were a god, social and sexual continuance increasingly comes under male management, and the problematic female body comes to seem merely the pliant material means to male ends[25]—as Mariana herself obligingly turns up only when the Duke needs her body to fill in for Isabella's. If Helena's pregnant body is the site of Bertram's honor and the sign of new life in *All's Well*, *Measure for Measure* makes male honor and even life itself dependent not on the pregnant female body but on the Duke's machinations; the last scene is constructed to make invisible male power, rather than the visibly pregnant female body, the site of revelation. In the end, the replacement of the bodily female by the spiritual male dispensation seems complete.

But it is not entirely complete. The play's very peculiar treatment of Juliet seems to me the sign of its deep equivocation about origins. Juliet's pregnant body is the originating site for this play's confrontation with sin and death; it itself is the "character too gross" (1.2.144) in which Claudio's sin is written[26] and hence the material cause of his subjection to death. As such, it is a visible reminder of maternal origins and of the danger that is their inheritance. But the body so prominent in the beginning is curiously effaced by the action of the play, as the relationship between Juliet and Claudio is effaced; and this effacement seems to me a sign of the play's uneasy relation to sexuality and to the pregnant female body as the site of origin. Silent, strikingly isolated from the other characters—never acknowledged by Claudio during their two appearances on stage together, virtually unmentioned after her brief encounter with the Duke in 2.3—Juliet functions less as a realized character in the social world of Vienna than as a figure for the problem they would all like to efface, the problem of maternal origins. Originating cause of the play's dilemmas, she is largely forgotten as the Duke increasingly commands center stage; her pregnant body— the visible sign of maternal origin and of female generative power—is replaced by his invisible and bodiless control. But at the end Juliet returns, silently entering with Claudio; and her return qualifies the Duke's control. Displaced but never quite effaced by his machinations, wordlessly present at the end as at the beginning, she haunts the play, her body making legible the origin that can never quite be suppressed, as it makes legible the play's originating sin.

The solution to the dilemma registered in Juliet's body at first seems to be Isabella: the life that one woman has ruined, another can repair— or so Claudio hopes. The relationship between the two women is in fact both curious and elusive; though Isabella apparently never gives Juliet a thought after she is drawn out of the convent by Lucio's news, her initial response stresses the former closeness between them:

> *Isab.* Someone with child by him? My cousin Juliet?
>
> *Lucio* Is she your cousin?
>
> *Isab.* Adoptedly, as schoolmaids change their names
>   By vain though apt affection.
>
> (1.4.45–48)

Though Isabella immediately attempts to disown the connection— *vain* though apt affection—it remains; Juliet's membership in Isabella's family comes first through her relationship with Isabella and only later through marriage to her brother. We glimpse here a bond like that of Hermia and Helena, or Rosalind and Celia: the fusion of identities between women that in the romantic comedies will be ruptured by relationship with men. But here the rupture is caused not by the entry into heterosexuality but by what seems to be the radical difference between the two women: one on the point of entering a convent, the other on the point of giving birth to the child of an illicit union. Isabella's response to Lucio acknowledges the difference, disowning not only Juliet but the whole mode of vain affection to which she belongs; in effect, Juliet becomes a part of the past that Isabella tries to leave behind in entering the convent. Yet the two have exchanged names; their identities remain more closely bound than Isabella knows or can later acknowledge. Juliet's pregnancy calls Isabella out of the convent; and later, Angelo will attempt to force Isabella to undo the distance between herself and Juliet by giving up her "body to such sweet uncleanness / As she that [Claudio] hath stain'd" (2.4.54–55).

How are we to understand the bond between the two women?[27] It seems to me to function less as a fact in Isabella's psyche than as an indication of the act of splitting that has produced these two characters and the act of violence that would undo the split, compelling Isabella once again to exchange names with Juliet, through the machinations either of Angelo or of the Duke. Isabella and the cloister she inhabits initially enter the play as the solution to the problem caused by Juliet and registered in her pregnant body; in effect, Isabella is imagined— by Claudio and by the play—as a response to Juliet. In that sense, the women share a common origin. Both derive from the same anxiety about sexuality and female generativity: the body of one—her presence mediated by Mistress Overdone, the bawd who first introduces her into the play—is the repository for the sense of sexual generation as illicit and dangerous; the body of the other—an unpolluted sanctuary about to be immured within another sanctuary—carries the promise of escape from sexuality and from the consequences of sexuality. But the split that initially promises to heal the sexual fault in fact reinforces it; the embodiment of sanctuary in the person of Isabella awakens the desire it would suppress, and the purported solution becomes the new problem. The play abruptly hurries us away from the relatively benign and mutual desire of Claudio and Juliet, transporting us instead into the dark region of Angelo's desire for Isabella. No longer mutual, desire now turns precisely on the destruction of the sanctuary that had seemed to promise escape. For Angelo's desire requires the presence of Isabella as a nun to be violated; having been created to embody an absolute purity, Isabella must be sacrificed to the split—in Angelo, in the play— that engendered her.

The psychic splitting in the play is, for the most part, localized in Angelo, who replicates and hence defines its psychic geography; his attempt to keep the portions of himself radically separate from one another is reproduced in the play's rigidly separated and confined spaces.[28] The battle within him between fierce repression of sexual desire and equally fierce outbursts of degrading and degraded desire is externalized in Vienna's convent and brothel, this play's version of Hamlet's two nunneries (*Hamlet*, 3.1.121, 130, 141); for Angelo as for Vienna, there is only a region of sexual soil below marriage and a region of absolute purity above it, with no middle ground for legitimate sexuality within marriage, no "moated grange" until the Duke magically calls one up through his dubious machinations. And even when it has been invoked by the Duke, this middle ground— spatially undefined except by its position outside the city—can no more be incorporated into the city than it can be incorporated into Angelo himself; he can neither inhabit it nor allow it to inhabit him. The violence with which Angelo carves himself up into separate spaces and attempts to keep them separate is released in the violence of his desire for Isabella:[29] violently separated, nunnery and brothel must be violently brought together. "Having waste ground enough, / Shall we desire to raze the sanctuary / And pitch our evils there?" (2.2.170–72): Angelo's question suggests the degree to which his desire turns on the confounding of places, the radical unmaking of distinctions. The "strumpet / With all her double vigor, art and nature" (2.2.183–84) could not tempt him because he can experience desire only as the remaking of the sanctuary as brothel /privy, only as the polluting of a sacred space by his own bodily wastes.[30]

In the violence of Angelo's sexual imagination, Shakespeare reworks the terrible paradox of male desire as he had presented it in *Troilus and Cressida* and in *Othello*. There, the fantasy of pollution had been the tragic side effect of desire; but here that fantasy is itself the motive-force of desire. Othello destroys Desdemona and himself because he cannot tolerate the contamination of her sanctified being; Angelo wills just this contamination, experiencing desire only in terms of the split it would vindictively undo. But why does *Measure for Measure* portray desire only thus, only through the exciting image of contaminating a sanctified female space? In part, I think, because this image casts male sexuality as a punitive response to original female betrayal: through intercourse, Angelo would vindictively rewrite the sanctified female body as corrupt as though to punish it for originally betraying him to desire.

From the start, the play vests the fantasy of escape from desire in Angelo and allies that fantasy with escape from the body and from sexual origin, the stinking dependence that governs ordinary human life. Withdrawing from visible authority, the Duke—and the play—set out to test Angelo's refusal to confess that "his blood flows; or that his appetite / Is more to bread than stone" (1.3.52–53), claims exaggerated in Lucio's comic contention that his "blood / Is very snow-broth" (1.4.57–58), his urine "congealed ice" (3.2.106–7). He is the *locus classicus* in Shakespeare for the fantasy of a body born exempt from appetite; and near the center of the play, Lucio associates his coldness specifically with his exemption from the ordinary means of procreation:

> Lucio They say this Angelo was not made by man and woman, after this downright way of creation: is it true, think you?
>
> Duke How should he be made, then?
>
> Lucio Some report, a sea-maid spawned him. Some, that he was begot between two stockfishes. . . . And he is a motion ungenerative; that's infallible.
>
> (3.2.99–108)

The underground logic of Lucio's joke depends on the assumption that one's sexuality is an inheritance from one's parents: being without appetite, Angelo must not have been conceived in the ordinary way. Angelo is "ungenerative" because he is, as Lucio later says, an "ungenitured agent" (3.2.167–68): not only lacking testicles, but himself unbegotten.[31] The Duke's unusual willingness to participate in Lucio's joke, even to entertain for a moment the possibility of an alternative to the "downright way of creation," marks the centrality of this fantasy in the creation of Angelo. But the play sets out ruthlessly to bring Angelo to the startled recognition that his blood does flow ("Blood, thou art blood" [2.4.15]), and hence to demonstrate the obverse of Lucio's joke: here, as in *Hamlet*, one's own sexual body is the sign of original sin, the sin inherited from one's parents.

The discovery of desire is for Angelo initially equivalent to the discovery that he has a body:

> it is I
> That, lying by the violet in the sun,
> Do as the carrion does, not as the flower,
> Corrupt with virtuous season.
> (2.2.165–68)

In answering his own questions ("What's this?. . .who sins most?" [2.2.163–64]), Angelo makes the equation "I am flesh," as though recognizing this about himself—"it is I"—here for the first time. And to have a body is to be bound to death: reiterating Hamlet's image for conception (*Hamlet*, 2.2.181–82), Angelo can speak his bodily desire to himself only as the stirring of maggots in dead flesh. Confronting his own sexuality, that is, he experiences the secular equivalent of original sin and the fall into death: hence the logic by which Angelo is eventually brought to enact his sexual desire in a garden. Entry into this garden— itself carefully described to evoke the double passage of the female genitalia[32]—doubly returns Angelo to the female body, the site of origin from which he had seemed to claim exemption.

When we next see Angelo after 2.2, he seems to be exactly where we had left him; though we know that time has passed, he has apparently been immobilized by the discovery that he has a body. The logic that governs the imagery of the meditation that opens 2.4 follows from this discovery:

> Heaven hath my empty words,
> Whilst my invention, hearing not my tongue,
> Anchors on Isabel: Heaven in my mouth,
> As if I did but only chew his name,
> And in my heart the strong and swelling evil
> Of my conception.
>
> (2.4.2–7)

His new awareness of his bodily self—his tongue, his mouth, his heart—blocks his access to the spiritual father on whom he has relied,[33] transforming God Himself into empty substance in a cruel parody of transubstantiation. And as in *Hamlet*, Angelo's horrified awareness of himself as body distances him from the idealized father and returns him to the moment of his own conception, the maternal site of his original sin. In place of the heavenly father who could protect him from his body, Angelo finds the overwhelming presence of his bodily parents in "the strong and swelling evil / Of [his] conception"; swollen with this conception, he replicates the swelling both of phallic potency and of pregnancy, hence reproduces within himself the downright way he was conceived. For his desire is the mark of this conception: Angelo can imagine his own sexuality only as a return to this point of origin, the point at which he was made flesh. In his own embodiedness, he becomes the sin his mother carried: idealized and bodiless male presence is lost to him and in him as he becomes equivalent to Juliet, female and soiled,[34] pregnant with his own sexuality. In *Measure for Measure*'s elaborately psychologized version of the fall, familiar from *Hamlet* and played out in Angelo, recognition of the fall and hence of original sin in oneself is thus equivalent to the loss of the spiritual father and the discovery of the indissoluble link to the maternal body.

The anger of this recognition is turned on Isabella. Angelo's determination to pollute the sanctuary within her is exciting to him in part because it replays his discovery of maternal corruption within himself. In polluting the sanctuary, he would dirty Isabella as he has been dirtied, punitively recording the discovery of corruption in her body, as though tracing his own corruption to its source;[35] in effect, he excitedly desires to replicate the shaming and exciting discovery of maternal sexuality in her. And if she acquiesces in her own corruption, Isabella can moreover assuage the guilt of his polluting desire: acquiescing, she demonstrates that there never was a sanctuary, that all women are the same, all equally subject to soil. Angelo's attempt to compel Isabella's acquiescence in her own pollution thus takes the form of forcing her to acknowledge her kinship with Juliet (2.4.55), hence her position as woman, where "woman" is no more than the sign of sexual frailty:

> Be that you are,
> That is, a woman; if you be more, you're none.
> If you be one—as you are well express'd
> By all external warrants—show it now,
> By putting on the destin'd livery.
>
> (2.4.133–37)

"Be that you are": Angelo would make Isabella woman with a vengeance,[36] binding her to the livery of a specifically female flesh and hence marking her as inescapably sexual; Isabella's later invocation of her mother's sexual guilt (3.1.140–41) demonstrates how fully she has understood his drift. In his attempt to seduce Isabella, that is, Angelo turns the horror of his self-recognition back toward her, binding her to her corrupt origin as he is newly bound to his.

If Angelo's confrontation with sexuality forces him back toward his sexual origins, Isabella's literally enmeshes her in family; the encounter between them is so explosive in part because her fantasies mesh so well with his. For Isabella is not merely a counter in Angelo's fantasy; when we first see her, she is vividly and independently alive, portrayed with fantasies of her own. Her initial flight to the nunnery and her desire for more restrictions there (1.4.4–5) suggest that she, like Angelo, wishes to be exempt from ordinary human sexuality and from the ordinary bonds so engendered. When Angelo asks her to embrace female frailty by "putting on the destin'd livery," he allows us to understand that this is precisely the livery Isabella had hoped to escape by putting on the livery of the nun. For the religious community promises to free her both from sexuality and from the bonds of the sexual family, replacing its relationships by those of a spiritual family, in which *sister, brother, mother, father* are freed from the taint of sexuality.[37] But just at the moment of Isabella's apparent escape, the sexuality of her natural family draws her back into the world, forcing its ties upon her appropriately through Lucio, emissary of the brothel.

In bringing her face to face with the conflict between her two kinds of sisterhood, the play binds her at once to family and to her female flesh; characteristically, she feels the temptation of this flesh as an inheritance from what Lucio would call the downright way of creation. She responds to Angelo's claim that women are frail—the preface to his invitation to show herself a woman—with an hysteria that voices her own sense of contaminating origins:

> Ang.   Nay, women are frail too.
>
> Isab. Ay, as the glasses where they view themselves,
> Which are as easy broke as they make forms.
> Women?—Help, heaven! Men their creation mar
> In profiting by them. Nay, call us ten times frail;
> For we are soft as our complexions are,
> And credulous to false prints.[38]
>
> (2.4.123–29)

In her shift from *they* to *us*, Isabella reenacts in miniature her attempt to escape from the condition of "woman" and her eventual entrapment in it. And that condition is inextricably bound to woman's role in reproduction: like Angelo, Isabella can understand her own potentiality for frailty only as the continuation of her mother's fault. Her bizarre response to Angelo fuses conventional commentary on woman's vanity with anxiety about reproductive sexuality, as the mirror becomes a trope for the woman's body, broken as it makes forms;[39] the impulse that has led her to the nunnery becomes visible here, in her image of the female body broken both in the act of penetration and in the act of giving birth. But Isabella turns the fear and shame of this moment against women, attempting to separate herself from "them" as she identifies with the aggressor, articulating her own version of the misogynistic fantasy of male parthenogenesis. "Men their creation mar / In profiting by them": here, in one more version of the fall, Isabella imagines a purely male creation spoiled by concourse with women. But in wishing, as Posthumus later will, that there might be "some way for men to be" without women as "half-workers" (*Cymbeline*, 2.4.153–54), Isabella in effect wishes herself out of bodily existence; and the failure of the fantasy—the inevitability of the female role in reproduction—brings her back to herself and to her woman's body. Within four words, she conspicuously marks the passage from "them" to "us," for the first time acknowledging her own involvement in the offending category, for the first time feeling woman's frailty as her own.

In the underground logic of Isabella's transition from "them" to "us," hereditary participation in the downright way of creation makes female frailty her inescapable legacy, binding her to her fate as a sexual being. Called out of the nunnery by her bodily family, Isabella is forced to confront her sexual origins and hence her complicity in what the play poses as original sin. The panic engendered by this incipient recognition is voiced in the hysteria with which she responds to Angelo and later to Claudio; the second encounter repeats and intensifies the terms of the first. Faced with the evidence not only of her brother's sexuality but of his desire to live, Isabella traces what she sees as his corruption back to his sexual origin, specifically back to his mother's fault; and Claudio's attempt to replicate that fault in her—to pull her into her mother's sphere—is at the center of her panic:

> Wilt thou be made a man out of my vice?
> Is't not a kind of incest, to take life
> From thine own sister's shame? What should I think?
> Heaven shield my mother play'd my father fair:
> For such a warped slip of wilderness
> Ne'er issued from his blood.
>
> (3.1.137–42)

Isabella begins by questioning the dependence of manhood on female shame, but her horror gives her question a particularly vivid anatomical cast: "wilt thou be made a man out of my vice?"[40] If Isabella were willing to rescue Claudio by sexual means, he would in effect be born from her; but this would make Isabella into his mother, the woman out of whose vice Claudio was literally made man. In duplicating the parental act that made Claudio man, intercourse with Angelo would incestuously bind Isabella to her family, replicating in Angelo the father who mars his creation in profiting by woman, and in Isabella the mother who is the site of corruption.[41] And in remaking her incestuously as her brother's mother, the act would cancel out Isabella's difference from her mother; revoking her escape from family, it would seal in her the inheritance that is anatomically the woman's part, identifying her vice as her maternal legacy.[42]

Isabella's desperate search for a means to defend herself against this contaminating identification with her mother is registered in the poignant question—"what should I think?"—that breaks her diatribe, calling our attention both to her inner processes and to the peculiarity of what she decides to think. The urgency of her need is underscored by her bizarrely inverted prayer: she calls on heaven to shield—or forbid—not her mother's infidelity but her fidelity, invoking a heavenly father in effect to guarantee the bastardizing of her brother. The idea of her mother's adultery seems to come to her as a saving remedy, offering her some respite from her panic. But how can it serve her to imagine her mother a whore and her father a cuckold? First of all, the very viciousness with which she turns on her mother serves in part to assuage the terrifying identification with her: here as in her partheno-genesis fantasy of 2.4, she allies herself with the male voices condemning female contamination,[43] as though to distance herself absolutely from the mother she attacks. And in the process, she rescues her father from degradation: by locating responsibility for Claudio's corruption entirely with her mother, she manages to maintain the purity of her father and hence the possibility of protection that she has imagined in him. Her image of her father has in fact functioned thus for her earlier, anticipating the logic of this moment. In 2.4, Isabella defends herself against Angelo's proposal in part by imagining in her brother a "mind of honour" that would gladly prefer his own death to his sister's pollution (2.4.178–82). When Claudio in fact speaks with the voice that she imagines there, she sees him as fully his father's son, speaking with his father's voice: "There spake my brother: there my father's grave / Did utter forth a voice" (3.1.85–86). For Isabella, he is his father's son and speaks with his father's voice insofar as he is willing to die to protect her from sexual contamination, allying himself with her against the female body and its frailty. When that protection fails— when his desire for life threatens her exemption from sexuality— Isabella reinvents his familial relationship, making him radically his mother's son rather than his father's: if Claudio is vicious, then her father had no part in his making. "Such a warped slip of wilderness / Ne'er issued from his blood": her brother's vice, like her own, is purely a maternal inheritance.[44] In response to Claudio's attempt to ally her with female frailty, that is, she rewrites the failed parthenogenesis fantasy of her earlier encounter with Angelo, rationalizing it and hence keeping it within the limits of the possible: once again, women are the source of corruption and men mar their creation in profiting by them; but Isabella manages to make an exception of her father by removing him bodily from the moment of conception. Exonerating her father at her mother's expense, she leaves her father free to remain an idealized presence, separated from the contaminated sphere of female sexuality and hence still available to protect her from it.

Threatened by identification with the mother who can exist for her only as a site of corruption, Isabella responds by invoking the protective image of a pure father who can serve as a buffer between her and the maternal legacy that both Angelo and Claudio bid her to assume. In her need for a saving father as in her flight from sexuality, Isabella resembles Angelo, who also attempts to invoke the pure father as a bulwark against his new bondage to his body and hence to the sexual family. Like Angelo unsuccessfully calling on heaven as he recoils in horror from his own conception (2.4.2), Isabella calls on a heavenly father both here and earlier, when enforced identification with female frailty had threatened her ("Women?—Help, heaven" [2.4.126]). Both Angelo and Isabella need a bodiless father to protect them from the consequences of their own bodily legacy—and this is the role the play assigns to the Duke, its "ghostly father" (4.3.47; 5.1.129). The distant heavenly father whom Angelo cannot reach is realized for him in the figure of the newly returned Duke: hence the ease with which Angelo identifies his unseen observation with that of "power divine" (5.1.367). The Duke's mid-play appearance to Isabella similarly follows out the logic of her need for a sanctified father. When the protection of Claudio and the father embodied in him fails, she attempts to invent a father dissociated from the troubling female region of sexuality; and the Duke appears to her magically as a nonsexual father-protector within ten lines. (Indeed, when Claudio had proclaimed his willingness to die, he had in fact been speaking with the voice of this father: it is of course the Duke who has reconciled him to death.) The congruence of this appearance suggests the degree to which the Duke as Friar is the embodiment of the fantasied asexual father who will protect Isabella from her own sexuality, the vice that is her inheritance from her mother. It is striking that Isabella calls him "good father" (3.1.238, 269) not in response to his appearance as friar *per se* but only after he has offered her a way to avoid the destined livery; he becomes the "good father" for her only insofar as he can take on her dead father's protective role.

Angelo needs the Duke as the heavenly father who comes back to judge him, condemning him to death for his manifold infractions against a sacred space and then forgiving him by demonstrating that the space has not been violated after all; Isabella needs the Duke as the heavenly father who can protect her from female frailty and provide her with a safely asexual family. But the play simultaneously needs the Duke to move these characters away from sexual disgust, to enable the marriages on which both social continuance and comic closure depend. For most audiences, I suspect, this conflict in his roles—and hence the ambivalence about sexuality throughout the play—is focused most clearly in his last-minute marriage proposal. The Duke who has protected Isabella from sexuality now invites, or perhaps coerces, her participation in it; and given both the ease with which the distinction between legitimate and illegitimate sexuality breaks down in this play and the suddenness with which the sainted Duke, like the sainted

Angelo, announces his desire, his proposal threatens disturbingly to reiterate Angelo's.[45]

Our uneasiness with the final marriage proposal underscores our uneasiness with the Duke's role throughout; he is on the face of it a very odd person through whom to attempt an accommodation to marriage and the life of the sexually created family. He enters 1.1 announcing his intention to withdraw from civic power and enters 1.3 announcing his disdain for what he calls "the dribbling dart of love" (1.3.2); by escaping into the role of friar, he manages to evade the expectation that he will use the paternal rod (1.3.26) either punitively or generatively, practicing a kind of self-castration in handing both sorts of potency on to Angelo. "Be thou at full ourself" (1.1.43), he tells Angelo: as the Duke becomes a friar, he makes Angelo the duke *in absentia*, in effect splitting himself into two figures—the Angelo whose potency he creates and who enacts the conflicts of carnal paternal power in his stead,[46] and the Friar whose status as an unproblematically ghostly father protects him from those conflicts. Through this device, the Duke—who is fully as fastidious about sexuality as Angelo himself—is spared the sort of testing that Angelo must undergo: the affiliation with "dark corners" (4.3.156) that we might be tempted to see in the Duke's voyeuristic fascination with the corruption that boils around him and in his role as virtual bawd to Angelo and Mariana is in effect dislocated from his psyche, given its locus only in Angelo's actions and in Lucio's treasonable slander; thus relocated, it is exorcised from the person of the Duke, who remains strikingly without bodily desires. In the figure of the Duke, that is, the play pulls in two directions at once: even while Shakespeare apparently uses him to reconcile the others to their own human nature, he reinstates in the Duke a fantasy of escape from that nature, allowing the Duke to become an ungenitured agent just as Angelo is forced to acknowledge his own origins.

This doubleness deeply compromises the play's ostensible attempt at cure; in fact it replicates the very split in Angelo—between sexuality and absolute purity, the brothel and the sanctuary—that the bed trick seems designed to heal. The play has throughout made its meaning through its radical divison into separate places—not only nunnery and brothel, but prison, moated grange, Angelo's garden—a division that cannot be canceled by ducal (or authorial) fiat any more than the bed trick can cancel the violence of the splittings that haunt Angelo's imagination, the violence that has split even the Duke himself. Throughout, as the Duke crosses boundaries, moving from monastery to prison and moated grange, apparently psychically in control of nunnery and brothel and the garden in which they meet in the bed trick, he carries the promise of a more fluid psychic geography. But instead of incorporating these locales into himself—hence incorporating the possibility of a renewed city—he remains aloof from them all, maintaining both his own and their separateness intact. In the last scene, Shakespeare (through the Duke) moves the play to the fluid open space outside the city walls, as though to break down the psychic rigidity that has immobilized Vienna's citizens; but instead of enabling the transformation of these places, or any kind of communication between them, the Duke seems only to reconstitute them through his intrusive management, simultaneously transgressing their boundaries and reinforcing their stability. Apparently married in prison (5.1.518–19) to the prostitute he has wronged, Lucio will become in effect a permanent inhabitant of the brothel; instead of redeeming marriage, the Duke's sentence makes it equivalent to the prison—or to a worse sentence—for him. For Angelo too, enforced marriage takes the place of a death sentence, binding him permanently to the fallen garden in which he discovered his mortality; even after he has discovered that he has bedded his virtual wife, he craves "death more willingly than mercy" (5.1.474), and can scarcely be persuaded to give up his new alliance with carrion, his conviction that death is the appropriate punishment for his original sin—a conviction unlikely to be changed by the technicality that Claudio turns out to be alive. Distrust of sexuality remains so much in force that Shakespeare deliberately minimizes his one chance for a conventional happy ending: though Claudio and Juliet enter together, there is no indication that they have noticed one another; they remain as separate at the end as at the beginning, unjoined by the Duke who specializes in joining only those who do not want to be together.[47] Instead of resolving the psychic impasse that has made the bed trick necessary—hence achieving even the half-hearted cure of *All's Well*—*Measure* reiterates that impasse in the Duke's final manipulations, in which the bed trick's coercion of desire seems to become not a momentary aberration but rather the law of marriage itself.

In *Measure for Measure*, the curative role of Helena is in effect shrunk to that of Mariana; Helena's vehement and dangerous love is now contained in her much more manageable person. She alone among the play's characters can express desire without a sense of contamination; she carries the fragile hope not only of reformation but of a healing reconciliation to origins and hence to the sins of the body: "They say best men are moulded out of faults" (5.1.437).[48] Both Shakespeare's habitual use of "moulded" and the play on *fault/foutre* throughout

Measure for Measure let us hear the fullness of the hope that she expresses: not only that Angelo may be improved by the confrontation with his own specifically sexual faults, not only that he will be able to tolerate his own sexuality as the legacy of the fault/foutre that moulded him, but that the sin of origin will be accepted as the common ground of human goodness.[49] "Best men are moulded out of faults," Mariana implies, because, in the downright way of creation, that is the only way men are moulded at all. But the wistful hope that she expresses here is frail indeed. There is little sign that Angelo has been remade by his confrontation with original sin in the garden of her body, and still less sign that Isabella's surrogate participation in Mariana's sexuality has made her any more willing to put on the destined livery. Moreover, as a vessel of cure, Mariana herself is a relatively unsubstantial character, introduced late in the play and as an obvious *corpus ex machina* to solve an unsolvable dilemma. Though her desires are vehement and her own, her very being in the play seems under the management of the Duke: conveniently forgotten by him early in the play, she turns up only when she is useful to him; in effect invented by his need of her, she serves entirely at his pleasure. In the relationship between them, Shakespeare redoes the problematic relationship between Helena and the King, and hence between male and female sites of authority. Now the male ranges freely while the female is impotent and confined: stuck helplessly in her moated grange, freed only by the Duke's intervention, Mariana epitomizes *Measure for Measure*'s restructuring of male/female relation.

In its own way, then, *Measure for Measure* takes back what *All's Well* has given Helena, assuaging the acute anxiety that she creates—"that man should be at woman's command, and yet no hurt done!" (*All's Well.* 1.3.89–90)—by relocating sexual and social power firmly in the male domain. Her bed trick is no longer the sign of female control over generation and hence over the passing on of male honor; it is now under male management, the sign of invisible male control over the work of generation itself.[50] So powerful that she must be dismembered in order to be remembered, Helena is in effect split into three in *Measure for Measure*, the better to be contained. Mariana inherits her active desire and her curative role, both now sternly subordinate to the Duke. Juliet inherits her pregnant body, now the sign of sin rather than the sign of generative power: imprisoned and immobilized by that body, always on the point of giving birth (2.2.15–16) but never reaching that fruition, utterly dependent on the Duke's authority for her release, silenced by Shakespeare as by the Duke, she reinscribes pregnancy as the site of female vulnerability and male control. And Isabella inherits Helena's status as sacred virgin, her virginity now the inciting cause of a sick male desire, not the source of a near-magical restoration: a sanctuary made only to be violated, invaded and shamed as much by the play as by Angelo and the Duke, her threatening power is in the end firmly subordinated to the imperatives of patriarchal marriage.[51] Initially self-enclosed, she becomes increasingly a common thoroughfare, in the imagination of whose body the desires of others meet; initially vividly defined by her own unbending selfhood and her articulate voice, she becomes increasingly unable to say what she wants, increasingly the tool of the Duke. By thus splitting Helena's power and revealing the controlling male presence that will finally put her in her place, *Measure for Measure* undoes the central movement of *All's Well*, enabling marriage by putting it under the aegis not of a sexual woman but of a sternly a-sexual man.[52]

In the final revelations of *Measure for Measure*, it is the pure father rather than the sexual mother who proves to have been everywhere unseen. Only in the presence of this father can sexuality and marriage be made safe; when he withdraws at the start of the play, sexuality bubbles and boils (5.1.316) like a witches' cauldron (*Macbeth*, 4.1.19) in Vienna, threatening to overwhelm both Angelo and Isabella in what they feel as their maternal legacy. But this is exactly the condition that obtains at the beginning of *Hamlet*, where the disappearance of Hamlet's father immerses Hamlet in the realm defined by his mother's sexuality; and it is the condition of *All's Well*, where a similar disappearance puts Bertram under the combined power of his mother and Helena. No wonder, then, that the Duke returns as a revised version of Hamlet's ghostly father,[53] a version in which that father proves to be all-powerful: the pattern of doing and undoing implicit in *All's Well* and *Measure for Measure*, and most visible in its repeated bed tricks— the one the mother's, the other the father's—responds to the crisis initiated by *Hamlet*. But the bodiless Duke is not finally an adequate solution to this crisis; as the persistence of Juliet reminds us, maternal origin cannot simply be wished away. In *King Lear*, *Macbeth*, and *Coriolanus*, Shakespeare returns to the vulnerability of the bodily father and hence to the world of paternal absence in which the mother is given full sway.

5

SUFFOCATING MOTHERS IN
KING LEAR

Troilus and Cressida, All's Well That Ends Well, Measure for Measure, and *Othello* are all to some degree exfoliations of Hamlet's spoiled relation with Ophelia, following out the consequences of his recognition that there can be no more marriage in a world contaminated by maternal sexuality. *King Lear* also plays out this recognition, excising any imaginable space in which legitimate sexuality might take place. But in *King Lear*, the marital plots are no longer central; here Shakespeare returns to the primary material of *Hamlet*, where the virtual abdication of the father from his position of power unleashes for his son a violent fear of unmediated maternal power. And here, father and son are collapsed into one figure: for Lear is simultaneously the father who abdicates and the son who must suffer the consequences of this abdication. In thus collapsing father and son into one figure, Shakespeare enables his story about a father's relationship with his daughters to carry the immense fear and longing of a son's relationship with a mother, investing it with infantile fantasies so unmediated in their intensity that they are relatively disorganized, not bound within the limits of a single fictional character or plot movement. For the collapse of father and son into one figure is only the first of many such collapses. If Hamlet must struggle to keep male and female apart, struggle against the horror of the "one flesh," at least his own identity remains relatively assured; but here all the traditional guarantees of identity itself dissolve in a terrifying female moisture in which mother and daughter, male and female, inner and outer, self and other, lose their boundaries, threatening a return to the primal chaos.[1] For here the fantasies are themselves wholly unbounded, and in their unboundedness return us to the maelstrom of what Freud called primary process thinking, making us lose our bearings as Lear loses his; in measuring these fantasies, we measure the distance between the literal mothers Tamora or Gertrude or Volumnia and the power of the storm.

It may at first seem merely perverse to understand *King Lear* as in part the adumbration of fantasies about maternal power, particularly given the entire absence of literal mothers in the play; at first glance, *Lear* seems overwhelmingly about fathers and their paternity rather than about mothers. The motherlessness of Lear's world is striking particularly if one comes to it from the source play, *The True Chronicle Historie of King Leir*, in which the emotional starting point is the king's dismay at the death of his wife and the motherlessness of his daughters; in that play, the king's decision to abdicate and divide the kingdom is presented in part as his response to her loss.[2] But our King Lear has no wife, his daughters no mother; nor, apparently, have they ever had one: Queen Lear goes unmentioned, except for those characteristic moments when Lear invokes her to cast doubt on his paternity. *Leir* starts with the fact of maternal loss; *Lear* excises this loss, giving us the uncanny sense of a world created by fathers alone.[3] But Lear's confrontation with his daughters (I will argue) repeatedly leads him back to the mother ostensibly occluded by the play:[4] in recognizing his daughters as part of himself he will be led to recognize not only his terrifying dependence on female forces outside himself but also an equally terrifying femaleness within himself—a femaleness that he will come to call "mother" (2.4.56). For this text about fathers insistently returns to mothers: discovering what he is father to, confronting the implications of his own paternity, Lear is brought to acknowledge their absent presence; and even Gloucester, unproblematically father to sons, is made the victim of their awesome power. I take as a central text of the play the fool's bitter "thou mad'st thy daughters thy mothers; . . . thou gav'st them the rod and putt'st down thine own breeches" (1.4.179–81), with its painfully literal suggestions of both generational and gender reversal, of infantile exposure and maternal punishment. Much of the play's power comes, I think, from its confrontation with the landscape of maternal deprivation or worse, from the vulnerability and rage that is the consequence of this confrontation and the intensity and fragility of the hope for a saving maternal presence that can undo pain. In the characteristic way of the return of the repressed, that is, the excision of the mother that seems initially to allow for a fantasy of male parthenogenesis ends by releasing fantasies far more frightening than any merely literal mother could be, fantasies that give emotional coloration to the entire play in part because they are not localized in (and hence limited to) any single character.

We can see this process of repression and terrifying return played out in miniature in the Gloucester plot. In the opening lines of the play, Edmund's mother is invoked only to be absented, apparently for the rest of the play. The opening exchange between Kent and Gloucester is full of nervousness about the biological relation between fathers and sons, and about the place of mothers; Edmund's mother appears in the text only in response to a pun that emphasizes the differing reproductive roles of men and women:

> *Kent*   Is not this your son, my Lord?
>
> *Glou.*   His breeding, Sir, hath been at my charge: I have so often blush'd to acknowledge him, that now I am braz'd to't.
>
> *Kent*   I cannot conceive you.
>
> *Glou.*   Sir, this young fellow's mother could; whereupon she grew round-womb'd. . . . Do you smell a fault?
>
> *Kent*   I cannot wish the fault undone, the issue of it being so proper.
>
>   (1.1.8–18)

Kent could not conceive, but this fellow's mother could. The pun doubly turns on the tenuousness of this father's biological relation to his son: Gloucester's terms for his part in the making of Edmund ("his breeding . . . hath been at my charge") are so evasive[5] that Kent does not at first understand what Gloucester means; and their evasiveness is a function not only of Gloucester's shame but also of the tenuousness of the male role in reproduction *per se*. But there is nothing tenuous about that round womb: Edmund is unequivocally his mother's child, the "issue" from her "fault."[6] As though in response to that unequivocal round womb, Gloucester then turns from Edmund to the absent Edgar: "But I have a son, Sir, by order of law, some year elder than this" (1.1.19–20). His shift from one son to the other—"but I have a son"—in effect distinguishes between Edmund as his mother's child and Edgar as his father's: if Edmund is the product of a mother's womb, Edgar is the product of patriarchal law, apparently motherless. In distinguishing between his legitimate and illegitimate sons, Gloucester manages to do away with the womb altogether, making Edgar all his.

The differences between these sons will be played out in the dynamic between them. But for the moment, let us ask what becomes of Edmund's mother in this transaction. Present only as a site of illegitimacy, she—and the round womb of maternal reproduction—are erased by Gloucester's reference to Edgar and by the rest of the play. She may make a brief and covert reappearance under the guise of "Nature" in

Edmund's apostrophe to her when he next appears; at least his dedication of himself to Nature's "law" (1.2.1–2) reminds us that there is more than one law and recalls the outlaw status of Edmund's mother. For the most part, however, her erasure seems total. But although exiled as a bodily presence or even as a figure to whom others allude, she returns in full force in the last moments of the play, when Edgar offers a moralized account of his father's history:

> My name is Edgar, and thy father's son.
> The Gods are just, and of our pleasant vices
> Make instruments to plague us;
> The dark and vicious place where thee he got
> Cost him his eyes.
>
> (5.3.169–73)

In Edgar's account, the play comes full circle and we are returned to its beginning. As legitimate Edgar identifies himself to his dying brother ("My name is Edgar, and thy father's son"), he stresses not their fraternity but his claim to his father, reiterating the distinction of the opening scene: once again, Edgar—the legitimate, the would-be rescuer of his father—is his "father's son"; once again, Edmund—the illegitimate, his father's scourge—is his mother's, derivative from her dark and vicious place. And now the vice lightly acknowledged—and dismissed—by Gloucester is revealed as the cause of all his suffering. But even as Edgar blames his father for his own blinding, he constructs an alternate version of the story in which the blinding is less the logical moral consequence of Gloucester's vicious action than it is the analogical extension of the place of vice; and in this version, the blinding is all the mother's fault. Wholly excising Cornwall's role in Gloucester's blinding, acknowledging even Edmund's only parenthetically ("where thee he got"), Edgar in effect names the female sexual "place" as the blinding agent, metonymically making the darkness of that place equivalent to the darkness into which Gloucester is plunged. And at this moment, the presence occluded throughout the play reinstates itself with a vengeance, and reinstates itself in Gloucester's body: blinded by his commerce with her darkness, he carries in himself the darkness of this "dark and vicious place" writ large.[7]

In simultaneously marking the mother's child as illegitimate and locating the place of female begetting as the father's scourge, the Gloucester plot plays out a bizarre fantasy in which social anxieties about illegitimacy and patriarchal inheritance are fused with psychological anxieties about sexuality and masculine identity. Patriarchal society depends on the principle of inheritance in which the father's identity—his property, his name, his authority—is transmitted from father to son; in the words of the Paphlagonian king who is Gloucester's prototype in *Arcadia*, the father of a true son need "envie no father for the chiefe comfort of mortalitie, to leave an other ones-selfe after me."[8] But this transmission from father to son can take place only insofar as both father and son pass through the body of a woman;[9] and this passage radically alters them both. This is the weak spot in patriarchal inheritance: maternal origin and illegitimacy are synonymous in the Gloucester plot—and throughout *Lear*—because sexuality *per se* is illegitimate and illegitimizes its children; whether or not the son is biologically his father's, the mother's dark place inevitably contaminates him, compromising his father's presence in him.[10] For the son who has traversed the maternal body cannot be wholly "an other ones-selfe" for his father; the mother's part in him threatens the fantasy of perfect self-replication that would preserve the father in the son. As Falstaff tells us, "the son of the female"—any female—"is the shadow of the male" (2 *Henry IV*, 3.2.126–28). And the father himself will be deeply compromised by the sexual concourse that produces the son. Edgar's bizarre metaphor for his father's blindness—"in this habit / Met I my father with his bleeding rings, / Their precious stones new lost" (5.3.188–90)—makes plain what his earlier equation of blindness with the place of female generation (5.3.172–73) had implied: both the secondary meaning of "stones" as testicles and the frequent association of rings with the female genitals rewrite Edgar's reassuringly cold and hard metaphor for loss as an image of castration, in effect registering the transformation of his father into a woman with a bleeding ring.[11] In Edgar's image, that is, the father bears the corrosive signs of his concourse with the female; the occluded maternal presence is in effect etched on his face.

The pattern of repression and return visible in Edmund's illegitimacy and in the blinding of Gloucester is played out again in the Lear plot, where the presence of daughters *per se*— daughters instead of sons— has a function equivalent to the presence of illegitimacy in the Gloucester plot, that of returning the father to the occluded maternal place. Shakespeare in fact arranges matters so that we will feel the presence of Lear's daughters as a slight disturbance, a perplexing substitution for the sons we expect him to have: in the play's opening lines, both Gloucester's reference to his own two sons and the talk of dividing the kingdom between two men we know nothing about predispose us to think of these men as Lear's sons; and Lear himself refers to Albany and Cornwall as his sons (1.1.41–42) before he mentions that he has daughters (1.1.44). Our carefully induced surprise at the sudden substitution of daughters—three of them for the two sons we had apparently been promised—registers something like Lear's unspoken problem:[12] by definition, his daughters disrupt the patriarchal ideal, both insofar as they disrupt the transmission of property from father to son and insofar as they disrupt the paternal fantasy of perfect self-replication. Even more clearly than the mother's son, the daughter is but "the shadow of the male," carrying within her the disruptive sign of the mother's presence. (Why does this father have only daughters?)

In its representation of Lear's problematic relation to his daughters, the Lear plot simultaneously replicates and analyzes the logic of illegitimacy in the Gloucester plot. If Gloucester's wicked son is literally illegitimate, Lear similarly imagines that his disobedient daughters are illegitimate, "degenerate bastard[s]" (1.4.262), the products of an adulterous womb (2.4.131–33). If the only mother of the Gloucester plot is Edmund's, the only mother of the Lear plot is the adulterous mother Lear thus imagines; and like Edgar,[13] Cordelia is motherless, purely her father's child. Once again, the female sexual place is necessarily the place of corruption, the "sulphurous pit" (4.6.130) that is Lear's equivalent to Edgar's "dark and vicious place";[14] present only as a site of illegitimacy, the mother once again transmits her faults to her issue, the children whose corrupt sexuality records their origin. And once again the plot sets the father's pure and a-sexual child[15] against the mother's, making his child the father's bulwark against her dark power as it is played out through her children.[16] But the logic of illegitimacy is played out with a difference in the Lear plot. For we know, as Lear comes to know, that Goneril and Regan are not in fact illegitimate; the whole of the play works to bring him to the recognition of his own complicity in their making. And this time the protective function of the fantasy of illegitimacy is made visible. Lear imagines his daughters illegitimate when he cannot tolerate their failure to meet his needs; he would rather imagine himself a cuckold than be forced to acknowledge that the female children who so imperfectly replicate him are part his. The fantasy of their illegitimacy is thus his pyrrhic solution to the larger problem of daughters: insofar as he can make their disruptive femaleness entirely derivative from their mother's sexual fault, he can dissociate himself wholly from it, in effect disowning them as he has earlier attempted to disown Cordelia.

But even while the logic of illegitimacy is thus stripped bare, the female site of generation nonetheless remains the site and sign of corruption in the Lear plot as in the Gloucester plot. For Lear's acknowledgment of complicity in the making of his daughters turns out to mean not so much his acknowledgment of his own sexual darkness as his acknowledgment that he too has been contaminated by the dark and vicious place. Far from recuperating the place of female sexuality by freeing it from blame, his recognition that his daughters are legitimate merely invests the horror of that place in him. Recognizing his part in Goneril and Regan entails recognizing their part in him; if they are his, then he is intolerably implicated in their femaleness.[17] Forced to acknowledge his own part in the making of Goneril, he identifies her as the disease in his own body:

> We'll no more meet, no more see one another;
> But yet thou art my flesh, my blood, my daughter;
> Or rather a disease that's in my flesh,
> Which I must needs call mine: thou art a boil,
> A plague-sore, or embossed carbuncle,
> In my corrupted blood.
>
> (2.4.222–27)

Even as he would disown her ("We'll no more meet"), he must acknowledge that she is inextricably his, and hence the sign of corruption in him. For if she is his, then he is complicit with the dark and vicious place that made her: both her name and the imagery of skin disease make her the sign of the specifically venereal disease that registers his own participation in the sexual fault.[18] And as he imagines her a swelling within him—"a boil, / A plague-sore, or embossed carbuncle" in his corrupted blood—he takes that dark place into himself; his language figures his body as grotesquely female, pregnant with the disease that is his daughter. Acknowledging Goneril his flesh and blood entails making his own body the site of her monstrous femaleness.[19]

Lear cannot ultimately sustain the protective fantasy that his daughters are bastards, wholly separate from him, and the collapse of this fantasy illustrates what it is designed to protect him from: if Goneril is his, then her female corruption is within him; in attempting to disown her, he finds her inside himself. Like Edgar's account of the blinding of Gloucester, this moment seems to me characteristic of the broader pattern of repression and return that governs the play's treatment of mothers: for the play that apparently excludes mothers simultaneously plays out a dark fantasy about the interior of the female body, about the position of the male who traverses that body, and about the traces the female body consequently leaves within the male. This fantasy everywhere shapes Lear's encounters with his daughters, the literally female flesh that he must needs call his. But it is most terrifyingly expressed not through them but through the storm that is their avatar; its traces in fact determine the logic that governs Lear's meditative reworking of the storm in his meeting with Gloucester in 4.6, the logic that links his greeting of Gloucester ("Goneril, with a white beard" [l.

97]), his recollection of the rain that came to wet him once (ll. 102–8), his bitter acknowledgment that his daughters were "got 'tween the lawful sheets" (l. 119), his recoil from the "sulphurous pit" (l. 130), and the smell of mortality on his own hands (l. 135). For he concludes his meditation by arriving at the place of his birth, acknowledging his mortality as he remembers his origins: "We came crying hither: / Thou know'st the first time that we smell the air / We wawl and cry" (ll. 180–82). Within the logic of these associations, the storm comes to function as the sign of the female place of origin; in remembering it, Lear records its traces in himself.

Initially, the storm seems to Lear to be the place of the male thunderer classically associated with its powers. In his initial response to it, he invokes this thunderer, rewriting his impotence in the face of the daughters who have thrust him into the storm—the daughters who can "shake [his] manhood thus" (1.4.306)—by imagining himself on the side of the "all-shaking thunder" (3.2.6) that makes the caitiff shake (3.2.55). And he invokes this masculine authority specifically against the female site of origin, "round-womb'd" as Edmund's mother (1.1.14): commanding the thunder to "Strike flat the thick rotundity o' th' world! / Crack Nature's moulds, all germens spill at once" (3.2.7–8), he cosmologizes his earlier attack on Goneril's womb ("Into her womb convey sterility! / Dry up in her the organs of increase" [1.4.287–88]). But Lear cannot reinstate his own masculine authority by joining with the thunderer in his destruction; he cannot command this or any other power. Recourse to male authority—his own or that of the gods—will not protect him; as the storm speaks his impotence, exposing him as "a poor, infirm, weak, and despis'd old man" (3.2.20), it reiterates not his lost power but his own helplessness in the face of his daughters' rage, and the elements themselves come to seem less the signs of male authority than the exfoliations of their power, "servile ministers / That will with two pernicious daughters join / . . . 'gainst a head / So old and white as this" (3.2.21–24).

For if the storm is classically the domain of the male thunderer, it is simultaneously the domain of disruptive female power: associated both with the storms that witches were commonly suspected of raising and with the storms that conventionally figure the turbulence of Fortune (the "arrant whore" who—like Lear's daughters—"ne'er turns the key to th' poor" [2.4.52–53]), this storm becomes in effect the signature of maternal malevolence, the sign of her power to withhold and destroy.[20] As Poor Tom reminds us, this storm is witch's turf, where "Swithold . . . met the night-mare, and her nine-fold; / . . . And aroint thee, witch, aroint thee!" (3.4.123–27). It is no accident, I think, that Poor Tom himself defines his place in this nightmare world by what he has been forced to eat: asked who he is, he answers with a catalogue that anticipates the "eye of newt, and toe of frog," the toad and dog and lizard, of *Macbeth* (4.1.6–17); he is

> Poor Tom; that eats the swimming frog, the toad, the todpole, the wall-newt, and the water; that... eats cow-dung for sallets; swallows the old rat and the ditch-dog; drinks the green mantle of the standing pool.
>
> (3.4.132–37)

This is the landscape of the witches' cauldron, the obverse of the landscape on Lear's map,[21] with its "plenteous rivers and wide-skirted meads" (1.1.65) reassuringly abundant and reassuringly under male control; here, the kind goddess nature whom Lear thought he could command (1.4.284) is revealed under the aspect of Hecate. No wonder that he should attempt to invoke the masculine authority of the gods against her, as though he could uproot her monstrous generativity.

Despite Lear's recurrent attempts to find a just Thunderer in the storm, that is, its violence ultimately epitomizes not the just masculine authority on which Lear would base his own but the dark female power that everywhere threatens to undermine that authority. No longer under the aegis of a male thunderer, the very wetness of the storm comes to seem a sexual wetness, a monstrous spilling of germens that threatens to undo civilization and manhood itself, spouting rain until it has "drench'd our steeples, drown'd the cocks" (3.2.3), its power an extension into the cosmos of Goneril's power to shake Lear's manhood. Fantasized site of Poor Tom's "act of darkness" (3.4.87–88), the storm takes on the aspect of the hellish "Lake of Darkness" in which Nero is an angler (3.6.7), becoming itself the dark and vicious place writ large.[22] Hence, I think, the logic according to which Lear's memory of the storm—"when the rain came to wet me once and the wind to make me chatter, when the thunder would not peace at my bidding" (4.6.102–4)—leads him to imagine that female place, and to imagine concentrated in it the dispersed elements of the storm:

> But to the girdle do the Gods inherit,
> Beneath is all the fiend's: there's hell, there's darkness,
> There is the sulphurous pit—burning, scalding,
> Stench, consumption; fie, fie, fie! pah, pah!
>
> (4.6.128–31)

For the "sulph'rous and thought-executing fires" (3.2.4) of that "hell-black night" (3.7.59) are replicated in the hell and darkness and burn-

ing and stench of this "sulphurous pit" (4.6.129–31); in arriving at
this pit, Lear in effect traces the elements of the storm back to their
origin.

The fantasy given darkest expression in the storm is of Lear's subjection to the realm of Hecate, in which masculine identity and the civilization that upheld it are dissolved in a terrifying female moisture. Hence,
I think, the logic behind the awful simultaneity of Lear's exposure on
the heath and Gloucester's blinding, instigated by Lear's daughters.
The oscillation of scenes throughout Act III—indoors and outdoors
equally brutal—serves to intensify the audience's pain, as each promises
momentary relief from the other and then drives in a different mode
toward the same dark place. For the one acts out the subjugation that
has been implicit in the other: in the blinding of Gloucester, the punitive
female power of the storm—the power of the dark and vicious place—
is given a local habitation and a name. We begin the rush into the
storm with the womanish tears Lear attempts to suppress, the tears
that threaten to stain his "man's cheeks" (2.4.280); we end with a
Gloucester vulnerable as a woman, a Gloucester whose man's cheeks
are stained with the blood and jelly of his weeping eyes. We begin with
the "eyeless" storm (3.1.8) and end with the blinded Gloucester. As
Lear is driven toward the nightmare state of the naked baby, exposed
to the rage of the punitive mother in the storm, Gloucester is transformed into a woman by the daughters who are her human agents:
her dark and vicious place newly recorded in his own eyelessness,
Gloucester is mistaken by Lear for that monster-woman herself, "Goneril, with a white beard" (4.6.97).

The storm as Lear recalls it is the testing place of masculine power,
the site of the punitive sexualized mother; in greeting the feminized
Gloucester as Goneril, Lear sees her signs in him. And as he traces the
elements of the storm back to their origin in her, he comes to find the
same elements in himself. This recoil onto the self is registered in part
through smell, the most primitive of infant senses, the one that Lear
later makes synonymous with breathing itself (4.6.181). Initially smell-
ing out the flattery of others in the storm ("there I found 'em, there I
smelt 'em out. Go to, they are not men o' their words" [4.6.105–6]),
he comes via the stench of the sulphurous pit to the smell of mortality
on his own hands:

> *Lear* There is the sulphurous pit—burning, scalding,
> Stench, consumption; fie, fie, fie! pah, pah!
> Give me an ounce of civet, good apothecary,
> To sweeten my imagination.
> There's money for thee.

> *Glou.*   O! let me kiss that hand.
>
> *Lear* Let me wipe it first; it smells of mortality.
>
> (4.6.129–35)

In tracing his mortality to its source, he revises the bravado of his triumphant "there I found 'em, there I smelt 'em out": the smell becomes specifically female and implicates him in its stench. Spitting out his words ("pah, pah!") as though he would violently expel the tormenting thought of that female stench within him, Lear finds it in his own body. For the stench of the sulphurous pit and the smell of mortality turn out to be one:[23] his own flesh—traditionally derivative from the woman's part in conception—carries that stench within it, as the mark of her female corruption in him.[24] This—his origin in and vulnerability to the sulphurous pit—is what Lear smells out in the storm.

Attempting to disown Goneril, Lear finds her a disease within his own body; attempting to separate himself from her corrupt femaleness, he finds himself pregnant with her. Attempting to escape his own feminizing emotions by rushing out into the storm, he finds himself caught in the female maelstrom; attempting to smell out the faults of others, he finds the stench of the sulphurous pit on his own hands. But despite his attempts to suppress its presence in himself, he has always known that that pit was within him; his rush out into the storm was in part one more attempt to avoid that knowledge. Lear wants to think that his daughters drive him out into the storm (3.4.17–19). But he is driven toward the storm less by his daughters' actions than by the intensity of feeling with which he responds to their actions; he invents his exposure to the storm (2.4.210–13) well before they close their doors against him. When the storm he imagines materializes, it announces itself as an externalization of his feelings, in effect a projection outward of everything he cannot tolerate within:

> You think I'll weep;
> No, I'll not weep:
> I have full cause of weeping, [*Storm and Tempest.*][25]
>   but this heart
> Shall break into a hundred thousand flaws
> Or ere I'll weep.
>
> (2.4.284–88)

Attempting to mobilize masculine rage against his intolerable feelings—as he will later attempt to invoke the male Thunderer in the storm—he identifies these feelings specifically as female: "touch me with noble anger, / And let not women's weapons, water-drops, / Stain my man's cheeks" (2.4.278–80). Rushing out into the storm made of his own tears, Lear rushes out to confront what is inside him: for if the storm is the embodiment of the female force that shakes his manhood, that force is from the start the enemy within.[26]

Earlier, before the storm, Lear has given this female force her proper name:

> O! how this mother swells up toward my heart;
> *Hysterica passio!* down, thou climbing sorrow!
> Thy element's below. Where is this daughter?
> (2.4.56–58)

The bizarreness of these lines has not always been appreciated; in them, Lear quite literally acknowledges the presence of the sulphurous pit within him. Suffocated by the emotions that he thinks of as female, Lear gives them the name of the woman's part, as though he himself bore that diseased and wandering organ within: for "mother" is a technical term for the uterus; "Hysterica passio" or "the suffocation of the mother" is the disease caused by its wandering.[27] Like Richard III, Lear discovers his origin in the suffocating maternal womb and traces his vulnerability to it: if he was once inside it, it is now inside him, and his suffocating emotions are its sign. Thus naming his pain, Lear localizes in himself the nightmare that Poor Tom will later evoke in the storm:[28] finding her within and calling her "mother," he traces his internal femaleness to her presence within him, the presence that now rises up to choke him. And at this moment, Shakespeare shows us the place of the repressed mother: her organ the epitome of the woman who refuses to stay in her proper place,[29] she turns up at the very center of masculine authority, in the king's own body; excluded outside, she returns within, undermining the gender divide and so shaking the foundations of masculine identity. It is no wonder that the storm seems a near-psychotic experience for us as for Lear, for it plays out the terror of this discovery: in the storm made of his own irrepressible femaleness, the storm that is the maternal signature, all boundaries dissolve, and Lear is once more inside what is inside him.

Insofar as the Lear plot insists on Lear's complicity in the making of his daughters and on the presence of the female within him, it scrutinizes, and criticizes, the scapegoating logic of the Gloucester plot—the logic that would make only the female the agent of darkness. In fact the play at one point thematizes the logic of this scapegoating, as though to distance itself from it. Faced with the hard evidence of Edgar's mutilated body, Lear invents wicked daughters to account for his suffering, as though only they could be to blame:

> *Lear*   Now all the plagues that in the pendulous air
> Hang fated o'er men's faults light on thy daughters!
>
> *Kent*   He hath no daughters, Sir.
>
> *Lear*   Death, traitor! nothing could have subdu'd nature
> To such a lowness but his unkind daughters.
> Is it the fashion that discarded fathers
> Should have thus little mercy on their flesh?
> Judicious punishment! 'twas this flesh begot
> Those pelican daughters.
>
> (3.4.66–75)

Inventing these wicked daughters, Lear in effect rewrites a tale of fraternal and paternal abuse as a tale of abuse by daughters. And this invention serves a patently defensive function: having invented them, he can righteously call punishment down upon them, deflecting onto them the plague that "hangs fated o'er men's faults." But this is the punishment that hangs specifically over Lear's own fault/foutre. In diverting the plagues that hang fated over men's faults onto the daughters who can be made to suffer in their stead, Lear attempts to insulate himself from acknowledgment of the "plague-sore, or embossed carbuncle" (2.4.226) in his own corrupted blood; relocating plague outside the boundaries of his body, in the wicked daughters he invents, he ensures that the daughters—rather than their fathers—are to be punished for the faults/foutres that have made them.

The mechanism of scapegoating is laid bare here, in Lear's attempt to redirect the plague from his own fault; but the plague nonetheless lights on his daughters. Even while the play enables us to see Lear's need for wicked daughters, and hence undermines the scapegoating logic, it nonetheless replicates that logic,[30] construing Lear's fault itself as the legacy of the female, the contaminating maternal inheritance that cannot be disowned or suppressed. And it moreover represents Goneril and Regan in accordance with the demands of that logic; in their portrayal, the play's dramaturgy is entirely complicit with the fantasy of the dark and vicious place. For the play simultaneously illuminates their genesis in Lear's need and embraces Lear's vision of them, making them as monstrous as he himself could have wished: as it progresses, they are increasingly identified as the source of evil; finally removed wholly from the realm of human sympathy—as Edmund never is—they die as monsters, consumed by their own excess.[31] And insofar as the play localizes plague in them, it collaborates in Lear's own attempt to transfer blame and punishment to daughters, who thus become the contaminating plague-source that can deflect blame away from him. "Is it the fashion that discarded fathers / Should have thus little mercy on their flesh?" Lear asks; and the question cuts both ways: for if they hurt Lear, Lear—and Shakespeare—hurt them.[32] If the play relentlessly returns Lear to the dark and vicious place initially occluded, forcing him to acknowledge his complicity in the stench of female corruption, it is nonetheless the women who pay the full cost of his return. And if the cost is high for Goneril and Regan, it is even higher for Cordelia. For the monstrous mother/daughters Lear finds in them are in part Cordelia's psychic progeny, generated out of his terrible need for her; and as a consequence, she must become the sacrificial antidote to maternal malevolence in them. Acting out Lear's fantasied relation to the occluded mother through all three of the daughters who are her projections, the play divides and conquers her, recontaining her in the daughters who are her derivatives, all three of whom die in an instant. The wheel indeed comes full circle and the play ends where it had begun, with the eradication of the problematic female body.[33]

Because Cordelia is the original site of vulnerability, the site from which Lear's need unfolds, the process of recontainment is most intensely played out in relation to her. For the fantasy of maternal contamination is, I think, the flip side of the longing for maternal presence expressed through Lear's relationship to her; it is in part the price required by the fantasy of merger with which the play begins. When Lear strips himself in 1.1, voluntarily giving up everything to embrace the nothing that is his traditional end—"Sans teeth, sans eyes, sans taste, sans everything," as Jaques would have it (As You Like It, 2.7.165–66)—he attempts in effect to bargain with the nothingness of death, embracing nothingness on his own terms and for his own ends.[34] And as he does so, Shakespeare psychologizes Jaques's familiar trope of old age as "second childishness": in giving his daughters control over the extended body that is his kingdom, Lear would make them his mothers, deliberately putting himself in the position of infantile need from which he will experience the rest of the play. His response to Cordelia after she has disappointed him shows us what is at stake for him in this bargain: he will trade in his all ("I gave you all" [2.4.252]) to secure Cordelia's all, exchanging both possessions and adult autonomy for the promise of her unconditional and undivided love, in order to make her nursery his final resting place ("I lov'd her most, and thought to set my rest / On her kind nursery" [1.1.123–

24]). Imagining himself an infant sleeping at her breast, he revisions as plenitude the death toward which he is crawling (1.1.41), attempting to replace its nothingness with the *all* that fusion with her idealized maternal body seems to promise.

In this exchange, Shakespeare reworks the fantasy of maternal plenitude as a stay against death that he had articulated briefly in *2 Henry VI*, when Suffolk imagined death separated from his beloved Margaret:

> . . . in thy sight to die, what were it else
> But like a pleasant slumber in thy lap?
> Here could I breathe my soul into the air,
> As mild and gentle as the cradle-babe
> Dying with mother's dug between its lips;
> Where, from thy sight, I should be raging mad,
> And cry out for thee to close up mine eyes,
> To have thee with thy lips to stop my mouth.
> (*2 Henry VI*, 3.2.388–95)[35]

Nothing we have seen of Suffolk or Margaret prepares for the bizarre intensity of this moment; its very extraneousness, the extent to which it is not assimilated to the text, marks it as urgently intrusive, not merely an instance of the youthful Shakespeare's stylistic experimentation (although it is certainly that) but an early eruption of the peculiarly Shakespearean fantasy that shapes the portrayal of sexual union and death in *Troilus and Cressida*, *Othello*, and *Antony and Cleopatra* as it shapes the portrayal of Lear's need. For Suffolk, lover and mother fuse; and death is tolerable only insofar as it is imagined as union with this ideally nurturant figure. Madness, he suggests, is the only alternative to this vision. But even at this early stage, the fantasy is self-consuming. Even as Suffolk articulates it, it rebounds upon itself, making of Margaret less a stay against death than an agent of death itself: she closes his eyes; she stops his mouth. Both in the nakedness with which it articulates the fantasy of maternal plenitude and in the transformation of Margaret into an agent of death, Suffolk's speech usefully anticipates the movement of *King Lear*: for in *King Lear*, Shakespeare elaborates both the madness Suffolk hints at and the danger inherent in this maternal body.

This danger initially emerges when Cordelia cannot meet Lear's need of her; at this point, maternal presence splits in two, as the benign and nurturant mother with whom Lear would merge generates her opposite, the annihilating mothers who seek his death.[36] For Cordelia cannot give Lear her *all*; her first word to him, reiterating the threat of death itself, is "Nothing."[37] Attempting to separate herself from her father by insisting on her duties as a wife, she partitions her love, rebuking his desire for *all* by using the language of arithmetical exactitude: "I love your Majesty / According to my bond; no more nor less. . . . That lord whose hand must take my plight shall carry / Half my love with him. . . . Sure I shall never marry like my sisters, / To love my father all" (1.1.92–104). But in the arithmetic of infantile need, there can be no *some*; anything less than all is nothing.[38] Her response shatters his dream of kind nursery, of the unconditional and undivided love that could turn death itself into blissful fusion; thrust back toward the nothingness of his own death, Lear discovers from Cordelia that he is not all, that he is a finite and mortal creature.[39]

Lear responds to this discovery with the rage of an abandoned infant, banishing her both in retaliation for her abandonment of him and in order to gain control over his loss, like a child closing his eyes against the dark—or like a Coriolanus shouting "I banish you!" to the Rome that has banished him. And in his rage, he calls up the mother she has become in his mind, invoking in her place those punitive mothers to whom he himself has given the rod (1.4.179–81). Cordelia clarifies this exchange as she bids her sisters farewell, setting her "better place" against their "professed bosoms" ("To your professed bosoms I commit him: / But yet, alas! stood I within his grace, / I would prefer him to a better place" [1.1.272–74]). Like Cordelia, the play strenuously insists on the difference between these two places—and yet at the same time reveals their common origin. For these monstrously punitive mothers are, I think, psychically generated by Lear's rage at Cordelia; they play out her abandonment of him. As Goneril and Regan develop into monsters, they become exfoliations of what Lear's imagination has made of Cordelia: it is Cordelia's sexuality, her insistence on her own separateness, that first strike Lear as monstrous. If she seems willing to cuckold him by choosing a husband in place of him, they "leave his horns without a case" (1.5.31–32); her troublesome sexuality is played out in their voracious appetite. If she seems to offer him nothing in place of all, they would reduce him to nothingness; her psychic abandonment of him is literalized in their opposing the bolt against his coming in (2.4.178–79), in their driving him into the storm that is the epitome of their annihilating power. If her muted strivings toward autonomy—her standing aside from her father's need—are the first challenge to Lear's omnipotence and hence the reminder of his finitude, Goneril and Regan become the principle of female autonomy run mad, playing out the logic through which female autonomy must mean the annihilation of the male.[40]

Mothers made monstrous by Lear's disappointed rage at Cordelia, Goneril and Regan enact the fantasies of abandonment and annihilation that her rejection has created in him; we see their genesis as he attempts to disown the mother/child who has disobeyed him, invoking the horrific landscape of maternal abandonment that he will then be forced to occupy.[41] Disclaiming his paternal care of Cordelia not only "by the sacred radiance of the sun" but also by "the mysteries of Hecate and the night" (1.1.109–13), Lear calls upon the dark female region of the storm as though it were his to command; but, once invoked, it will take on a life of its own, peopled by Goneril and Regan, the cannibalistic witch-children his own rage has made. For they are the distorted children of his own appetite, born from his hunger for Cordelia. Disowning her, he compares her to "the barbarous Scythian . . . that makes his generation messes / To gorge his appetite" (1.1.116–18). Just where we might expect a reference to a wicked child, we are given this monstrously devouring father;[42] and the illogic of the image suggests the psychic source of Lear's monster daughters. For the Scythian's grotesque appetite is a nightmare version of Lear's own desire to feed on Cordelia's kind nursery; and as though in talion punishment for this thwarted desire, her punitive surrogates turn cannibal in his imagination, becoming sharp-toothed (1.4.297, 2.4.136), the "pelican daughters" (3.4.75), the kites and wolves (1.4.271, 317), vultures and serpents (2.4.136, 162), who feed on him.

As Cordelia is the original site of vulnerability, only she can serve as reassurance against the dark mother Lear's rage releases into the play. Physically separated from the place of this mother—the place of the storm—through her long absence, she comes to epitomize the antidote against it; on her return, she is identified as the "one daughter, / Who redeems nature from the general curse / Which twain have brought her to" (4.6.206–8). —But which twain? The Gentleman's words construe Cordelia as the antidote not only to the curse of Goneril and Regan, but, behind them, to the curse of our first parents. In his extraordinary condensation of Goneril and Regan with Adam and Eve, the Gentleman makes both pairs equally responsible for the fall; in superimposing one "twain" on the other, he doubles Eve's role in Goneril and Regan and eliminates Adam. Through this condensation, Shakespeare in effect offers a revised version of the fall, making our fallen nature entirely derivative from Eve and her daughters, entirely the inheritance of the woman's part. In this revision, we are fallen insofar as we are hers; our fallen nature is her sign in us. And Cordelia can return—can redeem the nature that they have cursed—only insofar as she is exempt from this maternal inheritance, in essence remade as the second Eve, the Virgin Mother who can undo harm.

But the remaking is strenuous. Cordelia leaves Act I a loving but stubbornly self-righteous daughter, devoted equally to her own harsh truth and to her father, insisting on her right to give half her love to her husband; remade in her absence in the image of Lear's need, she returns in Act IV as a holy mother, surrounded by the nimbus of redemption. At least in the Quarto version of the play, Shakespeare works hard to prepare for her reappearance,[43] transforming her from a relatively naturalistically conceived character into a virtual icon of the *mater dolorosa*, the heavenly queen who shakes "the holy water from her heavenly eyes" (4.3.31); when she herself enters, going about her father's business (4.4.24), she confirms her assumption of this role, praying that "All bless'd secrets, / All you unpublish'd virtues of the earth, / Spring with my tears!" (4.4.15–17).[44] Hence, I think, the fate of France: for Cordelia can become the curative virgin mother only insofar as she gives up every sign of the marital sexuality that had epitomized her disturbing otherness in 1.1, the sexuality that in effect mobilized Lear's fantasy-creation of the malevolent mother. Transformed in Lear's mind into "the hot-blooded France, that dowerless took / Our youngest born" (2.4.214–15), France must be banished from the scene, however awkwardly ("Why the King of France is so suddenly gone back know you no reason?" [4.3.1]), before Cordelia can be reconstituted as Virgin Mother, exempt from the fault of Eve: we need only try to imagine where France might be in Lear's prison fantasy—"We three alone will sing like birds i' th' cage"?—to see how vital his absence is. And hence the logic that gives Cordelia no mother: she can play redeeming Mary to Goneril and Regan's offending Eve only insofar as she is radically isolated from their maternal heritage.

Only thus redefined as the holy mother can Cordelia safely return to love her father all, her kiss repairing "those violent harms that [her] two sisters / Have in [his] reverence made" (4.7.28–29); only thus redefined can she redeem the dark and vicious place of the storm, the place of Eve, and of Goneril and Regan. And with her return, the storm indeed fades, its landscape of deprivation replaced by the renewed vision of kind nursery that springs with her tears. With her return, something like trust in the natural world becomes possible again, for us and for Lear: though we do not return to the nature Lear thought he could command, the witch-nature of the storm is replaced by the figure of Cordelia as Ceres—the good mother searching "the high-grown field" (4.4.7) for her child, the mother whose care brings back spring to the earth.[45] Now, where there had been only "idle weeds"—the rank fumiter and furrow-weeds, the hardocks, hemlock, nettles and darnel that crown Lear—there is "our sustaining corn" (4.4.6). *Our* corn: Cordelia carries with her the possibility of a benign natural world, a world that can sustain us. This is the emotional landscape of Eden, nature redeemed from the curse that twain had brought her to.

Cordelia's return seems to give Lear everything that he had wanted in 1.1—indeed, everything that he had been punished for wanting—promising a return to *all*, hence enabling in him a renewed fantasy of the boundless fusion that can undo division and death. His awakening to Cordelia in 4.7 is literally an awakening from a dream of death as isolation and endless punishment, in which the tears he had tried to suppress have become instruments of torture: "I am bound / Upon a wheel of fire, that mine own tears / Do scald like molten lead" (4.7.46–48). At first her presence seems a faint continuation of that dream: for he can recognize her only by seeing in her the last vestige of the punitive mother his rage at her has released into the play ("If you have poison for me, I will drink it. / I know you do not love me" [4.7.72–73]); like a penitent child, he is willing to accept any punishment in order to earn her love. But Cordelia's "no cause" (4.7.75) kills the great rage in him (4.7.78–79), returning him to the dream of maternal plenitude, where love is outside the realm of deserving.[46] It is a short step from here to Lear's vision of their life together in prison, outside time and flux, endlessly reliving this flow of blessing and forgiveness in a space of undifferentiated union that itself seems to promise exemption from death:

> We two alone will sing like birds i' th' cage:
>   . . . so we'll live,
> And pray, and sing, and tell old tales, and laugh
> At gilded butterflies, and hear poor rogues
> Talk of court news; and we'll talk with them too . . .
> And take upon 's the mystery of things,
> As if we were Gods' spies: and we'll wear out,
> In a wall'd prison, packs and sects of great ones
> That ebb and flow by th' moon.
>
>   (5.3.9–19)

Recasting the walled prison in the image of the walled garden, complete with birds and butterflies, Lear in effect transforms it into a spatialized form of the unfallen maternal body in which he initially sought shelter, the representation of Cordelia's idealized virgin body. And as such, the prison he constructs is the antidote to the maternal body of the storm and the attendant horrors of mortality; sheltering in this undifferentiated space, wearing out packs and sects of great ones, Lear would unmake division and mortality itself, recapturing the kind nursery denied him in 1.1.

But the cost for Cordelia is too high: she can occupy this space, repairing the breach that twain have made, only by sacrificing her own

separateness, her own individuality; and Shakespeare makes it plain
that this sacrifice is no accident, that it is just what Lear requires. If
Cordelia's insistence on her separateness initially defines Lear's fall
into mortality, his fantasy of recovery requires that she give up her
separateness, along with the sexuality that is its sign. Lear's great prison
fantasy takes as its premise his need to deny her a separate voice; it in
fact emerges in response to her muted attempt to separate her voice
from his:

> *Cor.*   We are not the first
> Who, with best meaning, have incurr'd the worst.
> For thee, oppressed King, I am cast down;
> Myself could else out-frown false Fortune's frown.
> Shall we not see these daughters and these sisters?
>
> *Lear* No, no, no, no! Come, let's away to prison;
> We two alone will sing like birds i' th'cage. . . .
>   (5.3.3–9)

"No, no, no, no": Lear does not want to believe that Cordelia is cast
down for him, does not want to be reminded of those daughters and
sisters; more fundamentally, he does not want to hear her dividing *we*
into its constituent *thee* and *I*. Overriding the formal couplets that
threaten the intimacy of the moment he would construct, that suggest
division in the doubleness of their form,[47] his outburst enfolds her in
his relentless *we*, reconstructing her as part of himself. Only thus can
he recreate their life together in prison as a place outside time, flux,
and individual being, attempting to make of it an antidote to individual
mortality and hence to the vision of the storm.

In negating everything outside their union in prison—no, no, no,
no—Lear must necessarily negate Cordelia too; she can be made to
serve his vision only insofar as he can deny the possibility of difference
between them, dissolving Cordelia's identity into his own. For if Cordelia's insistence on her separateness in 1.1 casts Lear out of his dream
of fusion with maternal plenitude, only the sacrifice of her separateness
can allow for the fantasy of return. These are the terms of redemption
implicit even as the Gentleman names Cordelia the "one daughter, /
Who redeems nature from the general curse / Which twain have
brought her to" (4.6.206–8); *one* and *twain* themselves specify what
needs redeeming. For two is the first number, the beginning of the
counting and accounting that ends in Cordelia's giving away half her
love, the fall from the dream of union and the infantile *all*; two is the
sign of separation and division. Beginning in the play's opening lines,
with Gloucester's reference to the "division of the kingdom" (1.1.4),

this is everywhere a play of division; the violent harms that Cordelia's two sisters make in Lear's reverence (4.7.28–29)—what she calls the "breach" in his abused nature (4.7.15)—replicate internally all the external divisions that motivate the plot.[48] The very two-ness of Goneril and Regan makes them apt agents of division, particularly since they seem conspicuously divided versions of a single whole, conspicuously *twain* rather than simply two.[49] Twain, they come to stand for the fact of division itself, the fact that Lear relearns when Cordelia divides her love in half; in setting their *twain* against Cordelia's *one*, the Gentleman names the play's most primary loss: the fall into division, the loss of one-ness that only the return of the one can redeem.[50]

In the version of fall and redemption played out through Lear's daughters, Shakespeare seems to me to reiterate the organizing trope of Book I of *The Faerie Queene*, where the movement from Una to Duessa—from one-ness to two-ness—similarly signals the entrance into a fallen world, and only the recovery of the one promises redemption. And by beginning the play with Lear's fantasy of resting on Cordelia's kind nursery, Shakespeare psychologizes this trope, replaying in Cordelia's refusal and Lear's shocked response the child's fall into selfhood and finitude, the moment when self and world (in the shape of the mother) begin to divide. From Cordelia, Lear rediscovers the primal separation. And insofar as her "nothing" is the first agent of division, the immense longing for her that fills the whole space of her absence comes to stand for the longing to undo separation itself; in her absence, she becomes the bearer of the hope that twain can become one again. Although Cordelia is apparently excised from Lear's memory—he makes no direct reference to her during the play's middle acts—the longing for her reappears outside him, in the poignant song-fragment in which Edgar and the Fool speak with the voice of his loss:

Edg. Come o'er the bourn, Bessy, to me,—

Fool   Her boat hath a leak,
          And she must not speak;[51]
     Why she dares not come over to thee!
                 (3.6.26–29)

Present only in this riddling exchange, she is nonetheless intensely present: she is the beloved one on the other side of the water, the one who cannot speak. The dense complexity of "bourn"—alluding simultaneously to the watery boundary that separates Lear from Cordelia, to the fact of boundedness that marks us as separate individuals, and perhaps to the origin of finitude in birth—gathers up into itself all the inarticulate longing of the play's middle acts, recording at once all the boundaries that enforce human separateness, that divide Lear from his beloved mother/daughter.[52] "When we are born, we cry," Lear tells us at the end of his meditation on the storm, figuring birth itself as abandonment into mortality, the smell that we take in with our first breath (4.6.180–84).[53] In this fragmentary interchange in the storm, Shakespeare thus plays with the heart of loss, setting the longing that finitude be undone against the knowledge that it cannot—must not—be undone, that Cordelia can never come over to Lear. And then, against this knowledge at its center, the play sets the return of Cordelia.

The sacrifice of Cordelia's otherness is not an incidental requirement of the plot; it is the meaning of her return. She can only come over the bourn by losing herself; according to the terms of the fantasy of kind nursery, her selfhood *is* the bourn. Lear ends his prison speech by asking, "Have I caught thee?" (5.3.21), and Cordelia's response is silence, as it must be: caught in his *we*, there is no longer an *I* from which she can speak. Permanently silenced by Lear's *no*, she does not speak again. At this moment, Shakespeare seems to make clear the cost of her return, anticipating her death in her silence and enabling us to understand both as the consequence of Lear's psychic need. But at the same time as Shakespeare seems to analyze Lear's need, and hence to distance himself from it, his representation of Cordelia is deeply complicit with that need. The Cordelia he reconstructs in Act IV is largely the Cordelia of Lear's fantasy; and unless we strain against the bias of the text, no other Cordelia is readily available to us. As with *Troilus and Cressida*, Shakespeare's complicity with the dominant male fantasy is registered through a change not only in the character but in the mode of representation: the woman we thought we knew—or thought we could know—simply disappears from view as our access to her is blocked. In 1.1, Cordelia is very much a creature of flesh and blood, with her own psychic necessities, and the mode through which she is represented draws our attention to these necessities. The asides through which we are initially introduced to her and her exchanges with her father and her sisters make us keenly aware of her inner life: of her attempt to define or perhaps defend her nascent selfhood, her refusal to speak unless she can speak herself truly, her competitive struggle with her sisters, her need to separate herself from her father. We may well feel that we cannot fully know her; but there is no doubt that there is someone there to know. But when Cordelia returns, our questions no longer seem fully legitimate: she returns as the creature of Lear's need, changed utterly, and changed not only in her nature but in the mode through which Shakespeare allows us access to her.[54] Introduced to us initially as a subject, she returns as the object of our reverent gaze, her significance for us determined not by what she says or feels but by what others say and feel about her. We may see some vestiges of her old self in the poignance of her desire to see her father (4.4.29), in her familiar inarticulatenesss in the reunion scene, and perhaps especially in her troublesome desire to see "these daughters and these sisters" (5.3.7); we may even be able to construct the sense of her continuing subjectivity from these hints. But we are no longer invited to speculate about her motivation; except insofar as she murmurs her love for her father, what she feels seems no longer to matter. Even before her death, even before Lear silences her, she has died as a subject, the illusion of her inwardness, of her flesh-and-blood being, visibly sacrificed to the new business the play requires of her: she now exists to bring Lear to the promised end, and that is all.

Insofar as the Cordelia of 1.1 is silenced, insofar as we feel the Cordelia who returns more as an iconic presence answering Lear's terrible need than as a separate character with her own needs, Shakespeare is complicit in Lear's fantasy, rewarding him for his suffering by remaking for him the Cordelia he had wanted all along; Shakespeare too requires the sacrifice of her autonomy. This is a very painful recognition for a feminist critic, for any reader who reads as a daughter. As feminist critics, we may once again note wryly that this sacrifice is regularly required of Shakespeare's tragic women, and perhaps of women *per se*; and yet the cases of Cressida and Desdemona are not comparable. For how can we experience this play and not want Cordelia to return to Lear? And yet how can we want what Lear—what Shakespeare—does to her? It is easy enough simply to dissociate ourselves from Lear's need, to gender it male and thus escape its traces in ourselves; it is easy enough thus to mobilize anger against both the fathers—literal and literary—that require Cordelia's sacrifice. And yet, if we allow the anger we mobilize to cut us off from the heart of longing embedded in Lear's suffering, do we not replicate Lear's own attempt to mobilize anger against vulnerability (2.4.278–80)— this time our own? For the fantasies that determine the shape of Cordelia's return are, I think, only in part gendered; in part they spring from the ground of an infantile experience prior to gender.[55]

When Cordelia insists that she cannot love her father all, she creates a rage in Lear that we might agree to call oedipal, and to gender male, insofar as it seems to have its roots in the son's frustrated desire for the mother's exclusive sexual attention; this is, I think, the stratum of desire played out, for example, in Goneril's and Regan's voracious sexuality, especially insofar as that sexuality is triangulated, adulterous. But this (gendered) rage at female sexuality in part figures and in part covers over and defends against the more primitive pain of preoedipal betrayal,[56] the betrayal inherent in individuation itself; and though the expression of this pain will be inflected by gender, we cannot ultimately distance ourselves from it by gendering it male. For the fantasies enacted in Cordelia's loss and return—in Lear's terrible hunger and isolation, in the blissful fusion of his walled prison—derive from the very beginnings of nascent selfhood, before consciousness of the gender divide. Even while I understand the urgency of Cordelia's refusal to be all to her father, I share with Lear—and with Shake-speare—the stratum of desire that brings her back all his; and to the extent that I share in their desire, I cannot shelter in the anger that would allow me to make their need alien, gendering it male. For I too inhabit the terror of finitude and the desire for merger with the infinitely kind nursery that can undo the pain of separation; I too long for her return. And if so, then I participate with them in the destruction of Cordelia's selfhood; daughters as well as sons require this sacrifice from those we make our mothers.

Perhaps our task—if we read this play specifically as feminists—is simultaneously to acknowledge this place of common need and to measure its cost to the woman forced to bear its burden. It is by way of continuing to measure this cost that I want to turn finally to Corde-lia's death, understood not only as the ultimate silencing of her subjec-tivity but specifically as the response of a recuperative male rage against the power vested in her. Cordelia's death used to be read largely as a stage in Lear's spiritual development; it is now sometimes read as retribution for Lear's inappropriate desires, punishment for his failure to acknowledge her otherness.[57] The order for her death ("Come hither, captain; hark. / Take thou this note; Go follow them to prison" [5.3.27–28]) in fact comes immediately after Lear asks, "Have I caught thee?" as though in response to his question. But if her death is an answer to Lear's question, it is a deeply ambiguous answer: is it the final sign of separation, proof that Lear has not caught her, that Cordelia cannot come over the bourn no matter how much he wishes it? or is it the final stage in Lear's fantasy of fusion? Lear's is the lover's question; when Falstaff similarly asks "Have I caught thee, my heavenly jewel?" misquoting Astrophel, he adds, "Why, now let me die, for I have lived long enough" (Merry Wives of Windsor, 3.3.35).[58] Death is often the place of union for Shakespearean lovers; and Lear carries the dead Cordelia onto the stage like a bridegroom carrying his bride across the threshold;[59] is death their new home, the final version of prison as kind nursery? Or does the reversed pietà of his gesture—the mortal father/son now carrying the holy virgin mother, dead as earth—signal the permanent loss of this possibility, the final sepa-ration?[60]

No matter what our answers are, they play across—and require—

Cordelia's dead body. At the end, the play invites us to see this dead body as a prop for Lear's anguish, whatever the terms in which we would understand that anguish; having evacuated Cordelia's subjectivity, the play takes even her death from her. Without attempting to reconstruct that subjectivity, I want to try to read Cordelia's death, first of all, as something that happens specifically to her, not only to Lear, and then as something that happens to her because of the intensity of the emotions invested in her. —What literally kills Cordelia? Much of the play—including Cordelia's own "Shall we not see these daughters and these sisters?"—leads us to expect that Goneril and Regan will have a hand in her death; but the order for her death comes from Edmund, apparently in response to Lear's prison speech. But what exactly is he responding to? He is clearly enraged by Lear's attempt to redefine his punishment as bliss, defeating Edmund's control of him. But his order to the captain conspicuously musters the tropes of manliness—"know thou this, that men / Are as the time is; to be tender-minded / Does not become a sword" (5.3.31–33); and the captain responds, "If it be man's work I'll do't" (5.3.40). This exchange places Edmund and the captain in the psychic mode of Troilus at the end of *Troilus and Cressida*, where manliness depends on leaving the hermit pity with one's mother (5.3.45); and it makes the killing of Cordelia in effect into a recuperation of masculinity, as though it were the exercise of a male rage not only against Lear's redefinition but more specifically against the threat to masculinity inherent in Lear's vision of blissful fusion.[61]

If the timing and the terms of Edmund's command make Cordelia's death seem the recuperation of a threatened masculinity, the mode of her death itself enacts a metaphoric revenge. Like Desdemona, Cordelia is choked, her potentially troublesome voice silenced in her throat; her death by hanging thus invites reading as the logical extension of Lear's own silencing of her speech in order to build his prison fantasy. But the suffocation of Cordelia seems to me the product of a retaliatory rage directed less toward her voice than toward her heart—and toward her heart as the representative site of the overwhelming feelings that Lear genders female. Both in her first appearance, when she cannot heave her heart into her mouth (1.1.91–92), and in her return, pantingly heaving forth the name of father (4.3.27), Cordelia embodies the rising, choking heart (*cor*) that we half-hear in her name, the heart that Lear would attempt to beat down, the heart that suffocates him in the end ("Pray you, undo this button" [5.3.309]).[62] Her *cor* invokes the *cor* in him; and this heart is Lear's alternative name for the suffocating feeling rising within him, the feeling he first calls "mother" ("O! how this mother swells up toward my heart; / . . . down, thou climbing sorrow!" [2.4.56–57]; "O me! my heart, my rising heart! but, down!" [2.4.121]). As Lear imagines the internal presence that would suffocate him, "heart" and "mother" coalesce, and coalesce in the figure of Cordelia:[63] site of his deepest longings, she herself is revealed as the suffocating mother within, through the heart that is her sign. But this coalescence merely rejoins what Lear's initial act of splitting had attempted to sunder. For the idealized mother Lear seeks in Cordelia and the horrific mother he finds first in her sisters and then in himself are psychically one, merely flip sides of one another; they have a common origin in the developmental history of male identity as it is tenuously separated out from its originary matrix, the mother that it— like this text—would occlude.[64] As the site of both longing and loss, as the source of femaleness itself, the mother and her surrogates will be forced to pay the price of this history, not least in the stories told about her. For longing and terror interlock: in its longing for originary wholeness, the unstable masculinity that would escape its own finitude through a fantasy of merger with her recoils at finding the signs of her presence within, including the signs of his need for her,[65] and in its recoil transforms the dream of union into the nightmare of suffocation—as Suffolk does when he imagines Margaret stopping his mouth. This is the crime that Cordelia must pay for, and pay for with her breath: at the end, she—not he— has "no breath at all" (5.3.307). Insofar as she is the point of origin for Lear's desire, insofar as she therefore represents the source of Lear's choking emotion, her own death by choking enacts a talion punishment, the terrible recuperation of male individuality from the threat of the overwhelming mother within.[66]

King Lear is often seen as an extraordinary celebration of relatedness and emotional openness, of all the vulnerability that Lear has tried to gender female and deny in himself; and in this celebration, Cordelia must die so that Lear can die of love, "with his whole being launched toward another," in Maynard Mack's wonderful phrase.[67] But if Cordelia's death comes to Lear as the prerequisite for his new emotional openness, it comes to Cordelia herself as a punishment for the desire he has invested in her. For the mother that threatens to suffocate Lear by his sheer need of her must herself be suffocated: that is the price Cordelia pays for acquiring the power of the displaced and occluded mother. It seems to me not quite coincidental that Desdemona—who creates in Othello the same longing for wholeness, who has the same power to make men vulnerable to their own need—should also die by suffocation: if Othello too finds himself choked by his own emotion ("I cannot speak enough of this content, / It stops me here," *Othello*,

2.1.196–97), he too retaliates by suffocating his emotion at its source. In *King Lear* Edmund—and Shakespeare[68]—do to Cordelia what Othello does to Desdemona, and for the same reasons: acting on behalf of a threatened masculinity, they choke off the rising heart that is the source of danger. For the Shakespeare who wrote *King Lear*—unlike the Shakespeare who wrote *Antony and Cleopatra* or *The Winter's Tale*—could allow the expression of Lear's naked vulnerability only by simultaneously allowing the expression of the self-preserving and self-enclosing male rage that it provokes, the rage that Lear had earlier attempted to mobilize against his own female feeling (2.4.278–80): splitting off that rage, distancing and localizing it in Edmund's command, Shakespeare can simultaneously enact it in Cordelia's death and mourn its consequences. And if the celebration of Lear's vulnerability to Cordelia leads toward *Antony and Cleopatra* and the great reunions of the romances, the enactment of Cordelia's death leads toward *Macbeth*, *Coriolanus*, and *Timon of Athens*: toward the excision of the dangerous female presences—the mothers within and without—that threaten to overwhelm male authority and selfhood.

6

ESCAPING THE MATRIX: THE CONSTRUCTION
OF MASCULINITY IN *MACBETH*
AND *CORIOLANUS*

Just before Lear rushes out into the storm, he prays to the absent gods
to "touch [him] with noble anger, / And let not women's weapons,
water-drops, / Stain [his] man's cheeks" (2.4.278–80): threatened by
the "mother" within (2.4.56), he attempts to mobilize manly anger
against her. But Lear cannot sustain his anger; and in the end, after his
great rage has passed, he dissolves mercifully into relationship with the
mother he has made of Cordelia. The drive toward masculine autonomy diverted in him is in effect deflected onto Edmund, who becomes
the standard-bearer for masculinity as he orders Cordelia's death; and
it is resurrected in Macbeth and Coriolanus, each of whom similarly
constructs his exaggerated and blood-thirsty masculinity as an attempt
to ward off vulnerability to the mother.[1] For the cannibalistic witch-
mothers Lear finds in Goneril and Regan are resurrected in Lady
Macbeth and Volumnia; and fatherless, these sons are terribly subject
to their power. The initially defining act for both of them thus turns
on re-imagining the origin of masculine selfhood: both Macbeth's
early victory over Macdonwald and the conquest of Corioli that gives
Coriolanus his name figure the decisive masculine act as a bloody
rebirth, replacing the dangerous maternal origin through the violence
of self-creation. For both heroes, as for Troilus, heroic masculinity
turns on leaving the mother behind. Or on seeming to leave her behind:
for both plays construct the exaggerated masculinity of their heroes
simultaneously as an attempt to separate from the mother and as the
playing out of her bloodthirsty will; both enact the paradox through
which the son is never more the mother's creature than when he
attempts to escape her.

Maternal power in *Macbeth* is not embodied in the figure of a
particular mother (as it is in *Coriolanus*); it is instead diffused through-

130

out the play, evoked primarily by the figures of the witches and Lady Macbeth. Largely through Macbeth's relationship to them, the play becomes (like *Coriolanus*) a representation of primitive fears about male identity and autonomy itself, about those looming female presences who threaten to control one's actions and one's mind, to constitute one's very self, even at a distance. When Macbeth's first words echo those we have already heard the witches speak—"So foul and fair a day I have not seen" (1.3.38); "Fair is foul, and foul is fair" (1.1.11)— we are in a realm that questions the very possibility of autonomous identity. As with Richard III, the maternal constitutes the suffocating matrix from which he must break free; and as with Richard, his solution will be to hew his way out with a bloody axe.[2]

This fantasy of escape in fact haunts *Macbeth*. In its last moments, as Macbeth feels himself increasingly hemmed in by enemies, the stage resonates with variants of his repeated question, "What's he / That was not born of woman?" (5.7.2–3; for variants, see 5.3.4, 6; 5.7.11, 13; 5.8.13, 31.) Repeated seven times, Macbeth's allusion to the witches' prophecy—"none of woman born / Shall harm Macbeth" (4.1.80–81)—becomes virtually a talisman to ward off danger; even after he has begun to doubt the equivocation of the fiend (5.5.43), mere repetition of the phrase seems to Macbeth to guarantee his invulnerability. And as he repeats himself, his assurance seems to turn itself inside out, becoming dependent not on the fact that all men are, after all, born of woman but on the fantasy of escape from this universal condition.[3] The duplicity of Macbeth's repeated question—its capacity to mean both itself and its opposite—carries such weight at the end of the play, I think, because the whole of the play represents in very powerful form both the fantasy of a virtually absolute and destructive maternal power and the fantasy of absolute escape from this power; I shall argue in fact that the peculiar texture of the end of the play is generated partly by the tension between these two fantasies. For if the unsatisfactory equivocation through which Macduff defeats Macbeth seems to suggest that no man is not born of woman, the play nonetheless re-imagines autonomous male identity only through the ruthless excision of all female presence, its own peculiar satisfaction of the witches' prophecy.

In *Macbeth*, as in *Hamlet*, the threat of maternal power and the crisis it presents for individuated manhood emerge in response to paternal absence; once again, the death of the father figures the fall into the maternal realm. But if in *Hamlet* Shakespeare constructs this fall as the death of the ideally masculine father, here he constructs a revised version in which the fall is the death of the father as ideally androgynous parent. For Duncan initially seems to combine in himself the attributes of both father and mother: he is the center of authority, the source of lineage and honor, the giver of name and gift; but he is also the source of all nurturance, planting the children to his throne and making them grow. He is the single source from which all good can be imagined to flow, the source of a benign and empowering nurturance, the opposite of that imaged in the witches' poisonous cauldron and Lady Macbeth's gall-filled breasts. Such a father does away with any need for a mother: he is the image of both parents in one, threatening aspects of each controlled by the presence of the other.[4] When he is gone, "The wine of life is drawn, and the mere lees / Is left this vault to brag of" (2.3.93–94): nurturance itself is spoiled, as all the play's imagery of poisoned chalices and interrupted feasts implies. In his absence male and female break apart, the female becoming merely helpless or merely poisonous and the male merely bloodthirsty; the harmonious relation of the genders imaged in Duncan fails.

Or so the valorizing of Duncan suggests. But in fact masculinity and femininity are deeply disturbed even before his death; and he himself seems strikingly absent before his death. Heavily idealized, this ideally protective father is nonetheless largely ineffectual: even while he is alive, he is unable to hold his kingdom together, reliant on a series of bloody men to suppress an increasingly successful series of rebellions.[5] The witches are already abroad in his realm; they in fact constitute our introduction to that realm. Duncan, not Macbeth, is the first person to echo them ("When the battle's lost and won" [1.1.4]; "What he hath lost, noble Macbeth hath won" [1.2.69]). The witches' sexual ambiguity terrifies: Banquo says of them, "You should be women, / And yet your beards forbid me to interpret / That you are so" (1.3.45–47). Is their androgyny the shadow-side of the King's, enabled perhaps by his failure to maintain a protective masculine authority? Is their strength a consequence of his weakness? (This is the configuration of *Cymbeline*, where the power of the witch-queen-stepmother is so dependent on the failure of Cymbeline's masculine authority that she obligingly dies when that authority returns to him.) Banquo's question to the witches may ask us to hear a counter-question about Duncan, who should be man. For Duncan's androgyny is the object of enormous ambivalence: idealized for his nurturing paternity, he is nonetheless killed for his womanish softness, his childish trust, his inability to read men's minds in their faces, his reliance on the fighting of sons who can rebel against him. Macbeth's description of the dead Duncan—"his silver skin lac'd with his golden blood" (2.3.110)—makes him into a virtual icon of kingly worth; but other images surrounding his death make him into an emblem not of masculine authority but of feminine vulnerability. As he moves toward the murder, Macbeth first imagines himself the allegorical figure of Murder, as though to absolve himself of the responsibility of choice. But the figure of murder then fuses with that of Tarquin:

> wither'd Murther,
> ... thus with his stealthy pace,
> With Tarquin's ravishing strides, towards his design
> Moves like a ghost.
>   (2.1.52–56)

These lines figure the murder as a display of male sexual aggression against a passive female victim: murder here becomes rape; Macbeth's victim becomes not the powerful male figure of the king but the helpless Lucrece.[6] Hardened by Lady Macbeth to regard maleness and violence as equivalent, that is, Macbeth responds to Duncan's idealized milky gentleness as though it were evidence of his femaleness. The horror of this gender transformation, as well as the horror of the murder, is implicit in Macduff's identification of the king's body as a new Gorgon ("Approach the chamber, and destroy your sight / With a new Gorgon" [2.3.70–71]). The power of this image lies partly in its suggestion that Duncan's bloodied body, with its multiple wounds, has been revealed as female and hence blinding to his sons: as if the threat all along was that Duncan would be revealed as female and that this revelation would rob his sons of his masculine protection and hence of their own masculinity.[7]

In *King Lear*, the abdication of protective paternal power seems to release the destructive power of a female chaos imaged not only in Goneril and Regan but also in the storm on the heath. Macbeth virtually alludes to Lear's storm as he approaches the witches in Act IV, conjuring them to answer though they "untie the winds, and let them fight / Against the Churches," though the "waves / Confound and swallow navigation up," though "the treasure / Of Nature's germens tumble all together, / Even till destruction sicken" (4.1.52–60; see *King Lear*, 3.2.1–9). The witches merely implicit on Lear's heath have become in *Macbeth* embodied agents of storm and disorder,[8] and they are there from the start. Their presence suggests that the paternal absence that unleashes female chaos (as in *Lear*) has already happened at the beginning of *Macbeth*. That absence is merely made literal in Macbeth's murder of Duncan at the instigation of female forces: from the start, this father-king cannot protect his sons from powerful mothers, and it is the son's—and the play's—revenge to kill him, or, more precisely, to kill him first and love him after, paying him back for his excessively "womanish" trust and then memorializing him as the ideal androgynous parent.[9] The reconstitution of manhood becomes a central problem in the play in part, I think, because the vision of manhood embodied in Duncan has already failed at the play's beginning.

The witches constitute our introduction to the realm of maternal malevolence unleashed by the loss of paternal protection; as soon as Macbeth meets them, he becomes (in Hecate's probably non-Shakespearean words) their "wayward son" (3.5.11). This maternal malevolence is given its most horrifying expression in Shakespeare in the image through which Lady Macbeth secures her control over Macbeth:

> I have given suck, and know
> How tender 'tis to love the babe that milks me:
> I would, while it was smiling in my face,
> Have pluck'd my nipple from his boneless gums,
> And dash'd the brains out, had I so sworn
> As you have done to this.
>
> (1.7.54–59)

This image of murderously disrupted nurturance is the psychic equivalent of the witches' poisonous cauldron; both function to subject Macbeth's will to female forces.[10] For the play strikingly constructs the fantasy of subjection to maternal malevolence in two parts, in the witches and in Lady Macbeth, and then persistently identifies the two parts as one. Through this identification, Shakespeare in effect locates the source of his culture's fear of witchcraft in individual human history, in the infant's long dependence on female figures felt as all-powerful: what the witches suggest about the vulnerability of men to female power on the cosmic plane, Lady Macbeth doubles on the psychological plane.

Lady Macbeth's power as a female temptress allies her in a general way with the witches as soon as we see her. The specifics of that implied alliance begin to emerge as she attempts to harden herself in preparation for hardening her husband: the disturbance of gender that Banquo registers when he first meets the witches ("you should be women / And yet your beards forbid me to interpret / That you are") is played out in psychological terms in Lady Macbeth's attempt to unsex herself. Calling on spirits ambiguously allied with the witches themselves, she phrases this unsexing as the undoing of her own bodily maternal function:

> Come, you Spirits
> That tend on mortal thoughts, unsex me here,

And fill me, from the crown to the toe, top-full
Of direst cruelty! make thick my blood,
Stop up th'access and passage to remorse;
That no compunctious visitings of Nature
Shake my fell purpose, nor keep peace between
Th'effect and it! Come to my woman's breasts,
And take my milk for gall, you murth'ring ministers.

(1.5.40–48)

In the play's context of unnatural births, the thickening of the blood and the stopping up of access and passage to remorse begin to sound like attempts to undo reproductive functioning and perhaps to stop the menstrual blood that is the sign of its potential.[11] The metaphors in which Lady Macbeth frames the stopping up of remorse, that is, suggest that she imagines an attack on the reproductive passages of her own body, on what makes her specifically female. And as she invites the spirits to her breasts, she reiterates the centrality of the attack specifically on maternal function: needing to undo the "milk of human kindness" (1.5.17) in Macbeth, she imagines an attack on her own literal milk, its transformation into gall. This imagery locates the horror of the scene in Lady Macbeth's unnatural abrogation of her maternal function. But latent within this image of unsexing is the horror of the maternal function itself. Most modern editors follow Johnson in glossing "take my milk for gall" as "take my milk in exchange for gall," imagining in effect that the spirits empty out the natural maternal fluid and replace it with the unnatural and poisonous one.[12] But perhaps Lady Macbeth is asking the spirits to take her milk *as* gall, to nurse from her breasts and find in her milk their sustaining poison. Here the milk itself is the gall; no transformation is necessary. In these lines, Lady Macbeth focuses the culture's fear of maternal nursery—a fear reflected, for example, in the common worries about the various ills (including female blood itself) that can be transmitted through nursing and in the sometime identification of colostrum as witch's milk.[13] Insofar as her milk itself nurtures the evil spirits, Lady Macbeth localizes the image of maternal danger, inviting the identification of her maternal function itself with that of the witch. For she here invites precisely that nursing of devil-imps so central to the current understanding of witchcraft that the presence of supernumerary teats alone was often taken as sufficient evidence that one was a witch.[14] Lady Macbeth and the witches fuse at this moment, and they fuse through the image of perverse nursery.

It is characteristic of the play's division of labor between Lady Macbeth and the witches that she, rather than they, is given the imagery of perverse nursery traditionally attributed to witches. The often-noted alliance between Lady Macbeth and the witches constructs malignant female power both in the cosmos and in the family; it in effect adds the whole weight of the spiritual order to the condemnation of Lady Macbeth's insurrection.[15] But despite the superior cosmic status of the witches, Lady Macbeth seems to me finally the more frightening figure. For Shakespeare's witches are an odd mixture of the terrifying and the near-comic. Even without consideration of the Hecate scene (3.5) with its distinct lightening of tone and its incipient comedy of discord among the witches, we may begin to feel a shift toward the comic in the presentation of the witches: the specificity and predictability of the ingredients in their dire recipe pass over toward grotesque comedy even while they create a (partly pleasurable) shiver of horror.[16] There is a distinct weakening of their power after their first appearances: only in 4.1 do we hear that they themselves have masters (1. 63). The more Macbeth claims for them, the less their actual power seems: even their power over the storm—the signature of maternal malevolence in *King Lear*—is eventually taken from them. By the time Macbeth evokes the cosmic damage they can wreak (4.1.50–60), we have already felt the presence of such damage, and felt it moreover as issuing not from the witches but from a divinely sanctioned nature firmly in league with patriarchal order. The witches' displays of thunder and lightning, like their apparitions, are merely childish theatrics compared to what we have already heard: the serious disruptions of natural order—the storm that toppled the chimneys and made the earth shake (2.3.53–60), the unnatural darkness in day (2.4.5–10), the cannibalism of Duncan's horses (2.4.14–18)— are the horrifying but reassuringly familiar signs of God's displeasure, firmly under His—not their—control. Partly because their power is thus circumscribed, nothing the witches say or do conveys the presence of awesome and unexplained malevolence in the way that Lear's storm does. Even the process of dramatic represen- tation itself may diminish their power: embodied, perhaps, they lack full power to terrify; "Present fears"—even of witches—"are less than horrible imaginings" (1.3.137–38). They tend thus to become as much containers for, as expressions of, nightmare; to a certain extent, they help to exorcise the terror of female malevolence by localizing it.

The witches may of course have lost some of their power to terrify through the general decline in witchcraft belief. Nonetheless, even when that belief was in full force, these witches would have been less frightening than their Continental sisters, their crimes less sensational. For despite their numinous and infinitely suggestive indefinability,[17] insofar as they are witches, they are distinctly English witches; and most commentators on English witchcraft note how tame an affair it was in comparison with witchcraft belief on the Continent.[18] The most sensational staples of Continental belief from the *Malleus Maleficarum* (1486) on—the ritual murder and eating of infants, the attacks specifically on the male genitals, the perverse sexual relationship with demons—are missing or greatly muted in English witchcraft belief, replaced largely by a simpler concern with retaliatory wrongdoing of exactly the order Shakespeare points to when one of his witches announces her retaliation for the sailor's wife's refusal to share her chestnuts.[19] We may hear an echo of some of the Continental beliefs in the hint of their quasi-sexual attack on the sailor with the uncooperative wife (the witches promise to "do and do and do," leaving him drained "dry as hay") and in the infanticidal contents of the cauldron, especially the "finger of birth-strangled babe" and the blood of the sow "that hath eaten / Her nine farrow." The cannibalism that is a stable of Continental belief may be implicit in the contents of that grim cauldron; and the various eyes, toes, tongues, legs, teeth, livers, and noses (indiscriminately human and animal) may evoke primitive fears of dismemberment close to the center of witchcraft belief. But these terrors remain largely implicit. For Shakespeare's witches are both smaller and greater than their Continental sisters: on the one hand, more the representation of English homebodies with relatively small concerns; on the other, more the incarnation of literary or mythic fates or sybils, given the power not only to predict but to enforce the future. But the staples of Continental witchcraft belief are not altogether missing from the play: for the most part, they are transferred away from the witches and recur as the psychological issues evoked by Lady Macbeth in her relation to Macbeth. She becomes the inheritor of the realm of primitive relational and bodily disturbance: of infantile vulnerability to maternal power, of dismemberment and its developmentally later equivalent, castration. Lady Macbeth brings the witches' power home: they get the cosmic apparatus, she gets the psychic force. That Lady Macbeth is the more frightening figure—and was so, I suspect, even before belief in witchcraft had declined—suggests the firmly domestic and psychological basis of Shakespeare's imagination.[20]

The fears of female coercion, female definition of the male, that are initially located cosmically in the witches thus find their ultimate locus in the figure of Lady Macbeth, whose attack on Macbeth's virility is the source of her strength over him and who acquires that strength, I shall argue, partly because she can make him imagine himself as an infant vulnerable to her. In the figure of Lady Macbeth, that is, Shakespeare rephrases the power of the witches as the wife/mother's power to poison human relatedness at its source; in her, their power of cosmic coercion is rewritten as the power of the mother to misshape or destroy the child. The attack on infants and on the genitals characteristic of Continental witchcraft belief is thus in her returned to its psychological source: in the play these beliefs are localized not in the witches but in the great central scene in which Lady Macbeth persuades Macbeth to the murder of Duncan. In this scene, Lady Macbeth notoriously makes the murder of Duncan the test of Macbeth's virility;[21] if he cannot perform the murder, he is in effect reduced to the helplessness of an infant subject to her rage. She begins by attacking his manhood, making her love for him contingent on the murder that she identifies as equivalent to his male potency: "From this time / Such I account thy love" (1.7.38–39); "When you durst do it, then you were a man" (1.7.49). Insofar as his drunk hope is now "green and pale" (1.7.37), he is identified as emasculated, exhibiting the symptoms not only of hangover but also of the green-sickness, the typical disease of timid young virgin women. Lady Macbeth's argument is, in effect, that any signs of the "milk of human kindness" (1.5.17) mark him as more womanly than she; she proceeds to enforce his masculinity by demonstrating her willingness to dry up that milk in herself, specifically by destroying her nursing infant in fantasy: "I would, while it was smiling in my face, / Have pluck'd my nipple from his boneless gums, / And dash'd the brains out" (1.7.56–58). That this image has no place in the plot, where the Macbeths are strikingly childless, gives some indication of the inner necessity through which it appears. For Lady Macbeth expresses here not only the hardness she imagines to be male, not only her willingness to unmake the most essential maternal relationship; she expresses also a deep fantasy of Macbeth's utter vulnerability to her. As she progresses from questioning Macbeth's masculinity to imagining herself dashing out the brains of her infant son,[22] she articulates a fantasy in which to be less than a man is to become interchangeably a woman or a baby,[23] terribly subject to the wife/mother's destructive rage.

By evoking this vulnerability, Lady Macbeth acquires a power over Macbeth more absolute than any the witches can achieve. The play's central fantasy of escape from woman seems to me to unfold from this moment: for if Macbeth's bloodthirsty masculinity is partly a response to Lady Macbeth's desire, in effect an extension of her will, it simultaneously comes to represent the way to escape her power. We can see the beginnings of this process in Macbeth's response to her evocation of absolute maternal power. Macbeth first responds by questioning the possibility of failure ("If we should fail?" [1.7.59]). Lady Macbeth counters this fear by inviting Macbeth to share in her fantasy of omnipotent malevolence: "What cannot you and I perform upon / Th'unguarded Duncan?" (1.7.70–71). The satiated and sleeping Duncan takes on the vulnerability that Lady Macbeth has just invoked in the image of the feeding, trusting infant;[24] Macbeth releases himself from the image of this vulnerability by sharing in the murder of this innocent. In his elation at this transfer of vulnerability from himself to Duncan, Macbeth imagines Lady Macbeth the mother to infants sharing her hardness, born in effect without vulnerability; in effect, he imagines her as male and then reconstitutes himself as the invulnerable male child of such a mother:

> Bring forth men-children only!
> For thy undaunted mettle should compose
> Nothing but males.
>
> (1.7.73–75)

Through the double pun on *mettle/metal* and *male/mail*, Lady Macbeth herself becomes virtually male, composed of the hard metal of which the armored male is made.[25] Her children would necessarily be men, composed of her male mettle, armored by her mettle, lacking the female inheritance from the mother that would make them vulnerable. The man-child thus brought forth would be no trusting infant; the very phrase "men-children" suggests the presence of the adult man even at birth, hence the undoing of childish vulnerability.[26] The mobility of the imagery—from male infant with his brains dashed out, to Macbeth and Lady Macbeth triumphing over the sleeping, trusting Duncan, to the all-male invulnerable man-child—suggests the logic of the fantasy: only the child of an all-male mother is safe. We see here the creation of a defensive fantasy of exemption from the woman's part: as infantile vulnerability is shifted to Duncan, Macbeth creates in himself the image of Lady Macbeth's hardened all-male man-child; his murder of Duncan thus becomes the sign of his distance from the infant whom Lady Macbeth could destroy, the sign of the mettle that composes him.

Macbeth's temporary solution to the infantile vulnerability and maternal malevolence revealed by Lady Macbeth is to imagine Lady Macbeth the all-male mother of invulnerable infants and to imagine himself as such an infant, in effect doing away with vulnerability by doing away with the female site of origin. The final solution, both for Macbeth and for the play itself, though in differing ways, is an even more radical excision of the female site of origin: it is to imagine a birth entirely exempt from women, to imagine in effect an all-male family, composed of nothing but males, in which the father can be fully restored to power. Overtly, of course, the play denies the possibility of this fantasy: Macduff carries the power of the man not born of woman only through the equivocation of the fiends, their obstetrical joke that quibbles with the meaning of "born" and thus confirms circuitously that all men come from women after all. Even Macbeth, in whom, I think, the fantasy is centrally invested, knows its impossibility: his false security depends exactly on his common-sense assumption that everyone is born of woman. Nonetheless, I shall argue, the play curiously enacts the fantasy that it seems to deny: punishing Macbeth for his participation in a fantasy of escape from the maternal matrix, it nonetheless allows the audience the partial satisfaction of a dramatic equivalent to it. The equivocating ending of *Macbeth* seems to me to play out this dual process of repudiation and enactment, uncreating any space for the female even while it seems to insist on the universality of maternal origin.

The witches prophesy invulnerability for Macbeth insofar as all men are born of women:

> Be bloody, bold, and resolute: laugh to scorn
> The power of man, for none of woman born
> Shall harm Macbeth.
> (4.1.79–81)

But the prophecy has the immediate force of psychic relevance for Macbeth in part because it so perfectly fits with the fantasy constructions central to 1.7: even as it depends on the vulnerability of all others, it ambiguously constructs Macbeth as exempt from this vulnerability. For the witches here invite Macbeth to make himself into the bloody and invulnerable man-child he has created as a defense against maternal malevolence in 1.7. The creation of this man-child is recalled by the apparition of the Bloody Child that accompanies the witches' prophecy: the apparition alludes at once to the bloody vulnerability of the infant destroyed in fantasy by Lady Macbeth and to the bloodthirsty masculinity that seems to promise escape from this vulnerability, the bloodiness the witches urge Macbeth to take on. The doubleness of the image thus epitomizes exactly the doubleness of the prophecy itself, which constructs Macbeth's invulnerability in effect from the vulnerability of maternal origin in all other men. Macbeth does not question this prophecy, even after the experience of Birnam Wood should have taught him better, partly because it so perfectly meets his needs: in encouraging him to "laugh to scorn / The power of man," the prophecy seems to grant him exemption from the condition of all men, who bring with them the liabilities inherent in their birth. As Macbeth carries the prophecy as a shield onto the battlefield, his confidence in his own invulnerability increasingly reveals his sense of exemption from the universal human condition. Repeated seven times, the phrase "born to woman" with its variants begins to carry for Macbeth the meaning "vulnerable," as though vulnerability itself were the taint deriving from woman; his own invulnerability comes therefore to stand as evidence for his exemption from that taint. This is the subterranean logic of Macbeth's words to Young Siward immediately after Macbeth has killed him:

> Thou wast born of woman:—
> But swords I smile at, weapons laugh to scorn,
> Brandish'd by man that's of a woman born.
> (5.7.11–13)

Young Siward's death becomes in effect proof that he was born of woman; and in the logic of Macbeth's psyche, his own invulnerability is the proof that he was not. The "but" records this fantasied distinction: it constructs the sentence, "You, born of woman, are vulnerable; but I, not born of woman, am not."[27]

Insofar as this is the fantasy embodied in Macbeth at the play's end, it is punished by the equivocation of the fiends: the revelation that Macduff derives from woman, though by unusual means, musters against Macbeth all the values of ordinary family and community that Macduff carries with him. Macbeth, "cow'd" by the revelation (5.8.18),[28] is forced to take on the taint of vulnerability; the fantasy of escape from the maternal matrix seems to die with him. But although this fantasy is punished in Macbeth, it does not quite die with him; it continues to have a curious life of its own in the play, apart from its embodiment in him. Even from the beginning of the play, the fantasy has not been Macbeth's alone: as the play's most striking bloody man, he is in the beginning the bearer of this fantasy for the all-male community that depends on his bloody prowess. The opening scenes strikingly construct male and female as realms apart; and the initial descriptions of Macbeth's battles construe his prowess as a consequence of his exemption from the taint of woman.

In the description of his battle with Macdonwald, what looks initially like a battle between loyal and disloyal sons to establish primacy in the father's eyes is oddly transposed into a battle of male against female:

> Doubtful it stood;
> As two spent swimmers, that do cling together
> And choke their art. The merciless Macdonwald
> (Worthy to be a rebel, for to that

The multiplying villainies of nature
Do swarm upon him) from the western isles
Of Kernes and Gallowglasses is supplied;
And Fortune, on his damned quarrel smiling,
Show'd like a rebel's whore: but all's too weak;
For brave Macbeth (well he deserves that name),
Disdaining Fortune, with his brandish'd steel,
Which smok'd with bloody execution,
Like Valour's minion, carv'd out his passage,
Till he fac'd the slave;
Which ne'er shook hands, nor bade farewell to him,
Till he unseam'd him from the nave to th'chops,
And fix'd his head upon our battlements.

(1.2.7–23)

The two initially indistinguishable figures metaphorized as the swimmers eventually sort themselves out into victor and victim, but only by first sorting themselves out into male and female, as though Macbeth can be distinguished from Macdonwald only by making Macdonwald functionally female. The "merciless Macdonwald" is initially firmly identified; but by the time Macbeth appears, Macdonwald has temporarily disappeared, replaced by the female figure of Fortune, against whom Macbeth seems to fight ("brave Macbeth, . . . Disdaining Fortune, with his brandish'd steel"). The metaphorical substitution of Fortune for Macdonwald transforms the battle into a contest between male and female; in effect, it makes Macbeth's claim to his name—"brave Macbeth"—contingent on his victory over the female. We are prepared for this transformation by Macdonwald's sexual alliance with the tainting female, the whore Fortune;[29] Macbeth's identification as valor's minion redefines the battle as a contest between the half-female couple Fortune/Macdonwald and the all-male couple Valor/Macbeth. Metaphorically, Macdonwald and Macbeth take on the qualities of the unreliable female and the heroic male; Macbeth's battle against Fortune turns out to be his battle against Macdonwald because the two are functionally the same. Macdonwald, tainted by the female, thus becomes an easy mark for Macbeth, who demonstrates his own untainted manhood by unseaming Macdonwald from the nave to the chops: simultaneously castrating and performing a caesarian section on him, Macbeth remakes Macdonwald's body as female, revealing what his alliance with Fortune has suggested all along.

In effect, then, the battle that supports the father's kingdom plays out the creation of a conquering all-male erotics that marks its conquest by its triumph over a feminized body, simultaneously that of Fortune and Macdonwald. Hence, in the double action of the passage, the victorious unseaming happens twice: first on the body of Fortune and then on the body of Macdonwald. The lines descriptive of Macbeth's approach to Macdonwald—"brave Macbeth . . . Disdaining Fortune, with his brandish'd steel, / . . . carv'd out his passage"—make that approach contingent on Macbeth's first carving his passage through a female body, like Richard III hewing his way out (3 Henry VI, 3.2.181). The language here perfectly anticipates Macduff's birth by caesarian section, revealed at the end of the play: if Macduff is ripped untimely from his mother's womb, Macbeth here manages in fantasy his own caesarian section,[30] carving his passage out from the unreliable female to achieve heroic male action, in effect carving up the female to arrive at the male. Only after this rite of passage can Macbeth meet Macdonwald: this act of aggression toward the female body, with its accompanying fantasy of self-birth, marks Macbeth's passage to the contest that will define his maleness partly by attributing tainted femaleness to Macdonwald. For the all-male community surrounding Duncan, then, Macbeth's victory is allied with his triumph over femaleness; self-born, he becomes invulnerable, "lapp'd in proof" (1.2.55) like one of Lady Macbeth's armored men-children.[31] Even before his initial entry into the play, that is, Macbeth becomes the bearer of the shared fantasy that secure male community depends on the prowess of the man not born of woman, the man who can carve his own passage out, the man whose very maleness is the mark of his exemption from maternal origin and the vulnerabilities that are its consequence.[32]

Ostensibly, the play rejects the version of manhood implicit in the shared fantasy of the beginning. Macbeth himself is well aware that his capitulation to Lady Macbeth's definition of manhood entails his abandonment of his own more inclusive definition of what becomes a man (1.7.46); and Macduff's response to the news of his family's destruction insists that humane feeling is central to the definition of manhood (4.3.221). Moreover, the revelation that even Macduff had a mother sets a limiting condition on the fantasy of a bloody masculine escape from the maternal matrix and hence on the kind of manhood defined by that escape. Nonetheless, even at the end, the play enables one version of the fantasy that heroic manhood is exemption from the female even while it punishes that fantasy in Macbeth. The key figure in whom this double movement is vested at the end of the play is Macduff; the unresolved contradictions that surround him are, I think, marks of ambivalence toward the fantasy itself. In insisting that mourning for his family is his right as a man, he presents family feeling as central to the definition of manhood; and yet he conspicuously leaves his family vulnerable to destruction when he goes off to offer his services to Malcolm. The play moreover insists on reminding us that he has inexplicably abandoned his family: both Lady Macduff and Malcolm question the necessity of this abandonment (4.2.6–14, 4.3.26–28), and the play never allows Macduff to explain himself. This unexplained abandonment severely qualifies Macduff's force as the play's central exemplar of a healthy manhood that can include the possibility of relationship to women: the play seems to vest diseased familial relations in Macbeth and the possibility of healthy ones in Macduff; and yet we discover dramatically that Macduff has a family only when we hear that he has abandoned it. Dramatically and psychologically, he takes on full masculine power only as he loses his family and becomes energized by the loss, converting his grief into the more "manly" tune of vengeance (4.3.235); the loss of his family here enables his accession to full masculine action even while his response to that loss insists on a more humane definition of manhood.[33] The play here pulls in two directions; and it then reiterates this doubleness by vesting in Macduff its final fantasy of exemption from woman. The ambivalence that shapes the portrayal of Macduff is evident even as he reveals to Macbeth that he "was from his mother's womb / Untimely ripp'd" (5.8.15–16): the emphasis on untimeliness and the violence of the image suggest that he has been prematurely deprived of a nurturing maternal presence; but the prophecy construes just this deprivation as the source of Macduff's strength.[34] The prophecy itself both denies and affirms the fantasy of exemption from women: in affirming that Macduff has indeed had a mother, it denies the fantasy of male self-generation; but in attributing his power to his having been untimely ripped from that mother, it sustains the sense that violent separation from the mother is the mark of the successful male. The final battle between Macbeth and Macduff thus replays the initial battle between Macbeth and Macdonwald. But Macduff has now taken the place of Macbeth: he carries with him the male power given him by the caesarian solution, and Macbeth is retrospectively revealed as Macdonwald, the woman's man.

The doubleness of the prophecy is less the equivocation of the fiends than Shakespeare's own equivocation about the figure of Macduff and about the fantasy vested in him in the end. For Macduff carries with him simultaneously all the values of family and the claim that masculine power derives from the unnatural abrogation of family, including escape from the conditions of one's birth. Moreover, the ambivalence that shapes the figure of Macduff similarly shapes the dramatic structure of the play itself. Ostensibly concerned to restore natural order at the end,[35] the play bases that order upon the radical exclusion of the female. Initially construed as all-powerful, the women virtually disappear at the end. Increasingly cribbed and confined by the play, Lady

Macbeth's psychic power and subjectivity are increasingly written out of it. At first a source of terror, she increasingly becomes the merely helpless wife, alienated from her husband's serious business, pleading with him to come to bed, cooperatively dying offstage in her separate sphere, amidst a cry of women. Even when she is at the center of the stage, her own subjectivity is denied her: the broken object of others' observation in the sleep-walking scene, she has become entirely absent to herself. By the end, she is so diminished a character that we scarcely trouble to ask ourselves whether the report of her suicide is accurate or not. At the same time, the witches who are her avatars disappear from the stage and become so diminished in importance that Macbeth never alludes to them, blaming his defeat only on the equivocation of their male masters, the fiends. Even Lady Macduff exists only to disappear.

With the excision of all the female characters, nature itself can in effect be reborn male. The bogus fulfillment of the Birnam Wood prophecy emphasizes the extent to which the natural order of the end depends on this excision of the female. Critics sometimes see in the march of Malcolm's soldiers bearing their green branches an allusion to the Maying festivals in which participants returned from the woods bearing branches, or to the ritual scourging of a hibernal figure by the forces of the oncoming spring.[36] The allusion seems to me clearly present; but it serves I think to mark precisely what the moving of Birnam Wood is not. Malcolm's use of Birnam Wood is a military maneuver. His drily worded command (5.4.4–7) leaves little room for suggestions of natural fertility or for the deep sense of the generative world rising up to expel its winter king; not does the play later enable these associations except in a scattered and partly ironic way.[37] These trees have little resemblance to those in the Forest of Arden; their branches, like those carried by the apparition of the "child crowned, with a tree in his hand" (4.1.86), are little more than the emblems of a strictly patriarchal family tree.[38] This family tree, like the march of Birnam Wood itself, is relentlessly male: Duncan and sons, Banquo and son, Siward and son. There are no daughters and scarcely any mention of mothers in these family trees. We are brought as close as possible here to the fantasy of family without women.[39] In that sense, Birnam Wood is the perfect emblem of the nature that triumphs at the end of the play: nature without generative possibility, nature without women. Malcolm tells his men to carry the branches to obscure themselves, and that is exactly their function: insofar as they seem to allude to the rising of the natural order against Macbeth, they obscure the operations of male power, disguising them as a natural force; and they simultaneously obscure the extent to which natural order itself is here reconceived purely as male.[40]

If we can see the fantasy of escape from the female in the play's fulfillment of the witches' prophecies—in Macduff's birth by caesarian section and in Malcolm's appropriation of Birnam Wood—we can see it also in the play's psychological geography. The shift from Scotland to England is strikingly the shift from the mother's to the father's terrain.[41] Scotland "cannot / Be call'd our mother, but our grave" (4.3.165–66), in Rosse's words to Macduff: it is the realm of Lady Macbeth and the witches, the realm in which the mother *is* the grave, the realm appropriately ruled by their bad son Macbeth. The escape to England is an escape from their power into the realm of the good father-king and his surrogate son Malcolm, "unknown to woman" (4.3.126). The magical power of this father to cure clearly balances the magical power of the witches to harm, as Malcolm (the father's son) balances Macbeth (the mother's son). That Macduff can cross from one realm into the other only by abandoning his family suggests the rigidity of the psychic geography separating England from Scotland. At the end of the play, Malcolm returns to Scotland mantled in the power England gives him, in effect bringing the power of the fathers with him: bearer of his father's line, unknown to woman, supported by his agent Macduff (himself empowered by his own special immunity from birth), Malcolm embodies utter separation from women and as such triumphs easily over Macbeth, the mother's son.

The play that begins by unleashing the terrible threat of destructive maternal power and demonstrates the helplessness of its central male figure before that power thus ends by consolidating male power, in effect solving the problem of masculinity by eliminating the female. The play's recuperative consolidation of masculinity answers the maternal threat unleashed and never fully contained in *Hamlet* and *King Lear*: here, maternal power is given its most virulent sway and then handily abolished. In the end, we are in a purely male realm, founded—as Prospero's will be—on the excision of maternal origin; here, mothers no longer threaten because they no longer exist. But this solution is inherently unstable: the ending of *Coriolanus* will undo the ending of *Macbeth*, bringing back the mother with a vengeance.

The central psychological concerns of *Macbeth* are reiterated in *Coriolanus*: once again, masculinity is constructed in response to maternal power, and in the absence of a father;[42] and once again, the hero attempts to recreate himself through his bloody heroics, in fantasy severing the connection with his mother even as he enacts the ruthless masculinity that is her bidding. "Bring forth men-children only! / For thy undaunted mettle should compose / Nothing but males" (1.7.73–

75), Macbeth tells Lady Macbeth in response to her fantasy of infanticide; and Coriolanus initially seems to be the incarnation of this invulnerable "man-child" (*Coriolanus*, 1.3.17), the child who sucks only valiantness from the mettle/metal of his mother's breast (*Coriolanus*, 3.2.129). But as in *Macbeth*, his very pose as self-sufficient man-child marks his subjection to his mother: even more insistently than *Macbeth*, *Coriolanus* problematizes the construction of heroic masculinity, locating its source in the deprivation that is the maternal signature in both plays.

Maternal malevolence is never as horrific in *Coriolanus* as in *Macbeth*: *Coriolanus* localizes and domesticates the power of the witches and Lady Macbeth in the literal relation of mother and son. But although Volumnia does not make stews out of body parts or threaten to dash Coriolanus's brains out while he is nursing, her less melodramatic disruptions of the feeding situation give her a power over her son that is the psychic equivalent of theirs: "framed" (5.3.63) by her equation of starvation and masculinity, he becomes the man her fancy builds (2.1.198). By failing to feed him enough, she makes hunger the sign of his vulnerability, creating him as a virtual automaton who cannot tolerate his own ordinary human neediness and who thus is compelled to act out needs he can neither understand nor satisfy. Under her tutelage, any acknowledgment of need—starting with the acknowledgment that he, like the crowd he so despises, needs food—threatens to undermine his masculine autonomy, in effect returning him to the maternal breast from which he could never get enough. But finally self-starvation is no solution to the problem of human vulnerability; in the end, it returns him to the same place of deprivation. Framed by maternal insufficiency, Coriolanus can never successfully wean himself from what he has never truly had:[43] thrusting him out, Volumnia binds him to her. Despite his efforts at self-creation, this exiled son is utterly unable to separate from his mother; thus in the end he turns on Rome and his mother in an outraged attempt to stabilize his identity by eradicating his deprivation at its source. In its violence, his return takes on the configuration of a failed separation ritual, a final desperate attempt to separate himself from his mother by destroying her, forging a new name for himself in the fires that will burn Rome.

Coriolanus begins in the landscape of maternal deprivation.[44] It was written during a period of rising corn prices and the accompanying fear of famine; in May 1607, "a great number of common persons"— up to five thousand, Stow tells us in his *Annales*—assembled in various

Midlands counties, including Shakespeare's own county of Warwickshire, to protest the acceleration of enclosures and the resulting food shortages.[45] Shakespeare rewrites the popular uprising in Plutarch to make it reflect the contemporary threat: in Plutarch the people riot because the Senate refuses to control usury; in Shakespeare they riot because they are hungry. And if the specter of a multitude of hungry mouths, ready to rise and demand their own, is the exciting cause of *Coriolanus*, the image of the mother who has not fed her children enough is at its center. One does not need the help of a psychoanalytic approach to notice that Volumnia is not a nourishing mother. Her attitude toward food is nicely summed up when she rejects Menenius's invitation to a consolatory dinner after Coriolanus's banishment: "Anger's my meat: I sup upon myself / And so shall starve with feeding" (4.2.50–51). We might suspect her of having been as niggardly in providing food for her son as she is for herself, or rather suspect her of insisting that he too be self-sufficient, that he feed only on his own anger; and indeed, he is apparently fed only valiantness by her ("Thy valiantness was mine, thou suck'st it from me" [3.2.129]). He certainly has not been fed the milk of human kindness: when Menenius later tells us that "there is no more mercy in him than there is milk in a male tiger" (5.4.28–29), he seems to associate Coriolanus's lack of humanity not only with the absence of any nurturing female element in him but also with the absence of mother's milk itself.[46] Volumnia takes some pride in the creation of her son, and when we first meet her, she tells us exactly how she's done it: by sending him to a cruel war at an age when a mother should not be willing to allow a son out of the protective maternal circle for an hour (1.3.5–15). She elaborates her creation as she imagines herself mother to twelve sons and then kills all but one of them off: "I had rather had eleven die nobly for their country, than one voluptuously surfeit out of action" (1.3.24–25). To be noble is to die; to live is to be ignoble and to eat too much.[47] If you are Volumnia's son, the choice is clear.

But the most telling—certainly the most disturbing—revelation of Volumnia's attitude toward feeding comes some twenty lines later, when she is encouraging Virgilia to share her own glee in the thought of Coriolanus's wounds: "The breasts of Hecuba / When she did suckle Hector, look'd not lovelier / Than Hector's forehead when it spit forth blood / At Grecian sword contemning" (1.3.40–43). Blood is more beautiful than milk, the wound than the breast, warfare than peaceful feeding. But this image is more disturbing than these easy comparatives suggest. It does not bode well for Coriolanus that the heroic Hector doesn't stand a chance in Volumnia's imagination: he is transformed immediately from infantile feeding mouth to bleeding wound. For the unspoken mediator between breast and wound is the infant's mouth: in this imagistic transformation, to feed is to be wounded; the mouth becomes the wound, the breast the sword. The metaphoric process suggests the psychological fact that is, I think, at the center of the play: the taking in of food is the primary acknowledgment of one's dependence on the world, and as such, it is the primary token of one's vulnerability. But at the same time as Volumnia's image suggests the vulnerability inherent in feeding, it also suggests a way to fend off that vulnerability. In her image, feeding, incorporating, is transformed into spitting out, an aggressive expelling; the wound once again becomes the mouth that spits "forth blood / At Grecian sword contemning." The wound spitting blood thus becomes not a sign of vulnerability but an instrument of attack.

Volumnia's attitudes toward feeding and dependence are echoed perfectly in her son. Coriolanus persistently regards food as poisonous (1.1.177–78, 3.1.155–56); the only thing he can imagine nourishing is rebellion (3.1.68–69, 116). Among the patricians, only Menenius is associated with the ordinary consumption of food and wine without an allaying drop of Tiber in it, and his distance from Coriolanus can be measured partly by his pathetic conviction that Coriolanus will be malleable—that he will have a "suppler" soul (5.1.55)—after he has had a full meal. But for Coriolanus, as for his mother, nobility consists precisely in *not* eating: he twice imagines starving himself honorably to death before asking for food, or anything else, from the plebians (2.3.112–13; 3.3.89–91).[48]

Coriolanus incorporates not only his mother's attitude toward food but also the transformations in mode implicit in her image of Hector. These transformations—from feeding to warfare, from vulnerability to aggressive attack, from incorporation to spitting out—are at the center of Coriolanus's character and of our responses to him; for the whole of his masculine identity depends on his transformation of his vulnerability into an instrument of attack, as Menenius suggests when he tells us that each of Coriolanus's wounds "was an enemy's grave" (2.1.154–55). Cominius reports that Coriolanus entered his first battle a sexually indefinite thing, a boy or Amazon (2.2.91), and found his manhood there: "When he might act the woman in the scene, / He prov'd best man i'th'field" (2.2.96–97). The rigid masculinity that Coriolanus finds in war becomes a defense against acknowledgment of his neediness; he nearly succeeds in transforming himself from a vulnerable human creature into a grotesquely invulnerable and isolated thing. His body becomes his armor (1.3.35, 1.4.24); he himself becomes a weapon "who sensibly outdares his senseless sword, / And when it bows, stand'st up" (1.4.53–54), or he becomes the sword itself: "O me alone! Make you a sword of me!" (1.6.76). His whole life becomes a kind of phallic exhibitionism, devoted to disproving the possibility that he is vulnerable.[49] In the transformation from oral neediness to phallic aggression, anger becomes his meat as well as his mother's; Volumnia's phrase suggests not only his mode of defending himself against vulnerability but also the source of his anger in the deprivation imposed by his mother. We see the quality of his hunger and its transformation into aggression when, after his expulsion from Rome, he tells Aufidius, "I have . . . / Drawn tuns of blood out of thy country's breast" (4.5.99–100). Fighting here, as elsewhere in the play, is a poorly concealed substitute for feeding (see, for example, 1.9.10–11; 4.5.191–94, 222–24); and the unsatisfied ravenous attack of the infant on the breast provides the motive force for warfare. The image allows us to understand the ease with which Coriolanus turns his rage toward his own feeding mother, Rome.[50]

Thrust prematurely from dependence on his mother, forced to feed himself on his own anger, Coriolanus refuses to acknowledge any neediness or dependency: for his entire sense of himself depends on his being able to see himself as a self-sufficient creature. The desperation behind his claim to self-sufficiency is revealed by his horror of praise, even the praise of his general.[51] The dependence of his masculinity on warfare in fact makes praise (or flattery, as he must call it) particularly threatening to him on the battlefield: flattery there, where his independence has apparently been triumphant, would imply that he has acted partly to win praise, that he is not self-sufficient after all; it would ultimately imply the undoing of his triumphant masculinity, and the soldier's steel would grow "soft as the parasite's silk" (1.9.45). The juxtaposition of soldier's steel and parasite's soft silk suggests both Coriolanus's dilemma and his solution to it: in order to avoid being the soft, dependent, feeding parasite, he has to maintain his rigidity as soldier's steel; that rigidity would be threatened were he to be "dieted / In praises sauc'd with lies" (1.9.51–52). (The same fears that underlie Coriolanus's use of this image here are brought home to him by Aufidius's charges at the end of the play: that he broke "his oath and resolution, like / A twist of rotten silk" [5.6.95–96]; that he "whin'd and roar'd away" the victory [5.6.98]; that he is a "boy of tears" [5.6.101].)

The complex of ideas that determines Coriolanus's response to praise also determines the rigidity that makes him so disastrous as a political figure. As he contemptuously asks the people for their voices and later gives up his attempt to pacify them, the language in which he imagines his alternatives reveals the extent to which his unwillingness to ask for the people's approval, like his abhorrence of praise, depends on his attitude toward food: "Better it is to die, better to starve, / Than crave the hire which first we do deserve" (2.3.112–13); "Pent to linger / But with a grain a day, I would not buy / Their mercy at the price of one fair word" (3.3.89–91). Asking, craving, flattering with fair words are here not only preconditions but also equivalents of eating: to refuse to ask is to starve; but starvation is preferable to asking because asking, like eating, is an acknowledgment of one's weakness, one's dependence on the outside world. "The price is, to ask it kindly" (2.3.75), but that is the one price Coriolanus cannot pay. When he must face the prospect of revealing his dependence on the populace by asking for their favor, his whole delicately constructed masculine identity threatens to crumble. In order to ask, a harlot's spirit must possess him; his voice must become as small as that of a eunuch or a virgin minding babies; a beggar's tongue must make motion through his lips (3.2.111–18). Asking, then, like susceptibility to praise, would undo the process by which he was transformed on the battlefield from boy or woman to man. That he imagines this undoing as a kind of reverse voice change suggests the extent to which his phallic aggressive pose is a defense against collapse into the dependent oral mode of the small boy. And in fact, Coriolanus's own use of language constantly reiterates this defense. Instead of using those linguistic modes that acknowledge dependence, Coriolanus spits out words, using them as weapons. His invective is in the mode of Hector's wound, aggressively spitting forth blood: it is an attempt to deny vulnerability by making the very area of vulnerability into the means of attack.[52]

Coriolanus's abhorrence of praise and flattery, his horror lest the people think that he got his wounds to please them (2.2.147–50), his insistence that he be given the consulship as a sign of what he is, not as a reward (1.9.26), his refusal to ask— all are attempts to claim that he is *sui generis*. This attitude finds its logical conclusion in his desperate cry as he sees his mother approaching him at the end:

> I'll never
> Be such a gosling to obey instinct, but stand
> As if a man were author of himself
> And knew no other kin.
>
> (5.3.34–37)

The gosling obeys instinct and acknowledges his kinship with mankind;[53] but Coriolanus will attempt to stand alone. (Since his manhood depends exactly on this phallic standing alone, he is particularly susceptible to Aufidius's taunt of "boy" after he has been such a gosling as to obey instinct.) The relationship between Coriolanus's aggressive pose and his attempts to claim that he is *sui generis* is most dramatically realized in the conquest of Corioli; it is here that Coriolanus most nearly realizes his fantasy of standing as if a man were author of himself. For the scene at Corioli represents a glorious transformation of the nightmare of oral vulnerability ("to th'pot" [1.4.47], one of his soldiers says as he is swallowed up by the gates) into a phallic adventure that both assures and demonstrates his independence. Coriolanus's battlecry as he storms the gates sexualizes the scene: "Come on; / If you'll stand fast, we'll beat them to their wives" (1.4.40–41). But the dramatic action itself presents the conquest of Corioli as an image not of rape but of triumphant rebirth: after Coriolanus enters the gates of the city, he is proclaimed dead; one of his comrades delivers a eulogy firmly in the past tense ("Thou wast a soldier / Even to Cato's wish" [1.4.56–57]); then Coriolanus miraculously reemerges, covered with blood (1.6.22), and is given a new name. For the assault on Corioli is both a rape and a rebirth: the underlying fantasy is that intercourse is a literal return to the womb, from which one is reborn, one's own author.[54] The fantasy of self-authorship is complete when Coriolanus is given his new name, earned by his own actions.[55]

But despite the boast implicit in his conquest of Corioli, Coriolanus has not in fact succeeded in separating himself from his mother; even the very role through which he claims independence was designed by her—as she never tires of pointing out ("My praises made thee first a soldier" [3.2.108]; "Thou art my warrior: / I holp to frame thee" [5.3.62–63]). In fact, Shakespeare underlines Volumnia's point by the placement of two central scenes. In 1.3, before we have seen Coriolanus himself as a soldier, we see Volumnia first describe her image of her son on the battlefield and then enact his role: "Methinks I see him stamp thus, and call thus: / 'Come on you cowards, you were got in fear / Though you were born in Rome' " (1.3.32–34). This marvelous moment suggests not only the ways in which Volumnia herself lives through her son, but also the extent to which his role is her creation. For when we see him in the next scene, acting exactly as his mother had predicted, we are left with the impression that he is merely enacting her enactment of the role that she has imagined for him.

That Coriolanus is acting under Volumnia's direction even in the role that seems to ensure his independence of her helps to explain both his bafflement when she suddenly starts to disapprove of the role she has created ("I muse my mother / Does not approve me further" [3.2.7–8]) and his eventual capitulation to her demand that he shift roles, here and at the end of the play. For his manhood is secure only when he can play the role that she has designed, and play it with her approval.[56] He asks her, "Why did you wish me milder? Would you have me /

False to my nature? Rather say I play / The man I am" (3.2.14–16). But "I play the man I am" cuts both ways: in his bafflement, Coriolanus would like to suggest that there is no distance between role and self, but he in fact suggests that he plays at being himself, that his manhood is merely a role. Given that Volumnia has created this dilemma, her answer is unnecessarily cruel, but telling: "You might have been enough the man you are, / With striving less to be so" (3.2.19–20). Volumnia is right: it is the intensity and rigidity of Coriolanus's commitment to his masculine role that makes us suspect the intensity of the fears that this role is designed to hide, especially from himself. For the rigidity of the role and the tenuousness of the self that it protects combine to make acknowledged play-acting of any kind terrifying for Coriolanus, as though he can maintain the identity of self and role, and hence his integrity, only by denying that he is able to assume a role. Because he cannot acknowledge the possibility of role playing, Coriolanus must respond to his mother's request that he act a new role as a request that he be someone other than Coriolanus. When he finally agrees to take on the role of humble supplicant, he is sure that he will act badly (3.2.105–6), and that he will lose his manhood in the process (3.2.111–23).

The fragility of the entire structure by which Coriolanus maintains his claim to self-sufficient manhood helps to account for the violence of his hatred of the plebeians. For Coriolanus uses the crowd to bolster his own identity: he accuses them of being exactly what he wishes not to be.[57] He does his best to distinguish himself from them by emphasizing his aloneness and their status as multitude as the very grounds of their being.[58] Throughout, he associates his manhood with his isolation, so that "Alone I did it" becomes a sufficient answer to Aufidius's charge that he is a boy. Hence the very status of the plebeians as crowd reassures him that they are not men but dependent and unmanly things, merely children—a point of view that Menenius seems to confirm when he tells the tribunes: "Your abilities are too infant-like for doing much alone" (2.1.36–37). His most potent image of the crowd is as an appropriately infantile common mouth (3.1.22, 155) disgustingly willing to exhibit its neediness. Coriolanus enters the play identified by the plebeians as the person who is keeping them from eating (1.1.9–10); indeed, one of his main complaints about the plebeians is that they say they are hungry (1.1.204–7). Coriolanus himself has been deprived of food, and he seems to find it outrageous that others should not be. His position here is like that of the older brother who has fought his way into manhood and who is now confronted by an apparently endless group of siblings—"my sworn brother the people" (2.3.95), he calls them—who still insist on being fed by mother Rome, and whose insistence on their dependency threatens the pose of self-sufficiency by which his equilibrium is perilously maintained.[59] To disclaim his own hunger, Coriolanus must therefore disclaim his kinship with the crowd; "I would they were barbarians—as they are, / . . . not Romans—as they are not" (3.1.236–37). But the formulation of the disclaimer itself reveals the very tensions that it is designed to assuage. Insofar as he wishes the people non-Roman, he acknowledges their Romanness; but this acknowledgment of kinship must immediately be denied by the assertion that they are in fact not Roman. The very insistence on difference reveals the fear of likeness.

But the multitudinous mouth of the crowd is horrifying to Coriolanus not only insofar as it threatens to reveal his own oral neediness to him but also insofar as it makes the nature of his vulnerability uncomfortably precise. In this hungry world, everyone seems in danger of being eaten. The crowd suspects the senators of cannibalistic intentions: "If the wars eat us not up, they will; and there's all the love they bear us" (1.1.84–85). Since Coriolanus twice dismisses them as ignoble food ("quarry" [1.1.197]; "fragments" [1.1.221]), their fears seem not entirely without basis. But Coriolanus thinks that, without the awe of the Senate, the crowd would "feed on one another" (1.1.187). Given their choice, the tribunes would naturally enough prefer that the "present wars devour" Coriolanus (1.1.257) instead of the populace. The people's belief that the death of Coriolanus would allow them to have corn at their own price (1.1.9) is eventually sustained by the plot, insofar as Coriolanus opposes the giving of corn gratis (3.1.113–17). But at the start of the play, we are not in a position to understand the logic behind their association between killing Coriolanus and an unlimited food supply; and in the context of all the cannibalistic images, the mysterious association seems to point toward a fantasy in which the people, rather than the wars, will devour Coriolanus.[60] Menenius explicates this fantasy:

> Men. Pray you, who does the wolf love?
> Sic. The lamb.
> Men. Ay, to devour him, as the hungry plebeians would the noble Martius.
>
> (2.1.6–9)

And in the third act, as the people begin to find their teeth and rise against Coriolanus, his images of them as mouths begin to reveal not only his contempt for their hunger but also his fear of his own oral vulnerability, fear of being bitten, digested, pecked at: "You being their mouths, why rule you not their teeth?" (3.1.35); "How shall this bosom multiplied digest / The senate's courtesy?" (3.1.130–31); "Thus we debase / The nature of our seats, . . . / . . . and bring in / The crows to peck the eagles" (3.1.134–38). The fear of being eaten that lies just below the surface in these images is made explicit when Coriolanus tells Aufidius that the people have "devour'd" all of him but his name (4.5.77).

The crowd, then, is both dependent, unmanly, contemptible—and terrifyingly ready to rise up and devour Coriolanus. Through his portrayal of the crowd, Coriolanus can manage to dismiss the specter of his own hunger and insist on his identity as an isolated and inviolable thing ("a thing / Made by some other deity than nature" [4.6.91–92], as Cominius says). But he cannot dismiss the danger that exposure to their hunger would bring. His absolute horror of the prospect of showing his wounds to win the consulship depends partly, I think, on the complex of ideas that stands behind his characterization of the crowd. In Plutarch, Coriolanus shows his wounds; in Shakespeare, the thought is intolerable to him and, despite many promises that he will, he never does. For the display of his wounds would reveal his kinship with the plebeians in several ways: by revealing that he has worked for hire (2.2.149) as they have (that is, that he and his deeds are not *sui generis* after all); by revealing that he is vulnerable, as they are; and by revealing, through the persistent identification of wound and mouth,[61] that he too has a mouth, that he is a dependent creature. Moreover, the exhibition of his wounds to the crowd is impossible for Coriolanus partly because his identity is sustained by exhibitionism of another sort. Coriolanus is right in believing that he must not "stand naked" (2.2.137) before the crowd, asking for their approval; for this standing naked would reverse the sustaining fantasy by which he hoped to "stand / As if a man were author of himself" (5.3.35–36). For the phallic exhibitionism of Coriolanus's life as a soldier has been designed to deny the possibility of kinship with the crowd; it has served to reassure him of his potency and his aggressive independence, and therefore to sustain him against fears of collapse into the dependent mode of infancy. To exhibit the fruits of his soldiership as the emblems not of his self-sufficiency but of his vulnerability and dependence, and to exhibit them precisely to those whose kinship he would most like to deny, would transform his chief means of defense into a proclamation of his weakness: it would threaten to undo the very structure by which he lives. And finally, insofar as he would expose himself as vulnerable and dependent by displaying his wounds, he would invite the oral rage of the crowd to satisfy itself on him. "If he show us his wounds and tell us his deeds, we are to put our tongues into those wounds and speak for them" (2.3.5–8), the Third Citizen says; his grotesque image suggests that the sweet licked by the multitudinous tongue (3.1.155–56) would be "sweet" Coriolanus himself (3.2.107).[62]

During the first part of the play, Coriolanus uses his opposition to the crowd to define himself and to fend off his vulnerability. But after the exile from Rome, this source of definition fails, and Coriolanus turns toward his old enemy Aufidius to confirm himself. For if Coriolanus has throughout defined himself by opposition, he has defined himself by likeness as well; from the beginning, we have watched him create a mirror image of himself in Aufidius. As soon as he hears that the Volsces are in arms, Coriolanus announces the terms of his relationship with Aufidius: "I sin in envying his nobility; / And were I anything but what I am, / I would wish me only he" (1.1.229–31). But the noble Aufidius is Coriolanus's own invention, a reflection of his own doubts about what he is, an expression of what he would wish himself to be. Shakespeare takes pains to emphasize the distance between the Aufidius we see and the Aufidius of Coriolanus's imagination. The Aufidius invented by Coriolanus seems designed to reassure Coriolanus of the reality of his own male grandeur by giving him the image of himself; his need to create a man who is his equal is in fact one of the most poignant elements in the play and helps to account for his tragic blindness to his rival's true nature as opportunist and schemer. Immediately after Coriolanus has imagined himself Aufidius, he allows us to see the extent to which he is dependent on Aufidius for his self-definition in a nearly prophetic confession: "Were half to half the world by th' ears, and he / Upon my party, I'd revolt to make / Only my wars with him" (1.1.232–34). Later, the Coriolanus who shrinks violently from the praise of others eagerly solicits news of Aufidius's opinion of him; and his oddly touching "Spoke he of me?" (3.1.12) reveals the extent to which he needs to see himself in Aufidius's eyes.[63] As he approaches Antium after the exile, he pauses to reflect on the strangeness of his actions but succeeds only in suggesting that the issue driving him from Rome and toward Aufidius is a "trick not worth an egg" (4.4.21), as though for the moment the fact of his union with Aufidius is more important than the circumstances that drove him to it. His attempt to explain his actions begins and ends with the image of friends "who twin, as 'twere, in love / Unseparable" (4.4.15–16), who "interjoin their issues" (4.4.22). The movement of this soliloquy reveals the fantasy of twinship underlying his relationship with Aufidius both as foe and as friend.

The union with Aufidius is for Coriolanus a union with an alter ego; it represents a flight from the world of Rome and his mother toward a safe male world. Devoured in all but name by Rome (4.5.77), Coriolanus enters Antium afraid of being eaten: he fears that the Volscian wives will slay him with spits (4.4.5) and tells the Third Servingman that he has dwelt "i'th'city of kites and crows" (4.5.43), a city of scavengers. (That this city is both the wilderness and Rome itself is suggested by Coriolanus's echo of his earlier peril, the crows who will peck the eagles [3.1.138].) Here, far from Rome, Coriolanus at last allows his hunger and his vulnerability to be felt, and he is given food. He presents himself to Aufidius during a great feast, from which he is initially excluded: "The feast smells well, but I / Appear not like a guest" (4.5.5–6). But here in Antium, the play moves toward a fantasy in which nourishment may be safely taken because it is given by a male, by a father-brother-twin rather than a mother. Coriolanus is finally taken into the feast. In the safe haven provided by his mirror image, he will not be devoured; instead, he will eat.[64] Aufidius's servants give us the final development of this fantasy:

> *First Serv.* . . . Before Corioles he scotched him and notched him like a carbonado.
>
> *Second Serv.* And had he been cannibally given, he might have broiled and eaten him too.
>
> (4.5.191–94)

The scene moves, then, from hunger and the fear of being eaten to an image of Coriolanus triumphantly eating Aufidius. Since his mother will not feed him, Coriolanus will find in Aufidius the only nourishment that can sustain him; and insofar as Aufidius is his alter ego, he, like his mother, will sup on himself.

When Coriolanus is banished from Rome, he responds with an infantile fantasy of omnipotent control: "I banish you!" (3.3.123). He then attempts to ensure the reality of his omnipotence by wishing on his enemies exactly what he already knows to be true of them: "Let every feeble rumour shake your hearts! / . . . Have the power still / To banish your defenders" (3.3.125–28). Few curses have ever been so sure of instantaneous fulfillment. Having thus exercised his rage and assured himself of the magical power of his invective, Coriolanus finally makes his claim to true independence: "There is a world elsewhere!" (3.3.135). His encounter with Aufidius is an attempt to create this world, one in his own image; but even the union with Aufidius leads ultimately back to Rome and his mother. For Coriolanus's rage, like his hunger, is properly directed toward his mother; though it is deflected from her and toward the plebeians and Volscians for much of the play, it finally returns to its source. For Rome and his mother are finally one:[65] in exiling Coriolanus, Rome reenacts the role of the mother who cast him out. Although in his loving farewell his family and friends are wholly distinguished from the beast with many heads, by the time he has returned to Rome they are no more than a poor grain or two that must be consumed in the general fire (5.1.27). (Even in his loving farewell we hear a note of resentment when he consoles his mother by telling her: "My hazards still have been your solace" [4.1.28].) As he approaches Rome, the devouring populace becomes indistinguishable from his loving mother. But Menenius has already pointed toward the fantasy that identifies them:

> Now the good gods forbid
> That our renowned Rome, whose gratitude
> Towards her deserved children is enroll'd
> In Jove's own book, like an unnatural dam
> Should now eat up her own!
>
> (3.1.287–91)

The cannibalistic mother who denies food and yet feeds on the victories of her sweet son stands at the darkest center of the play, where Coriolanus's oral vulnerability is fully defined. Here, talion law reigns: the feeding infant himself will be devoured; the loving mother becomes the devourer. In this dark world, love itself is primitive and dangerous: both the First Citizen and Menenius suggest that here, to be loved is to be eaten (1.1.84–85; 2.1.6–9).[66]

Coriolanus's return to Rome is not ultimately a return to his mother; it is rather a last attempt to escape her love and its consequences. If Coriolanus can make himself a new name, forged in the fires of burning Rome (5.1.14–15), he can construct a new identity independent of his mother: an identity that will demonstrate his indifference to her, his separation from her. For he can stand as author of himself only by destroying his mother. The return to Rome is an act of retaliation against the mother on whom he has been dependent, the mother who has cast him out. But it is at the same time an acting out of the child's fantasy of reversing the roles of parent and child, so that the life of the parent is in the hands of the omnipotent child. The child becomes a god, dispensing life and death (5.4.24–25): becomes in effect the author of his mother, so that he can finally stand alone.

But Coriolanus can sustain neither his fantasy of self-authorship nor his attempt to realize a godlike omnipotent power. And the failure of both leaves him so unprotected, so utterly devoid of a sense of self that, for the first time in the play, he feels himself surrounded by dangers.[67] The capitulation of his independent selfhood before his mother's onslaught seems to him to require his death, and he embraces that death with a passivity thoroughly uncharacteristic of him:

> O my mother, mother! O!
> You have won a happy victory to Rome;

But for your son, believe it, O, believe it,
Most dangerously you have with him prevail'd,
If not most mortal to him. But let it come.
(5.3.185–89)

Volumnia achieves this happy victory partly because she makes the dangers inherent in his defensive system as terrifying as those it is designed to keep at bay. Her last confrontation with her son is so appallingly effective because she invalidates his defenses by threatening to enact his most central defensive fantasies, thereby making their consequences inescapable to him.

The very appearance of his mother, coming to beg him for the life of her city and hence for her own life, is an enactment of his attempt to become the author of his mother, his desire to have power over her. He has before found her begging intolerable (3.2.124–34); when she kneels to him here, making the role reversal of mother and child explicit (5.3.56), he reacts with an hysteria that suggests that the acting-out of this forbidden wish threatens to dissolve the very structures by which he orders his life:

> What's this?
> Your knees to me? to your corrected son?
> Then let the pebbles on the hungry beach
> Fillip the stars. Then let the mutinous winds
> Strike the proud cedars 'gainst the fiery sun,
> Murd'ring impossibility, to make
> What cannot be, slight work!
> (5.3.56–62)

At first sight, this speech seems simply to register Coriolanus's horror at the threat to hierarchy implied by the kneeling of parent to child. But if Coriolanus were responding only—or even mainly—to this threat, we would expect the threatened chaos to be imaged as high bowing to low; this is in fact the image we are given when Volumnia first bows to her son as if—as Coriolanus says—"Olympus to a molehill should / In supplication nod" (5.3.30–31). But Coriolanus does not respond to his mother's kneeling with an image of high bowing to low; instead, he responds with two images of low mutinously striking at high. The chaos imaged here is not so much a derivative of his mother's kneeling as of the potential mutiny that her kneeling seems to imply: for her kneeling releases the possibility of his mutiny against her, a mutiny that he has been suppressing all along by his exaggerated deference to her. His response here reveals again the defensive function of his hatred of the mutinous and leveling populace:[68] the violence of his images suggests that his mother's kneeling has forced him to acknowledge his return to Rome as a rising up of the hungry and mutinous forces within himself. With her usual acumen, Volumnia recognizes the horror of potential mutiny in Coriolanus's response and chooses exactly this moment to assert, once again, his dependence on her: "Thou art my warrior" (5.3.62).

Coriolanus's forbidden wish to have power over his mother was safe as long as it seemed impossible. But now that protective impossibility itself seems murdered, and he is forced to confront the fact that his wish has become a reality. Nor are the hungry and mutinous forces within him content to murder only an abstract "impossibility": the murderousness of the image is directed ultimately at his mother. And once again, Volumnia makes Coriolanus uncomfortably clear to himself: after she has enacted his terrifying fantasy by kneeling, she makes it impossible for him to believe that her death would be merely an incidental consequence of his plan to burn Rome.[69] For she reveals exactly the extent to which his assault is on both. Her long speech builds to its revelation with magnificent force and logic. She first forces him to see his attack on his country as an attack on a living body by accusing him of coming to tear "his country's bowels out" (5.3.103). Next, she identifies that body as their common source of nurture: "the country, our dear nurse" (5.3.110). Finally, as she announces her intention to commit suicide, she makes absolute the identification of the country with herself. After she has imagined him treading on his country's ruin (5.3.116), she warns him:

> Thou shalt no sooner
> March to assault thy country than to tread—
> Trust to't, thou shalt not—on thy mother's womb
> That brought thee to this world.
>
> (5.3.122–25)

The ruin on which Coriolanus will tread will be his mother's womb— a warning accompanied by yet another assertion of his dependence on her as she recalls to him the image of himself as a fetus within that womb.

If Coriolanus's mutinous fantasies are no longer impossible, if his mother will indeed die as a result of his actions, then he will have realized his fantasy of living omnipotently without kin, without dependency. In fact this fantasy, his defense throughout, is articulated only here, as he catches sight of his mother (5.3.34–37), and its expression is the last stand of his claim to independence. Throughout this scene, Volumnia has simultaneously asserted his dependence on her and made the dangers inherent in his defense against that dependence horrifyingly clear; and in the end, it is the combination of her insistence on his dependency and her threat to disown him, to literalize his fantasy of standing alone, that cause him to capitulate. Finally, he cannot "stand / As if a man were author of himself / And knew no other kin"; he must become a child again, a gosling, and admit his neediness. The presence of his own child, holding Volumnia's hand, strengthens her power over him. For Coriolanus seems to think of his child less as his son than as the embodiment of his own childhood and of the child that remains within him; even when we are first told about the son, he seems more a comment on Coriolanus's childhood than on his fatherhood. The identification of father and child is suggested by Coriolanus's response as he sees wife, mother, and child approaching: "My wife comes foremost; then the honour'd mould / Wherein this trunk was fram'd, and in her hand / The grandchild to her blood" (5.3.22–24). Here Coriolanus does not acknowledge the child as his and his wife's: he first imagines himself in his mother's womb and then imagines his child as an extension of his mother. Even Coriolanus's language to Menenius as he earlier denies his family reveals the same fusion of father and son: "Wife, mother, child, I know not" (5.2.80), he says, in a phrase that suggestively identifies his own mother as the mother of the child and the child he attempts to deny as himself. Volumnia had once before brought Coriolanus to submission by reminding him of himself as a suckling child (3.2.129); now virtually her last words enforce his identification with the child that she holds by the hand: "This fellow had a Volscian to his mother; / His wife is in Corioles, and his child / Like him by chance" (5.3.178–80). But at the same time that she reminds him of his dependency, she disowns him by disclaiming her parenthood; she exacerbates his sense of himself as a child, and then threatens to leave him—as he thought he wished—alone. And as his fantasy of self-sufficiency threatens to become a reality, it becomes too frightening to sustain. Just as his child entered the scene holding Volumnia's hand, so Coriolanus again becomes a child, holding his mother's hand.

In *Macbeth*, the fantasy of caesarian self-birth is the answer to the mother's power over her feeding infant: if vulnerability comes of having a mother, the solution is to be self-born, not born of woman. Although *Macbeth* punishes this fantasy in Macbeth himself, its creation of an all-male lineage and landscape keeps the caesarian solution available for its audience. *Coriolanus* enacts, exposes, and then punishes the fantasy of self-authorship much more ruthlessly than *Macbeth*: though

Coriolanus begins as Macbeth's heroic "man-child," he ends fully subject to the place of origin and to the mortality that place entails. In the end, neither Coriolanus nor *Coriolanus* can sustain the fantasy that he is motherless, the author of himself.

Initially, the play seems to grant Coriolanus the status he desires: renamed by his self-birth at Corioli, he apparently escapes the condition of his natural birth, becoming "Jove's statue" (2.1.264), "a thing / Made by some other deity than nature, / That shapes man better" (4.6.91–93). His determination to forge a new name in the fires that burn Rome plays out the logic of this escape: his renaming now will be the explicit sign of his destruction of the maternal body, the "country" that is simultaneously Rome and his mother's womb. But it is the work of the play's ending to demonstrate that he has not been made by some other deity than nature, hence to demonstrate his subjection to the "mother's womb / That brought [him] to this world (5.3.124–25). In fact the fantasy of self-authorship emerges explicitly only *in extremis*, only at the moment that marks its limitation—immediately after Coriolanus himself sees his mother approaching and identifies her, not by name or familial position, but as "the honour'd mould / Wherein this trunk was fram'd" (5.3.22–23). The fantasy of escape itself is the sign of his subjection: at the very moment that Coriolanus would stand alone, he is returned to the "natural" place of origin. Unable finally to destroy that place in himself, he must capitulate to it; and in the bleak psychological landscape of this play, this capitulation means his death.

At the moment of capitulation, the ending of *Coriolanus* undoes the ending of *Macbeth*: if *Macbeth* enacts the severing of maternal connection, *Coriolanus* brutally displays the failure of this attempt. If maternal power is excised from Scotland, it is triumphant in Rome— and its triumph inevitably means the failure of male autonomy, the death of the male self. "O mother, mother! / What have you done?" (5.3.182–83): Coriolanus is killed in Antium immediately after Volumnia is triumphantly welcomed to Rome; the action of *Coriolanus* in fact construes her triumph as his death. If Macbeth dies fighting, heroically mantled in his own self-sufficiency, Coriolanus dies helpless and unarmed, his multiply-penetrated body the sign of his mother's presence in him. The ending of *Coriolanus* thus revises the ending of *Macbeth* without offering any relief from its bleak alternatives. Between them, the two plays enact the logic of a terrible either/or: either the excision of the female or the excision of the male, either the death of the mother or the death of her son.

And with these two plays, Shakespeare's tragic art itself seems to have come to an impasse. Both plays deny us the traditional comforts of tragic theater; both protagonists die in terrible isolation, still in flight from the contamination that relationship to the female would bring. Moreover, both plays constitute the theatrical itself as the realm of disturbance: if both figure maternal presence as devastating to the masculine identity of the son, both strikingly figure theater as allied with this dangerous female presence. This figuration seems to me to shape the dramaturgy of the two plays: taken together, they constitute a theatrical doing and undoing, engaging their audiences theatrically in the central psychological dilemmas of their protagonists as they play out in their own dramaturgy first the dangers of merger with the female and then the recoil into an exaggerated autonomy.

The loss of masculine autonomy that is the psychological threat of *Macbeth* everywhere infects that play's dramaturgy: for the play's audience as for its hero, distinctions between inner and outer fail as discrete objects blur and fuse, overwhelmed by their own boundary instability. "Rapt" by the "horrid image" of Duncan's murder (1.3.57, 135), Macbeth is driven to enact it in the world; under the guidance of the witches who speak the voice of his own horrible imaginings, "be it thought and done" (4.1.149) becomes less his wish than his fate, as though he were doomed to have the firstlings of his heart become the firstlings of his hand (4.1.147–48). As in a dream, the images of his own desires and fears are projected outward into the world, so that he meets fantasy-versions of himself again and again: in the traitor to whom he clings (1.2.8), the bloody child arising from the witches' cauldron, the man not born of woman, perhaps especially in the final desolate landscape, emptied of generative potential. And except for the English interlude, the play insists that we share in his claustrophobic and phantasmagoric space:[70] meeting the witches that are ambiguously inside and outside of Macbeth, seeing the dagger that both is and is not a dagger of his mind, we do not know where we are, whose voice we hear, any more than Macbeth knows whose voice cries out "Sleep no more!" (2.2.34). This is the dramaturgy of the witches' cauldron, where function is smothered in surmise (1.3.141). And though the spectacular theater of the witches' cauldron ends in the vision of a triumphant male lineage (4.1.106–11), this spectacle nonetheless marks the space of the theatrical itself as female in origin: it erupts from the witches' cauldron as the play erupts from their first words, materializing as though called forth by them.

For *Macbeth*, participation in the theatrical means participation in the witches' realm; in the end, in the chastened realm of Malcolm, even theater must be robbed of its magic. When Malcolm commands his troops to carry the boughs of Dunsinane's trees, he simultaneously appropriates the "natural" and exposes the devices of the witches' theater, in effect ruining their theatrical effect by showing us the stage hands moving the props. Under his rule, the theater of spectacle is exorcised, and we are firmly on the ground of the literal, where objects stay themselves. And this antitheatrical territory is, I think, the ground upon which *Coriolanus* stands. In *Coriolanus* there are no supernatural beings, blurring boundaries by calling up their fantastic spectacles; this play, like Malcolm, seems deliberately to refuse what *Macbeth* constitutes as the theatrical.

Casting the theatrical as the feminine, Coriolanus himself refuses to participate in it: spectacle is for him the sign of boundary confusion, a dangerously feminizing self-exposure; acting is the province of the harlot, the eunuch, the virgin minding babies (3.2.112–15). Refusing theater, Coriolanus will not act for applause: he refuses to show himself to us as he refuses to show his wounds to the populace, as though he feared that we too would find him feminized by the display. Insisting on his own rigid integrity, Coriolanus enforces ours: if Macbeth invites our dangerous merger, Coriolanus courts our alienation, dismantling the relationship between actor and audience. Excluded by his exclusion of the theatrical, we are in effect denied our roles as spectators to his tragic scene. And this work of exclusion is carried out by the whole play, not simply by its protagonist; throughout, *Coriolanus* replicates in its audience Coriolanus's own isolation, his own claim to self-authorship. If the dramaturgy of *Macbeth* characteristically threatens boundaries, smothering function in its female element, the dramaturgy of *Coriolanus* characteristically reinforces boundaries, walling in cities and individuals. If the metamorphically fluid language of *Macbeth* works to merge and blur distinctions, incarnadining "the multitudinous seas," "Making the green one red" (2.2.61–62), the metallic language of *Coriolanus* works to define and separate, to limit, almost as rigidly as Coriolanus himself does.[71] In this world of isolates, we too become isolates, as rigid and separate as Coriolanus himself is.

The association of the theatrical with the feminine in both *Macbeth* and *Coriolanus* threatens to dismantle theater altogether: if Malcolm diminishes its effects by mastering and displaying its props, Coriolanus refuses to act and refuses us our role as spectators. Winnicott suggests that play can happen only in the transitional space established by trust in the good-enough mother;[72] here, in the absence of such trust, rigid autonomy seems the only antidote to terrifying boundary instability, and there can be no play. Shakespeare's capacity to re-imagine play, to turn toward the new theatrical art of the romances, will depend in part on his re-imagining the relationship of theater to the maternal; as Antony is recreated in the spacious theater of Cleopatra's imagination, Shakespeare will move beyond the impasse of *Macbeth* and *Coriolanus* into a region where play once more becomes possible.

7

MAKING DEFECT PERFECTION: IMAGINING MALE BOUNTY IN *TIMON OF ATHENS* AND *ANTONY AND CLEOPATRA*

At the end of *Macbeth*, the man born of woman has been defeated by the man exempt from her power, and women are excised from the realm; at the end of *Coriolanus*, the man who would be author of himself has been reduced to a boy and his mother is triumphant in Rome. In the scarcity economy of these plays, masculinity depends on the excision of the female: the mother's death is the price of the son's survival; if she wins, he loses. In *Antony and Cleopatra*, by nearly all accounts written between these two plays, Shakespeare momentarily imagines a new psychic economy that can undo these bleak alternatives: in the last act of *Antony and Cleopatra*, Cleopatra reigns triumphant on stage; and her triumph turns crucially on her capacity not to destroy but to recreate Antony, remaking him from her own imaginative amplitude. This moment is fragile: if Shakespeare opens up the possibility of escape from the either/or of psychic scarcity in *Antony and Cleopatra*, he immediately forecloses that possibility again in *Coriolanus*. Nonetheless, the psychic economy glimpsed in Cleopatra's monument will eventually lead Shakespeare to *The Winter's Tale*, where trust in maternal amplitude enables Shakespeare's own imaginative bounty. I want to approach this new psychic economy by way of the text that seems to me at the maximum distance from it: *Timon of Athens*. Insofar as *Timon* illustrates the alliance between psychic scarcity and distrust of the female with an almost allegorical purity, it can help to clarify the visions and revisions that stand behind Shakespeare's fragile recovery of amplitude in *Antony and Cleopatra*.

Timon of Athens is Shakespeare's most extreme vision of scarcity and his most ruthless exposure of the fantasy of male bounty; and it is not coincidentally the Shakespearean text most filled with a pure and raging disgust at sexuality—pure in that it is quite divorced from any considerations of plot and from any particular female characters, since women themselves have been virtually eliminated from the play. In part because of this purity, *Timon* allows us to see the formation and function of this disgust more clearly than Shakespeare's more fully populated texts, where it can seem to be motivated by the actual excesses of a Gertrude or a Goneril, the actual whoredom of a Cressida. In the absence of these characters or their like, the play's bewhoring of women is foregrounded and requires explanation: why should a play that exposes the limited resources of male selfhood and the failure of male community in its first half vent its rage in the second half on the act of generation and particularly on the female body? The answer lies, I think, in the defensive function of the fantasy of male bounty itself.

From the beginning, the play exposes in Timon the unmediated fantasy of an infinite male nurturance. In the figures of Lear dispensing all or Duncan planting his subjects and making them grow, the earlier plays have given us glimpses of the man who would make himself the dispenser of bounty in order to protect himself against its unstable female source: the mother who can betray, denying nurturance or life itself to her son.[1] But these figures are set in a social context that in fact makes them the source of all gifts; as kings, they are moreover able to participate in the ideology that makes the king the "nourish-father" to his people.[2] With Timon, we have arrived at the thing itself, unmasked by social position or political ideology. At the beginning, we see Timon's "magic of bounty" (1.1.6) drawing all toward him, nourishing all; and while the fantasy holds sway, we are not encouraged to question the social or material base for his wealth. Ventidius inherits from his father; but Timon's wealth initially seems to have no source outside himself: it is simply there until it is gone, magically coterminous with his body and apparently self-renewing.[3]

In not specifying a source for Timon's wealth, the play initially seems to cooperate in Timon's own fantasy of self-generating abundance. For Timon can allow nothing to be seen to come from outside the self. When Ventidius offers—however cynically—to repay Timon's gift, Timon insists on his position as sole giver:

> O by no means,
> Honest Ventidius. You mistake my love;
> I gave it freely ever, and there's none
> Can truly say he gives, if he receives.
> (1.2.8–11)

If he receives, he cannot say he gives. In order to sustain his fantasy, his giving must be unbounded, unconstrained by amount (free) or by time (ever); and above all, it must be self-generated. Despite his fantasy of friends like brothers, commanding one another's fortunes (1.2.101–3), his entire sense of himself turns on denying reciprocity, hence denying his dependence on others; even before his self-exile, he locates himself in a landscape of absolute isolation, with no renewing resources outside the self. The undeveloped characters and shadowy social relations of the play thus replicate Timon's own condition: for the social world is present to him only insofar as he can imagine that his own generosity has made that world, through a kind of parthenogenesis; as he contemplates his friends, they dissolve into the babes that spring up in his eyes as he weeps (1.2.103–8). Denying otherness, he can allow into himself only what he believes that he himself has made: even in the masque ostensibly designed to flatter him, he can recognize only his "own device" (1.2.146).[4]

In refusing to locate his wealth in its social context, both Timon and the play initially make that wealth identical with Timon's body. This identification serves to conceal both the terrible arbitrariness of wealth—in effect naturalizing it as the possessor's body, rather than as his accumulation—and the social relations on which wealth depends; and in this concealment, it enables the fantasy of a magically bountiful male body that can replace the female body by taking on its nurturant qualities. The first scenes figure Timon's body as the feast at which every man feeds, from Alcibiades who "feed[s] / Most hungerly on [his] sight" (1.1.251–52) to the lords who go in to "taste Lord Timon's bounty" (1.1.273). Apemantus's "O you gods! What a number of men eats Timon, and he sees 'em not!" (1.2.39–40) is the first hint that Timon's personal resources may not be infinitely renewable; but before the conversation with Flavius (1.2.153ff.) everything seems to support the fantasy of a magically endless supply generated out of Timon himself. In his self-congratulating pageant, Timon suggests how fully he himself participates in this fantasy:

> *Cupid* Hail to thee, worthy Timon, and to all that of his bounties taste! The five best senses acknowledge thee their patron, and come freely to gratulate thy plenteous bosom.
>
> (1.2.118–21)

In thus posing his own body as the source of an infinite nurturance, Timon transfers to himself the nurturant qualities of the female body, replacing her "plenteous bosom" with his own; in effect, he identifies his bounty with the infinitely renewable female resource of breast milk rather than with the male wealth that is finite and quantifiable.

The defensive function of this identification becomes clear when we recall the poet's initial description of Timon's position,[5] tenuously perched on Fortune's hill, coterminous with the earth itself, where "all kind of natures / . . . labour on the bosom of this sphere / To propagate their states" (1.1.67–69). There is no magical male bounty here, and no guarantees of a permanent supply from this unreliable bosom: Lord Timon himself is potent only because he is Fortune's beloved; his resources come from her and can—and the poet predicts, will—be withdrawn. The language of generation makes the point: if the female body is imagined as a "high and pleasant hill" (1.1.65), the source of endless riches, man must labor on her sphere, propagating only through the usury of accumulation, always subject to her controlling will. And her unreliability is figured as a feature of her immense generativity: in the joint composition of poet and painter, Fortune's spurning of Timon is conveyed in an overdetermined language of pregnancy ("A thousand moral paintings I can show / That shall demonstrate these quick blows of Fortune's / More pregnantly than words" [1.1.92–94]).[6] As Apemantus says, ladies "eat lords; so they come by great bellies" (1.1.206): men are swallowed up by the immense generative appetite of women. No wonder that Timon should want to replace the "bosom of this sphere" with his own "plenteous bosom," defending himself against dependence on the strumpet fortune.

The fantasy of a magical male bounty that can replace the unreliable female otherness of the world initially sustains Timon. But Timon cannot endlessly generate resources from himself; and his discovery of a limit to his own bounty thrusts him into the landscape of utter deprivation. As with Lear, there is no *some* for Timon: he is either full or empty, all or nothing.[7] Because his wealth is magically coterminous with his body, any ordinary fiscal accounting seems to him tantamount to cannibalistic dismemberment:

> *Phil.* [Here's] all our bills.
> *Tim.* Knock me down with 'em: cleave me to the girdle.
> *Luc. Serv.* Alas, my lord—
> *Tim.* Cut my heart in sums.
> *Tit.* Mine, fifty talents.
> *Tim.* Tell out my blood.
> *Luc. Serv.* Five thousand crowns, my lord.
> *Tim.* Five thousand drops pays that. What's yours? And yours?

First Var. Serv. My lord—

Second Var. Serv. My lord—

Tim. Tear me, take me, and the gods fall upon you!
(3.4.88–98)

To make him some by summing his resources is to tear him apart, rending and rendering his body as finite and partitionable as his wealth, making him nothing by cutting his heart in *somes*. Thus become nothing, he can give nothing—and he does so aggressively, displaying the failure of his fantasy of infinite nurturance in an elaborately staged feast:

For these my present friends, as they are to me nothing, so in nothing
bless them, and to nothing are they welcome.
Uncover, dogs, and lap.
[*The dishes are uncovered and seen to be full of warm water*].
(3.6.79–83)

After this display, Timon runs to the woods, as Lear to the heath, bearing only his nothingness with him ("Nothing I'll bear from thee / But nakedness" [4.1.32–33]).

Like Lear, Timon runs toward that which he would most escape; in the woods to which he bears his naked nothingness, he finds the whore-mother in all her treacherous fecundity, of which the gold he finds when he needs roots (4.3.26–28) is the sign. And if the failure of the fantasy of infinite male bounty is initially phrased as the tearing apart of Timon's body, it is ultimately phrased as confrontation with this mother. This progression—from the torn male body to the sexually corrupt female body—makes visible the logic behind the construction of the whore fortune and the bewhoring of women, here and elsewhere;[8] through it, I think, we can glimpse why women must be made whores to assuage the narcissistic wound in men.

While Timon's sustaining fantasy is intact, women are exiled from his psychic world, present only in the elaborately controlled form of the masque; even there, they exist only to enable other men to adore him. After the dance of the Amazons,

The Lords rise from table, with much adoring of Timon, and to show
their loves each single out an Amazon, and all dance, men with
women, a lofty strain or two to the hautboys, and cease.
(1.2.141)[9]

But as soon as the fantasy has collapsed, women are everywhere, both in the city he leaves and in the wilderness he flees to; and they are everywhere a source of sexual revulsion. The long soliloquy that constitutes 4.1 is the point of transition: evoked for the first time there, the women are *made* whores by Timon's curses ("Matrons, turn incontinent! . . . To general filths / Convert, o' th' instant, green virginity!" [4.1.3, 6–7]), as though he could not tolerate their chastity, as though he needed their whoredom to maintain his sense of himself. By the time we next see him, the conversion has been completed; the female has become the source of corruption, and her generativity the means to destroy the contaminated universe:

> O blessed breeding sun, draw from the earth
> Rotten humidity; below thy sister's orb
> Infect the air!
>
> (4.3.1–3)

The earth's rotten humidity is the source of infection: the sun's breeding merely returns to the earth the infection inherent in it. Even as Timon ostensibly condemns the breaking of bonds among men—the "twinn'd brothers of one womb" (4.3.3)—his discourse is generated and empowered by the idea of female corruption. The telling pun with which he concludes this stage of his diatribe makes the point: "Therefore be abhorr'd / All feasts, societies, and throngs of men" (4.3.20–21). They will be ab/whored: as he continues, misanthropy turns toward misogyny, specifically toward the discourse of the whore.

It is at this point that Timon finds the gold. The gold that magically appears as he is digging for roots becomes the central emblem of the play: not only the plot mechanism that drives the dramatic action—such as it is—of the play's second half, but the fantasy object of all Timon's hate. Despite the use to which various of Timon's visitors would put it, the gold seems strikingly removed from its ordinary social origin or function, almost purely an object in Timon's mind, magically appearing in response to his need for vituperation. And his response to it makes the turn toward misogyny clear; initially the sign of the wealth that has corrupted the men of Athens, it increasingly becomes the sign of the whore:[10]

> Why, this
> Will lug your priests and servants from your sides,
> Pluck stout men's pillows from below their heads.
> This yellow slave
> Will knit and break religions, bless th'accursed,

Make the hoar leprosy ador'd, place thieves,
And give them title, knee and approbation
With senators on the bench. This is it
That makes the wappen'd widow wed again:
She whom the spital-house and ulcerous sores
Would cast the gorge at, this embalms and spices
To th' April day again. Come, damn'd earth,
Thou common whore of mankind, that puts odds
Among the rout of nations, I will make thee
Do thy right nature.

(4.3.31–45)

This transition is mediated by the incipient pun on the "hoar leprosy ador'd"[11] and especially by the lovingly explicit description of the diseased female body made newly desirable by the gold. By the end, the gold has become entirely identified with female corruption; no longer the "yellow slave," it is now the "common whore of mankind."

But why should the gold—initially the sign of male wealth and therefore male corruptibility—be identified with the whore? The play puts this question to the test when it literalizes Timon's fantasy, obligingly giving him two whores to vent his anger on: immediately after he has identified the gold as a whore, Alcibiades enters with Phrynia and Timandra. Timon's repeated references to the women as a source of infection (4.3.63, 85–88, 143) seem initially to make the logic of the identification clear: gold corrupts, and whores corrupt; the two are therefore interchangeable in their effects.[12] Hence the logic through which Timon imagines that the gold, which might permit the whores to foreswear their trade (4.3.135), will instead make them even more effective whores (4.3.136–51), allowing them to achieve truly apocalyptic effects:

Consumptions sow
In hollow bones of man; strike their sharp shins,
And mar men's spurring. Crack the lawyer's voice,
That he may never more false title plead,
Nor sound his quillets shrilly. Hoar the flamen,
That scolds against the quality of flesh,
And not believes himself. Down with the nose,
Down with it flat, take the bridge quite away
Of him that, his particular to foresee,
Smells from the general weal. Make curl'd-pate ruffians bald,
And let the unscarr'd braggarts of the war
Derive some pain from you. Plague all,
That your activity may defeat and quell
The source of all erection. There's more gold.

(4.3.153–66)

Like Lear,[13] Timon would put an end to the sexuality that breeds ungrateful man (*King Lear*, 3.2.9; see *Timon*, 4.3.190); in effect, he would use the contaminated whores to end the society contaminated by gold. But as with the first address to the gold, the sexual disgust in this speech is so extreme that it displaces the logical equivalence between gold and whore, becoming less the vehicle for a comparison (gold operates as whores do in society; both are mediums of contagion) than a primary locus of feeling. The whores that initially seem to come on stage in order to literalize Timon's identification of gold as whorish eventually supersede the gold in his imagination, as his disgust shifts from the gold and the society it corrupts to the female body as the source of all contagion, like the earth of 4.3.1.

As in an hallucination, the infectious earth breeds the gold, the gold breeds whores, and the whores breed infection;[14] the imagery circles around to its starting point. The whole sequence plays out the logic of Timon's early apostrophe to the gold ("damn'd earth, / Thou common whore of mankind" [4.3.42–43]); and immediately after the women have left, Timon arrives back at this starting point, in his address to the earth as "common mother":

> Common mother, thou
> Whose womb unmeasurable and infinite breast
> Teems and feeds all; whose self-same mettle,
> Whereof thy proud child, arrogant man, is puff'd,
> Engenders the black toad and adder blue,
> The gilded newt and eyeless venom'd worm,
> With all th'abhorred births below crisp heaven
> Whereon Hyperion's quick'ning fire doth shine:
> Yield him, who all the human sons do hate,
> From forth thy plenteous bosom, one poor root.
> Ensear thy fertile and conceptious womb;
> Let it no more bring out ingrateful man.
> (4.3.179–90)

This is, I think, the root fantasy of the sequence, and the root of Timon's manic generosity: here is what that generosity was designed to deny. For the fantasy of infinite male bounty must end here, at the "plenteous bosom" of this mother. The transfer of the phrase from its original place in Timon's self-congratulatory masque suggests what is at stake: as Timon's "plenteous bosom" runs dry, unable to renew itself, he is brought face to face with the promiscuous and unreliable female source of nourishment outside himself, the "plenteous bosom" of the "common mother" on whom he must depend. And the gold— "damn'd earth, thou common whore of mankind"—leads him back to this whore-mother not only because it corrupts but because it is the sign of her unreliable bounty. As such, it cannot replenish his depleted resources and must remain utterly unusable by him. For it comes as a kind of insult to him, taunting him with his own inadequacy: as the gift of mother earth, or of the Fortune who was her avatar in the poet's description, it is the physical evidence that his wealth is not self-generated, and never was. No longer magically coterminous with his body, that wealth becomes the mark of his dependence on an unreliable source of nurturance outside himself, the mother who gives him gold when he needs food.

When Timon can no longer sustain the fantasy of self-generated nurturance, he responds by finding the world outside himself wholly unreliable and giving this unreliability the name of the whore-mother, as though to trace it to its first source. The gold thus comes to be the sign not of man's corruption but of the unreliable female body itself. And the very generativity of that body becomes the sign of the common-ness of this mother, the sign that she has betrayed her hated human son.[15] The instability of Fortune had previously been associated with her generativity; now the bitterness of Timon's discovery that he is not himself the source of bounty releases a terrible disgust at female fecundity, teeming and feeding. Under the aegis of this disgust, all births are equally ab-horred/ab-whored (4.3.185); hence I think the degree to which the cluster of ordinarily positive terms for fecundity—unmeasurable, infinite, plenteous, fertile, conceptious—here carries an enormous bitterness. For this mother's plenty becomes the sign of his poverty: no longer the unique generator of the world outside himself, Timon now finds himself merely one of the multitudinous and abhorred births, scrabbling among his siblings for one poor root.[16] Naming the otherness of the world "common mother," Timon shifts the blame for his starvation, his status as one among many, to her monstrous generativity; his narcissistic wound—the finitude of his body, its isola-tion and divisibility—is now transformed into her betrayal of him.

The play does not end here, with Timon's address to his common mother earth; and there is some attempt to recuperate the female after this moment. In attempting to demonstrate that he has a better claim to rage than Apemantus, Timon reinvents the fantasy of Fortune as loving mother whose "tender arm" clasped him (4.3.252–53); held by this mother, he "had the world as [his] confectionary" (4.3.262).[17] Perhaps under the aegis of this revived fantasy, the terms for natural abundance become much less equivocal in Timon's lecture to the thieves than in his address to his whore-mother earth ("The bounteous housewife nature on each bush / Lays her full mess before you" [4.3.423–44]); and Flavius's compassionate tears now demonstrate that he is a woman or at least born of woman (4.3.487, 498). But given the absence of any female character who might qualify Timon's vituperation, his ab/whoring of women is too insistent to be easily recuperable—particularly since it seems to be Shakespeare's as well as Timon's. Though the play punishes Timon's fantasy of self-generating male bounty, ruthlessly demonstrating the scarcity of his resources and the folly of his attempt to substitute the limited bounty of gold for the limitlessness of maternal provision, it nonetheless accepts his terms, narrowing its scope to the limits of his mind. The insistence on Timon's nobility and his aggrandizing difference from others, the absence of a fully realized social world, especially of fully realized female characters, the magical appearance of the gold and especially the whores as Timon requires them—all point toward Shakespeare's absorption in the fantasy expressed through Timon. For otherness is finally no more admissible to the play than it is to Timon: despite all the conversation, no one manages to talk back to Timon; even the landscape gives him only the image of his inner world.[18] And as in Timon's self-devised masque, the result is a radical narrowing of Shakespeare's own dramatic art: if the theatrical is associated with the disruptive female other in *Macbeth* and *Coriolanus*, here it seems largely to be banished along with her; shrunk to the limits of Timon's masculine self, founded in scarcity, the play itself becomes parsimonious.

If one comes to *Antony and Cleopatra* from *Timon*, the extent to which the one seems to answer the other is startling.[19] Timon's "Methinks I could deal kingdoms to my friends, / And ne'er be weary" (*Timon*, 1.2.219–20), a claim that excites contempt at his folly, recurs at the heart of Cleopatra's idealizing vision of Antony: "in his livery / Walked crowns and crownets: realms and islands were / As plates dropped from his pocket" (5.2.90–92). Timon learns the hard way that he has no "magic of bounty" (1.1.6), that his man-made resources are not renewable: as the servant of one of his creditors says, "a prodigal course / Is like the sun's, / But not, like his, recoverable. I fear / 'Tis deepest winter in Lord Timon's purse" (3.4.12–15). But Cleopatra's claim is precisely that Antony's resources are infinitely renewable; and she specifically disclaims the winter-scarcity of the servant's seasonal analogy:

> For his bounty,
> There was no winter in't: an autumn 'twas
> That grew the more by reaping.
> (5.2.86–88)

We may, of course, choose not to accept Cleopatra's vision of Antony; the play seems to me poised between acceptance and rejection of her claim, and it locates us in the same uneasy region.[20] But the claim of male bounty is no longer punitively mocked, as it is in *Timon*; and the play's own dramaturgy enacts the bountifulness she imagines: if *Timon* is shrunk to the limits of Timon's inner world, *Antony and Cleopatra* has the spaciousness and generosity that Cleopatra claims for Antony, whose "legs bestrid the ocean" (5.2.82).[21]

It is, I think, no accident that the dream of Antony's bounty is localized within the character of Cleopatra: Shakespeare in effect frees himself—and his dramatic art—from Timon's landscape of scarcity by re-imagining the relation of male selfhood and male bounty to the maternal.[22] Through its revaluation of female sexuality and generativity, *Antony and Cleopatra* recuperates *Timon*'s "common mother"; no longer purely the register of loss, she can become the potential site of an idealized male selfhood. Antony's "dungy earth" that "feeds beast as man" (1.1.35–36) and Cleopatra's "dung, / The beggar's nurse, and Caesar's" (5.2.7–8) condense the opening lines of Timon's address to this mother,

> Whose womb unmeasurable and infinite breast
> Teems and feeds all; whose self-same mettle,
> Whereof thy proud child, arrogant man, is puff'd,
> Engenders the black toad and adder blue,
> The gilded newt and eyeless venom'd worm.
> (4.3.180–84)

In effect, Egypt becomes the locus of the common mother's promiscuous generativity, indifferently producing figs and asps from its slime. And Egypt's Queen is virtually her avatar: when Cleopatra appears on stage, nursing the venomed worm whose bite is mortal to her, she literalizes the image of Timon's teeming and feeding mother earth.[23] And if Timon had made the claim to an endless supply partly in order to substitute himself for this mother, attempting to control her unreliability by recreating her bounty in himself, Antony embraces her in all her unreliability and finds in her a true source of supply. For the terrible generativity of this mother is revalued in Cleopatra, as female sexuality itself is revalued: the "infinite breast" of Timon's common mother, promiscuously feeding all, becomes Cleopatra's "infinite variety," endlessly renewing the appetites she feeds (2.2.236); her "womb unmeasurable"—which serves in the bleak landscape of *Timon* only as the register of male finitude and loss—becomes the model for Antony's own bounty, as he himself "o'erflows the measure" (1.1.2) and grows the more by reaping.

Once Timon's "common mother" has been revalued, scarcity will be revalued too. Timon's landscape of scarcity recurs in *Antony and Cleopatra*—Caesar's portrait of Antony starving after his defeat at Modena recapitulates its central elements[24]—but with a difference: it is now the consequence of denial of—not subjection to—the female. In *Timon*, female abundance exists only to demonstrate to Timon the poverty of his own "plenteous bosom," and male scarcity is psychologically the consequence of that unreliable abundance: the teeming of the common mother places her son in a landscape of deprivation, where endless siblings compete ruthlessly for limited resources, where he must be grateful even for one root. But in *Antony and Cleopatra*, scarcity is the sign of the state from which the female has been excised: there are virtually no women in Rome, there is no natural abundance. In effect, Caesar and his Romans have claimed Timon's scarcity as their own, institutionalizing it and making it the basis of their male selfhood, as though they could divorce themselves from subjection to the unreliable female and the problematics of her generativity by willfully embracing a condition of limited resources, in which measure is the means to success and any excess counts as waste. Thus localized as the emotional landscape of masculine selfhood in Rome, scarcity becomes the domain of its competing siblings, the rival brothers who cannot stall together in the whole world because the whole world is not large enough for them; no longer the mother's fault, hunger, rivalry, and the incompletion of the male self now seem intrinsic to the all-male society that has attempted to divorce itself from her.

Bounty and scarcity continue to be the key terms in *Antony and Cleopatra*, as they are in *Timon*; but in *Antony and Cleopatra*, Shakespeare succeeds in transvaluing them and hence in transfiguring their relation to male selfhood. *Antony and Cleopatra* is ostentatiously framed by its two memorializing portraits of Antony, Caesar's in act 1 and Cleopatra's in act 5. Caesar's locates Antony in the Timonesque landscape of absolute deprivation, where he must browse on the bark of trees and eat strange flesh to survive; and it figures his heroic masculinity as his capacity to survive in this wintry landscape. Cleopatra's locates him in a landscape of immense abundance with no winter in it; and it figures his heroic masculinity as his capacity to participate in the bounty of its self-renewing autumn. If Timon is driven from his fantasy of bounty to a landscape of absolute scarcity and is made to acknowledge that landscape as his psychic home, Antony begins in Caesar's landscape of scarcity but then finds himself in Cleopatra's bounty. And what is at stake in this trajectory is the relocation and reconstruction of heroic masculinity.[25]

The contest between Caesar and Cleopatra, Rome and Egypt, is in part a contest between male scarcity and female bounty as the defining site of Antony's heroic masculinity. Longing for that heroic masculinity is, I think, at the center of the play. Though Enobarbus's great set-piece on Cleopatra at Cydnus would seem to create Cleopatra as the play's ultimate unattainable erotic object, Antony himself is the primary absent object of desire for all the major characters.[26] Both Caesar and Cleopatra fill up the gap his absence makes by imagining him present, addressing him in the second person as though he were there, both at the beginning and at the end of the play (1.4.55–56, 1.5.27; 5.1.35, 5.2.286, 311);[27] and Enobarbus dies, speaking to him (4.9.18–23). No one is more keenly aware of his absence than Antony himself, who watches his status as "Antony" dissolve and become as indistinct as water is in water (4.14.11); his peculiar pain turns in part on his awareness of himself as the standard against which his own loss of heroic masculinity must be measured. Even when he is on stage, that is, his presence is suffused with a sense of absence or loss; except in his triumphant land battle, his heroic grandeur is always constructed retrospectively, in his—and its—absence.

In the figure of Antony and the complex longing that surrounds him, Shakespeare restages the loss of idealized masculinity that had initiated *Hamlet*; and in his recovery of Antony through Cleopatra's dream of bounty, Shakespeare brings that masculinity back to life. This recovery seems to me momentous in Shakespeare's career: through it, Shakespeare in effect undoes the conditions that have defined tragic masculinity since Old Hamlet's death. In the tragedies that follow from *Hamlet*, heroic masculinity has been constructed defensively, by a rigid separation from the dangerous female within and without; founded in the region of scarcity, the self-protective and niggardly manliness of Macbeth or Coriolanus illustrates the impasse at the end of this defensive construction. And Timon's defensive and self-delusive bounty offers no escape from this impasse; it merely brings him back to the same region of scarcity. By locating Antony's heroic manhood within Cleopatra's vision of him, Shakespeare attempts in effect to imagine his way beyond this impasse, recovering the generous masculinity of Old Hamlet in Antony by realigning it with its female source. In effect, Shakespeare returns masculinity to its point of origin, the maternal body; and without denying the potentially devastating effects of that return—indeed, the play is full of references to Cleopatra's emasculating effect on Antony—he rewrites that body as the source of male bounty. This rewriting is only tenuously achieved, but it nonetheless seems to me at the center of *Antony and Cleopatra*; and it is, I think, deeply bound up with Shakespeare's own recovery of theatrical play and hence with his move beyond tragedy and toward the manifold recoveries of *The Winter's Tale*.

From the beginning, Caesar is the spokesman for the realm of scarcity and the masculinity constructed on its model. His first words constitute Egyptian excess as an effeminizing threat to that masculinity:

> From Alexandria
> This is the news: he fishes, drinks, and wastes
> The lamps of night in revel; is not more manlike
> Than Cleopatra.
>
> (1.4.3–6)

According to Caesar's distinctly Roman economy of the self, plenty constitutes self-waste, compromising the stringent self-withholding that is his ideal. Satiety itself is suspect: Caesar imagines Antony's sexual exploits as a kind of voluptuous over-feeding in which bodily fullness becomes its own punishment ("If he fill'd / His vacancy with his voluptuousness, / Full surfeits, and the dryness of his bones / Call on him for't" [1.4.25–28]). And if fullness compromises a fragile Roman masculinity, emptiness guarantees it; womanly when he feasts with—and on—Cleopatra, voluptuously filling his vacancy, Caesar's Antony can be manly only when he is starving:

> Antony,
> Leave thy lascivious wassails. When thou once
> Was beaten from Modena, where thou slew'st
> Hirtius and Pansa, consuls, at thy heel
> Did famine follow, whom thou fought'st against,
> Though daintily brought up, with patience more
> Than savages could suffer. Thou didst drink
> The stale of horses, and the gilded puddle
> Which beasts would cough at: thy palate then did deign
> The roughest berry, on the rudest hedge;
> Yea, like the stag, when snow the pasture sheets,
> The barks of trees thou browsed. On the Alps
> It is reported thou didst eat strange flesh,
> Which some did die to look on: and all this—
> It wounds thine honor that I speak it now—
> Was borne so like a soldier, that thy cheek
> So much as lank'd not.
>
> (1.4.55–71)

This is a landscape of absolute deprivation, at the furthest possible remove from the emasculating excess Caesar associates with Egypt; as such, it—rather than the battlefield Philo evokes in the play's opening lines—serves as the test of Antony's heroic masculinity. Scarcity is the ground of masculine selfhood, as Caesar defines it: Antony proves himself the equal of the preeminently masculine stag when he survives the bleak winter of famine. As in *Coriolanus*, the hungry self is the manly self; not-eating permits the fantasy of entire self-sufficiency, the escape from the body and its effeminizing need.

The mixture of awe, longing, and envy in Caesar's reconstruction of the heroic Antony is unmistakable; and it seems to me to position Caesar in effect as a son in relation to the legendary father who constitutes the standard of masculinity. Caesar's need for such a figure rests in complex ways on his imagined relation with his own father, Julius Caesar, and on Antony's role in the oedipal dynamic between them. Inadvertently or not, Shakespeare rewrites history to make the fathers of both Caesar and Pompey Cleopatra's lovers.[28] Both Pompey and Caesar display a prurient interest in Antony's sexual life with Cleopatra; Antony himself asks Caesar, "My being in Egypt, / Caesar, what was't to you?" (2.2.35–36). What, indeed? For a generation of Romans that has successfully excised the female—in which there are no wives, in which mothers are apparently necessary only for the production of illegitimate children in Egypt—Egypt is the only place of sexual concourse, Cleopatra the only mother there is. For these unwomaned sons, she carries the taint of the whore-mother, site of the father's contamination; and through his liaison with her, Antony restages that contamination, becoming the focus both of longing for the father who might be exempt from woman and of disgust at the father who is not.[29]

Caesar's one oblique reference to his father in fact locates him precisely in Antony's position, condemning Rome by fathering illegitimate Egyptian issue:[30]

> Contemning Rome he has done all this, and more
> In Alexandria: here's the manner of't:
> I' the market-place, on a tribunal silver'd,
> Cleopatra and himself in chairs of gold
> Were publicly enthron'd: at the feet sat
> Caesarion, whom they call my father's son,
> And all the unlawful issue that their lust
> Since then hath made between them.
>
> (3.6.1–8)

And although other Romans are tolerant of Julius Caesar's liaison with Cleopatra—they in fact mythologize its details, as though creating a barroom legend—Caesar himself seems distinctly uncomfortable with it. His reference to Caesarion linguistically undoes his father's paternity of him, reducing it to the status of a rumor, as though he would undo the sign of his father's liaison with Cleopatra altogether if he could. For insofar as his father effortlessly brings together aspects of selfhood that Caesar works to keep separate—kissing Cleopatra's hand while musing on taking kingdoms in (3.13.82–85)—he destabilizes the distinctions through which Caesar has constructed his own niggardly masculinity; always already contaminated by Egypt, he can be of no service to his son in Rome.

In the intensity of its longing, Caesar's encomium of Antony seems to me to serve the function of recuperating the damaged image of paternal masculinity, in effect re-inventing the father-figure Caesar needs as the basis for his own stringent masculinity: if "Julius Caesar / Grew fat with feasting" in Egypt (2.6.64–65), at least this father-figure starves honorably. And his honorable starvation indicates his separation from the effeminizing realm of women and bodily need: this father could do without the nurturance everywhere associated with Egypt and Cleopatra, in effect do without maternal provision altogether; surviving the landscape of maternal deprivation—the spatial projection of Lady Macbeth's or Volumnia's withholding—Antony demonstrates his invulnerability to the female, thus over-mastering what over-mastered Julius Caesar. His masculinity is so secure that he can survive even the most dangerous sorts of feeding:

> On the Alps
> It is reported thou didst eat strange flesh,
> Which some did die to look on.

These are mysterious lines, and deliberately so: Shakespeare's lack of specificity—especially compared with Plutarch's much more matter-of-fact reference to "such beasts, as never men tasted of their flesh before"[31]—invokes the presence of the bizarre, even the tabooed. What is this strange flesh that some did die to look on? Cleopatra will soon recall that Pompey "would stand and make his eyes grow in my brow, / There would he anchor his aspect, and die / With looking on his life" (1.5.32–34); she herself is the locus of visual desire and visual danger[32] in the play, as well as the locus of dangerous feeding. Caesar's "strange flesh" leads back to Antony's "Egyptian dish," the "ordinary" wherein he "pays his heart / For what his eyes eat only" (2.6.123, 2.2.225–26). And the condensation of eating, looking, and dying in Caesar's image suggests what is at stake in Antony's heroic oral exemption: he can survive not only maternal deprivation but the danger inherent in maternal flesh itself. Caesar's deadly "strange flesh" seems to me to invoke the taboo against that flesh, returning us to the realm of infantile fantasy where looking and devouring the mother's body coalesce, and where both are punishable by death. Antony's importance for Caesar—and for the fantasy the play articulates through him—lies in his capacity to survive this death: to survive the confrontation not only with maternal deprivation but with the maternal body, the other/mother that is Egypt.

Midway between the generation of the fathers and the generation of the sons, the idealized Antony can serve as the repository of Roman masculinity, in effect recuperating the heroic father lost in Julius Caesar. But this is an inherently unstable position for Antony to occupy: by stressing Caesar's youth and Antony's age,[33] Shakespeare structures their relationship oedipally, making it resonate with the son's contest against the father he must idealize, possess, and, above all, subdue. From Caesar's first entrance, denying that he hates his "great competitor" (1.4.3), Shakespeare has insisted on the mix of awe and rivalry in Caesar's attitude toward Antony; and in fact Caesar does everything he can to undermine—not to recuperate—Antony's past heroism and seems positively gleeful when he can report the disgusting details of his captivity by Egypt. For like the oedipal father, Antony is the measure of Caesar's own stature: "When such a spacious mirror's set before him, / He needs must see himself" (5.1.34–35). And this rivalrous identification with Antony is dangerous to Caesar: in so spacious a mirror, how can he not see himself diminished? The impetus toward idealization that makes Antony the legendary father is consequently counterbalanced by the contrary impetus to cut him down to size: Caesar uses Antony simultaneously to recuperate the father destroyed in Julius Caesar and to master his prodigious presence, basing his own potency on that mastery.

The need to subdue Antony's magical presence—in effect to reduce him from an idealized father to an equal rival/brother— seems to me to govern Caesar's pursuit of Antony throughout. It is, I think, the impetus behind Caesar's initial gleeful relishing of the details of Antony's degradation: in his account, the effeminized Antony restages Julius Caesar's Egyptian revels in a diminished form, serving not as a spacious mirror but as a monitory image that confirms Caesar's own superiority. As a virtual case study in self-loss, this diminished paternal image rationalizes Caesar's self-withholding, his determination to possess himself and everything around him: xenophobia toward his father's Egypt, hatred of its bodily processes and their attendant wastes, fear of the gender transformations that they entail—all these become definitive of his new-style Roman masculinity, dependent on the news from

Alexandria to shore up its sense of itself. And in relation to this Antony, Caesar can constitute himself not as an awestruck son but as a righteous father, chiding him "as we rate boys" (1.4.31). We can see the operation of the same impetus at the end, in the speech with which Caesar responds to the news of Antony's death. He begins by acknowledging Antony's stature as a legendary figure equivalent to Julius Caesar and entitled to the same portents that heralded his death:[34]

> The breaking of so great a thing should make
> A greater crack. The round world
> Should have shook lions into civil streets,
> And citizens to their dens.
> (5.1.14–17)

But within a few lines, he has obliquely made the claim to equal stature (only "a moiety"—half—the world lay in Antony's name [5.1.19]; the rest is Caesar's); and as he continues, he carries the reduction of the spacious mirror even further:

> O Antony,
> I have follow'd thee to this, but we do launch
> Diseases in our bodies. I must perforce
> Have shown to thee such a declining day,
> Or look on thine: we could not stall together,
> In the whole world. But yet let me lament
> With tears as sovereign as the blood of hearts,
> That thou my brother, my competitor,
> In top of all design; my mate in empire,
> Friend and companion in the front of war,
> The arm of mine own body, and the heart
> Where mine his thoughts did kindle;—that our stars,
> Unreconciliable, should divide
> Our equalness to this.
> (5.1.35–48)

Even "moiety" turns out not to be enough: the brother-competitor must be rewritten first as a disease, and finally as a diminished part of Caesar's own gigantic body. Caesar—not the stars—has divided their "equalness" to this.[35]

"We could not stall together, in the whole world": the scarcity that is the landscape of Antony's Roman masculinity proves also to be the landscape of male bonds in Rome, where there is never enough to go around, where even the whole world is too small. And if the famine had not existed, Caesar would have had to invent it: only its psychic landscape could justify his version of Roman selfhood and the ruthless competition through which he defines himself. Moreover, Shakespeare's presentation of Casear's relation to Antony is less the exploration of an individual psyche than of an entire society: in this preeminently patriarchal city, rivalry itself is a hand-me-down from father to son.[36] And Cleopatra turns out to be oddly inessential to this father-son story: in his final version of Antony's story, Caesar never mentions her. If we read the play backwards from his response to Antony's death, then the official Roman line—that Antony was destroyed by Cleopatra's entrapment—begins to look like a cover-up: if Cleopatra had not been there, Caesar's Rome would have had to invent her too. With or without the existence of Cleopatra, Rome could not be the memorializing site of Antony's heroic masculinity: in the scarcity that rules its emotional economy, it must first establish, and then destroy, its legendary fathers.

Very shortly after Caesar cuts Antony down to size in the service of establishing his own gigantic stature, Cleopatra dreams her Emperor Antony, reconstructing him as the colossus of her abundant imagination. Claiming the right to Antony's memory, she in effect reinserts herself into the story from which she has just been occluded; furthermore, she makes herself—and not Caesar—the repository of his heroic masculinity. In thus giving Cleopatra the last word, Shakespeare robs Caesar of his "triumph," his attempt to arrange how these events will be remembered; in effect, she displaces his play with her own. And through this gesture, Shakespeare revises both the gender and the site of memory: although Shakespeare's own play is based on the historical record and concerned throughout with the judgments of history, memory in it is no longer purely the province of male history, which must subdue its objects, dismembering in order to remember; it now becomes the province of female desire, which "kiss[es] / The honour'd gashes whole" (4.8.10–11).

Cleopatra's monumental recreation of Antony seems to me the great generative act of the play; and it is unprecedented in Plutarch—or at least in Plutarch's "Life of Marcus Antonius." But it does have a precedent, I think, in another probable Plutarchian source for the play: Plutarch's "Of Isis and Osiris."[37] If in "The Life"—and in one Roman version of Antony's story in *Antony and Cleopatra*—the woman figures the destruction of a great man, in "Of Isis and Osiris" she is the agent of salvation; by inserting elements of "Of Isis and Osiris" into the more monovocal "Life," Shakespeare opens up interpretative possibility,[38] rewriting the female as the potential site of both generation and regeneration. As in *Antony and Cleopatra*, the loss and recovery of a charismatic male figure is at the center of Plutarch's Egyptian regeneration myth; like Antony, Osiris is the absence over which male and female rivals contend.[39] Typhon, Osiris's brother-rival, repeatedly pursues Osiris to his death, first locking him into a chest and throwing him into the sea, then cutting his body into fourteen parts and scattering them widely; Isis, Osiris's sister-wife, repeatedly performs the work of revival, first retrieving Osiris from the chest, then gathering up the scattered body parts and building memorials to them. This configuration of male rivalry and a saving female presence seems to me teasingly similar to *Antony and Cleopatra;*[40] in both, the male dismembers while the female remembers. Caesar in effect holds Typhon's place as the male destroyer in Shakespeare's text; his attempt to reduce Antony to an arm of his own body or to a disease that must be launched bears the traces of Typhon's persistent attempt to dismember Osiris. And if Caesar is Typhon to Antony's Osiris, Cleopatra takes on the role along with the "habiliments"[41] of the goddess Isis (3.6.17), "wandring heere and there, gathering together the dismembered pieces" of Osiris (p. 1309), restoring the memory and the sacramental generative potential of the scattered hero. When Typhon cuts off Osiris's "privy member" and feeds it to the fishes, Isis makes and consecrates a "counterfeit one, called Phallus" (p. 1294); when Caesar virtually dismembers—and dis-remembers—Antony, making him into the arm of his own gigantic body, Cleopatra restores his potent image in her dream-vision of him. Like Isis, Cleopatra finds and restores, memorializes and consecrates Antony's male identity: in the womblike receptive space of her female memory, suffused with sexual longing, he can live again.[42]

Shakespeare achieves his refiguration of Timon's "common mother" in part by aligning her with Plutarch's Isis; and he robes Cleopatra in her most numinous garments. In Plutarch's Isis, the promiscuous generativity of *Timon*'s "womb unmeasurable and infinite breast" (4.3.180) are the signs of her divinity: his Isis

> is the feminine part of nature, apt to receive all generation, upon which occasion called she is by Plato, the nurse and Pandeches, that is to say, capable of all: yea, and the common sort name her Myrionymus, which is as much as to say, as having an infinite number of names, for that she receiveth all formes and shapes. (p. 1310)

Cleopatra's "infinite variety" seems to me to have its source in Isis Pandeches; in her particolored nature, she replicates Isis's own multitudinousness:

> Moreover the habilliments of Isis, be of different tinctures and colours: for her whole power consisteth and is emploied in matter which

> receiveth all formes, and becommeth all maner of things, to wit, light, darknesse, day, night, fire, water, life, death, beginning, end. (p. 1318)

Like Isis—and unlike the more decorous Cleopatra of the "Life"—Shakespeare's Cleopatra is at home in the realm of becoming: "every thing becomes" her (1.1.49), as she becomes everything; even "vilest things / Become themselves in her" (2.2.238–39).[43] And like Isis, she acquires her restorative power from that realm: if Isis restores Osiris by immersing him in generation, Cleopatra would "quicken with kissing" (4.15.39).[44]

Transferred from the divine to the human plane in Cleopatra, Isis's restorative gesture will necessarily be incomplete and equivocal; Cleopatra herself reminds us that she does not have a goddess's power, that "wishers were ever fools" (4.15.33, 37). Nonetheless, the model of Isis may have partly enabled the opening out of trust in the female that leads Shakespeare toward *The Winter's Tale*: although Cleopatra cannot literally kiss the honored gashes whole, she can restore Antony's presence through her generative memory, assuaging his loss. From the beginning, her erotic longing has been the memorializing site of Antony's heroic masculinity: immediately after Caesar has located Antony's glory firmly in the past, in the landscape of starvation, Cleopatra recreates him as "the arm / And burgonet of men" (1.5.23–24), conflating him with Mars; when Mardian evokes "What Venus did with Mars," Cleopatra answers, "O Charmian, / Where think'st thou he is now?" (1.5.18–19). Antony's manhood is alive and well in her erotic recreation of him. And the play does not encourage us to dismiss this recreation merely as foolish wishing: Antony's one moment of represented martial heroism—his victorious land battle, greatly expanded from Plutarch's account[45]—issues from and returns to Cleopatra and to the specifically erotic energy she gives him.

Preparation for that battle begins on the familiar territory of the morning-after scenes in *Romeo and Juliet* and *Troilus and Cressida*, where the man arises, apparently feeling depleted by the sexual encounter and ready to reaffirm his manhood in the world outside the bed, while the woman tries to keep him with her; like Juliet's "Wilt thou be gone?" (3.5.1) or Cressida's "Prithee, tarry" (4.2.15), Cleopatra's "Sleep a little" (4.4.1) initially seems to register the dangerous pull toward dissolution in the female. But in a wonderful transformation of this motif, Cleopatra helps harden her man for that world, making him "a man of steel" (4.4.33); as she becomes not only "the armourer of [his] heart" but the armorer of his body, "a squire / More tight at this" than Eros (4.4.7, 14–15), she demonstrates in effect that Venus can arm as well as disarm Mars. For Shakespeare's other martial heroes—Troilus, Macbeth, Coriolanus—manliness means radical disavowal of the female; but Antony is never more manly than when he is armed by Cleopatra. Armed by her, he fights as well as ever in his idealized Roman past; and he returns his victory to her in language that suggests how fully he acknowledges her as the point of origin of his masculinity:

> O thou day o' the world,
> Chain mine arm'd neck, leap thou, attire and all,
> Through proof of harness to my heart, and there
> Ride on the pants triumphing!
>
> (4.8.13–16)

The enormous energy of these lines comes in part from the way in which they transform Roman threat into Egyptian triumph: images of entrapment and servitude are revised as boundary permeation itself becomes an expression of deep erotic delight. Despite the Roman conviction that Cleopatra has weakened Antony—a conviction that he himself sometimes shares—the entire sequence from 4.4 to 4.8 enfolds his martial heroism within her embrace.

These moments prepare us for the impassioned act of memory through which Cleopatra recreates her Emperor Antony in the last act. For that act comes in the most literal way from what Cleopatra herself has earlier called "the memory of my womb" (3.13.163), her own sexualized desire for what is absent. In her phrase, the sheltering space of female memory becomes one with the nurturant space of the womb itself: in context, "the memory of my womb" refers periphrastically to her children, as though they were what her womb remembered, as though they were made by its memorializing powers. Early in the play, Cleopatra imagines herself pregnant with the "idleness" Antony suspects her of ("'Tis sweating labour, / To bear such idleness so near the heart / As Cleopatra this" [1.3.93–95]. Mardian's later report of her pseudo-death makes her pregnant not with idleness—the womb-wishes the Soothsayer senses in Charmian (1.2.37)—but with Antony's name:

> . . . in the midst a tearing groan did break
> The name of Antony; it was divided
> Between her heart, and lips: she render'd life
> Thy name so buried in her.
>
> (4.14.31–34)

Given the frequency with which women rendered up their lives with their babies buried in them, it is hard not to hear in this pseudo-death the echo of an abortive birth; and of course the Romans would be happy to see Cleopatra's body as the burial ground of Antony's noble name. But Cleopatra's monumental recreation of Antony rewrites this abortive birth: in the protected female space of her own monument, the memory of her womb can at last bring Antony forth whole and undivided, rendering him life.

This is obviously an equivocal image, capable of multiple readings; the return to maternal origins is never unproblematic in Shakespeare. In casting Cleopatra as Plutarch's "mother of the world" (p. 1304) and bringing Antony to rest in her monument, Shakespeare evokes all the ambivalence of the mother-infant bond.[46] Antony has already told us that Cleopatra's "bosom was [his] crownet, [his] chief end" (4.12.27): through Cleopatra's final image, the end of the play returns him to Cleopatra's maternal body, the resting place from which he will no longer stray. In Cleopatra's final words, he becomes one with the asp, the baby at her breast, as she carries them both toward death ("O Antony! Nay, I will take thee too. / What should I stay—" [5.2.311–12]). Insofar as the play ends with the fantasy of a mutual sleep that undoes boundaries, it fulfills the dangerous desire at the heart of masculine selfhood, the dream of reunion with the maternal matrix. And fulfillment of this dangerous dream seems to require no less than all: Antony can be cured only with a wound (4.14.78).

And the play insists on the danger: for the male self in Rome, individuated selfhood is simultaneous with masculinity; both mark the self as distinct from the mother, not-female. The affiliation of "masculine" Rome with the solid and bounded, "feminine" Egypt with the fluid,[47] registers this simultaneity: from the Roman point of view, the melting of the boundaries of the self is necessarily its effeminization, its pull back toward that matrix. Hence, for example, Enobarbus's worry that dissolving into tears will make him a woman (4.2.36) or Antony's rewriting his self-dissolution as the loss of his sword when he sees the eunuch Mardian (4.14.23): for individuated masculinity as it is defined in Rome, castration is the price of merger, and death its promised satisfaction. Like most of the men in Shakespeare's tragedies, Caesar builds his masculinity on this threat: in attenuated form, he is the exemplar of defensive masculinity; and he demonstrates the dead end to which it leads. For the whole of his masculine selfhood as he defines it depends on his denial of the female, its reduction to the manageable proportions of his sister Octavia. From his first description of Antony in Egypt, he makes it plain that the female could only contaminate the male; from his point of view, there would be only one way to read the image of Antony dressed in Cleopatra's clothing. In his construction of masculinity, he belongs in the company of Richard

III, Troilus, Lear, Macbeth, Coriolanus—all those Shakespearean men who fear contamination from the mother within. And the Typhon who is his avatar provides the founding metaphor for this relation to the maternal: Plutarch tells us that Rhea "brought forth Typhon, but he came not at the just time nor at the right place, but brake thorow his mothers side and issued forth at the wound" (p. 1292).[48] Plutarch's account of Typhon's birth figures aggressive escape from the maternal body as the founding gesture of his male selfhood; as a radical metaphor for differentiation from the originary maternal matrix, Typhon's birth could serve as the model for all of Shakespeare's would-be Caesarian sons.[49]

These sons define themselves by their differentiation from that dangerous matrix; but Antony has allowed himself to be pulled back toward it from the start. From his first entrance, he knows that his love will require of him not only the dissolution of his Roman selfhood, but the dissolution of all such firm boundaries: the command that would undo his Roman selfhood—"Let Rome in Tiber melt!" (1.1.33)—follows from his claim that love is by nature unbounded ("There's beggary in the love that can be reckon'd" [1.1.15]). The love he seeks will necessarily entail the dissolving of the self into dangerous and fecund waters—into the Nile, if not the Tiber. Antony resists this pull for much of the play: from 1.2 until 4.14, he occupies himself in shoring up the boundaries of his masculine selfhood as Rome defines it. But the concealed accents of desire are audible even in his most plangent grieving for the dissolution of this self:

> *Ant.* Eros, thou yet behold'st me?
>
> *Eros*   Ay, noble lord.
>
> *Ant.* Sometime we see a cloud that's dragonish,
> A vapour sometime, like a bear, or lion,
> A tower'd citadel, a pendent rock,
> A forked mountain, or blue promontory
> With trees upon't, that nod unto the world,
> And mock our eyes with air. Thou hast seen these signs,
> They are black vesper's pageants.
>
> *Eros*   Ay, my lord.
>
> *Ant.* That which is now a horse, even with a thought
> The rack dislimns, and makes it indistinct
> As water is in water.
>
> *Eros*   It does, my lord.
>
> *Ant.* My good knave Eros, now thy captain is
> Even such a body: here I am Antony,

> Yet cannot hold this visible shape, my knave.
>
> (4.14.1–14)

No longer Herculean in his response to catastrophe, Antony contemplates his own dissolution with a quiet melancholy, letting go of his defining rage.[50] The very images of prominent manhood—dragon, bear, lion, citadel, rock, mountain, promontory, trees—now dissolve before his eyes, as though they had been illusory all along, merely temporary shapes wrested from vapor; in comparing himself to them, Antony acknowledges that he himself has mimicked the shapes of masculine identity only to dislimn, revealing his watery foundation.

As Antony imagines himself becoming indistinct as water is in water, he embraces the desire to lay it all down, to let go of the Roman selfhood maintained by such rigid vigilance.[51] For the masculinity of the sword—the masculine selfhood that defines itself by rigid differentiation from the female—has increasingly seemed too constraining for Antony's fluid desires. And so he greets Mardian's news that Cleopatra is dead with an odd sense of acquiescence and relief, as though he can at last stop struggling to bear the armor of a selfhood that has always been too heavy, too encasing:

> Unarm, Eros, the long day's task is done,
> And we must sleep. . . .
>   Off, pluck off,
> The seven-fold shield of Ajax cannot keep
> The battery from my heart. O, cleave, my sides!
> Heart, once be stronger than thy continent,
> Crack thy frail case! Apace, Eros, apace!
> No more a soldier: bruised pieces, go,
> You have been nobly born.
>
> (4.14.35–43)

Othello bids farewell to his military occupation (3.3.353–63) only with intense pain, as the sign of his loss of honor and of the heroic selfhood he had invested in Desdemona; but Antony gives up his bruised pieces willingly, as though he has finally gotten what he has wanted all along. His armor and his body coalesce as he lets both go, for both now seem to confine the desire that would overflow their boundaries. "Unarm, Eros, the long day's task is done, / And we must sleep": the langorousness of the language itself suggests the wished-for dissolution of the self into the unbounded state of sleep ("lie down and stray no farther" [4.14.47]) and the dream of unbounded fusion with Cleopatra.[52]

Shakespeare is acutely aware of the danger of this letting go; the play's repeated images of unmanning do not let us forget what is at stake. Nonetheless, in giving up the boundaries of his selfhood, Antony can be recreated in and through his merger with Cleopatra; and in her re-creation of him, the play reaches toward a new kind of masculinity. If Caesar's masculinity is founded on differentiation from the female— and on the psychic scarcity that is the consequence of that differentiation—Antony's is finally founded on incorporation of the female: in Cleopatra's vision of him, his bounty flows from him as though it were an attribute of his own body, as though he himself possessed the "plenteous bosom" with which mother earth mocked Timon.[53] In his capacity to give without being used up, he replicates the female economy of breast milk, self-renewing in its abundance; leaving behind Caesar's male economy of limited resources, he becomes like Cleopatra, feeding and renewing the appetite in an endless cycle of gratification and desire, making hungry where most he satisfies. Shakespeare begins the play by giving us an Antony whose compromised manhood allows him to be mistaken for Cleopatra (1.2.76); he ends it by giving us an Antony whose manhood rests on his return to her as the source of his own bounty.

Insofar as the memory of Cleopatra's womb becomes the nurturant space that holds the fullness of Antony's masculine bounty, insofar as she herself becomes the model and the source for that bounty, *Antony and Cleopatra* is Shakespeare's most strenuous attempt within the tragedies to redefine the relationship of masculinity to the maternal, hence to redefine tragic masculinity itself. Through her, Shakespeare allows himself to imagine a fully masculine selfhood that can overflow its own rigid boundaries, a masculinity become enormous in its capacity to share in the female mystery of an endlessly regenerating source of supply, growing the more it is reaped. But this imaginative act is hedged around with conditions. It is, first of all, deeply retrospective, as much a lament for a dream that is irrevocably gone as a recreation of it in the present. In fact, both of the protagonists must die in order for it to be safe: death is not only the image but also the detoxifying agent of merger and of the masculine selfhood achieved through its means.[54] And Cleopatra must, in particular, die for the right reason: she can become the repository of Antony's new masculinity only insofar as she is willing to die specifically for him, simultaneously validating their love and her vision of him. Throughout, she has been presented almost entirely in relation to Antony: although she is allowed far more dramatic force than Shakespeare's other tragic women—we more frequently see matters from her point of view, and the fourth act "female interlude"[55] in which the other women characteristically register their helplessness and self-abandonment is strikingly relocated to the fifth act, where it becomes potent enough to outwit Caesar and to redefine the tragedy in its own terms—the arena of her subjectivity and power has nonetheless been very carefully circumscribed.[56] Her queenship is largely implicit, her subjects invisible; she is one with her feminized kingdom as though it were her body, not her domain. Political power is reserved for the men; Cleopatra's royalty in the end consists of dying well. The entire drama is played out within the context of Caesar's final conquest of Egypt and the establishment of patriarchal rule there.[57] The serious threats to this rule—the Gonerils, Lady Macbeths, Volumnias—are in effect banished from this play; they make a brief cameo appearance under the guise of Fulvia and then are chased off the stage, as though Shakespeare could allow himself to re-imagine a masculinity founded on incorporation of the maternal only by first exorcising their destabilizing power.

But despite all these circumscriptions and qualifications, Shakespeare's imaginative achievement in this play seems to me extraordinary—and extraordinarily liberating. For one fragile moment, Shakespeare is able to imagine the possibility of a maternal space that is neither suffocating nor deforming; now, the memory of Cleopatra's womb becomes the site of her—and his—imaginative power to restore the heroic male whose loss has haunted Shakespeare's plays at least since *Hamlet*, which begins with a mother's sexualized failure to remember right. And unlike *Lear*, where maternal space can be imagined as protective only insofar as it is relentlessly separated from sexuality, here the nurturing female space is profoundly allied with generative process: Antony does not need to remake Cleopatra as the virgin mother in order to rest on her kind nursery. The old images of generation undergo transvaluation in *Antony and Cleopatra*: Hamlet's sun breeding maggots (2.2.181), Othello's "slime / That sticks on filthy deeds" (5.2.149–50), have become Antony's potentiating "fire / That quickens Nilus' slime" (1.3.68–69). The nightmare vision of female sexuality that initiates the tragedies and problem plays has its place in *Antony and Cleopatra*, but that place is partial:[58] the violent language of sexual loathing familiar from *Troilus and Cressida*—language of venereal disease, of fragmentation and spoiled food—makes a muted appearance in Roman accusations of Cleopatra (3.10.11; 3.13.117) but is finally dissolved as Cleopatra becomes a source of wholeness.[59] Through her, the baby cast violently away from Lady Macbeth's breast is restored to nurturance in the end;[60] and the witchcraft of *Macbeth* is recuperated in Cleopatra's enchantment, which makes defect perfection (2.2.231).

In thus realigning masculinity with the maternal, Shakespeare is able to see his way beyond the either/or of *Macbeth* and *Coriolanus*, and beyond the end-stopped genre of tragedy.[61] The whole of *Antony and*

Cleopatra overflows the measure; in its interpretative openness,[62] its expansive playfulness, its imaginative abundance, it seems to me to lead directly to *The Winter's Tale*, where trust in female process similarly bursts the boundaries of the tragic form.[63] Identified with Cleopatra in his longing for Antony, Shakespeare in effect locates the recuperative power of his own art in the female space of her monument, making her imaginative fecundity the model for his own; and in his imaginative alliance with her, he is able to recuperate theater itself, rewriting its dangerous affiliation with the female in *Macbeth* and *Coriolanus*.[64] In Caesar's theater of history—an extension of Malcolm's stripped-down and anti-theatrical theater, where there would be no room for illusion, where even Cleopatra would merely be boyed (5.2.219)—there is no space left for play; but in the spacious theater of Cleopatra's monument, we are given leave to play till doomsday.

8

MASCULINE AUTHORITY AND THE MATERNAL BODY: THE RETURN TO ORIGINS IN THE ROMANCES

Within Shakespeare's career, *Antony and Cleopatra* functions as a fragile pastoral moment. Its pastoral is shorn of the power to bring even its modest gains back to the dominating culture: as Egypt's female pastoral is in the end contained and colonized by Rome, so *Antony and Cleopatra*'s moment of festive possibility is largely contained by the surrounding texts. The generative maternal power celebrated in Cleopatra's recreation of Antony is severely curtailed in *Coriolanus*, where maternal presence is once again construed as paternal absence, where mothers are once again fatal to their sons. This construction is, I have argued, the legacy of *Hamlet*, where the mother's sexual body is itself poisonous to the father on whom the son would base his identity; its consequences are variously played out in the problem plays and tragedies that follow from *Hamlet*. Taken together, the romances can be understood as Shakespeare's final attempt to repair the damage of this legacy, in effect to reinstate the ideal parental couple lost at the beginning of *Hamlet*: the idealized mother is recovered in *Pericles* and *The Winter's Tale*, the idealized father in *Cymbeline* and *The Tempest*. But the attempt at recovery itself reinscribes the conditions of loss: in the plays of maternal recovery, the father's authority must be severely undermined and the mother herself subjected to a chastening purgation; in the plays of paternal recovery, the mother must be demonized and banished before the father's authority can be restored.

From beginning to end, the romances reiterate the terms of *Hamlet*, working and reworking his problematic confrontation with the sexualized maternal body: if *Pericles* begins where Hamlet does, in the psychic world poisoned by female sexuality, *The Tempest* answers his need for a bodiless father immune to the female, able at last to control her unweeded garden. Except for a moment in *The Winter's Tale*, when the generative female space of Cleopatra's monument recurs in Paulina's own sheltering monument, the mother and father lost in *Hamlet* cannot be fully recovered together. Instead, the romances oscillate between them, broadly structured by a series of gendered either/or's: either maternal or paternal authority; either female deity or male; either nature or art; either trust in processes larger than the self or the attempt to control these processes.[1] Each play is in effect written in defensive response to the one before it; each destabilizes the resolution previously achieved, working and reworking the problematic relationship of masculine authority to the female. *Pericles* ends with masculine identity tenuously achieved through recovered trust in (severely chastened) female powers; *Cymbeline* begins with the loss of masculine identity through excessive trust in women. *Cymbeline* ends with the recovery of male authority through distrust of women and the exorcising of their power; *The Winter's Tale* begins with the catastrophic results of that distrust. *The Winter's Tale* ends with the return of a masculine authority grounded in a benignly generative maternal presence; *The Tempest* begins by unmaking that presence, renaming it a witch and exorcising it in order to found its masculine authority in the excision of the female. As masculine identity is alternately defined as founded in, and founded in opposition to, the female, the good mothers of one play breed the bad mothers of the next: Marina and Thaisa give way to the wicked stepmother Queen; Hermione and Paulina give way to Sycorax. And the stakes grow clearer as the pairs duplicate themselves: the mother only tentatively recovered in *Pericles* returns in her full power in *The Winter's Tale*; the masculine authority only tentatively recovered in *Cymbeline* is virtually absolute in *The Tempest*. The last two plays confront one another as though across a vast: if *The Winter's Tale* reopens the possibility of *Antony and Cleopatra*'s pastoral, recreating a space for the sexualized maternal body, *The Tempest* forecloses that space, reinstating the image of absolute paternal authority only by exorcising the witch-mother. The repeated cycle of doing and undoing—*Pericles* to *Cymbeline*, *The Winter's Tale* to *The Tempest*—suggests the deep divisions in Shakespeare's psychic world: even at the end, he cannot fully join together what he has put asunder in *Hamlet*.

As the earliest of the romances, *Pericles* reiterates the terms of *Hamlet*'s dilemma with particular clarity: it begins with a condensed version of his unweeded garden, where everyone is "a little more than kin, and less than kind" and paternal authority is lost; and it ends with a wish-fulfillment satisfaction of what Hamlet most desired, the return of maternal presence purged of its sexual body. The Pericles of the text

Shakespeare inherits[2] is initially very much a son searching for a father: he asks the gods to aid him in his quest to marry Antiochus's daughter, "As I am son and servant to your will"; he phrases his desire for her first as his desire to "be son to great Antiochus" (1.1.24, 27). But his hope of a secure filial identity fixed by his relationship to great Antiochus is undone by his discovery of Antiochus's incestuous relationship with his daughter. This relationship confounds all familial roles, unmaking the distinctions on which they rest:

> I am no viper, yet I feed
> On mother's flesh which did me breed.
> I sought a husband, in which labour
> I found that kindness in a father.
> He's father, son, and husband mild;
> I mother, wife, and yet his child:
> How they may be, and yet in two,
> As you will live, resolve it you.
>   (1.1.65–72)

And its confusions are founded in the female body: though incest may in general be the logical extension of patriarchal power,[3] this particular incest is emphatically the woman's fault. In this version of the story, she—not the king—becomes the deadly answer to the riddle:[4] she is less the victim than the agent of incest ("I sought . . . I found"); her body is the site of the promiscuous mixture that dissolves masculine identity. Although the plot is ostensibly motivated by Pericles's fear of Antiochus's vengeance, imagistically she—not he—is the first bearer of death, the "fair Hesperides, / With golden fruit, but dangerous to be touch'd" (1.1.28–29), the "glorious casket stor'd with ill" (1.1.78). Pericles hopes to shore up his identity by becoming great Antiochus's son, but in her presence, the wished-for father himself turns monstrous: faced with a woman's body that confounds distinctions, unmaking the very identity he seeks and the father through whom he would seek it, he abandons his kingship and takes to the sea as a nameless wanderer.

By the time this text becomes fully "Shakespearean" in 3.1, the initial act of incest has been spectacularly punished (2.4.1–12) and apparently forgotten, and Pericles's identity and the familial relations upon which it is based have apparently stabilized: he has discovered his father's armor, magically plucked out of the sea, and has found a new father in Simonides ("Yon king's to me like to my father's picture" [2.3.37]); he has been furnished with a loving wife and is about to become a father himself. But the Shakespearean portion of the play nonetheless responds profoundly to that initial act, working and reworking the threat it represents;[5] though the incest is ostensibly forgotten, acts 3 through 5 are structured counter-phobically, as though all sexuality were tantamount to that initial act of incest and all families based in the sexual body were similarly contaminated. If the point of origin for the disasters of the first part of the play is the sexualized body of Antiochus's daughter, the point of origin for the disasters of the second is Thaisa's sexualized body, as the sailors half-intuit when they insist that she be thrown overboard; in effect returned to that first body by his wife, Pericles has to begin his wandering all over again. The repetition makes this new round of wandering seem a recapitulation of the first, a response to the original source of danger; and the resolution that allows Pericles's resumption of identity and return to his family entails so thorough a rooting out of sexuality that it confirms this point of origin: if the cure is the excision of the sexual female body, then the disease must have been that body in the first place. In the end Shakespeare will reestablish Pericles's masculine identity only by first detoxifying the contaminating female body and the family relations based on it, in effect undoing the initial trauma of the play and freeing the family from its sexual origin.

Perhaps because he was able to avoid acknowledging the play's initial things of darkness his—after all, he was merely filling out the story begun by Gower or by the unknown author of the first two acts—Shakespeare was able to confront and master the female sexual body more directly in *Pericles* than in any of his other plays. This mastery takes two forms. First of all, the play follows the riddle's directive—"As you will live, resolve it you"—by splitting and dispersing the female body. In the promiscuous mixture of Antiochus's daughter's body, identity had collapsed in on itself in a kind of primal soup; the prerequisites for healing that collapse are the separation of the roles dangerously compacted in her and the assignment of them to discrete persons, who are then forcibly separated from each other, and from their husband-father Pericles.[6] Then, after this separation is achieved, the play exorcises sexuality itself and remakes the sexual family by nonsexual means, permitting it to escape its origin in the problematic maternal body. In effect, the three brought together through the sexual act—mother, father, child—are violently put asunder, each to be desexualized and reborn purified. The wife/mother Thaisa is thrown dead into the sea and remade by benevolent male power in the form of Cerimon, Prospero's precursor; given life at his hands, she is inducted by him into her new role as Diana's vestal (3.4.7–9), ratifying her separation from ordinary generative process. The child Marina is relentlessly separated from her mother, her father, even her nurse; and though she movingly recalls her origins (4.1.13–20, 51–64; 4.2.63), she is not allowed to return to her family until both she and it have been cleansed. Reborn in effect by her double escape from Leonine and the pirates, she emerges from her trial by sea pure enough that she is "able to freeze the god Priapus, and undo a whole generation" (4.6.3–4); and once she has escaped the brothel that is the only space left for generation in this play, she becomes (in Gower's account) a virtual divinity, remaking herself through her art as she "with her neele composes / Nature's own shape" (5.ch.5–6). Thus remade, she can remake her father as well: in a formulation that neatly circumvents the need for any biological mothers, she becomes "thou that beget'st him that did thee beget" (5.1.195), the safely virginal mother that can make him new. Reborn from her, Pericles can emerge from his wandering, once again resuming his kingship and reclaiming the masculine identity initially lost in his confrontation with the sexualized body of Antiochus's daughter. And thus reborn, he can safely reclaim his now thoroughly purified wife: Diana herself appears in order to lead him to her.

The ending of *Pericles* is often read as a celebration of benign generativity and of the restored "natural" family that can replace Antiochus's sterile and "unnatural" one.[7] But what exactly is restored and celebrated? The sacred healing power of Marina is clearly an antidote to the poisonous monstrosity of Antiochus's daughter; her reunion with her father undoes the riddle,[8] offering a safe—and profoundly moving—satisfaction of the desire "to find the mother in the daughter,"[9] a desire at least as old as *Lear*. But this satisfaction is not precisely the same as the restoration of generativity and the sexual family, for the familial relationships initially based in the sexualized female body can be refound only when the family itself has been remade without sexual origin, in effect under the aegis of Diana. Finding the mother in the daughter in fact turns out to be a way of escaping the mother: in both *King Lear* and *Pericles*, maternal presence can be safely recovered in daughters because the daughters are not mothers; virginal and unequivocally subject to their fathers, the daughters protect against the sexualized maternal body, enabling the satisfaction of the desire for merger without its dangers. The deadly mergers of the beginning—the collapse of mother, wife, and daughter in Antiochus's daughter's body and the attendant collapse of Pericles's masculine identity—can be benignly rearticulated in the end, in Pericles's rebirth from his mother/daughter Marina and in his desire to "melt and no more be seen" (5.3.43) in the arms of his recovered wife, because the identities conflated in Antiochus's daughter have been separated out, and because their separation allows for the excision of sexuality from wife and daughter alike. For sexuality itself dangerously confounds distinctions, making—as Hamlet knew—man and wife one flesh; without its excision, the blissful mergers celebrated at the end of *Pericles* would inevitably take us back to the terrible boundary confusions of its beginning.[10]

In recovering the desexualized family, *Pericles* may recover a celebratory language of generation, phrasing its reunions as rebirths. But its language of generation has been purified of the sexual body, especially the sexual female body: in place of the literally pregnant Thaisa, we are given the metaphorically pregnant Pericles ("I am great with woe / And shall deliver weeping" [5.1.105–6]); in place of literal begetting, we are given Marina's symbolic begetting of Pericles. Literal begetting is not part of the celebratory design: whereas Gower counts the fecundity of Pericles and his wife as evidence that honest love thrives— "Honestly his love he spedde, / And had chyldren with his wife"— Shakespeare's couple have no more children and are apparently past begetting;[11] the "night-oblations" Pericles promises to pure Diana (5.3.68–70) seem distinctly a substitute for the resumed nightly rituals of marriage. It is not easy to incorporate marriage and babies back into the country from which sexuality has been banned: even the eventual husband of Marina can be introduced only as a frequenter of the brothel. The rather hugger-mugger betrothal of Lysimachus and Marina—a betrothal to which Marina is allowed no response—carries no celebratory weight at the end, no hint of heirs to rule in Tyre; and our unease about Lysimachus, our slight dismay at the marriage, register the extent to which sexuality of any sort has become taboo in the reformations celebrated at the end of *Pericles*.

What is celebrated, then, is the recuperation of the family, freed from the sexual body. In Barber's famous formulation, "where regular comedy deals with freeing sexuality from the ties of family, these late romances deal with freeing family ties from the threat of sexual degradation";[12] but in *Pericles*, the fact of sexual origin is itself the degradation from which family ties must be freed. Barber writes beautifully about the recovery of relation to sacred maternal presence in *Pericles* and *The Winter's Tale*; but *Pericles* suggests the cost of sacredness to the women made to bear its burden.[13] If Pericles—and Shakespeare—recover in Thaisa and Marina the mother Hamlet lost, the mother whose sacred presence can insure masculine identity, they recover her very much on Hamlet's—or on Lear's—terms: by the subduing of her dangerous body.

Like the Hamlet who sees in his mother's body the dissolution of the father on whom he would found his own identity, Pericles loses an idealized paternal presence and is cast from his moorings by his confrontation with the sexualized female body; and he can return to himself only after that body has been thoroughly desexualized. Whatever the overt sympathy extended to Thaisa in childbirth, the play proceeds to treat her as though her maternity had made her taboo or tainted, allowing her to return only after a long period of penitential cleansing. And her cleansing is managed by the idealized father recreated in Cerimon, the father whose benevolent control over nature and the female body enables this play's "miracle" (5.3.58); in the fantasy of restored paternal presence, final authority is his, as he leads the players off the stage (5.3.84). But masculine authority can be only tenuously recovered in *Pericles*: despite the desexualization of the maternal body, masculine identity remains dangerously fragile, dangerously subject to definition by the female. The riddle of Marina's chaste body replaces the riddle of Antiochus's nameless daughter's; but masculine identity still depends on solving the riddle of the female body.

As though recognizing that the solution of *Pericles* did not go far enough, Shakespeare reworks it in *Cymbeline*, this time exorcising not only the sexualized female body but all traces of the woman's part in men. At first glance, *Cymbeline* seems to move beyond the legacy of *Hamlet*, simultaneously restoring the idealized father lost in Old Hamlet and recuperating the sexualized female body through Imogen, whose supposed adultery is astonishingly dismissed as "wrying but a little" (5.1.5). But I shall argue that *Cymbeline* too replicates this legacy, enacting in its own dramatic disunity the continued incompatibility between paternal authority and the sexualized female body. For *Cymbeline* sets its parts against one another, enabling the restoration of marital harmony only through a defensive structure that protects its male protagonists, deflecting the dangers of one plot onto another where they can be safely managed; and through these displacements, Shakespeare founds masculine identity and authority in a fantasy of pure male family from which women can be wholly excluded. The masculine authority only tenuously reinstated at the end of *Pericles* in Pericles's return to his desexualized family is triumphantly recovered in *Cymbeline*, and its recovery depends specifically on the enactment of two interlocking fantasies: the achievement of the parthenogenetic family in Cymbeline's recovery of his sons, and the exorcism of the woman's part in Posthumus. Taken together, these fantasies seem to provide a secure basis for masculine identity, and hence for the limited return of the female allowed in Imogen. But they enable this return only by continually shifting ground: in the dispersal of plots and the doubling of characters necessary to achieve its defensive ends, *Cymbeline* suggests the radical instability of a masculine identity inevitably defined by the female.

Cymbeline has seemed to many a radically incoherent play.[14] Despite the deliberate bravura of the recognition scene, in which all the plots are yoked violently together, the play does not cohere: that final scene, in which the emotional force of one recognition is constantly being interrupted by another, is diagnostic of the play as a whole, in which the focus of our attention continually shifts, in which we are hard-pressed to decide on the play's dominant action or even its dominant characters. The title leads us to expect that Cymbeline will be at the play's center; and yet, despite his structural importance in the last scene, he is for the most part conspicuously marginal.[15] He is of course literally absent for a great many scenes, especially the most memorable scenes; and though his literal absence might not count for much— Henry IV is absent throughout his name-plays, and yet his role is genuinely central to them—this king is not memorable even when he is on stage. Marginal to the actions that most nearly concern him— the actions of Cloten, the lost sons, and the Roman invasion—he remains a pasteboard figure even when he becomes structurally central in the last scene; and the flatness of his character extends to the characters of those most intimately connected with him: his sons, his queen, her son. For the interest provided by psychological realism, we look to Imogen, Posthumus, and to some extent Iachimo; despite Cymbeline's titular status, the disrupted marriage is at the center of the play for most audiences, and, at least in the beginning, Cymbeline seems to matter chiefly as the initial blocking agent to that marriage. But the marriage plot provides only a very uncertain center: the plot that is virtually the play's only concern for the first two acts is literally marginalized, displaced from the center, nearly disappearing in acts 3 and 4, replaced by the question of the tribute due Rome, by Cloten's various attempts on Imogen, and by the wilderness education of Cymbeline's lost sons. This structural displacement is moreover reiterated in the last scene, where our anticipated pleasure in the reunion of husband and wife is first interrupted by another long account of the wicked Queen's wickedness (5.5.243–60)—an interruption that must be very difficult to stage—and finally displaced altogether by Cymbeline's regaining of his sons and by the business of Rome.

Cymbeline is conspicuously without a center; and its centerlessness seems to me related in ways not merely structural to the absence of Cymbeline himself as a compelling male figure.[16] His absence in the play is so prominent, I think, because he strikes us as absent even when present, absent to himself: as the first scene with Lucius (3.1) makes comically evident, he has simply been taken over by his wicked queen and her son. And the failure of male autonomy portrayed grotesquely in him is the psychological starting point of the play as well as the determinant of its structural weaknesses; despite the prominence of the marriage plot, the repair of that failure is the play's chief business. But this goal is ultimately disastrous for its emotional coherence, and not only because the characters of the marriage plot are far more engaging than the relatively pasteboard characters of the Cymbeline plot: in *Cymbeline*, a plot ostensibly about the recovery of trust in woman and the renewal of marriage is circumscribed by a plot in which distrust of woman is the great lesson to be learned and in which male autonomy depends on the dissolution of marriage. Moreover, the effect of the Imogen-Posthumus plot is everywhere qualified by the effect of the Cymbeline plot, and the two plots seem to be emotionally at cross-purposes: if one moves toward the resumption of heterosexual bonds in marriage, the other moves toward the renewed formation of male bonds as Cymbeline regains both his sons and his earlier alliance with an all-male Rome, the alliance functionally disrupted by his wife. Hence the emotional incoherence of the last scene: the resolution of each plot interrupts the other, leaving neither satisfactorily resolved.

The degree to which the two plots are apparently at cross-purposes— the degree to which their different psychological goals disturb the coherence of the play—is registered in the play's extraordinarily prob-lematic representation of Rome. For the Cymbeline plot, Rome is the ancient seat of honor, the place of the heroic father Caesar who knighted Cymbeline in his youth; for the marriage plot, Rome is the seat of a distinctly Renaissance and Italianate corruption, home to Iachimo's "Italian brain" (5.5.196), the place of a fashionable cynicism about the attemptability of all women. Fifteen centuries separate these places: hence our surprise at finding Lucius and Iachimo in the same army. But they are even further apart psychologically than chronologi-cally. Both Romes represent a male refuge from women: Posthumus's Rome of adolescent male competition over women serves as a defense against women as surely as Cymbeline's adopted fatherland does. But Posthumus must leave his Rome—psychologically as well as literally— before he can find Imogen; Cymbeline must in effect return to his as the sign that he has broken the bond with his wife, and his return will be part of his triumph. And as with the other plot elements, the differences here are not brought into dialogue; they are simply set side by side and ignored.

The different valuations of Rome required by the Cymbeline plot and the marriage plot are, I think, diagnostic of the apparently different valuations of women that govern the two plots. These different valua-tions recur strikingly in the play's contradictory articulations of the

parthenogenesis fantasy that is at its core. Embodied in a variety of
ways throughout the play, the fantasy of parthenogenesis is overtly
articulated twice: once in Posthumus's wish for an alternative means
of generation in which women need not be half-workers (2.4.153–54);
and again in Cymbeline's response to the regaining of his children
("O, what am I? / A mother to the birth of three?" [5.5.369–70]).
Posthumus's fantasy, I shall argue, is part of his brutal rage at Imogen's
power to betray him, to redefine him as his mother could redefine him
through her apparent act of infidelity; it is in effect the moment when
he discovers that he has a mother and that his identity is radically
contingent upon her sexuality. As such, it is the impediment to the
happy ending of the marriage plot; it must apparently be discarded
before Posthumus can recover Imogen and his harmonious sense of
family. But for Cymbeline, the parthenogenesis fantasy *is* the happy
ending.[17] By suggesting that Cymbeline has produced these children all
by himself, the fantasy here—after the death of his wife—makes the
regaining of his children into a reward for his renewed male autonomy:
having finally separated from the wicked stepmother of the play, he is
allowed to take on the power of the mothers and to produce a family
in which women are not half-workers. The fantasy apparently rejected
in the marriage plot is thus enshrined in the Cymbeline plot; to a
striking degree, I shall argue, its fulfillment determines the shape of
that plot.

The parthenogenesis fantasy is central to the Cymbeline plot because
it so perfectly answers the needs of that plot. The Cymbeline plot takes
as its psychological starting point Cymbeline's failure of authority and
his need to separate himself from the woman he trusts over-much. But
insofar as Shakespeare characterizes that woman repeatedly as mother
and stepmother, he infuses the play with the deep anxiety of the mother-
infant bond; Cymbeline's failure of autonomy here is thus associated
with the infant's failure to separate from the overwhelming mother.
And insofar as she inhibits male autonomy, this mother is by definition
evil; the play asks us to blame all Cymbeline's evil on her control over
him. Hence the extent to which everything in his kingdom—and in
Cymbeline himself—rights itself once she is dead and her wickedness
is exposed. She becomes the scapegoat for Cymbeline's misjudgment
and tyranny: her death magically restores what we are presumably
supposed to think of as his original goodness at the same time that it
restores his autonomy; her magical death in fact construes his new
moral stature as his renewed autonomy. Moreover, Cymbeline's recovered autonomy is instantly rewarded by his recovery of his family; and
as if to consolidate his new separation from her, that renewed family
is strikingly male. For despite our own interest in Imogen, despite the

expectations produced by *King Lear*, *Pericles*, and *The Winter's Tale*, even despite Cymbeline's last-minute protestation of his love for Imogen (4.3.5) and his instantaneous affection for her as Fidele (5.5.92ff.), little in the play defines either her loss or her recovery as central to him; the final and most deeply felt recovery is of his sons, not his daughter.[18] It is in fact striking that Cymbeline expresses much more immediate affection for his daughter when she is disguised as the boy Fidele than he has ever expressed for her as a girl; he accepts her more readily as a surrogate son than as a daughter ("Boy, / Thou hast look'd thyself into my grace, / And art mine own" [5.5.93–95]). That even Imogen is recovered first as a son underscores the extent to which the renewed family of the last scene is male. The final moments of the play in fact enact Cymbeline's recovery of three generations of all-male relation: the recovery not only of his lost sons, but also of the wronged Belarius as his "brother" (5.5.400), and of his psychic father, the Roman Octavian who had knighted him in his youth (3.1.70). Insofar as these recoveries are the consequence of his separation from his wicked queen, his triumphant articulation of the parthenogenesis fantasy as he recovers his children is perfectly appropriate: for that fantasy seeks to rob women of their fearful power by imagining sexual generation without mothers. In effect, Cymbeline celebrates his triumphant separation from the mother's power by appropriating that power for himself, consolidating his own power by claiming to absorb hers.

Cymbeline's recovery of his sons can serve as the sign of his separation from his queen and hence his renewed masculine autonomy partly because the sons function in the plot to literalize the transference of power from female to male: Imogen, heir to the kingdom at the beginning of the play (1.1.4), is displaced by them at the end (5.5.374).[19] These sons are particularly fitting agents of this displacement: throughout the play, they have served to define a realm decidedly in opposition to the female, a realm in which they preserve their father's royal masculinity more successfully than he can. Belarius steals the princes long before the wicked queen comes on the scene; nonetheless, these two actions seem causally related in the psychological if not the literal plot. Cymbeline's readiness to believe the worst of Belarius—whom he loved (3.3.58)—signals the breaking of a crucial male bond; and the vacuum caused by the breach of this bond—the loss both of Belarius and of his sons—in effect enables the intrusion of the queen and the implicit substitution of her son for his own. In their absence, the court becomes the site of female corruption, while the pastoral to which Belarius flees enables the continuation of the male bond *in absentia* in a landscape of idealized masculinity. Despite Belarius's brief invocation of "thou goddess, / Thou divine Nature" (4.2.169–70), that is, this is a relentlessly male pastoral,[20] sufficiently hostile to the female that the princes' nurse-mother dies, and Imogen, who can enter its landscape only in male disguise, also dies to them. For female nature in this play is dangerous, its poisonous flowers the province of the wicked stepmother; but here, the princes need fear no poison (3.3.77). Belarius's pastoral is thus constructed as a safe site for masculinity uncontaminated by women; and in this landscape, the masculinity weakened in Cymbeline can thrive. Belarius's rather fatuous and too often repeated assertions that Cymbeline's kingly blood flies out in the extreme martial masculinity of his hidden sons (3.3.79–98; 4.4.53–54) make a claim about Cymbeline's masculinity that we never see verified by the action; the effect is to make us feel that they are purer vials of their father's blood than Cymbeline himself is.

The sons can function as the sign of Cymbeline's recuperated masculine autonomy at the end of the play because they have functioned throughout as a split-off and hence protected portion of his masculinity. The familiar romance plot of the lost children here literalizes this psychic splitting: removed from their father and his susceptibility to corruption by his queen, the boys are raised in an all-male world, virtually uncontaminated by women and hence able to maintain Cymbeline's masculinity pure even while he himself is corrupted. The twice-repeated phrase with which Belarius re-introduces them to their father—"First pay me for the nursing of thy sons" (5.5.323, 325)—confirms their purely male lineage and suggests the extent to which that purity depends on Belarius's appropriation of the female, his capacity to take on female roles and so dispense with women.[21] Given this psychic configuration, it seems to me significant that the princes do not enter the stage for the first time until after Posthumus has ascribed all evil to the woman's part and has wished for a birth exempt from woman. Their mother virtually unmentioned, their nurse dead, reared by a male substitute for her, the princes come close to realizing a safe version of Posthumus's parthenogenesis fantasy; hence the appropriateness of Cymbeline's articulation of his own version of the fantasy—"O, what am I? A mother to the birth of three?"—when they return to him.

The Belarius who nursed Cymbeline's children and thus became the repository of his masculine lineage and his masculine selfhood is welcomed back in language that suggests the renewal of permanent male bonds: "Thou art my brother; so we'll hold thee ever" (5.5.400). Functionally, these bonds can be renewed only in the absence of the queen: Belarius's return (and hence the return of Cymbeline's sons) depends not on Cymbeline's revoking the initial charges of treason against Belarius (these are mentioned only to be ignored by Cymbeline

[5.5.334–36]) but on her death. And that death itself is complexly portrayed as the consequence of an encounter that anticipates and ensures Cymbeline's resumption of triumphant masculinity and true masculine lineage. Cymbeline tells us that the queen has "A fever with the absence of her son; / A madness, of which her life's in danger" (4.3.2–3); we first hear of her illness immediately after we have seen Guiderius kill Cloten. In effect, this encounter causes the death of the queen; and in itself it prefigures Cymbeline's own resumption of autonomous masculinity.

Guiderius clearly sees their contest as the test of his own masculinity ("Have not I / An arm as big as thine? a heart as big?" [4.2.76–77]); and—taking his cue from Cloten's own introduction of himself as "son to th' queen" (4.2.93)—he constructs Cloten's beheading as his return to the maternal matrix: "I have sent Cloten's clotpoll down the stream, / In embassy to his mother" (4.2.184–85). This return moreover follows out the logic of parentage in these two sons: if the princes are an experiment in male parthenogenesis, a portion of Cymbeline's own masculinity split off and preserved from the taint of women, Cloten is an experiment in female parthenogenesis—he is apparently made without a father, the product of his mother's will alone. The struggle between Guiderius and Cloten thus becomes emblematically a struggle between the mother's son and the father's, the false heir and the true. By his triumph over Cloten, Guiderius not only proves his own masculinity but begins the process of regaining his full identity, replacing Cloten as his father's heir, emblematically asserting the rights of the father's son here even as his return will later enact the return of power from female heir to male. But at the same time, the encounter between Guiderius and Cloten epitomizes the struggle within Cymbeline: as Cymbeline's potential heir, Cloten is the sign of his damaged masculinity, the sign of his subjection to female power; and Guiderius is the heir of Cymbeline's true masculine selfhood. The triumph of the true heir causes the queen's death because it signals the dissolution of her power; the princes' next act as the bearers of triumphant masculinity will be the literal rescue of their father. And this rescue simultaneously confirms their masculinity and his. Initially sexually ambiguous, "with faces fit for masks" (5.3.21), the princes are marked as decisively masculine by their military heroics: as Posthumus reports, they "could have turn'd / A distaff to a lance" (5.3.33–34).[22] When we next see them, Cymbeline is asking them to stand by his side (5.5.1), in the place of his dead queen.

In a strategy characteristic of this play's displacements of conflict away from its main characters,[23] Cymbeline's own magical regaining of male autonomy is thus figured through his sons: their participation in an all-male realm and their triumph over the mother's son enact the heroic masculinity that will rescue Cymbeline himself; and through them, the king's own masculine autonomy, preserved apart from the taint of woman, is returned to him. Cymbeline's last-minute decision to renew the payment of tribute to Rome at first seems a deflection from this action; but like the recovery of Belarius and his sons, it serves to ratify Cymbeline's autonomous masculinity by ratifying male bonds. His decision is, first of all, an undoing of his queen's will and hence the sign of his new separation from her:

> My peace we will begin: and Caius Lucius,
> Although the victor, we submit to Caesar,
> And to the Roman empire; promising
> To pay our wonted tribute, from the which
> We were dissuaded by our wicked queen,
> Whom heavens in justice both on her, and hers,
> Have laid most heavy hand.
>
> (5.5.460–66)

Heaven's justice to the queen in effect guarantees the rightness of his decison to resume the male bond disrupted by her wickedness. Cymbeline has already suggested the value of this bond when he tells Lucius, "Thy Caesar knighted me; my youth I spent / Much under him; of him I gather'd honour" (3.1.70–71). Having recovered his sons, and through them his own masculinity, Cymbeline now moves to recover the basis of that masculinity in the past, in the father-figure who enables and is the sign of separation from the overwhelming mother: through union with the imperial Caesar, Cymbeline reconstitutes his bond with that father. This is the bond functionally disrupted by the play's wicked stepmother: hence the need to insist on her wickedness—yet again— as a precondition of reunion.

But as Shakespeare surely knew, he was on tricky ground here, and not just because the Rome with which Cymbeline reunites is sometimes disturbingly Italianate. In the history plays, belief in the fierce independence of England—its autonomy behind its protective sea-barrier— had always been the sign of heroic masculine virtue; and even in this play, belief in patriotic self-sufficiency and hardihood is articulated not only by the villainous queen and her son, but also by Posthumus (2.4.15–26). English concern about lost autonomy is to some extent assuaged by Cymbeline's military victory over Lucius, but—despite the religious resonance of Augustus's Rome or the political resonance of James I's foreign policy and his self-promotion as Augustus— it is not easy to construe reunion with the Rome of this play as an unmitigated triumph for England or for Cymbeline's authority.[24] The troublesome reunion with Rome in fact suggests the conflicted desire for merger even at the root of the desire for autonomy. The soothsayer's words as he responds to Cymbeline—words given prominence by their position very close to the end of the play—suggest what is at stake in this psychologically complex moment:

> The fingers of the powers above do tune
> The harmony of this peace. The vision,
> Which I made known to Lucius ere the stroke
> Of yet this scarce-cold battle, at this instant
> Is full accomplish'd. For the Roman eagle,
> From south to west on wing soaring aloft,
> Lessen'd herself and in the beams o' the sun
> So vanished; which foreshadow'd our princely eagle,
> Th'imperial Caesar, should again unite
> His favor with the radiant Cymbeline,
> Which shines here in the west.
>
> (5.5.467–77)

Cymbeline demonstrates his autonomy—his independence from the will of his queen—by his submission to Caesar, his merger with a male will larger than his own. As at the end of *Hamlet*, the soothsayer registers the presence of a fantasy in which dangerous merger with the female is replaced by a benign and sanctified merger with the male. And that safe merger becomes the foundation of a triumphant male authority:[25] Cymbeline submits to Caesar; but the imperial Caesar vanishes into Cymbeline. Submission to the father rather than the mother miraculously turns out to be the way to increase the son's power and radiance, as the father lends his own radiance to his sun/ son: hence the fantasy registered in the soothsayer's words, the fantasy that reinterprets the son's submission to the father as the father's vanishing into the beams of the son.

The Cymbeline plot celebrates the return of male authority only by destroying the wicked mother and her son, clearing an imaginative space for an all-male family and hence for reunion with the father's Rome; in each of its elements, it realizes Cymbeline's parthenogenetic fantasy. The marriage plot ostensibly moves in the opposite direction, turning Posthumus away from the similar fantasy with which he responds to Imogen's apparent betrayal of him. If Cymbeline moves toward the resumption of male identity and male bonds only by destroying the heterosexual family based in the mother's body, Posthumus moves toward the resumption of that family as the basis for his own male identity, fully conferred on him by his vision in prison. Trust in woman is the key term in both plots,[26] but the two plots differ radically in their valuation of that term: if Cymbeline must learn to distrust—and hence to separate himself from—his wife, Posthumus must learn the trust that enables reunion with his. Not long before Cymbeline naively claims that it would have been vicious to have mistrusted his wife (5.5.65–66), Posthumus gives voice to his renewed trust in one of the most extraordinary moments in Shakespeare: extraordinary because Posthumus recovers his sense of Imogen's worth not—like Othello or Claudio or Leontes—after he has become convinced of her chastity, but before.[27] For once, the fundamental human worth of a woman has become disengaged from the question of her chastity; in the face of his own guilt in ordering her dead, her supposed adultery has become "wrying but a little" (5.1.5).

This extraordinary moment suggests that the reunion of Posthumus and Imogen is contingent psychologically on Posthumus's learning the lesson Imogen teaches Iachimo—"the wide difference / 'Twixt amorous and villainous" (5.5.194–95)—and hence accepting her sexuality as part of her goodness. Partly because such acceptance is rare among Shakespearean heroes—only Antony seems to achieve it, and then only intermittently—it is tempting to see Posthumus's new valuation of Imogen as the culmination of the marriage plot, and hence to see the marriage plot as radically opposed to the Cymbeline plot, as I have thus far argued. But how radical is their opposition in fact? Despite their apparently opposed goals, the marriage plot seems to me to participate strikingly in the conditions of the Cymbeline plot, conditions that insist on the subjugation of female power and the return of authority to the male; like the Cymbeline plot, it takes as its psychic premise the anxieties expressed through the parthenogenesis fantasy, anxieties about male identity and female power to define the male. These anxieties—manifest in Cymbeline's subjection to his queen—are initially encoded in the marriage plot through Posthumus's situation as Imogen's unacknowledged husband. Deprived at birth of the familial identifiers that would locate him, psychologically and socially, Posthumus defines himself and is defined for others largely by Imogen's choice of him.[28] She is "that which makes him both without and within" (1.5.8–9): "his virtue / By her election may be truly read" (1.1.52–53); "he must be weighed rather by her value than his own" (1.5.13–14). She can make or unmake him: radically deprived of family, dependent on her love for his position, he has no secure self; he cannot return any gift that is worth what he has received (1.2.50–52).

The marriage plot rejoins husband and wife; but it does so only through an action designed to reverse their initial positions. Posthumus begins the play radically placeless, radically subject to definition by his wife and queen; he ends the play an exemplar of heroic masculinity, upholder of the kingdom, rescuer of the king. The Imogen he leaves behind is a powerful and powerfully passionate woman, the only heir to a king; the Imogen he returns to is the faithful page of a defeated soldier, about to lose her kingdom to her brother. The structural chiasmus creates the suspicion that, as in the Cymbeline plot, Posthumus's gain requires Imogen's loss. Posthumus's return to Imogen is in fact thoroughly mediated by her victimization, as though that victimization were its precondition: he returns to her in imagination only when he thinks her dead, only when he is given safe passage by the bloody cloth that ambiguously signifies both her wounded sexuality and his punishment of her. And his act of violence toward her immediately before they are reunited disturbingly underscores this precondition: he strikes her, punishing her as the upstart he might initially have been mistaken for ("Thou scornful page, / There lie thy part" [5.5.228–29]). His violence here literally enables their reunion—Pisanio reveals Imogen's identity only because he thinks Posthumus may have killed her—and it suggests Posthumus's need to dominate Imogen physically, as he has dominated her psychologically, before that reunion can take place. Imogen's masochistic response—"Think that you are upon a rock, and now / Throw me again" (5.5.262–63)—moreover does little to qualify his domination: in fact the whole play has brought her to this moment of submission.[29]

Initially, Imogen is a wonderfully vivid presence, shrewd, impetuous, passionate, and very much the proprietress of her own will. Unlike the Posthumus who allows himself to be defined by events—including the event of his marriage—Imogen is extraordinarily forceful in defining herself and her relation to father and husband. Her initial election of Posthumus against her father's will, her contempt at his various attempts to bully her, her easy penetration of Iachimo's attempts at seduction, her initial anger when she hears Posthumus's charges against her (3.4.41–45): all demonstrate her extraordinary self-possession; though as fiercely loving and loyal as any of Shakespeare's idealized women, her self-determination is a far cry from their characteristic self-abnegation. But their self-abnegation is precisely what the play brings her to. The crucial moment in this process seems to me her turn from anger to a masochistic self-sacrifice in her response to Posthumus's accusation. As she moves from the righteous indignation of "False to his bed? What is it to be false?" (3.4.41) to "When thou see'st him, / A little witness my obedience. Look, / I draw the sword myself" (3.4.66–68), she charts the trajectory of her submission; a moment later, she will proclaim her heart "obedient as the scabbard" (3.4.81) to receive the sword. Newly practicing a masochistic self-abnegation phrased as obedience to male will, she bizarrely redefines even the grounds for her anger at Posthumus: now she chides him not for betraying her love but for having caused her "disobedience 'gainst the king my father" (3.4.90). Given her new emphasis on obedience to male authority, the action Imogen is about to undergo takes on the configuration of a punishment for her initial act of self-definition: her willingness now to obey Posthumus's sword becomes in effect the righting of her first disobedience of her father, the righting of the very vividness of selfhood that had attracted us to her in the first place.

In asking her to give up the habits of a princess as he counsels her to take on male disguise, Pisanio summarizes the process of submission: "You must forget to be a woman; change / Command into obedience" (3.4.156–57). Because she has commanded as a woman, Imogen must simultaneously give up her command and her femaleness, as though her male disguise were the sign of her penitential obedience to male power. And it is: by the end of the scene, her female selfhood has undergone a process of radical constriction. Helpless, she accepts Pisanio's plan to make herself into Lucius's page, doubly putting herself under male management; when we next see her, her femaleness itself will be submerged in her disguise. The degree to which similar disguises serve to enable the selfhood of the earlier women in the comedies emphasizes the reduction of Imogen's power here: far more than any of Shakespeare's other transvestite women, she will feel her own inadequacy as a man; the disguise reveals her not as a powerfully self-directing woman but as a hopelessly inadequate man. As she takes on the disguise, she gives up command with a vengeance, becoming uncharacteristically directionless, the nearly passive recipient of her brothers' kindness, Cloten's sexual fantasy, and the queen's poison. The masculine disguise that initially seemed a way for her to find Posthumus and hence perhaps regain him (3.4.150)—as her predecessors in the source stories do—becomes instead the sign of her passivity, her willingness to allow events to define her. Settling into helpless androgyny, she gives up her own powerful femininity, entering willingly into the realm from which women have been displaced, into the plot that has displaced her own: "I'ld change my sex to be companion with them, / Since Leonatus false" (3.7.60–61).[30] From this point on, she will no longer generate the action through her own will; that role increasingly passes from her to Posthumus, as his repentance, his vision, and his heroism become the focus and motivator of the action.

Imogen begins the play as its primary defining figure, defining herself, her husband, and the dramatic focus for the audience; by the end, she has learned her place. She virtually disappears between 4.2 and 5.5, displaced by the husband she had initially defined, the father she had initially defied. In its treatment of her, that is, the play enacts a revenge that in its own way parallels Posthumus's revenge, scourging her sexual body even while insisting that he repent of his violence. Her turn toward masochism may be psychologically plausible when read within the boundaries of her own subjectivity;[31] but it is nonetheless accompanied by something like the play's sadism toward her:[32] robbed of her own powerful selfhood, put entirely under male command, she becomes imaginatively the victim not only of Posthumus's revenge and Cloten's rape fantasy but also of her author's cruelty. During the play's penitential middle section, the woman who easily penetrated Iachimo's deceit cannot tell the body of Cloten from her husband's; the woman who had directed our perceptions becomes the object of our pity precisely for her helpless inability to see what we already know. Harried, degraded, she gives up command with a vengeance, becoming entirely subject to those around her. And despite the happy ending of the marriage plot, there is no sign that she will be allowed to regain her own powerful selfhood; indeed, the happy ending is radically contingent on her self-loss, on the ascendancy of male authority and the circumscription of the female. The tapestries of Imogen's bedchamber tell the story of "proud Cleopatra, when she met her Roman, / And Cydnus swell'd above the banks" (2.4.70–71); but *Cymbeline* is the undoing of that story, the unmaking of female authority, the curtailing of female pride, as much for Imogen as for the wicked queen.

In veiled form, then, both plots enact the recuperation of male power over the female. In this recuperation, the marriage plot oddly replicates the conditions governing Cymbeline's parthenogenetic fantasy: insofar as the play successfully turns Posthumus away from his rage at Imogen and redirects him toward heterosexual union, it does so only by first unmaking woman's power to form or deform man. And in this unmaking, it answers the conditions of Posthumus's own parthenogenesis fantasy: the radical uncertainty about male identity central to both plots is in fact distilled in his "woman's part" speech; and even while it is ostensibly the marker of the psychic place Posthumus must leave, that speech dictates the terms of his return. For Posthumus recovers his marriage at the end only through a series of defensive strategies designed to excise the woman's part in him: his fantasized revenge against Imogen, her harrying by events beyond her control, and the scapegoating of Iachimo and especially Cloten all serve to preserve his manhood intact, enabling his return by first confirming his pure masculine identity.

The woman's part speech cuts to the heart of anxiety about male identity and female power, associating both with the mother's capacity to unmake the son's identity through her sexual fault:

> Is there no way for men to be, but women
> Must be half-workers? We are all bastards,
> And that most venerable man, which I
> Did call my father, was I know not where
> When I was stamp'd. Some coiner with his tools
> Made me a counterfeit: yet my mother seem'd
> The Dian of that time: so doth my wife
> The nonpareil of this.
>
> (2.4.153–60)

Posthumus's logic takes as its starting point a rational uncertainty about male lineage and hence about the patriarchal structures on which identity is based: insofar as Posthumus's identity depends on his status as his father's son, his mother's infidelity would make him counterfeit. So far, so good: but the parthenogenesis fantasy of the opening lines makes bastardy contingent not on the mother's infidelity but on her mere participation in the act of procreation. The gap between the opening question—"Is there no way for men to be, but women / Must be half workers?"—and the answer—"We are all bastards"—contains a submerged *if*: if there is no way for men to come into being without the half-work of women, then we are all bastards. As in *King Lear*, bastardy is the sign of the mother's presence in the child: only the pure lineage of the father, uncontaminated by the mother, would guarantee legitimacy. The rational concern with patriarchal lineage thus covers a fantasy in which maternal sexuality *per se* is always infidelity, always a displacement of the father and a corresponding contamination of the son; in effect, through her participation in the procreative act, the mother makes the son in her own image. Hence Posthumus's hysterical desire to unmake her part in him:

> Could I find out
> The woman's part in me—for there's no motion
> That tends to vice in man, but I affirm
> It is the woman's part.
>
> (2.4.171–74)

But why should the supposed infidelity of his wife return Posthumus to his mother and hence to the woman's part in him? And what is this woman's part? The association of the beloved's sexual fault with the mother's is of course familiar from *Troilus and Cressida*, but here it functions less as a marker for the soiling of the idealized mother than as shorthand for the covert equation that makes female sexuality— legitimate or illegitimate—responsible for the sexual fault in man: as though Imogen's sexuality evoked the woman's part in Posthumus, making him acknowledge himself (for the first time) as born of woman. Posthumus will go on to associate the woman's part with all vices great and small, "all faults that name, nay, that hell knows" (2.4.179); but in his first articulation, it is associated specifically with the sexual fault, the "motion" that tends to "vice" in man.[33] In this formulation, sexuality itself is— familiarly—the inheritance from the woman's part in procreation; and as Posthumus recoils from that part in himself, the "part" takes on a specifically anatomical tinge, as though Posthumus— like Lear—catches a terrifying glimpse of the "mother"[34] within.

The signs of Imogen's sexuality return Posthumus to the woman's part in himself; and his—and the play's—response is to recast her sexuality in the nightmare image of her copulation with Iachimo, and then to exorcise it, remaking her in the image of a perfect chastity. As in *Othello*, the accusation of adultery gives Posthumus a locus for outrage and an occasion for revenge, permitting the excision of sexual danger. His letter to Pisanio suggests what is at stake:

> Thy mistress, Pisanio, hath played the strumpet in my bed: the testimonies whereof lie bleeding in me. I speak not out of weak surmises, but from proof as strong as my grief, and as certain as I expect my revenge. That part thou, Pisanio, must act for me, if thy faith be not tainted with the breach of hers.
>
> (3.4.21–27)

As in *Othello*, crime and punishment coalesce, and the locus of the crime is the marriage bed: like Othello's reference to the lust-stained bed (*Othello*, 5.1.36), Posthumus's charge that Imogen has played the strumpet in his bed can refer equally well to the supposed act of adultery and to the act of marital consummation.[35] The vivid physicality of his response to her strumpetry—"the testimonies whereof lie bleeding in me"—in fact conflates the two acts, as though this new evidence of her sexuality replayed an earlier scene in which he was left bleeding in bed. The incipient pun on "testimonies"[36] moreover specifies and localizes the attack: in this fantasy, Imogen has in effect reversed the traditional marriage-bed scene, inflicting sexual damage on him, marking his genitals with the blood she should have shed, as though literalizing the woman's part in him at the site of his maleness. No wonder that he should wish to make her bleed, and should look to a Pisanio "not tainted with the breach of hers" to accomplish his revenge: untainted and undamaged by her sexualized "breach,"[37] Pisanio can reenact Posthumus's part in the consummation, in effect redoing the sexual act so that he inflicts the damage and she lies bleeding. The "bloody cloth" (5.1.1) that is the "sign" of revenge (3.4.127) alludes, like Othello's handkerchief, to the bloodied wedding sheets, but it reverses the act that left Posthumus's testimonies bleeding there: in effect, it signals the excision of the woman's part in him and the punitive reinscription of it in Imogen. Enforcing her female wound, it reassuringly makes the violence all his: and through its allusion to menstrual blood, it reassures him that she—not he—is the bearer of the woman's part.

As the sign of this reassurance, the cloth mediates Posthumus's return to Imogen: when we next see him, he is fondling it, keeping it close to him, "for I wish'd / Thou shouldst be colour'd thus" (5.1.1–2). Colored thus, it is the sign that her dangerous sexuality has been subdued. And although the play protects Posthumus from the literal fulfillment of his revenge, it nonetheless achieves the same subduing through another route, carrying out his revenge in a mitigated form. I have already suggested the extent to which the vigorous and passionate woman we have seen in Imogen is subsumed and contained in her male disguise: as though complicit with Posthumus's wish, the play remakes for him an Imogen stripped of her vibrant sexuality, as she is stripped of her political and dramatic power. This is in fact the Imogen that Posthumus has wanted all along: well before the accusation of infidelity, virtually as soon as he has left her—a little too quickly, many feel[38]—he proclaims himself "her adorer, not her friend" (1.5.65–66), as though her sexuality were taboo even for him.[39] He enters Rome apparently already in the habit of proclaiming her "less attemptable" (1.5.58) than all other women; according to Iachimo, "He spoke of her, as Dian had hot dreams / And she alone were cold" (5.5.180–81). We have initially seen Imogen as a vibrantly passionate and faithful woman—a woman who (like Desdemona) disobeys her father to choose her husband and then publicly defends him, who pleads with that husband to "stay a little" (1.2.40) as Juliet, Cressida, and Cleopatra plead with their lovers, who imagines the parting kiss forestalled by her father's arrival. But in the "woman's part" speech, Posthumus splits Imogen apart, recasting her sexuality in the form of the strumpet who welcomes Iachimo's attack and her fidelity in the cold chastity that would forbid even lawful pleasure ("Me of my lawful pleasure she restrain'd, / And pray'd me oft forbearance. . . . I thought her / As chaste as unsunn'd snow [2.4.161–65]).[40] And the only Imogen who can return to Posthumus is the product of this split: though we might be tempted to read the discrepancy between the Imogen we have seen and the cold Imogen of Posthumus's imagination as the product of his psychic need, the play nonetheless embraces that need. Iachimo claims that he has learned from Imogen the "wide difference / 'Twixt amorous and villainous" (5.5.194–95), but the play itself fails to embody this distinction in the Imogen who returns: having exorcised her sexuality through the image of the whore, it allows her in the end only a helpless fidelity utterly purged of erotic power. Like the threatening femaleness permanently submerged in her disguise, her amorousness itself remains off-limits, its sacrifice a precondition of the happy ending.

This compliance with Posthumus's wishes is characteristic of the ways in which the play protects Posthumus, shielding him from the consequences of his own violent desires, while nonetheless permitting their satisfaction. Through a strategy of displacement and dispersal, the play persistently shifts these desires away from him, relocating them in Iachimo and especially Cloten. We can see this process in miniature in the "woman's part" speech, where Posthumus's vivid imaging of Iachimo's sexual villainy— "Perchance he spoke not, but / Like a full-acorn'd boar . . . / Cried 'O!' and mounted" (2.4.167–69)— falls between his portrayal of his own sexual arousal (2.4.162–64) and his desire to excise the woman's part in himself (2.4.171). In his response to the "rosy pudency" of Imogen's chastity, he in effect constructs himself a would-be rapist, "warm'd" like Saturn by her chaste coldness; and then he displaces his sexuality onto Iachimo, who mounts Imogen in his stead, enacting his desire. But this is the role that the play—not just Posthumus—assigns to Iachimo. For Iachimo becomes the bearer of Posthumus's sexual desires and the one unmanned by them (5.2.2); in effect, he acts out these desires for Posthumus, hence maintaining Posthumus's purity. In his approach to Imogen, he enacts the psychic splitting that governs Posthumus's relationship to her: his vivid fantasy of the whore with whom Posthumus slavers lips (1.7.105) replicates Posthumus's sense of the sexual woman as soiled whore; and Imogen herself becomes a forbidden holy object, "alone th'Arabian bird" (1.7.17), her eyes "azure lac'd / With blue of heaven's own tinct" (2.2.22–23), a "heavenly angel" (2.2.50). And like the Saturn whom Posthumus imagines in himself, Iachimo's desire is to spoil this chaste object, feeding his sight on her exposed body. As she lies exposed to his— and our—eyes, she is voyeuristically soiled by him: though full of the sense of awe her being creates, the scene is nonetheless the first stage in the play's humiliation of her. With Posthumus's desires thus deflected onto Iachimo, Posthumus himself can regain his purified manhood, easily triumphing over the Iachimo who has been his surrogate.[41]

But if the play initially locates Posthumus's desires in Iachimo, it ultimately locates them in Cloten, the play's literal rapist; through him, the woman's part in Posthumus is ritually defined and exorcised. The first business of the play seems to be to distinguish between Posthumus and Cloten (1.1.16–21); and yet the distinction between them keeps threatening to collapse. Cloten plans his rape of Imogen in part as an act of aggression against Posthumus, whose beheaded body is to serve him as a pillow during the act; that Cloten himself, rather than Posthumus, is beheaded suggests his nature as surrogate.[42] In effect, Posthumus's own violent sexuality is displaced onto the loathsome person of Cloten and given its appropriate punishment: hence the logic through which Cloten dresses in Posthumus's clothing as he attempts to rape Imogen, and hence Imogen's inability to tell their bodies apart. For Cloten *is* Posthumus's body, Posthumus's body without its head: through him, the play constructs the male sexual body itself as the woman's part that must be excised. Cloten is the play's purebred mother's son, the son whose traces Posthumus feared in himself; and as he approaches his beheading, he is increasingly identified with the male genitals, becoming a "walking phallus,"[43] "an arrogant piece of flesh" (4.2.127), finally interchangeable with his own head— "Cloten's clotpoll" (4.2.184)—at his beheading. And with the rigorous psychic justice exacted by this fantasy, his punishment amounts to a kind of castration: the father's son cuts off his flesh to send it back in embassy to his mother (4.2.150–53, 185). For that flesh was hers to begin with: as with Shakespeare's other mothers' sons—the rapists Charon and Demetrius at the beginning of his career, the would-be rapist Caliban at the end—his violent sexuality is construed as derivative from the woman's part, an extension of her will in him.[44] And insofar as Cloten becomes the surrogate for Posthumus's sexualized body, he takes the place of the woman's part that Posthumus seeks to find and destroy in himself; his beheading serves as the final exorcism of that part.

In the "woman's part" speech, Imogen's "rosy pudency" had threatened to turn Posthumus into a Cloten, registering the woman's part in him through his own sexual desire; her sexuality, like his mother's, would in effect mark him as a mother's son, no longer his father's legitimate heir. Without Cloten to take on the burden of his sexuality, Posthumus himself would collapse into Cloten, and the distinction on which the marriage—and the play—depends would be undone. But the play rescues Posthumus, displacing the male sexual body—the derivative of the woman's part—from him and relocating it in Cloten; and then it visits on Cloten the punishment deflected from Posthumus. Cloten's psychological function in relation to Posthumus thus takes as its starting point the same parthenogenesis fantasy that governs the Cymbeline plot: if Cloten's death serves in the Cymbeline plot as the point at which father's son triumphs over mother's, and hence as the point of origin for Cymbeline's restored masculinity, it serves in the marriage plot to liberate Posthumus from the woman's part by proxy. With Cloten's death, Posthumus is free to reenter the stage and begin his reconstruction as father's son; and as father's son, he can safely regain an Imogen who is powerless, an Imogen from whom there is no longer anything to fear.

This reconstruction is the business of the last act. Posthumus's decision to fight in disguise against the part he comes with is initially defined as one of his rites of penitence (5.1.24–26); but the disguise itself is designed to show him forth as one of the Leonati, worthy through his manliness to be his father's son ("Let me make men know / More valour in me than my habits show. / Gods, put the strength o' th' Leonati in me!" [5.1.29–31]). Fighting unknown, he can establish a secure masculine identity in no way indebted to Imogen's choice of him, dependent rather on his status as heroic warrior and his alliance with a series of patriarchal families: after easily defeating Iachimo, whose "manhood" has been "taken off" by his sexual guilt (5.2.1–2), his next action is to ally himself with the lost princes in rescuing the father from whom they are all estranged. And after this rescue, he is rewarded by a vision of the renewed patriarchal family,[45] a vision that systematically undoes the horror of the woman's part speech:

> Solemn music. Enter (as in an apparition) Sicilius Leonatus, father to Posthumus, an old man, attired like a warrior, leading in his hand an ancient matron (his wife, and mother to Posthumus) with music before them. Then, after other music, follow the two young Leonati (brothers to Posthumus) with wounds as they died in the wars. They circle Posthumus round as he lies sleeping.
>
> (5.4.29)

The woman's part speech had recorded the loss of both his chaste mother and his venerable father as ideal images through the action of an uncontrolled female sexuality; now—in the family asexually begotten by a "grandsire," Sleep (5.4.123)[46]—that sexuality is firmly under control. Posthumus's father—dressed in the garb that epitomizes his successful masculinity—now leads his mother by the hand; reconstructed as a matron, her sexuality is now in the service of the patriarchal family, producing warrior sons as the sign of male lineage. This righting of hierarchy is ratified by Jupiter's appearance: as the play's ultimate strong father, he reassures us that events have been under his control all along. Under the double guidance of two asexual fathers—grandsire sleep and the Jupiter who "coin'd" Posthumus's life (5.4.23)—Posthumus undoes the horrific vision of the "coiner with his tools" who made him counterfeit (2.4.157–58), establishing his new identity as father's son by establishing a pure male lineage, subduing the woman's part in his family and in himself.

The vision is troubling not only because of the oft-debated quality of its verse and the somewhat tacked-on quality of Jupiter's reassurances, but also because it condenses and hence makes visible the contrary impulses that govern the play. Posthumus falls asleep crying out for renewed intimacy with Imogen ("O Imogen, / I'll speak to thee in silence" [5.4.28–29]); when the audience hears the solemn music announcing the presence of the supernatural, surely the expectation is that Posthumus will be given what he has asked for, some form of communion with or reassurance about Imogen. Instead, he is given a graphic representation of the successfully patriarchal family. This shift epitomizes both the displacement of the marriage plot by the Cymbeline plot and the conditions that enable Imogen's return: by the end, according to Jupiter's prophecy, Imogen's sexual body has been unmade and she has been reduced to a "piece of tender air" (5.5.447), while Posthumus has been enlarged to a young lion.

The fragile recoveries of the marriage plot thus rest on a series of accommodations that radically reduce Imogen's power, displace both sexuality and its appropriate punishment away from Posthumus, and celebrate his renewed status as father's son; they rest, that is, on a thorough undoing of the fantasy of contamination by the "woman's part." If the Cymbeline plot magically does away with the problematic female body and achieves a family and a masculine identity founded exclusively on male bonds, the marriage plot manages somewhat less magically to achieve the same ends: in their very different styles, both enact versions of a world in which women need not be half-workers. Despite their ostensibly opposed goals, the plots interlock and are driven by the same anxieties: Posthumus's "woman's part" speech is apparently disowned by the play, and yet its terms generate the Cymbeline plot. Behind Posthumus's response to Imogen's imagined infidelity looms the figure of the father weakened or displaced by the overwhelming wife/mother: looms precisely Cymbeline and his queen. The son lost there—made counterfeit through the father's loss of authority—is epitomized by Cloten, who is the embodiment of the mother's son Posthumus fears in himself. And the pure father's son Posthumus wishes to be is localized in Guiderius and Arviragus, in alliance with whom Posthumus recovers his manhood. The elements of the Cymbeline plot thus function as two-dimensional projections of the fears condensed in the "woman's part" speech; the marriage plot is interrupted by the Cymbeline plot because the Cymbeline plot enacts in exaggerated form the fears about masculine identity and contamination by the female that disrupt marriage.

In the end, despite the violent yoking together of opposites in the recognition scene, *Cymbeline* acts out the oscillating pattern of the romances as a whole: the plot that would recover trust in the female is frustrated and baffled by the plot that would recover masculine authority; the two remain incompatible. And yet this very incompatibility allows the two plots to protect one another: the recovery of Imogen conceals the extent to which the Cymbeline plot grounds its masculine authority on the excision of the female; the Cymbeline plot provides the context in which Imogen can safely return. For the Cymbeline plot fulfills the conditions of her return, enabling the marriage by shielding the marriage plot from responsibility for those conditions: as the shadowy projections of the Cymbeline plot serve to protect Posthumus, exorcising the woman's part in him and enabling his pure manhood, they serve to chasten Imogen, punishing her for her sexuality and remaking her in boy's clothes, the woman's part in her utterly subdued.

These conditions are ultimately those set by *Hamlet*: in response to the sexualized maternal body's unmaking of paternal authority through its poisonous mixture, Hamlet had said "no mo marriage"; and marriage here becomes possible only with the undoing of that body and the resumption of an absolute masculine authority. If *Pericles* attempts to recover the possibility of marriage by splitting the wife into the asexual daughter and the asexual mother, hence doing away with the threat of sexuality, the fantasy solution of *Cymbeline* is more radical: it would attempt to do away with the female body altogether. Here marriage can be recovered only in the context of a parthenogenetic fantasy that denies the place of the maternal body, allowing safe satisfaction of Hamlet's or Macbeth's or Coriolanus's desire not to have been born of woman; even Posthumus turns out to have been untimely ripped from his mother's womb (5.4.45). But as the wild play of doubling and redoubling suggests, this fantasy is hard to sustain; and as though recognizing its hopelessness, Shakespeare returns in *The Winter's Tale* to the point of origin in the problematic female body. And though *The Winter's Tale* reiterates the shape of *Pericles*—separating husband, daughter, and wife/mother, allowing for reunion only after a sustained period of penitence—its ends are quite different: now the fear of the maternal body, not that body itself, is what must be cleansed; now the recovery of the virginal daughter proves to be an inadequate substitute for the recovery of the sexual mother and wife. For paternal authority must ultimately be founded in that recovery, whatever the dream-satisfactions of *Cymbeline*: initially Leontes could see in Paulina's management only the signs of her emasculating control; but in the end, he can find himself as husband and father only by giving himself into her hands, rediscovering his masculine potency and authority through trust in her and in the female processes she speaks for.

If *Cymbeline* ends with the magical restoration of paternal authority and the fantasy-accomplishment of a parthenogenetic family in which women need not be half-workers, *The Winter's Tale* begins with the pregnant female body. In its opening lines, the play seems initially to replicate aspects of Belarius's male pastoral, giving us the image of the "natural" male world from which women have been wholly excluded: in the dialogue between Camillo and Archidamus, the "rooted" affection (1.1.23) between the brother-kings and the healing powers of fathers' sons take center stage, with no mention of wives or mothers, and certainly no need for daughters. Though there is tension in this world[47]—the hospitality is distinctly competitive and leaves a residue of anxiety about indebtedness, the kings can "branch" into "great difference" from their common root—nonetheless there seems "not in the world either malice or matter to alter" their love (1.1.33–34). Hermione's entrance—perhaps literally between the two kings?—disrupts this male haven. The visual impact of her pregnant body[48] inevitably focuses attention on her, reminding the audience of what has been missing from the gentlemen's conversation; and her body immediately becomes the site of longing and terror, its very presence disruptive of male bonds and male identity.

Even before Leontes's jealousy makes Hermione's pregnant body the sign of betrayal between the brothers, Polixenes has recast the covert tensions of the first scene in its image:

> Nine changes of the watery star hath been
> The shepherd's note since we have left our throne
> Without a burden. Time as long again
> Would be fill'd up, my brother, with our thanks;
> And yet we should, for perpetuity,
> Go hence in debt: and therefore, like a cipher
> (Yet standing in rich place) I multiply
> With one 'We thank you' many thousands moe
> That go before it.
>
> (1.2.1–9)

"Nine changes," "watery star," "burden," "fill'd up": in Polixenes's opening lines, anxieties about indebtedness and separation are registered through the imagery of pregnancy,[49] as though Hermione's body provided the language for the rupture in their brotherhood. In fact, as Polixenes goes on to tell us in his mythologized version of the kings' childhood, the sexualized female body has already been assigned this role:

Pol. We were as twinn'd lambs that did frisk i' th' sun,
And bleat the one at th'other: what we chang'd
Was innocence for innocence: we knew not
The doctrine of ill-doing, nor dream'd
That any did. Had we pursu'd that life,
And our weak spirits ne'er been higher rear'd
With stronger blood, we should have answer'd heaven
Boldly 'not guilty', the imposition clear'd
Hereditary ours.

Her.   By this we gather
You have tripp'd since.

Pol.   O my most sacred lady,
Temptations have since then been born to's: for
In those unfledg'd days was my wife a girl;
Your precious self had not yet cross'd the eyes
Of my young play-fellow.

                            (1.2.67–80)

Once again, the female body disrupts the idealized male pastoral, becoming the sign of "great difference" between the kings: "crossing"[50] the eyes of the young playfellows, Hermione and the unnamed woman who will be Polixenes's wife unmake their symbiotic innocence, plummeting them simultaneously into adult differentiation—now there is "my" and "your" where there had been only "we" and "our"—and into their newly sexualized bodies, in effect recording the fall in them as their phallic spirits are higher reared with stronger blood.[51] Polixenes may call Hermione "most sacred lady," but he makes her body the locus and the sign of division and original sin, as Hermione herself is quick to note (1.2.80–82). Moreover, her visible pregnancy stages the submerged logic of his account of original sin: temptations have been born to us, her presence suggests, because we have been born to them, acquiring original sin at the site of origin.

Both in Polixenes's opening speech and in his pastoral myth, the sexualized female body is the sign of male separation and loss. Moreover, in its very fullness, that body becomes the register of male emptiness. The final metaphorics of Polixenes's opening speech bizarrely transform an expression of his indebtedness to Leontes into an expression of chronic male indebtedness to the female in the procreative act: "like a cipher / (Yet standing in rich place) I multiply / With one 'We thank you' many thousands moe / That go before it." Nothing in himself, he is able to multiply only when he stands in a rich place: his computational joke barely conceals anxiety about the male role in procreation, an anxiety made visible on stage in the rich place that is Hermione's body.[52] But in thus figuring male emptiness and female fullness, Polixenes allows for a transvaluation of sexuality and of the female body. If women are the first temptation, if the phallic rearing of the spirits with higher blood is the sign of the fall in Polixenes's mythologized account of childhood, here it is only by such standing in rich place that man becomes generative: the rich place itself confers value on him. These sharply contrasting attitudes toward sexuality and toward the female body that engenders it mark the trajectory of the play: from an idealized male pastoral to a pastoral richly identified with the generative potential of the female body; from a sterile court in which the maternal body and the progeny who bear its signs must be harried to death to a court in which that body can be restored, its regenerative sanctity recognized and embraced.

If Polixenes's initial speeches give us the image of what must be cured before the play can end happily and hint at the direction from which cure will come, Leontes's psyche is presented as the locus of the disease. Leontes's jealousy erupts out of nowhere and breaks his world apart, as it breaks the syntax and rhythms of his own speeches apart; in the violence and obscurity of its expression, it draws the audience into its own sphere, causing us to snatch at nothings, to reconstruct the world (as Leontes himself does) in a reassuringly intelligible image. Any attempt to explain its strangeness away or to make it wholly coherent violates the dramatic principles through which it communicates itself to us; Shakespeare has deliberately left its expression fragmentary and incoherent, the better to engage us in its processes, making us—like Leontes—communicate with dreams (1.2.140).[53] But whether or not we think we can pinpoint the onset of the jealousy or the exact progress of its etiology, it is far from the psychologically unmotivated "given" of the plot that it is sometimes taken to be.[54] For the jealousy erupts in response to the renewed separation from a mirroring childhood twin and the multiple displacements and vulnerabilities signaled by Hermione's pregnant body;[55] it localizes and psychologizes the myth of loss embedded in Polixenes's version of Eden. And through it, Shakespeare floods the play with the fantasies that have haunted his male protagonists since *Hamlet*, articulating with astonishing economy and force the anguish of a masculinity that conceives of itself as betrayed at its point of origin, a masculinity that can read in the full maternal body only the signs of its own loss. In Leontes, Shakespeare condenses the destructive logic of tragic masculinity itself; and then, wrenching the play out of the obsessional space of Leontes's mind, he moves beyond tragedy.

In the fantasies given a local habitation in Leontes's jealousy, the fall into original sin is once again registered through the rupture of an idealized mirroring relationship with the brother-twin; genital sexuality once again marks the moment of separation and contamination by women. Polixenes's fantasy of twinship functions in effect as Leontes's prehistory, the shaky foundation from which his jealousy erupts: it is his guarantee of a pure male identity, an identity unproblematized by sexual difference, shaped by a mirroring other who reassuringly gives back only himself;[56] its generative equivalent is the fantasy of male parthenogenesis, with its similar denial of otherness and the woman's part. The alternative to the masculine identity conferred through this mirror is the masculine identity originating in the female and everywhere marked by vulnerability to her: the conflicted identity for which Hermione's pregnant body comes to stand. Either the mirroring twin or the pregnant wife-mother: like Polixenes's fragile pastoral, Leontes's psychic world cannot contain both together. Hence the repeated insistence—visual and metaphoric—that Hermione's pregnant body comes between the two kings: as the emblem of a male identity always already contaminated at its source, that body is the limiting condition to the fantasy of an identity formed through male parthenogenesis or a pure male twinship. Its presence in effect forces Leontes to acknowledge his own maternal origins, immersing him in the dangerous waters—the contaminated "pond" (1.2.195)—of a female sexuality he can neither excise nor control.

The fantasy of twinship functions in effect to protect Leontes from immersion in those waters.[57] His jealousy erupts at the first sign of rupture in that protective mirroring relationship, as though its loss returned him to the site of his vulnerability to the female; "At my request he would not" (1.2.87) is the first sign of danger. As though newly cast out of his equivalent to the all-male Eden, he finds in Hermione's pregnant body the sign of all he stands to lose: remembering their courtship, he remakes her as the unreliable maternal object, capable of souring the entire world to death by withholding herself from him (1.2.102–4). And this withholding is in his imagination tantamount to annihilation: imagining himself excluded from her rich place, he responds as though he has become Polixenes's cipher, flooded with the sense of his own and the world's nothingness; as he later tells Camillo,

> Why then the world, and all that's in't, is nothing,
> The covering sky is nothing, Bohemia nothing,
> My wife is nothing, nor nothing have these nothings,
> If this be nothing.
>
> (1.2.293–96)[58]

But this nothingness is not tolerable: and Leontes retaliates against it, attempting through a monstrous birth of his own—the "something" born of his affection's copulation with nothing (1.2.138–43)[59]—to recreate himself and the world in the shape of his delusion. If the possibility of Hermione's betrayal first plunges him into the nothingness of maternal abandonment, it becomes his stay against nothingness as it hardens into delusion: the world is nothing, he tells Camillo, *if Hermione is not unfaithful.* Threatened by absolute loss, he seizes on the fantasy of Hermione's adultery as though it in itself could give him something to hold on to: better the "something" of cuckoldry than the nothingness into which he would otherwise dissolve. Naming himself a cuckold, insisting on his identity as cuckold and his community with other men (1.2.190–200), he finds in the culturally familiar fiction of female betrayal in marriage both an acceptable narrative for his sense of primal loss and a new adult selfhood. Through the self-born delusion of Hermione's betrayal, he thus gives himself a recognizable place to stand; without it, "the centre is not big enough to bear / A school-boy's top" (2.1.102–3).

The fantasy of Hermione's adultery initially seems to serve Leontes well, answering several of his psychic needs at once. Through it, Leontes can attempt to undo his subjection to the rich place of Hermione's body, making her—rather than himself—nothing and securing his "rest" by giving her to the fire (2.3.8). His monstrous birth in effect undoes hers: if she is unfaithful, then he can deny his connection to her body, both as husband and as son. Through his delusion, he can imagine her pregnant body as the sign of her infidelity, rather than the sign of his sexual concourse with her; and the baby she carries thus becomes no part of him. For in his mobile fantasy, her pregnant body threatens to display him in the fetus she bears; he keeps dissolving into that fetus. The delusion of Hermione's adultery affords Leontes secure ground in part because it helps him resist this regressive pull back toward her body; in its own way, it serves the same needs as the initial fantasy of twinship. But it is ultimately no more successful than that fantasy; in the end, it returns him to what refuses to stay repressed. In Leontes's fluid formulations, cuckoldry fuses with sexual intercourse and with birth, implicating him once again in the maternal origin he would deny. If Othello and Posthumus conflate adultery with marital sexuality,[60] Leontes conflates both with cuckoldry: all three "sully / The purity and whiteness" of his sheets (1.2.326–27). For the sexually mature male body is one with the cuckold's body, both marked by the deforming signs of female betrayal: differentiating himself from Mamillius—"thou want'st a rough pash and the shoots that I have / To be full like me" (1.2.128–29)—Leontes identifies the bull's horns with the cuckold's, as though the sexually mature male body were by definition the cuckold's body. And both sexuality and cuckoldry return

him to the original site of betrayal: imagining himself a cuckold—
"Inch-thick, knee-deep; o'er head and ears a fork'd one" (1.2.186)—
he simultaneously imagines himself sexually entering Hermione's body
between her forked legs[61] and immersed in that body, knee-deep, over
head and ears, as though returned to the fetal position. Cuckold,
adulterer and fetus fuse in their entry into the maternal womb, the
belly that "will let in and out the enemy, / With bag and baggage"
(1.2.205–6).[62] And the fetus itself becomes that enemy: in the most
bizarre and violent of Leontes's conflations—his brutal "let her sport
herself / With that she's big with" (2.1.60–61)—he imagines the unborn baby he would disown as the mother's illicit sexual partner,[63]
graphically literalizing the sexualized return to the womb.

Deprived of his protective mirroring relationship, thrust back to his
origin in the maternal body, Leontes attempts to escape that body
through the fantasy of his own cuckoldry; but the fantasy itself betrays
him, returning him to his source. But Leontes has simultaneously been
pursuing another strategy against nothingness: virtually as soon as
his jealousy erupts, Leontes turns toward Mamillius and attempts to
recreate a mirroring twin in him.[64] He begins with the familiar patriarchal worry that his son might not be his son: his thrice-repeated assertions of likeness (1.2.130, 135, 159) serve, first of all, to guarantee
his own paternity, as if it were in doubt. But—as in *King Lear* and
Cymbeline—worries about illegitimacy turn out to be in part a cover
for worries about the female role in procreation, legitimate or illegitimate. As Leontes makes clear when he violently separates the boy from
his mother—as though she were "infectious," Hermione says later
(3.2.98)—his fear is not that Mamillius resembles Polixenes, but that
he resembles his mother:

> Give me the boy: I am glad you did not nurse him:
> Though he does bear some signs of me, yet you
> Have too much blood in him.
>
> (2.1.56–58)

In this construction of likeness, the signs of Mamillius's difference
from him are signs not of an illegitimate father but of his mother's
contaminating presence in her son: if he is her child, then he is not
fully his father's. Hence the drive toward absolute identity in Leontes's
early assertions of the likeness between father and son: those assertions—especially the anxiety-filled assertion that they are "almost as
like as eggs" (1.2.130)[65]—move from a (just barely) rational concern
with paternity toward a deeply irrational attempt to replace the lost
twinship by reinstating the fantasy of male parthenogenesis in Mamil-

lius. Leontes's pet names for his son increasingly identify the child as a part—perhaps specifically a sexual part—of his own body, his "bawcock," a "collop" of his flesh (1.2.121, 137), as though he could be made without his mother's participation; in effect, those names would make him a split-off portion of his father's masculinity, hence a secure repository for Leontes's threatened identity.[66]

But this defensive fantasy cannot be sustained: like the fantasy of cuckoldry, the attempt at protective identification with Mamillius turns back on itself, ultimately returning Leontes to the corrupt maternal body. Seeing himself in his "unbreech'd" son may temporarily relieve Leontes of the guilt associated with the use of his own dangerous ornament (1.2.155, 158), but it must simultaneously recall the period when he himself was not securely differentiated from his mother.[67] For the inescapable fact of maternal origin is always there in Mamillius— as much a part of him as his name, with its unmistakable allusion to the maternal nursery Leontes so dreads.[68] Approaching the boy sitting by his mother's side, Leontes recoils as though he were seeing himself; and he immediately acts to remove the child from her infectious presence. Conflating his own danger with what he imagines to be Mamillius's, he figures Hermione's betrayal as the source of infection in his drink:

> There may be in the cup
> A spider steep'd, and one may drink, depart,
> And yet partake no venom (for his knowledge
> Is not infected); but if one present
> Th'abhorr'd ingredient to his eye, make known
> How he hath drunk, he cracks his gorge, his sides,
> With violent hefts. I have drunk, and seen the spider.
> (2.1.39–45)

"I have drunk, and seen the spider"; "I am glad you did not nurse him": only eleven lines apart, the phrases echo and explicate one another, identifying Hermione's maternal body with the spider in the cup.[69] In Leontes's infected imagination, maternal nursery is that spider, the infection taken in at the source; his spasmodic attempts to disown Hermione are the psychic equivalents of the violent hefts he images, violent attempts to heave out the internalized mother, the contaminated origin within, like a child spitting up infected—or soured—milk.[70]

Leontes's psychosis illustrates in its purest form the trauma of tragic masculinity, the trauma of contamination at the site of origin. Hermione's pregnant body in effect returns him to this point of origin, and to the sense of contamination culturally registered as original sin; and, despite all his best efforts, the Mamillius in whom he would see himself originally pure gives him back only the reflection of her taint in him. But this taint is ultimately epitomized for Leontes in the baby Hermione now carries; the drama of his expulsion and recovery of the female is thus played out through her. Like everyone else (2.1.17; 2.2.26), Leontes apparently expects this baby to be a boy; that she turns out to be a girl merely confirms her mother's presence in her and hence—according to the familiar logic of illegitimacy[71]—her status as a "female bastard" (2.3.174): for Leontes at this stage, "female" and "bastard" might as well be interchangeable terms. But her supposed illegitimacy nonetheless serves a defensive purpose. When Paulina brings the baby to him and attempts to make him see himself in her, he reacts with panic, summoning up all the cultural tropes for overpowering women—the shrew, the mannish woman, the husband-beating wife, the witch, the bawd, the midwife—with a nearly comic haste:[72] to see himself in his daughter would be the final blow to his threatened masculinity.[73] Paulina's strategy must therefore backfire: the more convincingly she can represent the baby girl as his likeness, the more desperately he will need to dissociate himself from her, hysterically naming her bastard (seven times within roughly forty lines) and casting her out "like to itself, / No father owning it" (3.2.87–88). He has already managed to isolate Hermione with her women, as though their femaleness were catching; now he phobically drives Paulina off the stage and refuses to go near his infant daughter, violently disowning her as though she too could contaminate him.

In casting her out, Leontes begins counter-phobically to remake himself in the shape of the overwhelming mother he most fears: he would dash his infant's brains out with his own hands (2.3.139–40) or abandon her in a landscape of absolute deprivation (2.3.175).[74] It is diagnostic of this play's radical re-valuation of the maternal that Leontes should thus appropriate the imagery of Lady Macbeth: here the ultimate source of danger is not the overwhelming mother but the tyrannical husband/father. Localizing tragic masculinity in Leontes and decisively moving beyond it, Shakespeare thus recasts the gendered etiology of tragedy as he had defined it in *Hamlet*, *King Lear*, *Macbeth*, and *Coriolanus*: no longer the province of maternal contamination, it is now the province of the male ego that fears such contamination, the ego that would remake the world in the image of its own desired purity. With the casting out of his baby girl, the death of the son too obviously born of woman, and the apparent death of his wife, Leontes has arrived at this point: he has in effect exorcised female generativity and achieved the all-male landscape he thought he wanted. But he discovers in it not the timeless spring of Polixenes's pastoral fantasy but the landscape of tragedy, an endless winter of barrenness and deprivation the psychic equivalent of the "barren mountain, and still winter / In storm perpet-ual" (3.2.212–13) that Paulina describes as the fitting setting for his repentance. But the same exorcism that locates Leontes in this psychic landscape allows Shakespeare to undertake a radical recuperation of the maternal body: exorcised and banished from the stage, it can in effect be reconstituted and revalued; and thus released from the con-fines of Leontes's obsessions, the play itself can begin the turn from tragedy to romance.

The first hints of this release come with the birth of Perdita, "lusty, and like to live" (2.2.27), herself "free'd and enfranchis'd" from the womb (2.2.61). The short scene in which her birth is reported is filled with the promise of release from the tyrannous hold of Leontes's mind. The entrance of Paulina brings not only a new character but a new voice—shrewd, self-assured, funny—strong enough to provide an au-thoritative countervoice to Leontes's; and from her we hear for the first time of the "great nature" (2.2.60), the "good goddess Nature" (2.3.103), who will become the presiding deity of recuperation.[75] Through her, Shakespeare begins the move toward romance, simulta-neously underscoring a new alliance between gender and genre: her husband allows himself to become the agent of Leontes's delusions (though he recognizes the sanctity of the Hermione who appears to him [3.3.23], he nonetheless believes her guilty); she becomes the advocate for mother and baby, aligning herself firmly with the female forces of recovery.[76] While Paulina sees birth as the promise of freedom and enfranchisement, Antigonus repeats the tragic paradigm linking birth and mortality: in what are virtually his last words—"poor wretch, / That for thy mother's fault art thus expos'd / To loss and what may follow!" (3.3.49–51)—he rewrites the baby's exposure not as the consequence of Leontes's phobic delusion but as a parable for birth itself, the exposure to loss that is always the mother's fault.[77] But Perdita lives, while he himself dies as the sacrificial (and gendered) representative of tragedy.[78] And with his death, the play turns decisively away from the tragic paradigm, increasingly aligning its own artistic processes with the good goddess whom Paulina invokes.

Shakespeare achieves the recuperation of the maternal body and the attendant turn from tragedy to romance by immersion in the fertile space of a decidedly female pastoral. Though the entrance to the pastoral domain is mediated by a series of male figures—Time, Poli-xenes and Camillo, Autolycus—that domain itself is deeply allied with the fecundity of "great creating nature" (4.4.88); filled with the vibrant energies of sexuality and seasonal change, it stands as a rebuke to

Polixenes's static and nostalgic male pastoral and to the masculine identity that would find itself there.[79] And it reaches back, behind Polixenes, toward the nightmare version of the female body that could provoke his consolatory dream: the circumstances of Antigonus's death at the entrance to this pastoral allude to Lear's great tragic pastoral, replicating its storm and literalizing its bear and sea (*King Lear*, 3.4.9–11), as though signaling that it too must be revised before the play can proceed. And through Florizel, Shakespeare hints at just such revision. Lear sees in his pastoral the emblem of an horrific female sexuality utterly beyond male control; like Leontes lashing out at the Hermione who "rounds apace" (2.1.16), he would attack the generative female body, "Strike flat the thick rotundity o' th' world! / Crack Nature's moulds, all germens spill at once" (3.2.7–8). Florizel recalls this body in his vow to Perdita:

> It cannot fail, but by
> The violation of my faith; and then
> Let nature crush the sides o' th' earth together,
> And mar the seeds within!
>
> (4.4.477–80)

But he would recuperate what Lear would destroy,[80] aligning his faith with its generative potential and cherishing the seeds within.

If Leontes founds his masculine identity on separation from the female, Florizel embraces the female. He has already told Perdita "I cannot be / Mine own, nor anything to any, if / I be not thine" (4.4.43–45); now he disowns the ordinary patriarchal identifiers: "From my succession wipe me, father; I / Am heir to my affection" (4.4.481–82). Mirrored not in an idealized male twin or in a father but in Perdita— Florizel to her Flora—he founds his identity in his relation to her, in the process recuperating the word—"affection"—that had figured Leontes's monstrous birth. And in return, Perdita promises him not the static eternity of Polixenes's pastoral but an aliveness that springs out of the very conditions of his mortality. She would "strew him o'er and o'er" with the "flowers o' th' spring" that Proserpina let "fall / From Dis's waggon" (4.4.113, 117–18, 129), flowers that allude to the seasonal cycles of birth and death. "What, like a corpse?" Florizel asks playfully, recapitulating the fears of all those men who find only death in love, only mortality in the sexual body; and Perdita replies,

> No, like a bank, for love to lie and play on:
> Not like a corpse; or if—not to be buried,
> But quick, and in mine arms.
>
> (4.4.130–32)

In these wonderful lines, Perdita encapsulates the whole process of regeneration enacted by the play, herself becoming the presiding deity of recuperation. Immersed in her pastoral, covered with the flowers that are her sign as Flora, Florizel is immersed in the mortal body: hence the pun on *corpse*. But Perdita does not let that body stay dead. She first rewrites it as the literal ground of love—the bank, for love to lie and play on—and then she revives it, making it "quick" by taking it into her embrace. *Quick* is the decisive word, in which all the anxieties about maternal origin can meet and be resolved: as he quickens in her embrace, she herself imagistically becomes quick with him, restoring him through the pregnant fecundity of her own body.

If Lear's anti-pastoral storm figures the horrific female body that teaches man his mortality, Perdita's pastoral refigures that body in Perdita herself. Imagining Florizel a bank for love to lie and play on, she remakes herself in the image of Love, the Venus genetrix who is one with great creating nature;[81] her words are in fact anticipated by Shakespeare's earlier Venus ("Witness this primrose bank whereon I lie" [*Venus and Adonis*, l. 151]). Polixenes will later equate the pastoral landscape itself with her body, forbidding his son entrance to both and threatening death to Perdita "if ever henceforth thou / These rural latches to his entrance open" (4.4.438–39).[82] But within her "rural latches," in the sheltering womb of her pastoral, the mortal body is refigured: death is not denied but embraced and redefined as the condition of the body's aliveness. Perdita's imagistic revival of Florizel turns crucially on her astonishing *or if*, with its acknowledgment that the body is indeed like a corpse: for only what can die can live. Perdita thus reverses the logic of tragedy, restoring aliveness to the mortal body: if Leontes's logic is "if alive, then dead," the logic of her pastoral is "if dead, then alive." As an extension of her body, Perdita's version of pastoral thus repairs the fall implicit in Polixenes's pastoral vision; through it, Shakespeare in effect returns to the source of original sin, rewriting it as the source of wholeness and life.

Florizel stakes his faith on the generative female body, and his extravagant gesture predicts the movement of the play: for with the recovery of the benign maternal body as a source of life comes the recovery of faith, the recovery that enables the play's final restitutions. In its most primitive form, Leontes's crisis has been a crisis of faith.[83] For him as for Othello, doubt is intolerable: the merest possibility of his wife's infidelity spoils her as a source of inner or outer goodness; doubt itself is tantamount to the loss of the sustaining object. Through his doubt, Leontes relives as though for the first time the infant's discovery that the world is separate from him and is not subject to his desires: if his wife can betray him, she is one with the mother who can seduce and betray, souring his inner world as he takes her into himself. All his fantasies of betrayal, of contamination by the female, of spoiling at the maternal site of origin, reflect this fear: in his loss of faith, he can locate only contamination and dread in the female space outside the self. Hence the logic through which he imagines Hermione's betrayal as the spoiling of nurturance: the spider in the cup condenses and epito- mizes the unreliable outer world that can contaminate the self, the world that is always figured first in the mother's body. Unable to trust in this world, he rejects it, reshaping it in its original form as a promiscuous woman and banishing it, reducing it to nothingness in order to stave off its capacity to hurt him and the contamination he fears from it.

But a world so reduced is a world from which no good can come. As Leontes increasingly manages to do away with the world—casting off wife, friend, children, counselors, reducing everything external to the level of his dreams (3.2.81)—he not only reflects but sustains and ensures his own inner hopelessness, his doubt that there is anything good out there. In his panic at the possibility of loss, he unmakes the world; and his cure can come only from the world's refusal to stay unmade. Hence, I think, the primary psychic significance of the play's radical break with Leontes's consciousness: though that break seems to court dramatic discontinuity, it is in fact the only possible antidote to his disease. If Leontes seems to have succeeded in reducing the world to the level of his dreams, what he—and we—need to learn is that the world will go on existing, that it will survive despite his best efforts at destroying it.[84] And the pastoral, first of all, signifies this fact: it is the place neither he nor we knew about, the place outside the sphere of his omnipotent control. Such a place is by definition dangerous: for Lear, it is epitomized by his monstrous daughter-mothers and by the overwhelming maternal body of the storm that shows him he is not ague-proof; and in his disease, Leontes too can see only betrayal there, in the region beyond his control. But if this place is dangerous, it is also the only place from which hope can come: blotting out the world, making it nothing, can lead only to the stasis of Leontes's winter's tale, in which there is no possibility of renewal. The pastoral of act 4 acknowledges the danger—hence its bear and storm—but it insists on the possibility of hope: here, the mother's body is full of promise. Through its association with the female and its structural position in the play—outside Leontes's control, outside his knowledge—the pastoral can figure this body, the unknown place outside the self where good things come from.

If the world's treachery is first figured in the maternal body, then the recovery of faith requires the recuperation of that body. The pastoral in effect initiates this recuperation: *The Winter's Tale* moves from tragedy to romance by demonstrating that this place of "otherness" can be the source of richness as well as poverty, making the promise that the world is worth having faith in. And in the end, Shakespeare's deep intuition makes Leontes's recovery of trust in the world tantamount to his recovery of the benign maternal body in the literal form of Hermione: if Leontes's attempt to control the world by banishing the female had unmade the world for him, locating him in his own dead inner spaces, Hermione's coming to life figures the return of the world to him and his capacity to tolerate and participate in its aliveness, with all its attendant risks.[85] This return is tellingly mediated by a series of female figures, each beyond the sphere of his control: by Paulina, the archetypically unruly woman; by Perdita, the daughter who outlives his destructive fantasies, growing beyond his knowledge; and by the "good goddess Nature," the "great creating nature" they both invoke. For the male effort to make the self safe by controlling the female body is what must be relinquished before Hermione can return:[86] in this play's gendering of doubt and faith, faith means willingness to submit to unknown processes outside the self, processes registered as female. Hence, I think, the shift in status of the play's ruling deity: though Apollo is at first clearly the god in charge, his authority diminishes as the play gathers toward an ending; named eleven times before the end of 3.3, he is mentioned only twice after, and not at all in the recognition scenes that ostensibly manifest his power by fulfilling his oracle. We too as audience must learn to trust in the female: control of the play is increasingly given over to the numinous female presence invoked by Paulina and Perdita, the goddess nature who is named eleven times in 4.4 and 5.2. The pastoral scene is again the point of transition: there the "fire-rob'd god" (4.4.29) becomes merely one of those subject to the erotic energies of great creating nature; the ceremonious solemnity and unearthliness (3.1.7) of his sacred habitat give way to the profound earthliness of hers, as sacredness itself is redefined and relocated in the female body of the natural world.

The shift from male to female deity thus epitomizes the movement of the play: for Apollo stands for the reassurances of male control, including artistic control, conventionally gendered male and set against a female nature;[87] and this control is what Leontes must be willing to give up. The conventional gendering of the art-nature debate thus suits the purposes of Shakespeare's gendering of the process of faith; and given that the crisis of faith is initiated by Hermione's pregnant body, it is no wonder that the debate turns crucially on the issue of breeding. For Polixenes, the prototypical artist is the gardener who manages nature's generativity, marrying "a gentler scion to the wildest stock," making her "bark of baser kind" conceive "by bud of nobler race" (4.4.92–95). And though he claims that this artist's power derives from and is subservient to nature herself (4.4.89–92), the incipient pun on "kind" tells a different story: the implicit fusion of class and gender terms—a fusion played out for Polixenes in Perdita's supposedly lower-class body— represents art as the masculine taming of nature's wildness, the ennobling of her base material. But of course Perdita's body turns out not to be base: Polixenes may seem to win this debate; but the structure of the play overturns his temporary victory. In the end, the play decisively rejects the artificial generation of another male artist—Julio Romano, who "would beguile Nature of her custom" (5.2.98), outdoing nature by making people in her place. In the context of the gendered art-nature debate, Paulina's introduction to the statue takes on a new emphasis: for the statue who can come alive "excels" specifically "whatever . . . hand of man hath done" (5.3.16–17). As Apollo gives way to nature, art gives way to her great creating powers: Leontes asks, "What fine chisel / Could ever yet cut breath?" (5.3.78–79).

In 2.1, Leontes's entrance had violently shattered the sheltering female space occupied by Hermione and her ladies; the death of Mamillius was the consequence of that shattering and the attendant loss of maternal presence, without which—his death tells us—we cannot live. Now that space is recreated in Paulina's refuge, which Leontes's long penitential submission entitles him to enter; and here maternal presence can be restored. And the restoration turns on bringing him face to face with exactly what he has done, so that he can undo it step by step, vesting Hermione with life as he has earlier deprived her of it. For the statue grants him what he thought he wanted: the unreliable female body reduced to an icon he could possess forever, static and unchanging; in Othello's words over the Desdemona he has similarly turned to alabaster, "No more moving" (*Othello,* 5.2.94). Now, in his wife's "dead likeness" (5.3.15), he sees the consequences of his inability to tolerate her difference, his attempt at absolute control:[88] confronting in its stoniness both the cold barrenness he has made of the world and the deadness of his own inner world—he has been "more stone than it" (5.3.38)—he is overwhelmed by longing for sheer aliveness—hers, and his own—whatever the risks. And in the end, his longing creates her alive for him, recreating aliveness in them both: for the process of her restoration to him has always been interior; all that is required is that he awaken his faith (5.3.95). Brought through Paulina's ministrations to accept what he knows cannot be true, what is beyond not only his control but his rational understanding, he gives himself over to a magic "lawful as eating" (5.3.111): as the spider in the cup had registered the loss of faith in the world, the sanctity of this moment is registered through an image of renewed nurturance. For now "greediness of affection" (5.2.102) can be fed in a world made newly trustworthy: in response to his desire, the statue moves, at once embodying and rewarding his faith.

If in his rage and fear Leontes had obliterated the maternal body of the world, his long submission to the female rewards him in the end by returning the world alive to him in the shape of his wife. And though Leontes has—from his point of view—created her aliveness, she is nonetheless alive beyond his need of her: she exists on her own terms, beyond the sphere of his omnipotence. Shakespeare signals her independent existence by insisting that we see her awakening into life from her point of view as well as his: for Hermione awakens only at Paulina's repeated urging ("'Tis time; descend; . . . approach; . . . / Come! . . . stir, nay, come away" [5.3.99–101]), as though unwilling to risk coming alive; "Be stone no more. . . . Bequeath to death your numbness" (5.3.99, 102) makes us feel what her transformation feels like to her. And once alive, she remains outside the sphere of Leontes's omnipotence; though she answers his desire with her embrace, she then turns away from him, turns toward Perdita, insisting on her own agency, her own version of her story: "Thou shalt hear that I . . . have preserv'd / Myself to see the issue" (5.3.125–28). This turning away seems to me extraordinary and wonderful; we need only try to imagine Cordelia turning thus from Lear to see what is at stake. For through it, Shakespeare marks and validates Hermione's separateness as the source of her value, accepting female separateness for himself as well as for Leontes; and he simultaneously opens up a space for the female narrative—specifically the mother-daughter narrative—his work has thus far suppressed. As the mark of his own renewed capacity to tolerate female separateness, he rewrites his own rewriting of one of the governing myths of his imagination, in the process restoring it to its original form: if in *Lear* he occludes the mother-daughter bond central to the story of Proserpina and Ceres, reshaping it as a mother-son or father-daughter narrative, here he restores that bond, as though acknowledging a female continuity and generativity outside the sphere of male desire.[89]

The Hermione who awakens is thus both the creation of Leontes's renewed desire and independent of that desire; she exists at the boundary between inner and outer, self and other. Situated thus, she epitomizes the recovery of fruitful relatedness with the world: the relatedness that Winnicott saw modeled in the infant's relation with its first not-me possession, the relatedness that enables creative and recreative play in the potential space that is neither self nor other.[90] And if Leontes is brought to this place, we are brought there, too:[91] in the last moments of the play, Shakespeare aligns his own theater with Paulina's female space, where we too can "sup" (5.2.103), where our desires can be safely fed in recreative play. For the female space of Hermione's recovery is also the space of Shakespeare's theater: as many have noted, Hermione's aliveness alludes to the risky aliveness of theater itself, with its moving actors; and like Paulina's, Shakespeare's is a participatory theater, in which the awakening of our faith is required.[92] Like Leontes, we must first be willing to relinquish control: Shakespeare requires us to give up our position as knowing audience while he transports us to the place we did not know about and gives us the recognition scene we were not looking for, asking that we recreate Leontes's faith in ourselves by our own willingness to believe in what we know cannot be happening. For just this willingness to suspend our own mistrust, to participate in the rich illusionistic play of Hermione's recovery without undue anxiety that we are being played upon, signals the recovery of potential space in us. In the first half of the play we had witnessed the shattering of this space in Leontes, who, in his inability to tolerate the unreliable world outside himself, had retreated to the space of his delusion. From this position of dread, free play across the boundary between inner and outer becomes impossible: any intrusion of the world merely bolsters his conviction that he is being played upon, that his wife's sexual play has forced him to play a role not of his own choosing (1.2.187–89). We witness the restored possibility of play in the rich festivity of pastoral;[93] now, as we choose with Leontes to make Hermione live, submitting ourselves both to our own desires and to Shakespeare's control of us, we participate in the restoration of the zone of trust, where we discover our own aliveness by allowing the world to come alive for us in the play of her return.

The Winter's Tale is, I think, an astonishing psychic achievement: through his nourishing art, Shakespeare figures the loss and recovery of the world in the mother's body, returning to us what we didn't know that we had lost. But there are, of course, limitations to this achievement. First of all, it takes place—not surprisingly—within a framework that is decidedly patriarchal. Leontes is fully restored to personal and political potency at the end; and the female agents of restoration turn out to have been good patriarchalists all along, working to permit the father's recovery of himself and of his heir.[94] Apollo's deity is emotionally displaced by nature's, his agency by Paulina's magic; and yet his control persists as a kind of psychic last resort, enabling the free play of the female forces because he is after all there to be called on if need be. The pastoral itself can seem an autonomous female space in part because reproductive female sexuality is excised from it: though it is identified with Perdita's regenerative body, it is literally the property of the old shepherd whose wife has died; entrance to it is gained only by our submission to Time, "the ultimate father-creator."[95] If Paulina is the agent of restoration, her own generativity must be excised before Leontes can be safely put under her control: since her own daughters go virtually unmentioned, her association with birth remains comfortably symbolic; indeed, her daughters seem to be created only so that their father can threaten to geld them (2.1.147). Hermione herself can return only when she is past childbearing, her dangerous generativity bequeathed to the next generation; and though Perdita's body is the locus of a revitalized and sanctified sexuality, that sexuality and its promised generativity are merely potential at the play's end. Female power of all sorts is contained because it is divided: reproductivity is split between Hermione and Perdita, deflected in one and deferred in the other; and female rage is located in the safely asexual Paulina.[96] In these respects, *The Winter's Tale* reiterates—though in a very much muted form—the solutions of the earlier romances: the exorcism of sexuality in *Pericles* and the reconstitution of paternal power in *Cymbeline*.

But the distance of *The Winter's Tale* from these romances seems to me far more impressive than its similarities to them. If *Cymbeline* could recover masculine authority and marital bonds only by killing off the mother and the mother's son, *The Winter's Tale* restores the mother to life and makes the father's generativity and authority contingent on her return. If *Pericles* could allow the mother back only by ruthlessly excising her sexual body, *The Winter's Tale* insists on the recovery—within patriarchal limits—of that body: it is Leontes's determination to kiss Hermione that precipitates her awakening.[97] And this time, she returns under the aegis of great creating nature, not Diana: structurally, the place of the brothel is taken by the pastoral, the place of Cerimon by Paulina.[98] If Shakespeare undoes the ending of *Othello* in *The Winter's Tale*—it is Hermione's movement, not her stillness, that is sanctified—he undoes the starting point of tragedy in *Hamlet* as well: Hamlet's unweeded garden is punningly rewritten in Perdita's unusual weeds (4.4.1) and in the pastoral for which she speaks; and through Hermione, Shakespeare celebrates the recovery of the mother who can bless. For now sacredness itself is compatible with the sexual body: Cordelia had to be separated from that body before she could return as Virgin Mother; but the miracle of this madonna is in her warm flesh (5.3.109).[99]

With the recovery of benign maternal presence in the flesh, Shakespeare is able, for a moment, to undo the legacy of *Hamlet*: for a moment, mother and father stand together, themselves a gracious couple begetting wonder (5.1.132–33). But the moment is fragile. Shakespeare does not rest long in the recreative space of *The Winter's Tale*: as though once more in recoil from an intolerable solution, he unmakes Paulina's female space in *The Tempest*, reinstating absolute paternal authority with a vengeance. Prospero's reappropriation of control at the beginning of *The Tempest* is nearly diagrammatic: even before the play has begun, the maternal body has been defined as dangerous and banished in the form of Sycorax—as though Paulina had turned out to be a witch after all; Prospero's use of Medea's words to describe his own magic suggests the extent to which his reappropriated control is based firmly on her banishment.[100] For now the maternal body of nature is dangerous and needs the father's benign management; only his art releases Ariel from confinement in her material body. Except for Caliban, Prospero's companions on his island are freed from that body through his appropriation of its generative power: he "made gape / The pine, and let [Ariel] out" (1.2.292–93) in a kind of pseudo-birth, releasing him to be his ideal bodiless son; and Miranda's passage to the island is similarly mediated by a birth-act, the fantasized pregnancy[101]—he "groan'd" under his "burthen"; her smiles "rais'd in [him] / An undergoing stomach, to bear up / Against what should ensue" (1.2.156–58)—that imagistically remakes her wholly her father's daughter. Thus able to control the maternal body, Prospero seems able to reshape the world in the image of his own mind, having achieved everything Leontes initially thought he wanted.

But the cost of banishing the world—even for Prospero—is high: although his isolation is less desperate than Leontes's, it is equally self-enclosed. The play turns on this recognition, on Prospero's learning from Ariel that it is less than human to refuse the vulnerabilities of human feeling (5.1.20); and in the end, he abjures his magical control, releasing Ariel and even Miranda (though to a marriage he has arranged for her) and returning to the maternal body of the world, where every third thought shall be his grave (5.1.311). And all the ambivalence of this return is focused in Caliban, the mother's son in whom Prospero must finally see himself. The last of Shakespeare's mother's sons—"hag-seed" (1.2.367) and "bastard" (5.1.273), according to the terms of the anxious patriarchal psyche—Caliban must finally be acknowledged; but he cannot be incorporated into that psyche. Acknowledged but unassimilated, in the end he is banished like his mother, left alone on her island when Prospero leaves. But now the body of that island has been spoiled for him, its "fresh springs, brine-pits, barren place and fertile" (1.2.340) named in the father's language and estranged from him. Like Mamillius, he has been violently separated from this maternal body by the father's intrusion; but he stays alive to bear witness to the cost. Perpetually excluded from the patriarchal world and the patriarchal psyche that cannot tolerate him, crying to dream again of a lost fusion with the place of plenitude (3.2.133–41), Caliban—in his violent love, his sexuality, and his unassuagable longing— is the final register of Shakespeare's ambivalence toward what it means—from *Hamlet* on—to be a mother's son.

NOTES

NOTES TO CHAPTER 1

1.   Among those who trace elements of Richard's character to his fantasized relationship with his mother and its derivatives, see especially Richard P. Wheeler ("History, Character and Conscience in *Richard III*," *Comparative Drama 5* [1971–72]: 313–15), Michael Neill ("Shakespeare's Halle of Mirrors: Play, Politics, and Psychology in *Richard III*," *Shakespeare Studies 8* [1975]: 105–7), Coppélia Kahn (*Man's Estate: Masculine Identity in Shakespeare* [Berkeley: University of California Press, 1981], pp. 63–66), and C. L. Barber and Richard P. Wheeler (*The Whole Journey: Shakespeare's Power of Development* [Berkeley: University of California Press, 1986], pp. 104–13). For a specifically non-psychoanalytic reading of the birth stories prominently associated with Richard, see Marjorie Garber's intriguing account of them as "an embodiment of the paradoxical temporality of history," always already deformed and belated (*Shakespeare's Ghost Writers: Literature as Uncanny Causality* [New York: Methuen, 1987], esp. pp. 44–46).

2.   Shakespeare's imagistic transformation catches the word *impale* in transition, capitalizing on the tension between its opposing meanings. *Impale* in the sense of "to enclose with pales, stakes or posts; to surround with a palisade" (*Oxford English Dictionary* [hereafter OED] 1) is dominant; OED 4, "to thrust a pointed stake through the body of, as a form of torture or capital punishment," is cited first only in 1613. But OED 4 was probably becoming familiar in speech before its first clear citation in print; it certainly seems to stand behind Richard's torment here.

3.   In fact, Richard's fantasized caesarian from the inside out is only an extreme form of what was commonly believed to be the fetus's role in labor. Many imagined the fetus "seeking for the outward air, or finding itself cramped and seeking release, or being driven by the insufficiency of the food supply to seek an alternative" (Audrey Eccles, *Obstetrics and Gynaecology in Tudor and Stuart England* [Kent, Ohio: Kent State University Press, 1982], p. 55)—all of

which sounds very much like Richard, toiling desperately to find the open air. Arguing specifically for the uterus's role in labor late in the seventeenth century, Mauriceau wrote that it is "not, as ordinarily believed, that the Infant (being no longer able to stay there for want of the nourishment and refreshment) useth his pretended indeavours to com forth thence, and to that purpose kicking strongly, he breaks with his feet the membranes" (cited in Eccles, p. 56). Robert N. Watson notes the imagery of caesarian birth in this passage and in *Macbeth* (*Shakespeare and the Hazards of Ambition* [Cambridge, Mass.: Harvard University Press, 1984], esp. pp. 19–20, 99–105, and 168–72); the metaphors of caesarian section and oedipal rape are central to his understanding of ambitious self-creation insofar as both imagine a usurpation of the defining parental acts of generation (see, e.g., pp. 3–5). Though it is frequently very suggestive, Watson's account tends too easily to blur the distinction between matricide and patricide: in fantasies of rebirth, the hero may symbolically replace the father to recreate himself, but he often does so by means of an attack specifically on the maternal body. In Shakespeare's images of caesarian birth, the father tends to be conspicuously absent; indeed, I shall argue, precisely his absence—not his defining presence—creates the fear of the engulfing maternal body to which the fantasy of caesarian section is a response. This body tends to be missing generally in Watson's account, as it is missing specifically in his discussion of Richard's caesarian fantasy here.

4.   "The real pleasure . . . comes through inflicting suffering on women. . . . The dramatic situation is polarized into a verbal battle between Richard . . . and a chorus of bereaved mothers" (Wheeler, "History, Character and Conscience," p. 314); see also Madonne M. Miner's extended analysis of Richard's attack on women, both through his scapegoating of them and through his attack on the roles that define them (" 'Neither mother, wife, nor England's queen': The Roles of Women in *Richard III*," in *The Woman's Part: Feminist Criticism of Shakespeare*, ed. Carolyn Ruth Swift Lenz, Gayle Greene, and Carol Thomas Neely [Urbana: University of Illinois Press, 1980], pp. 37–55).

5.   "Richard lives by sadomasochistic structuring of relationships so as to enforce separateness and autonomy, a pattern shaped by fixation at . . . the biting stage of infantile development" (Barber and Wheeler, *The Whole Journey*, p. 110).

6.   For these anxieties, see David M. Bevington ("The Domineering Female in *1 Henry VI*," *Shakespeare Studies* 2 [1966]: 51–58), Leslie A. Fiedler (*The Stranger in Shakespeare* [London: Croom Helm, 1972], pp. 47–54), and especially Kahn (*Man's Estate*, pp. 55–56), David Sundelson (*Shakespeare's Restorations of the Father* [New Brunswick, N.J.: Rutgers University Press, 1983], pp. 18–23), and Barber and Wheeler (*The Whole Journey*, pp. 93, 99, and 105–9).

7.   Given that Margaret wasn't even present at Rutland's death, the degree to which she is retroactively made responsible for that murder is astonishing: Clifford—the actual murderer—is scarcely mentioned by York in his long

lament (*3 Henry VI*, 1.4.111–49); by *Richard III*, Hastings can say to her, "O, 'twas the foulest deed to slay that babe" (1.3.183), as though she herself had done the deed.

8. With its reference to pregnancy, the "quick" of "eat him quick" says it all: buried alive, the men of these plays are returned to the womb in death. As though in response to Richard's fantasy of the thorny wood, the characteristic mode of death in *Richard III* is suffocation, not the stabbing of the earlier plays: see, e.g., Clarence's dream of his soul "smother'd . . . within [his] panting bulk" (1.4.40) and his actual death by drowning, the princes "smothered" in the Tower (4.3.17, 4.4.134), "Hastings, Rivers, Vaughan, Grey, / Untimely smother'd in their dusky graves" (4.4.69–70). Alan B. Rothenberg notes the preponderance of images of smothering in *Richard III* in his "Infantile Fantasies in Shakespearean Metaphor: 1. The Fear of Being Smothered" (*Psychoanalytic Review* 60 [1973]: 216–17).

9. My formulation here—and elsewhere—is deeply indebted to Richard Wheeler's wonderful paragraph on the disembodied "spectral woman" who haunts the tragedies (*Shakespeare's Development and the Problem Comedies* [Berkeley: University of California, 1981], pp. 150–51). Though Jungian critics use a similar language to describe this woman, they are too prone to replicate— rather than analyzing—the fantasy that creates her. See, e.g., Alex Aronson, for whom "Man's tortuous pilgrimage from the unconscious . . . to selfhood . . . corresponds to man's gradual deliverance from the Great Mother," and for whom "all the uncontrolled affects and primeval impulses . . . are the progeny of the Magna Mater"; in his account, Shakespeare's symbolism unproblematically points "to the victory of the masculine, conscious spirit over the power of the matriarchate. The mother, the wife, and the daughter have to be overcome so that order and consciousness may be re-established" (*Psyche and Symbol in Shakespeare* [Bloomington: Indiana University Press, 1972], pp. 255–56).

10. Lawrence Stone notes the high rate of stillbirths and deaths before one year of age (*The Family, Sex and Marriage in England, 1500–1800* [New York: Harper & Row, 1979], pp. 52, 55); Samuel X. Radbill thinks that the infant mortality rate under two years sometimes went as high as forty percent ("Pediatrics," in *Medicine in Seventeenth Century England*, ed. Allen G. Debus [Berkeley: University of California Press, 1974], pp. 252–53).

11. See Radbill, "Pediatrics," pp. 249–51, and Eccles, *Obstetrics and Gynaecology*, p. 99.

12. See the warnings in Thomas Phaire's *The Boke of Chyldren*, reprinted frequently throughout the sixteenth century (Edinburgh: E. & S. Livingstone, 1955), pp. 18–19; and see Eccles, *Obstetrics and Gynaecology*, p. 97.

13. See Radbill, "Pediatrics," p. 243, for the killing nurses. The estimate of deaths is Stone's (*The Family, Sex and Marriage*, p. 65); see also Eccles (*Obstetrics and Gynaecology*, pp. 97–99). William Clowes notes that children

catch syphilis "by sucking the corrupte mylke of an infected nursse" (*A Brief and Necessary Treatise, touching the cure of the disease called Morbus Gallicus* [London, 1585], p. 3). Murder in its more direct form—both by mother and by nurse—may not have been uncommon; see, e.g., Radbill on "accidental" overlaying of children ("Pediatrics," p. 252). There is some evidence that infanticide, or at least prosecutions for infanticide, increased after 1560; see J. A. Sharpe's assertion that England participated in the " 'infanticide craze' which affected much of western Europe" ("The History of Crime in Late Medieval and Early Modern England: A Review of the Field," *Social History* 7 [1982]: 200).

14. Stone several times asserts that weaning usually took place at around eighteen months but then says that children generally returned home from the wet nurse at two (*The Family, Sex and Marriage*, pp. 52, 83, and 84); Radbill thinks that weaning was sometimes delayed until three ("Pediatrics," p. 250). Infantile mobility was initially hampered by tight swaddling (Stone, p. 115), and children do not seem to have been encouraged to walk early. Especially in the seventeenth century, when rickets became common, bone deformation may have prevented them from walking before two or three (Radbill, pp. 255, 263). But *Romeo and Juliet* suggests that both weaning and walking took place as late as the age of three even before rickets became prevalent; Nurse is clearly proud that her precocious near-three-year-old charge "could stand high-lone" and "could have run and waddled all about" (1.3.36–37).

15. From Guazzo's *Civile Conversation*, cited in Stone (*The Family, Sex and Marriage*, p. 83).

16. James Guillimeau, *The Nursing of Children*, affixed to *Child-birth, or The Happy Delivery of Women* (London: Printed by Anne Griffin, for Ioyce Norton and Richard Whitaker, 1635); the quotations are from the "Preface" (I.i.2) and "The Preface to Ladies."

17. See Radbill, "Pediatrics," p. 250, and *Romeo and Juliet*, 1.3.26, 30.

18. See Howard R. Patch, *The Goddess Fortuna in Mediaeval Literature* (Cambridge, Mass.: Harvard University Press, 1927), p. 56.

19. Francis Quarles, *Emblems, Divine and Moral*, ed. Augustus Toplady and John Ryland (London: John Bennet, 1839), p. 44. I am indebted to Patricia Parker for calling my attention to this emblem.

20. See *OED* for *matter* (verb) 2, "to exude in the form of matter or pus"; derived from *matter* (substantive) 4, "purulent discharge, pus." (See *Troilus and Cressida*, 2.1.8, for this sense of *matter*.)

21. "Death's Duell," *The Sermons of John Donne*, ed. Theodore Gill (New York: Meridian Books, 1958), p. 265.

22. Belief that the mother contributed the matter and the father the spirit or form in conception was grounded both in Aristotle and in *Genesis*; see

Ian Maclean (*The Renaissance Notion of Woman* [Cambridge: Cambridge University Press, 1980], pp. 8, 32, 35, and 104, n. 33) and Marina Warner (*Alone of All Her Sex: The Myth and the Cult of the Virgin Mary* [New York: Random House, 1983], pp. 40–42). Even in the act of praising women, the standard English midwifery in the sixteenth century replicates this duality: "And although that man be as principall moover, and cause of the generation: yet (no displeasure to men) the woman doth conferre and contribute much more, what to the encrebement of the chyld in her wombe, and what to the nourishment thereof after the byrth, than doth the man. And doubtless, if a man would demaund to whom the childe oweth most his generation: Ye may worthily make aunswer, that to the mother, whether ye regarde the paines in bearing, other els the conference of most matter in begetting" (Thomas Raynalde, *The birth of mankinde otherwyse named The Womans Book* [London: Imprinted by Richard Watkins, 1598], p. 17; see also Raynalde's extensive comparison of the womb to the earth as the receptacle for seed, pp. 186–90). According to Maclean, the Galenist position—that "female seed" contributes both matter and form—was the one most commonly adopted in the medical community, but the matter was still hotly debated (pp. 36–37). In 1651—the same year that Harvey published his work on the *ovum*— the atomist Nathaniel Highmore ingeniously preserved the old association by conceiving of "two varieties of seminal atoms: spiritual atoms from the male and material atoms from the female" (cited in Charles W. Bodemer, "Materialistic and Neoplatonic Influences in Embryology," in Debus, *Medicine in Seventeenth Century England*, p. 189).

23. See Radbill ("Pediatrics," p. 246), Maclean (*The Renaissance Notion of Woman*, p. 41), and Eccles (*Obstetrics and Gynaecology*, pp. 46–47, 64–65). In *3 Henry VI*, Queen Elizabeth worries about blasting or drowning King Edward's fruit with her sighs and tears (4.4.23).

24. For labor as the fetus's response to the insufficiencies of the womb, see note 3. Raynalde's *The birth of mankinde*, which was a revision of Richard Jonas's 1540 translation of *De partu hominis*, was first published in 1545 and was reprinted thirteen times; until the 1612 publication of Guillimeau's *Childbirth, or the happy delivery of women*, it was the only midwifery in English (see Eccles, *Obstetrics and Gynaecology*, pp. 11–12).

25. *The Nursing of Children*, Preface, I.i.2. See Eccles on abortion, including the attempts of mothers to induce abortion through tight lacing (*Obstetrics and Gynaecology*, pp. 67–70).

26. Guillimeau, *The Nursing of Children*, Preface, I.i.2; see also, e.g., Eccles, *Obstetrics and Gynaecology*, pp. 51–52.

27. See, e.g., Maclean, *The Renaissance Notion of Woman*, pp. 39–40, and Eccles, *Obstetrics and Gynaecology*, pp. 49–50.

28. See Phaire, *The Boke of Chyldren*, pp. 17–18, and Radbill, "Pediatrics," p. 250.

29. In associating his son's likeness to his mother with her blood in him, Leontes seems to be echoing not only the relatively orthodox belief that the fetus fed on menstrual blood *in utero* (see, e.g., Raynalde, *The birth of mankinde*, p. 56, and Eccles, *Obstetrics and Gynaecology*, pp. 49–50) but also the less orthodox Aristotelian position that this blood transmitted the mother's likeness to the child (Maclean, *The Renaissance Notion of Woman*, p. 37).

30. See especially the work of Robert Stoller (especially "Conclusion: Masculinity in Males," *Sex and Gender*, Volume 2: *The Transexual Experiment* [New York: Jason Aronson, 1975], pp. 281–97) and Nancy Chodorow (*The Reproduction of Mothering* [Berkeley: University of California Press, 1978], and "Gender, Relation, and Difference in Psychoanalytic Perspective," in *The Future of Difference*, ed. Hester Eisenstein and Alice Jardine [New Brunswick, N. J.: Rutgers University Press, 1985], pp. 3–20); or see Kahn's wonderfully lucid and succinct summary of this work (*Man's Estate*, esp. pp. 9–12). I am grateful to Murray Schwartz for having introduced me to Stoller's work in 1976. The consequences of the masculine need to dis-identify from the female are very powerfully spelled out by Madelon Sprengnether (formerly Gohlke) in her classic essay, " 'I wooed thee with my sword': Shakespeare's Tragic Paradigms," in *Representing Shakespeare: New Psychoanalytic Essays*, ed. Murray M. Schwartz and Coppélia Kahn (Baltimore, Md.: Johns Hopkins University Press, 1980), pp. 170–87; I am deeply indebted to her work.

31. See Stone, *The Family, Sex and Marriage*, for the *rite de passage* of breeching (p. 258) and for the shift from women to men as caretakers (pp. 120, 258); Philippe Aries asks pointedly, "Why, in order to distinguish the boy from the man, was he made to look like the girl who was not distinguished from the woman?" (*Centuries of Childhood*, trans. Robert Baldick [New York: Random House, 1962], p. 58). (There was no comparable ceremony for girls, which meant not only that they were perpetually infantilized, but also—as Stoller and Chodorow suggest [see references in note 30]—that they were not defined through rigid differentiation from their mothers.) Both the use of the boy actor and the convention of Shakespeare's transvestite heroines play on the analogy between boys and women, perhaps especially on the perceived resemblance between their voices; see, e.g., *Two Noble Kinsmen*, 4.1.58–59 (" 'twas one that sung, and by the smallness of it / A boy or woman").

32. For fuller treatment of this moment, see Chapter 5, pp. 117.

33. See Wheeler, "History, Character and Conscience," pp. 314–15.

34. Neill reads Richard's acting as a way to invent a self out of the nothingness left by his mother's failure to mirror him ("Shakespeare's Halle of Mirrors," pp. 105–8, 112); though I find this reading very moving, it seems to me in tension with Richard's pride specifically in shape-shifting. My reading is closer to that of Wheeler, who sees Richard adopting the vice role "to avoid

facing the complicating demands of his inner self" ("History, Character and Conscience," p. 312).

35. Miner pointedly notes their absence at the end, but for her its effects are mitigated by a "counterprocess . . . that insists on the inherently positive value of women" (" 'Neither mother, wife, nor England's queen,' " pp. 51–52).

36. See Barber and Wheeler's wonderful account of her as the horrific omnipotent mother of infancy (*The Whole Journey*, pp. 105–9).

37. See David Willbern's brilliant reading of maternal malevolence in *Titus* ("Rape and Revenge in *Titus Andronicus*," *English Literary Renaissance* 8 [1978]: 159–82).

38. This absence becomes particularly striking when one notes the extent to which Shakespeare was surrounded by maternal older women; see Carol Thomas Neely's account of the demographics of his family ("Shakespeare's Women: Historical Facts and Dramatic Representations," in *Shakespeare's Personality*, ed. Norman N. Holland, Sidney Homan, and Bernard J. Paris [Berkeley: University of California Press, 1989], pp. 116–34). Shakespeare replicates these demographics only in *The Merry Wives of Windsor*; both in "Shakespeare's Women" and in "Constructing Female Sexuality in the Renaissance: Stratford, London, Windsor, Vienna" (in *Feminism and Psychoanalysis*, ed. Richard Feldstein and Judith Roof [Ithaca, N. Y.: Cornell University Press, 1990], pp. 209–29), Neely speculates brilliantly on the conditions that enable the anomalies of this play, "in which anxieties about women are in abeyance" ("Shakespeare's Women," p. 134), in which wives and mothers are not only present but cheerfully dominant. But even in this anomalous play, I would note, only daughters have mothers; even here, sons are shielded from their presence.

NOTES TO CHAPTER 2

1. My sense of the shape of Shakespeare's career and of the defensive construction of both the comedies and the histories is deeply indebted to Richard P. Wheeler; see *Shakespeare's Development and the Problem Comedies* (Berkeley: University of California Press, 1981), esp. pp. 46–50, 155–64.

2. Shakespeare generalizes this guilt by suppressing the rumor that Brutus was Caesar's illegitimate son; *2 Henry VI* testifies to his knowledge of it ("Brutus' bastard hand / Stabbed Julius Caesar," 4.1.137–38). *Hamlet* has often been understood as a reworking of the father-son conflict in the histories and *Julius Caesar*; see, for example, Norman Holland (*Psychoanalysis and Shakespeare* [New York: Octagon Books, 1979], pp. 286–87) and C. L. Barber and Richard P. Wheeler (*The Whole Journey: Shakespeare's Power of Development* [Berkeley: University of California Press, 1986], esp. pp. 11–12, 236–38). For the relationship between *Hamlet* and *Julius Caesar*, see also Ernest

Jones (*Hamlet and Oedipus* [Garden City, N.Y.: Doubleday, 1954], pp. 137–40); for that between *Hamlet* and the *Henriad*, see also Peter Erickson (*Patriarchal Structures in Shakespeare's Drama* [Berkeley: University of California, 1985], pp. 63–67), Wheeler (*Shakespeare's Development and the Problem Comedies*, pp. 161, 190–91), and Linda Bamber (*Comic Women, Tragic Men* [Stanford, Calif.: Stanford University Press, 1982], pp. 154–58). Though these accounts all acknowledge the eroticizing presence of women in *Hamlet*, they do not all emphasize the significance of that presence; in this emphasis, my account is closest to Wheeler and to Bamber, for whom tragedy turns on the encounter with woman as Other.

3. See René Girard ("Hamlet's Dull Revenge," in *Literary Theory/Renaissance Texts*, ed. Patricia Parker and David Quint [Baltimore, Md.: Johns Hopkins University Press, 1986], pp. 280–302) and especially Joel Fineman ("Fratricide and Cuckoldry: Shakespeare's Doubles," in *Representing Shakespeare*, ed. Murray M. Schwartz and Coppélia Kahn [Baltimore, Md.: Johns Hopkins University Press, 1980], pp. 86–91) for the threat of collapse into No Difference. In Girard's reading, Old Hamlet and Claudius are the enemy twins between whom there is never any difference; Hamlet consequently has to try to make a difference where none exists and then to fire up his dull revenge mimetically when that difference cannot be sustained. Girard locates the no-difference in his myth of sacralizing violence; like most psychoanalytically oriented critics, I locate it in the common origin of both Old Hamlet and Claudius in the ambivalently regarded father of childhood. Though based in Girard, Fineman's account seems to me both richer and more far-reaching than his, in part because he engages with the "drama of individuation" through which Shakespeare represents the failed myth of differentiation and hence with misogyny as an expression of the fear of No Difference; in his account, as in mine, Gertrude's sexuality becomes the mark of No Difference.

4. This is the likeness registered stunningly, for example, in Hamlet's "How stand I then, / That have a father kill'd, a mother stain'd" (4.4.56–57), where *have* can indicate either possession or action. This likeness is the staple of most oedipal readings of the play, in which—in Ernest Jones's formulation—Claudius "incorporates the deepest and most buried part of [Hamlet's] own personality" (*Hamlet and Oedipus*, p. 100); see Holland's useful discussion of this and other oedipal readings (*Psychoanalysis and Shakespeare*, pp. 163–206). These readings have been extended and challenged by Avi Erlich (*Hamlet's Absent Father* [Princeton, N.J.: Princeton University Press, 1977]), who sees the basic motive of the play not in Hamlet's covert identification with Claudius but in his desperate need for a strong father who can protect him from his own incestuous impulses and from the castrating mother they would lead to: "Much more than he wants to have killed his father, Hamlet wants his father back" (p. 260). Although most oedipal accounts begin by acknowledging that Hamlet is initially more obsessed with his mother's remarriage than with his father's death, they usually go on to focus on the father-son relationship, discussing the mother merely as the condition that occasions the son's struggle with—or need for—his father (but see Irving I. Edgar, *Shakespeare, Medicine*

and Psychiatry [London: Vision, 1971], pp. 288–311, for an exception). Without entirely discounting oedipal motives in the play, I want to restore what seems to me the mother's clear primacy in her son's imagination; I consequently emphasize preoedipal motives, in which fantasies of merger with and annihilation by the mother are prior to genital desire for her, and in which the strong father is needed more as an aid to differentiation and the establishment of masculine identity than as a superego protecting against incestuous desire. The extraordinary oral valence of both sex and killing in *Hamlet*—the extent to which both are registered in the language of eating and boundary diffusion— seems to me evidence of the extent to which even the more purely oedipal issues are strongly colored by preoedipal anxiety. My emphasis on Gertrude has to some extent been anticipated by those who stress matricidal impulses in the play, implicitly or explicitly making Orestes—rather than Oedipus—the model for *Hamlet*; see, for example, Gilbert Murray (*Hamlet and Orestes*, [London: Oxford University Press, 1914), Frederic Wertham ("The Matricidal Impulse: Critique of Freud's Interpretation of Hamlet," *Journal of Criminal Psychopathology* 2 [1941]: 455–64), J. M. Moloney and L. Rockelein ("A New Interpretation of *Hamlet*," *International Journal of Psychoanalysis* 30 [1949]: 92–107), Harry Levin (*The Question of Hamlet* [New York: Oxford University Press, 1959], p. 65), Theodore Lidz (*Hamlet's Enemy*, [London: Vision, 1975]), and Maurice Charney ("The 'Now Could I Drink Hot Blood' Soliloquy and the Middle of *Hamlet*," *Mosaic* 10 [1977]: 77–86). Jones (pp. 106–7), Edgar (pp. 294–98) and Erlich (p. 152) see matricidal rage primarily as a derivative of oedipal desire; in the accounts of Moloney and Rockelein (pp. 99, 106) and of Lidz (pp. 183, 231), it is also derived—at least incipiently— from the relationship to the overwhelming preoedipal mother. For more explicitly preoedipal readings of *Hamlet*, see, for example, accounts of the play's oedipal issues as covers for preoedipal masochism (Edmund Bergler, "The Seven Paradoxes in Shakespeare's 'Hamlet,' " *American Imago* 16 [1959]: 379–405) or narcissism (Kaja Silverman, "*Hamlet* and the Common Theme of Fathers," *Enclitic* 3 [1979]: 106–21), or of Hamlet's sarcasm as oral aggression (M. D. Faber, "Hamlet, Sarcasm, and Psychoanalysis," *Psychoanalytic Review* 58 [1968]:79–90); see especially Wheeler's account of Hamlet's attempt to build a self both by incorporating the image of an ideal father and by recovering the trust shattered by disillusionment with his mother (*Shakespeare's Development and the Problem Comedies*, pp. 161, 190–200). Although I share many details of interpretation with Avi Erlich, whose work I learned from and reacted against in my earliest days at Berkeley, my account of the play is most deeply indebted to Wheeler's.

5.   Ophelia's contamination by association has been a commonplace of *Hamlet* criticism for a long time; among the legions, see, for example, A. C. Bradley (*Shakespearean Tragedy* [New York: Meridian Books, 1955], p. 101), John Dover Wilson (*What Happens in Hamlet* [Cambridge: Cambridge University Press, 1951], p. 133), and Harley Granville-Barker (*Prefaces to Shakespeare* [Princeton, N.J.: Princeton University Press, 1946], p. 79).

6.   Most apparently do: see, for example, Bradley (*Shakespearean Tragedy*,

p. 136), Wilson (*What Happens in Hamlet?*, pp. 251–53), Bertram Joseph (*Conscience and the King: A Study of Hamlet* [London: Chatto and Windus, 1953], p. 94), Carolyn Heilbrun ("The Character of Hamlet's Mother," *Shakespeare Quarterly* 8 [1957]: 204), Rosamond Putzel ("Queen Gertrude's Crime," *Renaissance Papers, 1961*, ed. George Walton Williams [Southern Renaissance Conference, 1962], p. 44), Rebecca Smith ("A Heart Cleft in Twain: The Dilemma of Shakespeare's Gertrude," in *The Woman's Part: Feminist Criticism of Shakespeare*, ed. Carolyn Ruth Swift Lenz, Gayle Greene, and Carol Thomas Neely [Urbana: University of Illinois Press, 1980], p. 202) and Roland Mushat Frye (*The Renaissance "Hamlet": Issues and Responses in 1600* [Princeton, N.J.: Princeton University Press, 1984], p. 151), all of whom think that her response demonstrates her innocence. Others note that her involvement—particularly in comparison with the sources—is left ambiguous (see, e.g., William Empson, "*Hamlet* When New," *The Sewanee Review* 61 [1953]: 37, and Lidz, *Hamlet's Enemy*, pp. 78, 81); and at least one critic is sure that she knows of the murder (Richard Flatter, *Hamlet's Father* [New Haven, Conn.: Yale University Press, 1949], pp. 30–31, 59–80, and 153–60).

7. Ever since Joseph (*Conscience and the King*, pp. 17–18) pointed out that "adulterate" in Shakespeare's time could apply to sexual sin generally, not just to what we moderns narrowly call adultery, critics have cautioned against assuming that Gertrude and Claudius were adulterous in our sense (see, e.g., Putzel, "Queen Gertrude's Crime," p. 39; Smith, "A Heart Cleft in Twain," pp. 209–10, n. 11; and Frye, *The Renaissance "Hamlet"*, p. 323). But the definitions Joseph cites all seem to add a more inclusive definition to a word more commonly—or, as the homily *Against Whoredom and Uncleanness* puts it, "properly"—understood in the narrower sense (Joseph, p. 17); and the ghost's emphasis on the marriage vow (1.5.49) suggests that Gertrude's crime was specifically against marriage. As usual with Gertrude, the matter is far from settled.

8. See Smith's fine discussion of the discrepancy between the monstrously sensual Gertrude portrayed by Hamlet, the ghost, and many critics, and the "careful mother and wife" Gertrude appears to be in her brief appearances on stage ("A Heart Cleft in Twain," pp. 194–201); R. A. Foakes notes specifically that Hamlet's attack in 3.4 "proceeds more from his imagination than from anything the audience has seen or heard" ("Character and Speech in 'Hamlet,'" in *Shakespeare Institute Studies: Hamlet*, ed. John Russell Brown and Bernard Harris [New York: Schocken Books, 1963], p. 158). For G. Wilson Knight, this discrepancy illustrates the degree to which our judgment is independent of Hamlet's ("The Embassy of Death," in *The Wheel of Fire* [New York: Meridian Books, 1957], pp. 32, 43–44). But in Linda Bamber's reading of misogyny as a consequence of the tragic hero's decentering confrontation with the Other, Gertrude is simply "a vessel for Hamlet's feelings," not an independent character in whom we have an investment; since we "adopt his feelings as long as he displays them," we think of her as vaguely redeemed once he has given up his sexual disgust (*Comic Women, Tragic Men*, pp. 72–83). While I largely concur in Bamber's assessment, I note that the generations

of critics who have struggled to define Gertrude suggest that the play promotes some investment in her; her ambiguous status as Other seems to me the mark of Shakespeare's ambiguous investment in the fantasies localized in Hamlet.

9. Bradley (*Shakespearean Tragedy*, p. 137), Joseph (*Conscience and the King*, pp. 96–97), and Putzel ("Queen Gertrude's Crime," p. 43) think that Gertrude repents and gives her allegiance to Hamlet; Eleanor Prosser (*Hamlet and Revenge* [Stanford, Calif.: Stanford University Press, 1967], p. 196), Baldwin Maxwell ("Hamlet's Mother," *Shakespeare Quarterly* 15 [1964]: 242), and Smith ("A Heart Cleft in Twain," p. 205) think that she is unchanged.

10. Gertrude drinks the cup knowingly in Olivier's *Hamlet*.

11. T. S. Eliot, "Hamlet," *Selected Essays* (New York: Harcourt Brace, 1932), p. 124. In Eliot's view, the discrepancy between Gertrude and the disgust she arouses in Hamlet is the mark of "some stuff that the writer could not drag to light, contemplate, or manipulate into art" (p. 123) and hence of artistic failure; but, in concluding that Gertrude needs to be insignificant to arouse in Hamlet "the feeling which she is incapable of representing" (p. 125), he inadvertently suggests the aesthetic power of fantasy disengaged from its adequate representation in a single character. For a brilliant analysis of the way in which the feminine stands for the failure of all kinds of representational stability in Eliot's aesthetic, in various psychoanalytic attempts to master the play, and in *Hamlet* itself as the representative of Western tradition, see Jacqueline Rose, "Hamlet—the *Mona Lisa* of Literature," *Critical Quarterly* 28 (1986): 35–49.

12. Critics of all sorts agree that Gertrude's remarriage disturbs Hamlet more profoundly than his father's death: in addition to the "Orestes" and preoedipal critics cited in note 4, see, for example, Bradley (*Shakespearean Tragedy*, p. 101), Eliot ("Hamlet," p. 123), Wilson (*What Happens in Hamlet?*, pp. 42–43), Jones (*Hamlet and Oedipus*, p. 68), Granville-Barker (*Prefaces to Shakespeare*, pp. 94–95), Flatter (*Hamlet's Father*, pp. 62–63), and Smith ("A Heart Cleft in Twain," p. 197). For the opposing point of view, see, e.g., Arthur Kirsch's account of Hamlet's impeded work of mourning, in which Hamlet's father's death has explanatory primacy ("Hamlet's Grief," *English Literary History* 48 [1981]: 17–36). Though Kirsch refers to Freud's "Mourning and Melancholia," he does not foreground the ambivalence toward the lost and introjected object that is the crux of that essay; this ambivalence toward the father is at the center of Barber and Wheeler's account of the play (*The Whole Journey*, p. 254).

13. *Rank* is evocative of sexual disgust in *Hamlet* and elsewhere in Shakespeare: Claudius's offense is "rank" (3.3.36); he and Gertrude live "in the rank sweat of an enseamed bed, / Stew'd in corruption" (3.4.92–93). For other uses of *rank*, see, for example, Desdemona's "will most rank" (*Othello*, 3.3.236) or Posthumus's description of the woman's part ("lust, and rank thoughts, hers, hers," *Cymbeline*, 2.4.176). Burgundy describes a France "corrupting in it own fertility," in which "the even mead . . . / Wanting the scythe,

all uncorrected, rank, / Conceives by idleness" (*Henry V*, 5.2.40, 48–51); in its depiction of a monstrous female fecundity that is out of control, his "rank" is very close to Hamlet's unweeded garden. In his fine early discussion of the stench of corrupting flesh pervasive in *Hamlet*, Richard D. Altick notes the association of *rank* specifically with the smell of sexuality ("*Hamlet* and the Odor of Mortality," *Shakespeare Quarterly* 5 [1954]: 173–4).

14. Hamlet's sexual disgust and allied hatred of the flesh have been widely recognized; see, for example, Knight (*The Wheel of Fire*, p. 23), Prosser (*Hamlet and Revenge*, p. 175), and especially L. C. Knights ("Prince Hamlet," *Scrutiny* 9 [1940–41]: 151; *An Approach to "Hamlet"* [London: Chatto and Windus, 1960], esp. pp. 50–60). Most trace his recoil from the flesh to his shock at his mother's sensuality: "Is he not . . . her very flesh and blood?" Granville-Barker asks (*Prefaces to Shakespeare*, p. 235; see also, e.g., Wilson, *What Happens in Hamlet?*, p. 42; Knights, *An Approach to "Hamlet"*, p. 60; and Karl P. Wentersdorf, "Animal Symbolism in Shakespeare's *Hamlet*: The Imagery of Sex Nausea," *Comparative Drama* 17 [1983–84]: 375); in some ways my reading of *Hamlet* is an attempt to unfold the implications of Granville-Barker's question. For Jones, as for most oedipal critics, this recoil comes more indirectly from his mother: it is Hamlet's defensive response to the incestuous desire her remarriage fosters in him (*Hamlet and Oedipus*, pp. 88–89, 95). But John Hunt sees the source of Hamlet's contempt for the body not in his mother but in the ghost, the "memento of all that rots" ("A Thing of Nothing: The Catastrophic Body in *Hamlet*," *Shakespeare Quarterly* 39 [1988]: 32–35).

15. After giving the reasons for preferring Quarto 1 and 2's "sallied" (= sullied) to Folio's "solid," Jenkins concedes that Shakespeare may have intended a pun (see Arden *Hamlet*, pp. 436–37).

16. In Bamber's formulation, "What we see in Hamlet is not the Oedipal drama itself but the unraveling of the resolution to the Oedipus complex" (*Comic Women, Tragic Men*, p. 156); Rose understands femininity as the scapegoated sign of this unraveling ("Hamlet—the *Mona Lisa* of Literature," esp. pp. 40–41, 46–47). Traditional Freudian theory locates the father's protective function at the point of this resolution (see, for example, Erlich's account of Hamlet's fantasy-search for the father who can protect him from his own incestuous impulses [*Hamlet's Absent Father*, esp. pp. 23–37, 185–94]). But in object-relations theory, the father's protective role comes much earlier, when he helps the son in the process of differentiation from the potentially overwhelming mother of infancy (see, e.g., Nancy Chodorow, *The Reproduction of Mothering* [Berkeley: University of California Press, 1978], pp. 71, 79–82; the father's role in the process of individuation was first pointed out to me by Dr. Malcolm Pines at a meeting of the British Psychoanalytical Society in 1977). Both sorts of paternal protection seem to me to be lost at the beginning of *Hamlet*; but the distinctly oral valence of the unraveling of the oedipal resolution here (see note 4, above) suggests the primacy of the earlier crisis in the play's structuring fantasy.

17. The sense that Old Hamlet is somehow guilty has been most vigorously registered through the suspicion that the ghost is up to no good, that he is— as Protestant theology would insist and as Hamlet himself suspects when it is convenient for him to do so—a diabolic agent conducing to damnation. (The classic account of this view is Prosser's *Hamlet and Revenge*; in my view, it has been largely refuted by those who insist on the ghost's mixed nature [e.g., Charles A. Hallet and Elaine S. Hallet, *The Revenger's Madness: A Study of Revenge Tragedy Motifs* (Lincoln: University of Nebraska Press, 1980), pp. 184–89] and on the extent to which his nature is deliberately left ambiguous [e.g., Robert H. West, *Shakespeare and the Outer Mystery* (Lexington: University of Kentucky, 1968), pp. 56–68] and Frye, *The Renaissance "Hamlet"*, pp. 14–29).

18. See Erlich's similar reading of this passage as expressing the wish for a nonsexual birth that can defend against female danger (*Hamlet's Absent Father*, pp. 201–4). Though they do not specifically allude to this passage, Barber's and Wheeler's comments on the transformation of religious need into tragic theater are, I think, especially pertinent to the filial identity imaged through it: "The play is a version of the family romance of which Jesus's conviction that he is the son of God, that 'My father and I are one,' is the ultimate extreme" (*The Whole Journey*, p. 29).

19. The place of this dream-technique in the creation of Old Hamlet and Claudius was identified by Jones (*Hamlet and Oedipus*, p. 138) and Maud Bodkin (*Archetypal Patterns in Poetry* [London: Oxford University Press, 1934], pp. 13–14) and has since been widely accepted by psychoanalytic critics; see especially Barber and Wheeler's account of its devastating effects on the son who thus loses the capacity to move toward independent selfhood by coming to terms with his father's imperfections (*The Whole Journey*, pp. 249, 254–55). The over-idealized father must be destructive to Hamlet's own selfhood (see Wheeler, *Shakespeare's Development*, pp. 143, 193–94); in discussing Hamlet's need to escape "from the shade of the dead hero," Levin strikingly anticipates more recent formulations of the problem (*The Question of Hamlet*, pp. 57–58).

20. Critics often note that Old Hamlet's crimes seem to be of the same kind as Claudius's (see, for example, Rebecca West, *The Court and the Castle* [New Haven, Conn.: Yale University Press, 1957], pp. 27–28; P. J. Aldus, *Mousetrap: Structure and Meaning in "Hamlet"* [Toronto: University of Toronto Press, 1977], pp. 47–48; David Leverenz, "The Woman in Hamlet: An Interpersonal View," in *Representing Shakespeare*, p. 117; and Margaret W. Ferguson, "Hamlet: Letters and Spirits," in *Shakespeare and the Question of Theory*, ed. Patricia Parker and Geoffrey Hartman [New York: Methuen, 1985], pp. 296–97); the recent mini-tradition of doubling the roles of Claudius and the ghost seems to respond to this likeness (see Ralph Berry, "Hamlet's Doubles," *Shakespeare Quarterly* 37 [1986]: 209–10). But critics like West or Girard (see note 3, above) who begin by noting the likeness seem to me to obscure its force: the shock of noticing the likeness works on us, I think, only

if we have first accepted the difference between them; the play thus replicates in its audience the disillusionment Hamlet continually tries to defer.

21.   Elizabeth Abel first called my attention to the implicit presence of a controlling male gardener in Hamlet's image; since she has been a great help to me at virtually every stage of this book, it is a particular pleasure to record this specific debt to her. The father's place in controlling the mother's sexuality for the (oedipal) son is familiar in psychoanalysis; see, e.g., Lidz (*Hamlet's Enemy*, pp. 54, 83). Rose forcefully poses the broader social question this formulation partly occludes: "What happens . . . to the sexuality of the woman, when the husband dies, who is there to hold its potentially dangerous excess within the bounds of a fully social constraint?" ("Hamlet—the *Mona Lisa* of Literature," pp. 38–39).

22.   When "grossly" is glossed, editors generally apply it to Old Hamlet's spiritual state; see, e.g., Jenkins (Arden edition), Willard Farnham (in *William Shakespeare: The Complete Works*, gen. ed. Alfred Harbage [Baltimore, Md.: Penguin Books, 1969]), and G. R. Hibbard (*The Oxford Shakespeare: Hamlet* [Oxford: Oxford University Press, 1987]). But "grossly" modifies Claudius's action before it modifies Old Hamlet's state; in virtually all Shakespeare's other uses of it, it describes an action both bodily and palpable (see, e.g., *All's Well*, 1.3.173; *Measure*, 5.1.470; *Othello*, 3.3.401).

23.   Given my reading of this passage, Warburton's famous emendation of *good* to *god* is nearly irresistible; but I have nonetheless resisted it, staying with the Arden's *good* on the grounds that the word does not, strictly speaking, require emendation.

24.   According to John E. Hankins, Hamlet is quite orthodox here; see his account of the Aristotelian and post-Aristotelian theories that made generation of all kinds dependent on putrifying matter ("Hamlet's 'God Kissing Carrion': A Theory of the Generation of Life," *PMLA* 64 [1949]: 507–16).

25.   "Marrow" is unusual in Shakespeare; three of its four other occurrences are in a sexual context (see *All's Well*, where Parolles cautions Bertram against "spending his manly marrow" in the arms of his kicky-wicky [2.3.276–77]; see also "Venus and Adonis," l. 142, and *3 Henry VI*, 3.2.125).

26.   See John H. Astington, " 'Fault' in Shakespeare," *Shakespeare Quarterly* 36 (1985): 330–4, for *fault* as a slang term for the female genitals; he does not note its use in this passage. But *fault* could apparently carry the more general suggestion of sexual intercourse as well: as the language lesson in *Henry V* makes clear, French *foutre* was available to corrupt good English words (3.4.47–49), and Shakespeare routinely takes advantage of this potentiality in his use of *fault*. Among many instances, see especially Sonnet 138 ("Therefore I lie with her and she with me, / And in our faults by lies we flattered be"), *Othello* ("oft my jealousy / Shapes faults that are not," 3.3.151–52), *Measure* ("some condemned for a fault alone," 2.1.40), and *The Winter's Tale* ("Th' offenses we have made you do, we'll answer, / If you first sinn'd

with us, and that with us / You did continue fault," 1.2.83–85). Stephen Booth hears *false* in the *faults* of Sonnet 138 and cites an apparent faults/fall echo (*Othello*, 4.3.86–87); see his note on the complex issue of pronunciation (*Shakespeare's Sonnets* [New Haven, Conn.: Yale University Press, 1977], p. 481). Whether or not the "l" was audible in *faults*, the word could clearly serve as a nexus for the sense of sexual corruption.

27. Critics often portray Hamlet's world as infected by original sin (see, e.g., West, *The Court and the Castle*, p. 28; Levin, *The Question of Hamlet*, p. 58; Robert B. Bennett, "Hamlet and the Burden of Knowledge," *Shakespeare Studies* 15 [1982]: 77–97; Donald V. Stump, "Hamlet, Cain and Abel, and the Pattern of Divine Providence," *Renaissance Papers 1985* [The Southern Renaissance Conference], pp. 29–30). Hankins associates original sin generally with the flesh of Hamlet's "good kissing carrion" ("Hamlet's 'God Kissing Carrion,' " pp. 515–16), Walter N. King specifically with Hamlet's own sullied flesh (*Hamlet's Search for Meaning* [Athens: University of Georgia Press, 1982], p. 44); but Hamlet's anatomy of original sin is more precise than they suggest. And it is also accepted orthodoxy: see Marina Warner (*Alone of All Her Sex: The Myth and the Cult of the Virgin Mary* [New York: Random House, 1983], pp. 54, 57) for the Augustinian view that original sin was transmitted in the womb through the act of conception. Hence the logic that led eventually to the doctrine of Immaculate Conception for the Virgin (Warner, pp. 236–54) and also to her exemption from death (Warner, pp. 97–98; see also Julia Kristeva, "Stabat Mater," in *The Female Body in Western Culture*, ed. Susan Rubin Suleiman [Cambridge, Mass.: Harvard University Press, 1986], p. 102).

28. Without noting the pun on *fault* or the allusion to original sin, Erlich comes to a similar conclusion about this passage; see his use of it to explicate the "to be or not to be" soliloquy as a meditation on whether or not to be born (*Hamlet's Absent Father*, esp. pp. 182–85). Erlich understands the play's emphasis on birth primarily in relation to the oedipally castrating mother (e.g., p. 187); I am nonetheless indebted to his explication of the various forms of *bear* in the soliloquy and elsewhere (see esp. p. 183). The soliloquy similarly asks "how he or anyone lets himself be born as the one he is" in Stanley Cavell's meditation on Hamlet's refusal to accept his birth, which means his refusal "to take [his] existence upon [him]" ("Hamlet's Burden of Proof," *Disowning Knowledge in Six Plays of Shakespeare* [Cambridge: Cambridge University Press, 1987], p. 187). In Cavell's complex account, acceptance of one's birth is acceptance of one's own separateness, hence acceptance of the sexually independent mother and the sexually dependent father shadowed in the fantasy of the primal scene; I locate the problematics of birth in more specifically preoedipal and gendered terms, as a register of fears of male contamination by the female at the point of origin of subjectivity as well as in the primal scene.

29. The allusion to the fall in garden and serpent is commonly recognized (see, e.g., Arthur M. Eastman, "*Hamlet* in the Light of the Shakespearean

Canon," in *Perspectives on Hamlet*, ed. William G. Holzberger and Peter B. Waldeck [Lewisburg, Pa.: Bucknell University Press, 1975], p. 53; Kirsch, "Hamlet's Grief," p. 25; and Stump, "Hamlet, Cain and Abel," p. 29); the anomalous position of Eve in this version of the fall is not.

30.   Few critics share Flatter's conviction that Gertrude was literally complicit in Old Hamlet's murder (see note 6), but some note the sense of murderous culpability nonetheless associated with her; they attribute it to her (naturalistically conceived) failure to love her husband enough (Lora Heller and Abraham Heller, "Hamlet's Parents: The Dynamic Formulation of A Tragedy," *American Imago* 17 [1960]: 417–20), to the specifically male fantasies that equate female betrayal with death (Madelon [Sprengnether] Gohlke, " 'I wooed thee with my sword': Shakespeare's Tragic Paradigms," in *Representing Shakespeare*, p. 173; A. Andre Glaz, "*Hamlet*, Or the Tragedy of Shakespeare," *American Imago* 18 [1961]: 139) or to fantasies of the primal scene in which the mother damages the father (Erlich, *Hamlet's Absent Father*, pp. 62–63, 115; Cavell, *Disowning Knowledge*, pp. 183–85). Others note the more generalized nexus of sexuality and death without addressing the specific issue of Gertrude's culpability (e.g., Levin, *The Question of Hamlet*, pp. 59, 64; Moloney and Rockelein, "A New Interpretation of *Hamlet*," p. 94; Aldus, *Mousetrap*, pp. 108–13). In thinking of the story of fratricidal rivalry in effect as a cover for the more primary story of male subjection to the female, I am implicitly quarreling with the assumptions of Girard and others, for whom woman takes on meaning only insofar as she functions as a sign of differentiation between men; Girardian No-Difference seems to me at its most dangerous—at least to the Shakespearean (male) subject—when it threatens to obliterate the difference between male and female on which manhood is founded.

31.   The shift of blame from male to female that is the subtext of *Hamlet* is modeled in little by the Player's speech on the death of Priam, where the strumpet Fortune stands in for Pyrrhus at the crucial moment of the murder (2.2.488–89); see Erlich, *Hamlet's Absent Father*, p. 118, and Chapter 3, p. 43, above.

32.   See Kay Stockholder (*Dream Works: Lovers and Families in Shakespeare's Plays* [Toronto: University of Toronto Press, 1987], pp. 52–53) for a similar formulation. *OED* 1 (e) gives "sexual intercourse" as one of the meanings for *mixture*. Holland cites several psychoanalytic critics who see the poisoning "as a childishly confused account of the sexual act" (*Psychoanalysis and Shakespeare*, p. 194); see also Erlich (*Hamlet's Absent Father*, p. 93), and especially Cavell, who reads the dumb-show poisoning as Hamlet's dream-version of a primal scene fantasy (*Disowning Knowledge*, p. 185).

33.   Skin eruptions of the sort the ghost describes were one of the symptoms of syphilis (see James Cleugh, *Secret Enemy: The Story of a Disease* [London: Thames and Hudson, 1954], pp. 46–50); Thersites wishes "tetter" on the "masculine whore" Patroclus (*Troilus and Cressida*, 5.1.16, 22). Both the ghost's "crust" and his odd "bark'd about" are anticipated in early descriptions of the disease: Francisco Lopez de Villalobos notes the "very ugly eruption of

crusts upon the face and body," Josef Grunbeck the wrinkled black scabs, "harder than bark" (cited in English translation in Cleugh, pp. 48, 49). The description of the poison as a "leperous distilment" that courses through his body like "quicksilver" (1.5.64, 66) might also further the association of the poison with syphilis, since quicksilver was a routine treatment for syphilis (Cleugh, pp. 59, 61) and leprosy itself was associated with venereal disease (see Cleugh, pp. 53–55, and Charles Clayton Dennie, *A History of Syphilis* [Springfield, Ill.: Charles C. Thomas, 1962], pp. 13, 32; for Shakespearean uses of this association, see Timon's punning "Make the hoar leprosy ador'd" [*Timon*, 4.3.36] and Antony's wishing leprosy on "yon ribbaudred nag of Egypt," *Antony*, 3.10.10).

34. See Erlich's similar speculations on this pun (*Hamlet's Absent Father*, pp. 62–63).

35. The descriptions of hell and of Gertrude's body coalesce in the burning characteristic of venereal disease; see Timon ("Be strong in whore, allure him, burn him up" [4.3.143]) and especially Thersites ("Lechery, lechery, still wars and lechery! . . . A burning devil take them!" [*Troilus*, 5.2.193–95]). For the female genitals as burning hell, see Booth, *Shakespeare's Sonnets*, pp. 499–500.

36. An incipient pun on matter and *mater* seems to run just below the surface of *Hamlet*, emerging only when Hamlet wittily asks his mother, "Now, mother, what's the matter?" (3.4.7) and perhaps in the "baser matter" of 1.5.104 (Fred Crews long ago electrified a Berkeley colloquium by speculating on this latter possibility after a talk by Avi Erlich). For extended commentary on the pun, see Erlich (*Hamlet's Absent Father*, p. 215) and Ferguson ("*Hamlet*: Letters and Spirits," p. 295); for the anatomical association of matter and *mater*, see Chapter 1, p. 6. Shakespeare toys with this association even in casual use: see, for example, *Twelfth Night*, where Sebastian's proclamation that he is a spirit indeed, "but . . . in that dimension grossly clad / Which from the womb I did participate" (5.1.229–30) anticipates *Hamlet's* genesis of gross flesh. Given this association, even the gravedigger's reference to a corpse as "your whoreson dead body" (5.1.166) may not be wholly casual.

37. Hamlet's famous pun to Ophelia—"Do you think I meant country matters?" (3.2.115)—clarifies the use of "country" here. Erlich first called my attention to this pun in the soliloquy (see *Hamlet's Absent Father*, p. 188; and see the same page, and Booth, *Shakespeare's Sonnets*, p. 526, for the possibility that the *conscience* that makes cowards of us all (3.1.83) similarly puns on the female genitals).

38. The pun associating the poison with marriage and sexual union has been noted at least since Bradley (*Shakespearean Tragedy*, p. 126); Faber sees in Hamlet's forcing Claudius to drink his "union" specifically the playing out of Hamlet's oral aggression ("Hamlet, Sarcasm and Psychoanalysis," p. 89).

39. See note 36 for the pun on *mater*/matter.

40. In this paragraph, as elsewhere, I am drawing on ideas expressed by D. W. Winnicott in a series of essays on the interface between inner and outer in earliest infantile development, especially on the ways in which a developing core of selfhood can meet with a reliable world in a transitional zone that makes creative interaction between inner and outer possible, and on the ways in which this zone can be destroyed (see especially "Transitional Objects and Transitional Phenomena," *Through Paediatrics to Psycho-Analysis* [London: The Hogarth Press and the Institute of Psycho-analysis, 1975], pp. 229–42; "Ego Distortion in Terms of True and False Self," *The Maturational Processes and the Facilitating Environment* [London: The Hogarth Press and the Institute of Psycho-analysis, 1972], pp. 140–52; and "Communicating and Not Communicating Leading to a Study of Certain Opposites," *The Maturational Processes*, pp. 179–92; and see Chapter 8, notes 83, 84, and 90, for further discussion of Winnicott). See also Wheeler on Hamlet's "excruciating efforts to establish a self while hiding it from others" for a similarly Winnicottian account (*Shakespeare's Development*, p. 198). Many have noted the troubled relationship between inner and outer in Hamlet: for particularly interesting accounts, see, e.g, Marvin Spevack on Hamlet's "self-conceived inner realm" ("Hamlet and Imagery: The Mind's Eye," *Die Neueren Sprachen* n.s.25 [1966]: 203–12), David Pirie on Hamlet's retreat into soliloquy (*"Hamlet* without the Prince," *Critical Quarterly* 14 (1972): 293–314), and Holland on Hamlet's "tendency to turn inner life into outward" (*Psychoanalysis and Shakespeare*, p. 204); Brent Cohen notes the extent to which even the distinction between inner and outer is problematized as Hamlet's claims to interiority become merely another role (" 'What is it you would see?': *Hamlet* and the Conscience of the Theatre," *ELH* 40 [1977]: 240–42). The vexed relationship between inner and outer in *Hamlet* makes for some odd readings of the play, in which anything distantly resembling plot or character is dissolved. For extreme instances, see Glaz, for whom the whole play acts out a conversation between Gertrude and Hamlet confirming Hamlet's—or maybe Shakespeare's—illegitimacy ("*Hamlet*, Or the Tragedy of Shakespeare," pp. 129–58), and Aldus, who sees in all the male characters a single mythic man encountering sex and death in a single woman (*The Mousetrap*, e.g., pp. 115, 146, and 159); for a less extreme instance, see Stockholder, for whom plays are always the dreams of their protagonists, in this case the oedipally tinged dream of Hamlet's conflicted move toward maturity (*Dream Works*, pp. 12–16, 40–64). The entire collapse of what he dismisses as the literal perspective on the play is especially frustrating in Aldus's account, since it prevents his sometimes fascinating intuitions from becoming fully coherent.

41. See Erickson's account of Horatio's defensive function for Hamlet (*Patriarchal Structures*, pp. 66–80); in his account, the imperviousness of Horatio helps Hamlet to ward off the psychic demands of his overwhelming father (pp. 68–69) and allows Hamlet safely to replicate the affectionate bond he cannot have with his mother or Ophelia (pp. 74–78).

42. Critics who use the model of Freud's "Mourning and Melancholia" (see note 12, above) generally assume that the lost object is Hamlet's father;

but Hamlet's discovery of the whore inside himself suggests that the lost, introjected, and then berated object is his mother (see, e.g., Paul A. Jorgensen, "Hamlet's Therapy," *The Huntington Library Quarterly* 27 [1964]: 254–55, and Stephen A. Reid, "Hamlet's Melancholia," *American Imago* 31 [1974]: 389–92). Psychoanalytic critics sometimes note Hamlet's difficulty in reconciling what they see as the masculine and feminine elements within him; see, for example, Murray M. Schwartz ("Shakespeare through Contemporary Psychoanalysis," in *Representing Shakespeare*, p. 27) and especially Winnicott, in his not wholly successful attempt to gender the development of the objective subject ("Creativity and its Origins," in *Playing and Reality* [London: Tavistock Publications, 1971], esp. pp. 79–84; see also Rose's critique of Winnicott, "Hamlet—the *Mona Lisa* of Literature," p. 45). Holland points toward the same difficulty in Shakespeare (*Psychoanalysis and Shakespeare*, p. 142). The fullest account of Hamlet's relation to his own "femaleness" is David Leverenz's "The Woman in Hamlet: An Interpersonal View" (in *Representing Shakespeare*, pp. 110–28). Despite its suggestive use of double-bind theory and its wonderful account of Ophelia as an empty repository for other people's voices, this essay seems to me to some extent vitiated by its attempt to locate the female as a positive source of value within Shakespeare's text; it is much more successful in demonstrating Hamlet's revulsion against the female than in suggesting Shakespeare's critique of his revulsion. In *Macbeth* and *Coriolanus*, Shakespeare will foreground the consequences of constructing masculinity as the not-female; here he seems to me largely to replicate Hamlet's sense of the female as the source of weakness and contamination. For the basis of this construction of the masculine self in the theories of object-relations psychoanalysis, see Chapter 1, p. 7; for *Hamlet* specifically, see Madelon Gohlke, " 'I wooed thee with my sword': Shakespeare's Tragic Paradigms," in *Representing Shakespeare*, pp. 172–73.

43.   In an attempt to preserve Hamlet's nobility, several critics have attributed his behavior in 3.4 to his high-minded and altogether selfless reformist impulses toward his mother (see, for example, Bradley, *Shakespearean Tragedy*, p. 115; Joseph, *Conscience and the King*, pp. 95–97; Frye, *The Renaissance "Hamlet"*, pp. 152, 162); but Knights notes that he "seems intent not so much on exposing lust as on indulging an uncontrollable spite against the flesh" ("Prince Hamlet," p. 151). I would add that he shows very few signs of interest in his mother as a real person who might be won to repentance; in my view, she remains almost entirely a fantasy-object for him in this scene.

44.   As Charney notes, "Hamlet characteristically displaces the expected plot interest from the king . . . to his mother" in the middle of the play; the "crucial prayer scene occurs, as it were, in passing" ("The 'Now Could I Drink Hot Blood' Soliloquy," pp. 82–83).

45.   Although Barber does not specifically discuss this moment in *Hamlet*, my sense of the importance of the sacred as a psychic category in Shakespeare is greatly indebted to him. His work—which I first saw in 1976—locates the tragic need to find the sacred in familial relationships in the context of the

Protestant dismantling of the Holy Family, especially of the Holy Mother "whose worship could help meet the profound need for relationship to an ideal feminine figure, unsullied either by her own sexuality or by the sexual insecurities of men and unlimited in maternal solace and generosity" (Barber and Wheeler, *The Whole Journey*, p. 32; see also "On Christianity and the Family: Tragedy of the Sacred," in *Twentieth Century Interpretations of "King Lear"*, ed. Janet Adelman [Englewood Cliffs, N.J.: Prentice-Hall, Inc., 1978], pp. 117–19, and "The Family in Shakespeare's Development: Tragedy and Sacredness," in *Representing Shakespeare*, pp. 188–202, for earlier formulations of these ideas). Although Barber and Wheeler's full discussion of *Hamlet* in *The Whole Journey* foregrounds the father-son relationship, they characterize relationship to the mother as the "anguished center of Hamlet's experience" in discussing the needs the Holy Mother is no longer available to fulfill (p. 31). Wheeler's earlier account of *Hamlet* in *Shakespeare's Development and the Problem Comedies* powerfully foregrounds this anguished center: in it, he draws on the work of Erik Erikson (especially pp. 82–83, 161) and Winnicott (especially pp. 195–99) to explicate Hamlet's "need to repurify and rediscover himself in the trustworthy, internalized maternal presence that Gertrude has contaminated" (p. 196); in his view, Hamlet can begin to imagine that blessed presence only after his matricidal impulse is "released and deflected onto Polonius" (p. 197).

46.   See Meredith Skura's account of the ways in which Hamlet's world embodies (and hence justifies) what he feels (*The Literary Use of the Psychoanalytic Process* [New Haven, Conn.: Yale University Press, 1981], p. 47). Though she seems to me too quick to dismiss the locus of fantasy in the character of Hamlet—"*Hamlet* recreates the fantasy, not the fantasizer" (p. 48)—and though she stresses oedipal to the exclusion of preoedipal fantasy, her account of the presence and status of fantasy in *Hamlet* and in other literary works seems to me extraordinarily rich and compelling (see the whole of Chapter 3, "Literature as Fantasy," pp. 58–124; and see especially pp. 47–50, 97–98, for *Hamlet*).

47.   See Eastman, "*Hamlet* in the Light of the Shakespearean Canon," for a striking explication of *Hamlet* via its exfoliations in *Othello* and *King Lear*; this essay anticipates my own formulations at several points (see esp. pp. 55–56, on Lear's vagina/hell-mouth, and p. 65, on the "deep desire for spiritual rapprochement" in the blessing of parent and child).

NOTES TO CHAPTER 3

1.   See L. C. Knights's fine description of Hamlet's "desire to lapse back from the level of adult consciousness" toward sleep and consummation ("Prince Hamlet," *Scrutiny* 9 [1940–41]: 152–3).

2.   Both Ronald Bates ("Shakespeare's 'The Phoenix and Turtle,' " *Shakespeare Quarterly* 6 [1955]: 19–30) and K.T.S. Campbell (" 'The Phoenix and

the Turtle' As a Signpost of Shakespeare's Development," *The British Journal of Aesthetics* 10 [1970]: 169–79) note in passing the importance of the context *Hamlet* provides for the poem; Bates especially associates this context with its insistence on chastity (p. 30). Muriel Bradbrook (" 'The Phoenix and the Turtle,' " *Shakespeare Quarterly* 6 [1955]: 356–58) takes exception to Bates, insisting that "married chastity" is not equivalent to abstinence here (p. 357). But it's hard to see why "married chastity" should be cited as the reason this couple left no progeny unless "married chastity" here means abstinence. William Empson, responding to the same issues, posits a composition date of 1598–99 specifically in order to dissociate the poem from *Hamlet* and hence from any taint of sexual nausea: "Shakespeare did not write 'The Phoenix and the Turtle' while Hamlet was saying he could not bear to think what his mum did in bed" but during the period of *Henry V* (" 'The Phoenix and the Turtle,' " *Essays in Criticism* 16 [1966]: 148). His conjecture about the date has not been widely accepted.

3. Robert Chester's *Loves Martyr*, the volume in which Shakespeare's poem was first printed, sets the subject of this odd union for all the poems (*Loves Martyr*, ed. Alexander B. Grosart for The New Shakspere Society, London: N. Trubner & Co., 1878). The union would seem to defeat the possibility of ordinary sexuality; but the matter is not as simple as Bradbrook assumes when she writes that "the Phoenix and Turtle could not mate, for they were not of a species" (" 'The Phoenix and the Turtle,' " p. 357). Bates's assertion that the other poems in the collection celebrate sexual union ("Shakespeare's 'The Phoenix and Turtle,' " pp. 29–30) has been challenged by Empson (" 'The Phoenix and the Turtle,' " pp. 149–50) and G. Wilson Knight, who finds the phoenix throughout the symbol for a love beyond consummation, especially heterosexual consummation (*The Mutual Flame* [London: Methuen, 1955], pp. 155, 199, and 219). But despite the vow of chaste love undertaken by Chester's birds, his own long and puzzling poem celebrates their sexual consummation in a union on Paphos (pp. 17, 32, and 89), managed by Venus herself (p. 20); in the appended "Cantoes Alphabet-wise to faire Phoenix," the dove specifically urges the phoenix not to make "a Iewell of nice Chastity." Despite Empson and Knight, that is, Shakespeare's emphasis on chastity does not necessarily come with the turf of Chester's poem.

4. "The reference is to the belief that the crow . . . engendered by the mouth" (Grosart, cited in *The Poems*, Arden Edition, ed. F. T. Prince [London: Methuen, 1960], p. 180).

5. Although he does not specify *Troilus and Cressida*, Daniel Seltzer posits a general relation between the poem and the love tragedies, noting especially the centrality of a "potential metamorphosis of an 'identifying' property" to tragedy (" 'Their Tragic Scene': *The Phoenix and the Turtle* and Shakespeare's Love Tragedies," *Shakespeare Quarterly* 12 [1961]: 95). See also Susan Snyder's account of the ways in which "the dead-end quality [of the poem] illuminates tragic love in *Othello*" (*The Comic Matrix of Shakespeare's Tragedies* [Princeton, N.J.: Princeton University Press, 1979], p. 88).

6. See Chapter 2, pp. 25–30. Kenneth Palmer, in his note on "mixture" in the Arden *Troilus and Cressida*, specifies the sexual pun and comments that "sexual intercourse [is] often implied punningly in respect of planetary conjunction" (p. 128).

7. See, for example, the way in which 2.2 initially establishes Priam's authority by having him open the scene and pose the question of Helen's return, only to have his voice silenced by the voices of his squabbling sons; even his sensible assessment of Paris (ll. 143–46) is virtually ignored. His silencing here, in the council he has called, epitomizes his displacement from authority throughout the play.

8. References to venereal disease—and its accompanying skin disease (see Chapter 2, n. 33)—are rampant (see, for example, 2.3.76, 5.1.16–22, 5.3.105, and 5.10.35–57). The insistence on venereal disease may owe much to the leprosy Henryson assigned to Cressida as punishment for her sexual crimes, since leprosy and syphilis were routinely associated (see Chapter 2, n. 33). W. S. C. Copeman notes that syphilis was often confused with plague as well (*Doctors and Disease in Tudor Times* [London: Dawsons of Pall Mall, 1960], p. 129). Cressida herself may allude to Henryson's Cressida's fate when she says, "I shall be plagu'd" (5.2.104). In the end, Pandarus implies, we too will be plagued: he bequeaths his disease to us, as though we could catch it through our lust of the eye, the scopophilia that Hamlet associates with the desire to see plays (*Hamlet*, 3.2.140–43); Pandarus thus metaphorically confirms the charges of the anti-theatrical tracts, which often associated attendance at plays with illicit sexuality (see, for example, Jonas Barish, *The Antitheatrical Prejudice* [Berkeley: University of California Press, 1981], p. 85).

9. The play continually frustrates our expectation that plot matters and that endings are final; hence, for example, the fizzling of the much-vaunted Hector-Ajax encounter and of Ulysses's scheme to rouse Achilles, and the almost offhand death of Hector. Barbara Everett powerfully associates these plot discontinuities with "the fragmentation and atomism that we think peculiar to modern life" ("The Inaction of *Troilus and Cressida*," *Essays in Criticism*, 32 [1982]: 30).

10. Thersites's first words about the "matter" of Agamemnon's boils associate meaninglessness with the corrupted body (2.1.2–9). The only matter here is the pus of the play's pervasive infection.

11. Once the illusion of individuated wholeness is gone, the psychic alternatives are bleak: either the isolation of warring fragments or annihilating fusion. Fragmentation is figured, for example, in Ulysses's depiction of a world broken into parts that meet "in mere oppugnancy" (1.3.111), in the descriptions of Cressida or Ajax or Troilus as random collections of unrelated fragments (1.1.54; 1.2.19–31; 1.2.257–61), in the frequent lists of unrelated nouns (1.2.287; 1.3.179–83; 2.2.1–5) that characterize the play; it is dramatically enacted in Hector's myriad wounds and in the Myrmidons who substitute themselves for Achilles's single heroic action. (See J. Hillis Miller's discussion

of stylistic fragmentation in the play ["Ariachne's Broken Woof," *The Georgia Review* 31 (1977): 54] and Charles Lyons's analysis of the gap "between the pure and constant identity of desire and the despoiled and complex fragmentation of identity in reality" ["Cressida, Achilles, and the Finite Deed," *Études Anglaises* 20 (1967): 233].) Annihilation is figured most powerfully in Ulysses's depiction of "appetite," the "universal wolf" who "must make perforce an universal prey, / And last eat up himself" (1.3.121–24) and in the play's other frequent references to eating and being eaten up: war (2.2.6), lechery (5.4.35), pride (2.3.156), time (3.3.148), and fortune (4.5.292) are all voracious eaters, consuming or self-consuming. (R. J. Kaufmann identifies "self-consumption" as the deep theme of the play and notes the presence of eating and cookery images, "subversive of ideals of wholeness and permanence," in connection with this theme ("Ceremonies for Chaos: The Status of *Troilus and Cressida*," *ELH* 32 [1965]: 142, 155.)

12.   In the course of the play, Cressida merges with Helen, both in her sexual soiling and in her status as debased and desired foreign woman. The lovers' first meeting (3.2) and their morning-after scene (4.2) are both symbolically mediated by Helen, literally present in 3.1 and figuratively present through Diomedes's description of her "soilure" in 4.1; variants of "soil" are insistently used in reference to Helen (2.2.71, 2.2.149, 4.1.57) in preparation for Cressida's soiling (5.2.133). Marianne Novy powerfully analyzes the treatment of both Helen and Cressida as pawns or property, symptomatic of flawed gender relations (*Love's Argument: Gender Relations in Shakespeare* [Chapel Hill: University of North Carolina Press, 1984], p. 110).

13.   See, for example, Henri Fluchère in response to Troilus's words: "Tortured love here presents a problem of identity which the play fails to solve" (*Shakespeare*, trans. Guy Hamilton [Longmans: London, 1953], p. 216). Other critics are also troubled by Cressida's failure to achieve a stable identity. Derek Traversi finds Cressida characteristic of a play in which many characters fail to have "consistent status as persons" because they are all subject to time (*An Approach to Shakespeare* [Garden City, N. Y.: Doubleday, 1956], pp. 328–29); John Bayley brilliantly extends Traversi's view in his "Time and the Trojans" (*Essays in Criticism* 25 [1975]: 55–73), understanding Troilus's horror at the two Cressida's as "a recognition not so much of falsity as of the fact that she is not a single coherent person" in a play in which Shakespeare dissolves the "assurances of selfhood" (p. 70). Jonathan Dollimore locates the play's value in just this decentering of the subject; in his reading, the shift in Cressida becomes an instance of the ultimately liberating insight that "identity is a function of position, and position of power" (*Radical Tragedy* [Chicago, Ill.: University of Chicago Press, 1984], p. 48). But Dollimore's reading seems to me ultimately to obscure the extent to which incoherence of identity is not shared equally among the characters; even Bayley seems uneasily aware that Cressida bears more than her fair share (pp. 63, 67). His uneasiness is, I think, characteristic of much of the most acute critical commentary on Cressida, which registers less the dissolution of selfhood than the inconsistency of its presentation. L. C. Knights, for example, comments both on Cressida's position

as a stereotypical wanton and on the note of sincerity we sometimes hear in her exchanges with Troilus ("The Theme of Appearance and Reality in *Troilus and Cressida*," *Some Shakespearean Themes* [Stanford, Calif.: Stanford University Press, 1959], p. 69); Arnold Stein analyzes Cressida both as a full character motivated by her belief that "what is precious is what the masculine 'particular will,' unsatisfied, imagines" and as an incomplete character whose dramatized reserve "prevents her from ever saying or doing what might register the feeling of her full presence" (*"Troilus and Cressida*: The Disjunctive Imagination," *ELH* 36 [1969]: 157–58); Gayle Greene acknowledges that Cressida's "sudden and complete violation of declared intentions damages her coherence in 'realistic' terms" but then goes on to read this violation in realistic terms as Cressida's response to her valuation by others ("Shakespeare's Cressida: 'A kind of self,' " in *The Woman's Part: Feminist Criticism of Shakespeare*, ed. Carol Ruth Swift Lenz, Gayle Greene, and Carol Thomas Neely [Urbana: University of Illinois Press, 1980], pp. 135). But see Linda Charnes's account, where these disjunctions—in Cressida and others—point less toward Shakespeare's inconsistent representation of Cressida than toward his cunning solution to the problems of representing a story so overdetermined: "Rather than trying to make these figures 'new' to his audience, Shakespeare's strategy is to portray their desire, and their inability, to be new even to themselves; to represent their struggle to produce subjective self-representations that can in fact only be realized at the *expense* of their notorious identities" (" 'So Unsecret to Ourselves': Notorious Identity and the Material Subject in Shakespeare's *Troilus and Cressida*," *Shakespeare Quarterly* 40 [1989]: 418).

14. The phrase is L. C. Knights's, yet he himself notes the inadequacy of this characterization and comments tantalizingly that "she exists mainly in the imagination of Troilus" (*Some Shakespearean Themes*, p. 69). See Carolyn Asp ("In Defense of Cressida," *Studies in Philology* 74 [1977]: 406–17), Grant L. Voth and Oliver H. Evans ("Cressida and the World of the Play," *Shakespeare Studies* 8 [1975]: 231–39) and Gayle Greene ("Shakespeare's Cressida: 'A kind of self' ") for accounts of Cressida's critical history. These critics all attempt to rehabiliate Cressida, as do R. A. Yoder (" 'Sons and Daughters of the Game': An Essay on Shakespeare's *Troilus and Cressida*," *Shakespeare Survey* 25 [1972]: 11–25), M. M. Burns (*"Troilus and Cressida*: The Worst of Both Worlds," *Shakespeare Studies* 13 [1980]: 105–30), and Stephen J. Lynch ("Shakespeare's Cressida: 'A Woman of Quick Sense,' " *Philological Quarterly* 63 [1984]: 357–68); they all stress her vulnerable position, specifying her subjection to Troilus's idealism (Voth and Evans, Lynch), to a capitalist society in which there is no intrinsic value (Asp and Greene), to a fragmented society at war (Yoder and Burns), or to the unadorned lust of the Greeks (Lynch). Robert Ornstein anticipates this trend in his powerful early comment on the masculine ego that makes Cressida what she is: "She is a daughter of the game which men would have her play and for which they despise her" (*The Moral Vision of Jacobean Tragedy* [Madison: University of Wisconsin Press, 1960], p. 245). These rehabilitating critics have taught us to see Cressida as the victim of her world, and insofar as I understand Cressida

as a full character, my understanding of her is close to theirs; but, valuable as they are, these readings of Cressida all seem to me to founder because, at the crucial moment of betrayal, the text does not give us sufficient grounds for understanding Cressida fully in their terms. E. Talbot Donaldson's sympathetic reading of the ambiguity of both Criseyde and Cressida is finally more helpful insofar as it acknowledges the gaps in our knowledge of these characters (*The Swan at the Well: Shakespeare Reading Chaucer* [New Haven, Conn.: Yale University Press, 1985], pp. 74–118). (Though Donaldson taught me Chaucer, not Shakespeare, at Yale, I came to realize while reading his book how much my understanding of Shakespeare owes to his understanding of Chaucer.)

15. Lynch, for example, celebrates her wit and finds her the most clear-sighted and trustworthy commentator in the play ("Shakespeare's Cressida: 'A Woman of Quick Sense,' " pp. 357–58, 367). Emil Roy comments more broadly on Cressida's defensive use of language to acquire phallic power and to deny her vulnerable situation ("War and Manliness in Shakespeare's *Troilus and Cressida*," *Comparative Drama* 7 [1973]: 112).

16. The Prologue introduces us to the "expectation" that tickles the "skittish spirits" of audience and characters alike throughout the play (l. 20). The gap between expectation and performance becomes definitive of sexual experience when Troilus defines the "monstruosity in love" (3.2.79) and of war when Agamemnon speaks to his demoralized commanders of the "protractive trials of great Jove" (1.3.20); it governs our aesthetic experience as the play refuses to meet our expectation that its heroes will be heroic or that its plot will be consequential, that its ending will end anything.

17. Gayle Greene comments on Cressida's "uncustomary loss of self-control"; she sees Cressida throughout 3.2 as struggling both to maintain and to relinquish the defenses she has so carefully constructed ("Shakespeare's Cressida: 'A kind of self,' " p. 140).

18. Elizabeth Freund sees in these characters' identifications with their names a demonstration of the extent to which the self is "always already another, a self-alienated iterable citation" (" 'Ariachne's broken woof': The Rhetoric of Citation in *Troilus and Cressida*," in *Shakespeare and the Question of Theory*, ed. Patricia Parker and Geoffrey Hartman [New York and London: Methuen, 1985], pp. 25, 26); for Charnes, the notorious figures of the play "can be present neither to themselves nor to others without recourse to narrative reference, without referring to their own legendary citationality" (" 'So Unsecret to Ourselves,' " p. 429). These are persuasive arguments; but the generalizing of self-alienation runs the risk of obscuring gender differences as they are played out in literary representation, obscuring specifically here the extent to which Cressida's reduction to her name is much more final than Troilus's. Perhaps we are all equally iterable citations; but Shakespearean representation tends frequently—particularly in the tragedies—to create the illusion that men are subjects, and women citations. Moreover, as Carol Cook suggests in her wonderful Lacanian analysis of the play, the self-alienated female helps to

stabilize the illusory wholeness of the male: "the instability and fictionality of identity is finally located and exorcised in Cressida" ("Unbodied Figures of Desire," *Theatre Journal* 38 [1986]: 46).

19. Several critics blame Pandarus for the failure of Troilus's love without noting the implicit alliance between them here and elsewhere; see, for example, Richard D. Fly (" 'I cannot come to Cressid but by Pandar': Mediation in the Theme and Structure of *Troilus and Cressida*," *English Literary Renaissance* 3 [1973]: 153–56) and R. J. Kaufmann ("Ceremonies for Chaos," p. 149).

20. Robert Kimbrough (*Shakespeare's "Troilus and Cressida" and Its Setting* [Cambridge, Mass.: Harvard University Press, 1964], p. 56), Stephen A. Reid ("A Psychoanalytic Reading of 'Troilus and Cressida' and 'Measure for Measure,' " *Psychoanalytic Review* 57 [1970]: 267), Yoder ("Sons and Daughters of the Game," p. 21), Lynch ("Shakespeare's Cressida: 'A Woman of Quick Sense,' " pp. 360–63), Burns ("*Troilus and Cressida*: The Worst of Both Worlds," pp. 120–22), Novy (*Love's Argument*, p. 118), René Girard ("The Politics of Desire in *Troilus and Cressida*," in *Shakespeare and the Question of Theory*, pp. 188–89), and Donaldson (*The Swan at the Well*, pp. 79, 98, and 107–8), among others, note Troilus's weariness and the near-relief with which he gives her up.

21. Girard sees Troilus's desire, reawakened from satiety by Cressida's allusion to the "merry Greeks" who are his potential competitors, as the epitome of "mimetic desire"; he rests his argument partly on the (inaccurate) claim that Troilus does not suspect her fidelity until this moment ("The Politics of Desire in *Troilus and Cressida*," pp. 194–96, 198). In my view, Diomedes— who clearly wants Cressida only because Troilus wants her— presents a more clear-cut instance of pure Girardian desire.

22. Critics have responded to Ulysses's speech in ways that are predictably various. At one end of the spectrum is Kimbrough, for whom the speech is "almost a stage direction to one playing Cressida's role" (*Shakespeare's "Troilus and Cressida" and Its Setting*, p. 79); at the other are Lynch, Burns, and Donaldson, who analyze Ulysses's speech as the consequence of Cressida's rejection of him ("Shakespeare's Cressida: 'A Woman of Quick Sense,' " p. 364–65; "*Troilus and Cressida*: The Worst of Both Worlds," p. 124; *The Swan at the Well*, p. 113).

23. At issue here is, I suspect, a primitive fantasy in which separation *is* infidelity: for the infant, the mother's separateness constitutes the first betrayal; insofar as she is not his, she is promiscuously Other. This sense of otherness itself as promiscuous betrayal may antedate the more specifically triangular oedipal jealousies and be retrospectively sexualized by them; in this (implicitly anti-Girardian) model, the early sense of betrayal itself may create the need for a rival on whom to lay the blame. The whole process seems to be condensed in the play's conflation, in the character and characterization of Cressida, of separation, opaque otherness, and sexual betrayal with a rival.

24. Joel Fineman writes powerfully about the consequences of the loss of distinction, or Difference, in *Troilus and Cressida*, expanding on Girard's brief commentary on Ulysses's "degree" speech (Fineman, "Fratricide and Cuckoldry: Shakespeare's Doubles," in *Representing Shakespeare: New Psychoanalytic Essays*, ed. Murray M. Schwartz and Coppélia Kahn [Baltimore, Md.: Johns Hopkins University Press, 1980], pp. 94–100; Girard, *Violence and the Sacred* [Baltimore, Md.: Johns Hopkins University Press, 1977], pp. 50–51).

25. The extraordinary frequency of references to feeding, palates, tasting, and distasting, suggests that the other characters share Troilus's tastes: see, for example, 1.3.337–38, 389; 2.2.67, 124; 2.3.218; 3.2.90, 158; 3.3.13, 49; 4.1.60; 4.4.3, 7, 47; 4.5.230; 5.2.126; 5.3.111; 5.8.19. Emil Roy comments on the Trojans' urge for oral merger and their fears of engulfment, noting Troilus's insatiable desire for the mother's breast in 3.2; he sees both Helen and Cressida as contested mother-figures ("War and Manliness," pp. 109–10).

26. Roy similarly suggests that strategies of splitting in the play derive from failed attempts to regain the nurturing mother ("War and Manliness," pp. 118–19); his wonderfully suggestive and maddeningly chaotic essay anticipates my understanding of the play at several points. He does not, however, see the extent to which union with the nurturing mother is ultimately as threatening as the loss of her.

27. Terence Eagleton says, more charitably, "Cressida to him is the Cressida of their relationship; she has no meaning or existence for him outside this context" because reality and identity are social, shared creations (*Shakespeare and Society* [London: Chatto & Windus, 1967], p. 17). This is all very well but, again, obscures gender differences; would Eagleton seriously propose that Antony ceases to be Antony at the moment that he becomes Octavia's Antony rather than Cleopatra's?

28. "Ariachne" is a famous crux, especially delightful to deconstructionists. J. Hillis Miller finds in it a symptom of the play's challenge to Western logocentric monological metaphysics insofar as it asks us to hold two incongruent myths in our heads at once ("Ariachne's Broken Woof," p. 47); his argument has a powerful—and characteristically unassuming—antecedent in L. C. Knights's discussion of the same passage (*Some Shakespearean Themes*, p. 71). In Freund's complex extension of Miller's argument, Ariachne, "child of écriture," becomes the muse for the play's (and the period's) "sustained meditation on the parasitism of texts and on the plight of a belated writer who knows that all the stories have already been told" ("Ariachne's Broken Woof," p. 34). I see in the composite Ariachne less the signs of fractured metaphysics or citational belatedness than the signs of the play's split treatment of Cressida, who is both Arachne (the treacherous spider-woman) and Ariadne (the archetypal woman betrayed—in this case by the plot as well as by Troilus).

29. Shakespeare frequently associates "subtle" with sexuality; see, for

example, Othello's "subtle whore" (4.2.21) or Temperance, "a delicate wench, / Ay, and a subtle" (*Tempest*, 2.1.43–44). My somewhat bizarre reading here depends in part on Cressida's virginity, never certain in the play. Shakespeare's revision of his heroine's marital status—in Chaucer, she is a widow—at least allows for the possibility; her morning-after response to Troilus—"You men will never tarry" (4.2.16)—may be second-hand schoolgirl wisdom, or it may be evidence that she is "already an experienced coquette" (Fluchère, *Shakespeare*, p. 214).

30. Donaldson notes that Troilus's "favorite subject, . . . his own high potential for maintaining constancy in love," is characteristically accompanied by doubts about Cressida's capacity for fidelity (*The Swan at the Well*, pp. 98–99); he further notes that Troilus welcomes "the separation—even Cressida's possible infidelity—as providing the most favorable circumstances in which to exhibit his fidelity" (p. 111).

31. In teaching this play, I have often found myself "correcting" students who assume that Troilus is announcing his impending union with Cressida; see Daniel Seltzer's footnote to this passage for a similar correction (The Signet Classic Shakespeare, *Troilus and Cressida* [New York: New American Library, 1963], p. 85). We all know that Troilus is simply inventing an analogy. But I think that the naive students are, as so often happens, at least partly right: they can teach us to notice Troilus's breath-taking capacity to compartmentalize, so that he can use this analogy apparently without registering its relevance. Critical response to this passage suggests that Troilus's capacity to compartmentalize is catching.

32. Derek Traversi's wonderful intuition that sexuality seeks union but always entails a sense of separation seems to me very near the heart of the play; he too sees the plot as in effect a rationalization for this inevitable movement (*An Approach to Shakespeare*, p. 325–37). See also L. C. Knights ("The actual separation of the lovers . . . only emphasizes what is in fact intrinsic to their relationship" ["The Theme of Appearance and Reality in *Troilus and Cressida*," p. 67]) and Everett ("Troilus and Cressida are hostile lovers, for whom love is a way of proving human separateness" ["The Inaction of *Troilus and Cressida*," p. 126]). These critics do not analyze the sense of separateness in any detail, nor do they analyze it psychoanalytically. Such an analysis is promised by Stephen Reid, who notes Troilus's worry that the sexual act will be disappointing as a result of "the gap between the sense of boundlessness in his desire and the limitation of the sexual act" ("A Psychoanalytic Reading," p. 264). But although his essay generally locates the source of sexual dissatisfaction where Freud does, in the deflection of desire from its original incestuous objects and in the repression of pre-genital components of sexuality, he attributes this particular gap only to the temporal limitations of the sexual act, noting neither the oral valence of Troilus's desire nor his association of Cressida with his mother.

33. Act 3, scene 3, the scene in which the trade of Cressida for Antenor is

arranged, occurs between 3.2, in which the lovers move toward the bedchamber under the guidance of Pandarus, and 4.2, the morning-after scene. Act 3, scene 3 thus occurs during what we think of as the lovers' night together; and yet it is obviously an outdoor daytime scene. But which day? The lovers awaken in 4.2 on the morning of the non-battle between Ajax and Hector; in 3.3, the battle is still "tomorrow" (l. 246). Judging from the exchange of dismissive salutations (3.3.62–69), 3.3. takes place early on the day before the non-battle. Act 3, scene 2 seems to take place later the same day: Pandarus's comment— "how loath you are to offend daylight!" (l. 47)—specifies that the lovers meet during the day; nonetheless, given the lovers' departure for bed and their awakening in 4.2 the next morning, there is a strong presumption that they are meeting late in the day. The simultaneity of consummation and separation thus requires some temporal disjunction, since 3.2 apparently takes place after 3.3. Norman Rabkin notes that arrangements for the separation are being made while the lovers are enjoying their night together; he does not note this disjunction (*Shakespeare and the Common Understanding* [New York: The Free Press, 1967], p. 50).

34. I do not mean to imply that Troilus's fear of engulfment is "really" castration anxiety, rather that castration anxiety itself may work to rationalize and localize a more general and overwhelming fear of engulfment derivative from pre-genital phases of development.

35. Shakespeare often sexualizes variants on *stand*; see Eric Partridge, *Shakespeare's Bawdy* (New York: E. P. Dutton, 1960), p. 194, for numerous examples. The reference in the nearly contemporaneous *All's Well That Ends Well* is especially germane: the Clown tells the Countess that Bertram will live longer now that he has left his wife to go to war, since "the danger is in standing to't; that's the loss of men, though it be the getting of children" (3.2.40–41).

36. Both of the men seem to want to turn her into a baby; Troilus's wish to infantilize Cressida is curiously echoed in Pandarus's teasing baby-talk after the consummaton ("Has't not slept tonight? Would he not—ah, naughty man—let it sleep? A bugbear take him!" (4.2.32–33).

37. For other references to Troilus's youth, see, for example, 1.2.113–19, 238; 2.2.167; 4.2.77; 4.5.96; 5.2.164; these references prepare for Hector's developmental narrative here.

38. Shakespeare's need for a Troilus who is at least marginally heroic throughout additionally complicates the portrayal of him as warrior: despite Troilus's sense of himself as disarmed by love, he re-arms himself at the end of 1.1, exiting the scene with Aeneas, bound for the "sport abroad" (1.1.115); and in 1.2 Cressida watches him return from the battle with a bloodied sword (11. 235–36). Moreover, Ulysses's panegyric in 4.5 claims that he is as "manly as Hector, but more dangerous" (l. 104) well before his disillusionment with Cressida. But this panegyric sounds premature, partly because we never see

Troilus as a warrior after 1.2, and partly because both 5.2 and 5.3 suggest in different ways that Troilus's ruthless masculinity is a new development.

39. Richard P. Wheeler (*Shakespeare's Development and the Problem Comedies* [Berkeley: University of California Press, 1981], p. 200) and Marianne Novy (*Love's Argument*, pp. 100 and 111), among others, similarly note Troilus's construction of ruthless masculinity as leaving womanish weakness behind. Although she does not discuss *Troilus and Cressida* specifically, Madelon Gohlke (now Sprengnether) sees this renunciation of the female as the characteristic founding gesture of tragic masculinity in Shakespeare (" 'I wooed thee with my sword': Shakespeare's Tragic Paradigms," in *Representing Shakespeare*, pp. 170–87); as always, I am indebted to her here.

40. The play does not wholly endorse Troilus's view of ruthless masculinity, as the exchange with Hector ("O, 'tis fair play" [5.3.42]) makes plain. But Ulysses clearly prefers Troilus's style of masculinity (4.5.104–9); and Hector himself is too compromised a figure to give us a strong alternative. Moreover, Shakespeare constructs the scene dramatically so that even Hector's manhood depends on his leaving the women behind, ignoring Andromache's and Cassandra's requests that he disarm (5.3.3, 25), in order to maintain his honor on the field.

41. Many critics, following G. Wilson Knight, see Troilus's love as in some sense idealizing, an attempt to achieve the infinite and spiritual by finite sensual means (*The Wheel of Fire* [New York: Meridian, 1957], pp. 63–65); see, e.g., Traversi (*An Approach to Shakespeare*, p. 331), Lynch ("Shakespeare's Cressida: 'A Woman of Quick Sense,' " p. 362), and especially Cook on the tension between desire and the representability and corporality of its objects ("Unbodied Figures of Desire," p.p. 34–42).

42. Though he does not discuss *Troilus and Cressida* at any length, my account of Troilus's movement here is very much indebted to Richard Wheeler's account of the oscillation between "extreme situations either of destructive merger or desperate isolation" (p. 157) in Shakespeare's tragedies and romances; see " 'Since first we were dissevered': Trust and Autonomy in Shakespeare's Development," the wonderfully rich concluding chapter to his *Shakespeare's Development and the Problem Comedies*, especially pp. 200–221.

43. On his way to establishing the presence of mimetic desire everywhere in this text, Girard constructs an argument very similar to mine in its understanding of the ways in which the plot covers for Troilus here, fulfilling "his secret wish" without making him take responsibility for it ("The Politics of Desire in *Troilus and Cressida*," p. 194). But since his Troilus suffers only temporarily from sexual satiety (his desire is restored mimetically, through Cressida's well-timed allusion to the "merry Greeks"), Girard does not see the extent to which Cressida's final betrayal serves the same wish.

44. This is the logic according to which Pandarus blames Cressida for the separation (4.2.88–89) even before she has left Troy. This shift of blame may

partly account for an habitual oddity in critical response to the play: even those critics who do not question Troilus's apparently unflagging devotion to Cressida after the consummation tend to find Cressida's "things won are done; joy's soul lies in the doing" an apt summary for the play; see, for example, Stein, "*Troilus and Cressida*," p. 158; Kaufmann, "Ceremonies for Chaos," p. 155; and Rabkin, *Shakespeare and the Common Understanding*, p. 44. Charles Lyons argues persuasively that the self-consuming sexual act, in which "the very consummation which appetite demands destroys the appetite and so disintegrates the source of value," is the model for all action and all valuation in the play ("Cressida, Achilles, and the Finite Deed," p. 233). His argument founders only when he turns specifically to Troilus, as his uneasiness about the point at which Troilus revalues Cressida indicates: "He conceives of her as a sexual object, uses her, and—when he suffers knowledge of her common behavior—he discards her" (p. 241). His uneasiness indicates the point at which he replicates—rather than analyzing—the play's shift of blame from Troilus to Cressida.

45. Iago is very largely absent in the account that follows. Like most analysts of Othello's susceptibility to Iago, I see the stunning success of Iago's tutoring as an indication of Iago's status as the psychic repository for Othello's own unrecognized doubts, the "shadow-side of Othello," as Maud Bodkin calls him (*Archetypal Patterns in Poetry* [London: Oxford University Press, 1934], p. 245); I consequently focus on these doubts in Othello. Nonetheless, Iago has his own distinctive solutions to the problems that torment Othello. If Othello is destroyed at least in part by his pain at having desecrated an idealized maternal body, Iago has disavowed that body from the start. His determination to serve only himself, his fundamental distrust of the world, his need to destroy whatever goodness or beauty he sees in it: all seem adult equivalents of infantile rage at a mother who has failed him. The degree to which his attack is ultimately on maternal presence is registered largely through his appropriation of a perverted form of female generativity: fantasizing his plot as a dark pregnancy (1.3.401–2), he makes its success the consequence of his own parthenogenetic power. Thus its anti-generative force: initially directed toward anyone who seems full in the face of his emptiness, his hatred of the idealized maternal body is ultimately directed toward Desdemona, driving him toward the tragic lodging of the bed as the goal that he can never quite acknowledge. In him the relationship between hatred of maternal power and fantasies of male parthenogenesis—a relationship elaborated in *King Lear*, *Macbeth*, *Cymbeline*, and *The Tempest*—is explored for the first time in the tragedies.

46. Three extraordinary critics explored the dynamics of the male sexual imagination in essays published in 1979 and 1980: Stanley Cavell ("*Othello* and the Stake of the Other," *Disowning Knowledge in Six Plays of Shakespeare* [Cambridge: Cambridge University Press, 1987], pp. 125–42; originally published in 1979 both in *Daedalus* and as the concluding section of *The Claim of Reason* [Oxford: Oxford University Press]), Edward A. Snow ("Sexual Anxiety and the Male Order of Things in *Othello*," *English Literary Renais-*

sance 10 [1980]: 384–412), and Stephen Greenblatt ("The Improvisation of Power," *Renaissance Self-Fashioning* [Chicago, Ill.: The University of Chicago Press, 1980], pp. 232–52). While strikingly different in emphasis, these essays nonetheless established and elaborated the psychological dynamic of Othello's jealousy: for each of these critics, Othello's readiness to believe his wife a whore depends in large measure on his own sexual revulsion, whether that revulsion is understood as one of the signs of his dismay at human finitude and imperfection (Cavell) or as the consequence of his enforced identification with the punitive father-superego of patriarchal society (Snow) or his dependence in his fragile self-fashioning on the Christian doctrine condemning sexual pleasure as adulterous (Greenblatt). Though I finally disagree with important elements of the argument in each of these essays—with Snow's romanticizing of sexual passion and consequent assumption that the superego and its agents and institutions in patriarchal society are entirely to blame for the tragedy; with Greenblatt's underplaying the psychic processes that make Christian sexual revulsion congenial to Othello; and to a lesser extent with Cavell's wanting to take what seems to me Othello's decidedly male dilemma as a test case for "the way human separateness is turned equally toward splendor and toward horror" (p. 137)—the following discussion relies heavily on their work; because they collectively demonstrate so fully the mechanisms through which Othello finds his own guilt in Cassio, I have not found it necessary to do so in any detail. I owe a particular debt to Edward Snow, whose essay I saw in various early forms long before it was published and whose many brilliant formulations doubtless helped to reshape my understanding of much in Shakespeare even when I was not immediately aware of the debt. Though each of these critics anticipates my argument at several points, none foregrounds either the relationship with *Troilus and Cressida* or the maternal subtext that I find essential to the play. This subtext is in part the subject of Arthur Kirsch's reading of *Othello*, initially published in 1978 and reprinted in his *Shakespeare and the Experience of Love* (Cambridge: Cambridge University Press, 1981), pp. 10–39; he finds the currents of idealization and debasement, consequences of the male child's first relationship with his mother, central to the play. Kirsch's essay is particularly good at identifying the fusion of erotic and spiritual ecstasy in Othello's love; his account of the processes of debasement is less satisfying, partly because his own idealization of Othello's love and its object in Desdemona—and his laudable desire to rescue Othello from charges that he is merely spiritually or psychologically pathological—keep him from discussing with much exactness how it is that Othello comes to kill his wife. For other essays that anticipate the more recent studies of male sexual pathology, see, for example, Bodkin's wonderful early statement of the interrelation between romantic idealization and sexual cynicism in Othello (*Archetypal Patterns in Poetry*, pp. 221–23), Leo Kirschbaum's comments on Othello's attempt to disclaim sexual feeling in his love for Desdemona (*Character and Characterization in Shakespeare* [Detroit, Mich.: Wayne State University Press, 1962], pp. 150–58), Stephen Shapiro's claim that Othello sets Desdemona up as a "virginal but maternal idol to worship" and then hates her for inhibiting his sexual instincts ("Othello's Desdemona," in *The Design Within*, ed. M. D. Faber [New York: Science House, 1970], pp. 185–92; originally published in *Literature and Psychology* in 1964), Hugh Richmond's analysis of Othello's absolutism ("Love and Justice: *Othello*'s Shakespearean Context," in *Pacific Coast Studies in Shakespeare*, ed. Waldo F. McNeir and Thelma N. Greenfield [Eugene: University of Oregon Books, 1966], pp. 148–72), Stephen Reid's account of Othello's repressed oedipal rage ("Othello's Jealousy," *American Imago* 25 [1968]: 274–93), Leslie Fiedler's brilliant intuition that Iago—and the Iago in Othello—is what happens when the dark attraction to and revulsion from sexuality is no longer exorcised by comedic laughter (*The Stranger in Shakespeare* [London: Croom Helm, 1973], esp. pp. 155–64), Michael Long's discussion of Othello as victim and representative of a Venetian society that attempts to ignore the wild world of natural appetite (*The Unnatural Scene* [London: Methuen and Company, 1976], pp. 37–58), Carol Thomas Neely's now classic account of the women in the play as failed comic heroines, unable to cure the men of their murderous tendency to idealize and degrade women ("Women and Men in *Othello*: 'What should such a fool / Do with so good a woman?' " in *The Woman's Part*, pp. 211–39; first published in *Shakespeare Studies* in 1978), Andre Green's complex Lacanian reading of Othello's transgression of the law of the father ("*Othello*: A Tragedy of Conversion," *The Tragic Effect: The Oedipus Complex in Tragedy*, trans. Alan Sheridan [Cambridge: Cambridge University Press, 1979], pp. 88–136), and Gayle Greene's exploration of tragically interlocking gender roles (" 'This That You Call Love': Sexual and Social Tragedy in *Othello*," *Journal of Women's Studies in Literature* 1 [1979]: 16–32). Among more recent accounts of the play, those by Marianne L. Novy, Peter Erickson, and Richard P. Wheeler are closest to my own concerns: see Novy, *Love's Argument*, pp. 125–49; Erickson, *Patriarchal Structures in Shakespeare's Drama* (Berkeley: University of California Press, 1985), esp. pp. 89–97; and Wheeler, " ' ... And my loud crying still': The *Sonnets*, *The Merchant of Venice*, and *Othello*," in *Shakespeare's "Rough Magic": Renaissance Essays in Honor of C. L. Barber*, ed. Peter Erickson and Coppélia Kahn (Newark, N.J.: University of Delaware Press, 1985), pp. 193–209, and *Shakespeare's Development and the Problem Comedies*, esp. pp. 18, 125, and 128.

47. Until relatively recently, most critics seem to have assumed that the consummation took place as planned (2.3.9–10). This assumption has recently been challenged at length by T. G. A. Nelson and Charles Haines ("Othello's Unconsummated Marriage," *Essays in Criticism* 33 [1983]: 1–18), who assume that the consummation is first interrupted by the brawl and then indefinitely deferred by Othello's tending to Montano's wounds, Desdemona's badgering him about Cassio, and Cassio's well-meant morning music. They are very literal-minded about all this, assuming not the intervention of any psychological process but rather that the lovers simply didn't have time. But given the play's more famous problem with time, it seems dangerous to base so

significant a speculation on exact time-keeping here; if Iago has had time to get three lads of Cyprus drunk before he begins on Cassio (2.3.54), then the lovers have had time for their intimacies. Moreover, even exact time-keeping does not support their assumption. This is a long night; Shakespeare specifies both that the General has "cast" Cassio and Iago early for love of Desdemona (2.3.14) and that the interruption comes well over an hour after the lovers leave the stage (Iago tells us that the lovers leave before 10 P. M. and that the watch is not due to be set until 11 [2.3.13]. After the drinking scene, Montano marks the time by offering—at l. 113—to set the watch; since it is therefore presumably nearing 11 P. M., the drinking scene has taken roughly an hour. At this point, there is still the brawl to come before the lovers are awakened.) Nor is it at all clear that Othello leaves to tend to Montano, despite his offer to be surgeon to his wounds: he ends the scene by ordering others to lead Montano off (l. 246) at the same time as he twice tells Desdemona to come— not go—to bed (ll. 244, 249); the strong implication is that he leaves with Desdemona, not with Montano. The play thus allows time for the consumma- tion. More seriously, the hypothesis of Nelson and Haines depends not on such dubious evidence as they adduce but on a rather naive sense of psychological plausibility: they find Othello's surrender to jealousy "inconceivable, whether by the standards of dramatic convention or by those of realism and common sense" in a man "who has just completed a blissful union with a loved and admired wife" (p. 2); in their view, the jealousy becomes plausible only once we understand that Othello is suffering from an unbearable sexual frustration that clouds his rational faculties (p. 3). Since consummation is followed by revulsion in three of the plays written in proximity to Othello—Troilus, All's Well, and Measure—it is clear that Shakespeare does not share their view of what is plausible. Their interpretation fails to account for the particulars of Othello's misjudgment, especially for the part that his ambivalence toward sexuality plays in that misjudgment; it moreover outrageously glorifies the strength of the male sexual impulse by making its frustration for one night adequate (that is, credible) grounds for a man's murder of his wife. This seems to me morally as well as psychologically dubious. It is of course possible to doubt the consummation on other grounds: Greene (" 'This That You Call Love,' " p. 23), Neely ("Women and Men in Othello," p. 233), Randolph Splitter ("Language, Sexual Conflict, and 'Symbiosis Anxiety' in Othello," Mosaic 15 [1982]: 23), Michael Neill ("Changing Places in Othello," Shake- speare Survey 37 [1984]: 116), Peter L. Rudnytsky ("The Purloined Handker- chief in Othello," in The Psychoanalytic Study of Literature, ed. Joseph Reppen and Maurice Charney [Hillside, N.J.: The Analytic Press, 1985], pp. 181–82), and Julia B. Holloway ("Strawberries and Mulberries: Ulysses and Othello," in Hypatia, ed. William M. Calder, III, Ulrich K. Goldsmith, and Phyllis B. Kenevan [Boulder: Colorado Associated University Press, 1985], pp. 125–36) all express such doubts, though they do not always make their basis entirely clear; Pierre Janton ("Othello's Weak Function," Cahiers Elisabethains 7 [1975]: 43–50) and Marjorie Pryse ("Lust for Audience: An Interpretation of Othello," ELH 43 [1976]: 465–68) assume that Othello is—or is made to be—impotent. In Joel Kovel's brilliant dialectical reading of the intersection of psychic process and cultural circumstance in what he takes to be the unconsummated marriage, Othello's phallic power is given him by the state that simultaneously demands its repression, maintaining sexuality as a "goad" and readying it "for the turn into hate" in the service of the state ("*Othello*," *American Imago* 35 [1978]: 117–18); see also Kay Stockholder's account of the "Venetian view" of Othello "that forces him to repudiate his sexuality" ("Form as Metaphor: *Othello* and Love-Death Romance," *Dalhousie Review* 64 [1984–85]: 738). In Cavell's beautiful inquiry, doubt about the consummation is not a matter that the audience can or should be able to resolve; it is rather a sign of Othello's own inability to tolerate the knowledge of consummation and its attendant contamination (*Disowning Knowledge*, pp. 131–37). In the end, this issue cannot be settled with absolute certainty. Nonetheless, both the abruptness of Othello's belief that his wife is a whore and the terms in which that belief expresses itself point toward a fantasy of contaminating consummation immediately before Iago's poison begins to work in 3.3; that this psychic event is at the center of the play is given added plausibility by its reiteration in the plays surrounding *Othello*—*All's Well*, *Troilus and Cressida*, and *Measure for Measure*—each of which embeds a morning-after fantasy in its plot.

48. Othello's need for Desdemona to remain intact is partly the measure of his own sense of himself as empty and fragmented; no longer intact, she loses her potency as a source of wholeness for him. Critics have understood what I am here calling Othello's sense of the gaps in his being in a variety of ways, most commonly as a consequence of his perception of his status as black outsider; for good recent accounts, see, for example, Erickson's discussion of Othello's unstable position as the marginalized man who must protect Venice's margins (*Patriarchal Structures*, pp. 85–86) and Neill's discussion of Desdemona as the "place" of Othello's vulnerable identity ("Changing Places," pp. 126–28). For others, Othello's sense of lack is more broadly diagnostic of the ways in which we construct our identities and relationships; see especially Kenneth Burke, who in an extraordinary early essay finds the triad of Othello, Desdemona, and Iago representative of the estrangement inherent in the idea of property ("*Othello*: An Essay to Illustrate a Method," *The Hudson Review* 4 [1951]: 165–203), Greenblatt, who uses Lacan to explicate the self-alienation inherent in narrative self-fashioning (*Renaissance Self-Fashioning*, pp. 244–45), and Cavell, who understands Othello's investment of perfection in Desdemona as a consequence of his (skeptical) inability to tolerate human finitude and imperfection (*Disowning Knowledge*, pp. 9, 137–38). Like Cavell, I find the fact of separateness itself at the root of Othello's sense of gap or loss; but I understand Othello's pain as the adult reworking of the infant's sense of his mother as separate. (This possibility is only implicit in Cavell's original essay, but see *Disowning Knowledge*, where he specifically invokes—and then partially disowns—this psychoanalytic interpretation [p. 13].) Splitter finds preoedipal anxiety about merger and hence identity, rather than preoedipal separa-

tion anxiety, central to the play ("Language, Sexual Conflict and 'Symbiosis Anxiety' in *Othello*," especially p. 24).

49.   It's hard for me not to hear in this conjunction an echo of what the ceremony of breeching might have felt like to the boy-child not quite yet ready to leave his mother's embrace; see Chapter 1, p. 7.

50.   Kirsch (*Shakespeare and the Experience of Love*, p. 33), Snow ("Sexual Anxiety," p. 404), Erickson (*Patriarchal Structures*, p. 190, n. 15), and Novy (*Love's Argument*, pp. 132, 146–47) all comment on the maternal valence of this passage, and hence of Othello's relation with Desdemona. Though they do not comment at length on this passage, both Wheeler and C. L. Barber find the fusion of wife and mother in Desdemona central to the tragedy: see especially Wheeler, *Shakespeare's Development*, pp. 18, 125; Wheeler, " ' . . . And my loud crying still,' " pp. 201–3; and C. L. Barber and Richard P. Wheeler, *The Whole Journey: Shakespeare's Power of Development* (Berkeley: University of California Press, 1986), pp. 34–35, 277–78. My reading of this passage, and of much else in *Othello*, is indebted to conversations with Brent Cohen and to his unpublished PhD. dissertation, "Sexuality and Tragedy in *Othello* and *Antony and Cleopatra*" (University of California, Berkeley, 1981); see especially pp. 71–72.

51.   The imagery here is anticipated—and illuminated—by Othello's previous fantasy of toad, dungeon, and sexual contamination, in which he himself is the toad: "I had rather be a toad, / And live upon the vapour in a dungeon, / Than keep a corner in a thing I love, / For others' uses" (3.3.274–77). This imagery would have been especially pointed for a Renaissance audience, for whom the association between toads and lust was conventional: as Karl P. Wentersdorf notes in connection with this passage, "In pictorial art, *Luxuria* may be depicted as a naked man or woman with a toad at the breast or genitals" ("Animal Symbolism in Shakespeare's *Hamlet*: The Imagery of Sex Nausea," *Comparative Drama* 17 [1983–84]: 370); he reproduces a stunning example (*Les Amants Trépassés*, a sixteenth-century painting by the Master of the Upper Rhine in which a toad crouches at a naked woman's genitals).

52.   As many have noted, the timing of Othello's readiness to believe his wife a whore immediately after their consummation is both crucial and problematic: crucial to understanding the role his own sexual shame plays in the tragedy; and problematic insofar as it makes absurd Othello's belief that Cassio and Desdemona have had time to commit the act of shame a thousand times (5.2.211–13). But since Shakespeare revises Cinthio's more plausible temporal arrangement, he must have wanted the juxtaposition of consummation and debasement enough to be willing to put up with the risk of absurdity: in Cinthio, Iago's insinuations begin only after Othello has been married for some time; as A. C. Bradley notes, all the famous problems with time arise only because the temptation begins on the morning after the consummated marriage (*Shakespearean Tragedy* [New York: Meridian Books, Inc., 1955], p. 342). In

fact the literal absurdity makes the psychological point: it is easier for Othello to imagine his beloved as already soiled, and soiled innumerable times, than for him to imagine himself as the soiling agent.

53. This process has already been elaborated in 3.3: "My name, that was as fresh / As Dian's visage, is now begrim'd, and black / As mine own face" (ll. 392–94). Whether we accept Folio's "my" or Second Quarto's "her," the lines point toward the mutuality of contamination: Othello sees his begrimed face as it is reflected in the blackening of Desdemona's chaste purity by his own black desire. (See Snow, "Sexual Anxiety," pp. 401–2, and Cavell, *Disowning Knowledge*, pp. 130, 136, for particularly fine readings of the process in this passage; in Cavell's words, he is "black with desire, which she desires.") Othello's finding only his own face the adequate measure for the contamination of his Diana has always seemed to me the most poignant moment in the play considered as a tragedy of race. And it must be so considered: Othello's status as an outsider and his inevitable participation in the metaphoric system of a culture that equates black with foul and white with fair are crucial elements in his tragedy, predisposing him both to seek a mirror for himself in the fair Desdemona and to believe that she must be foul for having chosen him. Particularly given the degree to which the play turns on stereotypes of the black Moor or African, it is obviously inadequate to see Othello as merely Everyman (see, e.g., Eldred Jones, *Othello's Countrymen: The African in English Renaissance Drama* [London: Oxford University Press, 1965], esp. pp. 86–109, or Karen Newman, " 'And wash the Ethiop white': Femininity and the Monstrous in *Othello*," in *Shakespeare Reproduced: The Text in History and Ideology*, ed. Jean E. Howard and Marion F. O'Connor [New York: Methuen, 1987], pp. 143–62). Nonetheless, Shakespeare does not "other" the psychological processes explored in the play by making them only the consequences of Othello's race; instead, he uses Othello's blackness to bring particular poignance and intensity to dilemmas commonly shared. Part of Shakespeare's special genius here is to make us feel simultaneously Othello's exotic uniqueness and his representativeness, what Burke early on called "the 'black man' in every lover" ("*Othello*: An Essay to Illustrate a Method," p. 182). But see also Michael Neill's important corrective to this "liberal" view; in his most recent account, the play turns on the horror of miscegenation that it pruriently provokes ("Unproper Beds: Race, Adultery, and the Hideous in *Othello*," *Shakespeare Quarterly* 40 [1989]: 383–412).

54. In Lydna E. Boose's classic essay, "Othello's Handkerchief: 'The Recognizance and Pledge of Love' " (*English Literary Renaissance* 5 [1975]: 360–74), the handkerchief is a "visually recognizable reduction of Othello and Desdemona's wedding-bed sheets" (p. 363). This reading of the handkerchief has been almost universally accepted by recent psychoanalytically oriented critics, displacing (or perhaps combining) earlier attempts to identify the handkerchief with the breast (Martin Wangh, "*Othello*: The Tragedy of Iago," in *The Design Within*, p. 166; Robert Fliess, *Erogeneity and Libido* [New York: International Universities Press, 1956], pp. 66–69) or the penis (Gordon Ross Smith, "Iago the Paranoiac," in *The Design Within*, pp. 176–77). But a Lacan-

ian counter-tradition reads the handkerchief as the fetishistic sign of the missing maternal phallus; see Green ("*Othello*: A Tragedy of Conversion," especially pp. 99–100, 110, and 126) and Rudnytsky ("The Purloined Handkerchief," pp. 185–86).

55.   Some version of this tension is at the center of many recent psychoanalytically oriented accounts of Othello, where the crux of the tragedy is seen as his inability to unite the affectionate/spiritual and the sensual trends in his love for Desdemona. These readings depend ultimately on Freud's account of the dual processes of idealization and debasement of women as strategies for dealing with the anxieties of oedipal desire ("On the Universal Tendency to Debasement in the Sphere of Love," *The Standard Edition of the Complete Psychological Works of Sigmund Freud*, vol. 11 [London: The Hogarth Press, 1957] pp. 179–90); see, for example, Shapiro ("Othello's Desdemona," p. 187), Reid ("Othello's Jealousy," pp. 287–88), Robert Rogers ("Endopsychic Drama in *Othello*," *Shakespeare Quarterly* 20 [1969]: 213), and especially Kirsch (*Shakespeare and the Experience of Love*, pp. 33, 37–39) and Wheeler (*Shakespeare's Development*, p. 128). The twin processes of idealization and debasement are central even where Freud is not explicitly invoked: see, for example, Bodkin (*Archetypal Patterns*, pp. 222–33), Kirschbaum (*Character and Characterization*, pp. 152–55), Neely ("Women and Men in *Othello*," pp. 216–17), Greene (" 'This That You Call Love,' " pp. 17, 21–22), Snow ("Sexual Anxiety," p. 394), W. D. Adamson ("Unpinned or Undone?: Desdemona's Critics and the Problem of Sexual Innocence," *Shakespeare Studies* 13 [1980]: 181–82), Novy (*Love's Argument*, pp. 132–33), and especially Cavell, for whom "the pivot of *Othello*'s interpretation of skepticism is Othello's placing of a finite woman in the place made and left by Descartes for God," with his consequent surprise at finding that she is flesh and blood (*Disowning Knowledge*, pp. 35, 126, and 136). I owe my general sense of the investment of the sacred in familial relationships to C. L. Barber (see Chapter 2, n. 45; and see Barber and Wheeler's *The Whole Journey*, pp. 33–35, for discussion specifically of the sacred in relation to Desdemona).

56.   See particularly Barber and Wheeler's comments on the degree to which the handkerchief demonstrates both "Othello's need to sanctify [sexuality] and keep it virginal" and his identification of wife with mother (*The Whole Journey*, pp. xxi, 278); Novy similarly finds in the handkerchief "suggestions of Othello's fantasy of love as fusion with a woman both maternal and virginal" (*Love's Argument*, p. 133). Snow notes that the handkerchief is "a nexus for the three aspects of woman—chaste bride, sexual object, and maternal threat—which the institution it represents seeks to separate" ("Sexual Anxiety," pp. 391, 392). My formulation here is in a sense an extension of a potential contradiction in Neely's rich account of the handkerchief: she identifies it with "women's civilizing power," specifically with the "middle ground [the women find] between lust and abstinence," hence with "sexuality controlled by chastity"; but she adds in a note that this power "belongs almost always to maidens" and is in abeyance in married women ("Women and Men," pp. 228, 229, and 238). But if it is in abeyance in married women, then there is no

middle ground, and the handkerchief represents the control that virginity, not chastity, exercises over sexuality.

57.   See note 23, in this chapter; the frustrated desire of the oedipal complex gives a local habitation and a name to the crisis of the mother's otherness—her unpossessability—that precedes it.

58.   "Her" refers equally to the mother and to the wife; insofar as the mother is vividly present and the wife there only by implication, as the syntactically nonexistent object of the intransitive verb "wive," "her" might be said to refer more clearly to the mother than to the wife. Snow notes the fusion of mother and wife in "her" and the circular transmission of the handkerchief ("Sexual Anxieties," p. 404); but he does not specify the centrality of death in this process. Although Erickson does not comment on this fusion or the return specifically to the dead mother, he anticipates my account of the handkerchief: his Desdemona "lives implicitly under the sign of the maidens whose hearts supply the mummy" and is killed when Othello acts out this association (*Patriarchal Structures*, pp. 94, 95).

59.   In her discussion of adultery, Emilia oddly anticipates the psychoanalytic terms here: "I might do it as well in the dark . . . By my troth, I think I should, and undo't when I had done it" (4.3.66–71). Shapiro ("Othello's Desdemona," pp. 189–90), Boose ("Othello's Handkerchief," p. 373), Holloway ("Strawberries and Mulberries," pp. 131–34), and Stockholder ("Form as Metaphor," p. 737), among others, discuss Othello's murder of Desdemona as a substitute consummation; Neely ("Women and Men in *Othello*," pp. 217–18), Snow ("Sexual Anxiety," pp. 392–94), Neill ("Changing Places," p. 128), and Leonard Tennenhouse (*Power on Display: The Politics of Shakespeare's Genres* [New York, London: Methuen, 1986], p. 127) stress its function as an act of purification (in Tennenhouse's case, purification of the authority of the monarch). Cavell sees the murder as simultaneous doing and undoing: it is both an enactment of "the thing *denied our sight* throughout the opening scene," "our ocular proof of Othello's understanding of his two nights of married love," and a denial "that he scarred her and shed her blood" (*Disowning Knowledge*, pp. 132, 134).

60.   Cavell (*Disowning Knowledge*, p. 135), Snow ("Sexual Anxiety," p. 393) and Greenblatt (*Renaissance Self-Fashioning*, p. 252; p. 306, n. 67) all comment powerfully on the hint of necrophilia here.

61.   Among the critics who discuss the threats to Othello's masculinity and his resumption of masculinity and male bonds via violence, see Greene (" 'This That You Call Love,' " pp. 19, 22–23), Neely ("Women and Men," p. 222), and especially Erickson (*Patriarchal Structures*, pp. 95–97) and Novy (*Love's Argument*, pp. 126, 130, and 134–39). In Wheeler's very suggestive discussion of Shakespeare's developing representation of conflicting needs for autonomous manhood, merger with an idealized nurturant femininity, and sexuality, death becomes the only available resolution once the suspensions and displace-

ments of the *Sonnets* and *Merchant of Venice* have been abandoned in *Othello*; see " ' . . . And my loud crying still,' " especially pp. 196, 201–6.

62.   Smith notes this vow as a "grim parody of the marriage ceremony" in his early discussion of Iago's homosexual love for Othello ("Iago the Paranoiac," pp. 179); it has since become a trope of criticism, recently understood less in terms of homosexual erotics than as the shoring up of homosocial male bonds. See especially Novy (*Love's Argument*, pp. 135–36), Erickson (*Patriarchal Structures*, pp. 96–97), and Coppélia Kahn's important discussion of cuckoldry as a way of formulating bonds between men (*Man's Estate: Masculine Identity in Shakespeare* [Berkeley: University of California Press, 1981], pp. 140–44).

63.   Among the many who comment on Othello's longing for death here, see especially Greenblatt's fine discussion of this passage as an evocation both of Othello's experience of desire and of his longing for release from desire (*Renaissance Self-Fashioning*, p. 243).

64.   Cassio and Iago share responsibility for this fantasy insofar as they participate in Othello's idealization and debasement of women, the split that makes Desdemona's warm sexuality intolerable to him: as has often been noted, the contrast between Cassio's and Iago's greetings to Desdemona (2.1.81–87; 2.1.118–60) is virtually a textbook illustration of the two processes; and the same split is enacted in Cassio himself, who reserves Desdemona for idealization and Bianca for debasement. (See, for example, Burke ["*Othello*: An Essay to Illustrate a Method," p. 180], Rogers ["Endopsychic Drama in *Othello*," pp. 210–13], Fiedler [*The Stranger in Shakespeare*, p. 156], Shirley Nelson Garner ["Shakespeare's Desdemona," *Shakespeare Studies* 9 (1976): 239], Neely ["Women and Men in *Othello*," p. 216], and Greene [" 'This That You Call Love,' " pp. 20–21]; though Adamson sees this split in the play, she is unusual in finding Cassio the representative of a balanced sexuality ["Unpinned or Undone?" p. 180].)

65.   This difference is reflected initially in the contrast between her passionate request that she be allowed to accompany Othello to Cyprus and his nervous denial of sexual excess in response to her request (1.3.248–74). Among the many who note this difference in the lovers' exchange on Cyprus, see especially the accounts by John Bayley (*The Characters of Love* [London: Constable, 1960], pp. 159–61), Richmond ("Love and Justice", p. 154), Neely ("Women and Men," p. 217), Novy (*Love's Argument*, pp. 128–29), and Greenblatt, who compellingly identifies Othello's longing for closure with his desire for control over the narrative of his life, the narrative chronically threatened by Desdemona's "vision of unabating increase" (*Renaissance Self-Fashioning*, p. 243). (For a minority reading on this issue, see Julian Rice's rather capricious attempt to portray a Desdemona who priggishly denies her sexuality, refusing to face her inherently whorish nature ["Desdemona Unpinned: Universal Guilt in *Othello*," *Shakespeare Studies* 7 (1974): 209–26].) Both Richmond ("Love and Justice," pp. 153–54) and Snow ("Language and

Sexual Difference in *Romeo and Juliet*," in *Shakespeare's Rough Magic*, esp. pp. 172–73) see the difference between Othello and Desdemona as already incipient in the lovers of *Romeo and Juliet*. Insofar as critics minimize Shakespeare's careful gender distinction in *Othello*, they tend to universalize Othello's erotic fantasy, thus undoing Shakespeare's own attempt to dissociate himself from it. Kirsch, for example, writes very movingly of Othello's ecstasy at this moment (*Shakespeare and the Experience of Love*, p. 26) and of Desdemona as "the life, not only the imago, of that union of tenderness and desire, that unconditional love toward which all men aspire" (p. 35), but he does not take his implicit gender distinction seriously; the consequence is that he can refer both to Othello's rage as reaching "back to the elemental and destructive triadic fantasies that at one stage in childhood govern the mind of every human being" (p. 34) and to Othello's enactment of "the primitive energies that are the substance of our erotic lives" (p. 39). But whose erotic lives does he mean? Throughout, Kirsch's account tends to make Desdemona merely that "toward which all men aspire," without seeing Desdemona's attempt to qualify that aspiration; partly as a consequence of this identification with Othello's fantasy, he seems to find her death more moving as the suicidal destruction of a part of Othello himself (pp. 30, 35) than as *her* death, the sacrifice of her to Othello's needs.

66.　Though very different in its focus, Patricia Parker's important discussion of the valence of "dilation" in *Othello* similarly associates the need to limit dilation both with mysogyny and with the play's tragic momentum, as contrasted with the "second chance" of *The Winter's Tale*; see "Shakespeare and Rhetoric: 'Dilation' and 'Delation' in *Othello*," in *Shakespeare and the Question of Theory*, p. 68.

67.　Cheerful obedience is of course central to this ideal: "The tryall of obedience is, when it crosseth her desires. . . . This declares conscionable submission, when shee chuseth to doe what her selfe would not, because her husbands [sic] wils it. . . . But it sufficeth not that her obedience reach to all things that are lawfull, vnlesse it bee also willing, ready, without brawling, contending, thwarting, sowrenesse" (William Whately, *A Bride-Bush, or Wedding Sermon: Compendiously describing the duties of Married Persons* [London, 1617], p. 42). Many comment on Desdemona's final status as model wife; see, for example, Margaret Loftus Ranald, who emphasizes Desdemona's deviations from the contemporary ideal and notes the change at the end ("The Indiscretions of Desdemona," *Shakespeare Quarterly* 14 [1963]: 127–39). Greene ("This That You Call Love," pp. 19, 25–26), Snow ("Sexual Anxiety," pp. 407–9), Irene G. Dash (*Wooing, Wedding and Power: Women in Shakespeare's Plays* [New York: Columbia University Press, 1981], pp. 119–26), and Diane Elizabeth Dreher (*Domination and Defiance: Fathers and Daughters in Shakespeare* [Lexington: University Press of Kentucky, 1986], pp. 88–95), among others, emphasize the extent to which her final conformity to this wifely ideal is catastrophic for her. The shift in Desdemona from active and independent to passive and dependent is a commonplace of criticism; see Paula

S. Berggren's excellent early account ("The Woman's Part: Female Sexuality as Power," in *The Woman's Part*, p. 24). But it is to some extent contested by Neely ("Women and Men," pp. 218–21) and Ann Jennalie Cook ("The Design of Desdemona: Doubt Raised and Resolved," *Shakespeare Studies* 13 [1980]: 193), both of whom stress her strength in the end; see also Eamon Grennan's fine analysis of the continuing moral power of her deictic speech ("The Women's Voices in *Othello*: Speech, Song, Silence," *Shakespeare Quarterly* 38 [1987]: 275–92). Bernard J. Paris qualifies the shift in Desdemona from the opposite direction, maintaining that she shows the configurations of Horney's "self-effacing personality" throughout (" 'His Scorn I Approve': The Self-Effacing Desdemona," *American Journal of Psychoanalysis* 44 [1984]: 413–24).

68.   Unlike Cressida's, Desdemona's transformation can be largely explicated from within her character; see especially Garner ("Shakespeare's Desdemona," pp. 245–47) and Jane Adamson (*Othello as Tragedy* [Cambridge: Cambridge University Press, 1980], pp. 217–56) for rich and convincing accounts of her bewilderment and her attempt to maintain an idealized view of Othello. Psychoanalytic accounts of Desdemona tend to explain her transformation as a consequence of her overwhelming oedipal guilt (Robert Dickes, "Desdemona: An Innocent Victim?" *American Imago* 27 [1970]: 279–97; Stephen Reid, "Desdemona's Guilt," *American Imago* 27 [1970]: 245–62; and Green, "*Othello*: A Tragedy of Conversion," p. 107). Kay Stockholder writes particularly well about the ways in which Desdemona's identification with and desire for Othello's violence lead to her transformation; in her view, Desdemona is fully in collusion with Othello's destruction of her ("Form as Metaphor," pp. 744–45). But several critics argue that the change in Desdemona is not a product of her selfhood: see, for example, Madelon (Sprengnether) Gohlke (" 'All that is spoke is marred': Language and Consciousness in *Othello*," *Women's Studies* 9 [1982]: 157–76) and Linda Bamber (*Comic Women, Tragic Men* [Stanford, Calif.: Stanford University Press, 1982], pp. 6–9), both of whom argue that Desdemona, like the other women in the tragedies, does not possess full interiority or selfhood; for Kathleen McLuskie, Desdemona's status throughout is "iconic, exemplary, the site of meanings generated by others," hence typical of the representation of women on the Renaissance stage (*Renaissance Dramatists* [Atlantic Highlands, N.J.: Humanities Press International, 1989], p. 150). Whether or not Shakespeare successfully creates the illusion that the change in Desdemona proceeds from within her character, that change clearly serves Shakespeare's ends, however we define them: in Fiedler's account, it is "motivated by no probabilities of the waking world, only by the exigencies of Shakespeare's dream, in which the women whom men destroy, on the verge of their deaths, declare the men guiltless, white not black" (*The Stranger in Shakespeare*, p. 190); in Tennenhouse's account, it indicates Shakespeare's collaboration in removing patriarchal authority from the female and returning it to the male (*Power on Display*, p. 126). In Peter Stallybrass's brilliant account of the mapping of cultural tensions on the body, the transformation of Desdemona into "aristocratic enclosure"

is the cost of rescuing her honor and the sign of the play's participation in the "problematic of the enclosed body" ("Patriarchal Territories: The Body Enclosed," in *Rewriting the Renaissance*, ed. Margaret W. Ferguson, Maureen Quilligan, and Nancy J. Vickers [Chicago: University of Chicago Press, 1986], pp. 123–42, esp. p. 141).

69. Bradley's responses most tellingly explicate this connection. In his paean to Desdemona, he speaks of the "heavenly sweetness and self-surrender" that makes us almost forget her earlier self-assertion, the "love which, . . . when bruised, only gave forth a more exquisite fragrance" (*Shakespearean Tragedy*, pp. 165, 166)); the difficulty is of course that this love calls out to be bruised. Fortified by Desdemona's "heavenly sweetness," Bradley is nonetheless able to translate the ending into a sign of the power of love and to exult in it: "when he dies upon a kiss the most painful of all tragedies leaves us for the moment free from pain, and exulting in the power of 'love and man's unconquerable mind' " (*Shakespearean Tragedy*, p. 162).

NOTES TO CHAPTER 4

1. The term is Arthur Kirsch's (*Shakespeare and the Experience of Love* [Cambridge: Cambridge University Press, 1981], p. 136). Kirsch's account of both plays stresses the centrality of the bed trick as cure (see, for example, pp. 84, 98–99, and 141–42); though he finds the plays more celebratory of sexuality and procreation than I do, his argument anticipates mine at several points. For another reading of the bed trick that minimizes its problematic nature, see Eileen Z. Cohen ("Virtue is Bold": the Bed-Trick and Characterization in *All's Well That Ends Well* and *Measure for Measure*," *Philological Quarterly* 65 [1986]: 171–86). Both Richard P. Wheeler (*Shakespeare's Development and the Problem Comedies* [Berkeley: University of California Press, 1981], esp. pp. 12–13, 55) and Carol Neely (*Broken Nuptials in Shakespeare's Plays* [New Haven, Conn.: Yale University Press, 1985], esp. pp. 71–74, 78–79, and 92–95) have written on the bed trick as a problematic attempt to recuperate sexuality in these plays; their understanding of what needs recuperating is very close to mine. I am deeply indebted to them both, not only for many specifics of interpretation in these plays but also for long ago introducing me to the interpretative power of a method that understands the plays comparatively, as developments and redevelopments of the same set of issues; along with C. L. Barber, they liberated me from the constraints of a New Critical practice that tended to think about these texts in isolation from one other.

2. See Geoffrey Bullough, *Narrative and Dramatic Sources of Shakespeare*, vol. 2 (London and New York: Routledge and Kegan Paul, Columbia University Press, 1958), p. 395.

3. Instead of legitimizing desire, the descriptions of the bed trick make even legitimate sexuality illicit in fantasy, a "wicked meaning in a lawful deed," where technically "both not sin" and yet we are left with a "sinful fact"

(3.7.45–47). Helena's musings on Bertram's "sweet use" of what he hates (4.4.21–25) similarly work to make defilement and loathing central to the sexual act, whether licit or illicit. Helena's language here both hides and declares the sexual act at the center of the play: in her account, both actors disappear, their bodily relation expressed by the interaction of a series of abstractions ("Saucy trusting of the cozen'd thoughts / Defiles the pitchy night"). One is left only with a sense of disembodied but mutual defilement. In her condensation of night with her own body, Helena perfectly explicates this mutuality: the body in that bed is already defiled, already "pitchy," before Bertram comes to defile it; and as Shakespeare frequently reminds us (see, for example, *Much Ado*, 3.3.57, or *1 Henry IV*, 2.4.394), pitch defiles. In this representation of the bed trick, that is, Bertram defiles a body that is already defiled, and is himself defiled in turn; the act that should incorporate desire into marriage succeeds instead in making the marriage bed itself both defiled and defiling.

4.   Michel de Montaigne, *The Essayes of Michael Lord of Montaigne*, trans. John Florio (London, New York: J. M. Dent, E. P. Dutton, 1928), p. 72. Kirsch identifies this essay as a source for *All's Well* (*Shakespeare and the Experience of Love*, pp. 38, 122–27); I am very much indebted to his account. The essay seems to have been central to Shakespeare's imagination during this period; Cavell notes the similarity of its topics to those of *Othello* (*The Claim of Reason* [Oxford: Oxford University Press, 1979], p. 474).

5.   For some, the play's failure to satisfy desire is the source of its value. See, for example, Joseph Westlund's argument that the play tempers the dangerous tendency of its characters—and its critics—to idealize ("*All's Well That Ends Well*: Longing, Idealization, and Sadness," *Shakespeare's Reparative Comedies: A Psychoanalytic View of the Middle Plays* [Chicago: University of Chicago Press, 1984], pp. 121–46) and David Scott Kastan's congruent argument that it exposes the danger (especially to the autonomy of others) inherent in the desire for a comic ending ("*All's Well That Ends Well* and the Limits of Comedy," *ELH* 52 [1985]: 575–89).

6.   The continuity between the beginning of *Hamlet* and the beginning of *All's Well* is signaled by several odd verbal resemblances, as well as by the paternal death and the surviving mother common to both. Helena's riddling first speech (1.1.50), for example, echoes Hamlet's (1.2.65), as the Countess's advice to Bertram (1.1.60–64) echoes Polonius's to Laertes (1.3.59–68). Many note the similarities between *Hamlet* and *All's Well*; see, for example, Wheeler (*Shakespeare's Development*, p. 54), Neely (*Broken Nuptials*, p. 66), Barbara Hodgdon ("The Making of Virgins and Mothers: Sexual Signs, Substitute Scenes and Doubled Presences in *All's Well That Ends Well*," *Philological Quarterly* 66 [1987]: 49), and Ruth Nevo ("Motive and Meaning in *All's Well That Ends Well*," in *"Fanned and Winnowed Opinions": Shakespearean Essays Presented to Harold Jenkins* [London: Methuen, 1987], p. 35).

7.   Kirsch notes the "conspiracy of women whose nurturing affections

threaten to control" Bertram but chooses not to emphasize the threatening aspects of this maternal alliance, foregrounding instead the miraculous cure that they achieve (*Shakespeare and the Experience of Love*, p. 141). Seen from the women's point of view, this alliance is empowering, not threatening; see Neely's convincing discussion of the differing valences of male and female bonds in this play (*Broken Nuptials in Shakespeare's Plays*, pp. 74–78) and Carolyn Asp's suggestive account of Helena's increasing turn toward female bonds ("Subjectivity, Desire and Female Friendship in *All's Well That Ends Well*," *Literature and Psychology* 32 [1986]: esp. 59–60).

8.   In Richard Wheeler's account of the play, Bertram's flight from Helena and his attraction to a woman decidedly outside the family structure become intelligible as attempts to escape the dominion of the infantile family and its threats to adult masculine identity (*Shakespeare's Development*, esp. pp. 40–45, 55); see also Kirsch's brief discussion of Helena as incestuous object (*Shakespeare and the Experience*, p. 141).

9.   These are the distinctions Helena attempts to preserve in her anxious responses to the Countess's claim to be a mother to her (1.3.133–61). As in *Hamlet*, anxiety about mother-son incest is in part expressed and in part concealed by overt concern with brother-sister incest here; also as in *Hamlet*, the confounding of distinctions by incest reiterates the confounding of the more primary distinctions on which individuated identity is based.

10.   As many have noted, the language surrounding Helena's cure of the king sexualizes it: left alone with him by a Lafew who compares himself with Pandarus ("I am Cressid's uncle / That dare leave two together" [2.1.96–97]), the woman "whose simple touch / Is powerful to araise King Pippen" (2.1.74–75) does succeed in raising this king up. See, for example, Wheeler (*Shakespeare's Development*, pp. 75–76), Kirsch (*Shakespeare and the Experience*, p. 135), Neely (*Broken Nuptials*, p. 69), and Nevo ("Motive and Meaning," pp. 31–33). For Lisa Jardine, this sexualizing is indicative of the cultural ambivalence that is always prone to understand the woman with knowledge as a sexually "knowing" woman ("Cultural Confusion and Shakespeare's Learned Heroines: 'These are old paradoxes,' " *Shakespeare Quarterly* 38 [1987]: esp. 8–10).

11.   The King's image will not do much to comfort Bertram; in *The Winter's Tale*, it becomes Leontes's image for the corrupt sexual mixture that undoes distinction ("To mingle friendship far, is mingling bloods" 1.2.109).

12.   Such ring-play is of course familiar; see, for example, the end of *Merchant of Venice*. For an early account of the sexualization of the rings here, see John F. Adams, "*All's Well That Ends Well*: The Paradox of Procreation," *Shakespeare Quarterly* 12 (1961): 268–69.

13.   This confusion seems to be carefully cultivated by Shakespeare, not only when Helena sets off as Saint Jaques's pilgrim to cure her ambitious love (3.4.5–6) and ends up in Florence promoting an astonishingly ambitious

scheme, but nearly everywhere that her intentions are at issue; it is, I think, indicative of Shakespeare's—and his culture's—anxiety about female agency. Helena's dangerous power is constantly being contained, not only by her own assertions ("I dare not say I take you, but I give / Me and my service . . . / Into your guiding power" [2.3.102–4]) and by the ascription of her gifts to her father or to heaven, but also by a plot obscurity that keeps her intentions—and thus the degree of her control—undefined. But see Richard A. Levin, who reads the play in effect from the position of Bertram, unwriting its willed obscurity and insisting on Helena's manipulative control of virtually every detail in the plot, including the unmasking of Parolles ("*All's Well That Ends Well* and 'All Seems Well,' " *Shakespeare Studies* 13 [1980]: 131–44); though dubious as a reading of Helena's agency, the essay usefully reproduces the paranoia that the presence of a strong woman can create. Without rewriting the plot, Wheeler notes Helena's increasing strength—and Bertram's increasing weakness—as the play progresses (*Shakespeare's Development*, p. 55); his view of Helena's frightening power anticipates my own.

14.   The play is filled with images of man drained, spent, overwhelmed, or contaminated by sexual contact with women: see, for example, Parolles's warning against "spending his manly marrow in her arms" (2.3.275–79) or Lavatch's "the danger is in standing to't" (3.2.40); Parolles's long exchange with Lavatch on his disastrous fall into "Fortune's close-stool," his muddying in "the unclean fishpond of her displeasure" (5.2.1–26), is an extreme example, where even his punishment at the hands of men is rewritten as the woman's fault.

15.   We miss the point, I think, if we see this shaming as only or largely a theatrical ruse. Public shaming was the ordinary means through which church and community regulated misbehavior, especially sexual misbehavior; and it was inherently theatrical. See Paul Hair (*Before the Bawdy Court: Selections from the Church Court and Other Records Relating to the Correction of Moral Offences in England, Scotland, and New England, 1300–1800* [London: Elek, 1972], pp. 44–45, 119, 169, 197, and 256) and especially F. G. Emmison (*Elizabethan Life: Morals and the Church Courts* [Chelmsford: Essex County Council, 1973], pp. 280–87) for examples of the church courts' shame punishments for fornication and adultery; see John R. Gillis (*For Better, For Worse: British Marriages, 1600 to the Present* [Oxford: Oxford University Press, 1985], pp. 77–81) for community regulation through rough music. Emmison stresses the theatricality of the church penances (p. 280); in this context, it becomes difficult to distinguish between the theatrical and bogus (because undeserved) shame punishments of Diana or Isabella and the "real" thing: shame is shame.

16.   Though muted in this text, the topic of virgin birth was apparently on Shakespeare's mind as he wrote the problem comedies, with their obsessive interest in virginity and procreation; its presence is signaled by Pompey's small joke about Claudio and Juliet near the beginning of *Measure for Measure*:

Mis. Is there a maid with child by him?

Pom. No: but there's a woman with maid by him.

(1.2.84–85)

See, for example, Marc Shell's account of the end of *Measure for Measure*, where Isabella becomes mother to the reborn Claudio through a virgin birth (*The End of Kinship: "Measure for Measure," Incest, and the Idea of Universal Siblinghood* [Stanford, Calif.: Stanford University Press, 1988], pp. 143–44), or Ruth Nevo's wonderful intuition that the language of *Measure for Measure* "is haunted by a yearning for an unfleshed birth" (" 'Measure for Measure': Mirror for Mirror," *Shakespeare Survey* 40 [1988]: 122).

17.   See Lawrence Stone (*The Family, Sex and Marriage in England, 1500– 1800* [New York: Harper and Row, 1979], pp. 30–31) for consummation as the final stage in marriage; Margaret Loftus Ranald assumes that Bertram tries to avoid consummation in order to keep the marriage dissolvable (" 'As Marriage Binds, and Blood Breaks': English Marriage and Shakespeare," *Shakespeare Quarterly* 30 [1979]: 80). The doubleness of the benefit the Duke intends to accomplish via the bed trick in *Measure* turns in part on this understanding of consummation, insofar as consummation makes Angelo's contract with Mariana—whether *de praesenti* or *de futuro*—final.

18.   Many note the implicit conflict in Helena's various roles; see, for example, Neely's especially fine discussion (*Broken Nuptials*, esp. pp. 65, 67– 70, 72, and 78). I read these conflicts as signs of the play's deep ambivalence toward female power, especially sexual and maternal power; though Neely is always aware of the use the play makes of Helena (see especially p. 78), she tends to see Helena's conflicting roles naturalistically as the products of her complex character and situation (p. 67). Asp and Nevo similarly read the conflicts from within: for Asp, they are inherent in the development of Helena's specifically female subjectivity ("Subjectivity, Desire and Female Friendship," pp. 48, 52–61); for Nevo, they are a consequence of Helena's struggle with her own oedipal desires ("Motive and Meaning," pp. 35–40). Jardine and Wheeler read Helena's conflicting roles largely from without: for Jardine, they are the means by which "Helena is made a kind of wish-fulfillment solution to the paradox of the two-faced learned lady" who must act out her atonement for her forwardness ("Cultural Confusion and Shakespeare's Learned Heroines," p. 12); for Wheeler, they are the consequence of the ways in which "distinct modes of comic drama—one pointing back to the festive comedies, the other forward to the late romances— tend to interfere with each other in *All's Well*" (*Shakespeare's Development and the Problem Comedies*, p. 86).

19.   Several critics see the union of Venus and Diana as one of the governing tropes of the play, but they de-problematize it by asserting that married chastity and virginity are equated or that procreation legitimizes sexuality, in effect making Venus into Diana; see, for example, Adams ("*All's Well That Ends Well*: The Paradox of Procreation," pp. 262–64), James L. Calderwood ("Styles of Knowing in *All's Well*," *Modern Language Quarterly* 25 [1964]:

281, 290), and Hodgdon ("The Making of Virgins and Mothers," pp. 50, 64). But Alexander Welsh argues that the social and biological imperative of procreation is the problem from the start; instead of unproblematically transforming sexuality, it is what Bertram must be brought to accept ("The Loss of Men and the Getting of Children: *All's Well That Ends Well* and *Measure for Measure*," *Modern Language Review* 73 [1978]: 17–22). I see the final splitting off of Diana from Helena as a sign that the split between Venus and Diana remains irreparable.

20.   Many critics note that Diana functions as Helena's double, retaining Helena's virginity after she herself has given it up. See, for example, Hodgdon's comments on Diana in her suggestive account of the doublings and substitutions that pervade the play ("The Making of Virgins and Mothers," esp. pp. 50, 64–66). My reading of Diana as both substitute strumpet and repository for Helena's virginity is closest to Neely's (*Broken Nuptials*, esp. pp. 78, 86, and 93); but for Neely, Diana's double role serves to mute—not to exacerbate—the polarized traits implicit in Helena (p. 78).

21.   After we have met Mariana, the play works hard to reinforce the distinction that has been obliterated—in effect, to clear a space for legitimate sexuality. Hence the Duke's assurance that the sexual union of Angelo and Mariana is legal and no sin, despite its close resemblance to the sin of Claudio and Juliet. But the very insistence of his assurance—an assurance that he feels compelled to give, although Mariana shows no signs of needing it—should remind us that this apparently crucial distinction would be apt to disappear, and not just in the minds of modern audiences, were it not insisted on. The degree to which modern scholars disagree in assigning degrees of legitimacy to the two relationships suggests the flimsiness of the distinction. See, for example, S. Nagarajan ("*Measure for Measure* and Elizabethan Betrothals," *Shakespeare Quarterly* 14 [1963]: 116–18) and Ranald (" 'As Marriage Binds and Blood Breaks': English Marriage and Shakespeare," pp. 77–79); A. D. Nuttall wisely dissolves the distinction (" 'Measure for Measure': The Bed Trick," *Shakespeare Survey* 28 [1975]: 52–53). Margaret Scott notes that neither *de futuro* nor *de praesenti* contracts would have been held valid under the Tridentine decree of 1563 in force in Catholic Vienna; she sees the difficulty in distinguishing between Claudio's and Angelo's act as characteristic of a play in which differences often lie only in the eye of the beholder (" 'Our City's Institutions': Some Further Reflections on the Marriage Contracts in *Measure for Measure*," *ELH* 49 [1982]: 790–804).

22.   Critics often comment on Shakespeare's structural use of the pun in *Measure*. See especially Meredith Skura's analysis both of the fantasy linking sexuality and death and of the ways in which the play ultimately counters this fantasy (*The Literary Use of the Psychoanalytic Process* [New Haven, Conn.: Yale University Press, 1981], pp. 260–66), Kirsch's account of Claudio's confrontation with sexuality and hence mortality (*Shakespeare and the Experience of Love*, pp. 90–91), and Neely's discussion of the witty equation of love and death in *All's Well* and the very different valence of the pun in *Measure* (*Broken*

Nuptials, pp. 92–93, 99–100). For these critics, and many others, the pun expresses sexual anxiety; for Darryl J. Gless, it expresses the "unconventional *imitatio Christi*" through which Isabella is asked "to 'die' in order to 'redeem' Claudio from the 'law' " (*"Measure for Measure," the Law, and the Convent* [Princeton, N.J.: Princeton University Press, 1979], p. 126).

23. Wheeler tellingly notes not only the congruence between these two speeches—a congruence prior to any considerations of legitimacy or illegitimacy—but also the degree to which the Duke arranges matters so that he speaks his disgust in the first person in both cases ("Reason thus with life: / If I do lose thee . . . "; "Say to thyself . . . I drink, I eat") (*Shakespeare's Development and the Problem Comedies,* pp. 121–22).

24. Many critics understand the play in part as a testing of Isabella and Angelo that is designed to bring them to acknowledge their repressed bodily impulses and hence their places in the human community; see especially Kirsch's sensitive (though in my view overly optimistic) account of the curative process (*Shakespeare and the Experience of Love,* pp. 80–89).

25. This is of course a perfectly orthodox rendering of the Aristotelian position on generation; see Chapter 1, p. 6. Angelo's imagery of sexual commerce as coining (2.4.45) reiterates this orthodoxy: in it the male stamps his will—and his image—upon an unresisting female matter. Given the extent to which Angelo feels contaminated by the prospect of sexual exchange, this must be a consoling image for him; in transferring power over generation to the Duke, the play reproduces Angelo's metaphor in another register.

26. In assessing the possibilities of a resisting counter-hegemony in *Measure,* Anthony B. Dawson comments suggestively on the imagery of inscription that makes sex "ambiguously semiotic" throughout and hence foregrounds the dubiousness of the final resolution (*"Measure for Measure,* New Historicism, and Theatrical Power," *Shakespeare Quarterly* 39 [1988]: 336–39).

27. Not many critics bother to try. Ralph Berry specifically notes the alliance only to dismiss it ("Language and Structure in *Measure for Measure,*" *University of Toronto Quarterly* 46 [1976–77]: 156); in an unpublished paper, Maurice Charney implies—without quite stating—a relation between the two women when he notes that Angelo's dismissal of the "fornicatress" is followed immediately by the entrance of the "very virtuous maid" (" 'Be That You Are, / That is, a Woman': The 'Prenzie' Angelo and the 'Enskied' Isabella," ms. pp. 7–8). In her very suggestive analysis of the many splittings and doublings that make the play a "masterly study of repression, and of the repressed, and of its Hydra-headed return," Ruth Nevo reads the relation in terms very close to my own; for her, Juliet is Isabella's "alter ego, . . . the woman in Isabella which Isabella . . . has not chosen to be" (*"Measure for Measure:* Mirror for Mirror," pp. 112, 115).

28. Many note the play's psychic and geographic rigidity; see, for example, Berry's suggestive account of overworld and underworld as fragments both of

a body politic and of a single mind ignorant of its separate parts ("Language and Structure in *Measure for Measure*," pp. 147–49). For Skura, this rigidity is symptomatic of the overly rigid psychic organizations that the play must work through (*The Literary Use of the Psychoanalytic Process*, p. 247); for Gless, the play's various claustrophobic confinements point to its participation in the tradition of anti-monastic satire (*"Measure for Measure," the Law, and the Convent*, pp. 94–98).

29. See Wheeler (*Shakespeare's Development and the Problem Comedies*, p. 100) for a very similar account of this process.

30. See J. W. Lever's helpful note for the presence of the privy in Angelo's lines (Arden *Measure for Measure*, p. 50). Angelo's shocked recognition here is a tragic reworking of Montaigne's much cooler meditation on the mixture of delight and disgust in sexuality, where "our joyes and filthes" are "pell-mell lodged together" ("On Some Verses of Virgil," p. 105). But what amuses and repels Montaigne attracts Angelo.

31. Lever notes that "ungenitured" is a Shakespearean formation, used only here (Arden *Measure*, p. 89). The word is usually glossed as "sexless" or "without genitals," but "unbegotten" seems equally plausible and follows from Lucio's previous joke on the subject. Among the relevant meanings current for "geniture," *OED* lists (1) "begetting, generation; birth," (3) "that which is generated; offspring, product," and (5) "genitals"; its citation of Fulke (1579) in support of (3)—"he is a geniture, that is a thing begotten"— is particularly germane.

32. The resemblance is often noted; see, for example, Berry ("Language and Structure," p. 151), Rupin W. Desai ("Freudian Undertones in the Isabella-Angelo Relationship of *Measure for Measure*," *Psychoanalytic Review* 64 [1977]: 490), Neely (*Broken Nuptials*, p. 95), and Nevo ("*Measure for Measure*: Mirror for Mirror," p. 119). The enclosed garden—traditionally associated with the virgin body—is Shakespeare's addition here, not found in the play's sources.

33. For Wheeler, the disappearance of the protective father here reiterates and reveals the consequences of the Duke's earlier disappearance; see his rich discussion of Angelo's reliance on the Duke as externalized father/superego (*Shakespeare's Development*, esp. pp. 93–97, 110).

34. For David Sundelson, anxiety about the precariousness of male identity is at the heart of *Measure*; he notes the pun on "conception" and comments extensively on Angelo's fear both of female potency and of his own feminization (*Shakespeare's Restorations of the Father* [New Brunswick, N.J.: Rutgers University Press, 1983], pp. 91–92).

35. Both Richard A. Levin ("Duke Vincentio and Angelo: Would 'A Feather Turn the Scale'?" *Studies in English Literature, 1500–1900* 22 [1982]: 263) and Wheeler (*Shakespeare's Development*, p. 100) understand Angelo's vindictiveness toward Isabella in part as his attempt to replicate his own shame

in her. My emphasis on the corrupting of a specifically maternal body here is particularly indebted to Wheeler, who reads Angelo's rigid separation of the ideal and the sexual—and the devastating collapse of that separation when Angelo confronts Isabella—as the consequence of Angelo's imperfect resolution of oedipal desire for the mother (see especially pp. 96–97; see also Stephen A. Reid, "A Psychoanalytic Reading of 'Troilus and Cressida' and 'Measure for Measure,' " *The Psychoanalytic Review* 57 [1970]: 278). One name for Angelo's exciting desire is thus incest. This is in fact the name that Isabella gives to their proposed sexual concourse (3.1.138) in her rage at Claudio; here again, as in *Hamlet* and *All's Well*, the more visible threat of brother-sister incest seems to function partly as a displacement for the threat of mother-son incest. Isabella herself repeatedly asks Angelo to identify his desires with Claudio's (2.2.64–66, 137–42; see also Escalus at 2.1.8–16). It seems to be in response to this proposed identification with Claudio that Angelo first feels desire, signaled by his abruptly telling Isabella to leave (2.2.66) or attempting to leave himself (2.2.143); does Angelo feel desire only insofar as the object of desire is constructed incestuously as a sister/mother?

36. Charney notes the coerciveness of Angelo's attempt but on the whole seems to approve of it; in his view, it is disappointing that the play does not reward Angelo for "educating Isabella and bringing her out" by giving her to him in the end (" 'Be That You Are,' " ms. p. 14).

37. *Measure* frequently plays on the doubleness of these familial terms; the ambiguities coalesce in *sister* (see especially 1.4.19; 2.2.19–21; 2.4.18) because Isabella is most centrally "in probation of a sisterhood" (5.1.75), but they also affect *brother* (the earliest of the play's great many uses of the word refers to the Duke as spiritual brother [1.3.44]; the latest is the Duke's proposal that Claudio become his brother [5.1.491]), *mother* (1.4.86), and *father* (see p. 98). In his powerful meditation on incest in *Measure for Measure*, Marc Shell notes Isabella's ultimately futile attempt to replace the physical with the spiritual family; in his view, her attempt "merely relocates the problem of incest from the consanguinous family to the Christian Family" (*The End of Kinship*, p. 54). Although Shell is more concerned with the metaphysics and social theory of incest than with its psychological implications, his understanding of the incestuous subtext of the chief relationships in the play is frequently close to mine; see, for example, his discussions of Claudio and Juliet (pp. 37–38), Isabella and Claudio (pp. 51, 61, and 102), Isabella and Angelo (pp. 105–9), and Isabella and the Duke (pp. 92, 163–67).

38. As with so much of Isabella's language, the terms in which she expresses her fear—calling attention both to her softness and to her capacity to conceive—could hardly be more effective in stirring Angelo's desire, particularly since her phrase "false prints" echoes one of Angelo's favorite tropes for generation (2.4.45–46).

39. Lever notes "the traditional association of glass and virginity" (Arden *Measure for Measure*, p. 61).

40. The anatomical cast of "vice" here is often noted; see Reid ("A Psycho-analytic Reading," p. 279), Wheeler (*Shakespeare's Development*, p. 111), and Neely (*Broken Nuptials*, p. 99). The pun is frequently incipient in the play's other uses of "vice"; see especially Lucio's "the vice is of a great kindred" (3.2.97), which immediately precedes his meditation on the alternate means through which Angelo was created, and Isabella's "There is a vice that most I do abhor" (2.2.29), with its evocation of both *whore* and *Abhorson*.

41. Sexual union with Angelo would in effect force Isabella to take her mother's place in a fantasied act of incest with her father, from which union her brother Claudio would be made a man; the Duke's proposal of marriage at the end is so disturbing partly because it replicates the threat of father-daughter incest that shapes Isabella's response here. (See Wheeler, who under-stands Isabella's desire to become a nun as a perpetuation of her imperfect resolution of oedipal desire [*Shakespeare's Development*, pp. 111–12, 130]; see also Reid, "A Psychoanalytic Reading," p. 278.) But given the intensity of Isabella's response to Claudio, there are undercurrents of brother-sister incest here as well. Isabella has earlier attempted to identify Angelo with her brother (see note 35) as Angelo has attempted to make Isabella into Juliet; and insofar as Juliet and Isabella have exchanged names (1.4.47), Claudio's union with Juliet may carry elements of a fantasied union with Isabella. Isabella's incestu-ous desire for her brother is central to Nevo's argument that the play, from 3.1 on, is "the replay . . . in Isabella's wishful fantasy, of the traumatic events that are happening to her"; in her view, the sequence of surrogates in the bed trick allows for the satisfaction of Isabella's repressed desire, while Isabella's exposure and repudiation serve as punishment for her guilt ("*Measure for Measure*: Mirror for Mirror," pp. 118–21). I understand Isabella's use of "incest" in this context to signal not only her fear of a specifically incestuous alliance with Claudio as brother or Angelo as father but also her fear of becoming her mother; here, as in *Pericles*, incest threatens to confound all the distinctions that confirm identity. Insofar as Isabella's participation in any sexual act would undermine the distinction between her and her mother, any sexual act is for her potentially incestuous in its collapsing of necessary categories.

42. *All's Well* twice invokes this legacy, when Parolles tells Helena that "to speak on the part of virginity is to accuse your mothers" (1.1.134–35), and when Bertram asks Diana to model herself on her mother ("Now you should be as your mother was / When your sweet self was got" [4.2.9–10]).

43. Wheeler's account of this moment is very close to my own; see espe-cially his analysis of Isabella's participation "in the defense against sexual contamination through the ideal of male honor" as she shifts the blame to her mother (*Shakespeare's Development*, p. 114).

44. Logically, of course, Claudio's bastardy requires the presence of a father, albeit an illegitimate one; but Isabella here elides his role, making Claudio purely his mother's child.

45.   This reiteration is by now a critical commonplace, as is more general uneasiness with the Duke's relation to his own sexuality; see, for example, Levin ("Duke Vincentio and Angelo," pp. 259–60), Berry ("Language and Structure," p. 153), Marvin Rosenberg ("Shakespeare's Fantastic Trick: *Measure for Measure*," *Sewanee Review* 80 [1972]: 64–67), and Sundelson (*Shakespeare's Restorations of the Father*, pp. 98–100). Westlund finds the Duke's value precisely in his distance from the ideal, insofar as his failings—and his acceptance of them—induce tolerance in us and so limit our tendency toward idealization (*Shakespeare's Reparative Comedies*, esp. pp. 153, 156, and 168).

46.   Many critics read the opening action of the play as the Duke's substitution of Angelo for an aspect of himself, though they do not always agree on which aspect; see, for example, Berry ("Language and Structure," pp. 153, 159), Nancy S. Leonard ("Substitution in Shakespeare's Problem Comedies," *English Literary Renaissance* 9 [1979]: 296–97), Levin ("Duke Vincentio and Angelo," pp. 259–60), Sundelson (*Shakespeare's Restorations of the Father*, p. 90), Alexander Leggatt ("Substitution in *Measure for Measure*," *Shakespeare Quarterly* 39 [1988]: 345–46), and Nevo ("*Measure for Measure*: Mirror for Mirror," pp. 111–12). In Bernard J. Paris's Horneyan analysis of the play, the Duke's deputizing of Angelo perfectly serves the Duke's conflicting trends toward perfectionism and self-effacement ("The Inner Conflicts of *Measure for Measure*: A Psychological Approach," *Centennial Review* 25 [1981]: 274); in Jonathan Goldberg's account, it initiates the series of substitutions that represents "the endless refiguration of the king in representative acts of substitution" and hence analyzes James's absolutist mode of "presence-in-absence" (*James I and the Politics of Literature* [Baltimore, Md.: Johns Hopkins University Press, 1983], pp. 234–35). In Wheeler's brilliant argument about the structure of the play, the substitution is Shakespeare's, not the Duke's: Shakespeare preserves Vincentio as an ideal figure by displacing "conflict away from [him] and into the world around him"; "Shakespeare ... uses Angelo as a scapegoat who suffers in his person the consequences of a conflict Vincentio is thereby spared" (*Shakespeare's Development*, pp. 133, 138).

47.   Claudio's image of rat poison (1.2.120–22) suggests that even Claudio and Juliet want to be together only ambivalently. Lever argues that the "thirsty evil" is liberty rather than lust (Arden *Measure*, p. 15); but given the striking resemblance of Claudio's "when we drink, we die" to *The Faerie Queene*, 2.1.55, where Acrasia's poison works on Mordant as soon as he drinks, lust seems the more obvious choice. But the distinction is probably unnecessary, since in this play sexuality is the mark of excess liberty.

48.   See Neely's fine discussion of Mariana's potential as the instrument for comic rejuvenations and resolutions that remain largely undramatized (*Broken Nuptials*, pp. 96–98).

49.   Shakespeare often associates "mould" and its variants with the shaping of the body in the womb: see, for example, *Richard II*, 1.2.22–23 ("That bed, that womb, / That metal, that self mould that fashioned thee"); *1 Henry IV*,

1.1.23 ("whose arms were moulded in their mother's womb"), and *Pericles* 3. chorus 10–11 ("By the loss of maidenhead, / A babe is moulded"); Coriolanus calls his mother "the honour'd mould / Wherein this trunk was fram'd" (5.3.22–23). Other uses of the term are more broadly associated with generative process; see *King Lear* 3.2.8, *Cymbeline* 5.4.49, and *The Winter's Tale* 2.3.102. For *fault/foutre*, see Chapter 2, note 26. "Fault" in *Measure* often carries the weight of the double meaning; see particularly Escalus's "some condemned for a fault alone" (2.1.40) and Isabella's "ask your heart what it doth know / That's like my brother's fault" (2.2.138–39). Though he does not work with Mariana's series of puns, Lawrence W. Hyman sees the play as an attempt to bring its characters to the sardonic recognition that life "not only can but *must* come out of vice, shame, and dishonor" ("The Unity of *Measure for Measure*," *Modern Language Quarterly* 36 [1975]: 12).

50. See Marilyn L. Williamson's full discussion of Jacobean attempts to regulate sexual behavior—especially of the poor—through government control; in her view, the play "exposes the limits of public power and the fantasy of intruding power into the personal realm" (*The Patriarchy of Shakespeare's Comedies* [Detroit, Mich.: Wayne State University Press, 1986], pp. 74–110). Both Wheeler (*Shakespeare's Development*, pp. 12–13) and Neely (*Broken Nuptials*, p. 94) note specifically the shifting of the bed trick from female to male control; my understanding of the relationship between the two plays is very much indebted to theirs.

51. In the context of the other arranged marriages of 5.1, it makes sense to ask what crime in Isabella the Duke proposes to punish through marriage. Though the marriage proposal might be supposed to bring Isabella back to the world, and has usually been interpreted thus, its more fundamental function is to re-contain her dangerous desire to define a self outside the sphere of marriage and hence beyond the reach of male power as it is embodied in the state. (In this formulation—and doubtless elsewhere—I am indebted to a brilliant unpublished paper by Laura Camozzi Berry, written for my graduate Shakespeare seminar in May 1988; she sees the threat of independent female desire— embodied in Isabella and in Juliet's unauthorized pregnancy—as that which the play seeks to control, both through the Duke's appropriation of the powers of generation and through his management of marriage, which encloses and erases women.) Interpretations—and productions—that have Isabella refusing the Duke, even perhaps slapping his face (see Rosenberg, "Shakespeare's Fantastic Trick," p. 71), do a disservice to the play by undermining its portrayal of the impasse to which Isabella has been brought—an impasse that in effect acts out the closing of the nunneries and the loss of that option for women. In her full account of the constricting of Isabella's power—especially in comparison with the earlier comic heroines—as she comes under the Duke's control, Marcia Riefer notes the closing off of this option (" 'Instruments of Some More Mightier Member': The Constriction of Female Power in *Measure for Measure*," *Shakespeare Quarterly* 35 [1984]: 162); in her view, Shakespeare's concentration of dramaturgical control in the Duke illuminates both the incompatibility between patriarchy and comedy and Shakespeare's tendency to drain

life out of the women in the tragedies (pp. 159, 168–69). Wheeler understands the diminishing of Isabella's power as a defensive response to the fear of women that will become rampant in the tragedies (*Shakespeare's Development*, esp. pp. 116, 147–51); for Sundelson, the play repeatedly exposes and then tames the threat of women (*Shakespeare's Restorations of the Father*, pp. 92–96). But Kathleen McLuskie argues in effect that there is no real change: from the start, Isabella is "defined theatrically by the men around her for the men in the audience"; any attempt to see from her point of view "involves refusing the pleasure of the drama and the text" ("The Patriarchal Bard: Feminist Criticism and Shakespeare: *King Lear* and *Measure for Measure*," in *Political Shakespeare: New Essays In Cultural Materialism*, ed. Jonathan Dollimore and Alan Sinfield [Ithaca, N.Y.: Cornell University Press, 1985], pp. 96–97).

52.   Leonard Tennenhouse historicizes the shift from female to male, reading *Measure for Measure* as one of several disguised ruler plays that mark the transitional period between Elizabeth and James by revealing the true king as the idealized patriarch and source of law, hence participating in the "master narrative . . . of a return to origins in which the monarch is restored to a natural position of supremacy as a father over a family" ("Representing Power: *Measure for Measure* in its Time," in *The Forms of Power and the Power of Forms*, ed. Stephen Greenblatt, *Genre* 15 [1982]: 139–56). Despite my disagreement with Tennenhouse's assumption that Shakespeare's representation of women, sexuality, and the family arises from "anxiety in the political realm" (p. 154), this seems to me a brilliant reading of a particular cultural moment; though operative throughout Shakespeare's career—as early as the transition from *Venus and Adonis* to *The Rape of Lucrece* and as late as the transition from *The Winter's Tale* to *The Tempest*—the representation of the shift from female to male control must have had a particular piquancy in 1604. (See Jonathan Dollimore, "Transgression and Surveillance in *Measure for Measure*," in *Political Shakespeare*, pp. 72–87, for the more general argument that anxiety about sexuality is an ideological displacement in *Measure*.) The particular parents of the new father-king must have made it especially attractive to vest in the male ruler not only control over marriage and generation (see Tennenhouse, p.153) but also the fantasy of exemption from the woman's part in generation. This fantasy, elaborated and rejected in Angelo, returns in a muted and disguised form in the Duke and will become very signficant in *Macbeth*, another play associated with James (see Chapter 6, note 39).

53.   Both Wheeler (*Shakespeare's Development*, p. 143) and Sundelson (*Shakespeare's Restorations of the Father*, pp. 98, 102) note the incipient pun on Old Hamlet in *Measure*'s ghostly father.

NOTES TO CHAPTER 5

1.   Stephen Booth sees loss of boundaries, especially of intellectual categories, as the signature of Shakespearean tragedy (*King Lear, Macbeth, Indefinition and Tragedy* [New Haven, Conn.: Yale University Press, 1983], pp. 5–

57). For psychoanalytic critics, this boundary confusion frequently signals Lear's re-entry into the archaic, often persecutory, world of infantile need; see, for example, Murray M. Schwartz ("Shakespeare through Contemporary Psychoanalysis," in *Representing Shakespeare: New Psychoanalytic Essays*, ed. Murray M. Schwartz and Coppélia Kahn [Baltimore, Md.: The Johns Hopkins University Press, 1980], p. 27), and C. L. Barber and Richard P. Wheeler (*The Whole Journey: Shakespeare's Power of Development* [Berkeley: University of California Press, 1986], p. 291).

2. See *The True Chronicle Historie of King Leir*, 1.1.1–31, reproduced in Geoffrey Bullough, *Narrative and Dramatic Sources of Shakespeare*, vol. 7 (London: Routledge and Kegan Paul, 1973), pp. 337–38.

3. This uncanniness of course serves ideological ends; see, for example, Jonathan Goldberg's account of the extent to which "the natural event of procreation becomes an extension of male prerogative and male power in Stuart portraiture of families" ("Fatherly Authority: the Politics of Stuart Family Images," in *Rewriting the Renaissance: the Discourses of Sexual Difference in Early Modern Europe*, ed. Margaret W. Ferguson, Maureen Quilligan, and Nancy J. Vickers [Chicago, Ill.: University of Chicago Press, 1986], esp. pp. 16–25). Many have noted the absence of mothers specifically in *Lear*; see, for example, Stephen Greenblatt's suggestive comparison of *Lear* with Francis Wayland's (successful) attempt to "displace the nurturing female body" ("The Cultivation of Anxiety: King Lear and His Heirs," *Raritan* 2 [1982]: 105). For psychoanalytic critics, this absence often functions as a "decoy" (Peter Erickson, *Patriarchal Structures in Shakespeare's Drama* [Berkeley: University of California Press, 1985], p. 110), serving "to highlight her psychological presence" (Coppélia Kahn, "Excavating 'Those Dim Minoan Regions': Maternal Subtexts in Patriarchal Literature," *Diacritics* 12 [1982]: 37; amplified in "The Absent Mother in *King Lear*," in *Rewriting the Renaissance*, pp. 33–49).

4. It is by now a familiar trope of psychoanalytically informed criticism to note that Lear makes his daughters into mothers; see, for example, Marianne L. Novy (*Love's Argument: Gender Relations in Shakespeare* [Chapel Hill: University of North Carolina Press, 1984], pp. 152–53), Marvin Rosenberg (*The Masks of King Lear* [Berkeley: University of California Press, 1972], p. 120), and Diane Elizabeth Dreher (*Domination and Defiance: Fathers and Daughters in Shakespeare* [Lexington: University Press of Kentucky, 1986], pp. 7, 64–65). Many see in this exchange Lear's specifically incestuous and oedipal desire for his daughters; for full accounts, see especially Norman N. Holland (*Psychoanalysis and Shakespeare* [New York: Octagon Books, 1979], p. 343) and William H. Chaplin ("Form and Psychology in *King Lear*," *Literature and Psychology* 19 [1969]: 32). Like other critics who ground their work in object-relations psychoanalysis, I read in Lear's relationship to his daughters-made-mothers a reiteration of dynamics that are primarily preoedipal rather than oedipal; my account is, as always, heavily indebted to the

combined work of Richard Wheeler, C. L. Barber, Madelon (Gohlke) Spreng-nether, Murray Schwartz, Peter Erickson, and Coppélia Kahn.

5. "Breeding" can imply either biological reproduction or upbringing, "charge" either financial or moral responsibility: either "I have paid for his rearing" or "I have been blamed for his begetting," or some combination of the two. No wonder Kent is confused.

6. For "fault," see Chapter 2, note 26. Astington (cited in that note) argues for its use as slang for the female genitals both generally and specifically here. But the term seems to me to carry the meaning of the pun on *foutre* as well: Edmund the Bastard is the proper (=fitting) issue not only of his mother's anatomical fault, but of any fault/*foutre*, since all faults turn out to be equally illegitimate.

7. Many readers are uncomfortable with both the tone and the substance of Edgar's judgment and would not permit him to speak for the play: for a representative sample, see, for instance, A. C. Bradley, *Shakespearean Tragedy* (New York: Meridian Books, Inc., 1955), p. 244; William Empson, *The Structure of Complex Words* (London: Chatto & Windus, 1952), p. 150; S. L. Goldberg, *An Essay on King Lear* (Cambridge: Cambridge University Press, 1974), pp. 80, 82; Stephen Booth, *King Lear, Macbeth, Indefinition and Tragedy*, p. 47; and James R. Siemon, *Shakespearean Iconoclasm* (Berkeley: University of California Press, 1985), pp. 274–75. But others disagree; see, for instance, Maynard Mack's strong defense of the play's homiletic character at this moment: "The blindness is not what will follow from adultery, but what is implied in it. Darkness speaks to darkness" (*King Lear in Our Time* [Berkeley: University of California Press, 1965], p. 70). Mack would dissociate these words from Edgar conceived as a naturalistic character with motives, partly to preserve the play's homiletic nature; although I find Edgar's words of a piece with his anger at his father (see "Introduction," *Twentieth Century Interpretations of "King Lear"*, ed. Janet Adelman [Englewood Cliffs, N.J.: Prentice-Hall, Inc., 1978], pp. 8–20), my formulation here and elsewhere is very much indebted to Mack's. For the logic Edgar expresses is not isolated in him: Edmund's status as second son would have sufficed to motivate his plot against his brother (as in *As You Like It*, *Hamlet*, and *The Tempest*); Shakespeare's insistence on his bastardy traces both his outlaw viciousness and his father's blinding to the dark and vicious place where he was got. Moreover, Edgar's judgment relies on cultural commonplaces linking blindness with sexuality. The "blind Cupid" that Lear sees in Gloucester (4.6.139) is the sign of the brothel (see Muir's note, Arden *King Lear*, p. 178) partly because blindness was thought to be a consequence of sexuality: according to the pseudo-Aristotelian *Aristotle's Masterpiece*, excess sexuality "destroys the sight, dries the body, and impairs the brain" (cited by Vern L. Bullough, *Sex, Society, and History* [New York: Science History Publications, 1976], p. 94); according to Bacon, "It hath been observed by the ancients, that much use of Venus doth dim the sight" (cited by Stephen Booth in his rich commentary on "expense of spirit" in Sonnet 129, *Shakespeare's Sonnets* [New Haven, Conn.: Yale University

Press, 1977], p. 442). Loss of the eyes or blindness was moreover sometimes recognized as a symptom of syphilis; see, for example, Charles Clayton Dennie (*A History of Syphilis* [Springfield, Ill.: Charles C. Thomas, 1962], pp. 17, 36), and James Cleugh (*Secret Enemy: The Story of a Disease* [London: Thames and Hudson, 1954], pp. 47, 66). Whether or not this symptomology was commonly known, the association between sexual excess and blindness was familiar to Shakespeare; see Pompey's pitying description of Mistress Overdone as "you that have worn your eyes almost out in the service" (*Measure for Measure*, 1.2.101–2).

8.   Cited in Bullough, *Narrative and Dramatic Sources in Shakespeare*, vol. 7, p. 404. Anxiety about the transmission of paternal identity and property is played out when Edmund the Bastard is made Earl of Gloucester (3.5.17–18) and the designation "Gloucester" is abruptly emptied of fixed meaning: after Cornwall renames Edmund (3.5.17–18), "Gloucester" refers both to father and son, most strikingly within two lines (see 3.7.13, 15). This confusion raises primary questions about who— or what—is "Gloucester": not only what that identifier means, but who has the right to it, and who confers that right. (Naming in the speech-headings is conservative, locating the right to name only in the king: they designate as Gloucester the man Lear recognizes as Gloucester.) Anxiety about names and legitimacy is of course at the heart of the Gloucester plot; see, for example, William C. Carroll's meditation on legitimacy and the natural body in Edgar (" 'The Base Shall Top Th'Legitimate': The Bedlam Beggar and the Role of Edgar in *King Lear*," *Shakespeare Quarterly* 38 [1987]: 426–41). But by giving one of his fathers sons and one daughters, Shakespeare is able to play out anxieties inherent in each of the two different systems of property inheritance operating in the play. The father-son plot operates under the rules of primogeniture, where the replication of patriarchal identity is at stake; illegitimacy is thus its central anxiety. But the love test of the father-daughter plot seems to operate under the system that became increasingly common in the sixteenth century as the entails maintaining strict primogeniture were broken and the father became increasingly capable of disposing of his property as he saw fit, rewarding or punishing his children at will (see Lawrence Stone, *The Family, Sex and Marriage in England, 1500–1800* [New York: Harper and Row, 1979], pp. 112–13). It makes sense that the central anxieties of this system—anxieties about sincerity and insincerity, about bribery and misplaced trust—should be played out in relation to daughters, especially daughters whose impending marriage threatens the fantasy that they love their fathers all.

9.   This is the dilemma played out in the travels of Bertram's father's ring in *All's Well*; see Chapter 4, pp. 81–82.

10.   In *King John*, however, bastardy serves the function of a classic family romance, allowing the son to replace his "real" and decidedly unheroic father with Cordelion, the play's mythic Ur-father. It can serve this function partly because the fantasy is written decidedly from the perspective of the son, not

the father, and partly because disruptive maternal presence is invoked only to be contained and almost comically dismissed (4.2.120–23).

11. See Eric Partridge, *Shakespeare's Bawdy* (New York: E. P. Dutton, 1960) for sexualized instances of both "stones" (pp. 195–96) and "rings" (p. 179). (Partridge omits *Midsummer Night's Dream*, 5.1.188, a comic *locus classicus* for "stones.") Without commenting on these puns, David Willbern sees in Gloucester's bleeding eyes a traumatic mask of the "nothing" that is the female—or the castrated male—genitals ("Shakespeare's Nothing," in *Representing Shakespeare*, pp. 247, 253). The equivalence of blindness and castration is familiar to psychoanalysis and to psychoanalytic criticism, where it is usually read as punishment for oedipal crime: see, for example, Sigmund Freud ("The Uncanny," *The Standard Edition of the Complete Psychological Works of Sigmund Freud*, vol. 17, trans. James Strachey [London: Hogarth Press, 1955], p. 231); Alexander Grinstein ("King Lear's Impending Death," *American Imago* 30 [1973]: 135); Mark Kanzer ("Imagery in *King Lear*," in *The Design Within: Psychoanalytic Aproaches to Shakespeare*, ed. M. D. Faber [New York: Science House, 1970], p. 223); Holland (*Psychoanalysis and Shakespeare*, p. 344); and Chaplin ("Form and Psychology in *King Lear*," pp. 38, 39).

12. In *Leir*, the dilemma of the king's sonlessness is not unspoken (1.1.21, 44). I am indebted to Zan Marquis's wonderful undergraduate honors thesis on Lear's fear of female fertility (1978) for the perception that Lear's daughters arrive on stage in place of sons.

13. Characteristically, Edgar's mother is mentioned only obliquely, and only when Gloucester believes Edgar false and hence attempts to disown him ("I never got him," 2.1.78).

14. The play makes a small move toward recuperating sexual origin in Kent's musing that "one self mate and make" have begotten both Goneril and Regan and Cordelia (4.3.35); this is the only place in which sexuality is imagined as an indifferent force, not one that necessarily breeds monsters, and the only place in which it is hinted that even Cordelia might have had a mother. (But see Robert H. West for a recuperative reading of sexuality in *Lear* ["Sex and Pessimism in *King Lear*," *Shakespeare Quarterly* 11 (1960): 55–60].)

15. The extent to which their exemption from sexuality is structurally important can be gauged by the extent to which we find Tate's inclusion of a sexual relation between them utterly alien to the play Shakespeare wrote.

16. Like Edmund, Goneril and Regan seem complicit with her dark and vicious place as they initiate Gloucester's blinding (3.7.4–5); Regan may in fact imagine that she is blinding her own father in blinding him (see Stanley Cavell, "The Avoidance of Love," *Disowning Knowledge in Six Plays of Shakespeare* [Cambridge: Cambridge University Press, 1987], p. 53). She and her sister are, in any case, the agents of a similar unmanning of their father: the Fool repeatedly interprets the "nothing" to which they bring him as castra-

tion; see especially the dense series of images at his first entrance in 1.4, where Lear is "an O without a figure" (ll. 200–201), "a sheal'd peascod" (208), a hedge-sparrow that "had it head bit off by it young" (225). (See Willbern's "Shakespeare's Nothing," especially pp. 245–46, on the fantasized equivalence of femaleness and castration here.)

17.   My formulation here, and in the pages that follow, is heavily indebted to Madelon [Gohlke] Sprengnether's classic essay, " 'I wooed thee with my sword': Shakespeare's Tragic Paradigms," in which she argues that Shakespeare's tragic heroes struggle against the signs of "femininity" in themselves and see these signs especially in their powerlessness, "specifically in relation to a controlling or powerful woman" (*Representing Shakespeare*, p. 175); she notes, for example, that Lear reads his own tears—evoked by his daughters— as dangerously feminine. Many recent critics comment on Lear's fear of his own feminization: see, for example, Patrick Colm Hogan ("*King Lear*: Splitting and Its Epistemic Agon," *American Imago* 36 [1979]: 40); Carolyn Asp, for whom Lear himself becomes a type of the (French) feminine (" 'The Clamor of Eros': Freud, Aging, and *King Lear*," in *Memory and Desire*, ed. Kathleen Woodward and Murray M. Schwartz [Bloomington: Indiana University Press, 1986], pp. 196–97); and especially Coppélia Kahn, whose formulations are closest to my own, especially in her emphasis on Lear's identification with his daughters and his fear of the mother within ("Excavating 'Those Dim Minoan Regions,' " pp. 37–39; "The Absent Mother in *King Lear*," pp. 36, 43–44). Paul Jorgensen tends to replicate—rather than analyze—Lear's fear; for him, Lear's progress toward self-knowledge necessarily entails his sex-nausea and mysogyny because "only woman's body could suffice to illustrate the full depravity of man" (*Lear's Self-Discovery* [Berkeley: University of California Press, 1967], p. 126); his is nonetheless a good early account of these elements in the play.

18.   By naming Goneril a disease in Lear's flesh, Shakespeare characteristically takes a name that he found lying inert in his sources and transforms it into a dense center of meaning. The term "gonorrhea" was current. Before 1767, it referred to one of the symptoms of syphilis rather than to a separate disease (see James Cleugh, *Secret Enemy: The Story of a Disease*, p. 136); William Clowes, for example, writes of a syphilitic patient who had "a stinking Gonorrhea and running of the reines" (*A Brief and Necessary Treatise Touching the Cure of the Disease called Morbus Gallicus* [London, 1585], p. 195). The skin eruptions Lear describes were characteristic of syphilis in the early stages (see Chapter 2, note 33): Cleugh describes boils and other swellings very much like Lear's embossed carbuncles (pp. 46–49); the Spanish in fact named the disease *bubas* from these swellings (Cleugh, p. 57). "Plague sore" may be a general term, or it may reflect an association between syphilis and specifically Black Plague; see Chapter 3, note 8, and see Frankie Rubenstein for the relation between (generalized) plague and pox ("They Were Not Such Good Years," *Shakespeare Quarterly* 40 [1989]: 70–74). Rubenstein identifies the "good years" Lear wishes on Goneril and Regan (5.3.24) as venereal disease; if she is right, then Lear is attempting to retaliate specifically for the disease he

imagines in his flesh. Insofar as blindness was associated specifically with venereal disease (see this chapter, note 7), it makes sense that it should be Goneril who first suggests blinding Gloucester.

19. Recognition of his own flesh in his daughters may again lead to Lear's sense of himself as feminized in 3.4.74–75, where Lear figures himself as a grotesque version of the maternal pelican; Muir cites several instances of the pelican who feeds or revives her children with her blood (Arden *King Lear*, pp. 118–19). Perhaps in response to Lear's apparent gender confusion, Edgar/ Poor Tom immediately transforms the pelicans into decidedly male pillicocks (3.4.76).

20. As *Macbeth*'s witches imply (1.3.10–25), witches were traditionally able to raise storms. See, for example, *The Malleus Maleficarum of Heinrich Kramer and James Sprenger*, trans. Montague Summers (New York: Dover Publications, 1971), pp. 147–49; Reginald Scot, *The Discoverie of Witchcraft* (London, 1584; reprint, with an introduction by Hugh Ross Williamson [Carbondale: Southern Illinois Press, 1964], p. 31); King James's *Daemonologie* (London, 1603), p. 46; and the failure of the witches to raise a storm in Jonson's *Masque of Queens*, ll. 134–37, 209–20. Jonson's learned note to l. 134 gives his classical sources for the witches' association with storm and chaos; see *Ben Jonson: The Complete Masques*, ed. Stephen Orgel (New Haven, Conn.: Yale University Press, 1969), pp. 531–32. For the association of Fortune with storms, especially in the visual arts, see Frederick Riefer, who reproduces some spectacular instances in his *Fortune and Elizabethan Tragedy* (The Huntington Library, 1983), p. 287; he comments specifically on the presence of this traditional association in Lear's storm.

21. Mack, *King Lear in Our Time*, p. 94; for him, the play is "the greatest anti-pastoral ever penned" (p. 65).

22. This lake is identified with the female sexual place by Shakespeare's other uses of fishing for sexual intercourse; see *Measure for Measure*, 1.2.83, and especially *The Winter's Tale*, 1.2.195. Many understand the storm as sexual: see, for example, Kanzer ("Imagery in *King Lear*," p. 223), Rosenberg (*The Masks of King Lear*, pp. 126, 191–92), and Lisa Miller ("A View of 'King Lear,' " *Journal of Child Psychotherapy* 4 [1975]: 102); for Chaplin, it is specifically female, "Nature's womb-like upheaval," which is "given a new location and iconology" in the sulphurous pit ("Form and Psychology in *King Lear*," pp. 40–41).

23. Rosenberg (*The Masks of King Lear*, p. 271), Novy (*Love's Argument*, p. 157), and Kay Stockholder (*Dream Works: Lovers and Families in Shakespeare's Plays* [Toronto: University of Toronto Press, 1987], pp. 135–36) note this connection.

24. See Chapter 1 (p. 6, and n. 22) for the attribution of flesh to the woman's part in generation. This nexus of ideas informs Erickson's account of Lear's "mortification of the flesh" in the storm: "Lear punishes his body in

order to purify it while at the same time destroying the universal power of procreation that corrupted him" (*Patriarchal Structures in Shakespeare's Drama*, p. 110).

25.   This is Folio's stage direction; Muir uses Capell's "Storm heard at a distance" (Arden *King Lear*, p. 99).

26.   See Kahn's powerful insight that Shakespeare's portrayal of the storm as the "breaking open of something enclosed" makes it resemble "Lear's heart cracking, letting out the hungry, mother-identified part of him in a flood of tears" ("The Absent Mother in *King Lear*," p. 46).

27.   See Edward Jorden, *A Briefe Discourse of a Disease called the Suffocation of the Mother* (London, 1603): "This disease is called by diverse names amongst our Authors. Passio Hysterica, Suffocatio, Prasocatio, and Strangulatus uteri, Caducus matricis, etc. In English the Mother or the Suffocation of the Mother, because most commonly it takes them with choaking in the throat: and it is an affect of the Mother or wombe" (pp. 5–6); the suffocation is caused by "the rising of the Mother wherby it is sometimes drawn upwards or sidewards above his natural seate, compressing the neighbour parts" (p. 6). Not surprisingly, all Jorden's victims are women. According to The Right Honorable Lord Brain, this passage makes Shakespeare the first person to describe hysteria in a man ("The Concept of Hysteria in the Time of William Harvey," *Proceedings of the Royal Society of Medicine*, 56 [1963]: 321); but Samuel Harsnett notes that Richard Maynie "had a spice of the *Hysterica passio*, as seems from his youth, he himselfe terms it the Moother" (cited in Kenneth Muir, "Samuel Harsnett and *King Lear*," *Review of English Studies* N.S. 2 [1951]: 14). Maynie does not, however, think that he has a uterus; he says that a Scottish doctor in Paris told him that the disease "riseth . . . of a wind in the bottome of the belly" (Muir, p. 14). By 1667, Thomas Willis had dissociated the disease from the womb, partly on the basis of its occurrence in men (see Brain, "The Concept of Hysteria," pp. 321–22, and L. R. Rather, "Pathology at Mid-Century: A Reassessment of Thomas Willis and Thomas Sydenham," in *Medicine in Seventeenth Century England*, ed. Allen G. Debus [Berkeley: University of California Press, 1974], p. 107). But *hysterica passio* remained overwhelmingly associated with women: Harsnett notes that "a thousand poore girles in England" had the disease worse than Maynie (Muir, p. 14), Willis that "women of every age, and condition, are obnoxious to these kinds of Distempers . . . yea, sometimes the same kind of Passions infest Men" (Brain, p. 322). Moreover, whether or not Shakespeare knew from Harsnett or elsewhere that the disease could occur in men, Lear's words imply not only that he has the disease but also that he has the female organ (the "mother") itself: even if one wants to make this passage less bizarre by reading "this mother" (2.4.56) as the name of the disease rather than the organ, Lear's reference to the mother's swelling upward associates it unmistakably with the rising womb itself. Despite Muir's note pointing out the connection with Jorden (Arden *King Lear*, p. 85), most recent commentators have missed the precision of the anatomical reference; see, for example, Mark S. Shearer, for whom the

term functions vaguely as a birth metaphor ("The Cry of Birth: King Lear's Hysterica Passio," *Postscript* 1 [1983]: 60–66), and Margaret Hotine, who thinks that it refers to abdominal pain like that suffered by King James ("Lear's Fit of the Mother," *Notes and Queries* N.S. 28 [1981]: 138–41). The bizarreness of the anatomical reference is noted by Lisa Jardine (*Still Harping on Daughters: Women and Drama in the Age of Shakespeare* [Sussex: Harvester Press, 1983], p. 110) and especially by Kahn, whose account most fully anticipates my own; but even in Kahn's account, the bizarreness of the reference tends to be displaced by the speed with which the "mother" becomes metaphorical, serving simultaneously to indicate Lear's sense of loss of maternal presence ("Those Dim Minoan Regions," p. 38; "The Absent Mother in *King Lear*," p. 40), his repressed identification with the mother ("Minoan," p. 37; "Absent Mother," p. 36), and the female domain of feeling that refuses to stay in its place ("Minoan," pp. 38–39; "Absent Mother," p. 36).

28. Suffocation was the primary sign of the nightmare's or incubus's presence as it was the primary symptom of *hysterica passio*; inside (as the "mother") or outside (as the nightmare), the female remains the cause of suffocation. See Robert Burton, who notes that such sleepers "as are troubled with Incubus, or witch-ridden (as we call it); if they lie on their backs, they suppose an old woman rides, & sits so hard upon them, that they are almost stifled for want of breath" (*The Anatomy of Melancholy*, ed. Floyd Dell and Paul Jordan-Smith [New York: Tudor Publishing Company, 1948], p. 220). Though etymologically "nightmare" is derived from Old English *mare* and "has no connection with the word meaning a female horse" (Muir, Arden *King Lear*, p. 124), the linguistic accident that combines woman and horse in "nightmare" may have helped to shape Lear's horrific portrayal of woman as centaur (4.6.126).

29. Lear asks "Where is this daughter?" as though she too could suddenly turn up inside him. The conjunction of "Thy element's below" and "Where is this daughter?" moreover connects the medical discourse of hysteria with the social discourse of hierarchy, making the rising female element the center of anxiety for both social and bodily instability; see Kahn ("The Absent Mother," pp. 33–34, 36) and Lisa Jardine (*Still Harping on Daughters*, p. 110). Lear's discovery that he has a uterus seems to invert the Galenic model that would make the female body merely an inverted version of the male (see Thomas Laqueur's description of this model, "Orgasm, Generation, and the Politics of Reproductive Biology," *Representations* 14 [1986]: esp. 2–6); it thus serves to destabilize the reassuring primacy of the male. Moreover, the conception of the female body that would allow for the rising womb might in any case partly destabilize the hierarchical tidiness and stability implicit in the Galenic model; the body in which a womb can wander—what Edgar imagines as the "indistinguish'd space of woman's will" (4.6.273)—may figure not a comfortable homology with the male but rather a fearful interior and exterior chaos, as I think it does in Lear's storm. According to Foucault, mobility and permeability remain the keynotes of hysteria even when etiology has passed from the wandering womb to the wandering animal spirits; he asks, "If the body is firm and resistent, if internal space is dense, organized, and solidly heterogeneous

in its different regions, the symptoms of hysteria are rare. . . . Is this not exactly what separates female hysteria from the male variety?" (Michel Foucault, *Madness and Civilization: A History of Insanity in the Age of Reason*, trans. Richard Howard [New York: Random House, 1965], p. 149).

30. The scapegoating mechanism has frequently been noted; see, for example, Herbert Coursen ("The Death of Cordelia: A Jungian Approach," *Hebrew University Studies in Literature* 8 [1980]:7), Novy (*Love's Argument*, p. 156), Leonard Tennenhouse (*Power on Display: The Politics of Shakespeare's Genres* [New York: Methuen, 1986], p. 138), and especially Kahn ("Those Dim Minoan Regions," p. 38; "The Absent Mother in *King Lear*," p. 44) and Erickson ("Displaced from the male body and projected exclusively onto the female, sexuality becomes female sexuality," *Patriarchal Structures*, p. 109). Coursen and Novy exempt Shakespeare from this mechanism, locating it only in his male characters; but for Tennenhouse and Erickson, Shakespeare is clearly complicit in it.

31. See Kathleen McLuskie's discussion of the ideological weight Goneril and Regan are made to bear ("The Patriarchal Bard: Feminist Criticism and Shakespeare: *King Lear* and *Measure for Measure*," in *Political Shakespeare*, ed. Jonathan Dollimore and Alan Sinfield [Ithaca, N.Y.: Cornell University Press, 1985], pp. 98–99). For Bradley, there is no question that they are more monstrous than Edmund, "for Edmund, not to mention other alleviations, is at any rate not a woman" (*Shakespearean Tragedy*, p. 239). Stephen Reid's attempt to make Goneril and Regan plausible and perhaps even sympathetic by constructing numerous childhood setbacks for them is not markedly successful ("In Defense of Goneril and Regan," *American Imago* 27 [1970]: 226–44); but see Harry Berger's more sophisticated attempt to derive their characteristic stance toward the world from the Lear family dynamics ("*King Lear*: The Lear Family Romance," *The Centennial Review* 23 [1979]: 357). Claudette Hoover wisely notes that the text "teases us with explanations that consistently prove inadequate to our questions and that each of these hints involves traditions and myths about the nature of women" ("Goneril and Regan: 'So Horrid as in Woman,' " *San Jose Studies* 10 [1984]: 62).

32. My reading of this question turns on the lability of "flesh" as a marker both of the father's own body and of what he begets: throughout, Lear literalizes the trope of children as one's flesh and blood (see Gloucester, 3.4.149–50), identifying flesh as the junction point of father and daughters, hence as the place where his loathing of them turns masochistically toward his own body (2.4.223–24, 3.4.74–75). The three simultaneous and incompatible questions embedded here mark this lability: are fathers so cruel to their own bodies (=flesh)? are offspring (=flesh) so cruel to their fathers? are fathers so cruel to their offspring (=flesh)? Editors and directors usually foreground the first of these questions. See, for example, Rosenberg (*The Masks of King Lear*, p. 220) and the gloss provided by the following editions: *The Variorum King Lear*, ed. Horace Howard Furness (Philadelphia: Lippincott Company, 1880); Muir's Arden edition; *William Shakespeare: The Complete Works*, ed. Alfred Harbage

(Baltimore, Md.: Penguin Books, 1969); and *The Complete Works of Shakespeare*, ed. David Bevington (Glenview, Ill.: Scott, Foresman and Company, 1980). The Signet edition (*The Tragedy of King Lear*, ed. Russell Fraser [New York: New American Library, 1963]) is virtually alone in foregrounding the second ("*on*, i.e., shown to," p. 114). Despite its syntactical clarity, the third question seems to have been largely ignored by editors and commentators; but see Booth, who notes the "fusion and confusion of agents" here (*King Lear, Macbeth, Indefinition, and Tragedy*, p. 36). All three versions of Lear's question seem to me present and important: each follows from one element in the preceding speech (the masochism implicit in Poor Tom's body; Lear's assumption that daughters are to blame; the visibility of his attempt to transfer blame to daughters); together they illustrate the fusion of masochism and sadism through the nexus of *flesh*.

33.   Erickson similarly attributes the female deaths at the end to the need to separate "male spirit from female flesh" and hence to end "the threat posed by the female body" (*Patriarchal Structures in Shakespeare*, p. 110).

34.   Lear's rush toward nothingness may be in part an attempt to discover what he can command on his own, without the institutional potency he has had all his life. But—as many have noted—it nonetheless has a decidedly masochistic edge, understood variously, for example, as punishment for his oedipal desires (Chaplin, "Form and Psychology in *King Lear*," pp. 32, 38), as a "masochistic prepayment" for love (Holland, *Shakespeare and Psychoanalysis*, pp. 343–44), as an attempt to fend off self-knowledge by maintaining his status as victim (Berger, "*King Lear*: The Lear Family Romance," pp. 359ff.), or as a mortification of the flesh intended to free male soul from female matter (Erickson, *Patriarchal Structures*, p. 110). For Cavell, death itself is the "payment or placation for the granting of love" (*Disowning Knowledge*, p. 70).

35.   See Chapter 1, p. 8, for additional discussion of this passage.

36.   Bradley notes "the tendency of imagination to analyse and abstract, to decompose human nature into its constituent factors" (*Shakespearean Tragedy*, p. 212); the prevalence of this tendency in *Lear* allows the play to be read simultaneously as a return to a more primitive mode of drama (for example, in Mack's reading of its homiletic morality roots [*King Lear in Our Time*, p. 58]) and as a return to a more primitive stage of mental life (for example, in Maud Bodkin, *Archetypal Patterns in Poetry* [London: Oxford University Press, 1934], p. 15, or Kanzer, "Imagery in King Lear," p. 222). There are many analyses of the characters as split-off aspects of a single personality; for extreme versions, see Patrick Colm Hogan's "*King Lear*: Splitting and its Epistemic Agon," pp. 32–44, and Lisa Miller's little-known Kleinian analysis, in which all the characters become Lear's part-objects ("A View of 'King Lear,' " pp. 93–124).

37.   Both in *Othello* and in *The Tempest*, Shakespeare figures the daughter's marriage as tantamount to the father's death; here Cordelia's "nothing" seems

to reiterate what will be left for the father after she marries. In combining a testamentary with a marital occasion in 1.1, Lear himself seems to play out the association; his own use of will—"We have this hour a constant will to publish / Our daughters' several dowers" (1.1.43–44)—hovers between funeral and marriage. Freud famously argues that Cordelia represents the goddess of death ("The Theme of the Three Caskets," *The Standard Edition*, vol. 12, p. 301); among the recent critics who use Freud's identification of Cordelia with death as a starting point, see especially Asp (" 'The Clamor of Eros': Freud, Aging, and *King Lear*," pp. 192–203) and Arthur Kirsch ("The Emotional Landscape of *King Lear*," *Shakespeare Quarterly* 39 [1988]: esp. 164). I am resistant to the uncritical acceptance of this equation partly insofar as it is complicit in depriving Cordelia of her status as a character; specifically, I would argue that Lear's equation of Cordelia with death in the form of maternal plenitude—Freud's "Mother Earth who receives him once more"— costs her her life.

38. All and nothing are set against one another throughout the play; their opposition helps to locate the place of the fool as a spokesman for *some*, especially in the storm (see, for example, 3.2.10–12, 3.2.80–94, 3.4.65). Rosenberg notes Lear's "infant wish for *all*," though his characteristic method does not allow him to explore it at length (*The Masks of King Lear*, p. 77); Leonard Shengold, elaborating the "all-or-nothing system of values of the early narcissistic period," sees in Lear the "portrayal of a child who wants milk and sexual gratification from the mother and is presented with 'nothing'—the castrated genital" ("More about the Meaning of 'Nothing,' " *Psychoanalytic Quarterly* 43 [1974]: 116, 117). Without using psychoanalytic terms, Siemon associates Lear's *all* with the totalizing "desire for absolute plenitude" that makes "the idolatrous abbreviation [of emblem] so compellingly attractive" (*Shakespearean Iconoclasm*, pp. 265–66); he does not, however, notice Lear's investment of this *all* in the idol he (and the play) would make of Cordelia.

39. Noting that Cordelia echoes the marriage service in her response to Lear, C. L. Barber reads 1.1 as a failed marriage ritual ("The Family in Shakespeare's Development: Tragedy and Sacredness," in *Representing Shakespeare*, pp. 197–98; amplified and extended by Barber and Richard Wheeler in *The Whole Journey: Shakespeare's Power of Development*, pp. 284–88); see also Linda Boose's fine discussion of failed wedding ritual in *King Lear* ("The Father and the Bride in Shakespeare," *PMLA* 97 [1982]: 333). Social analysts tend to see Lear's anger at Cordelia's response as a function of her success in making the ideology of patriarchal marriage visible, exposing the "realities of property marriage" (Jonathan Dollimore, *Radical Tragedy* [Chicago: University of Chicago Press, 1984], p. 199) or the rival demands of patriarchy and the price of ideological coherence (Claire McEachern, "Fathering Herself: A Source Study of Shakespeare's Feminism," *Shakespeare Quarterly* 39 [1988]: 273–74, 280–81); see Alan Sinfield's related analysis of the (Laingian) double-bind in which Lear places Cordelia ("Lear and Laing," *Essays in Criticism* 26 [1976]: 5).

40. My formulation here is in part indebted to a wonderful paper by Beth Howlett, written for a graduate course in 1988. The peculiar horror of Goneril and Regan's representation—perhaps especially for those of us who are daughters—seems to me to lie in the inevitability of the logic through which their initial gesture of standing aside to criticize their father becomes their active attempt to emasculate, abandon, and, if we can believe Gloucester, murder him, all in the service of an insatiable sexuality, as though that first gesture of autonomy could lead only here. I became aware of the extent to which I felt implicated by this logic when I realized that my own standing aside from this most patriarchal text caused me intense anxiety and guilt, as though by that gesture I was attempting to kill not only Shakespeare but all the much-loved fathers who first gave him to me. John Donnelly thinks that some such mechanism works for everyone: he derives the play's power from the audience's initial identification with Goneril and Regan and from its consequent guilt, assuaged by the final retribution ("Incest, Ingratitude, and Insanity: Aspects of the Psychopathology of King Lear," *The Psychoanalytic Review* 40 [1953]: 152).

41. Both Shengold ("II. More about the Meaning of 'Nothing,' " p. 117) and Erickson (*Patriarchal Structures in Shakespeare*, p. 111) discuss Lear's creation of the malevolent mother in terms close to my own. For Stockholder, each of the characters is Lear's creation insofar as the entire play is Lear's dream (*Dream Works*, pp. 118–47); though this formulation does not always permit maximum clarity, several of her insights anticipate mine (see especially her account of the genesis of Goneril and Regan, p. 129). The association of Cordelia with a benignly maternal nature and the transformation of that nature by Lear's own rage might have come to Shakespeare (in a rather pallid form) from *The True Chronicle Historie of King Leir*, where Leir despairs of kindness at Cordella's court because "the causeless ire of my respectlesse brest, / Hath sowrd the sweet milk of dame Natures paps: / My bitter words have gauld her honey thoughts, / And weeds of rancour chokt the flower of grace" (ll. 2059–62, in Bullough, *Narrative and Dramatic Sources* vol. 7, p. 387). One could hardly ask for a more clinical description of the genesis of what Kleinians would call the "bad breast" (see, for example, Lisa Miller's allusions to Cordelia and her sisters as good and bad breast, "A View of 'King Lear,' " pp. 97–98, 114).

42. Muir, citing Craig's gloss of *generation* as *parents*, hears in these lines a reference to the (expectedly) monstrous child (Arden *King Lear*, p. 11); most other editors gloss it as "offspring." Insofar as the father's cannibalism in this image may be understood as derivative from Lear's infantile desire to feed on Cordelia-as-mother, the confusion seems appropriate.

43. Too hard, perhaps. Act 4, scene 3, present in the Quarto but not in the Folio, is full of signs of strain, both in the opening allusion to France's absence that calls attention to that absence in the course of excusing it and in the artificial and (to most modern tastes) saccharine imagery surrounding Cordelia's happy smilets and ample tears. The scene is sometimes cut in performance (see Rosenberg, *The Masks of King Lear*, p. 257); if Warren and

Urkowitz and company are right in believing that the Folio *Lear* represents Shakespeare's own revisions of Quarto *Lear*, Shakespeare may also have felt the excessiveness of the scene. (See Michael J. Warren, "Quarto and Folio *King Lear* and the Interpretation of Albany and Edgar," in *Shakespeare: Pattern of Excelling Nature*, ed. David Bevington and Jay L. Halio [Newark, N.J.: University of Delaware Press, 1978], pp. 95–107; Steven Urkowitz, *Shakespeare's Revision of King Lear* [Princeton, N.J.: Princeton University Press, 1980]; and the essays collected in *The Division of the Kingdoms: Shakespeare's Two Versions of "King Lear"*, ed. Gary Taylor and Michael Warren [Oxford: Oxford University Press, 1983].) Whether or not we think of Folio as Shakespeare's revision of Quarto, this scene remains significant in assessing his construction of Cordelia: although he may have finally felt that it was unnecessary—that he could trust the audience to see Cordelia as a redemptive presence without it—its presence in Quarto suggests that Shakespeare initially felt that he could not let Cordelia back on stage without first strenuously instructing the audience on how to see her; the very excessiveness that may have caused its omission in Folio signals his initial anxiety about her return. (Since most of the passages that my reading of the play depends on are virtually identical in Quarto and Folio, I have not had to decide on the revision hypothesis. In fact, pace Jonathan Goldberg, for whom the fact that "in the two *Lears* different characters may speak the same lines, that the same characters . . . speak different lines, suggests the radical instability of character as a locus of meaning in the Shakespearean text" ["Textual Properties," *Shakespeare Quarterly* 37 (1986): 215], I am struck by how little difference there is in the major characters, how peripheral the changes are to the central familial confrontations.)

44. See Marina Warner's suggestive discussion of the Virgin as Mater Dolorosa (*Alone of All Her Sex: The Myth and the Cult of the Virgin Mary* [New York: Random House, 1983], pp. 206–23). As the virginal nursing mother of Lear's fantasy in 1.1, Cordelia always has the potential to become infused with the sacredness of the Virgin; the queenliness and especially the tears stressed in 4.3—both familiar attributes of the Virgin Mary—make the identification irresistible. I am deeply indebted to C. L. Barber's understanding of Cordelia as tragic stand-in for the Virgin Mother, which was from the first central to his reading of the family and the sacred in Shakespearean tragedy (see Chapter 2, n. 45; and see Barber and Wheeler, *The Whole Journey*, pp. 284–97, for the most extended discussion of Cordelia in these terms).

45. The Virgin Mary's traditional power to calm storms (Warner, *Alone of All Her Sex*, pp. 265–66) is the appropriate opposite of the witches' traditional power to raise them. Cordelia can serve simultaneously as Virgin Mother and as fertility goddess in part because the Virgin herself was often associated with natural fecundity and specifically with Demeter (see Warner, *Alone of All Her Sex*, pp. 273–84). Shakespeare evokes these associations when Cordelia prays that the unpublished virtues of the earth spring with her tears; given the association of Goneril and Regan with winter (2.4.46, 2.4.68), the seasonal reference in "spring with my tears" seems inevitable. Shakespeare knew the myth of Ceres and Proserpina in its Ovidian form and used it in *The Winter's*

Tale (see 4.4.116–18). The "darnel" that crowns Lear may in fact be taken from the *lolium* in Ovid's account of Ceres's revenge on Sicily for the loss of her daughter (*Metamorphoses* V, 485); *OED* notes that *darnel* was "known first as the English name for the *lolium* of the Vulgate." Golding's translation, according to which "the Tines and Briars did overgrow the Wheate, / And other wicked weedes the corn continually annoy" (*Shakespeare's Ovid, Being Arthur Golding's Translation of the Metamorphoses*, ed. W. H. D. Rouse [London: Centaur Press, 1961], Book 5, ll. 602–3) is reminiscent of Cordelia's list of the "idle weeds that grow / In our sustaining corn." As both mother and daughter, Cordelia combines in herself aspects of both Ceres and Proserpina: she is simultaneously the mother who searches for her child and the child who is lost and then found. Insofar as Shakespeare's use of this myth makes Lear into Cordelia's lost child ("poor perdu" [4.7.35]), he significantly revises it, turning this mother-daughter tale into a mother-son tale, hence occluding the female bond at its heart.

46. The emotional grammar of cause and effect has been so devastating in this play that we must welcome Cordelia's attempt to escape its confines; nonetheless, her response short-circuits Lear's fragile attempt to assume full responsibility for what he has done to her. There seems to be no middle ground in which these two can meet as adult father and daughter: if she is not the punitive mother who would give him poison, she is the all-loving and all-forgiving mother of "no cause." The very fullness of her forgiveness protects Lear from the specificity of his guilt; hence in part Lear's desire to relive this delicious moment endlessly in his prison fantasy. See S. L. Goldberg (*An Essay on "King Lear"* [Cambridge: Cambridge University Press, 1974], pp. 32–33), Berger ("*King Lear*: The Lear Family Romance," pp. 372–33), and Asp ("The Clamor of Eros," p. 200) for similar analyses of the effect of Cordelia's "no cause."

47. See Sigurd Burckhardt's fine analysis of the ways in which Cordelia's speech warns us that the idyll cannot last (*Shakespearean Meanings* [Princeton, N.J.: Princeton University Press, 1968], pp. 255–56). Cordelia's loss of subjectivity is not at issue for Burckhardt as it is for those who note the repetition of the "kind nursery" of 1.1 in Lear's prison fantasy and consequently hear in it his continuing attempt to deny her separateness; see, for example, Coursen ("The Death of Cordelia," p. 11), Erickson (*Patriarchal Structures*, p. 114), Cavell ("The Avoidance of Love," pp. 68–73), Richard P. Wheeler (" 'Since first we were dissevered': Trust and Autonomy in Shakespearean Tragedy and Romance," in *Representing Shakespeare*, p. 163), Barber ("The Family in Shakespeare's Development," in *Representing Shakespeare*, p. 199), and Kahn, who nonetheless notes the reciprocal gestures of the prison fantasy ("The Absent Mother in *King Lear*," pp. 48–49). Rosenberg reads Cordelia's tears as a sign of her separateness, specifically as a reminder of her love for her husband; he describes one successful Cordelia who stood "uncomfortably here, arms at her side, not returning her father's caresses" (*The Masks of King Lear*, p. 300).

48.   Bonds are "crack'd" (1.2.113), Cordelia's coronet is parted (1.1.139), there is rumored division between the Dukes (3.1.19, 3.3.8); throughout the play, "division" is virtually synonymous with danger. Both Lear and Gloucester enter the play with the word or its cognate on their lips (1.1.4, 1.1.37); Edmund can successfully parody fear of division (1.2.144, 153) because we have heard the word so often. Both Lear's command to Kent ("Come not between the Dragon and his wrath" [1.1.122]) and his banishment of him because he has "come betwixt our sentence and our power" (1.1.170) seem to be attempts to fend off knowledge of impending division in himself.

49.   Shakespeare sometimes uses *twain* to mean simply "two"; but he often uses the word to register not simply two-ness, but unnatural or violent division in which what should be one is cleft (*Hamlet*, 3.4.158; *Measure*, 3.1.62), divided (*1 Henry VI*, 4.5.49; *Troilus and Cressida*, 2.3.245), broken (*2 Henry VI*, 1.2.26), riven (*Troilus and Cressida*, 1.1.35), cut (*Romeo and Juliet*, 5.3.99), or shorn (*Othello*, 5.2.207) in twain. Sonnet 36 beautifully illustrates the distance between *two* and *twain*: "Let me confess that we two must be twain / Although our undivided loves are one."

50.   Many diverse critics sense a desire for wholeness in this play. See, for example, Siemon's account of the "insistent pursuit of completeness," the "desire for the 'all' [that] makes idolatry possible" (*Shakespearean Iconoclasm*, pp. 261, 265), or S. L. Goldberg's account of Gloucester's simultaneous "help-lessness in the face of his deepest feelings" and hankering for "the integrity, the fullness, they could give" (*An Essay on King Lear*, p. 80). For Cavell, the splitting and doubling of characters—so that Lear meets himself in Gloucester, his shadow in the fool—"taunts the characters with their lack of wholeness, their separation from themselves"; in his account, the inability to tolerate our separateness from each other is—for both characters and audience—at the heart of our failures of acknowledgment, and hence of our avoidance of love ("The Avoidance of Love," pp. 79, 109). (See also "Othello and the Stake of the Other," Cavell's beautiful meditation on Othello's tragic inability to toler-ate his own finitude [*Disowning Knowledge*, pp. 125–42].) Although we often use quite different terms, my debt to Cavell's work is immense. When I first saw "The Avoidance of Love" in Cavell's *Must We Mean What We Say* (Cambridge: Cambridge University Press, 1976), it struck me—as it did many others—with revelatory force, as much for the intense relatedness Cavell de-mands of himself and his readers as for the brilliance of his insights; it seemed to me then, and still seems to me now, astonishing in its absolutely freshly felt and deeply thought-through responsiveness to the play.

51.   I prefer the quarto punctuation, which gives a comma after "speak," to Muir's semi-colon, because it permits more enjambment, hence the possibil-ity that we will hear "she must not speak why she dare not come over": read thus, the lines seem to allude not only to the fact of Cordelia's initial silence in 1.1. but also to the whole anguished complex of love and separateness that silences her.

52.   Lisa Miller similarly identifies Cordelia as the beloved on the other

side of the bourn ("A View of 'King Lear,' " p. 108). "Bourn" is Capell's emendation of Quarto's "broome"; the song is not in the Folio. The emendation is given force by numerous references to versions of the same song. Muir (Arden *King Lear*, p. 132) cites Wager's use of it—"Com ouer the Boorne beese to me"—in *The Longer thou Livest the More Fool thou Art*. The lover's refrain was sufficiently capacious that it could be filled with all kinds of desire. Arthur R. Kinney notes that Skelton's use of it in *Speke, Parrot* derives from a popular Tudor ballad in which Christ calls to mankind with the words "Come over the burn, Besse, to me" (*John Skelton, Priest as Poet: Seasons of Discovery* [Chapel Hill: University of North Carolina Press, 1987], p. 26; I am grateful to Professor Kinney for directing me to this reference). The version in *The Harleian Miscellany* (ed. Thomas Park [London, 1813], vol. 10, pp. 260–62) is "A Songe betwene the Quene's Majestie and Englande," a dialogue in which England invites Elizabeth to become queen with the words "Come over the born Bessy, / Sweete Bessy come over to me." These desires—for union of infinite with finite, for union with a virgin queen—both seem to me germane to the desire for Cordelia evoked by the song in its place here.

53. According to Freud, this first smell of mortality may also be the proto-typical experience of suffocation: he derives the sensation of choking character-istic of anxiety—our contemporary equivalent to the Suffocation of the Mother—from the physiology of birth, the first separation (*Introductory Lectures on Psychoanalysis, Standard Edition*, vol. 16, pp. 396–97). On the other hand, Otto Fenichel notes that "fears of suffocation are often specially directed against fantasies of being in the mother's womb" (*The Psychoanalytic Theory of Neurosis* [New York: Norton & Company, 1945], p. 202). Either by abandoning the infant to separate existence or by overwhelming him/her in suffocating closeness, the mother remains the site of suffocation in these apparently contrary formulations.

54. Attempts to demonstrate Cordelia's consistency often require baroque and not always convincing readings of her motives in 1.1 and on her return, even among the best critics: Cavell's Cordelia is consistent because she is trying to protect Lear even in 1.1 ("The Avoidance of Love," pp. 62–66); Boose's Cordelia returns in order to win Lear's blessing so that she can go on to complete the marriage ritual ("The Father and the Bride," pp. 334–35). The most convincing case for Cordelia's consistency is, I think, made by Berger, who argues that she retains her initial smugness after her return, when she has "triumphantly refined the victim's role to a Christ-like perfection" ("*King Lear*: The Lear Family Romance," p. 372); he can construct this case only by overlooking the extent to which the play—rather than Cordelia herself—sanctifies her. But McLuskie notes Cordelia's inconsistency and sees in her return as icon a deeply problematic attempt to restore patriarchy by resolving its ideological contradictions ("The Patriarchal Bard," pp. 99–101). Other critics note the change in Cordelia but do not find it problematic: D. G. James, because it serves Shakespeare's "abstractive imagination" (*The Dream of Learning* [Oxford: Oxford University Press, 1965], pp. 100–101, 110–17); Jungians, because Cordelia is Lear's anima and hence an aspect of him from

the start (see, for example, Alex Aronson, *Psyche and Symbol in Shakespeare* [Bloomington: Indiana University Press, 1972], pp. 185, 188; but Coursen simultaneously sees the anima in her and faults Lear for not responding to her otherness ["The Death of Cordelia," pp. 5, 8, and 11]).

55. McLuskie says, "The most stony-hearted feminist could not withhold her pity even though it is called forth at the expense of her resistance to the patriarchal relations which it endorses" ("The Patriarchal Bard," p. 102). For McLuskie, pity means the failure of resistance: either we exclude ourselves from the pleasure of the text, or we allow ourselves to be entrapped by its ideological misogyny (p. 98). In distinguishing between the (relatively gendered) fantasies of the oedipal period and the (relatively ungendered) fantasies of the preoedipal period, I attempt to articulate another alternative.

56. Insofar as the fantasy of oedipal betrayal allows the son both to mobilize an individuating rage and eventually to model himself on the father who has power, it may be a distinct improvement on the less mediated longings and terrors of the preoedipal period; it is in this sense that I see oedipal rage as a potential defense against a more primitive vulnerability. Received Freudian wisdom would in general construe this the other way around: for both Ella Freeman Sharpe ("From *King Lear* to *The Tempest*," *International Journal of Psychoanalysis* 27 [1946]: 29) and Chaplin ("Form and Psychology in *King Lear*," p. 32), Lear's regression to oral fantasies of merger represents a defense against genital/oedipal desire.

57. Bradley read Cordelia's death as the last stage of the poem called "The Redemption of King Lear" (*Shakespearean Tragedy*, p. 228). For updated versions of Bradley's reading, see, for example, Dreher's *Dominance and Defiance* (pp. 74–75) and especially Susan Snyder's "*King Lear* and the Psychology of Dying," where Cordelia's death is an aspect of Lear's and allows him "to experience his own death" (*Shakespeare Quarterly* 33 [1982]: 459). Among recent critics who read her death as the logical consequence of Lear's obliterating need for her, see especially Cavell ("The Avoidance of Love," pp. 72–73), Barber and Wheeler (*The Whole Journey*, pp. 38, 293–94), Erickson (*Patriarchal Structures*, p. 115), and Asp ("The Clamor of Eros," p. 201).

58. As Muir points out (Arden *King Lear*, p. 200) the line—"Have I caught my heavenly jewel?"—is from "Stella Sleeping," the second song of Sidney's *Astrophel and Stella*.

59. The Variorum *Coriolanus* has a long note to 4.5.123–24 speculating about Shakespeare's familiarity with the Roman custom of lifting the bride over the threshold of the husband's house (*The Tragedie of Coriolanus*, ed. Horace Howard Furness [Philadelphia and London: J. B. Lippincott Company, 1928], p. 437). But the issue may be moot: John R. Gillis suggests that the custom was still current in England (*For Better, For Worse: British Marriages, 1600 to the Present* [New York, Oxford: Oxford University Press, 1985], p. 75).

60. In this formulation, I am deeply indebted to Barber's identification of this moment as a reversed pietà and his reading of it as registering both sacredness and tragic loss: "The sacredness in Shakespeare's tragedy goes with recognition of the human impossibility of being divine, realized by the dread attempt, which brings destruction" ("The Family in Shakespeare's Development," pp. 200–201).

61. From the start, Edmund's masculinity has depended on his aggressive individuation; see, for example, the phallic force behind his "I grow, I prosper" (1.2.21). Since Stockholder sees Edmund as an aspect of Lear, she reads Cordelia's death as a reflection of Lear's—not Shakespeare's—ambivalence; nonetheless, her understanding of the threat Cordelia poses to masculine identity is in some respects close to mine (*Dream Works*, pp. 124, 145).

62. Shakespeare uses "heart" more often in *King Lear* than in any other play (forty-four times), and with special intensity; four strong uses of the term within thirty-five lines register the whole of the initial conflict with Cordelia, who cannot heave her heart into her mouth (1.1.91), but who nonetheless tells her father that her heart goes with her speech (1.1.104), and whose father responds by holding her as a stranger to his heart, giving his heart from her (1.1.115, 125–26).

63. Lear's association of heart and womb may have been traditional: according to *The Birth of Mankinde*, the most popular English gynecological handbook of the time (see Chapter 1, nn. 22 and 24), the "bottome of the matrix is not perfectly round bowlwise, but rather like the forme of a mans harte" (p. 27).

64. For this developmental history, see Chapter 1, p. 7, and n. 30).

65. Though I have earlier characterized preoedipal fantasies as in part ungendered, here they seem to me distinctly inflected by gender. For though the preoedipal girl may well feel overwhelmed by the mother's presence within her, she will not ordinarily feel contaminated specifically by the femaleness of that presence; though the internal mother may compromise her individuality, she will not compromise her core gender identity.

66. And perhaps not only male individuality, though Edmund's words have led me to construe Cordelia's choking thus. This play's portrayal of suffocating longing and dread are neither wholly "male" nor wholly academic for me; I read it as a childhood asthmatic, and often speak of it with one hand at my throat.

67. Mack, *King Lear in Our Time*, p. 100. (Though Mack emphasizes *esse* rather than *Existenz* in the characters and disdains the claim to "any form of psychic 'life' fluctuating among 'motives' " [p. 66], his own moving account of relatedness in the play [esp. pp. 110–13] touches on the emotions that I find central to it.)

68. The play's first audiences would have been shocked by Cordelia's

death, not only because it is a gratuitous accident that happens after victory seems assured but also because in the stories they knew she had always lived; Shakespeare's willfulness in killing her off would probably have been more apparent to them than it usually is to us.

NOTES TO CHAPTER 6

1. This chapter largely replicates two essays published separately in 1978 and 1987, each of which deals with the construction of a rigid male identity as a defense against overwhelming maternal power (" 'Anger's My Meat': Feeding, Dependency, and Aggression in *Coriolanus*," in *Shakespeare: Pattern of Excelling Nature*, ed. David Bevington and Jay L. Halio [Newark, N.J.: University of Delaware Press, 1978], pp. 108–24, reprinted in slightly altered form in *Representing Shakespeare: New Psychoanalytic Essays*, ed. Murray M. Schwartz and Coppélia Kahn [Baltimore, Md.: Johns Hopkins University Press, 1980, pp. 129–49; " 'Born of Woman': Fantasies of Maternal Power in *Macbeth*," in *Cannibals, Witches, and Divorce: Estranging the Renaissance* [Selected Papers from the English Institute, 1985], ed. Marjorie Garber [Baltimore, Md.: Johns Hopkins University Press], pp. 90–121). I have tinkered very slightly with the *Macbeth* essay but have left the bulk of the *Coriolanus* essay unchanged. Insofar as my formulations of the dilemmas of masculinity shifted between the two essays, the shift reflects what I have learned from feminist object-relations psychoanalysis, and from a group of critics engaged with its terms: especially Richard Wheeler, Madelon Gohlke (now Sprengnether), Coppélia Kahn, Carol Neely, Peter Erickson, and Murray Schwartz. For the specific connections between *Macbeth* and *Coriolanus*, see especially Gohlke (" 'I wooed thee with my sword': Shakespeare's Tragic Paradigms," in *Representing Shakespeare*, pp. 176–77), Kahn (*Man's Estate: Masculine Identity in Shakespeare* [Berkeley: University of California Press, 1981], pp. 151–92), and Wheeler (*Shakespeare's Development and the Problem Comedies* [Berkeley: University of California Press, 1981], pp. 203–13), each of whom notes that the plays share a common concern with establishing a defensive masculinity; in particular, Kahn's chapter title—"The Milking Babe and the Bloody Man in *Coriolanus* and *Macbeth*"—indicates the similarity of our arguments. Linda Bamber also analyzes the two plays together but interprets their similarity differently: for her, the absence of a true feminine Other in both plays prevents the development of true manliness in their heroes *(Comic Women, Tragic Men: A Study of Gender and Genre in Shakespeare* [Stanford, Calif.: Stanford University Press, 1982], pp. 20, 91–107).

2. See Chapter 1 for suffocation and the caesarian solution in Richard. In his classic preoedipal account of the failure of differentiation in *Macbeth*, David B. Barron associates the cutting and breaking imagery throughout the play with Macbeth's attempt to "cut his way out of the female environment which chokes and smothers him"; he notes that the choking/suffocating/smothering images find their realization in the witches' "birth-strangled babe" ("The

Babe That Milks: An Organic Study of *Macbeth*," originally published in 1960 and reprinted in *The Design Within*, ed. M. D. Faber [New York: Science House, 1970], p. 268). For similar preoedipal readings of the play, see Marvin Rosenberg's *The Masks of Macbeth* (Berkeley: University of California Press, 1978), pp. 81–82, 270–72, and especially Kahn's *Man's Estate*, pp. 151–55, 172–92, Wheeler's *Shakespeare's Development*, pp. 144–49, and David Willbern's "Phantasmagoric *Macbeth*," *English Literary Renaissance* 16 (1986): 520–49, an essay that I saw in an earlier form in 1981.

3. Oddly, this fantasy is present in the report of the Earl of Gowrie's attempt to kill King James in 1600, a report that may have influenced Shakespeare in *Macbeth*. James Weimis of Bogy, testifying in 1600 about the earl's recourse to necromancy, reported that the earl thought it "possible that the seed of a man and woman might be brought to perfection otherwise then by the *matrix* of the woman" ("Gowries Conspiracie: A Discoverie of the unnaturall and vyle Conspiracie, attempted against the Kings Maiesties Person at Sanct-Iohnstoun, upon Twysday the Fifth of August, 1600," in *A Selection from the Harleian Miscellany* [London: C. and G. Kearsley, 1793], p. 196). The account goes on to suggest the kind of invulnerability the earl sought from the necromancer: searching the dead earl's pockets, James found nothing in them "but a little close parchment bag, full of magicall characters, and words of inchantment, wherin, it seemed, that he had put his confidence, thinking him selfe never safe without them, and therfore ever carried them about with him; beeing also observed, that, while they were uppon him, his wound whereof he died, bled not, but, incontinent after the taking of them away, the blood gushed out in great aboundance, to the great admiration of al the beholders" ("Gowries Conspiracie," p. 196). Stanley J. Kozikowski argues strenuously that Shakespeare knew either this pamphlet, printed in Scotland and London in 1600, or the abortive play on the conspiracy, apparently performed twice by the King's Men and then canceled in 1604 ("The Gowrie Conspiracy Against James VI: A New Source for Shakespeare's *Macbeth*," *Shakespeare Studies* 13 [1980]: 197–211). Although I do not find his arguments entirely persuasive, it seems likely that Shakespeare knew at least the central facts of the conspiracy, given both James's annual celebration of his escape from it and the apparent involvement of the King's Men in a play on the subject. But whether or not Shakespeare knew of and deliberately recalled the conspiracy in *Macbeth*, the pamphlet's figuration of the connection between recourse to necromancy, invulnerability, and escape from maternal origin suggests that this connection would have been culturally and psychically resonant for many in Shakespeare's audience. (See also Steven Mullaney's suggestive use of the Gowrie material as analogous to *Macbeth* in its links between treason and magical riddle ["Lying Like Truth: Riddle, Representation and Treason in Renaissance England," *ELH* 47 (1980): 32, 38].)

4. David Sundelson (*Shakespeare's Restorations of the Father* [New Brunswick, N.J.: Rutgers University Press, 1983], p. 3), Harry Berger, Jr. ("The Early Scenes of *Macbeth*: Preface to a New Interpretation," *ELH* 47 [1980]: 26–28), and Willbern ("Phantasmagoric *Macbeth*," pp. 522–23) all see Dun-

can as an androgynous parent. Murray M. Schwartz and Wheeler note specifically the extent to which the male claim to androgynous possession of nurturant power reflects a fear of maternal power outside male control (Schwartz, "Shakespeare through Contemporary Psychoanalysis," in *Representing Shakespeare*, p. 29; Wheeler, *Shakespeare's Development*, p. 146). My discussion of Duncan's androgyny is indirectly indebted to Peter Erickson's rich account of the Duke's taking on of nurturant function in *As You Like It*, an account that I first heard in 1979, now a chapter in his *Patriarchal Structures in Shakespeare's Drama* (Berkeley: University of California Press, 1985); see especially pp. 27–37.

5. Many commentators note that Shakespeare's Duncan is less ineffectual than Holinshed's; others note the continuing signs of his weakness. See especially Harry Berger's brilliant account of the structural effect of Duncan's weakness in defining his (and Macbeth's) society ("The Early Scenes of *Macbeth*," pp. 1–31).

6. Many note the appropriateness of Macbeth's conflation of himself with Tarquin, given the play's alliance of sexuality and murder. See, for example, Ian Robinson, "The Witches and Macbeth," *The Critical Review* 11 (1968): 104; Dennis Biggins, "Sexuality, Witchcraft, and Violence in *Macbeth*," *Shakespeare Studies* 8 (1975): 269; and Robert N. Watson, *Shakespeare and the Hazards of Ambition* (Cambridge, Mass.: Harvard University Press, 1984), p. 100. Arthur Kirsch works extensively with the analogy, seeing the Tarquin of *The Rape of Lucrece* as a model for Macbeth's ambitious desire ("Macbeth's Suicide," *ELH* 51 [1984]: 269–96). Commentators on the analogy do not in general note that it transforms Macbeth's kingly victim into a woman; Norman Rabkin is an exception (*Shakespeare and the Problem of Meaning* [Chicago: Chicago University Press, 1981], p. 107).

7. Wheeler sees the simultaneously castrated and castrating Gorgon-like body of Duncan as the emblem of the world Macbeth brings into being (*Shakespeare's Development*, p. 145); I see it as the emblem of a potentially castrating femaleness that Macbeth's act of violence reveals but does not create. For an interesting counter-reading, see Marjorie Garber ("Macbeth: The Male Medusa," *Shakespeare's Ghost Writers: Literature as Uncanny Causality* [New York: Methuen, 1987], pp. 87–123); in her account, the gorgon functions throughout *Macbeth* not as the sign of a terrifying femaleness but as the sign of a (more terrifying) gender undecidability *per se*.

8. See Chapter 5, note 20, for the witch's traditional ability to raise storms.

9. Many commentators, following Freud, find the murder of Duncan "little else than patricide" ("Those Wrecked by Success," *The Standard Edition of the Complete Psychological Works of Sigmund Freud*, ed. James Strachey [London, The Hogarth Press, 1957], vol. 14, p. 321); see, for example, Rabkin (*Shakespeare and the Problem of Meaning*, pp. 106–9), Kirsch ("Macbeth's Suicide," pp. 276–80, 286), and Watson (*Shakespeare and the Hazards of Ambition*, esp. pp. 85–88, 98–99). (The last two are particularly interesting

insofar as they understand parricide as an ambitious attempt to redefine the self as omnipotently free from limits.) In standard oedipal readings of the play, the mother is less the object of desire than "the 'demon-woman,' who creates the abyss between father and son" by inciting the son to parricide (Ludwig Jekels, "The Riddle of Shakespeare's *Macbeth*," in *The Design Within*, p. 240); see also, for example, L. Veszy-Wagner (*"Macbeth*: 'Fair Is Foul and Foul Is Fair,'" *American Imago* 25 [1968]: 242–57), Norman N. Holland (*Psychoanalysis and Shakespeare* [New York: Octagon Books, 1979], p. 229), and Patrick Colm Hogan ("Macbeth: Authority and Progenitorship," *American Imago* 40 [1983]: 385–95). For Janis Krohn, Lady Macbeth is simultaneously the oedipal mother who incites her son to parricide and the preoedipal mother who betrays him ("Addressing the Oedipal Dilemma in *Macbeth*," *The Psychoanalytic Review* 73 [1986]: 333–37). By emphasizing the degree to which Duncan is absent even before his murder, I mean to suggest the extent to which maternal power—including the power to incite parricide—is a consequence as well as a cause of paternal absence.

10.   For those recent commentators who follow Barron in seeing preoedipal rather than oedipal issues as central to the play, the images of disrupted nurturance define the primary area of disturbance: see, for example, Barron ("The Babe That Milks," p. 255); Schwartz ("Shakespeare through Contemporary Psychoanalysis," p. 29); Kahn (*Man's Estate*, pp. 172–78); Wheeler (*Shakespeare's Development*, pp. 147–48); Berger ("The Early Scenes of *Macbeth*," pp. 27–28); Joan M. Byles ("Macbeth: Imagery of Destruction," *American Imago* 39 [1982]: 149–64); Kirsch ("Macbeth's Suicide," pp. 291–92); Susan Bachmann (" 'Daggers in Men's Smiles'—The 'Truest Issue' in *Macbeth*," *International Review of Psycho-Analysis* 5 [1978]: 97–104); and Willbern ("Phantasmagoric *Macbeth*," pp. 526–32). Among these, Barron, Bachmann, and Kahn see the abrupt and bloody weaning imaged by Lady Macbeth here as the root cause of Macbeth's failure to differentiate himself from the maternal figure and his consequent susceptibility to female influence; Willbern locates in it the psychological point of origin for the failure of potential space that Macbeth enacts. In Peter Erickson's suggestive account, patriarchal bounty itself fails in *Macbeth* in part because it depends on the maternal nurturance that is here disturbed (*Patriarchal Structures*, pp. 116–21). Each of these critics constructs Lady Macbeth as the destructive mother in relation to whom Macbeth is imagined as an infant; Rosenberg notes intriguingly that *Macbeth* has twice been performed with a mother and son in the chief roles (*Masks of Macbeth*, p. 196).

11.   Despite some over-literal interpretation, Alice Fox and particularly Jenijoy La Belle usefully demonstrate the specifically gynecological references of "passage" and "visitings of nature," using contemporary gynecological treatises: see Fox ("Obstetrics and Gynecology in *Macbeth*," *Shakespeare Studies* 12 [1979]: 129) and La Belle (" 'A Strange Infirmity': Lady Macbeth's Amenorrhea," *Shakespeare Quarterly* 31 [1980]: 382) for the identification of "visitings of nature" as a term for menstruation; see La Belle (p. 383) for the identification of "passage" as a term for the neck of the womb. See also Barron,

who associates Lady Macbeth's language here with contraception ("The Babe That Milks," p. 267).

12. "For" is glossed as "in exchange for" in the following editions, for example: *The Complete Signet Classic Shakespeare*, ed. Sylvan Barnet (New York: Harcourt, Brace, Jovanovich, 1972); *The Complete Works of Shakespeare*, ed. Hardin Craig (Chicago, Ill.: Scott, Foresman, 1951), rev. ed. edited by David Bevington, 1973; *The Riverside Shakespeare*, ed. G. Blakemore Evans (Boston, Mass.: Houghton Mifflin, 1974); *William Shakespeare: The Complete Works*, ed. Alfred Harbage (Baltimore, Md.: Penguin, 1969); *The Complete Works of Shakespeare*, ed. George Lyman Kittredge (Boston: Ginn, 1936), rev. ed. edited by Irving Ribner, 1971). Muir demurs, preferring Keightley's understanding of "take" as "infect" (see the Arden *Macbeth*, p. 30).

13. See Chapter 1 (pp. 4, 7, and notes 12, 13, and 28) for these ills; and see Samuel X. Radbill for the identification of colostrum with witch's milk ("Pediatrics," in *Medicine in Seventeenth Century England*, ed. Allen G. Debus [Berkeley: University of California Press, 1974], p. 249). The topic was of interest to King James, who claimed to have sucked his Protestantism from his nurse's milk; his drunkenness was also attributed to her (see Henry N. Paul, *The Royal Play of Macbeth* [New York: The Macmillan Company, 1950], pp. 387–88).

14. Many commentators on English witchcraft note the unusual prominence given to the presence of the witch's mark and the nursing of familiars; see, for example, Barbara Rosen's introduction to her collection of witchcraft documents (*Witchcraft* [London: Edward Arnold, 1969], pp. 29–30). She cites contemporary documents on the nursing of familiars, e.g., on pp. 187–88 and 315; the testimony of Joan Prentice, one of the convicted witches of Chelmsford in 1589, is particularly suggestive: "At what time soever she would have her ferret do anything for her, she used the words 'Bid, Bid, Bid, come Bid, come Bid, come suck, come suck, come suck" (p. 188). Katherine Mary Briggs quotes a contemporary (1613) story about the finding of a witch's teat (*Pale Hecate's Team* [New York: Arno Press, 1977], p. 250); see also Wallace Notestein, *A History of Witchcraft in England from 1558 to 1718* (Washington, D.C.: The American Historical Association, 1911), p. 36, and George Lyman Kittredge, *Witchcraft in Old and New England* (New York: Russell and Russell, 1956), p. 179. Though he does not refer to the suckling of familiars, King James believed in the significance of the witch's mark, at least when he wrote the *Daemonologie* (London, 1603; see p. 33). M. C. Bradbrook notes that Lady Macbeth's invitation to the spirits is "as much as any witch could do by way of self-dedication" ("The Sources of *Macbeth*," *Shakespeare Survey* 4 [1951]: 43); see also Leslie A. Fiedler, *The Stranger in Shakespeare* (London: Croom Helm, 1973), p. 72.

15. In a brilliant essay, Peter Stallybrass associates the move from the cosmic to the secular realm with the ideological shoring up of a patriarchal state founded on the model of the family ("*Macbeth* and Witchcraft," in *Focus*

on Macbeth, ed. John Russell Brown [London: Routledge and Kegan Paul, 1982], esp. pp. 196–98).

16. Wilbur Sanders notes the extent to which "terror is mediated through absurdity" in the witches (*The Dramatist and the Received Idea* [Cambridge: Cambridge University Press, 1968], p. 277); see also Harry Berger's fine account of the scapegoating reduction of the witches to comic and grotesque triviality ("Text Against Performance in Shakespeare: The Example of *Macbeth*," in *The Forms of Power and the Power of Forms in the Renaissance*, ed. Stephen Greenblatt, *Genre* 15 [1982]: 67–68). Harold C. Goddard (*The Meaning of Shakespeare* [Chicago, Ill.: The University of Chicago Press, 1951], pp. 512–13), Robinson ("The Witches and Macbeth," pp. 100–103), and Stallybrass ("*Macbeth* and Witchcraft," p. 199) note the witches' change from potent and mysterious to more diminished figures in act 4. For Fiedler, the witches are "always on the verge of shifting from satanic to grotesque to fully comic"; Lady Macbeth is "the sole substantial reality behind the shadow play of stage convention, hallucination, and delusion" in them (*The Stranger in Shakespeare*, pp. 71–72).

17. After years of trying fruitlessly to pin down a precise identity for the witches, critics are increasingly finding their dramatic power precisely in their indefinability. The most powerful statements of this critical topos are those by Sanders (*The Dramatist and the Received Idea*, pp. 277–79), Robert H. West, (*Shakespeare and the Outer Mystery* [Lexington: University of Kentucky Press, 1968], pp. 78–79), and Stephen Booth (*"King Lear", "Macbeth", Indefinition, and Tragedy* [New Haven, Conn.: Yale University Press, 1983], pp. 101–3).

18. For their "Englishness," see Stallybrass, "*Macbeth* and Witchcraft," p. 195. Alan Macfarlane's important study of English witchcraft, *Witchcraft in Tudor and Stuart England* (New York: Harper and Row, 1970), frequently notes the absence of the Continental staples: if the witches of Essex are typical, English witches do not fly, do not hold Sabbaths, do not commit sexual perversions or attack male potency, do not kill babies (see pp. 6, 160, and 180, for example).

19. Macfarlane finds the failure of neighborliness reflected in the retaliatory acts of the witch the key to the social function of witchcraft in England; see *Witchcraft in Tudor and Stuart England*, especially pp. 168–76, for accounts of the failures of neighborliness—very similar to the refusal to share chestnuts—that provoked the witch to act. James Sprenger's and Heinrich Kramer's *Malleus Maleficarum* (trans. Montague Summers [New York: Benjamin Blom, 1970]) is the *locus classicus* for Continental witchcraft beliefs: for the murder and eating of infants, see pp. 21, 66, 99, and 100–101; for attacks on the genitals, see pp. 47, 55–60, and 117–19; for sexual relations with demons, see pp. 21, 112–14. Or see Reginald Scot's convenient summary of these beliefs (*The Discoverie of Witchcraft* [London, 1584; reprinted, with an introduction by Hugh Ross Williamson, Carbondale: Southern Illinois University Press, 1964], p. 31).

20. The relationship between cosmology and domestic psychology is similar in *King Lear*; even as Shakespeare casts doubt on the authenticity of demonic possession by his use of Harsnett's *Declaration of Egregious Popish Impostures*, Edgar / Poor Tom's identification of his father as "the foul Flibbertigibet" (3.4.118) manifests the psychic reality and source of his demons. Characteristically in Shakespeare, the site of blessing and of cursedness is the family, their processes psychological.

21. In an early essay that has become a classic, Eugene Waith established the centrality of definitions of manhood and Lady Macbeth's role in enforcing Macbeth's particularly bloodthirsty version, a theme that has since become a major topos of *Macbeth* criticism ("Manhood and Valor in Two Shakespearean Tragedies," *ELH* 17 [1950]: 262–73). Among the legions, see, for example, Robert B. Heilman, "Manliness in the Tragedies: Dramatic Variations," in *Shakespeare 1564–1964: A Collection of Modern Essays by Various Hands*, ed. Edward A. Bloom (Providence, R.I.: Brown University Press, 1964), p. 27; Mathew N. Proser, *The Heroic Image in Five Shakespearean Tragedies* (Princeton, N.J.: Princeton University Press, 1965), pp. 51–91; Michael Taylor, "Ideals of Manhood in *Macbeth*," *Études Anglaises* 21 (1968): 337–48 (an early foregrounding of cultural complicity in defining masculinity as aggression); D. W. Harding, "Women's Fantasy of Manhood: A Shakespearean Theme," *Shakespeare Quarterly* 20 (1969): 245–53; Paul A. Jorgensen, *Our Naked Frailties: Sensational Art and Meaning in "Macbeth"* (Berkeley: University of California Press, 1971), esp. pp. 147ff.; Jarold Ramsey, "The Perversion of Manliness in *Macbeth*," *SEL* 13 (1973): 285–300; Carolyn Asp, " 'Be bloody, bold, and resolute': Tragic Action and Sexual Stereotyping in *Macbeth*," *Studies in Philology* 25 (1981): 153–69; Harry Berger, Jr., "Text Against Performance," esp. pp. 67–75; Robert Kimbrough, "Macbeth: The Prisoner of Gender," *Shakespeare Studies* 16 (1983): 175–90; King-Kok Cheung, "Shakespeare and Kierkegaard: 'Dread' in *Macbeth*," *Shakespeare Quarterly* 35 (1984): 437–38; and Krohn, "Addressing the Oedipal Dilemma," pp. 334–37. Virtually all these essays recount the centrality of 1.7 to this theme; most see Macbeth's willingness to murder as his response to Lady Macbeth's nearly explicit attack on his male potency. Dennis Biggins ("Sexuality, Witchcraft, and Violence," pp. 255–77) and James J. Greene ("Macbeth: Masculinity as Murder," *American Imago* 41 [1984]: 155–80) see the murder as a sexual act consummating the union of Macbeth and Lady Macbeth; see also Watson, *Shakespeare and the Hazards of Ambition*, p. 90. My account differs from most of these largely in stressing the infantile components of Macbeth's susceptibility to Lady Macbeth.

22. Although "his" was a common form for the as-yet unfamiliar possessive "its," Lady Macbeth's move from "while it was smiling" to "his boneless gums" nonetheless seems to register the metamorphosis of an ungendered to a gendered infant exactly at the moment of vulnerability, making her attack specifically on a male child. That she uses the ungendered "the" a moment later ("the brains out") suggests one alternative open to Shakespeare had he wished to avoid the implication that the fantasied infant was male; Antony's

crocodile, who "moves with it own organs" (*Antony and Cleopatra*, 2.7.42) suggests another. (*OED* notes that, although "its" occurs in the Folio, it does not occur in any work of Shakespeare published while he was alive; it also notes the various strategies by which authors attempted to avoid the inappropriate use of "his.")

23. Lady Macbeth maintains her control over Macbeth through 3.4 by manipulating these categories: see 2.2.53–54 (" 'tis the eye of childhood / That fears a painted devil") and 3.4.57–64 ("Are you a man? . . . these flaws and starts . . . would well become / A woman's story"). In his response to Banquo's ghost, Macbeth invokes the same categories and suggests their interchangeability: he dares what man dares (3.4.98); if he feared Banquo alive, he could rightly be called "the baby of a girl" (3.4.105).

24. Willbern notes the extent to which the regicide is re-imagined as a "symbolic infanticide," so that the image of Duncan fuses with the image of Lady Macbeth's child murdered in fantasy ("Phantasmagoric *Macbeth*," p. 524). Macbeth's earlier association of Duncan's power with the power of the "naked new-born babe, / Striding the blast" (1.7.21–22) prepares for this fusion: whatever their symbolic power, the literal babies of this play and those adults who sleep and trust like infants are hideously vulnerable. That Duncan is simultaneously female (Lucrece or Gorgon) and infantile suggests the degree to which these categories fuse in defining adult masculinity by opposition.

25. Kahn's reading of this passage is very similar to mine (*Man's Estate*, p. 173); for Jan Groen, the passage indicates Macbeth's attempt to identify with the split-off bad-mother part of himself, which is then defined as masculine ("Women in Shakespeare with Particular Reference to Lady Macbeth," *The International Review of Psycho-Analysis* 12 [1985]: 476). Cheung notes the puns, seeing in them the signs not of Lady Macbeth's fantasied maleness but of Macbeth's own equation of masculinity and aggression ("Shakespeare and Kierkegaard," p. 438).

26. Shakespeare's only other use of "man-child" is in *Coriolanus*, when Volumnia tells Virgilia, "I sprang not more in joy at first hearing he was a man-child, than now in first seeing he had proved himself a man" (1.3.16–18); this isolated repetition suggests the extent to which Shakespeare reworks similar concerns in that play.

27. De Quincy seems to have intuited this process: "The murderers are taken out of the region of human things, human purposes, human desires. They are transfigured: Lady Macbeth is 'unsexed'; Macbeth has forgot that he was born of woman" ("On the Knocking at the Gate in 'Macbeth,' " in *Shakespeare Criticism: A Selection, 1623–1840*, ed. D. Nichol Smith [London: Oxford University Press, 1946], p. 335). Critics who consider gender relations central to this play generally note the importance of the witches' prophecy for the figure of Macduff; they do not usually note its application to Macbeth. But see Kahn's suggestion that the prophecy sets Macbeth "apart from women as well as from men" (*Man's Estate*, p. 187) and Gohlke/Sprengnether's central

perception that, "To be born of woman, as [Macbeth] reads the witches' prophecy, is to be mortal" (" 'I wooed thee with my sword,' " p. 176).

28. See Kahn's rich understanding of the function of the term "cow'd" (*Man's Estate*, p. 191).

29. Many comment on this contamination: see, for example, Berger, "The Early Scenes of *Macbeth*," pp. 7–8; Hogan, "*Macbeth*," p. 387; Rosenberg, *The Masks of Macbeth*, p. 45; and Biggins, "Sexuality, Witches, and Violence," p. 265.

30. Watson notes the suggestion of caesarian section here (*Shakespeare and the Hazards of Ambition*, p. 100) and in *Coriolanus*; but in part because he understands self-birth in oedipal rather than preoedipal terms, he fails to note the aggression toward the female at its root (see Chapter 1, n. 3). I am specifically indebted to Willbern's reading of the caesarian implications of the unseaming from nave to chops ("Phantasmagoric *Macbeth*," p. 528–29).

31. The reference to Macbeth as "Bellona's bridegroom" anticipates his interaction with Lady Macbeth in 1.7: only the murderous man-child is fit mate for either of these unsexed, quasi-male figures.

32. To the extent that ferocious maleness is the creation of the male community, not of Lady Macbeth or the witches, the women are scapegoats who exist partly to obscure the conflicts in that male community. For fuller accounts of this process, see Veszy-Wagner ("Macbeth," p. 244), Bamber (*Comic Women*, pp. 19–20), and especially Berger ("Text Against Performance," pp. 69–75); for a more recent version, see Dianne Hunter ("Doubling, Mythic Difference, and the Scapegoating of Female Power in *Macbeth*," *The Psychoanalytic Review* 75 [1988]: 129–52). But whether or not the women are scapegoats falsely held responsible for Macbeth's murderous maleness, fear of the female power they represent remains primary (not secondary and obscurantist) insofar as the male community and to some extent the play itself construct maleness as violent differentiation from the female.

33. A great many critics, following Waith ("Manhood and Valor," pp. 266–67), find the play's embodiment of healthy masculinity in Macduff. They often register some uneasiness about his leaving his family, but they rarely allow this uneasiness to complicate their view of him as exemplary. But critics interested in the play's construction of masculinity in part as a defense against the fear of femaleness tend to see in Macduff's removal from family a replication of the central fear of women that is more fully played out in Macbeth. See, for example, Wheeler (*Shakespeare's Development*, p. 146), Berger ("Text Against Performance," p. 70), and Krohn ("Addressing the Oedipal Dilemma," p. 343). For these critics, Macduff's flight is of a piece with his status as the man not born of woman.

34. Critics interested in gender issues almost invariably comment on the centrality of Macduff's fulfillment of this prophecy, finding his strength here in his freedom from contamination by or regressive dependency on women:

see, for example, Harding ("Women's Fantasy," p. 250), Barron ("The Babe That Milks," p. 272), Fiedler (*Stranger*, p. 53), Myra Glazer Schotz ("The Great Unwritten Story: Mothers and Daughters in Shakespeare," in *The Lost Tradition: Mothers and Daughters in Literature*, ed. Cathy N. Davidson and E. M. Broner [New York: Frederick Ungar, 1980], p. 46), Berger ("The Early Scenes," p. 28), Bachmann ("Daggers," p. 101), Kirsch ("Macbeth's Suicide," p. 293), Kahn (*Man's Estate*, pp. 172–73), Wheeler (*Shakespeare's Development*, p. 146), and Victor Calef ("Lady Macbeth and Infanticide or 'How Many Children Had Lady Macbeth Murdered?' " *Journal of the American Psychoanalytic Association* 17 [1969]: 537). For Barron and Harding, Macduff's status as the bearer of this fantasy positively enhances his manhood; but for many of these critics, it qualifies his status as the exemplar of healthy manhood. Perhaps because ambivalence toward Macduff is built so deeply into the play, several very astute critics see the fantasy embedded in Macduff here and nonetheless continue to find in him an ideal manhood that includes the possibility of relatedness to the feminine. See, for example, Kahn (*Man's Estate*, p. 191) and Kirsch ("Macbeth's Suicide," p. 294).

35. The triumph of the natural order has of course been a commonplace of criticism since the classic essay by G. Wilson Knight ("The Milk of Concord: an Essay on Life-Themes in *Macbeth*," *The Imperial Theme* [London: Methuen, 1965], especially pp. 140–53). The topos is so powerful that it can cause even critics interested in gender issues to praise the triumph of nature and natural sexuality at the end without noting the exclusion of the female; see, for example, Greene ("Macbeth," p. 172). But Rosenberg, for example, notes the qualifying effect of this exclusion (*Masks of Macbeth*, p. 654).

36. See, for example, Goddard (*The Meaning of Shakespeare*, pp. 520–21); Jekels ("Riddle," p. 238); John Holloway (*The Story of the Night* [London: Routledge and Kegan Paul, 1961], p. 66); Rosenberg (*Masks of Macbeth*, p. 626); and Watson (*Shakespeare and the Hazards of Ambition*, pp. 89, 106–16). Even without sensing the covert presence of a vegetation myth, critics often associate the coming of Birnam Wood with the restoration of spring and fertility; see, for example, Knight ("Milk of Concord," pp. 144–45) and Greene ("Macbeth," p. 169). Only Bamber demurs: in her account Birnam Wood rises up in aid of a male alliance, not as the Saturnalian disorder of the Maying rituals (*Comic Women*, p. 106). My view coincides with hers.

37. When Malcolm refers to planting (5.9.31) at the play's end, for example, his comment serves partly to reinforce our sense of his distance from his father's generative power.

38. Paul attributes Shakespeare's use of the imagery of the family tree here to his familiarity with the cut of the Banquo tree in Leslie's *De Origine, Moribus, et Rebus Gestis Scotorum* (*Royal Play*, p. 175). But the image is too familiar to call for such explanations; see, for example, the tree described in *Richard II* (1.2.12–21).

39. As Wheeler notes, the description of Malcolm's saintly mother makes

him "symbolically the child of something approximating virgin birth" (*Shakespeare's Development*, p. 146)—in effect another version of the man not quite born of woman. Stallybrass calls attention to the structure of antithesis through which "(virtuous) families of men" are distinguished from "antifamilies of women" ("*Macbeth* and Witchcraft," p. 198). Berger comments on the aspiration to be "a nation of bachelor Adams, of no woman born and unknown to women" ("Text Against Performance," p. 72) without, however, noting the extent to which this fantasy is enacted in the play; for Krohn, the solution to the oedipal dilemma—"eliminate mothers"—is repeatedly portrayed by Shakespeare ("Addressing the Oedipal Dilemma," pp. 334–35). The fantasy of escape from maternal birth and the creation of all-male lineage would probably have been of interest to King James, whose problematic derivation from Mary, Queen of Scots, must occasionally have made him wish himself not born of (that particular) woman, no matter how much he was publicly concerned to rehabilitate her image. See Jonathan Goldberg's account of James's complex attitude toward Mary (*James I and the Politics of Literature* [Baltimore, Md.: The Johns Hopkins University Press, 1983], pp. 11–17, 25–26, and 119) and his later speculations on Mary and the fantasy of parthenogenesis in *Macbeth* ("Speculations: *Macbeth* and Source," in *Shakespeare Reproduced: The Text in History and Ideology*, ed. Jean E. Howard and Marion F. O'Connor [New York and London: Methuen, 1987], p. 259); the later essay came to my attention only after my own speculations on this subject were published. Stephen Orgel finds a similar configuration in *The Tempest*: James "conceived himself as the head of a single-parent family," as a paternal figure who has "incorporated the maternal," in effect as a Prospero; the alternative model is Caliban, who derives his authority from his mother ("Prospero's Wife," *Representations* 8 [1984]: 8–9). Perhaps *Macbeth* indirectly serves a cultural need to free James from entanglement with the problematic memory of his witch-mother (portrayed thus, for example, by Spenser in Book 5 of *The Faerie Queene*), tracing his lineage instead from a safely distanced and safely male forefather, Banquo.

40. Although neither Berger nor Stallybrass discuss the function of Birnam Wood specifically, I am indebted here to their discussions of the ideological function of the play's appeal to cosmology in the service of patriarchy, Berger seeing it as "a collective project of mystification" ("Text Against Performance," p. 64), Stallybrass as "a returning of the disputed ground of politics to the undisputed ground of Nature" ("*Macbeth* and Witchcraft," pp. 205–6). If, as Bradbrook suggests, witches were thought able to move trees ("Sources," p. 42), then we have in Malcolm's gesture a literal appropriation of female power, an act of making the unnatural natural by making it serve patriarchal needs.

41. See Erickson's fine discussion of this geographic distinction (*Patriarchal Structures*, pp. 121–22).

42. Coriolanus's father is in fact extraordinarily absent from the play; he is never mentioned. That Menenius repeatedly is identified as Coriolanus's father at the end of the play (5.1.3; 5.2.62, 69; 5.3.10) merely underscores this

absence. The father's role in the process of individuation and the consequent significance of Coriolanus's fatherlessness were first pointed out to me in 1976 by Dr. Malcolm Pines, when I read an early version of this essay to the Applied Section of the British Psychoanalytical Society.

43. See D. W. Winnicott on weaning: weaning goes well if "the baby really has had something to be weaned from" (*The Child, the Family, and the Outside World* [Harmondsworth: Penguin Books, 1964], p. 80).

44. From this point until p. 161, this chapter reproduces "Anger's My Meat: Feeding, Dependency, and Aggression in *Coriolanus*" (1980) unchanged, except for condensation of its opening paragraphs, some minor rearrangements of the notes, and deletion of its closing paragraphs. That essay was largely written in 1975–76, when I was just beginning to become interested in feminism and object-relations psychoanalysis; since it was the founding essay for this book, it seemed to me appropriate to leave it unchanged. (Where I have not been able to tolerate the difference that fourteen years has made in my reading of the play, I have registered my objections in square brackets in the notes.) Since 1980, the usefulness of these perspectives for *Coriolanus* has been amply demonstrated in work by Kahn (*Man's Estate*, pp. 151–72), Wheeler (*Shakespeare's Development and the Problem Comedies*, pp. 211–13), Richard P. Wheeler and C. L. Barber (*The Whole Journey: Shakespeare's Power of Development* [Berkeley: University of California Press, 1986], pp. 303–5), Madelon Sprengnether ("Annihilating Intimacy in *Coriolanus*," in *Women in the Middle Ages and the Renaissance*, ed. Mary Beth Rose [Syracuse, N.Y.: Syracuse University Press, 1986], pp. 89–111), and Page Dubois ("A Disturbance of Syntax at the Gates of Rome," *Stanford Literature Review* 2 [1985]: 185–208). (But see also Lisa Lowe's important corrective to all readings that isolate Volumnia as the cause of Coriolanus's impossible position [" 'Say I play the man I am': Gender and Politics in *Coriolanus*," *The Kenyon Review* 8 (1986): 86–95]. In her view, these readings—like object-relations psychoanalysis itself—scapegoat the mother, blaming her for the broader social structures that make it impossible to achieve unambiguous masculine identity; I would answer only that the play, as well as the critics, performs this scapegoating, though I agree with her that it is important to notice its effects.)

45. John Stow, *Annales* (London, 1631), p. 890. See Sidney Shanker, "Some Clues for *Coriolanus*," *Shakespeare Association Bulletin* 24 (1949): 209–13; E. C. Pettet, "*Coriolanus* and the Midlands Insurrection of 1607," *Shakespeare Survey* 3 (1950): 34–42; and Brents Stirling, *The Populace in Shakespeare* (New York: Columbia University Press, 1949), pp. 126–28, for discussions of this uprising and its political consequences in the play. See Edwin F. Gay, "The Midland Revolt and the Inquisitions of Depopulation of 1607," *Transactions of the Royal Historical Society*, N.S. 18 (1904): 195–244, for valuable contemporary commentary on the uprising and an analysis of it in comparison with earlier riots of the sixteenth century.

46. Menenius's words point to the rigid and ferocious maleness so prized

by Rome. Phyllis Rackin, in an unpublished paper entitled "*Coriolanus*: Shakespeare's Anatomy of *Virtus*" and delivered to the special session on feminist criticism of Shakespeare at the 1976 meeting of the Modern Language Association, discusses the denial of female values in the play as a consequence of the Roman overvaluation of valor as the chiefest virtue. Rackin's analysis of the ways in which the traditionally female images of food, harvesting, and love are turned to destructive purposes throughout the play is particularly revealing. [This essay has since been published in *Modern Language Studies* 13 (1983): 68–79.] The ideal Roman woman is in fact one who denies her womanhood, as we see not only in Volumnia but in Coriolanus's chilling and beautiful description of Valeria (5.3.65–67). (Indeed, Valeria seems to have little place in the intimate gathering of 5.3; she seems to exist there largely to give Coriolanus an excuse to speak these lines.) The extent to which womanhood is shrunken in Roman values is apparent in the relative unimportance of Coriolanus's wife Virgilia; in her, the female values of kindly nurturing have become little more than a penchant for staying at home, keeping silent, and weeping. (Given the extreme restrictions of Virgilia's role, one may begin to understand some of the pressures that force a woman to become a Volumnia and live through the creation of her exaggeratedly masculine son. In "Authoritarian Patterns in Shakespeare's *Coriolanus*," *Literature and Psychology* 9 [1959]: 49, Gordon Ross Smith comments perceptively that, in an authoritarian society, women will either be passive and subservient or will attempt to live out their thwarted ambition via their men.)

47. The association of nobility with abstinence from food—and of the ignoble lower classes with excessive appetite for food, in connection with their traditional role as the embodiment of appetite—was first demonstrated to me by Maurice Charney's impressive catalog of the food images in the play. See "The Imagery of Food and Eating in *Coriolanus*," in *Essays in Literary History*, ed. Rudolf Kirk and C. F. Main (New Brunswick, N.J.: Rutgers University Press, 1960), pp. 37–54.

48. In fact, Coriolanus frequently imagines his death with a kind of glee, as the badge of his noble self-sufficiency. See, for example, 3.2.1–5, 103–4; 5.6.111–12.

49. [Here and elsewhere in this essay, I would now foreground the extent to which vulnerability and oral neediness are figured as female throughout the play: for Coriolanus, to be a boy is to be a woman, and eating is the sign of this femaleness. The battlefield, where he proves himself specifically not a woman by becoming his sword, is thus the ground of his separation from his mother; it is where he proves that he has no more milk in him than a male tiger and hence that he has not been contaminated by her femaleness. But if he were to feed on praise or on the people's favor, he would become a woman again (an effeminate parasite, a harlot, a virgin minding babies).] The extent to which Coriolanus becomes identified with his phallus is suggested by the language in which both Menenius and Aufidius portray his death. For both, it represents a kind of castration: "He's a limb that has but a disease: / Mortal,

to cut it off; to cure it, easy" (3.1.293–94): "You'll rejoice / That he is thus cut off" (5.6.137–38). For discussions of Coriolanus's phallic identification and its consequences, see Robert J. Stoller, "Shakespearean Tragedy: *Coriolanus*," *Psychoanalytic Quarterly* 35 (1966): 263–74, and Emmett Wilson, Jr., "Coriolanus: The Anxious Bridegroom," *American Imago* 25 (1968): 224–41. In "An Interpretation of Shakespeare's *Coriolanus*," *American Imago* 14 (1957): 407–35, Charles K. Hofling sees Coriolanus as a virtual embodiment of Reich's phallic-narcissistic character. Each of these analysts finds Coriolanus's phallic stance to some extent a defense against passivity (Stoller, pp. 267, 269–70; Wilson, *passim*; Hofling, pp. 421, 424).

50. David B. Barron sees Coriolanus's oral frustration and his consequent rage as central to his character. See "*Coriolanus*: Portrait of the Artist As Infant," *American Imago* 19 (1962): 171–93. This essay anticipates mine in some of its conclusions and many of its details of interpretation.

51. Most critics find Coriolanus's abhorrence of praise a symptom of his pride and of his desire to consider himself as self-defined and self-sufficient, hence free from the definitions that society would confer on him. See, for example, A. C. Bradley, "Coriolanus," reprinted in *Studies in Shakespeare*, ed. Peter Alexander (London: Oxford University Press, 1964), p. 229; G. Wilson Knight, *The Imperial Theme* (London: Methuen, 1965), p. 169; Irving Ribner, *Patterns in Shakespearean Tragedy* (London; Methuen, 1960), p. 190; Norman Rabkin, *Shakespeare and the Common Understanding* (New York: Free Press, 1967), p. 131; and James L. Calderwood, "*Coriolanus*: Wordless Meanings and Meaningless Words," *Studies in English Literature, 1500–1900* 6 (1966): 218–19.

52. In his discussion of Coriolanus's cathartic vituperation, Kenneth Burke suggests that invective is rooted in the helpless rage of the infant. See "*Coriolanus*—and the Delights of Faction," *Hudson Review* 19 (1966): 200.

53. [Here again I would foreground gender. The "mankind" Coriolanus wishes to deny kinship with is specifically female; like Macbeth, Coriolanus wants to imagine himself not born of woman, hence self-authored.]

54. To see Corioli as the mother's womb here may seem grotesque; the idea becomes less grotesque if we remember Volumnia's own identification of country with mother's womb just as Coriolanus is about to attack another city (see discussion elsewhere in this chapter). Wilson ("Coriolanus: The Anxious Bridegroom," pp. 228–29) suggests that the attack on Corioli represents defloration—specifically, that it expresses the equation of coitus with damaging assault and the resultant dread of a retaliatory castration.

55. The force of this new name is partly corroborated by Volumnia, who delights in reminding her son of his dependence on her: she has trouble learning his new name from the start (2.1.173) and eventually associates it with the pride that keeps him from pity for his family (5.3.170–71). But several critics have argued convincingly that the self-sufficiency implicit in Coriolanus's ac-

quisition of his new name is ironically undercut from the beginning by the fact that naming of any kind is a social act, so that Coriolanus's acceptance of the name conferred on him by Cominius reveals his dependence on external definition just at the moment that he seems most independent. See, for example, Rabkin, *Shakespeare and the Common Understanding*, pp. 130–32; Lawrence Danson, *Tragic Alphabet: Shakespeare's Drama of Language* (New Haven, Conn.: Yale University Press, 1974), pp. 150–51; and Calderwood, "*Coriolanus*," pp. 219–23. [What Coriolanus wants, I think, is a name conferred on him specifically by men, and through masculine action: a name dissociated from his mother.]

56. Volumnia's place in the creation of her son's role, and the catastrophic results of her disavowal of it here, have been nearly universally recognized. For a particularly perceptive discussion of the consequences for Coriolanus of his mother's shift in attitude, see Derek Traversi, *Shakespeare: The Roman Plays* (Stanford, Calif.: Stanford University Press, 1963), pp. 247–54. In an interesting essay, D. W. Harding suggests Shakespeare's preoccupation during this period with the disastrous effects on men of their living out of women's fantasies of manhood. See "Women's Fantasy of Manhood," *Shakespeare Quarterly* 20 (1969): 252–53. Psychoanalytically oriented critics see Coriolanus as the embodiment of his mother's masculine strivings, or, more specifically, as her longed-for penis. See, for example, Ralph Berry, "Sexual Imagery in *Coriolanus*," *Studies in English Literature* 13 (1973): 302; Hofling, "An Interpretation," pp. 415–16; Stoller, "Shakespearean Tragedy," pp. 266–67, 271; and Wilson, "Coriolanus," p. 239. Several critics have noticed the importance of acting and the theatrical metaphor in the play. See, for example, William Rosen, *Shakespeare and the Craft of Tragedy* (Cambridge, Mass.: Harvard University Press, 1960), pp. 171–73, and Kenneth Muir, *Shakespeare's Tragic Sequence* (London: Hutchinson, 1972), pp. 184–85. Harold C. Goddard in *The Meaning of Shakespeare* (Chicago: University of Chicago Press, 1951), pp. 216–17, discusses acting specifically in relation to the role that Volumnia has cast for her son. Berry points to the acting metaphors as a measure of Coriolanus's inner uncertainty and his fear of losing his manhood if he shifts roles (pp. 303–6).

57. Goddard (*The Meaning of Shakespeare*, p. 238), Hofling ("An Interpretation," p. 420), and Smith ("Authoritarian Patterns," p. 46), among others, discuss Coriolanus's characterization of the crowd as a projection of elements in himself that he wishes to deny, though they do not agree on the precise nature of these elements. Barron associates Coriolanus's hatred specifically of the people's undisciplined hunger with his need to subdue his own impulses; here, as elsewhere, his argument is very close to my own ("Coriolanus," pp. 174, 180). The uprising of the crowd is in fact presented in terms that suggest the same transformation of hunger into phallic aggression that is central to the character of Coriolanus himself. In Menenius's belly fable, the people are "th'discontented members, the mutinous parts," and "the mutinous members" (1.1.110, 148); an audience for whom the mutiny of the specifically sexual member was traditionally one of the signs of the Fall would be prone to hear

in Menenius's characterization a reference to a part other than the great toe (1.1.154). When the first citizen tells Menenius, "They say poor suitors have strong breaths: they shall know we have strong arms too" (1.1.58–60), his image of importunate mouths suddenly armed in rebellion suggests the source of Coriolanus's rebellion no less than his own.

58. And so does Shakespeare. In Plutarch, Coriolanus is accompanied by a few men both when he enters the gates of Corioli and when he is exiled from Rome. Shakespeare emphasizes his isolation by giving him no companions on either occasion. Eugene Waith (*The Herculean Hero* [New York: Columbia University Press, 1962], p. 124) and Danson (*Tragic Alphabet*, p. 146) emphasize Coriolanus's position as a whole man among fragments.

59. Coriolanus himself is generationally ambiguous: though the populace considers him prime among the fathers who forbid access to food, we see him very much as a son, and he himself seems to regard the patricians as his fathers. His position midway between father and sons suggests the position of an older sibling who has made a protective alliance with the fathers and now fears the unruliness of his younger brothers: instead of fighting to take possession of the undernourishing mother, he will deny that he has any need for food. The likeness of the plebeians to younger siblings was first suggested to me by David Sundelson in conversation.

60. In his suggestive essay on the people's voices in *Coriolanus*, Leonard Tennenhouse notes that "Coriolanus, the child denied love in the service of patrician ideals, is perceived by the mob as the one who denies. The mysterious source of the cannibalistic rage directed against him is the recognition by the plebeians that he would withhold from them what the patrician mother would withhold from her son—nurturance and thus life itself" ("*Coriolanus*: History and the Crisis of Semantic Order," *Comparative Drama* 10 [1976]: 335). I saw this essay only after the 1978 version of my essay was already published; it and the comments of Zan Marquis in an undergraduate class resulted in my exploration of cannibalism in this paragraph and the next in the 1980 version.

61. See, for example, 1.3.40–43 and 2.3.5–8. Exposed, Coriolanus's wounds would become begging mouths, as Julius Caesar's do (*Julius Caesar*, 3.2.225–26). [In the 1978 version of this essay, I associated the wounds with castration and hence effeminization—an association that I rejected in the 1980 version. I now think that rejection was premature: displayed wounds and mouths both seem to me to function as the sign of the female in this play. In constructing the plebeians as all mouth, Coriolanus constructs them as feminized; in displaying his wounds/mouths, he would display himself as similarly feminized.]

62. The Third Citizen's image points also toward the possibility that Coriolanus would be inviting homosexual rape by standing naked before the crowd. Dr. Anne Hayman—to whom I am indebted for her many helpful comments on an early version of this essay—has suggested to me in conversation that Coriolanus's fear of his unconscious homosexual desires, especially of a passive

feminine kind, is central to his character; she sees his fear of the wish for passive femininity as part of his identification with his mother, who shares the same fear. Her interpretation is to some extent borne out by Coriolanus's relationship with Aufidius, which is presented in decidedly homosexual terms (see, for example, 4.4.12–16, 22; 4.5.110–19, 123–24); but ultimately—as I argue later in this chapter—that relationship seems to me more an expression of Coriolanus's need for a mirror image of himself than an expression of his homosexual desires.

63. That Coriolanus's identity is at issue in the turning toward Aufidius is made uncomfortably clear by the scene in which he comes to Antium. Despite the servingmen's comic and belated assertions that they had nearly pierced Coriolanus's disguise (4.5.150–64), they clearly had no inkling of his stature before he revealed himself. Furthermore, Coriolanus's gradual unmasking before Aufidius suggests that he wants to be known as himself before he names himself (4.5.55–66). The scene is in part a test of the power of Coriolanus's identity to make itself known without external definition; the results are at best ambiguous.

64. [Coriolanus in effect asks the male bond with Aufidius to do the work that should be done by the missing father: to reflect him back to himself whole, and male, and hence enable the process of separation from the mother. His creation of Aufidius as mirroring twin simultaneously protects him from and substitutes for merger with his mother, permitting a safer form of nurturance than any she would allow. I discuss this use of the male bond further in "Male Bonding in Shakespeare's Comedies," in *Shakespeare's Rough Magic: Renaissance Essays in Honor of C. L. Barber*, ed. Peter Erickson and Coppélia Kahn (Newark, N.J.: University of Delaware Press, 1985), esp. pp. 94–95.]

65. Donald A. Stauffer, in *Shakespeare's World of Images* (New York: W. W. Norton, 1949), p. 252, points out that Rome is less *patria* than *matria* in this play; he discusses Volumnia as a projection of Rome, particularly in 5.3. Virtually all psychoanalytic critics comment on the identification of Volumnia with Rome; Barron comments specifically that Coriolanus turns the rage of his frustration in nursing toward his own country at the end of the play ("Coriolanus," p. 175).

66. [See Stanley Cavell's powerful meditation on love, cannibalism, failed sacrifice, and theater in *Coriolanus* (*Disowning Knowledge* [Cambridge: Cambridge University Press, 1987], pp. 143–77).]

67. It is a mark of the extent to which external dangers are for Coriolanus merely a reflection of internal ones that he feels himself in no danger until the collapse of his defensive system. Unlike Coriolanus, we know that he is in danger before its collapse; Aufidius plans to kill him no matter what he does (4.7.24–26, 56–57).

68. Participants in the Midlands uprising were commonly called "levelers," in startling anticipation of the 1640s (see, for example, Stow [*Annales*, p. 890]

and Gay ["The Midland Revolt," p. 213, n. 2; p. 214, n. 1; p. 216, n. 3; and p. 242]); Shakespeare presents his uprising in relentlessly vertical terms and plays on fears of leveling when Cominius warns, "That is the way to lay the city flat, / To bring the roof to the foundation, / And bury all which yet distinctly ranges / In heaps and piles of ruin" (3.1.202–5).

69. Rufus Putney, in "Coriolanus and His Mother," *Psychoanalytic Quarterly* 21 (1962): 368–69, 372, finds Coriolanus's inability to deal with his matricidal impulses central to his character; whenever Volumnia threatens him with her death, he capitulates at once.

70. If the boundary between inner and outer is dangerous for Hamlet (see pp. 28–30, above), it is virtually nonexistent for Macbeth. I borrow the word "phantasmagoric" from David Willbern in order to register my debt to his rich exploration of these issues (see "Phantasmagoric *Macbeth*," esp. pp. 532–35; and see also Holland, *Shakespeare and Psychoanalysis*, p. 328); but Willbern's imagined audience is less claustrophobically engaged with Macbeth than mine is (pp. 535–40, 549). Although Macbeth's response to maternal threat is crucially inflected by his gender, I do not distinguish between male and female in imagining an audience trapped inside his head: much of the primary fantasy material of the play seems to me to derive from infantile vulnerabilities prior to fixed gender organization. The ungendered nature of this material may in fact make the ending of the play particularly bleak for women, who are positioned inside Macbeth's fantasy for much of the play but then are written out of its resolution. (For a very powerful account of gendered reading and cross-gender identification in *Macbeth*, see Madelon Sprengnether's "Reading as Lady Macbeth," in *Women's Re-Visions of Shakespeare*, ed. Marianne Novy [Urbana: University of Illinois Press, 1990], pp. 227–41. The central perceptions of this essay have influenced my thinking since 1981, when I saw it in an earlier version; its insistence on gendered reading was anticipated by Sprengnether's own " 'And when I love thee not': Women and the Psychic Integrity of the Tragic Hero," published under the name of Gohlke in *The Hebrew University Studies in Literature* 8 [1980]; see especially pp. 57–65.)

71. G. Wilson Knight discusses the hard metallic quality of the language at length; he associates it with the self-containment of the hostile walled cities and distinguishes it from the fusions characteristic of *Antony and Cleopatra* (*The Imperial Theme*, p. 156). In a particularly interesting discussion, Danson associates the rigidity and distinctness of the language with the play's characteristic use of metonymy and synecdoche, which serve to limit and define, in place of metaphor, which serves to fuse diverse worlds (*Tragic Alphabet*, pp. 155–59).

72. See the essays collected in *Playing and Reality* (London: Tavistock Publications, 1971), especially "Transitional Objects and Transitional Phenomena," pp. 1–25; and for fuller discussion of Winnicott, see Chapter 2, n. 40, and Chapter 8, nn. 83, 84, and 90. My understanding of Winnicott and of Shakespeare has been deeply influenced by Schwartz, whose wonderfully

rich reading of Shakespeare through Winnicott ("Shakespeare through Contemporary Psychoanalysis") traces the loss and recovery of play space in
his tragedies and romances; the fullest Winnicottian reading of *Macbeth* is
Willbern's brilliant account of the play's violations of this space ("Phantasmagoric *Macbeth*").

NOTES TO CHAPTER 7

1. Most recent psychoanalytic readings of the play have depicted Timon's
excessive generosity as a defensive attempt to identify with the all-providing
mother: see, for example, Stephen A. Reid's Kleinian account of the play (" 'I
am Misanthropos'—A Psychoanalytic Reading of Shakespeare's 'Timon of
Athens,' " *Psychoanalytic Review* 56 [1969]: esp. 446); Minerva Neiditz's
analysis of Timon's and Alcibiades's divergent responses to "the loss of a life-
sustaining object" ("Primary Process Mentation and the Structure of *Timon
of Athens*," *University of Hartford Studies in Literature* 11 [1979]: esp. 28,
32); Susan Handelman's exploration of Timon's—and *Timon*'s—refusal of
consolatory substitutes for the lost object ("*Timon of Athens*: The Rage of
Disillusion," *American Imago* 36 [1979]: esp. 53, 61); and Coppélia Kahn's
account of Timon's fantasy of maternal bounty as it intersects with Jacobean
patronage practices and contractual social organization (" 'Magic of Bounty':
Timon of Athens, Jacobean Patronage, and Maternal Bounty," *Shakespeare
Quarterly* 38 [1987]: 35–40); see also the briefer accounts of C. L. Barber
("The Family in Shakespeare's Development," in *Representing Shakespeare*,
ed. Coppélia Kahn and Murray M. Schwartz [Baltimore, Md.: Johns Hopkins
University Press, 1980], p. 191) and Richard Wheeler (*Shakespeare's Development and the Problem Comedies* [Berkeley: University of California Press,
1981], pp. 17–8, 216), both extended in Barber and Wheeler's *The Whole
Journey: Shakespeare's Power of Development* [Berkeley: University of California Press, 1986], pp. 305–9). Avi Erlich notes that Timon's final masochistic
identification is not with the nurturing mother but with the cruel withholding
mother ("Neither to Give nor to Receive: Narcissism in *Timon of Athens*,"
CUNY English Forum, vol. 1 [New York: AMS Press, 1985], pp. 229). (As
always, I am particularly indebted to Kahn, Barber, and Wheeler.)

2. See Kahn's discussion of the relevance to *Timon* of James's deployment
of this role (" 'Magic of Bounty,' " pp. 41–47).

3. The scene with the usurer (2.1) comes as a shock partly because it so
thoroughly countermands this fantasy; like the reference to Timon's land
(2.2.149–55), it comes only after the fantasy has collapsed.

4. H. J. Oliver thinks that the prologue to the masque is "not the kind of
address a man would compose to himself" and consequently understands
"device" as a reference to the feast, not the masque (Arden *Timon*, p. 29). But
all Timon's giving seems to me to turn on such self-congratulation; and the

usual Shakespearean use of "device" for something ingeniously made or planned makes the term more appropriate to the masque than to the feast.

5. The identification of the poet's Fortune with the unreliable mother is familiar to psychoanalytic criticism; see especially Handelman's and Kahn's descriptions of the ways in which Timon is represented as infantilized in comparison with Fortune's massive body (*"Timon of Athens,"* pp. 56–57; " 'Magic of Bounty,' " pp. 36–37).

6. *Quick, blow,* and *pregnantly* all carry secondary associations of sexual intercourse or pregnancy; see Eric Partridge's entries under each (*Shakespeare's Bawdy* [New York: E. P. Dutton, 1960]).

7. Neiditz notes Timon's resemblance to Lear's all-or-nothing and its basis in early object relations ("Either one is the bountiful breast which cannot be depleted or one is the empty, powerless babe," "Primary Process Mentation," p. 32); Erlich posits this alternation as characteristic of the narcissist ("Neither to Give," p. 218). Among the many who invoke comparison with *Lear,* I find Handelman's formulation the most suggestive; in her view, the play asks, "How do we go on living *after* Cordelia is dead?" (*"Timon of Athens,"* p. 47).

8. Several critics note the turn toward vituperation of women, surprising especially given the absence of women characters; among these, my formulations are closest to those of Handelman (*"Timon of Athens,"* p. 61), Wheeler (*Shakespeare's Development,* pp. 17–18), and Kahn (" 'Magic of Bounty,' " pp. 51–52). Although none of these critics notes specifically the imagery of the torn male body, both Handelman (p. 49, 56) and Kahn (p. 37) write powerfully of the mechanisms of projection and scapegoating through which male insufficiency and vulnerability are attributed to the mother. Erlich vacillates, sometimes making the horrific mother the first cause, sometimes understanding her as the infant's own creation ("Neither to Give," pp. 223, 226).

9. The unusually elaborate stage direction makes it plain that the men dance with the women to show their love to Timon. That the ladies so elaborately controlled are dressed as Amazons—often the representatives of a dangerous female autonomy outside the control of men—focuses the degree to which masculine control of the female is at issue here. See Robert C. Fulton, III ("Timon, Cupid, and the Amazons," *Shakespeare Studies* 9 [1976]: 287–92), Handelman (*"Timon of Athens,"* p. 62), and Erlich ("Neither to Give," p. 222) for discussion of these specific Amazons; and see Louis Montrose's far-reaching discussion of the Amazon in "*A Midsummer Night's Dream* and the Shaping Fantasies of Elizabethan Culture: Gender, Power, Form" (*Rewriting the Renaissance: The Discourses of Sexual Difference in Early Modern Europe,* ed. Margaret W. Ferguson, Maureen Quilligan, and Nancy J. Vickers [Chicago: University of Chicago Press, 1986], pp. 70–82).

10. The connection between the gold and the whore is noted by Reid (" 'I am Misanthropos,' " p. 449), Barber and Wheeler (*The Whole Journey,* pp. 307–8), and Kahn (" 'Magic of Bounty,' " p. 52).

11. The pun is so nearly irresistible that Oliver finds it necessary to note that the Folio distinguishes between *hoar* and *whore* in order to "forestall emendation" to *whore* (Arden *Timon*, p. 91). But whatever the practices of the Folio, a theater audience would be hard-pressed to hear the difference.

12. This is, in effect, the logic Marx derives from the play; see Kenneth Muir's extensive citation and discussion in " 'Timon of Athens' and the Cash Nexus," *Modern Quarterly Miscellany* 1 (1947): 73.

13. Timon would achieve through venereal disease the destruction Lear imagines cosmologically: if Timon would quell the source of all erection, Lear would drench the steeples and drown the cocks (*Lear*, 3.2.3); if Lear cries out "strike flat the thick rotundity o' th' world! Crack Nature's moulds" (3.2.7–8), Timon cries out "strike their sharp shins," "Crack the lawyer's voice," "Down with the nose, / Down with it flat." The startling recurrence of key terms—*strike, flat, crack*—suggests both the extent to which Timon's imagination is apocalyptic here and the extent to which a submerged fantasy of diseased sexual intercourse underwrites Lear's image of cosmological destruction. (See also the less precise echoings in down/drown and shrill/spill.)

14. This formulation is indebted to Erlich ("Neither to Give," p. 224). Several critics stress the dreamlike or hallucinatory quality of the play; see, for example, Erlich (p. 216) and Neiditz ("Primary Process Mentation," pp. 24–25).

15. The syntax leaves open the possibility that the sons are hated by the common mother earth ("thou, who") as well as Timon ("him, who").

16. See Kahn's description of the play's "core fantasy": "A male self is precipitated out of a profound and empowering oneness with the mother into a treacherous group of men in which he is powerless" (" 'Magic of Bounty,' " p. 35); I would add that the treachery of the men is figured as a function of the mother's ultimate unreliability, her indiscriminate breeding.

17. In preparing his grave "where the light foam of the sea may beat / [His] grave-stone daily" (4.3.381–82), Timon may be attempting to return to the ambivalent embrace of this mother; see Kahn (" 'Magic of Bounty,' " p. 54) and Erlich ("Neither to Give," p. 229) for discussion of this possibility.

18. Following L. C. Knights's early perception that Timon looks within "and, finding himself hateful, what he finds within he projects onto the world at large" (*An Approach to "Hamlet"* [Stanford, Calif.: Stanford University Press, 1961], p. 28), several critics understand the landscape as a projection of Timon's inner world, without, however, discussing Shakespeare's complicity in providing him this landscape; see especially Handelman (*"Timon of Athens,"* p. 63) and Kahn (" 'Magic of Bounty,' " p. 51). For Erlich, however, the correspondence between the landscape and Timon's inner world suggests Shakespeare's conscious desire to have "the form of his play . . . reflect the

nature of the psychology he is exploring" rather than his investment in Timon ("Neither to Give," p. 219).

19. This conversation between the plays does not depend on the order in which they were written; whatever the order of composition, Shakespeare seems to have associated the two stories. He would have found in Plutarch's "Life of Marcus Antonius" a reference to Antony's living apart on the sea's edge on the model of Timon, similarly disappointed in his friends (see Geoffrey Bullough, *Narrative and Dramatic Sources of Shakespeare*, vol. 5 [London: Routledge and Kegan Paul, 1964], p. 304); and in the absence of much detailed information about Timon, he grafted Plutarch's descriptions of Antony's extravagance (see Bullough, p. 235–36) onto the figure of Timon. This, and the expansion of the story of Alcibiades in *Coriolanus*, may suggest that *Timon* was written late, after *Antony*, or at any rate after Shakespeare had started thinking about Antony. On the other hand, *Timon*'s strong resemblance to *Lear* makes an earlier date equally plausible. In the absence of firm evidence, I suspect that *Timon* was written before *Antony*: since Plutarch emphasizes Antony's purely self-destructive generosity, I suspect that Shakespeare would have explored this trait in his Antony if he had not already done so in *Timon*. Though my language will often reflect this suspicion, I am in fact more interested in what sorts of things go together—distrust of the female with male scarcity and a niggardly dramatic form, acceptance of the female with male bounty and a generous dramatic form—than with the chronological relation between the plays. Though the common source is generally acknowledged, the two plays are not often discussed together; but see Handelman's brief but suggestive comments setting *Timon*'s "identity as sameness" against *Antony*'s metamorphic "identity-in-difference" (*"Timon of Athens,"* pp. 56, 67).

20. The claim that we are poised between belief and skepticism is central to my earlier work on the play (*The Common Liar: An Essay on "Antony and Cleopatra"* [New Haven, Conn.: Yale University Press, 1973], esp. pp. 11–12, 102–68). Most critics want to assert that Cleopatra's vision is at least partially true, usually on the grounds that the immense bounty she imagines is in fact congruent with the magnanimous Antony we have seen: of the many, see, for example, Eugene M. Waith, *The Herculean Hero in Marlowe, Chapman, Shakespeare and Dryden* (New York: Columbia University Press, 1962), pp. 114–15; Barbara L. Estrin, " 'Behind a Dream': Cleopatra and Sonnet 129," *Women's Studies* 9 (1982): 183–85; Bernard Beckerman, "Past the Size of Dreaming," in *Twentieth Century Interpretations of "Antony and Cleopatra"*, ed. Mark Rose (Englewood Cliffs, N.J.: Prentice-Hall, Inc., 1977), p. 111; and Anne Barton, " 'Nature's Piece 'Gainst Fancy': The Divided Catastrophe in *Antony and Cleopatra*," and Rosalie L. Colie, "The Significance of Style," both reprinted in *Modern Critical Interpretations: William Shakespeare's Antony and Cleopatra*, ed. Harold Bloom (New York: Chelsea House Publishers, 1988), pp. 54, 71–72. But this view is strenuously contested, for example, by Richard L. Nochimson ("The End Crowns All: Shakespeare's Deflation of Tragic Possibility in *Antony and Cleopatra*," *English* 26 [1977]:

120–21), J. Leeds Barroll (*Shakespearean Tragedy: Genre, Tradition and Change in "Antony and Cleopatra"* [Washington, D.C.: Folger Books, 1984], pp. 140–41, 172–73), and John Alvis ("The Religion of Eros: A Re-Interpretation of *Antony and Cleopatra*," *Renascence* 30 [1978]: 185–98).

21. The play's imaginative generosity and spaciousness are reflected in the boldness and fluidity of its style and in the enormous scale of its dramatic design, both frequently noted by critics in a language that replicates Antony's own overflowing of limits; see, for example, J. I. M. Stewart (*Character and Motive in Shakespeare* [New York: Barnes and Noble, 1949], p. 66) and Beckerman ("Past the Size of Dreaming," p. 99).

22. As his title ("Identification with the Maternal in *Antony and Cleopatra*") indicates, Peter Erickson has explored this relationship thoroughly (*Patriarchal Structures in Shakespeare's Drama* [Berkeley: University of California Press, 1985], pp. 123–47). "Bounty" is the key term in his argument, as in mine; he emphasizes Antony's finding "the maternal in the self" (p. 135) as the basis for his bounty, thus enabling Shakespeare's "experiment in alternative masculinity" (p. 133). My own emphasis is less on Antony's characteristic generosity than on Shakespeare's realignment of masculinity and the maternal, his choice of the heterosexual and maternal plot—rather than the male bonding plot—as the final resting place for Antony's heroic image. Despite this difference in emphasis, my work on the play is indebted to Erickson's in numerous particulars.

23. The woman with a snake at her breast was a traditional symbol for Terra; see Adelman, *Common Liar*, pp. 64, 205. Because Plutarch and Daniel have the asp at Cleopatra's arm and Garnier does not mention its location, I assumed in *The Common Liar* that this position was a Shakespearean innovation. But I have since found two earlier references to the asp at Cleopatra's breast, both of which were probably known by Shakespeare: Thomas Nashe's 1593 *Christs Teares ouer Ierusalem* (*The Works of Thomas Nashe*, vol. 2, ed. Ronald B. McKerrow [Oxford: Basil Blackwell, 1958], p. 140); and the 1601 volume in which "The Phoenix and the Turtle" first appeared, Robert Chester's *Loves Martyr* (ed. Alexander B. Grosart for the New Shakespeare Society [London: N. Trubner & Co., 1878], p. 114/122). Nashe's reference furthermore implies that this position was a commonplace: he warns female pride that "At thy breasts (as at *Cleopatras*), Aspisses shall be put out to nurse" after death. Dolabella's scrupulosity locates the asp's vent on her arm as well as her breast (5.2.346–48), thus enabling Shakespeare to maintain both traditions.

24. The scenes may have a common source in Plutarch: "It was a wonderfull example to the souldiers, to see Antonius that was brought up in all finenes and superfluitie, so easily to drink puddle water, and to eate wilde frutes and rootes: and moreover it is reported, that even as they passed the Alpes, they did eat the barcks of trees, and such beasts, as never men tasted of their flesh before" (Bullough, *Narrative and Dramatic Sources*, vol. 5, pp. 267–68). Antony does not eat roots, but Timon does. Moreover, Plutarch's contrast

between Antony's upbringing and his endurance of hardship is echoed by *Timon*, 4.3.252–69.

25.   It is by now a truism to say that a new kind of masculinity is represented in Antony; Eugene M. Waith's "Manhood and Valor in Two Shakespearean Tragedies" (*ELH* 17 [1950]: 268–73), Robert Ornstein's "The Ethic of the Imagination: Love and Art in 'Antony and Cleopatra' " (*Later Shakespeare*, Stratford-upon-Avon Studies 8 [London: Edward Arnold, 1966], pp. 36–37), and R. J. Dorius's little-known "Shakespeare's Dramatic Modes and *Antony and Cleopatra*" (*Literatur als Kritik des Lebens* [Heidelberg: Quelle & Meyer, 1975], pp. 91–93) seem to me the best early statements of the theme. One name for this new masculinity is "androgyny," as Dorius hints; see, for example, Raymond B. Waddington ("Antony and Cleopatra: 'What Venus did with Mars,' " *Shakespeare Studies* 2 [1963]: 223), Barton (" 'Nature's Piece 'Gainst Fancy,' " pp. 39–40), James J. Greene ("*Antony and Cleopatra*: The Birth and Death of Androgyny," *University of Hartford Studies in Literature* 19 [1987]: 25–44), and especially Erickson (*Patriarchal Structures*, pp. 131–34). But see Carol Thomas Neely's powerful argument that the lovers enlarge, but do not exchange or transcend, gender roles (*Broken Nuptials in Shakespeare's Plays* [New Haven, Conn.: Yale University Press, 1985], pp. 137–39, 150). Both sides in this debate seem to me right: insofar as Shakespeare grounds this new masculinity in acceptance of and relation to the female, he allows it to take on some of the qualities characteristically called female and hence to become, relatively speaking, "androgynous"; but insofar as Shakespeare claims that Antony is no less "manly" for this redefinition, he shores up (by enlarging) the category of manliness.

26.   In his rich account of the interplay of actor and character, William E. Gruber stresses the extent to which the audience participates in this desire, identifying with Cleopatra as she waits for Antony to appear on stage ("The Actor in the Script: Affective Strategies in Shakespeare's *Antony and Cleopatra*," *Comparative Drama* 19 [1985]: 31–36).

27.   Caesar enters the play ambiguously announcing (by denying) his hatred of Antony; but his longing for Antony—reflected both in his obsessive focus on Antony and in the accents of betrayal that often accompany his criticism—seems to me the deepest unacknowledged current of feeling in the play. This longing is implicitly eroticized as he gives his sister—"a great part of myself"—to Antony in marriage, with the ambiguous injunction that he "use me well in't" (3.2.24–25). When he imagines the reception Octavia should have had as Antony's wife and his own sister—"The trees by the way / Should have borne men, and expectation fainted / Longing for what it had not" (3.6.46–48)—the intense phallic giddiness of his language (so like Troilus's fainting expectation at 3.2.16–25) seems to me directed as much toward the Antony whom he reaches through Octavia as toward Octavia herself.

28.   In Cleopatra's account, her lover is "great Pompey" (1.5.31); in Antony's, he is (historically) Pompey the Great's son, Gnaeus Pompey (3.13.118).

Ridley notes that Cleopatra's "epithet is misleading" (Arden *Antony and Cleopatra*, p. 42); but it seems to me nearly irresistible for an audience accustomed to associating Cleopatra with legendary masculine presences. Her other grand lover, Julius Caesar, is Octavius Caesar's father only by adoption; but Octavius Caesar refers to him as "father" in his one oblique reference to him here (3.6.6), although he never does so in *Julius Caesar*.

29. Pompey in fact makes his own phallic potency depend on his capacity to wrest Antony away from this woman: if Antony returns to Rome, Pompey will "rear / The higher our opinion, that our stirring / Can from the lap of Egypt's widow pluck / The ne'er-lust-wearied Antony" (2.1.35–38). Like Pompey's, Caesar's contest with Cleopatra for possession of Antony has overtones of the negative oedipal complex, in which the father—rather than the mother—is both the object of desire and the measure of masculine success.

30. In fact, the ambiguity introduced by "since then" nearly succeeds in fusing Julius Caesar and Antony in their illicit paternity: the phrase simultaneously assigns Caesarion's paternity to Antony, not Julius Caesar (he is the first of the unlawful issue Antony and Cleopatra have since then made between them) and assigns paternity of all the other unlawful issue (since Caesarion) to Julius Caesar.

31. Bullough, *Narrative and Dramatic Sources*, vol. 5, pp. 267–68.

32. Looking and dying: their conjunction is the emotional terrain of both Diana/Acteon and the Gorgon—on the one hand, the desire to see that is punished by death; on the other, the woman so dangerous that the very sight of her kills. Part of the intense pleasure of spectacle in this play depends on Cleopatra's final satisfaction of this dangerous desire: when Cleopatra stages herself to our view in the last scene, she feeds our visual desire, allowing us to witness the scene at Cydnus from which we have been excluded; and, at the same time, she makes our desire to see safe, undoing the Acteon/Gorgon paradigms.

33. See Adelman, *Common Liar*, pp. 137–39, for a more extended discussion of Antony's position between the generations of father and son.

34. See *Julius Caesar*, 1.3.3–4, 20, 75; many members of Shakespeare's audience would probably have noted the allusion.

35. In the course of discussing the play's demonstration that *virtus* is an ideological effect of power, Jonathan Dollimore notes this typically mystifying appeal to necessity, as well as Caesar's eagerness to stress Antony's inferiority (*Radical Tragedy: Religion, Ideology and Power in the Drama of Shakespeare and His Contemporaries* [Chicago: University of Chicago Press, 1984], p. 212).

36. Pompey models this dangerous inheritance in miniature. The quarrel he inherits from his father first seems to make a man of him (the people "throw / Pompey the Great, and all his dignities / Upon his son, who high in name and power, / Higher than both in blood and life, stands up / For the main soldier"

[1.2.185–89]); but it finally leads to his destruction when he proves too small for his father's role (2.6.82–83).

37. "Of Isis and Osiris" was published in London in 1603, in Philemon Holland's translation of the *Moralia*; critics frequently assume that Shakespeare consulted it while working on *Antony and Cleopatra*, often without making explicit the basis for this assumption (see, for example, Harold Fisch, " 'Antony and Cleopatra': The Limits of Mythology," *Shakespeare Survey* 23 [1970]: 61; Frank Kermode, *The Riverside Shakespeare*, ed. G. Blakemore Evans [Boston: Houghton Mifflin Company, 1974], p. 1345; and Walter R. Coppedge, "The Joy of the Worm: Dying in *Antony and Cleopatra*," *Renaissance Papers* [1988]: 41–50). The fullest accounts of Shakespeare's possible indebtednesss to Plutarch's essay are those of Michael Lloyd ("Cleopatra as Isis," *Shakespeare Survey* 12 [1959]: 91–94) and Barbara Bono (*Literary Transvaluation: From Vergilian Epic to Shakespearean Tragicomedy* [Berkeley: University of California Press, 1984], pp. 199–213), both of which seem to me more suggestive than conclusive. My own sense of Shakespeare's indebtedness to this essay turns specifically on Shakespeare's use of "habiliments" to describe Cleopatra's clothing when she is dressed as Isis (3.6.17). The word is unusual in Shakespeare, occurring only five times in its various forms. In the comparable passage in the *Life*, North's Plutarch uses "apparell": "Now for Cleopatra, she did not onely weare at that time (but at all other times els when she came abroad) the apparell of the goddess Isis, and so gave audience unto all her subjects" (Bullough, *Narrative and Dramatic Sources*, vol. 5, p. 291). But in "Of Isis and Osiris," Holland's Plutarch uses "habilliments" specifically to refer to the clothing of Isis: "the habilliments of Isis, be of different tinctures and colours" (*The Philosophie, commonlie called The Morals*, trans. Philemon Holland [London, 1603], p. 1318). Since Shakespeare otherwise follows the passage in the *Life* quite closely, his use of "habiliments" seems to me strong evidence that he consulted "Of Isis and Osiris" while writing *Antony and Cleopatra*.

38. *Antony and Cleopatra* is a notoriously "open" text; I have written elsewhere of the degree to which the play sets contrary interpretative possibilities side by side (*The Common Liar*, esp. pp. 14–52, 99–171). "Of Isis and Osiris" is similarly full of contradictory interpretations of its central story. Bono argues that these contradictions are resolved into a syncretistic neo-platonic oneness (*Literary Transvaluation*, p. 203); but whether or not the contradictions are thus philosophically resolved, the sheer number of diverse interpreters in "Of Isis and Osiris," as in the play, foregrounds the process of interpretation itself. Even in the course of constructing his neo-platonic reading, Plutarch points toward the degree to which interpretation is both arbitrary and self-serving: "Of such fables as these we must make use, not as of reasons altogether really subsisting: but so, as we take out of ech of them, that which is meet and convenient to our purposes" ("Of Isis and Osiris," p. 1310). Fables may be veils for philosophy (p. 1291), but in Plutarch's account, we half-create what we think we see under the veil.

39.   Curiously indeterminate in Plutarch's text, Osiris shifts his meaning according to the company he keeps: construed, for example, as the generative moon in relation to Typhon as destructively hot sun (p. 1304), he becomes the sun "as the visible matter of a spirituall and intellectuall substance" in relation to Isis's female moon (p. 1308); construed as the principle of generative moisture in relation to Typhon's destructive heat (p. 1300), he becomes the Platonic Idea in relation to Isis's moist and receptive matter (p. 1310). If in the myth Isis and Typhon vie for possession of Osiris's body, in Plutarch's text they vie in effect for interpretative control over his significance; and in this they resemble Caesar and Cleopatra, each of whom imagines an Emperor Antony, each of whom wants to establish his meaning only in relation to his or her own story.

40.   This double resemblance has been noted in a general way by both Kermode ("Introduction," p. 1346) and Fisch ("Antony and Cleopatra," p. 61); neither treats it extensively or discusses its structural importance for the play. Neither Coppedge nor Erickson comments on the Typhon/Caesar analogy; but both note that Cleopatra resembles Isis in her rescue of the mutilated Antony ("The Joy of the Worm," p. 45–47; *Patriarchal Structures*, p. 141).

41.   Aside from its significance in establishing Shakespeare's probable use of Plutarch's essay (see note 37), the word "habiliments" is interesting in itself: unlike Plutarch/North's "apparell," it could carry the sense of abilities and faculties (see *OED* 6); how many of Isis's habiliments does Cleopatra put on?

42.   Although neither Wheeler's *Shakespeare's Development and the Problem Comedies* nor Madelon Gohlke's" 'I wooed thee with my sword': Shakespeare's Tragic Paradigms" (in *Representing Shakespeare*) contains full accounts of *Antony and Cleopatra*, both works have been (as always) seminal for my own; see, for example, Wheeler's reference to Antony "reborn through the fertile womb of [Cleopatra's] imagination" (p. 201) and Gohlke's to Cleopatra's "conception" of Antony (p. 179).

43.   The word "becomes," like "habiliments," seems to me to register the presence of Plutarch's Isis in Shakespeare's Cleopatra. Virtually absent from "The Life," it is central to Plutarch's characterization of Isis, and Shakespeare's of Cleopatra (see 1.3.96, 2.2.239; and see Adelman, *Common Liar*, pp. 144–45); Bono elliptically notes its importance in both texts (*Literary Transvaluation*, p. 212 n. 73).

44.   In Plutarch's neo-platonic myth, Isis (receptive matter) restores Osiris (the Platonic Idea) by immersing him in the generative world: "dying and being buried, [the Ideas] doe many times revive and rise againe fresh by the means of generations" (p. 1311). Plutarch generally valorizes the generative realm as the site of immanence and regeneration; he reports that Isis once cut Jupiter's legs apart when they had grown together, "which fable giveth us covertly thus to understand, that the understanding and reason of God in it selfe going invisibly, and after an unseene maner, proceedeth to generation by the meanes

of motion" (p. 1312). Critics who comment on Cleopatra's resemblance to Isis generally do so on the basis of her immersion in the generative world, noting especially her association with Isis's "motion" (Lloyd, "Cleopatra as Isis," p. 91 with her moon (Waddington, "Antony and Cleopatra," p. 216; Kermode, "Introduction," pp. 1345–46), and with her variability and multitudinous garments (Colie, "The Significance of Style," p. 74). But for Coppedge ("The Joy of the Worm," pp. 49–50), Fisch ("Antony and Cleopatra," p. 63), and Bono (*Literary Transvaluation*, pp. 5, 209–13), the resemblance rests also on Cleopatra's final transcendence of the natural world. Bono in fact sees Plutarch's resolution of the contradictory naturalistic interpretations of the myth into the One of neo-platonic interpretation as analogous to both Isis's and Cleopatra's turning from the many to the one (pp. 204, 211–13). But in my reading of Plutarch, Isis's role in the neo-platonic interpretation rests on her continued identification with the generative realm—as does Cleopatra's role in the play.

45. Bullough, *Narrative and Dramatic Sources*, vol. 5, p. 307; see Neely's fine discussion of Shakespeare's version of this battle and its aftermath (*Broken Nuptials*, pp. 146–47).

46. Stephen A. Shapiro finds ambivalence of all kinds characteristic of the play ("The Varying Shore of the World: Ambivalence in *Antony and Cleopatra*," *Modern Language Quarterly* 27 [1966]: 18–32). There has been very little full-scale psychoanalytic work done on *Antony and Cleopatra*, perhaps because Antony's emasculation is so transparent that it does not need much explication (but see Janis Krohn's explication of it: "The Dangers of Love in *Antony and Cleopatra*," *The International Review of Psychoanalysis* 13 [1986]: 89–96) or because the play's relatively high valuation of the lovers' deadly union does not fit well with psychoanalysis's usual negative stance toward such matters. The classic (and to my mind, still the richest) psychoanalytic account of the play is Constance Brown Kuriyama's reading of the interplay between its oedipal and preoedipal components ("The Mother of the World: A Psychoanalytic Interpretation of Shakespeare's *Antony and Cleopatra*," *ELR* 7 [1977]: 324–51); Roberta Hooks's suggestive reading follows Kuriyama's account of the dangers of regressive symbiotic union, but without her emphasis on why that union is so profoundly satisfying to the audience ("Shakespeare's *Antony and Cleopatra*: Power and Submission," *American Imago* 44 [1987]: 37–49). For virtually all psychoanalytic critics, Cleopatra is identified with the mother of infancy: see Cynthia Kolb Whitney's striking early formulation, "The War in 'Antony and Cleopatra,' " *Literature and Psychology* 13 (1963): 66; Kuriyama, "The Mother of the World," pp. 330–38; Shapiro, "The Varying Shore," pp. 29–30; Erickson, *Patriarchal Structures*, p. 135; Kay Stockholder, *Dream Works: Lovers and Families in Shakespeare's Plays* (Toronto: University of Toronto Press, 1987), pp. 153–57, 166; and Hooks, "Shakespeare's *Antony and Cleopatra*," pp. 42–45). For most of these critics, and many others, the final *Liebestod* represents satisfaction of the desire to be merged with this mother (see, e.g., Hooks, "Shakespeare's *Antony and Cleopatra*," pp. 44, 46); in Kuriyama's complex terms, it is simultaneously

the acting-out of the desire for union with the mother and the punishment for that desire ("The Mother of the World," pp. 344–46).

47. This set of affiliations is by now commonplace; see, for example, Ornstein ("The Ethic of the Imagination," p. 36), Adelman (*Common Liar*, pp. 127–31, 147–49), Michael Payne ("Erotic Irony and Polarity in *Antony and Cleopatra*," *Shakespeare Quarterly* 24 [1973]: 266–69), Dorius ("Shakespeare's Dramatic Modes," p. 93), Kuriyama ("The Mother of the World," p. 338), and Susan Snyder ("Patterns of Motion in 'Antony and Cleopatra,' " *Shakespeare Survey* 33 [1980]: 115–21). For these critics, and many others, Antony's turn toward a more "fluid" way of being is at least as positive as it is negative.

48. By contrast, Osiris seems to be in no hurry to leave Rhea's womb: Plutarch reports that "Isis and Osiris were in love in their mothers bellie before they were borne, and lay together secretly and by stealth" (p. 1292), perhaps elliptically signaling the extent to which generative harmony rests on a benign relationship to the maternal matrix.

49. Does Caesar's name locate him in the company of these sons? Although *OED* lists the first occurence of *caesarian* as an obstetrical term in English in 1615, the term may well have been creeping toward common usage ten years earlier; it was first used in France in an obstetrical handbook in 1581 (Rousset's *Traite nouveau de l'hysterotomokie ou Enfantement Caesarienne*, cited in J. H. Young, *The History of Caesarian Section* [London: H. K. Lewis, 1944], pp. 4, 23) and became commonplace in obstetrical literature thereafter. The obstetrical procedure itself, by whatever name, had a long association with the Caesars. Pliny the Elder thought that the first of the Caesars was so named because he had been cut from his mother's uterus ("Scipio Africanus prior natus, primusque Caesareum, a caeso matris utero dictus," *The Natural History*, bk. 7, chap. 9, cited in Young, pp. 2–3). Partly because Pliny's formulation allowed for a certain amount of confusion, a long (and unhistorical) tradition had Julius Caesar born by caesarian section (see J. Paul Pundel, *Histoire de L'Operation Caesarienne* [Brussels: Presses Academiques Européenes, 1969], pp. 15–39, *passim*); in one Arabic manuscript, even Octavius Caesar was born by caesarian (Pundel, p. 40). Pliny attributed particular good fortune to caesarian children, whose mothers invariably died at their birth; does his attitude stand behind Macduff and the full-fortuned Caesar?

50. See Eugene M. Waith's classic discussion of Antony's Herculean rage (*The Herculean Hero in Marlowe, Chapman, Shakespeare and Dryden* [New York: Columbia University Press, 1962], pp. 115–21).

51. In "Manliness in the Tragedies: Dramatic Variations" (*Shakespeare 1564–1964: A Collection of Modern Essays by Various Hands* [Providence, R.I.: Brown University Press, 1964], Robert B. Heilman notes that "man is always struggling to be of his own sex" (p. 20); Robert Stoller locates this struggle psychologically, in the male infant's need to dissociate from his mother (see Chapter 1 n. 30). David Kaula ("The Time Sense of *Antony and Cleopa-*

tra," *Shakespeare Quarterly* 15 [1964]: 217–18) and Erickson (*Patriarchal Structures*, p. 140) both write powerfully about Antony's relief at giving up the struggle as he disarms himself. For Dollimore, we witness in these scenes the dissolution not of Antony's selfhood or his masculinity but of his "essentialist fixedness" (*Radical Tragedy*, p. 211).

52.   That this mutual sleep is also imaged as orgasm—"I come, my queen" (4.14.50); "Husband, I come" (5.2.286)—suggests the deeply oral valence of genital sexuality in the play (see Kuriyama, "The Mother of the World," pp. 342–43; Hooks, "Shakespeare's *Antony and Cleopatra*," p. 37). Though the play initially celebrates phallic sexuality in Julius Caesar's ploughing (2.2.228), Antony's seedsman scattering his grain (2.7.21–22), and especially Cleopatra's cheerfully vulgar "Ram thou thy fruitful tidings in mine ears" (2.5.24), the aim of that sexuality is boundary dissolution; the play ends in a *Liebestod* that celebrates merger through Cleopatra's final image of the baby at her breast. As Stockholder notes, the "love-death fantasy . . . permits erotic fulfillment without taint from the world, the flesh, or sexuality" (*Dream Works*, p. 166); in effect, death replaces genital sexuality as the imagined means to fusion, for the audience as well as for the lovers. Philo has early on invited our voyeurism ("Look, where they come" [1.1.10]), but the play thwarts it until the last scene; instead of the sexually climactic moment Philo invites us to see, we are given repeated near-misses. In fact, by locating the great central scene of reunion only within Caesar's report of it (3.6.1–19, 65–67), Shakespeare puts us in Caesar's position, as one of the conspicuously excluded parties: only the mutual death of the lovers answers our desire to witness their union.

53.   See Erickson's discussion of Antony's identification with this maternal body (*Patriarchal Structures*, pp. 134–36).

54.   In effect, death becomes the safe solvent of masculine identity, enabling the fantasy of fusion that proved so dangerous for Troilus; see especially Neely's account of the ways in which "death renders female sexuality benign" (*Broken Nuptials*, p. 161).

55.   I am thinking of such moments as Ophelia's mad scene and drowning (reported by Gertrude), Desdemona's willow song and conversation with Emilia, and Lady Macbeth's sleep-walking, each of which shows its protagonist in a state at once intimate and self-alienated, stabilizing our image of her and allowing us to say farewell as we move on to the hero's tragedy.

56.   L. T. Fitz argues strenuously and wittily that Cleopatra is a tragic hero in her own right and sees the signs of sexism in the refusal to recognize her full subjectivity ("Egyptian Queens and Male Reviewers: Sexist Attitudes in *Antony and Cleopatra* Criticism," *Shakespeare Quarterly* 28 [1977]: esp. 307–14). While I agree that criticism has tended to grant Cleopatra much less subjectivity than Shakespeare does, I nonetheless find, with Linda Bamber, that she lacks the full privileges of the Self in comparison with Antony (*Comic Women, Tragic Men: A Study of Gender and Genre in Shakespeare* [Stanford, Calif.: Stanford University Press, 1982], esp. pp. 55–59, 66–69).

57. The dwindling into patriarchy of Cleopatra's realm is in part anticipated by Charmian's final placing of her as "a princess / Descended of so many
royal kings" (5.2.325–26); until that moment, she had seemed—virtually alone
of Shakespeare's women—to be *sui generis*.

58. Many critics note that Shakespeare revalues sexuality in *Antony and
Cleopatra*; see, for example, Ornstein's account of Shakespeare's shift from a
masculine to a feminine perspective on sexuality ("The Ethic of the Imagination," pp. 34–35) and Erickson's fine account of the ways in which the dark
lady of the sonnets is reclaimed in Cleopatra (*Patriarchal Structures*, pp. 125–
27). As far as I know, the longest and most serious account of this revaluation
is Brent Cohen's wonderful meditation on sexuality in *Antony and Cleopatra*
in his unpublished Ph.D. dissertation, "Sexuality and Tragedy in *Othello* and
Antony and Cleopatra" (University of California, Berkeley, 1981).

59. Through its dramatic structure, the play encourages our participation
in this fantasy of wholeness. The play is from the beginning obsessed with
gaps, absences, lacks (the word *lack* and its variants occur seven times), defects,
fragmentation. And its dramatic structure plays out this fragmentation in its
violent wrenchings from place to place, its numerous short scenes. Particularly
after the bustle of act 4, we (like Antony) long for a resting place; and we are
given such a place in the luxurious last scene, where we (again like Antony)
can come to rest in Cleopatra's monument. In this way, as in many others,
Antony and Cleopatra undoes *Troilus and Cressida*: Troilus is punished for
investing wholeness in Cressida, and the audience is made to undergo his
punishment as the play becomes increasingly fragmented; but we and Antony
are gathered up together in the recreative maternal space of Cleopatra's imagination.

60. See Wheeler, *Shakespeare's Development*, p. 209, for a very similar
formulation.

61. See Chapter 3, pp. 73–74, for speculations on the link between tragic
form and suspicion of female sexual process. Insofar as Cleopatra succeeds in
taking Antony with her into her own place of generative renewal, the love-
death of *Antony and Cleopatra* undoes that of *Othello*.

62. The interpretative openness of *Antony and Cleopatra* is particularly
striking if it is measured in relation to the plays around it: *Macbeth* and
Coriolanus both attempt to restrict interpretative possibilities for their audiences sharply in the end, as they narrow the options for their protagonists. Is
it purely coincidental that these are also the plays most deeply and explicitly
suspicious of female power? Near the beginning of "Of Isis and Osiris,"
Plutarch suggestively associates the inaccessibility of truth (and hence instability of interpretation) with the female body: fables are veils for truth, but what
is under Isis's veil remains a mystery ("I am all that which hath beene, which
is, and which shall be, and never any man yet was able to drawe open my
vaile" [p. 1291]). Perhaps Shakespeare's acceptance of difference—including
interpretative difference—in *Antony and Cleopatra* turns in part on his new

tolerance for the mystery of what lies beneath the veil, in effect his new capacity to trust in the female other.

63.   The deep playfulness of this text has long been noted; see, for example, Maynard Mack ("*Antony and Cleopatra*: The Stillness and the Dance," in *Shakespeare's Art: Seven Essays*, ed. Milton Crane [Chicago: University of Chicago Press, 1973], p. 84) and David Kaula ("The Time Sense of *Antony and Cleopatra*," p. 223). In linking this expansive playfulness to renewed trust in maternal presence, I am following the logic of Winnicott's work on "transitional phenomena" (see Chapter 2, n. 40, and Chapter 8, nn. 83, 84, and 90). Most psychoanalytic accounts of the play are forced to adopt a stern tone toward pleasures they are bound to define as "regressive" (Hooks refers to the play's "psychosis" ["Shakespeare's *Antony and Cleopatra*," p. 37]); Winnicott seems to me to permit a richer understanding of the play's manifold recoveries (see, e.g., Murray M. Schwartz, "Shakespeare through Contemporary Psychoanalysis," in *Representing Shakespeare*, pp. 29–30). In her most recent work on the play, Madelon Sprengnether argues the opposite point of view: for her, the playfulness of *Antony and Cleopatra* depends less on Shakespeare's recovery of trust in the female than on his construction of Cleopatra as not-female (through her reference to the boy actor) and the attendant diminution of her threat ("The Boy Actor and Femininity in *Antony and Cleopatra*," in *Shakespeare's Personality*, ed. Norman N. Holland, Sidney Homan, and Bernard J. Paris [Berkeley: University of California Press, 1989], pp. 201–2).

64.   Many have speculated about Shakespeare's identification with Cleopatra through her desire for Antony (G. Wilson Knight, *The Mutual Flame* [London: Methuen, 1955], pp. 30–31; Leslie A. Fiedler, *The Stranger in Shakespeare* [London: Croom Helm, 1972], pp. 74–75), her power as an imaginative artist (Ornstein, "The Ethic of the Imagination," pp. 44–45), and her theatrical virtuosity (Phyllis Rackin, "Shakespeare's Boy Cleopatra, the Decorum of Nature, and the Golden World of Poetry," *PMLA* 87 [1972]: 204; since Rackin's fine essay came out too late to be included in *The Common Liar* and since it anticipated many of my points in that book, I want to draw special attention to it here). Others find evidence of Shakespeare's more general identification with maternal cherishing, especially in the Sonnets (Norman Holland, *Shakespeare and Psychoanalysis* [New York: Farrar, Straus and Giroux, 1979], p. 84; Barber and Wheeler, *The Whole Journey*, pp. 167–74). Shakespeare's alliance with Cleopatra may also turn on the association of theater with the feminine (Jonas Barish, *The Antitheatrical Prejudice* [Berkeley: University of California Press, 1981], p. 50): see, for example, theatrical space as womb in David Willbern's "Shakespeare's Nothing," in *Representing Shakespeare*, pp. 256–59; actor as woman and woman as actor in Marianne Novy's *Love's Argument: Gender Relations in Shakespeare* (Chapel Hill: University of North Carolina Press, 1984), pp. 92–98; and the boy actor as female and not-female in Sprengnether's "The Boy Actor and Femininity," pp. 192–96. For Barish, Cleopatra is a figure for the theatrical (*The Antitheatrical Prejudice*, pp. 127–30); see also Hooks's suggestive account of the fusions common

to Cleopatra and theater ("Shakespeare's *Antony and Cleopatra,*" p. 41). Theatricality and female orgasm are allied in Stanley Cavell's reading of the play: Cleopatra repairs the withdrawal of the world from Antony (his crisis of skepticism) by giving herself and the world back to him in and through theater, thus presenting her orgasmic satisfaction by him (*Disowning Knowledge in Six Plays of Shakespeare* [Cambridge: Cambridge University Press, 1987], pp. 31–37). Cleopatra's affiliation with theater was first bought home to me in 1986 by some wonderful pages in Katherine Eggert's Masters thesis ("Deceit, Desire and Cleopatra: Creating the Woman Ruler," pp. 50–57).

NOTES TO CHAPTER 8

1. My account of this oscillation, like much else in this chapter, is deeply indebted to Richard Wheeler, specifically to his powerful description of the oscillation between trust/merger and autonomy/isolation throughout Shakespeare's tragedies and romances (*Shakespeare's Development and the Problem Comedies* [Berkeley: University of California Press, 1981], esp. pp. 156–57, 200–208, and 213–14). In his view, as in mine, this oscillation demonstrates "the resolution Shakespeare can never fully dramatize" (p. 88); the incompatibility of trust and autonomy has its origin in the destruction of the "half-mythic paradigm of stable family harmony" in *Hamlet* (p. 208).

2. The textual status of *Pericles* is still debated. Scholars generally attribute the "non-Shakespearean" quality of the first two acts either to poor reporting of a Shakespearean text or to the work of an inferior dramatist, whose play Shakespeare took in hand in 3.1. The second of these alternatives seems to me the most plausible: the carefully worked-out but flat imagery and wooden couplets of the first two acts sound to me more like the work of a thorough and accomplished hack than the mistakes of a reporter misremembering Shakespeare. The latest computer technology seems to support my suspicions; see M. W. A. Smith, "The Authorship of Acts I and II of *Pericles*: a New Approach Using First Words of Speeches," *Computers and the Humanities* 22 (1988): 35–37.

3. See especially Carol T. Neely's powerful reading of Antiochus's relationship with his daughter in these terms (*Broken Nuptials in Shakespeare's Plays* [New Haven, Conn.: Yale University Press, 1985], pp. 167–69). The Gower of *Pericles* supports Neely's reading, locating blame in Antiochus (1.Ch.26; 2.Ch.1–2). But in comparison with its sources and analogues, the incest in *Pericles* is initiated by the daughter: she is portrayed as a merely helpless victim of her father—rather than as the active seeker of incest that the riddle makes of her—in Chaucer, Gower, Twine, and Wilkins (see Geoffrey Bullough, *Narrative and Dramatic Sources of Shakespeare*, vol. 6 [London: Routledge and Kegan Paul, 1966], pp. 353, 377, 426, and 496).

4. See P. Goolden's account of the riddle's various permutations and its change of referent in *Pericles* ("Antiochus's Riddle in Gower and Shakespeare,"

Review of English Studies N.S. 6 [1955]: 245–51). Phyllis Gorfain puts the matter very neatly: "The solution to the riddle is not 'Incest,' but the name of Antiochus's nameless daughter" ("Puzzle and Artifice: The Riddle as Metapoetry in 'Pericles,' " *Shakespeare Survey* 29 [1979]: 13). Gorfain associates the daughter with the deadly female monsters who typically pose riddles ("Puzzle and Artifice," p. 14); for R. E. Gadjusek, she is equivalent to the Triple Goddess herself, pulling Pericles toward sex, death, matter, and unconsciousness ("Death, Incest, and the Triple Bond in the Later Plays of Shakespeare," *American Imago* 31 [1974]: 117–25). In an account that partly anticipates mine, Myra Glazer Schotz reads *Pericles* and the other romances as a response to this horrific figure: "In the great Romances, . . . Shakespeare wards off the power of the consolidated feminine archetype by doing what Lear could not. He separates her into mother and daughter and . . . keeps the two carefully apart" ("The Great Unwritten Story: Mothers and Daughters in Shakespeare," in *The Lost Tradition: Mothers and Daughters in Literature*, ed. Cathy N. Davidson and E. M. Broner [New York: Frederick Ungar, 1980], p. 49).

5. Among the many who read the story of Pericles's wanderings as a reworking of the initial incest, see especially C. L. Barber (" 'Thou That Beget'st Him That Did Thee Beget': Transformation in 'Pericles' and 'The Winter's Tale,' " *Shakespeare Survey* 22 [1969]: 61, 63; extended in Barber and Richard Wheeler, *The Whole Journey: Shakespeare's Power of Development* [Berkeley: University of California Press, 1986], pp. 310–28), Coppélia Kahn (*Man's Estate: Masculine Identity in Shakespeare* [Berkeley: University of California Press, 1981], p. 213), and Ruth Nevo (*Shakespeare's Other Language* [New York: Methuen, 1987], pp. 42–59). Each of these accounts foregrounds Pericles's own potentially oedipal desire and the oedipal father's punitive response; without denying their force, I want to stress the degree to which the father is spoiled by the sexualized female body; in my view, this body—rather than the castrating father—is the danger initially represented and phobically countered in the Shakespearean portion of the text.

6. See Barber and Wheeler (*The Whole Journey*, pp. 318, 328) for these prerequisites; they see Pericles's separation from Marina specifically as a preventative against his oedipal desire. Both Charles Frey and Cyrus Hoy similarly understand the separation of fathers and daughters throughout the romances as a response to the threat of incest (Frey, " 'O sacred, shadowy, cold, and constant queen': Shakespeare's Imperiled and Chastening Daughters of Romance," in *The Woman's Part: Feminist Criticism of Shakespeare*, ed. Carol Ruth Swift Lenz, Gayle Greene, and Carol Thomas Neely [Urbana: University of Illinois Press, 1980], p. 301; Hoy, "Fathers and Daughters in Shakespeare's Romances," in *Shakespeare's Romances Reconsidered*, ed. Carol McGinnis Kay and Henry E. Jacobs [Lincoln: University of Nebraska Press, 1978], pp. 84–88).

7. See, for example, Barber ("Thou That Beget'st Him That Did Thee Beget," p. 64), W. B. Thorne ("*Pericles* and the 'Incest-Fertility' Opposition," *Shakespeare Quarterly* 22 [1971]: 52–54), Gorfain ("Puzzle and Artifice," p.

16), and Kahn (*Man's Estate*, p. 214). For a view that anticipates my own in its insistence on qualifying the celebration, see Kay Stockholder, for whom "the visionary conclusion conceals the conflicts that shaped the tragedies" ("Sex and Authority in *Hamlet, King Lear*, and *Pericles*," *Mosaic* 18 [1985]: 28).

8. Although Kenneth Muir wrote in 1960 that there was "no integral connexion" between the wooing of Antiochus's daughter and the episodes that follow (*Shakespeare as Collaborator* [London: Methuen, 1960], p. 79), many critics since then have noted that the final father-daughter reunion answers the initial incestuous pair; see, for example, Barber (" 'Thou That Beget'st Him,' " p. 61; *The Whole Journey*, pp. 313–14, 328), Gadjusek ("Death, Incest, and the Triple Bond," pp. 125–26), Gorfain ("Puzzle and Artifice," pp. 14–15), Kahn (*Man's Estate*, pp. 212, 214), Neely (*Broken Nuptials*, p. 170), and Diane Elizabeth Dreher (*Domination and Defiance: Fathers and Daughters in Shakespeare* [Lexington: University Press of Kentucky, 1986], p. 149).

9. This is Barber's wonderful phrase (see Barber and Wheeler, *The Whole Journey*, p. 313); my use of it here is intended to register my deep indebtedness to his work on the romances and on *Lear*, which I have known and used in its various forms since roughly 1971. Like Barber, both D. W. Harding and Hoy note the importance of idealized female presences in the romances; but for Harding, these purified women are specifically dissociated from their mothers (Harding, "Shakespeare's Final View of Women," *Times Literary Supplement*, November 30, 1979, p. 59; Hoy, "Fathers and Daughters," pp. 81, 84).

10. In Nevo's reading, it does return us to this starting point (*Shakespeare's Other Language*, pp. 60–61).

11. Gower writes his tale explicitly to demonstrate the difference between good and bad love (Bullough, *Narrative and Dramatic Sources*, vol. 6, p. 422); in Shakespeare, all sexual love in effect becomes bad. The fact that both Twine and Wilkins also give the reunited couple an additional child (Bullough, pp. 480, 545) makes Shakespeare's failure to mention their generative prospects more visible. (But see Harding, who argues that Pericles resumes a fully sexual relationship with Thaisa ["Shakespeare's Final View of Women," p. 59].) The absence of predicted issue for either Pericles/Thaisa or Marina/Lysimachus perhaps vitiates David Bergeron's claim that royal lineage is central to all the romances, including *Pericles* (*Shakespeare's Romances and the Royal Family* [Lawrence: University Press of Kansas, 1985], e.g., p. 136).

12. " 'Thou That Beget'st Him,' " p. 61; extended in Barber and Wheeler, *The Whole Journey*, pp. 18, 301.

13. See Barber's " 'Thou That Beget'st Him,' " pp. 59–67, extended in Barber and Wheeler, *The Whole Journey*, esp. pp. 320–28, 332–34. In analyzing the recovery of relationship to "hallowed presences," Wheeler is particularly sensitive to the cost; he notes that the women of the romances must "survive violent attacks on them" in order to "provide the sacred context in

which the resolutions of these plays can take place" (*Shakespeare's Development*, pp. 83–84). Neely powerfully specifies the process through which death and mock-death enable the "desexualization and sanctification of good mothers" (*Broken Nuptials*, p. 174); see particularly her wonderful account of the links between "birth and the death of mothers" (pp. 171–74), an account to which I am much indebted. In the withdrawal and sanctified return of mothers after they give birth, Shakespeare found a dramatic equivalent for the customs surrounding churching, popularly regarded as a necessary purification after childbirth (see Keith Thomas, *Religion and the Decline of Magic* [New York: Scribners, 1971], pp. 38–39, 59–60).

14. See, for example, Harley Granville-Barker (*Prefaces to Shakespeare*, vol. 1 [Princeton, N.J.: Princeton University Press, 1946], pp. 461–62), J. M. Nosworthy ("Introduction," the Arden *Cymbeline*, p. lxxvii), and Howard Felperin (*Shakespearean Romance* [Princeton, N.J.: Princeton University Press, 1972], p. 178). Some see in the incongruities of plot, style, or character the signs of Shakespeare's deliberate experimentation with plot causality (R. A. Foakes, "Character and Dramatic Technique in *Cymbeline* and *The Winter's Tale*," *Studies in the Arts: Proceedings of the St. Peter's College Literary Society* [Oxford: Basil Blackwell, 1968], p. 123), with the portrayal of intense and isolated states of emotion (Roger Warren, "Theatrical Virtuosity and Poetic Complexity in 'Cymbeline,'" *Shakespeare Survey* 29 [1976]: 41–42), with the inclusive form of romance (R. S. White, *"Let wonder seem familiar": Endings in Shakespeare's Romance Vision* [Atlantic Highlands, N.J.: Humanities Press, 1985], pp. 143–44), or with the conventions of fictionality (Judiana Lawrence, "Natural Bonds and Artistic Coherence in the Ending of *Cymbeline*," *Shakespeare Quarterly* 35 [1984]: 444).

15. Simon Forman's summary of the play suggests that Cymbeline was no less absent for contemporary audiences than for us: Forman begins with Cymbeline but rapidly moves on to the erotic plot, clearly of more interest to him; as cited in the Arden edition, Cymbeline gets a scant six lines and the erotic plot fifteen (Nosworthy, "Introduction," pp. xiv–xv). His account seems to me to qualify the claim that a Stuart audience would have understood the play chiefly through the analogy between James and Cymbeline (see, for example, Emrys Jones, "Stuart Cymbeline," *Essays in Criticism* 11 [1961]: 87, 89, and Bergeron, *Shakespeare's Romances*, p. 137).

16. G. Wilson Knight hints at this analogy, noting that Cymbeline "is less a man than a centre of tensions" (*The Crown of Life* [London: Methuen, 1947], p. 130); and Wheeler makes the analogy explicit (*Shakespeare's Development*, p. 14). In Nevo's very suggestive account of the play, Cymbeline is the "central ego" of *Cymbeline*, but "that ego is in abeyance, in temporary suspension . . . behind the three plots" (*Shakespeare's Other Language*," p. 67); in her view, the conflict played out through the other characters is his "deeply repressed desire for his daughter" (p. 94). I read her essay only after this chapter was in its final stages; and though I would locate the central

psychic conflict elsewhere, in the construction of masculine identity itself, I am happy to note that we are in agreement about much in the play.

17.   Critics do not in general discuss the relation between the two partheno-genesis fantasies; but Leslie A. Fiedler hints at the connection (*The Stranger in Shakespeare* [London: Croom Helm, 1973], pp. 154–55), and Murray M. Schwartz notes that Cymbeline at the end fulfills Posthumus's desire for procreation without women ("Between Fantasy and Imagination: A Psychological Exploration of *Cymbeline*," in *Psychoanalysis and Literary Process*, ed. Frederick Crews [Cambridge: Winthrop Publishers, 1970], p. 280). (Fiedler's account of the play is fragmentary, but in its identification of the function of the witch-stepmother and of Cloten as mother's son, it anticipates mine. Schwartz's essay remains in my view the fullest psychoanalytic account of the play, and the one that I have learned the most from; though I don't always agree with the formulations and emphases of his largely oedipal reading, I am always struck upon rereading it by its comprehensiveness and interpretative richness, and by its deep fidelity to the play's tonal and structural peculiarities.) Posthumus's specifically parthenogenetic fantasy is not usually foregrounded by critics, though the "woman's part" speech is noted for its misogyny (see, e.g., Carolyn Ruth Swift Lenz, Gayle Greene, and Carol Thomas Neely, "Introduction," *The Woman's Part*, pp. 13–14), its projection of Posthumus's self-hatred (see, e.g., Harry Zuger, "Shakespeare's Posthumus and the Wager: From Delusion to Enlightenment," *Shakespeare Jahrbuch* 112 [1976]: 138), or its vague oedipal guilt (see, e.g., Arthur Kirsch, *Shakespeare and the Experience of Love*, [Cambridge: Cambridge University Press, 1981], p. 148); as far as I know, this parthenogenesis fantasy has not been seen as structurally central to the marriage plot. The significance of Cymbeline's parthenogenesis fantasy is more often noted, generally as a sign of Cymbeline's ideological resemblance to James (Jonathan Goldberg, *James I and the Politics of Literature* [Baltimore, Md.: Johns Hopkins University Press, 1983], p. 240; Bergeron, *Shakespeare's Romances*, p. 155) or of the renewal of fecundity—spiritual or literal—at the end (Bergeron, "Sexuality in *Cymbeline*," *Essays in Literature* 10 [1983]: 167; Dreher, *Domination and Defiance*, p. 157). Marianne L. Novy sees in it the signs of the transformed manhood of the romances, in which men are much more willing to incorporate traditionally female qualities into themselves (*Love's Argument: Gender Relations in Shakespeare* [Chapel Hill: University of North Carolina Press, 1984], p. 171); Marilyn L. Williamson reads it in terms closer to mine, as a patriarchal appropriation of procreative language in the service of the need for "asexual reproduction of heirs" (*The Patriarchy of Shakespeare's Comedies* [Detroit, Mich.: Wayne State University Press, 1986], pp. 164–65). Again, the structural centrality of the parthenogenesis fantasy to the Cymbeline plot is not often noted explicitly, though it is certainly implicit in Schwartz's reading of the play's search for the strong father (see, e.g., pp. 247, 259, and 276).

18.   The displacement of the daughter by the recovery of the sons (and the larger displacement of the female) is so out of kilter with the other romances that *Cymbeline* awkwardly compromises generalizations about their endings

(or would, if its awkwardness were acknowledged). See, for example, Hoy on the redemptive power of the romance daughters ("Fathers and Daughters," p. 78); Dreher on the "benevolent anima" as the concluding image of romance (*Domination and Defiance*, p. 157); and Williamson on the romance ruler's recovery of his "woman's part" through his wife or daughter (*Patriarchy*, p. 150).

19. The play thus constitutes a counterclaim to the frequently made claim that inheritance in the romances is through the female line; see, for example, Frey (" 'O sacred,' " p. 304) and Bergeron (*Shakespeare's Romances*, p. 116). Harding ("Shakespeare's Final View," p. 61) and Williamson (*Patriarchy*, p. 161) specifically note the play's deviation from the usual pattern of inheritance in the romances; in Williamson's account, the "natural" family Cymbeline recovers is thoroughly patriarchal (*Patriarchy*, p. 127). Imogen's oft-repeated desire to be free of her political position (1.2.79–81, 1.7.5–7, and especially 3.7.48–51) prepares the audience for this displacement; in its repetitiousness, it may also signal Shakespeare's uneasy awareness that Imogen's acquiescence in her displacement requires preparation. (See Nancy K. Hayles, "Sexual Disguise in *Cymbeline*," *Modern Language Quarterly* 41 [1980]: 239, for discussion of 3.7.48–51.)

20. In Rosalie L. Colie's terms, "This is unmitigated hard pastoral, a rocky, difficult terrain training its inhabitants to a spare and muscular strength sufficient to wrest their nutriment from its minimal, ungenerous, exiguous resources" (*Shakespeare's Living Art* [Princeton, N.J.: Princeton University Press, 1974], p. 295). But see Schwartz, for whom the pastoral is a maternal environment ("Between Fantasy and Imagination," p. 253), Novy, for whom the pastoral undermines rigid sex roles and "does not in principle exclude women" (*Love's Argument*, p. 170), and Nevo, for whom it represents the "denial of adult differentiation," especially gender differentiation (*Shakespeare's Other Language*, p. 84).

21. For Nevo, Belarius is a "substitute father-mother" (*Shakespeare's Other Language*, p. 63); in Schwartz's account, his pastoral permits its all-male community defensive identification with the good mother ("Between Fantasy and Imagination," pp. 253, 257–58).

22. In his Jungian account of *Cymbeline* as the rescue of the incestuous father from the Triple Goddess to whom he is bound, Gadjusek notes that the sexual transformation of the sons restores the father-king to his power ("Death, Incest," p. 141).

23. Many have noted the dreamlike displacements and condensations of this play, though more frequently in the erotic plot than in the Cymbeline plot; see, for example, Schwartz ("Between Fantasy and Imagination," p. 231), Kirsch (*Shakespeare and the Experience of Love*, p. 153), D. E. Landry ("Dreams as History: The Strange Unity of *Cymbeline*," *Shakespeare Quarterly* 33 [1982]: 70), and Nevo (*Shakespeare's Other Language*, p. 66).

24. For the centrality of Christ's birth during the *pax romana* and Cymbeline's reign, see, for example, Hugh M. Richmond ("Shakespeare's Roman Trilogy: The Climax in Cymbeline," *Studies in the Literary Imagination 5* [1972]: 129–39), Felperin (*Shakespearean Romance*, pp. 180–85, 187–88), and Marjorie Garber ("*Cymbeline* and the Languages of Myth," *Mosaic* 10 [1977]: 113–14); for the significance to *Cymbeline* of James's self-styling as the peaceful Augustus, see, for example, Jones ("Stuart Cymbeline," pp. 88–92, 96) and Goldberg (*James I and the Politics of Literature*, pp. 240–41). But neither of these analogies entirely solves the problem of union with Rome: England's assumption of Christianity is only problematically read through that union; nor would it have served as the most reassuring image for James's peacemaking proclivities.

25. In Schwartz's formulation, "submission to the father Caesar is a safeguard against the evil mother's feared powers" ("Between Fantasy and Imagination," p. 280).

26. See Wheeler's rich discussion of Ericksonian "basic trust" in the festive comedies and romances (*Shakespeare's Development*, esp. pp. 82–84); and see Harding's discussion of trust and distrust specifically in *Cymbeline* ("Shakespeare's Final View," p. 60).

27. According to Homer Swander, this recovery is unique not only in Shakespeare but also in the sources and analogues to the wager plot ("*Cymbeline* and the 'Blameless Hero,' " *English Literary History* 31 [1964]: 267–69); see also Kirsch's comparison of Posthumus's repentance with Claudio's (*Shakespeare and the Experience of Love*, pp. 151, 158).

28. I am very much indebted to Nora Johnson's ongoing work on *Cymbeline*—and especially to her masters thesis, "Posthumus and Selfhood in *Cymbeline*," University of California, Berkeley, 1986—for this formulation.

29. Fiedler notes her submissiveness (*The Stranger in Shakespeare*, p. 154); in Granville-Barker's phrase, "It is something of a simulacrum that survives" (*Prefaces to Shakespeare*, p. 542).

30. As Neely notes, she "puts aside her marriage, her sexuality, and even her sharp tongue"; she "is relieved to participate in this asexual family" (*Broken Nuptials*, p. 181). Hayles similarly notes her new passivity, but sees it as essential to her role as androgynous emblem of psychic wholeness and contact with the unconscious ("Sexual Disguise," pp. 238, 241–42). If so, then her progress can be construed to illustrate the cost of such emblematization.

31. See, for example, Nevo's reading of Imogen's "disharmony with her sexuality" and her turn toward masochism (*Shakespeare's Other Language*, pp. 79–83).

32. Granville-Barker chivalrously takes exception to her treatment: she is "put, quite needlessly, quite heartlessly, on exhibition. . . . Surely it is a faulty art that can so make sport of its creatures. . . . It is a pretty damnable practical

joke" (*Prefaces to Shakespeare*, pp. 539, 541). Schwartz ("Between Fantasy and Imagination," p. 266), Michael Taylor ("The Pastoral Reckoning in 'Cymbeline,' " *Shakespeare Survey* 36 [1983]: 99), and Neely (*Broken Nuptials*, p. 182) similarly feel the traces of Shakespeare's own punitiveness toward Imogen.

33.   The phrase is anatomically exact in tracing desire to the woman's part: "motion" is associated with sexual desire, "vice" with the female genitals (see Eric Partridge's entries under each in *Shakespeare's Bawdy* [New York: E. P. Dutton, 1948]).

34.   See Chapter 5, note 27, for "mother" as a term for the uterus. Iachimo's claim that he will enjoy "the dearest bodily part" of Imogen (1.5.146–47) increases the likelihood that we will hear the anatomical reference when Posthumus refers to the "woman's part" in himself; "vice *in man*" may also reinforce the image of the female genitals in the male. Schwartz ("Between Fantasy and Imagination," p. 246) and Nevo (*Shakespeare's Other Language*, p. 78) note the anatomical reference in "woman's part"; Schwartz reads it specifically oedipally, as an expression of Posthumus's castration anxieties.

35.   Schwartz speculates ("Between Fantasy and Imagination," p. 232), and Nevo concludes (*Shakespeare's Other Language*, p. 70), that the marriage is unconsummated. But Posthumus's assertion that Imogen "pray'd me oft forbearance" (2.4.162) suggests repeated opportunities for sexual contact; and both his sense that the adultery was specifically an affront to his bed (3.4.22) and his fantasy of the revenge as punishment for the damage done there seem to me to require the image of matrimonial consummation. But as in *Othello*, the question is ultimately unanswerable; the play works on us not by giving answers but by engaging our guilty speculation.

36.   The pun is reinforced by Cloten's later use of the relatively uncommon word "testiness" in his description of his mother's hold over Cymbeline ("my mother, having power of his testiness" [4.1.20–21]). Nevo notes the pun on "testimonies"; in her view, Posthumus "incorporates the woman's part" in the letter to Pisanio, playing the "violated virgin since he cannot be the violator that . . . he would wish to be" (*Shakespeare's Other Language*, p. 79). Schwartz does not note the pun, but he does more generally see the revenge as a punishment for sexual mutilation: "Since genital sex is mutilation, Imogen must be mutilated" ("Between Fantasy and Imagination," p. 252).

37.   See Partridge (*Shakespeare's Bawdy*, p. 78) for the equation of "breach" with the female genitals.

38.   Ever since Swander pointed out the myriad ways in which Posthumus is not "the blameless hero" ("*Cymbeline* and the 'Blameless Hero,' " pp. 260–65), critics have been noting his "assent to the forces of separation" (Schwartz, "Between Fantasy and Imagination," p. 234) and his eagerness to embrace Iachimo's design (Kirsch, *Shakespeare and the Experience of Love*, p. 147; see also, e.g., Zuger, "Shakespeare's Posthumus," pp. 134, 137–38, and Nevo, *Shakespeare's Other Language*, pp. 71–73).

39. See Novy's fine discussion of the element of "taboo" in Posthumus's relationship with Imogen; but she thinks that the taboo is broken and fecundity restored in the course of the play (*Love's Argument*, pp. 181–83).

40. For some, Posthumus's words record not his retrospective attempt to remake Imogen but the literal facts of their marriage and hence his hidden motive for revenge (see, e.g., Zuger, "Shakespeare's Posthumus," pp. 135–36, and White, *"Let wonder seem familiar"*, p. 134).

41. Iachimo is sometimes identified as Posthumus's surrogate (see, e.g., Felperin, *Shakespearean Romance*, pp. 186–87, Neely, *Broken Nuptials*, pp. 182–83, and Williamson, *Patriarchy*, p. 127), but the relationship is rarely analyzed at length; but see Schwartz's rich account of it ("Between Fantasy and Imagination," pp. 227–31, 238–45).

42. In Stephen Booth's wonderful speculations on the effects of doubling in the theater, the potential doubling of the roles of Cloten and Posthumus illustrates "the fusion and confusion of absolutely distinguishable identities [that are] of the essence of *Cymbeline*" ("Speculations on Doubling," *King Lear, Macbeth, Indefinition, and Tragedy* [New Haven, Conn.: Yale University Press, 1983], p. 151). It has become a trope of *Cymbeline* criticism to see Cloten as Posthumus's double, the scapegoated bearer of Posthumus's sexual violence and desire for revenge; see, among the many, Schwartz ("Between Fantasy and Imagination," pp. 226, 262), James Siemon ("Noble Virtue in 'Cymbeline,' " *Shakespeare Survey* 29 [1976]: 56–59), Warren ("Theatrical Virtuosity," pp. 44–45), Felperin (*Shakespearean Romance*, p. 186), Landry ("Dreams as History," pp. 70–72), Kirsch (*Shakespeare and the Experience of Love*, pp. 53–56), Neely (*Broken Nuptials*, pp. 182–83), and Nevo (*Shakespeare's Other Language*, pp. 74–75). In Fiedler's succinct phrase, *"all* men are Clotens" in their sexuality (*The Stranger in Shakespeare*, p. 243); but see Bergeron, who thinks that Cloten is a eunuch ("Sexuality in *Cymbeline*," pp. 160–63).

43. The phrase is Fiedler's (*The Stranger in Shakespeare*, p. 243).

44. In Schwartz's powerful phrase, "Cloten is the penis of that phallic woman" ("Between Fantasy and Imagination," p. 268); as Nevo notes, "the Queen, bereft . . . of her male organ, declines and dies" (*Shakespeare's Other Language*, p. 86). Fiedler's account of Shakespeare's lustful mother's sons— Demetrius and Charon, Cloten and Caliban—strikingly anticipates my own; though I don't think that I had read his account in 1981, when this aspect of Shakespeare first took shape for me, I am happy to acknowledge my general indebtedness to his method and insight.

45. See Meredith Skura's lovely meditation on the ways in which the shadowy presence of family "flicker[s] on the surface" of *Cymbeline*, "neither a psychoanalytic skeleton behind the surface, nor . . . quite part of the literal meaning"; although she does not foreground issues of gender, hers remains the richest account of the extent to which Posthumus is unable "to find himself

as husband until he finds himself as son, as part of the family he was torn from long ago" ("Interpreting Posthumus's Dream from Above and Below: Families, Psychoanalysts, and Literary Critics," in *Representing Shakespeare: New Psychoanalytic Essays,* ed. Murray M. Schwartz and Coppélia Kahn [Baltimore, Md.: Johns Hopkins University Press, 1980], p. 207).

46. As Schwartz points out, "the powers of generation now reside completely in a masculine figure" ("Between Fantasy and Imagination," p. 276); I am specifically indebted to him for this point.

47. The tension is noted by many; see especially Erickson on the corruption of the male entertainment on which patriarchy rests (*Patriarchal Structures,* pp. 149–51) and Nevo on the reversible images of estrangement in the kings' togetherness (*Shakespeare's Other Language,* pp. 100–101).

48. Among those who stress the centrality of Hermione's pregnancy, see especially Erickson (*Patriarchal Structures,* pp. 148–49), Neely (*Broken Nuptials,* pp. 191–92), and Stanley Cavell (*Disowning Knowledge* [Cambridge: Cambridge University Press, 1987], pp. 208–13). I am particularly indebted to Neely's account here.

49. For many, the pregnancy imagery here primes the audience for Leontes's suspicions; see, e.g., Charles Frey (*Shakespeare's Vast Romance: A Study of "The Winter's Tale"* [Columbia: University of Missouri Press, 1980], p. 120) and Nevo (*Shakespeare's Other Language,* pp. 101–3). Cavell's extraordinary account of telling, counting, indebtedness, and revenge turns complexly on the imagery of pregnancy and indebtedness here (*Disowning Knowledge,* p. 209): "The debt seems to be for the fact of separation itself, for having one's own life. . . . And this sense of the unpayable, the unforgivability of one's owing, as it were for being the one one is, for so to speak the gift of life, produces a wish to revenge oneself upon existence, on the fact, or facts, of life as such" (pp. 210–11).

50. For *cross,* see *OED* 12, *to cross the path of*: "to come in the way of; often implying obstruction or thwarting," and *OED* 14, "to thwart, oppose, go counter to." Shakespeare often uses the word in this general sense: of numerous uses, see, e.g., *3 Henry VI,* 3.2.127; *Much Ado,* 1.3.59; *Antony and Cleopatra,* 1.3.9; and *Pericles,* 5.1.229. (Joel Fineman would have had something wonderful to say about crossing eyes; I wish he were here to talk to.)

51. For the specifically phallic connotations of *spirit,* see Stephen Booth (*Shakespeare's Sonnets* [New Haven, Conn.: Yale University Press, 1977], pp. 441–43) and *Romeo and Juliet,* 2.1.24. Many have noted that Polixenes's version of Eden unorthodoxly exempts the boys from original sin, figuring the sexual woman as temptation and making phallic sexuality equivalent to the fall; see, e.g., Murray M. Schwartz ("Leontes' Jealousy in *The Winter's Tale,*" *American Imago* 30 [1973]: 257), Mark Taylor (*Shakespeare's Darker Purpose: A Question of Incest* [New York: A.M.S., 1982], pp. 35–38), and Peter

Lindenbaum ("Time, Sexual Love, and the Uses of Pastoral in *The Winter's Tale*," *Modern Language Quarterly* 33 [1972]: 7–8). For Schwartz, "The myth of childhood affection . . . preserves in masculine form a narcissistic and idealized version of the mother's dual unity with the son" (p. 256); he consequently foregrounds the fall into difference and the "splitting of their masculine egos" (p. 257). Kahn (*Man's Estate*, pp. 215–16) and W. Thomas MacCary similarly stress the equation of differentiation with heterosexuality in this fall: in MacCary's formulation, Polixenes's Eden recreates nostalgia for the period of primary narcissism that comes to an end with knowledge of sexual difference, making women "a sure sign of man's irremediable division from his god and therefore from himself" (*Friends and Lovers: The Phenomenology of Desire in Shakespearean Comedy* [New York: Columbia University Press, 1985], p. 203).

52.   Howard Felperin notes the imagery of copulation implicit in Polixenes's "standing" and finds in it evidence of the play's contagious suspicion, its self-conscious representation of the fall from verbal innocence into multivocality or linguistic indeterminacy (" 'Tongue-tied our queen?': The Deconstruction of Presence in *The Winter's Tale*," in *Shakespeare and the Question of Theory*, ed. Patricia Parker and Geoffrey Hartmann [New York: Methuen, 1985], p. 9). In Nevo's wonderfully suggestive account, Polixenes's phrase registers Leontes's "nothingness, the emptiness of exclusion from a once experienced plenitude" (*Shakespeare's Other Language*, p. 103).

53.   This fragmentariness of course presents some danger to critics, who will almost inevitably find their own obsessions reflected in Leontes, botching up the words "fit to their own thoughts" (*Hamlet*, 4.5.10). But Freud notes its efficacy as a technique of engagement in his comments on *Richard III*: Richard's soliloquy "merely gives a hint, and leaves us to fill in what it hints at"; by withholding open and complete expression of motives, Shakespeare "obliges us to supplement them . . . and keeps us firmly identified with his hero" ("Some Character-Types Met with in Psycho-Analytic Work," *Standard Edition*, vol. 14, ed. James Strachey [London: Hogarth Press, 1957], pp. 314–15). But see Barbara Mowat, who thinks that the ignobility of Leontes's passion and the intrusion of distancing comic perspectives keep us from engagement with him (*The Dramaturgy of Shakespeare's Romances* [Athens: University of Georgia Press, 1976], pp. 9–20).

54.   Among the many who find the jealousy unmotivated and see in it evidence of Shakespeare's declining interest in verisimilitude and individualistic character, see, e.g., Colie (*Shakespeare's Living Art*, p. 266) and Frey (*Shakespeare's Vast Romance*, pp. 28, 45); Frey's dismissal of motivation is especially odd, given his sensitive treatment of Leontes's psychic state elsewhere (e.g., p. 130). But several critics find Leontes's jealousy more fully represented than Othello's precisely because of the suppression of ordinary motivation (see, e.g., Knight, *The Crown of Life*, pp. 84, 96; Felperin, *Shakespearean Romance*, pp. 214, 216; and especially J. I. M. Stewart, *Character and Motive in Shakespeare* [New York: Barnes and Noble, 1949], pp. 30, 36–37). Psychoanalytic and

feminist critics have of course found motive a-plenty. Many see in the jealousy primarily Leontes's generalized fear of sexuality, displaced onto women (e.g., Lindenbaum, "Time, Sexual Love," pp. 10–11; Patricia Southard Gourlay, " 'O my most sacred lady': Female Metaphor in *The Winter's Tale*," *English Literary Renaissance* 5 [1975]: 376, 380; Carol Thomas Neely, "Women and Issue in *The Winter's Tale*," *Philological Quarterly* 57 [1978]: 182–83, extended in *Broken Nuptials*, pp. 193–94; Taylor, *Shakespeare's Darker Purpose*, pp. 38–39; Frey, *Shakespeare's Vast Romance*, p. 130; Dreher, *Domination and Defiance*, pp. 150–52). Many follow Stewart in attributing the jealousy specifically to Leontes's attempt to suppress his homoerotic bond with Polixenes (Stewart, *Character and Motive*, pp. 31–36; John Ellis, "Rooted Affection: the Genesis of Jealousy in *The Winter's Tale*," *College English* 25 [1964]: 525–27; Fiedler, *The Stranger in Shakespeare*, pp. 151–52); for some, that bond itself is a response to oedipal desires and fears (Barber, " 'Thou That Beget'st Him,' " p. 65, extended in Barber and Wheeler, *The Whole Journey*, pp. 18, 329–30; Stephen Reid, "*The Winter's Tale*," *American Imago* 27 [1970]: 266–74) or to an underlying narcissistic crisis (Kahn, *Man's Estate*, pp. 214–17; MacCary, *Friends and Lovers*, pp. 203, 206). For René Girard, the jealousy reflects Leontes's realistic appraisal of the mimetic desire upon which such bonds are based ("Jealousy in *The Winter's Tale*," in *Alphonse Juilland: D'une passion l'autre*, ed. Brigitte Cazelles and René Girard [Saratoga, Calif.: Anma Libri, 1987], pp. 47–57). For others, the motivational center is less in the male bond than in the fantasized relationship with the mother *per se*: see especially Schwartz's account of Leontes's response to the fear of separation from an idealized maternal presence and the recovery of that presence through sanctioned communal bonds ("Leontes' Jealousy," pp. 256–73; "*The Winter's Tale*: Loss and Transformation," *American Imago* 32 [1975]: 145–99); Wheeler's account of the loss and recovery of trust in the "hallowed presence" on which sustained selfhood can be based (*Shakespeare's Development*, pp. 82–84, 214–21); Erickson's account of the patriarchal transformation and appropriation of an untrustworthy maternal bounty (*Patriarchal Structures*, pp. 148–70); and Nevo's account of the fears of maternal abandonment and annihilation played out in Mamillius's death (*Shakespeare's Other Language*, pp. 104–14). (Among these, Schwartz's seems to me still the fullest and most nuanced psychoanalytic account of the play; I am deeply indebted to it, and to the work of Barber, Wheeler, Neely, Kahn, and Erickson, all of which has influenced my thinking about the play.) All these reconstructions of Leontes's psychic state are vigorously dismissed by White (*"Let wonder seem familiar"*, pp. 148–49) and Maydee Lande ("*The Winter's Tale*: A Question of Motive," *American Imago* 43 [1986]: 57–59), who see in Leontes's jealousy merely his response to challenges to his political authority (White) or to his sense of omnipotence (Lande).

55. In Erickson's elegant formulation, "The place of Iago is here filled by Hermione's pregnancy" (*Patriarchal Structures*, p. 148).

56. See Schwartz, Kahn, and MacCary, as cited in note 51, for similar readings of the narcissism implicit in the fantasy of twinship.

57. In "Male Bonding in Shakespeare's Comedies," I argued for this defensive function: the fantasy of twinship "allows for a new sense of self based on separateness from the mother while maintaining the fluidity of boundaries between self and other characteristic of that first relationship. In that sense it offers protection against engulfment by the mother while allowing for the comforts of union" (in *Shakespeare's Rough Magic: Renaissance Essays in Honor of C. L. Barber*, ed. Peter Erickson and Coppélia Kahn [Newark, N.J.: University of Delaware Press, 1985], p. 92).

58. Leontes is ostensibly proclaiming the world something, not nothing, in his speech to Camillo: the world dissolves into nothingness only if he is mistaken in his reading of the signs of Hermione's guilt. But despite this ostensible logic, any audience subjected to the relentless *nothing* of these lines will probably hear in them the pull toward annihilation more clearly than the initial if-clause. For me, at any rate, they are terrifying. See Nevo (*Shakespeare's Other Language*, p. 114), for a similar reading of these lines.

59. The distorted copulative and birth imagery of Leontes's "affection" speech has often been noted; see especially Schwartz ("Leontes' Jealousy," pp. 264–65), Carol Neely ("*The Winter's Tale*: The Triumph of Speech," *Studies in English Literature, 1500–1900* 15 [1975]: 325–27), and MacCary (*Friends and Lovers*, pp. 204–6). In his suggestive comments on Shakespeare's ambiguously generative nothing, David Willbern notes Leontes's creation of "destructive progeny" out of "nothing" here ("Shakespeare's Nothing," in *Representing Shakespeare*, pp. 248–49). My reading of Leontes's delusion as a way of staving off nothingness is very much indebted to Schwartz's wonderful account of Leontes's paranoia as "a defense which fails at the moment of its enactment," "a grotesque parody of creation itself" ("Leontes' Jealousy," pp. 263–65); see also Lande's account of the ways in which his delusion gives him a sense of authority and control ("*The Winter's Tale*," p. 60).

60. See p. 213.

61. See *King Lear*, 4.6.121.

62. Nevo notes the conflation of birth and intercourse here (*Shakespeare's Other Language*, p. 109).

63. See Partridge, *Shakespeare's Bawdy*, p. 192, for the sexualization of "sport."

64. Neely ("Women and Issue," p. 183), Kahn (*Man's Estate*, p. 216), and Erickson (*Patriarchal Structures*, pp. 154–55) all note this attempt.

65. Although medical science did not attribute the *ovum* to women until well after Shakespeare's time (see Audrey Eccles, *Obstetrics and Gynaecology in Tudor and Stuart England* [Kent, Ohio: Kent State University Press, 1982], pp. 30–32), common observation in the barnyard would suffice to ensure the association of eggs with female generativity.

66. Schwartz notes that Leontes would identify with Mamillius as a "symbol of phallic integrity" ("Leontes' Jealousy," p. 268).

67. For the custom of breeching, see Chapter 1, p. 7. As Maynard Mack notes, the unbreeched Mamillius would have been "wearing a costume very like [his] mother's" ("Rescuing Shakespeare" [Oxford: Oxford University Press, 1979], p. 11).

68. As Neely says, "Mamillius, since not created by some variety of male parthenogenesis, . . . is declared infected by his physical connection with Hermione" ("Women and Issue," p. 183). Latin *mamilla* = breast or teat; Schwartz ("Leontes' Jealousy," p. 268) and Kahn (*Man's Estate*, p. 216), among others, note the maternal valence of Mamillius's name.

69. Schwartz's account is the *locus classicus* for the identification of the spider with the catastrophic preoedipal mother, specifically here in the nursing situation ("Leontes' Jealousy," pp. 269–72; Erickson too associates the spider with "oral contamination" (*Patriarchal Structures*, p. 155). But for MacCary, the spider is the "sexually insatiable oedipal mother" (*Friends and Lovers*, pp. 209, 215). Whatever their precise interpretations, most psychoanalytically oriented critics—and G. Wilson Knight, for that matter (*The Crown of Life*, p. 81)—find this speech central to Leontes's character. But Anne Barton surprisingly chooses it to illustrate her claim that Shakespeare deliberately destroyed "the close relationship between language and dramatic character" in his last plays; in her view, the speech does not "focus attention upon Leontes's central self" ("Leontes and the Spider: Language and Speaker in Shakespeare's Last Plays," in *Shakespeare's Styles*, ed. Philip Edwards, Inga-Stina Ewbank and G. K. Hunter [Cambridge: Cambridge University Press, 1980], p. 135).

70. Knight notes this quality in Leontes's linguistic style: "The spasmodic jerks of his language reflect Leontes' unease: he is, as it were, being sick; ejecting . . . something he has failed to digest, assimilate" (*The Crown of Life*, p. 81).

71. See Chapter 5, pp. 106–7, and this chapter, p. 212..

72. See Gourlay's fine analysis of their interchange and of the negative stereotypes Leontes invokes (" 'O my most sacred lady,' " pp. 282–83). D'Orsay W. Pearson argues that Shakespeare invokes and refutes Paulina's association specifically with the stereotypical urban witch throughout the play ("Witchcraft in *The Winter's Tale*: Paulina as 'Alcahueta y un Poquito Hechizera,' " *Shakespeare Studies* 12 [1979]: 195–213). Mowat notes the comedy in Leontes's "dread of the scolding but powerless female" as evidence that we cannot be consistently engaged with him as tragic hero (*Dramaturgy*, p. 25); while I agree with her sensitive analysis of this scene, the problems of engagement—especially of gendered engagement—seem to me more complex than she allows for here.

73. Schwartz similarly notes Leontes's difficulty in "equat[ing] himself with his feminine issue" ("*The Winter's Tale*," p. 150). For Frey, daughters

always betoken "a guilty loss of patrilineal procreative power" (*Shakespeare's Vast Romance*, p. 87).

74. Schwartz notes Leontes's identification with the orally catastrophic mother and his echo of Lady Macbeth ("Leontes' Jealousy," p. 268; "*The Winter's Tale*," p. 153).

75. This view has been widely accepted since Knight's powerful expression of it (*The Crown of Life*, esp. pp. 88–90). But there have been at least two important recent *caveats* against the sentimentalizing of nature's power in the play: Erickson's analysis of the ways in which the associations of women with "natural" generative and nurturing processes secure patriarchy and limit gender roles (*Patriarchal Structures*, esp. pp. 158–64), and Williamson's demonstration of the ideological use of the construct "nature" to mythologize patriarchal power (*Patriarchy*, esp. pp. 116–21, 129–30, and 161–64).

76. Of the many who recognize that women and the generative forces associated with them are the agents of recovery in this play, see Gourlay (" 'O my most sacred lady,' " pp. 377–93) and especially Neely, to whose rich account, both in its original form ("Women and Issue," pp. 181–93) and in its revised form (*Broken Nuptials*, pp. 191–209), I am deeply indebted.

77. For the incipient pun on *fault*, see Chapter 2, note 26. Hermione playfully evokes the same pun in her dangerous conversation with Polixenes ("If you first sinn'd with us, and that with us / You did continue fault," 1.2.84–85).

78. Among the many who see Antigonus as Leontes's scapegoat, see especially Schwartz ("Leontes' Jealousy," p. 260; "*The Winter's Tale*," pp. 156–59), Erickson (*Patriarchal Structures*, pp. 156, 159), and Nevo (*Shakespeare's Other Language*, pp. 116–18); all three see his fate as a complex reworking of Leontes's delusion.

79. The pastoral is generally seen as a corrective to Leontes's court; Lindenbaum sees it specifically as a corrective to Polixenes's pastoral in its embracing of sexuality and change ("Time, Sexual Love," pp. 14–20).

80. Both Lindenbaum ("Time, Sexual Love," p. 18) and Frey (*Shakespeare's Vast Romance*, p. 73) note Florizel's implicit reversal of Lear's position.

81. Perdita is often identified with nature, Venus Genetrix, or Mother Earth (see, e.g., Lindenbaum, "Time, Sexual Love," p. 18; Gourlay, " 'O my most sacred lady,' " pp. 387–88; Kahn, *Man's Estate*, p. 219). But Williamson notes wryly that the natural processes embodied in Perdita are trustworthy because her noble birth proves them "socially acceptable" (*Patriarchy*, p. 130).

82. Leontes has already prepared for Polixenes's equation by identifying "gates" with the female genitalia (1.2.197).

83. Leontes's crisis of faith is often noted; see, e.g., Frey, *Shakespeare's*

Vast Romance, pp. 78–80. Book I of *The Faerie Queene* suggests how readily the loss and regaining of a beloved woman could serve as an analogy for the loss and regaining of faith. But I am thinking less of the loss of any specific religious faith than of the loss of faith in the world outside the self: what Cavell calls "skepticism's annihilation of the world" (*Disowning Knowledge*, p. 214); my debt to him in what follows will be obvious to anyone who knows his work. In associating this crisis of faith specifically with the mother's body and with the loss of interior aliveness, and the resolution of this crisis with the return of the capacity to play, I am following the insights of Winnicott, for whom the mother's reliable response to the infant's needs, especially in the nursing situation, creates "a belief that the world can contain what is wanted and needed, with the result that the baby has hope that there is a live relationship between inner reality and external reality, between innate primary creativity and the world at large" (*The Child, the Family, and the Outside World* [Harmondsworth: Penguin Books, 1964], p. 90). (Cavell's formulations are of course congruent with Winnicott's: in his reading of *The Winter's Tale*, birth stands for primary separation, what the skeptical annihilation of the world—like the paranoid's refilling of it with his own projections—is attempting to deny [*Disowning Knowledge*, esp. pp. 206–13].) C. L. Barber first told me to read Winnicott; I am deeply indebted to his and Wheeler's various formulations of the need "for recovering benign relationship to feminine presences" (Barber and Wheeler, *The Whole Journey*, p. 298) in order to restore "the core of the self that originates in relations to a trustworthy maternal presence" (Wheeler, *Shakespeare's Development*, p. 83). Wheeler's wonderfully rich account of the loss and recovery of trust in that "hallowed presence" (*Shakespeare's Development*, pp. 82–84) is very suggestive for all the romances and is worked out in detail for *The Winter's Tale* (pp. 214–19).

84. My formulation here follows from Winnicott's sense that the mother's survival of the infant's voracious attack on her allows the infant to discover the difference between inner and outer, fantasy and reality, and thereby makes the mother "usable" as an object outside the self. The object becomes "usable" only when it survives destruction and thus is placed outside the sphere of omnipotence; its "use" comes from the recognition of its otherness, which then enables it to contribute to interior richness: "The subject says to the object: 'I destroyed you,' and the object is there to receive the communication. From now on the subject says: 'Hello object!' 'I destroyed you.' 'I love you.' 'You have value for me because of your survival of my destruction of you.' . . . In these ways, the object develops its own autonomy and life, and (if it survives) contributes-in to the subject, according to its own properties" ("The Use of an Object and Relating through Identifications," *Playing and Reality* [London: Tavistock Publications, 1971], p. 90). Hermione is obviously the primary object that survives destruction; here I am arguing that her return is mediated for Leontes (who recovers her through Perdita) and for the audience by the position of pastoral as the place that Leontes's destruction of the world did not destroy, the place therefore "usable" because it is outside the sphere of omnipotent control. See Wheeler's closely related discussion of these processes

as they shape Shakespearean tragedy and romance (*Shakespeare's Development*, pp. 214–18).

85. The last scene presents something of a challenge to those who would see in the play primarily the recuperation of male bonds (e.g., Kahn, *Man's Estate*, pp. 218–19) or the recovery of control over patriarchal issue (e.g., Williamson, *Patriarchy*, pp. 150–52). Keeping us hungry by refusing to show us the reconcilations with Polixenes and Perdita, Shakespeare creates in us the sense that something is missing, so that we too will be ready to go to Paulina's house with "all greediness of affection" (5.2.102); and what is missing and longed for is focused in the report of Leontes's cry: "O, thy mother, thy mother" (5.2.52–53).

86. The (implicitly gendered) contrast between control and emotion is central to Novy's understanding of Shakespeare (see *Love's Argument*, pp. 9–10, 16–17); she finds the relinquishing of control characteristic of the romance protagonists and essential to the "transformed images of manhood" in them (pp. 172–74). See especially her moving account of the statue's awakening, where "imagery of warm flesh and cold stone . . . identifies the contrast between emotion and control with that between life and death" (p. 180).

87. The *locus classicus* for this formulation is Sherry Ortner's "Is Female to Male as Nature is to Culture?" in *Woman, Culture, and Society*, ed. Michelle Zimbalist Rosaldo and Louise Lamphere (Stanford, Calif.: Stanford University Press, 1974), pp. 67–87. The art-nature debate is a standard *topos* of criticism of the play; see, for example, Knight (*The Crown of Life*, pp. 122–23), Colie (*Shakespeare's Living Art*, pp. 274–83), and especially Leonard Barkan (" 'Living Sculptures': Ovid, Michelangelo, and *The Winter's Tale*," *English Literary History* 48 [1981]: 661–64).

88. My formulation here is very close to Novy's (*Love's Argument*, p. 180) and Neely's ("Women and Issue," p. 191); see also Taylor (*Shakespeare's Darker Purpose*, p. 45) and MacCary (*Friends and Lovers*, pp. 214–15).

89. For the Proserpina-Ceres story in *King Lear*, see Chapter 5, p. 120 and note 45. Of the many who note the relevance of that story to *The Winter's Tale*, Neely's account seems to me the richest, in part because she foregrounds the importance of the mother-daughter bond ("Women and Issue," pp. 186–87); see also Schotz's Jungian account of their reunion ("The Great Unwritten Story," pp. 52–53).

90. The "first not-me possession," Winnicott's "transitional object," provides "an intermediate area of *experiencing*, to which inner reality and external life both contribute. It is an area which is not challenged, because no claim is made on its behalf except that it shall exist as a resting-place for the individual engaged in the perpetual human task of keeping inner and outer reality separate yet inter-related" ("Transitional Objects and Transitional Phenomena," *Through Paediatrics to Psycho-Analysis* [London: Hogarth Press, 1975], p. 230). The existence of this space rests on the intersection of the infant's desire

with a world (in the form of the good-enough mother) adequately responsive to that desire (see "Transitional Objects," esp. pp. 237–41); as "potential space," it is the foundation for play and for creative living of all sorts (see the essays collected in *Playing and Reality*, esp. "The Location of Cultural Experience"). I find Winnicott's idea of potential space more useful than the older psychoanalytic concept of "wish-fulfillment," which implies both that there is a rigid boundary between inner and outer and that the reality principle has caved in to the demands of the pleasure principle; by establishing a middle zone between the two (see "Transitional Objects," pp. 230, 237–39), Winnicott seems to me to allow for a much richer formulation both of the value of art and of our everyday existence, where we half-perceive and half-create the world outside ourselves. For additional discussion of Winnicott, see Chapter 2, note 40, and notes 83 and 84 in this chapter; and see Chapter 2, p. 29, Chapter 6, pp. 163–64, and Chapter 7, pp. 192–93, for accounts of the loss of potential space in Hamlet, Macbeth, and Coriolanus, and its recovery in Cleopatra. I am very grateful to Murray Schwartz for helping to make this perspective available to me; see his "Shakespeare through Contemporary Psychoanalysis" (in *Representing Shakespeare*, pp. 21–32), for a beautiful reading of the loss and recovery of potential space in Shakespeare's tragedies and romances.

91.   I use *we* here to register my sense not only of the degree to which Shakespeare demands his audience's participation but also of the degree to which the deepest restorations of the end are relatively uninflected by gender. The most primitive losses and recoveries are prior to gender differentiation: though daughters will probably be less prone than sons to use the language of female contamination to register their sense that the world is alien and potentially overwhelming, both daughters and sons can find in the recovery of the benign maternal body a figure for the recovery of trust in the world. (See pp. 125–26 for a related discussion of Cordelia's return in *King Lear*.)

92.   Among the many who see in Hermione's awakening an allusion to Shakespeare's specifically theatrical art, see especially Barkan ("Living Sculptures," pp. 661–62) and Cavell (*Disowning Knowledge*, p. 218). The force of this allusion may be curiously confirmed by Gemma Jones, who uses language apparently drawn from the statue's awakening to describe the difference between rehearsing the part of Hermione and performing it before a live audience: "The shell, the shape and the form have been rehearsed, but the flesh and blood are revealed in front of an audience" ("Hermione in *The Winter's Tale*," in *Players of Shakespeare*, ed. Philip Brockbank [Cambridge: Cambridge University Press, 1985], p. 164). The role of the audience's faith in bringing the statue to life is commonly acknowledged: see, e.g., Felperin (*Shakespearean Romance*, p. 242), Frey (*Shakespeare's Vast Romance*, p. 161), White (*"Let wonder seem familiar"*, pp. 156–57), Bruce McIver ("Shakespeare's Miraculous Deception: Transcendence in *The Winter's Tale*," *Moderna Sprak* 73 [1979]: 341–51), William C. Carroll (*The Metamorphoses of Shakespearean Comedy* [Princeton, N.J.: Princeton University Press, 1985], pp. 213, 222–

23), and especially Nevo (*Shakespeare's Other Language*, p. 127) and Cavell (*Disowning Knowledge*, pp. 218–21).

93. Many note the healing of play in 4.4; see especially Frey's lovely description of pastoral play and of the ways in which the pastoral restores our faith as audience, reversing the theater of suspicion that had preceded it (*Shakespeare's Vast Romance*, pp. 138–44).

94. In different ways, Barber (" 'Thou That Beget'st Him,' " p. 66), Schwartz ("*The Winter's Tale*," pp. 153, 163–65, and 177–81), Kahn (*Man's Estate*, p. 219), and Erickson (*Patriarchal Structures*, pp. 164–67) all stress that the recovery of male bonds and patriarchal authority is a precondition of Hermione's return; for Erickson and Williamson (as cited in note 75) recourse to a female "nature" itself turns out to be a way of securing male control.

95. The phrase is Neely's ("Women and Issue," p. 185).

96. Feminist critics frequently note that Paulina is Hermione's surrogate, safely able to express her rage (Marilyn Williamson, "Doubling, Women's Anger, and Genre," *Women's Studies* 9 [1981]: 114–17; Erickson, *Patriarchal Structures*, p. 162) and to lead the way back to Hermione because she is asexual (Neely, "Women and Issue," p. 188; extended in *Broken Nuptials*, pp. 175, 200–201).

97. I am indebted to Neely for this observation ("Women and Issue," p. 191).

98. Like Cerimon, Paulina is given the authority not only to shape the plot but also to end the play by leading its characters offstage; Leontes's "Good Paulina, / Lead us from hence . . . hastily lead away" answers Pericles's "Sir, lead's the way" to Cerimon. Since none of Shakespeare's other plays end with this formula, the repetition is particularly striking.

99. See Barber's classic account of the resemblance between the statue's movement and medieval miracles of the Virgin (" 'Thou That Beget'st Him,' " pp. 59–60; extended in *The Whole Journey*, pp. 332–33); he stresses that "discovery of the Holy Mother in the wife" includes recovery of "the particular human identity of the long lost one" (" 'Thou That Beget'st Him,' " pp. 66, 60). In a very interesting essay, Cynthia Marshall sets Hermione's return in the context of grave statuary and the doctrine of bodily resurrection, with its "intense valuation of the human body" and of the individual identity founded in the body ("Dualism and the Hope of Reunion in *The Winter's Tale*," *Soundings* 69 [1986]: 294–309). Wheeler (*Shakespeare's Development*, p. 90), Neely (*Broken Nuptials*, p. 191), and Novy (*Love's Argument*, pp. 180–81) similarly stress the bodiliness of this miracle.

100. See Frank Kermode's appendix on Ovid and Golding (the Arden *Tempest*, pp. 147–50) for Shakespeare's use of Ovid's Medea in its various forms.

101. Jonathan Brennan first pointed this imagery out to me during a class

on *The Tempest*. It is a particular pleasure to end this book with a footnote to one of my students: all along, I have been blessed by my students, who have had a wonderful ability to ask me the right—that is, the unanswerable— question at the right time, and then have shown me what I needed to think my way toward an answer. I hope that Jonathan's name can stand for the many— some of whose names I didn't even know—who have helped me at every stage in writing this book and who have continually made Shakespeare a pleasure to think about. (The most recent help came from Nora Johnson, whose wonderful wit and judgement made the tasks of proof-reading and indexing not only bearable but a pleasure.)

Author Index

Abel, Elizabeth, 252
Adams, John F., 283, 285
Adamson, Jane, 280
Adamson, W.D., 276, 278
Adelman, Janet, 295, 333, 334, 336, 337, 338, 340
Aldus, P.J., 251, 254, 256
Altick, Richard D., 250
Alvis, John, 334
Aries, Philippe, 244
Aronson, Alex, 241, 310
Asp, Carolyn, 262, 283, 285, 298, 304, 307, 310, 318
Astington, John H., 252, 295

Bachmann, Susan, 315, 321
Bacon, Sir Francis, 295
Bamber, Linda, 246, 248, 250, 280, 312, 320, 321, 341
Barber, C.L., 198, 239, 240, 245, 249, 251, 257–58, 274, 276, 281, 294, 295, 304, 306, 307, 310, 311, 323, 330, 331, 343, 345, 346, 355, 359, 362
Barish, Jonas, 260, 343
Barkan, Leonard, 360, 361
Barnet, Sylvan, 316
Barroll, J. Leeds, 334
Barron, David B., 312–13, 315, 316, 321, 325, 326, 328
Barton, Anne, 333, 335, 357
Bates, Ronald, 258–59, 259
Bayley, John, 261, 278
Beckerman, Bernard, 333, 334

Bennett, Robert B., 253
Berger, Harry, 302, 303, 307, 309, 313, 314, 315, 317, 318, 320, 321, 322
Bergeron, David, 346, 347, 348, 349, 352
Berggren, Paula S., 279–80
Bergler, Edmund, 247
Berry, Laura Camozzi, 292
Berry, Ralph, 251, 287, 287–88, 288, 291, 326
Bevington, David M., 240, 302–3, 316
Biggins, Dennis, 314, 318, 320
Boccaccio, Giovanni, 78, 80
Bodemer, Charles W., 243
Bodkin, Maud, 251, 269, 270, 276, 303
Bono, Barbara, 337, 338, 339
Boose, Lynda E., 275, 277, 304, 309
Booth, Stephen, 253, 255, 293–94, 295, 295–96, 303, 317, 352, 353
Bradbrook, Muriel, 259, 316, 322
Bradley, A.C., 247, 247–48, 249, 255, 257, 274, 281, 295, 302, 303, 310, 325
Brain, The Right Honorable Lord, 300
Brennan, Jonathan, 362–63
Briggs, Katherine Mary, 316
Bullough, Geoffrey, 281, 294, 296, 305, 333, 334, 336, 337, 339, 344, 346
Bullough, Vern L., 295
Burckhardt, Sigurd, 307
Burke, Kenneth, 273, 275, 278, 325
Burns, M.M., 262, 264
Burton, Robert, 301
Byles, Joan M., 315

Index to Shakespeare's Works

Subject Index

Aristotelian theories of generation, 242, 244, 252, 287

birth: caesarian, 3, 7–8, 131, 140–44, 161, 188, 239, 240, 320, 340; desire for virgin, 18, 85, 197, 251, 284–85, 322; as betrayal, separation, and loss, 69, 110, 123–24, 173, 228, 309; as contamination by female, 30, 36, 253; as site of mortality and original sin, 6, 24, 27, 110, 221; revalued, in Cleopatra, 175–76, 186–87, in Perdita, 228, 230. See also *parthenogenesis*.
breeching, 7, 226, 244, 274, 357

Ceres and Proserpina, 120, 234, 306–7, 360
"country" as womb, 27, 160, 162, 255, 325

Elizabeth I, 293, 309
Eriksonian interpretations, 258, 350

Fall, 6, 17, 23–24, 27, 36, 41, 78, 92–93, 95, 100, 119, 122, 123, 221–22, 230, 253–54: Adam and Eve, 24, 30, 119; Eve, 6, 30; original sin as inheritance from maternal origin, 23–24, 36, 87–88, 89, 92–93, 96, 101, 221–21, 230, 253
fathers: paternal absence, 3, 10, 17–18, 30, 35, 43, 79, 81, 93, 98, 102, 103, 130, 131, 133, 146, 177, 179–81, 191, 193, 194–95, 198–99, 200, 212,

217, 218, 240, 260, 288, 315, 322, 328; creation of bodiless father, 18, 19, 34, 35, 97–98, 102, 146, 193, 207, 237; idealized presence protects against overwhelming mother, 3, 17–18, 22, 30, 35, 79, 81, 97–98, 206, 247, 250, 252, 323, 328
father's son, vs. mother's son, 97, 105–6, 146, 205, 215–17, 218, 220, 237–38, 348, 352
"fault"/*foutre*, and female genitals, 23–24, 100–101, 105, 109, 115, 228, 252–53, 292, 295, 358; and fall, 23–24, 253
Fortune, as whore-mother, 5, 23, 26, 29, 35, 43, 57, 110, 142–43, 168, 169, 173, 254, 299, 331

Galenic theories of generation, 243, 301
gendered vs. ungendered reading, 125–26, 305, 310, 311, 329, 361
Gowrie, Earl of, 313

Horneyan interpretations, 280, 291

illegitimacy, as maternal inheritance, 45, 97, 105–9, 212, 225, 227, 237, 290, 295
incest, 28, 78–79, 80, 83, 96, 195–96, 246–47, 250, 266, 283, 289, 290, 294; and boundary confusion, 28, 80, 195–95, 283, 290; brother-sister, 283, 289, 290
infantile vulnerability, fantasies of, 3–7,